GREAT EVENTS
FROM
HISTORY II

GREAT EVENTS FROM HISTORY II

Arts and Culture
Series

Volume 4
1955-1969

Edited by

FRANK N. MAGILL

SALEM PRESS

Pasadena, California   Englewood Cliffs, New Jersey

Library of Congress Cataloging-in-Publication Data
Great events from history II. Arts and culture series / edited by Frank N. Magill.
      p.   cm.
   Includes bibliographical references and index.
   1. Arts, Modern—20th century. 2. Arts and society—History—20th century. I. Magill, Frank Northen,
1907-   II. Title: Great events from history. 2. Arts
and culture series.

NX456.G72   1993
700′.9′04—dc20
ISBN 0-89356-807-4 (set)   93-28381
ISBN 0-89356-811-2 (volume 4)   CIP

LIST OF EVENTS IN VOLUME IV

xli

GREAT EVENTS
FROM
HISTORY II

BERRY'S "MAYBELLENE" POPULARIZES ROCK AND ROLL

Category of event: Music
Time: 1955
Locale: Chicago, Illinois, and New York, New York

Chuck Berry's "Maybellene" unexpectedly rocketed to the top of the music charts and set the stage for the rock-and-roll era

Principal personages:

CHUCK BERRY (1926-   ), a singer, songwriter, and guitarist who created a series of influential songs that defined early rock and roll and influenced generations of popular musicians

LEONARD CHESS (?-1969), a Chicago-based independent record producer who recorded many rhythm-and-blues acts and early rock-and-roll stars

ALAN FREED (1922-1965), a pioneer rock-and-roll radio disc jockey who championed the music of black artists

BILL HALEY (1925-1981), a singer, guitarist, and bandleader who fashioned a number of early hit rock-and-roll songs

Summary of Event

"Maybellene" was Chuck Berry's first hit and arguably, despite Elvis Presley's considerable fame, the most important initial reference point in the history of rock and roll. Berry melded rhythm and blues and country-western music with his special brand of guitar playing to fashion witty, defiant songs that have influenced virtually every rock musician. In his best work—including "Sweet Little Sixteen," "Carol," "Brown Eyed Handsome Man," "Roll Over Beethoven," "Living in the USA," and "Little Queenie"—Berry successfully melded resonant teen concerns with a blues base and country rhythms to fashion the basis of rock and roll.

Berry grew up in legally segregated St. Louis, Missouri. His teen years were troubled, and he spent time in a reform school; as a young adult, he tried working as a beautician and on a General Motors assembly line.

Making music, though, was his real love. By the early 1950's, he and pianist Johnny Johnson were leading a blues trio in clubs in and around St. Louis. In the process, Berry struggled to find a sound that appealed to both black and white audiences.

In this period, Berry melded a wide range of influences. Among guitarists, he favored the works of technical innovator Les Paul and jazz virtuoso Charlie Christian. Above all, though, T-Bone Walker's improvisational guitar stylings provided the source for Berry's highly danceable, insistent rhythms. Berry's vocal style owed much to Nat "King" Cole and Louis Jordan.

Berry's break came in the spring of 1955, when he made his way to Chicago to record a well-known song entitled "Ida Red" for Leonard Chess of independent Chess Records. Through club dates, Berry had revised "Ida Red," adding lyrics that he spit out in a rapid-fire fashion that perfectly complemented the song's narrative, which concerned a car chase.

"Ida Red," though, was in the public domain and thus could not be copyrighted, meaning that a recording of the song would generate no songwriting royalties. In the process of recording, Leonard Chess thus asked Berry to provide new words and an alternative title. Out came "Maybellene," a paean to an automobile; the recording was highlighted by Berry's unusual guitar lines. Noted bluesman Willie Dixon played stand-up bass in the session.

Berry later recalled that "Maybellene" was his effort to meld country and western with his own teen laments of trying to get girls to ride in his 1934 V-8 Ford. The name "Maybellene," came, Berry claimed in his autobiography, from a book he had read in the third grade.

Leonard Chess and his brother Phil Chess were creating an independent record company in Chicago that assembled most of the major artists of the blues. The brothers had arrived in the United States in 1928 from Poland and had made their way into the club business on the black South Side of Chicago. After World War II, they hit their stride with recordings of Muddy Waters, Howlin' Wolf, and John Lee Hooker. It would be Chuck Berry and Bo Diddley, though, who would give Chess Records national prominence through the 1950's.

Leonard Chess interested innovative disc jockey Alan Freed (who was listed as a cowriter) in helping to popularize "Maybellene." Freed, who was then in the process of trying to make rhythm and blues accessible to a burgeoning middle-class, suburban, white teen audience, liked the unusual record. Working for an independent Cleveland, Ohio, radio station, Freed had earlier championed rhythm-and-blues artists the Clovers, Johnny Ace, and Ruth Brown with some success. "Maybellene," though, worked better than any song Freed had promoted before.

"Maybellene" jumped onto the record charts midway through 1955. *Billboard*, the influential bible of the record industry, praised it as "fine jockey and juke wax." The song entered the rhythm-and-blues charts and soared to number one by mid-August of 1955; it stayed atop the rhythm-and-blues charts until mid-October.

"Maybellene" took no longer to crack the pop music charts. Tops that summer of 1955 was Bill Haley's own crossover song, "Rock Around the Clock." Haley's style was also influenced by rhythm and blues. The white Haley heavily accented his music's beat, and his pioneering songs educated white audiences in black rhythms. Berry's "Maybellene" would take advantage of this.

By the November of 1955, Berry had been named *Billboard*'s most promising rhythm-and-blues artist. Rock and roll was poised to explode on the music scene, but the new genre still lacked an identity; that same year, Elvis Presley was named *Billboard*'s most promising country-western star.

That neither Chuck Berry nor Leonard Chess nor Alan Freed was sure what had worked to attract the mass teenage audience to "Maybellene" could be seen in

Berry's next few records. In 1956, only Berry's magnificent hymn to the new music, "Roll Over Beethoven," proved a hit; his other follow-up tracks, including "No Money Down," "Thirty Days," "Brown Eyed Handsome Man," and "You Can't Catch Me," sold little.

Berry, though, was ever the adapter, and he and Chess worked to create a follow up. He traveled continually to promote himself. In January, 1957, impresario Irvin Feld premiered a musical revue that featured Clyde McPhatter, Fats Domino, the Moonglows, and Berry, among others. Before the tour closed five months later, its fourteen acts had appeared in every part of the United States, including places such as Colorado where no rock-and-roll show had ever been.

All this public-relations work paid off. During 1957 and 1958, Berry had five top-twenty successes, and six more of his tracks reached lower rungs on the charts. The late 1950's would prove to be Berry's golden age. In such hits as "School Day" (number eight on the pop charts and number one on the rhythm-and-blues charts in 1957), "Rock and Roll Music" (number eight on the pop charts and number six on the rhythm-and-blues charts in 1957), and "Sweet Little Sixteen" (which reached number two on the pop charts and number one on the rhythm-and-blues charts in 1958), Berry disseminated his lyrically sophisticated yet danceable style.

The secret, in retrospect, seems to have been Berry's unique ability to combine his insistent beat and catchy tunes with themes resonant to a white adolescent audience. "Johnny B. Goode" tells the story of the rise of a rock-and-roll star; "School Day" laments forced instruction; "Carol" and "Sweet Little Sixteen" celebrate teenage love; and "Rock and Roll Music" was both a hymn to and anthem for the latest teen craze. Berry even did "Run Rudolph Run," a Christmas novelty song in which Rudolph the Red-Nosed Reindeer, with the speed of a Sabre jet, runs Santa Claus down a freeway to deliver a doll to a girl and a guitar to a boy.

Impact of Event

Chuck Berry's blend of rhythm and blues and country music, his songwriting style, and his innovative guitar picking proved enormously influential. The biggest rock stars of the next generation, including the Beatles, Bob Dylan, the Rolling Stones, and the Beach Boys, all paid tribute to Berry's importance. Although Berry's own career had its ups and downs and was damaged by brushes with the law and by poor professional management, his effect on the course of popular music continued to be felt decades after he had ceased to be a major star. In short, Chuck Berry may be the most important name in the history of rock and roll.

One can forget how revolutionary Berry's approach was. In 1954, sanitized pop music was the rage. Patti Page was breaking "Young at Heart" on television's popular *The Colgate Comedy Hour*. Bing Crosby was a major star. It was only four years earlier that *Billboard* had dropped the term "race records" in favor of "rhythm and blues." Bill Haley's "Rock Around the Clock" was considered scandalous when it was introduced in the 1955 teen film *The Blackboard Jungle*, and Elvis Presley was still considered a country-western music star trying to sound like Dean Martin.

Berry toured the world, and his famous "duck walk" (a crouching near-run across the stage Berry would make during intricate solo guitar passages) brought audiences to their feet. His live performance was captured on film in the unlikely setting of the Newport Jazz Festival in the motion picture *Jazz on a Summer's Day* (1960) as well as in a more sanitized form in the Alan Freed-produced rock films *Rock, Rock, Rock* (1956), *Mr. Rock and Roll* (1957), and *Go, Johnny, Go!* (1958).

In the 1960's, Berry's influence became apparent in the work of many leading rock bands. In Great Britain, the Beatles acknowledged his centrality by placing Roll Over Beethoven" and "Rock and Roll Music" on early albums, and the Rolling Stones often ended their live performances with a rousing version of Berry's "Bye Bye Johnny." In the United States, the Beach Boys based their hit "Surfin' USA" directly on Berry's "Sweet Little Sixteen." More offbeat was Bob Dylan's 1965 single "Subterranean Homesick Blues," which sounded much like Berry's "Too Much Monkey Business."

In 1959, the bottom dropped out of Berry's life; he was convicted on an immorality charge concerning a teenage girl employed at his St. Louis club. Berry's conviction was initially reversed on appeal, but eventually authorities were able to send him to jail for two years. The prosecution of Berry's case has been widely held to have been racially motivated; nevertheless, the incident ended the remarkable early career of a master popular musician.

Berry would go on recording after serving his jail term, but he never recaptured the popularity of his 1950's peak. The intervening years, though, have given ample testimony to his enormous effect on the evolution of rock music; decades after his first success, he remains revered as one of the genre's true icons.

Bibliography

Berry, Chuck. *Chuck Berry: The Autobiography.* New York: Simon & Schuster, 1987. There is no better way to appreciate the far-reaching mind of Chuck Berry than look to his own words. This is the most important work on one of the most important figures in the history of rock and roll.

Gillett, Charlie. *The Sound of the City: The Rise of Rock 'n' Roll.* New York: Dell, 1970. A pioneering work on the roots and rise of rock and roll that remains helpful despite its relative age. An insightful sociological treatment.

Reese, Krista. *Chuck Berry: Mr. Rock and Roll.* London: Proteus, 1982. A well-produced but superficial biography, with wonderful color pictures and an adequate discography. Useful, though not entirely reliable.

Sanjek, Russell. *American Popular Music and Its Business.* Vol. 3, *From 1900 to 1984.* New York: Oxford University Press, 1988. Rock and roll survived because its products made money. This book, part of a three-volume series, illuminates the economic dimensions of the early rock-music business. There is little on Berry himself, but a great deal of vital information on the business he so powerfully affected.

Taylor, Paul. *Popular Music Since 1955.* Boston: G. K. Hall, 1985. This fine annotated bibliography tells of the growing literature on rock-and-roll artists. A good place to start researching the history of rock and roll.

Ward, Ed, Geoffrey Stokes, and Ken Tucker. *Rock of Ages: The Rolling Stone History of Rock and Roll*. New York: Rolling Stone Press, 1986. Offers the reader a fine survey history of the rock-and-roll era and places Berry at the center of the development of the rock genre. A good place to start.

Douglas Gomery

Cross-References

Presley Becomes a Rock-and-Roll Sensation (1956), p. 1705; Gordy Founds Motown Records (1959), p. 1790; The Beatles Revolutionize Popular Music (1963), p. 1944; The Rolling Stones Release *Out of Our Heads* (1965), p. 2027; Dylan Performs with Electric Instruments (1965), p. 2038; Brown Wins a Grammy for "Papa's Got a Brand New Bag" (1966), p. 2059; Hendrix Releases *Are You Experienced?* (1967), p. 2092.

DEAN BECOMES A LEGEND IN *REBEL WITHOUT A CAUSE*

Category of event: Motion pictures
Time: 1955
Locale: The United States

James Dean exemplified troubled youth in Rebel Without a Cause

Principal personages:
> JAMES DEAN (1931-1955), an actor who became a mythic figure on the basis of three films
> NATALIE WOOD (NATASHA GURDIN, 1938-1981), an actress who gave a memorable performance in *Rebel Without a Cause*
> NICHOLAS RAY (RAYMOND NICHOLAS KIENZLE, 1911-1979), a director with a personal style who captured Dean's charisma

Summary of Event

When *Rebel Without a Cause* was released on October 29, 1955, at the Astor Theatre in New York, it was not considered to be a major release. Although *East of Eden* had opened in March of that year to favorable reviews and James Dean generally had been applauded for his performance as Cal Trask, *Rebel Without a Cause* was considered a "B" picture and had no major publicity campaign. Dean had been buried just three weeks previously after a fatal automobile crash. The Warner Bros. studio, which released the film, was leery about it because the death of an actor was not often a stimulus for box-office success.

If a star had been born in *East of Eden*, *Rebel Without a Cause* made Dean a legend. His sudden death only added to his myth. As Jim Stark, the troubled adolescent, Dean embodied the very essence of a rebel without a cause; the phrase became synonymous with Dean.

Rebel Without a Cause is a story of three frustrated teenagers looking for love from families that did not understand them and for identities in a society that demanded conformity. Jim Stark and his family had to move from town to town because of the trouble the boy got into. His father and mother constantly bickered, and his father would not stand up and be the man his son needed him to be. Judy (Natalie Wood) desperately sought acceptance, especially from her repressed father. Failing to find acceptance there, she tried to fit in with the popular high-school crowd. Plato (Sal Mineo) was a psychologically damaged boy whose parents were divorced. He lived in a big house, alone except for his maid.

Early in the film, Jim is challenged to a "chicken run" by Buzz, Judy's boyfriend. The challenge was to see who would jump first from his car as each boy drove a car toward a cliff. Buzz is unable to escape from his car and is killed when it crashes. Jim, Judy, and Plato form a sort of family and go to a deserted mansion, but they are pursued by friends of Buzz. The gang and the police chase Plato, who flees into a nearby planetarium. Jim and Judy go after him, and Jim convinces Plato to come out. The police shoot Plato as Jim tries to save him. At the end, Jim's father and mother seem to have a new understanding of him. He now has Judy and finally belongs to someone.

The plot touched on many of the themes of the 1950's: conformity, status, middle-class values, the conflict between generations, the conflict between youth and authority, and the search for identity in an insensitive world. Dean brilliantly captured the frustration and insecurity of an individual trying to find himself within that world. He was knowing, confused, and innocent, all at the same time. *Rebel Without a Cause* is a melodrama and has some flawed sequences, such as the contrived ending of familial understanding, but Dean transcended the form. He infused the formula with originality and passion.

Dean displayed a variety of talents in the film, convincingly portraying a conflicted character. He acted out a range of emotions, kicking and pummeling a desk, reaching out for the fingers of Judy, kissing her sweetly, railing in frustration, kicking a hole in the painting of his mother, calming his friend Plato, laughing absurdly at the sad image of Plato's mismatched socks, and tenderly zipping up his jacket to warm his dead friend's body.

Dean's very inarticulateness was eloquent—it spoke to young audiences everywhere. He was restless, moody, and vulnerable. He was, in a word, youth. One of the ironic things about Dean's genuine perfomance as a teenager is that he was twenty-four years old when he made *Rebel Without a Cause*. Age gave his performance an edge that came from experience. Despite his age, he is considered to be the embodiment of adolescence. Dean, like J. D. Salinger's Holden Caulfield, is eternal youth. The fact of his death suspended him in time and gave him an eternal identity.

Dean emphasized insecurity, but he also was cool, offering a role model attractive to teens. His performance had flashes of humor, such as when he used the voice of the cartoon character Mr. Magoo in a line of dialogue in the mansion. This was an especially clever touch, because Jim Backus, who played Jim's father, was the voice of Mr. Magoo in the cartoons.

Surprisingly, his performance in *Rebel Without a Cause* was the only one of Dean's that did not get an Academy Award nomination. Dean received nominations for both *East of Eden* and *Giant* (1956), but Ernest Borgnine won for *Marty* (1955), and Yul Brynner won for *The King and I* (1956).

Director Nicholas Ray, whose own favorite film was *Rebel Without a Cause*, was recognized by the French as a leading auteur. He was affirmed for his personality as a socially conscious director who had a distinctive visual style. Ray's restless camera and vivid color were apt tools for Dean's sensitivity.

Dean embodied a young man trying to grow into manhood. He did not need a switchblade or a pistol to show his manhood. What is the everlasting appeal of Dean is his humanity—the rebel putting his red jacket on a dead friend and zipping it up, making a gesture of decency in a cold world. The rebel without a cause had a very basic, unspoken cause—to be as human as possible.

Impact of Event

If Marlon Brando had died at the same age that James Dean died, there would be no Brando films. Brando did not debut in films until *The Men* (1950) when he was twenty-six years old. That fact places Dean's death at the age of twenty-four and his accomplishments at that young age in stark perspective. With only three major roles in films, Dean's unfulfilled potential was incredible.

One can only imagine what Dean might have accomplished if he had lived beyond sixty years of age, as Brando did. It is almost certain that Dean would have directed because of his interest in photography and filmmaking and his creative instincts. One can compare him to Dennis Hopper, who had a minor role in *Rebel Without a Cause* and who went on to direct such films as *Easy Rider* (1969) and *Colors* (1988). Even Brando had a short-lived career as a director. One effect of his brief career is that, starring in only three films, Dean did not make any failures. Each Dean film is precious to his fans.

Dean made a major contribution to the theory of acting called method acting, of which Brando was the most famous proponent. In the Method, one is a personal actor finding himself in the part and finding the part in himself. One often hears that an actor *is* the part he is playing, but with James Dean it was true; James Dean *was* Jim Stark in *Rebel Without a Cause*. Despite being identified with youth, Dean also was able to age credibly in *Giant*, which he made the same year as *Rebel Without a Cause*, finishing shortly before his death.

Dean's sudden death in his silver Porsche Spyder as he was driving with his mechanic to take part in a race in Salinas, California, added to his image. His reckless life-style—his quest after speed—was his tragic flaw. Fate abruptly ended his quest, and audiences could relate to the glamour and horror of his death. A James Dean cult emerged that rivaled that of Rudolph Valentino after that actor's death. The adulation of Dean became an enduring phenomenon.

The three films Dean left behind are a remarkable legacy. Cal Trask in *East of Eden*, Jim Stark in *Rebel Without a Cause*, and Jett Rink in *Giant* each was a piece of Dean, but Stark was the most universal. Audiences could identify most with him since they too had gone to high school, grown up in conflicted families, and grappled with identity crises.

After his death, Dean became an icon. He had the nonconformity of John Garfield, the sensitivity of Montgomery Clift, and the smoldering sensuality of Valentino. The camera loved him and transformed him into something special and magical. Each appearance on the screen transformed him into something different from what the people who knew him expected.

Although most people idealized Dean's image, others—including Brando; Elia Kazan, who directed Dean in *East of Eden*; and George Stevens, who directed him in *Giant*—did not view Dean as heroic but as sick, self-pitying, and destructive. That only added to the image, introducing elements of impulsiveness and unpredictability. All over the world, people worshiped his memory and sought relics that were related to him.

One lasting by-product of *Rebel Without a Cause* was the curious "curse" surrounding the film. Many of its young stars died unnatural deaths: Dean died in an automobile accident, Sal Mineo was murdered, Nick Adams died of a drug overdose, and Natalie Wood drowned. This made *Rebel Without a Cause* even more provocative.

The myth of James Dean has fascinated filmmakers and critics. After Dean's death, François Truffaut, a leading French critic and subsequently a major international filmmaker, celebrated Dean, as did the critics of England, Japan, and countries all over the world. At the start of his career, director Robert Altman codirected the documentary *The James Dean Story* (1957). After leaving Hollywood, thirty years later he directed *Come Back to the Five and Dime, Jimmy Dean, Jimmy Dean*, Ed Graczyk's play about mythmaking and illusion. The play failed, but Altman got some rave reviews for his 1982 film version. *September 30, 1955* (1978) commemorates the date of Dean's death, offering a fictional account of Dean's mystique and his fans' reactions to his death.

James Dean is an American myth made in the 1950's but reaching out to other times and places. Reared in Fairmount, Indiana, educated in theater in Santa Monica, California, trained on the stage in New York City, successful in Hollywood, and buried in Fairmount, Dean was of the Midwest, the East, and the West. His career was brief, but his myth is vast.

Rebel Without a Cause focuses on the social problems of the 1950's, but it also captures the universal human condition. It is about youth, but it also is about lack of communication, a theme relevant to all times, places, and people. What makes Dean's myth enduring is his mystery. He was many things to many people. His deceptive age, his neurosis, and his moodiness gave his image an endless, fascinating ambivalence.

Bibliography

Adams, Leith, and Keith Burns, ed. *James Dean: Behind the Scenes.* Secaucus, N.Y.: Carol Publishing Group, 1990. Contains photographs from original negatives in the Warner Bros. Archives of the University of Southern California School of Cinema-Television, still photographs from Dean's three films, plus some photos that Dean took himself. Adulatory introduction by Dennis Hopper, who shares advice Dean gave to him about acting. More personal than factual.

Dalton, David. *James Dean, the Mutant King: A Biography.* San Francisco, Calif.: Straight Arrow Books, 1974. Treats Dean as a cult figure, comparing him to Osiris. Cites other cult figures, such as Elvis Presley and Bob Dylan, who were influenced by Dean. Uses sources as dissimilar as French cineast André Bazin and gossip columnist Hedda Hopper. Sometimes contrived, sometimes overwrought, but often thought-provoking.

Herndon, Venable. *James Dean: A Short Life.* Garden City, N.Y.: Doubleday, 1974. An intelligent book that transcends the traps of most movie-star biographies, although one sop to movie fans is the inclusion of an astrological reading of Dean.

Generally, Herndon's tone adds to his credibility. He studies both the myth and the factual reality of James Dean.

Stock, Dennis. *James Dean Revisited.* New York: Viking Press, 1978. Photos taken by a friend of James Dean on assignment from *Life* magazine. Includes an unpretentious introducton by Stock. Thematic photos include austere images of Dean as an Indiana farm boy and a haunting photo of the live Dean sitting in a coffin.

Vineberg, Steve. *Method Actors: Three Generations of an American Acting Style.* New York: Schirmer, 1991. A study of how the Method style was a foundation of American acting. Vineberg connects Dean to a Freudian sensibility and discusses why Dean's style affected teenagers. Relates Dean to Montgomery Clift, John Garfield, and Marlon Brando.

Tony Macklin

Cross-References

"Angry Young Men" Express Working-Class Views (1950's), p. 1454; *A Streetcar Named Desire* Brings Method Acting to the Screen (1951), p. 1487; Young Readers Embrace *The Catcher in the Rye* (1951), p. 1493; Marilyn Monroe Climbs to Stardom (1953), p. 1567; *Easy Rider* Captures the Spirit of 1960's Youth (1969), p. 2158.

O'CONNOR'S *A GOOD MAN IS HARD TO FIND* IS PUBLISHED

Category of event: Literature
Time: 1955
Locale: New York, New York

A Roman Catholic with an unerring eye for pretense and self-deception, Flannery O'Connor wrote blackly comic stories with a wicked grotesquery that unsettled her characters' and readers' complacencies

Principal personages:
> FLANNERY O'CONNOR (1925-1964), a writer of expertly crafted short stories who added several grotesque characters to Southern literature
> ROBERT FITZGERALD (1910-1985), a noted classicist and early literary friend of O'Connor
> ROBERT GIROUX (1914-), the editor at Harcourt Brace Jovanovich who encouraged O'Connor and brought *A Good Man Is Hard to Find* to print
> ROBERT LOWELL (1917-1977), a noted modern poet and literary friend who introduced O'Connor to Robert Giroux in 1949
> ELIZABETH MCKEE, the literary agent who helped to get *A Good Man Is Hard to Find* published

Summary of Event

A Roman Catholic from Milledgeville, Georgia, who was plagued most of her adult life with the disease of lupus (which caused her death at the age of thirty-nine), Flannery O'Connor was well on her way to becoming a successful writer by the time her collection of ten stories entitled *A Good Man Is Hard to Find* was published in 1955.

Having been graduated with a master's degree from the prestigious Iowa Writers' Workshop in 1947, O'Connor had already published several stories. In 1947 and 1948, she resided at the Yaddo writer's colony in upstate New York, where she met Robert and Sally Fitzgerald, Robert Lowell, and other writers and intellectuals who helped the young author to develop her craft as well as her unique vision, which combined an orthodox Catholic faith with a modern existential sense of things. In June, 1948, she took the important step of securing a literary agent, Elizabeth McKee, who helped O'Connor to publish her first novel, *Wise Blood* (1952). With the support of Robert Giroux of Harcourt Brace Jovanovich, O'Connor published her first collection of stories, *A Good Man Is Hard to Find*.

The recurrent theme of the stories in *A Good Man Is Hard to Find* involves the characters' discovery of the mystery of actuality, whether that mystery be described spiritually or existentially. In often bizarre and violent events, O'Connor's characters are shocked out of their placid, taken-for-granted worlds and into a discovery of the truth of things that often destroys forever, both spiritually and physically, their formerly secure havens of existence. The characters' prideful, rationalistic frameworks of certainty and explanation are shattered, and often, too, are their lives, as they are pushed into the harsh light of what for O'Connor was the ultimate mystery of being.

This experience is often brought about by the penetration of a grotesque, violent outsider into the smug, predictable lives of O'Connor's self-righteous characters. The invader (who often carries with him a strange aura of the religious, the holy), with his irrational perversity, challenges and calls into question their rationally organized worlds. In so doing, he undercuts their self-righteous values and forces the naïve characters to deal with him.

Nowhere is O'Connor's formula of penetration, shock, and discovery more apparent than in "A Good Man Is Hard to Find," the title story of the volume. In the opening passages, readers can well see the characteristics of the closed, self-satisfied mind. A typical Georgia family is going on vacation to Florida, and the family's grandmother sets the tone with her endless, vapid chatter. As they drive along, she babbles on monotonously, noting the sights, recalling events of her youth, and entertaining the children. In typical O'Connor fashion, this is all comically entertaining, but the grandmother and her family are ultimately portrayed as self-centered fools who are somehow asleep in their existence. They follow accepted patterns of behavior and avoid anything that calls accepted ways of living and seeing into question.

Like so many O'Connor characters in this collection of stories, however, they must lose themselves if they are ever to find themselves. When the family heads off the main road into the deep woods, the car overturns in the middle of nowhere. Upon them almost immediately is a murderous escapee from the state penitentiary. While his companions methodically and grotesquely lead the other members of the family off into the dark woods to be shot, the eerily calm, maniacally thoughtful killer begins to challenge the grandmother's heretofore safe and predictable world. Like Jesus—also a social misfit, who attacked the complacent money changers at the temple and shocked the rational Pharisees by irrationally suggesting that they should love their enemies—O'Connor's killer (who ruminates on how Jesus had "thrown everything off balance") causes the grandmother to enter a moment of spiritual and existential crisis. Her vapid mentality is arrested for a moment as she faces the cruel possibility of her own death. Suddenly, she is forced to vacate her private world and to see the killer as one of her own children. The moment she reaches out to touch him—the moment her shotgun death is delivered by the murderer—she perhaps sees into the mystery of being that had always been covered over by the dull tameness of her day-to-day existence. The quality and meaning of that experience are left unexplained and for the reader's speculation by O'Connor.

"A Good Man Is Hard to Find" is typical of the stories in the collection in that the discovery of something beyond the mundane comes in the experience of violence. The presentation is made all the more powerful by O'Connor's characteristic yoking of this radical (and cruel) event with the comic. This formula is again apparent in another story from the collection, "Good Country People." Rather than a silly, simpleminded grandmother, the protagonist who gets the shock of reality in this story is a brooding, arrogant young lady named Hulga who has a heart condition, an artificial leg, and a Ph.D. in philosophy. She has nothing but disdain for her mother and other "good country people" she finds too stupid and thoughtless to be tolerated.

Into Hulga's intellectually superior (and rather sterile) feminine world of order and certainty comes a traveling Bible salesman, aptly named Manly Pointer. Though she considers him a stupid bumpkin, she agrees to accompany him on a picnic with the intention of seducing him (sexually and intellectually) out of his innocence and into what she feels is her own honest knowledge of the nature of things. Ironically, and in typical O'Connor fashion, it is Hulga who is seduced by the young man. While in a hayloft, he gets her to remove her artificial leg, which he promptly appropriates. At that moment, like the grandmother in "A Good Man Is Hard to Find," Hulga is left in a state of startled discovery. The loss of the leg is a loss of the crutch of artificiality that had supported the pretense and arrogance that kept her from truly seeing. She is no longer in control and is painfully freed to experience pristine actuality, no matter how agonizing or destructive the experience may be.

The dramatic pattern of a violent outsider shocking a closed-minded protagonist into a discovery—all in a comic mode—characterizes every story in O'Connor's first collection. The pattern would continue to appear in almost all the fiction she consequently produced.

Impact of Event

In explaining her style and purpose as a writer, Flannery O'Connor once stated that "to the hard of hearing you shout, and for the almost-blind you draw large and startling figures." She also noted that "it is what is left over after everything explainable has been explained that makes a story worth writing and reading." Such remarks suggest that the violent alterations of perspective her characters experience in *A Good Man Is Hard to Find* are similar to what she expected her readers to experience when they are drawn into her comic world and its unexpected, and often illogical violence and grotesquery. Readers, too, are to be drawn out of their taken-for-granted perspectives and thrust into an awareness of the "realm of mystery which is the concern of the prophets."

Yet while most serious readers of O'Connor's fiction today perceive this intent, initial reaction to the publication of *A Good Man Is Hard to Find* revealed a tentativeness, a perplexity in the face of such strangely violent yet comic stories populated by misfits, displaced persons, and other lurid grotesques that seemed anything but realistic. Early reviews often merely focused on the surface of the tales, failing to address "the realm of mystery" that each story finally insists the characters and readers confront. One reviewer, for example, simply noted that "Miss O'Connor, with a direct, detached style, manages to preserve the complexity of the lives she takes up." Another cautiously observed that the author had "an unerring eye in the selection of detail" and an "exquisite ear . . . for the cadences of everyday speech."

While these remarks are sound, they do not go near to delineating the unique qualities of the stories.

Those reviewers who did attempt to comment on the grotesque, violent, and comic eccentricities of the tales were sometimes critical that the stories did not fit expected "realistic" fictional conventions. Said *The New Yorker:*

> There is a brutality in these stories, but since the brutes are as mindless as their victims, all we have, in the end, is a series of tales about creatures who collide and drown, or survive to float passively in the isolated sea of the author's compassion, which accepts them without reflecting anything.

Louis Rubin, on the other hand, saw in the stories what later readers would come to celebrate. Unlike realistic writers who were out "to make a social point" with their characters' lives, Rubin wrote, O'Connor's people "confront spiritual and moral problems, not economics." She is "in essence a religious writer," and "Knowledge of good and evil is at the heart of her stories." By 1962, sensitive readers such as Robert Fitzgerald were noting, for example, that a story such as "The Displaced Person" was about the modern "human Person displaced." "Almost all her people are displaced and some are either aware of it or become so," Fitzgerald observed. This "displacement" is the condition of contemporary humanity, lost because of its estrangement from the mystery that, for O'Connor, underpins all life. It is the burden of her stories to bring that mystery to light in the lives of her characters and readers; it is that mystery that is, finally, the essence of all of her fiction.

Modern writers who have been influenced directly by O'Connor's *A Good Man Is Hard to Find* are few. Yet her work, in its steadfast refusal to be merely realistic, its insistence on respect for a dimension of mystery (even religious mystery) in a secular age, and its biting and grotesquely comic satire of human arrogance and self-certainty has cleared the way for other writers with similar concerns, both thematic and stylistic. As different as they are from O'Connor, such writers as Walker Percy, Joyce Carol Oates, Alice Walker, John Barth, Thomas Pynchon, John Updike, and Saul Bellow come to mind.

Moreover, such contemporary writers surely admire, and in their own ways seek to emulate, the artistic qualities of her fiction so aptly noted by Frederick Crews: "her extravagant yet piercingly apt imagery, her subtle wit, her eye for the maliciously revealing detail, her infallible sense of pace and timing, [and] her knack of sliding seamlessly between the petty and the sinister."

Bibliography

Asals, Frederick. *Flannery O'Connor: The Imagination of Extremity.* Athens: University of Georgia Press, 1982. One of the best books on O'Connor's work. Asals admires her ability to balance terror and laughter, the grotesque and the understated commonplace. He sees a progression in O'Connor's work, from her early disdain for everything physical to a more ironic control of that disdain in her later fiction.

Brinkmeyer, Robert H. *The Art and Vision of Flannery O'Connor.* Baton Rouge: Louisiana State University Press, 1989. Brinkmeyer argues that O'Connor's artistic vision entertained two radically different Christian visions; fundamentalism and Catholicism. Her fictions are a constant dialogue between the two perspectives, with neither taking total control. The tension between these two forces creates the power of her writing.

Browning, Preston M. *Flannery O'Connor.* Carbondale: Southern Illinois University Press, 1974. A fine reading of O'Connor's fiction, with Søren Kierkegaard and Paul Tillich's existential notions of Christianity as a base.

Orvell, Miles. *Invisible Parade: The Fiction of Flannery O'Connor.* Philadelphia, Pa.: Temple University Press, 1972. Orvell discusses the fiction as an example of tragicomedy and notes O'Connor's debt to Edgar Allan Poe, Nathaniel Hawthorne, William Faulkner, and Nathanael West. Argues that O'Connor is at her best when she is not being religiously didactic.

Walters, Dorothy. *Flannery O'Connor.* New York: Twayne, 1973. Walters sees the fiction as falling in the broad category of "Christian tragicomedy." A good overview of O'Connor's career and work.

Richard M. Leeson

Cross-References

Cather's *My Ántonia* Promotes Regional Literature (1918), p. 452; *The Sound and the Fury* Launches Faulkner's Career (1929), p. 805; *The Diary of a Country Priest* Inspires Readers (1936), p. 1026; Pynchon's *Gravity's Rainbow* Is Published (1973), p. 2283.

POITIER EMERGES AS A FILM STAR IN
THE BLACKBOARD JUNGLE

Category of event: Motion pictures
Time: 1955
Locale: The United States

In The Blackboard Jungle *and succeeding films, Sidney Poitier helped to redefine the on-screen image of black Americans*

> *Principal personages:*
> SIDNEY POITIER (1924-   ), an American actor who rose to stardom with *The Blackboard Jungle*
> RICHARD BROOKS (1912-   ), the director of *The Blackboard Jungle*
> GLENN FORD (1916-   ), an American actor who costarred with Poitier in *The Blackboard Jungle*

Summary of Event

As late as 1954, success as an actor still eluded the young Sidney Poitier, who had to take nonacting jobs to make ends meet. True, he had come far, considering his lack of formal education. Born in the United States in 1924, he had spent his childhood in the Bahamas before returning to the United States as a teenager. Starting out in New York City as a dishwasher, he had begun taking acting lessons after answering an advertisement by the American Negro Theatre in a Harlem newspaper; with great effort, he had eliminated his West Indian accent. Stage roles were followed by an appearance in an Army Signal Corps film, *From Whence Cometh My Help* (1949).

In 1949, Poitier, despite his meager film experience, was chosen by director Joseph L. Mankiewicz to appear in *No Way Out* (1950). In the film, Dr. Luther Brooks (Poitier), a black intern in a Northern city hospital, is accused by white racist Ray Biddle (Richard Widmark) of murder after Biddle's brother dies while under Brooks's care. A race riot erupts and, ultimately, Brooks is cleared of all wrongdoing; when Biddle is injured, Brooks cares for him. Though *No Way Out* was a break for Poitier, the film was a financial failure. Poitier's next film, *Cry the Beloved Country* (1952), explored South Africa's racial problems at the family level and was a critical but not a box-office success. Between 1951 and 1954, Poitier played in only two other films: *Red Ball Express* (1952), a story about black U.S. Army soldiers in World War II; and *Go, Man, Go!* (1954), about the Harlem Globetrotters basketball team. Neither film reaped the critical and popular acclaim Poitier sought.

In 1954, however, Poitier was offered a role in a film about a young teacher's ordeal in a New York City high school. The director, Richard Brooks, a nonconformist by nature, wanted Poitier despite Poitier's rumored association with left-wing entertainers, a disadvantage in the anti-Communist climate of the times. Glenn Ford played Richard Dadier, who teaches rebellious older teenagers, too young to join the Army or get full-time jobs. Playing Gregory Miller, an intelligent but troubled youngster, Poitier, the only black in the cast, skillfully makes the viewer feel Miller's alienation and anger; here, as in later films, he projects passion without seeming menacing. Although Miller at first joins the other pupils in harassing Dadier, he is ultimately won over by Dadier's arguments and example; when the school bully attacks Dadier with a knife, Miller steps in to defend Dadier.

The scenes of student violence in *The Blackboard Jungle* shocked audiences when the film was released in 1955. In the relatively prosperous and tranquil 1950's, many film viewers could not believe that such chaotic schools actually existed. The film's vision of big-city schools, educators insisted, was exaggerated. The American ambassador to Italy pressured judges into dropping the film from the Venice Film Festival. Censors in the South objected not merely to the film's depiction of violence but also to the racial integration of Dadier's classroom.

Yet *The Blackboard Jungle* was a hit, not only because of Poitier's fine acting but also because it was released when juvenile delinquency was attracting nationwide attention. The confused and angry teenager was appearing in other films of the day, most notably the 1955 James Dean classic *Rebel Without a Cause*. Poitier played a character with whom millions of young Americans, black and white, could identify. The pulsating rhythms of "Rock Around the Clock," included as background music, made the film unforgettable.

The furor over *The Blackboard Jungle* made agents and directors aware of Poitier. An aggressive new agent found Poitier a role in the television play *A Man Is Ten Feet Tall*. In this play, and in the film version, *Edge of the City* (1957), a black dockworker dies defending a white coworker against a bullying white foreman. In *The Defiant Ones*, a big hit of 1958, Poitier played one of two escaped convicts—one black, the other (played by Tony Curtis) white—who come to depend on each other during their flight from the law. At the film's end, the black prisoner forgoes a chance to avoid recapture when his white partner cannot join him. After 1958, Poitier played in at least one film a year for an entire decade.

Later films included *A Raisin in the Sun* (1961), about a struggling Chicago black family; the Oscar-winning movie *Lilies of the Field* (1963), in which a wandering black handyman helps German nuns in the Southwest to build a chapel; and *A Patch of Blue* (1965), in which a black journalist befriends a poor, blind white girl. In 1967, Poitier was in three hits. *In the Heat of the Night* showed a bigoted Southern white sheriff coming to respect the Northern black detective who helps him to crack a murder case; in *Guess Who's Coming to Dinner*, a wealthy white newspaper publisher is shocked to learn that his daughter plans to marry a black man but eventually approves the match; and in *To Sir with Love*, a black London schoolteacher wins his white pupils' respect.

From 1955 to the late 1960's, Poitier was almost the sole black male playing serious roles in American films (Harry Belafonte and Sammy Davis, Jr., who acted sporadically in films, were primarily singers and dancers). From 1968 on, Poitier's near-monopoly was broken; more and more black actors (some playing in violence-filled "blaxploitation" films) made their way in films. In the 1970's, Poitier, now both actor and director, turned out such films as 1972's *Buck and the Preacher* (about ex-slaves' migration to the West), 1973's *A Warm December*, and 1975's *Let's Do It Again*. In the late 1970's, his influence waning, he retired from acting to write his autobiography; he continued to direct and did not act again until 1988.

Impact of Event

As late as the 1930's, most Hollywood films portayed blacks as buffoons, servants, athletes, dancers, or musicians. World War II made white filmmakers more sensitive to racial injustice; some began to produce films treating racial issues more openly and giving blacks a more dignified screen image. Stanley Kramer, who brought out *Home of the Brave* (1949), about a troubled black war veteran, directed Poitier in the racial "message" movies *The Defiant Ones, Pressure Point* (1962), and *Guess Who's Coming to Dinner*. From the appearance of *The Blackboard Jungle* in 1955 onward, Poitier benefited from this trend toward fairer treatment of blacks on the screen; he also did much himself to promote the trend.

In only one post-1955 film, a 1959 remake of *Porgy and Bess*, did Poitier play an obviously stereotypical role. In most films, Poitier's screen persona was that of a competent, likable black man who channels whatever racial resentments he has into productive activity, helping whites who are either no smarter than he is or are his intellectual or moral inferiors. In *No Way Out*, the black intern played by Poitier is almost saintly; his white accuser (and later patient) is a small-time crook. Although the racial issue is muted in *Lilies of the Field*, its hero's efficiency is a clear refutation of stereotypes of black incompetence. In *In the Heat of the Night*, the intellectual superiority of Poitier's character to the redneck sheriff played by Rod Steiger is obvious. Even in *The Blackboard Jungle*, the troubled youth played by Poitier is intelligent and salvageable; the incorrigible school bully who attacks Dadier with a knife is played by white actor Vic Morrow.

In many films (although not in *The Blackboard Jungle*), Poitier presents an image of a well-trained professional black man articulate in standard English; this was new for the time. In *No Way Out*, he plays a medical intern; in *All the Young Men* (1960), a black officer commanding white troops in the Korean War; in the suspense drama *The Slender Thread* (1965), a suicide hotline worker; in *Pressure Point*, a prison psychiatrist who interrogates a Nazi; in *A Patch of Blue* and *The Bedford Incident* (1965), a journalist; and in *To Sir with Love*, a teacher. Poitier's character in *Guess Who's Coming to Dinner*, a young white woman's fiancé, is a world-famous black physician.

In two films, Poitier crossed a barrier by playing roles originally designed for whites. In *The Bedford Incident*, he is a journalist trapped in a submarine with a trigger-happy anti-Soviet zealot of a commander (Richard Widmark). In *Duel at Diablo* (1966), Poitier portrays a cowboy gunfighter.

Yet one barrier was hard to break; that of portraying a black man, on the screen, as both sexual and romantic. In *No Way Out*, Poitier's character is happily married;

in his other films up to 1965, including *The Blackboard Jungle*, Poitier's characters have no love interest at all. In *A Patch of Blue*, Poitier's character ends a budding love interest by having the blind white girl sent away to a special school. In *Guess Who's Coming to Dinner*, the viewer catches only a brief glimpse, through the rear-view mirror of a taxicab, of a kiss exchanged between Poitier's character and his white fiancée; the couple leaves the country shortly after their marriage. The man upon whom Poitier's character in *To Sir with Love* was based had had an interracial romance with a fellow teacher, but the romance was omitted from the film. A frank interracial love scene occurs in *The Lost Man* (1969), but that film failed. *For Love of Ivy* (1968) was the first film in which Poitier had a frankly sexual romance (with bedroom scene) with a black woman.

After the release of *Edge of the City* and *The Defiant Ones*, Poitier came to symbolize for many moviegoers the dream of interracial harmony. Six feet, two inches tall, he was considered handsome by blacks and whites alike. To many blacks eager to see one of their own in dignified roles on the silver screen, Poitier's success seemed a confirmation of their faith in a fairer and more racially integrated future. For, while other black actors had played nonstereotypical roles on film before, none had had Poitier's staying power or drawing power.

If Poitier shunned the old stereotype of the black as servile buffoon, he was slow to adopt the newer stereotype of the black as revolutionary. While the racial angle in *The Blackboard Jungle* is not ignored, Poitier's Gregory Miller is more a rebellious youth than a rebellious black. The black militant played by Poitier in *Buck and the Preacher* is safely remote in time (the 1870's); the black militants he plays in *Something of Value* (1957) and *The Mark of the Hawk* (1958) are safely remote in space (British colonial Africa). When, in *The Lost Man*, Poitier did play a violent black militant in modern urban America, the film failed financially. Poitier's reluctance to play militants on screen, a reluctance that alienated some blacks in the late 1960's, reflected a need to make films palatable to white viewers.

The question of to what extent Poitier promoted black progress in American films, and in America as a whole, is hard to answer. Having made progress himself, Poitier opened a path for others. From 1969 onward, he pushed to get blacks hired on film-crew jobs for his films. Poitier's example encouraged younger black actors such as James Earl Jones, Louis Gossett, Jr., and Danny Glover to try for success in Hollywood. Yet four decades after Poitier rose to stardom, blacks were still struggling to achieve equal opportunities in American films.

Bibliography

Bergman, Carol. *Sidney Poitier.* New York: Chelsea House, 1988. Concise and richly illustrated; one of few easily available Poitier biographies. Written for young adults; useful for general readers of all ages. Provides details on Poitier's early life and his struggles in the early years. Attention paid to individual films varies. List of films, one-page chronology, bibliography, index.

Bogle, Donald. *Toms, Coons, Mulattoes, Mammies, and Bucks: An Interpretive His-

tory of Blacks in American Films. New York: Continuum, 1989. This survey discusses (among other things) Poitier's role in *The Blackboard Jungle* and his career as a whole. Offers insights into why Poitier succeeded while other black screen actors of the post-World War II years failed. Sees Poitier's characters as confirming some stereotypes while refuting others. Photographs; index.

Cripps, Thomas. "The Dark Spot in the Kaleidoscope: Black Images in American Film." In *The Kaleidoscopic Lens: How Hollywood Views Ethnic Groups,* edited by Randall M. Miller. Englewood, N.J.: Jerome S. Ozer, 1980. An interesting comparison of Poitier to Harry Belafonte, Sammy Davis, Jr., and 1930's film comic Stepin Fetchit. Sees Poitier playing a helper of whites, even in *The Blackboard Jungle*; as embodying a "culture of professionalism" spanning the racial divide; and as benefiting from Hollywood's post-World War II "conscience liberalism." Photographs, notes, index.

Keyser, Lester. *The Cinema of Sidney Poitier.* San Diego: A. S. Barnes, 1980. Discusses all Poitier's pre-1977 films, even the most obscure. Especially informative on the public's response to *The Blackboard Jungle* in 1955. Photographs, detailed filmography, bibliography, chapter notes, index. Based on interviews and printed sources.

Leab, Daniel J. *From Sambo to Superspade: The Black Experience in Motion Pictures.* Boston: Houghton Mifflin, 1975. This survey places Poitier's career in the context of Hollywood's well-meaning efforts to correct demeaning racial stereotypes. Sees Poitier as creating a new stereotype, the "ebony saint." Stresses the importance of *The Blackboard Jungle* as a turning point in Poitier's career. Photographs, endnotes, index, bibliography.

Poitier, Sidney. *This Life.* New York: Alfred A. Knopf, 1980. This autobiography, toughly realistic in outlook, is peppered with salty language. Contains details on both private and public life. Provides a detailed account of how Poitier got the role in *The Blackboard Jungle* and of the problems caused by his associations with left-wing entertainers. Includes photographs.

Walker, Alexander. "Black Is Box-Office: Ethnic Stars." In *Stardom: the Hollywood Phenomenon.* New York: Stein & Day, 1970. Written just as Poitier's popularity had crested. A British critic offers valuable insights into the reasons for Poitier's appeal to white moviegoers. The treatment of sexuality in Poitier's films is also discussed. Compares Poitier with newer black actors of late 1960's. Index of actors and films.

Zinman, David H. "The Blackboard Jungle (1955)." In *Fifty from the Fifties: Vintage Films from America's Mid-Century.* New Rochelle, N.Y.: Arlington House, 1979. Presents a detailed plot summary and photographs of scenes from the film. Provides interesting information, gleaned from *The New York Times,* on contemporary reaction to the film. List of film credits, including full cast of characters and names of performers, index of actors and film titles, and a selected bibliography.

Paul D. Mageli

Cross-References

Hallelujah Is the First Important Black Musical (1929), p. 772; *Stormy Weather* Offers New Film Roles to African Americans (1940's), p. 1159; Berry's "Maybellene" Popularizes Rock and Roll (1955), p. 1635; *I Spy* Debuts to Controversy (1965), p. 2044; *Do the Right Thing* Establishes Lee as a World-Class Director, p. 2641.

BOULEZ'S *LE MARTEAU SANS MAÎTRE* PREMIERES IN BADEN-BADEN

Category of event: Music
Time: June 18, 1955
Locale: Baden-Baden, West Germany

The premiere of Pierre Boulez's nine-movement serial work Le Marteau sans maître, *with text by René Char, catapulted Boulez to world attention*

Principal personages:
PIERRE BOULEZ (1925-   ), a French composer, conductor, and spokesman for musical modernism
RENÉ CHAR (1907-1988), a French modernist poet who supplied Boulez with texts for *Le Visage nuptial* and *Le Marteau sans maître*

Summary of Event

Sometimes acclaimed as the greatest French composer since Claude Debussy, Pierre Boulez has inspired controversy in his roles as composer, conductor, and champion of musical modernism. As a composer, he sided with the serialism of the German composers Arnold Schoenberg and Anton von Webern against his native French tradition. As a conductor, he succeeded the extrovert romantic Leonard Bernstein as music director of the New York Philharmonic, where his advocacy of modernist works failed to garner audience enthusiasm but where his clear, precise approach earned critical respect. As a polemicist and spokesman for modernism, he has been unsparing in his criticism of composers whose works he sees as unprogressive (such as Johannes Brahms and Giuseppe Verdi) or who have been seen to betray modernism by making use of or reverting to earlier musical styles (such as Richard Strauss and Igor Stravinsky).

An enigmatic intellectual, Boulez has been intensely private about his personal life and has been contemptuous of bourgeois French culture, although he has received numerous honors and positions from his country's government. It is not surprising that he would adopt some of the characteristic attributes of French theorists, such as clarity and rationality; but in Boulez's case, despite the charm and affability he has shown on social occasions, he has been accused of a general coldness and guardedness. Boulez, both as man and artist, has valued theory and system over imagination and invention.

Although Boulez has been extravagantly admired by a coterie of intellectual musicians, his own compositions have failed to generate much popular enthusiasm or to make concessions to popular taste. Because of its intellectual severity, Boulez's music could be said to provide more pleasure to the eye than to the ear. As biographer Joan Peyser has noted, "as ungratifying as it is to the ear, the Third Sonata is beautiful to the eye." Boulez is said to be largely indifferent to recordings of serious music, preferring instead to enjoy music by the reading of scores.

Unlike other avant-garde composers since World War II, however, Boulez has been thoroughly engaged with all aspects of modern music, as a composer, pianist, conductor, and polemicist. His biographers have routinely complained about his refusal to discuss details of his personal life, although other celebrities might envy his success in keeping his past a closed book. He garnered early attention for the severity of his rejection of the past. He has always professed a hatred for the music of such pillars of the symphonic and operatic repertory as Brahms, Verdi, and Peter Ilich Tchaikovsky—not necessarily because of the natural jealousy of the theorist for the melodic warmth and popular appeal of these old masters, but because of their unprogressive qualities as composers; it is the experimenter's natural dislike of consolidators.

Despite his youthful passion for twelve-tone music, which he first heard in 1945, Boulez later turned against the giants of musical modernism, Arnold Schoenberg and Igor Stravinsky—the latter for reverting to neoclassicism in works following the groundbreaking *The Rite of Spring* (1913) and the former for not extending the implications of the abandonment of tonality into a total theoretical system. The composer who retained Boulez's admiration was Anton von Webern, who best and most rigorously put the precepts of Schoenberg into practice.

Boulez regarded his discovery of serialism, or twelve-tone music, as a revelation. Under the guidance of his two teachers, Olivier Messiaen and René Leibowitz, Boulez came to grasp the need for a new theoretical system; as Peyser explains it, he "was obsessed with the formulation of a theoretical system that would serve composers in the future as tonality had served them in the past." Since both Stravinsky and Schoenberg had capitulated to tradition, it remained for Webern to create a totally serial music, in which pitch, timbre, rhythm, and color were all organized by rigorous discipline and logic. Boulez spoke of wanting to clean up Western music since the Renaissance by doubting the systems of the past and putting music on a more rational basis, as René Descartes had done for philosophy. (If Boulez is modern music's Descartes, the sensuous Catholic composer Messiaen, Boulez's teacher, would be its Blaise Pascal.)

The youthful Boulez proclaimed an ultrarational post-Webernian serialism. He asserted his credo in a 1952 article, "Eventuellement": "Our first determination will be to give it [his technique] autonomy, and, furthermore, to link rhythmic structures to serial structures by common organizations, which will also include the other characteristics of sound: intensity, mode of attack, timbre."

Boulez and his former teacher Messiaen collaborated in a performance of his landmark early work for piano, *Structures I* (1952); although Stravinsky was impressed by the integrity of this hard, clean work, he could not resist complaining of its "arrogance." Yet within two years, Boulez had moved dramatically beyond the theoretical severity of *Structures I* to his first undisputed masterpiece, *Le Marteau sans maître* (the hammer without a master). Set to a 1934 poem by the French modernist poet René Char, four of the work's nine movements involve the voice. Only the third movement can be considered a "song," and the vocal settings are actually surrounded by unusual instrumental commentaries. The work goes beyond the rigidly interpreted serialism of *Structures I* and beyond the dry abstraction of most of the academic serial compositions of the 1950's. In keeping with his admiration for the early revolutionary works of Schoenberg, Boulez called *Le Marteau sans maître* "my *Pierrot Lunaire*," referring to Schoenberg's comparably innovative treatment of voice and unusual instrumental combinations. Boulez's exotic use of the contralto voice, alto flute, viola, guitar, vibraphone, xylorimba, and percussion in various combinations has been widely imitated.

Char's poems had previously provided Boulez with texts for his vocal music, beginning with *Le Visage nuptial* (1950; the nuptial face). The apparent impersonality of the verse (as typified by a key line from *Le Visage nuptial*, "Leave me, let me wait unspeaking") must have appealed to the guarded Boulez, who utilized Char's verse again in *Le Marteau sans maître*. Its message is again impersonal and obscure but seems to propose the doom of civilization; the impersonal implication of its title, "the hammer without a master," fits in with Boulez's determination to remove personality from musical expression. For his later masterpiece *Pli selon pli* (1960; fold according to fold), Boulez turned to the work of the nineteenth century Symbolist Stéphane Mallarmé, precisely because of the tightness and obscurity of that poet's verse.

Impact of Event

Le Marteau sans maître marked the end of Pierre Boulez's early period of compositional creativity. Despite his youthful polemics against his erstwhile heroes Schoenberg and Stravinsky, Boulez paid implicit homage to both in his early vocal masterwork. Its organization and inventive use of instrumental combinations is comparable to Schoenberg's *Pierrot Lunaire* (1912), and its complex notation and frequent changes in tempo owe something to the example of Stravinsky, especially to *The Rite of Spring*.

Since Boulez was determined to forge a new musical system based on the rigorous application of theory rather than on imagination and subjective invention, it is difficult to assess the extent of influences on Boulez's compositional strategy or the influence of Boulez on others. His clarity, coldness, and rationality have been frequently noted; he himself sought a hard, clean, impersonal, and nonrhetorical music. His biographers have frequently been tempted into Freudian interpretations of his personality and music. Peyser cites the composer's sister, who has said that "my brother is completely closed"; Peyser tentatively alludes to the Freudian theory that a child who succeeds a dead sibling will be guarded and impersonal (Boulez is actually the second Pierre in his family, since he followed a deceased sibling by that name). Boulez gained a reputation for living in a succession of spare and tidy apartments with few bourgeois comforts, for being neat and for never shopping, and for generally living with the austerity of the sternly self-disciplined philosopher Ludwig Wittgenstein, who similarly avoided creature comforts.

Although she admires his music and finds him personally affable, Peyser admits the truth of the general perception of Boulez as cold and aloof and concludes her study with a criticism: "Boulez's inability to engage in a genuine dialogue with whatever is different from himself—whether people or earlier musical periods— seems to be the flaw that pulls him down." Boulez's outspoken dislike of many major composers of the past has been explained as the reflexive distaste of the natural innovator for those such as Brahms and Verdi, who consolidate older styles; even more culpable, in his view, are those who, like Stravinsky and Richard Strauss, retreat from experimentation into neoclassicism.

He has been equally unsparing of his compositional contemporaries. He turned against his youthful teachers, Messiaen and René Leibowitz. He overcame his initial attraction to John Cage, whose experiments with serialism and chance music (for which Boulez coined the term "aleatory music") he had found appealing, with a characteristically unkind dismissal: "He was refreshing but not very bright. His freshness came from an absence of knowledge." Although Cage's passion for the music of chance seems totally at odds with Boulez's belief in systematic rigor, both shared the anti-Romantic determination to remove the individual personality from composition. (Cage's famous 1952 celebration of total silence, *4' 33"*, was as thorough an attack on the musical past as was Boulez's determination to "clean up" Western music since the Renaissance.) Boulez has spoken contemptuously of those American academic serial composers (except for Milton Babbitt, whose rigor he admires) who were inspired by Boulez's theoretical integrity. His career has been shadowed by a kind of professional double, the German composer Karlheinz Stockhausen, and the two have alternated as the most visible spokesmen for their generation of avant garde composers.

Boulez has also been criticized for his lack of enthusiasm for native French tradition, a disinterest illustrated most obviously by his abandonment of his country for Germany in 1958 and by later moves to England and America.

When his interest in conducting expanded after his first period of compositional creativity had crested in the wake of *Le Marteau sans maître*, Boulez was rewarded with the music directorships of the British Broadcasting Corporation (BBC) and, later, the New York Philharmonic. The contrast of Boulez's conducting style with those of his predecessor, Leonard Bernstein, and successor, Zubin Mehta, is polar. Where Bernstein was romantic, impetuous, gregarious, and vulnerable, Boulez was clear, analytical, and precise; Bernstein was theatrical and warm, but he seemed not to have Boulez's remarkable sense of pitch and instrumental balance. Bernstein was beloved; Boulez was admired but scarcely regarded with audience passion. The orchestra members admired his precision, but the general audience, in one apt critical phrase, "found him a dry dog," although he raised the general standard of performance.

What one critic has written of Schoenberg is equally true of Boulez as a composer and conductor: "The artist and his public each conceived the other as a threat." If

Boulez was critical and often contemptuous of the musical past, the concert audience repaid the compliment; concert attendance and subscriptions declined under Boulez's tenure as music director of the New York Philharmonic. Nevertheless, Boulez has been credited with having provided high-quality performances, even when performing works of composers he disliked.

As a composer, he has not endeared himself to the popular audience. Yet he can certainly be commended for his theoretical rigor, for stretching his listeners' perception of musical forms and structures, and for the clarity and integrity of his vision. Whereas his early *Structures I* pursues the logic of total serialism, *Le Marteau sans maître* boldly moves beyond it to an intriguing set of experiments with form, timbre, and color. For most listeners, these experiments are more appealing to the eye or the mind than the ear, but the fact that Boulez will probably never win broad popular enthusiasm does not minimize his integrity as a theorist or his astonishing creativity as a visionary figure.

Bibliography

Boulez, Pierre. *Boulez on Music Today.* Translated by Susan Bradshaw and Richard Rodney Bennett. Cambridge, Mass.: Harvard University Press, 1971. Fascinating, if forbiddingly technical, discussion of the composer's own musical goals and technique.

Caws, Mary Ann. *René Char.* Boston: Twayne, 1977. Good critical study of the elusive French poet who supplied the texts for several of Boulez's vocal works. Caws chooses a fine single line to illustrate the teasing and opaque nature of Char's verse: "The poem is the fulfilled love of desire as it remains desire."

Glock, William, ed. *Pierre Boulez: A Symposium.* London: Eulenberg Books, 1986. Collects a variety of assessments of Boulez as composer, conductor, and ceaseless musical experimenter. Peter Heyworth's biographical sketch briskly surveys the composer's first fifty years; Susan Bradshaw analyzes *Le Marteau sans maître.*

Griffiths, Paul. *Boulez.* New York: Oxford University Press, 1978. Includes a helpful analysis of *Le Marteau sans maître* and a good assessment of its pivotal nature. In Griffith's view, the work is genuinely free of "the quasi-narrative forms of tonality" and the severe theoretical calculation of *Structures I.*

Johnson, Robert Sherlaw. *Messiaen.* Rev. ed. Berkeley: University of California Press, 1980. Good critical study of one of Boulez's two most important teachers.

Peyser, Joan. *Boulez: Composer, Conductor, Enigma.* New York: Schirmer, 1976. Controversial biography of the composer, by a specialist in "debunking" biographies who later revealed intimate secrets about Leonard Bernstein and George Gershwin. Written toward the end of Boulez's tenure as music director of the New York Philharmonic, the book is admiring of Boulez's integrity as a musical experimenter but more critical of his personal severity and aloofness.

Salzman, Eric. *Twentieth-Century Music: An Introduction.* Englewood Cliffs, N.J.: Prentice-Hall, 1967. Concisely traces Boulez's movement from a "totally organized, totally serial super-rationalist" to the much more expansive composer of

Le Marteau sans maître, who sought to manipulate "fluctuating masses, colors, densities, and intensities of sound."

Byron Nelson

Cross-References

Schoenberg Breaks with Tonality (1908), p. 193; Webern's *Six Pieces for Large Orchestra* Premieres in Vienna (1913), p. 367; Schoenberg Develops His Twelve-Tone System (1921), p. 528; Berg's *Wozzeck* Premieres in Berlin (1925), p. 680; Cage's *4'33"* Premieres (1952), p. 1546.

DICKINSON'S POEMS ARE PUBLISHED IN FULL FOR THE FIRST TIME

Category of event: Literature
Time: September, 1955
Locale: Cambridge, Massachusetts

The publication of Thomas H. Johnson's edition of Emily Dickinson's poems finally gave readers a complete and accurate text and led to an even higher echelon in American literature for this popular poet

Principal personages:
> EMILY DICKINSON (1830-1886), the celebrated Amherst, Massachusetts, poet
> THOMAS HERBERT JOHNSON (1902-1985), the editor of *The Poems of Emily Dickinson* (1955), the first complete and definitive edition
> THEODORA WARD (1890-1974), a granddaughter of two of Dickinson's favorite correspondents and Johnson's assistant
> R. W. FRANKLIN (1937-   ), the editor of *The Manuscript Books of Emily Dickinson* (1981)

Summary of Event

Of the many poems Emily Dickinson wrote between the 1850's and the time of her death in 1886, only a handful were published in her lifetime, and even those were published locally and anonymously. Even her sister Lavinia, who lived with her, was amazed at the bulk of Emily's poetry when she examined it after Emily's death. Mabel Loomis Todd, the wife of an Amherst College professor, and Thomas Wentworth Higginson, a man of letters to whom the poet had sent selected poems as far back as 1862, were enlisted to prepare some of them for publication.

They selected 115 from the sixty bundles of poems that the poet had sewn together, including two of the earliest Higginson had seen, "Safe in Their Alabaster Chambers," a wry poem about the faithful dead, and one beginning

> I'll tell you how the Sun rose—
> A Ribbon at a time—
> The Steeples swam in Amethyst—
> The news, like Squirrels, ran—

but Higginson, apparently apprehensive about their readability, attempted to improve various aspects of the poems: capitalization and punctuation, meter, rhyme, even the vocabulary itself.

Despite its editorial imperfections, the popularity of the book, when issued in 1890, encouraged a second volume in 1891. Todd, working alone, included more poetry in an edition of Dickinson's letters in 1894 and a further batch of poems in

1896, but even at that point, more than two-thirds of these short but striking poems remained unpublished at century's end.

In the early decades of the twentieth century, Martha Dickinson Bianchi, the poet's niece, transcribed—not always accurately—and published more poems, and in 1945 *Bolts of Melody*, the result of further labors by Todd and by her daughter Millicent Todd Bingham, essentially completed the task of bringing Dickinson's poems to the public. Clearly, a complete and freshly edited compilation was called for, and after the Dickinson manuscripts passed to Harvard University's Houghton Library in 1950, Thomas H. Johnson undertook the task.

Johnson, a secondary school teacher in New Jersey, was a well-qualified scholar. He held a Harvard University doctorate and had discovered and edited the long-forgotten poetry of Edward Taylor, who, as a result of Johnson's work, became generally recognized as America's foremost colonial poet. Johnson also considered the fact of his own Connecticut Valley origins as an important qualification; to his way of thinking, the valley had shaped Dickinson, who had lived her whole life in Amherst, Massachusetts, even more than it had Taylor, who came there as an adult. Johnson found a valuable assistant in Theodora Ward, who was then completing an edition of Dickinson's letters to her grandparents, Dr. and Mrs. Josiah Gilbert Holland.

Because Dickinson had left alternative versions of words, lines, and sometimes whole poems, often making determination of her final intention impossible, Johnson decided upon a variorum edition. Because Dickinson most often employed dashes rather than commas and periods, Johnson restored them where previous editors had substituted conventional punctuation. Because he thought that the edition should reflect Dickinson's poetic development, he endeavored to organize the poems chronologically as nearly as possible, relying on internal evidence, handwriting, and any other available means, instead of the typically thematic organizational schemes of previous editors.

Johnson and Ward did not find their task an easy one. Dickinson wrote a legible hand, but the editors were faced with many variants, and even in a variorum edition, priority must be assigned to one reading. In the poem beginning "Blazing in Gold and quenching in Purple," for example, the sun is described as "stooping as low as" a certain window, which is variously described as a "kitchen," "oriel," and "Otter's." Johnson favored "Otter's," doubtless on the grounds that having achieved it, a person as imaginative as Dickinson would certainly not have discarded it for "kitchen" and probably not for "oriel." Any reader of this edition, however, would know that Emily had considered all three possibilities.

For each poem, a conjectural year of composition was supplied; sometimes, as in the case of the favorite anthology poem "Safe in Their Alabaster Chambers," Johnson could determine that Dickinson had composed different versions of the same poem in different years. Sometimes he had to decide whether two similar poems represented variations of the same poem or two distinct poems. He numbered the poems, for Dickinson had rarely supplied titles. He dated number 1 "1850," when

Dickinson had turned twenty, and number 1648 "c. 1886," the year of her death. There remained 127 more poems and fragments, mostly undated, which he placed at the end, bringing the total to 1775 poems and substantial fragments. For five years, during which time Johnson chaired the English department in his preparatory school, he worked out solutions to these and numerous other problems, and in 1955 the edition, in three volumes, was ready for publication by the Harvard University Press.

Although the work over which he and Theodora Ward had labored would radically alter the relationship between Dickinson and her enthusiastic readers, Johnson knew that few people other than scholars and advanced students would consult these volumes with their scholarly apparatus, and three years later he issued a general reader's edition of the complete poems in which only a few of the more interesting variants were given. Thus, sixty-eight years after Todd and Higginson's first selection, and seventy-two years after the poet's death, it was possible for lovers of Emily Dickinson to consult a complete, reliable, and convenient edition of her poetry.

Impact of Event

Reviewers of the 1955 edition of Dickinson's complete poems recognized it as a major publishing event. The work of Johnson and Ward now permitted a look at the development of Dickinson's art over a period of thirty-five years in a text more visually suggestive of the Dickinson manuscripts. With her capitalization of important nouns and the characteristic dashes restored, the poems now looked different on the page. Other less immediately obvious differences, however, mattered much more. Dickinson's imagination had so far outstripped that of her earlier editors that they had made totally unwarranted verbal "corrections." For example, Todd and Higginson had printed the subsequent anthology favorite "I never saw a Moor," with its final line expressing the poet's sureness of the location of a heaven she had never seen, as "As if the chart were given" instead of "As if the Checks were given." Having conventional minds, they did not see that Dickinson, always fascinated by railroads, had based her metaphor on the checks the conductor distributes to indicate passengers' destinations.

The first editors had made more flagrant changes in "Dare you see a Soul *at the White Heat?*" Dickinson's line "It quivers from the Forge" became "Its quivering substance plays" for the sake of a rhyme with "blaze," although Dickinson, who loved slant rhymes, had deliberately rhymed "Blaze" and "Forge" not once but twice in the poem (the second time, Todd and Higginson let it stand, presumably because they could not think of an improvement). In the same poem, Dickinson's "Anvil's even ring" was altered to "anvil's even din" for the sake of a rhyme with "within." Yet these same editors altered the fifth line of the poem, "Has vanquished Flame's conditions," to "Has sated flame's conditions," thus demonstrating how very poor an ear they had for the sound effects that the poet had wrought. Dozens of similar editorial offenses might be cited.

The most important aspect of Johnson's work, then, was restoration. Dickinson enthusiasts could read what she wrote in essentially the order of composition, not what amateur editors thought she wrote or thought she should have written. In addition, the new edition went a long way to dispel the long-prevalent notion that Dickinson's poetry was haphazard, eccentric, and extravagant. Students could see the evidence of her precision and deliberation. For the first time, it became clear that Dickinson would reject adequate but facile rhymes in favor of more powerful diction, that she would violate conventions of mechanics and sometimes even grammar for the sake of something that felt poetically right.

Of course, the close study that Johnson's variorum and general readers' editions encouraged and deserved led to further insights, some of them resulting in challenges. In one of the most important, R. W. Franklin argued in a series of books and articles that Johnson, like his predecessors, had downgraded the importance of Dickinson's carefully arranged fascicles (pages of poems fastened together) in his concentration on a chronological ordering of the poems and thus had actually violated the integrity of her work. In addition, he also doubted the capacity of print to simulate visual features such as punctuation. In 1981, Franklin issued a two-volume facsimile edition of the fascicles. While valuable as a supplement to Johnson's text, this edition was incomplete, for Dickinson had not gathered all of her poems into bundles, and some of them had actually been written on backs of envelopes and other scraps of paper.

By focusing attention on the fascicles, however, which Mabel Todd had disassembled (fortunately not without prudent notations permitting later reconstruction), Franklin made another important contribution. He established that although Dickinson—perhaps disappointed by the professional critic Higginson's decidedly qualified approval of her work, perhaps intuiting that few or none of her contemporaries would be likely to appreciate it better—had left her poetry unpublished, she had, in grouping her poetry according to a plan, done the kind of work that poets do when readying their poems for publication. Franklin went as far as maintaining that the sixty sequences, each containing from eleven to twenty-five poems, constituted an organic structure somewhat like that of Walt Whitman's "Song of Myself" (1855) or T. S. Eliot's *The Waste Land* (1922).

Although Franklin's conclusions have not won anything like universal agreement, he put to rout the argument that because Dickinson's poems are short and discrete, she cannot be accorded the status of a major poet. Whether the nearly eighteen hundred poems constitute an "organic structure" or not, they form a body of work remarkable not only for its fertile images, astonishing diction, and flashes of insight but also for its coherence and integrity.

The legacy of Thomas H. Johnson is the virtually unanimous acceptance of Emily Dickinson alongside the erstwhile all-male American literary greats of the nineteenth century: Ralph Waldo Emerson, Nathaniel Hawthorne, Edgar Allan Poe, Henry David Thoreau, Herman Melville, Walt Whitman, Mark Twain, and Henry James. As one of the chief editors of the influential *Literary History of the United States* (1948, with several later revisions), Johnson might have been expected to ensure Dickinson more attention than literary history had accorded her before, but it is interesting that the more recent *Columbia Literary History of the United States* (1988) devotes even more space to her. The greatness of Emily Dickinson had always been there, but full recognition waited upon an edition worthy of her and upon the ensuing editorial and critical work of those in Johnson's debt. Johnson himself published a biography of Dickinson in the same year that his variorum edition appeared, and Theodora Ward became his associate in a later edition of the poet's letters.

In or around Dickinson's most prolific year, 1862, when she averaged nearly a poem a day, she wrote a poem beginning, "This is my letter to the World/ That never wrote to Me. . . . " Nearly a century later, the letter was delivered.

Bibliography

Dickinson, Emily. *The Complete Poems of Emily Dickinson.* Edited by Thomas H. Johnson. Boston: Little, Brown, 1960. A convenient and authoritative one-volume edition with a subject index as well as an index of first lines. Follows the arrangement of the variorum edition. Gives variants in some of the more interesting instances. The best source of Dickinson's poetry for the specialist.

_____. *The Manuscript Books of Emily Dickinson.* Edited by Ralph W. Franklin. 2 vols. Cambridge, Mass.: Harvard University Press, 1981. Carrying out the logic of his previous work, Franklin argues that Dickinson's poetry so far resists reduction to printed form that the appropriate edition is a facsimile one, which he provides as a further step in acquainting the reader with the essential Emily Dickinson. Since she did not gather all her poems into fascicles, however, this edition necessarily omits some of the poems of the Johnson edition.

_____. *The Poems of Emily Dickinson.* Edited by Thomas H. Johnson. 3 vols. Cambridge, Mass.: Harvard University Press, 1955. Consulted directly mainly by scholars and advanced students, but directly or indirectly the medium through which most readers now encounter one of America's greatest poets. Contains separate introductions on the creation and editing of the poems and on Dickinson's handwriting as well as notes on the text. Indispensable for serious students of the poet.

Franklin, R. W. *The Editing of Emily Dickinson: A Reconsideration.* Madison: University of Wisconsin Press, 1967. An examination of the work of previous editors of Dickinson leading to a reevaluation of Johnson's work. Criticizes Johnson's decision to organize the poems chronologically instead of retaining the poet's fascicle structure. Contains reproductions of selected Dickinson manuscripts. Franklin's sometimes supercilious tone toward his predecessors can be annoying.

Miller, Ruth. *The Poetry of Emily Dickinson.* Middletown, Conn.: Wesleyan University Press, 1968. A long, sometimes incoherent book marred by unnecessary sniping at other critics but containing a valuable eighty-five-page section on Dickinson's fascicle groupings. One of the earliest critics to consider closely the manuscript evidence in interpreting Dickinson's poetry, Miller argues for a symbolic narrative thread in each of the fascicles.

Rosenbaum, S. P., ed. *A Concordance to the Poems of Emily Dickinson.* Ithaca,

N.Y.: Cornell University Press, 1964. An inevitable outgrowth of Johnson's work and one of the most valuable tools for the analysis of Dickinson's poetry. While Johnson's indexes facilitate considerable study of the poet's vocabulary and patterns of imagery, the concordance is a handier and more thorough aid to such investigations.

Robert P. Ellis

Cross-References

Harriet Monroe Founds *Poetry* Magazine (1912), p. 314; The Imagist Movement Shakes Up Poetry (1912), p. 326; Yeats Publishes *The Wild Swans at Coole* (1917), p. 440; Pound's *Cantos* Is Published (1917), p. 445; Melville Is Rediscovered as a Major American Novelist (1920), p. 502; The New Criticism Holds Sway (1940's), p. 1169; Pound Wins the Bollingen Prize (1949), p. 1443; Plath's *The Colossus* Voices Women's Experience (1960), p. 1850.

GUNSMOKE DEBUTS, LAUNCHING
A POPULAR TELEVISION GENRE

Category of event: Television and radio
Time: September 10, 1955
Locale: The United States

Introduced as the first of the "adult" Westerns on television, Gunsmoke *became the longest-running network dramatic show with continuing characters*

Principal personages:
JAMES ARNESS (1923-   ), the star of *Gunsmoke*, who played the part of Marshal Matt Dillon
MILBURN STONE (1904-1980), the actor who played the town's doctor, the only supporting character to appear throughout the entire run of the show
AMANDA BLAKE (BEVERLY LOUISE NEILL, 1929-1989), the actress who played Miss Kitty, the owner of the Longbranch Saloon and friend of Marshal Dillon
DENNIS WEAVER (1924-   ), the actor who played Chester Goode, Matt Dillon's deputy
BURT REYNOLDS (1936-   ), the actor who played the town blacksmith during early years of the show
KEN CURTIS (CURTIS GATES, 1916-   ), the actor who replaced Weaver in the role of deputy
GLENN STRANGE (1899-1973), the actor who played the town's bartender, Sam

Summary of Event

Early television Westerns were patterned much like those shown in the theaters as matinees and were primarily children's shows that emphasized fantasy. Since it was expected that these shows would not hold any appeal for adults, few were broadcast during prime-time hours.

By the mid-1950's, however, a craze for Westerns began to sweep the country, a trend made clear by the 1954 prime-time success of a series of Walt Disney-produced made-for-television films about frontier hero Davy Crockett. The networks soon decided that Westerns that appealed to an adult audience could be successful during adult viewing hours. The result was that three Westerns for prime-time showing made their debut in the fall of 1955: *Frontier* on the National Broadcasting Company (NBC), *Cheyenne* on the American Broadcasting Company (ABC), and *Gunsmoke* on the Columbia Broadcasting System (CBS).

The first telecast of *Gunsmoke* took place September 10, 1955. By the time of the last original airing in 1975, the series had run for twenty years, longer than any other series that contained the same characters had run in the history of television.

Gunsmoke originated as a radio program in 1952, with William Conrad playing the role of Matt Dillon. When CBS decided to air a Western that would appeal to adult viewers, the show was a logical choice. Since the stocky Conrad did not fit any stereotype for a Western marshal, the first choice of the show's producers for the television role was Hollywood star John Wayne. Wayne, however, did not want to commit himself to a weekly television series, and instead suggested a friend of his, James Arness, for the part.

Arness was an authentic hero who had been wounded during the fighting around Anzio in World War II. He had appeared in a number of B-films after the war, most notably *The Thing* (1951), but was still relatively unknown. At six feet seven inches in height, he towered over even Wayne, and he proved to be a perfect choice for the role. Wayne did agree to introduce the first show when it aired in 1955, and he informed the viewing audience how they were about to see a new kind of Western program.

The show initially relied on radio scripts, which the writers adapted to the television series. The marshal was portrayed as a sad, lonely man; unlike most film lawmen, he sometimes made mistakes. Marshal Dillon had no family and few friends. His job, and indeed his life, was centered around Dodge City, Kansas, in the 1880's.

The writers of *Gunsmoke* attempted to capture some of the real feeling of the Old West. Horse tricks and fancy riding were out, as were long horse chases. Comic relief was found in the show, but comedian sidekicks often used in films were not in the cast. Sometimes the heroes were shot or took a beating, both physically and mentally. The town's doctor, though, was usually there to patch them up, either with the tools of his trade or by lending a sympathetic ear.

Marshal Dillon spent much of his spare time at the Longbranch Saloon, owned and operated by his friend Kitty Russell (or Miss Kitty, as she was known). Though on the radio version of the show Miss Kitty was clearly a prostitute, on television she remained merely a romantic interest for the marshal. Though they exchanged winks and nods on the show, the relationship between the marshal and the saloon-keeper was never precisely defined. Nevertheless, Miss Kitty exhibited a strong, businesslike appearance and had no compunction at laying down the law when customers were out of line.

The only actor besides Arness who remained on the show throughout its run was Milburn Stone, who played Doc Adams, the town's kindly yet crusty doctor. Doc was always ready with an insult, particularly as it applied to Festus Haggen (Ken Curtis), but he was one of Marshal Dillon's few true friends.

Through the first half of the show's run, Marshal Dillon's deputy was Chester Goode, portrayed by Dennis Weaver. Chester walked with a decided limp, which served to keep him around the marshal's office. Chester's limp and the twang in his voice developed into well-known, and often imitated, characteristics.

Gunsmoke was not an immediate success; in its initial season, it did not crack television's top fifteen. During its second season, though, the show jumped dramatically in popularity, and from 1957 to 1961, it was consistently the top-rated program on television.

In 1961, the program was expanded from thirty minutes to a full hour. Over the next six years, the show's ratings began a precipitous decline. Changes were made in the supporting cast. In 1964, Dennis Weaver left *Gunsmoke*, and the character of Chester was replaced by that of Festus (Ken Curtis), who remained with the show during the rest of its run. Other characters came and went.

In 1967, the CBS program council canceled the show but was overruled by William Paley, the network's chairman of the board. The show was moved to Monday night, and it returned to being among the ten top-rated programs; it remained in the top ten for another six seasons. During the last years of the program, Marshal Dillon appeared on fewer of the shows. Plots revolved around the other characters or around guest stars, with Dodge City merely as the setting.

When the show finally ended on September 1, 1975, some 233 half-hour shows and more than four hundred hour-long shows had been filmed. Despite the deaths of several of the show's actors, special hour-long episodes were filmed during ensuing years.

Impact of Event

Westerns represented a major form of viewing entertainment for children during the early years of network television. In general, the heroes of these shows were popular film stars, including Gene Autry, Roy Rogers, and Hopalong Cassidy. Such shows were low-budget productions and were often old films or serials fitted into thirty- or sixty-minute time slots. Production studios in many cities frequently converted buildings into "Western" frontiers and interspersed new footage with the material from old movies.

These programs were usually placed into midafternoon or weekend time slots and were targeted at children. Such shows were popular with young viewers, but represented simplistic fantasies of the Old West.

With the election of a "Westerner," Dwight Eisenhower, to the White House in 1952 and the successful showing of the Davy Crockett television films in 1954, a Western craze began sweeping the country. President Eisenhower himself enjoyed watching Westerns, and the networks decided to go after the adult audience during prime-time viewing hours with Westerns that appealed to adults.

The earliest and most successful of these shows was *Gunsmoke*. The adult Western was not new to production; Hollywood had earlier paved the way with films such as *My Darling Clementine* (1946), with Henry Fonda, and *Red River* (1948), with John Wayne. *Gunsmoke*, though, represented the introduction of the genre into television. Though the show was not an immediate huge success, its long-term popularity demonstrated that a well-written Western could appeal to adult audiences.

The choice of James Arness in the starring role had as much to do with the success of the show as the plots themselves. Arness simply looked the part of a western marshal. It was not long before other networks and sponsors introduced their own versions of the show; ABC began its long-running (eight years) *Cheyenne* series also in 1955. *Cheyenne* starred Clint Walker, like Arness more than six and a half feet in height. The hero of the show, Cheyenne Bodie, was a scout and drifter rather than a marshal, but the larger-than-life character with a lonely existence was the same image as Arness' Marshal Dillon.

An anthology series, *Frontier*, was NBC's entry into the adult Western genre. The show proved unsuccessful, probably because of the absence of any central characters, and lasted only a single season. ABC was to prove more successful in 1957, with the tongue-in-cheek adult Western *Maverick*; one *Maverick* episode even served to parody *Gunsmoke.*

Prime-time Westerns proved to be quite popular among adult viewers well into the 1960's. Shows such as *The Life and Legend of Wyatt Earp, Wagon Train,* and even *Have Gun Will Travel* were innovative and realistic in their own way. The stars of many of these shows, among them Hugh O'Brian, Ward Bond, and Richard Boone, became well known.

Not least among the effects of *Gunsmoke* and the other adult Westerns was on the way viewers saw themselves and their culture. The star was no longer always the clear-thinking and straight-shooting hero and the Indian no longer the villain of the piece. As *Gunsmoke* evolved, social issues began to appear on the show. With the arrival of Burt Reynolds in 1962 as the part-Indian Quint Asper, the show had to deal with the question of racial prejudice. Other plots dealt with such topics as rape and the rights of minorities.

During the 1957-1958 season, six Westerns were among the fifteen top-rated shows of the year. *Gunsmoke* was number one; close behind were *Tales of Wells Fargo* and *Have Gun Will Travel.* If one counted the top twenty-five shows, an additional three Westerns could be included. Some sixteen Westerns were shown in prime time during that season, and other shows such as *Zorro* could arguably be classified as Westerns. Clearly, the genre had become extremely popular.

The popularity continued for several more years. Six of the top seven shows in the 1958-1959 season were Westerns. (One show in the 1959-1960 season that did not enter the top twenty-five was a newcomer, *Bonanza.*)

The popularity of *Gunsmoke* was not limited to the viewing public in America. When the British Broadcasting Corporation (BBC) filmed a documentary on the first twenty-five years of television, viewers were observed watching the program in areas as diverse as the jungles in Africa, along the Ganges River in India, and in the deserts of the Middle East.

The innovative format associated with *Gunsmoke* soon became absorbed into the cultural mainstream. The Western in general became passé during the turbulent 1960's, and few of the shows survived the decade. Even the survival of *Gunsmoke* became a chance thing. Nevertheless, the show endured for two decades of changes in cultural fashion, influencing television and society at large with its depiction of steadfast Marshal Dillon and his devotion to "justice, sincerity, and truth."

Bibliography

Barabas, Suzanne, and Gabor Barabas. *Gunsmoke: A Complete History and Analysis of the Legendary Broadcast Series.* Jefferson, N.C.: McFarland, 1990. Contains the most complete discussion of *Gunsmoke.* Both the radio and television programs are described in an episode-by-episode program guide. Well written and well researched, the book makes for enjoyable reading.

Brooks, Tim, and Earle Marsh. *The Complete Directory to Prime Time Network TV Shows, 1946-Present.* 5th ed. New York: Ballantine Books, 1992. Among the best program guides available. The authors provide complete broadcasting histories for all prime-time network shows; an excellent description of *Gunsmoke* is included. Also included are programming charts and an early history of television, as well as a brief history of television Westerns in general.

McCrohan, Donna. *Prime Time, Our Time.* Rocklin, Calif.: Prima Publishing, 1990. A decade-by-decade description of television programming as reflected in the lifestyles of Americans. Highlights include stories about individual stars and programs and the legacy that those shows left behind.

McNeil, Alex. *Total Television.* 3d ed. New York: Penguin Books, 1991. Provides descriptions of all major programs shown on television. Included is a short history of programming, a list of top shows of each year, and a programming guide. More comprehensive than the volume by Brooks and Marsh, and equally enjoyable to thumb through.

Marc, David, and Robert J. Thompson. *Prime Time Prime Movers.* Boston: Little, Brown, 1992. An informal guide to what the authors have referred to as the creators of television. Stories and styles are discussed as related to individual performers and producers. Though the book does not deal specifically with *Gunsmoke,* the look at the origins of various genres of television programming makes for interesting reading.

Rose, Brian G., ed. *TV Genres: A Handbook and Reference Guide.* Westport, Conn.: Greenwood Press, 1985. Such television genres as Westerns and variety shows are examined with respect to elements that explain their popularity. A well-written history of television runs throughout the book. Extensive notes and a videography are provided for each chapter.

Richard Adler

Cross-References

Grey's *Riders of the Purple Sage* Launches the Western Genre (1912), p. 304; Ford Defines the Western in *Stagecoach* (1939), p. 1115; Westerns Dominate Postwar American Film (1946), p. 1313; Seven of the Top Ten Television Series Are Westerns (1958), p. 1768; *Bonanza* Becomes an American Television Classic (1959), p. 1800; Leone Renovates the Western Genre (1964), p. 1984.

THE HONEYMOONERS ENCHANTS AUDIENCES OF ALL AGES

Category of event: Television and radio
Time: October 1, 1955-May 9, 1971
Locale: New York, New York

The Honeymooners *expanded the parameters of situation comedy, accelerated the practice of syndication, and became one of the major artistic achievements of television history*

Principal personages:

JACKIE GLEASON (1916-1987), the driving creative force behind *The Honeymooners* and the actor who portrayed the show's protagonist, Ralph Kramden

ART CARNEY (1918-), a consummate comedy actor who brought Ralph's best friend, Ed Norton, to life

AUDREY MEADOWS (1924-), an actress who made the transition from glamor to comedy in order to portray Alice Kramden, Ralph's wife, during the show's golden era

Summary of Event

In 1955, Jackie Gleason, the Columbia Broadcasting System (CBS), and the Buick automobile company entered into a $14 million deal that would make television history and produce an enduring landmark of American culture. The deal created headline news immediately, not only because of the amount of money involved but also because Buick dumped Milton Berle, a popular variety-show host known as "Mr. Television," rather unceremoniously in order to sponsor the up-and-coming Gleason. Also notable was the nature of the show or, more accurately, shows that Gleason was to produce for Buick and CBS. The first half hour of each weekly program would be in the standard variety format of the show Gleason had been doing for CBS since 1952 and would feature singing, dancing, and performances by guest stars. The second half hour would be devoted to a situation comedy based on skits Gleason and his staff had developed over the preceding three years. Entitled *The Honeymooners*, the situation comedy would feature the trials, tribulations, and misadventures of a Brooklyn bus driver named Ralph Kramden, his wife Alice, and their best friends and neighbors, the Nortons. This second half hour would be filmed by means of an innovative technique and with the express purpose of syndication. Though the experiment lasted only one season (thirty-nine shows), it was long enough to make Ralph Kramden and Ed Norton household names for generations to come.

The Honeymooners was largely the brainchild of Gleason himself and reflected many of his personal experiences. During his formative years, Gleason lived in the Bushwick section of Brooklyn in an apartment building much like the one inhabited by the Kramdens and the Nortons. Gleason's family background was not so ordinary as that of his fictional characters, however; when Gleason was nine, his father had simply disappeared. Partly as a result, his mother's health went into decline, and she died shortly after Gleason turned nineteen. By that time, Gleason had decided on a career in show business. Starting as a comedic master of ceremonies in local theaters and clubs, he advanced, in time, to a film career, which, however, proved disappointing. His first major break came in 1949, when he took over William Bendix's radio role as Chester A. Riley in *The Life of Riley*. Like Ralph Kramden, Chester Riley was Brooklyn born, minimally educated, and given to conspicuously male sorts of foolishness. Gleason played the role with un-Gleason-like (and un-Kramden-like) restraint, but he was quietly effective. The show, however, was quickly canceled. (Bendix did ultimately become available for the television version of *The Life of Riley*, which was moderately successful.)

While performing at a club date, Gleason came to the attention of the short-lived DuMont network, and in 1950 he was asked to host its *Cavalcade of Stars* program. During the two years that he did the show, he began to invent some of the characters he would play during his glory years on CBS, including, briefly, a precursor to Ralph Kramden. He also worked with Art Carney, who would immortalize Ed Norton, for the first time. In 1952, Gleason got his own show on CBS. It was during this time that *The Honeymooners* was conceived, developed, and cultivated to a point where, in the eyes of Gleason and his staff, it deserved a life of its own. It also was the period during which Audrey Meadows came on board to portray Alice Kramden.

With the 1955 contract, *The Honeymooners* became a feature in its own right. Gleason's goal was to create weekly masterpieces of situation comedy, using the already-established characters of the original skits. A top-notch writing team was brought in to produce fresh scripts, which sometimes built on previous material. On the other hand, Gleason was notoriously hesitant about rehearsing material (he thought it took the spontaneous wit out of his performance) and was apt to improvise at a moment's notice. His costars knew what to expect and grew confident in their ability to work within this loose environment, largely because the show's characters were so well developed. Whether one's lines were entirely correct was less important than staying in character—and the characters were unforgettable: Ralph, fat, temperamental, sulky, and lovable; Alice, patient but willing to stand toe-to-toe with Ralph anytime; Ed Norton, Ralph's loyal, skinny friend with an endless appetite and a talent for driving Ralph up the wall; and, to a lesser extent, Trixie Norton (played by Joyce Randolph), who never played the central role or got many of the punch lines, but who nevertheless had her part down pat. Ralph Kramden, in particular, was a rich combination of ego, excess, affection and, in his own manner, loyalty. To many observers, such a description might seem an accurate reflection of Gleason himself. Unlike Gleason, however, Kramden managed to preserve a stable (if occasionally tumultuous) marriage, rarely drank, and never managed to hatch the scheme that would make him fabulously wealthy.

So the ingredients were there: a creative genius—Gleason—at the helm, good story lines, and actors who had a rapport with one another and a breathtakingly sure sense of their respective characters. The first show was broadcast on October 1, 1955, and, suitably enough, involved a plot in which Alice tries to get Ralph to buy a television set. The show ran through June 2, 1956, before reruns commenced for the summer season. The last three of the original thirty-nine episodes were broadcast in September, 1956, before the Gleason show returned to its original variety format. The shift took place partly because of less-than-spectacular ratings, but mostly because Gleason feared that the quality of the show would inevitably erode if production continued for another season.

Episodes of *The Honeymooners* continued to be made and broadcast on an occasional basis until 1966, when hour-long episodes of the series became a regular feature of Gleason's variety show. (Some of these episodes, minus Audrey Meadows and Joyce Randolph, also became available for syndication, but the later versions proved less popular than the originals.) CBS canceled *The Jackie Gleason Show* after the 1970 season, but episodes of *The Honeymooners* continued to be produced as specials, including musical versions, in the mid-1970's. In 1984, a number of early sketches of the show, recorded by the relatively primitive means of the times, were released as "lost" episodes. Though these early sketches evoke nostalgia and are of historical interest, they do not measure up to the thirty-nine episodes of the program's first feature run. It is these latter shows, filmed before live audiences by means of the innovative "electronicam," that made *The Honeymooners* enduringly popular.

Impact of Event

The impact of *The Honeymooners* can be gauged along a number of lines. For the show's stars, the program provided the centerpiece of their careers. Audrey Meadows and Joyce Randolph, in particular, are remembered almost exclusively for their work on the show. While Art Carney and Jackie Gleason went on to have notable careers apart from the show, they, too, remain closely identified with each other and with the characters they portrayed so poignantly. For Gleason, in particular, *The Honeymooners* provided the high note of a dynamic but sometimes disappointing career. It was, moreover, an achievement of lasting power, as the show's broadcast history and continuing popularity and critical acclaim indicate.

The Honeymooners also had an important effect on subsequent television productions. On the most apparent level, the show has often been imitated and parodied. For example, the families in *The Flintstones*, an animated comedy originally produced in 1960, are based on the Kramdens and Nortons. Less obvious, perhaps, is the role played by the *The Honeymooners* in laying the foundation for a particular genre of situation comedy. While all situation comedies explore personal relationships, they do so in a variety of ways. Some, such as *Mork and Mindy*, *Mr. Ed*, *The Beverly Hillbillies*, and even, in some of its incarnations, *The Lucy Show*, are predominantly farcical. Some, including *Ozzie and Harriet*, *Father Knows Best*, *The Donna Reed Show*, *My Three Sons*, and *The Cosby Show*, are essentially idealized depictions of family life. *The Honeymooners* falls into a third category that might be called "tempered realism." The drabness of the Kramdens' apartment, set on a real street in Brooklyn and filled with real people, illustrates not only some of the quirks of working-class America but also the fact that such a class exists—something the more sanitized situation comedies often failed to reveal.

This realism is tempered, however, by *The Honeymooners'* sentimental affirmation of bonds. Ralph always learns his lesson and ends many episodes by telling Alice that she is "the greatest." Likewise, though Ralph is always threatening to send Alice "to the moon," he never lays an angry hand on her. Thus, the irony of the show's title and of its beautifully romantic (even sentimental) theme music—written by Gleason himself—is not a bitter one. The program accepts reality and shows how it can be transformed, tolerated, or perhaps simply survived. This realism opened the way for such shows as *All in the Family* (which replaced the Gleason variety show and which was written by one of *The Honeymooners'* old writers) and other topical 1970's comedies. While the show was not used as a political vehicle, it did present a less upwardly mobile side of American society than did most programs of the time. (On the other hand, both *The Honeymooners* and *All in the Family* avoided problems of ethnic identity by making their central characters ethnically unidentifiable.)

The Honeymooners also helped to establish the great American pastime of watching reruns. Some shows (for example, *Star Trek*) would be long forgotten if not for their second lives in syndication. Syndication allows viewers to watch shows they might otherwise have missed and also presents an alternative to current programming. On the performer's side, residuals—the income generated by syndication income—is often quite lucrative. (Gleason, however, sold the syndication rights to *The Honeymooners* for a relatively low figure, two million dollars, and the show's performers did not have generous residual rights in their contracts.)

Through its long run and its even longer life in syndication, *The Honeymooners* became a cultural landmark. The program influenced the evolution of television programming and gave birth to characters who became American archetypes. Perhaps the most enduring legacy of *The Honeymooners*, however, is the show itself, which represents American television at its artistic and humorous best.

Bibliography

Berle, Milton, with Haskel Frankel. *Milton Berle: An Autobiography.* New York: Delacorte, 1974. Provides a spirited account of the early days of network television. Includes observations on Gleason's career from his start (when he allegedly borrowed material from Berle) to his subsequent rise to prominence at Berle's expense.

Bishop, Jim. *The Golden Ham: A Candid Biography of Jackie Gleason.* New York: Simon & Schuster, 1956. A surprisingly frank portrait of Gleason composed during *The Honeymooners'* heyday. Used as a primary source by later biographers, this book provides an early indication of Gleason's depth and complexity, qualities clearly reflected in the program.

Elliot, Marc. *American Television: The Official Art of the Artificial.* Garden City,

N.Y.: Doubleday, 1981. Elliot's book, a chronological summary of every television series from the early days of television to 1976, helps to put *The Honeymooners* into a larger context.

Henry, William A., III. *The Great One: The Life and Times of Jackie Gleason.* Garden City, N.Y.: Doubleday, 1992. A commentator on popular culture for *Time* magazine, Henry offers a critical biography of Gleason, focusing equally on his enormous talents and his self-destructive excesses. More detailed and analytic than the Weatherby book listed below.

McCrohan, Donna. *"The Honeymooners'" Companion: The Kramdens and Nortons Revisited.* New York: Workman, 1978. A tribute by a longtime fan, this book provides abundant information on the genesis of *The Honeymooners*, its golden period, when the classic thirty-nine episodes were broadcast, and the show's subsequent history. Full of interesting anecdotes and pictures.

Slater, Robert. *This . . . Is CBS: A Chronicle of Sixty Years.* Englewood Cliffs, N.J.: Prentice-Hall, 1988. Provides insight into the corporate context that helped to spawn *The Honeymooners.* Chapters 6 through 11 are particularly relevant.

Weatherby, W. J. *Jackie Gleason: An Intimate Portrait of the Great One.* New York: Pharos Books, 1992. Less profound than the Henry biography, but highly accessible. A veteran writer of popular biographies, Weatherby eschews fine details and heavy analysis. Instead, he provides numerous quotations, including several from personal interviews with Gleason.

Ira Smolensky
Marjorie Smolensky

Cross-References

Television Enters Its Golden Age (1950's), p. 1465; Television Family Comedy Becomes Extremely Popular (1950's), p. 1470; *I Love Lucy* Dominates Television Comedy (1951), p. 1525; *The Flintstones* Popularizes Prime-Time Cartoons (1960), p. 1840; *All in the Family* Introduces a New Style of Television Comedy (1971), p. 2234.

CAPTAIN KANGAROO DEBUTS

Category of event: Television and radio
Time: October 3, 1955
Locale: New York, New York

A new orientation in television that respected children's intelligence was demonstrated by the long-lasting, highly popular, and much-praised Captain Kangaroo *program*

Principal personages:
BOB KEESHAN (1927-   ), the cocreator, with Jack Miller, of the Captain Kangaroo concept
HUGH BRANNUM (1910-1987), the regular on the program known as Mr. Green Jeans
GUS ALLEGRETTI (1927-   ), the puppeteer who acted the parts of many of the show's recurring characters

Summary of Event

With high hopes but with no fanfare, as there were no well-known stars in the low-budget program, Bob Keeshan made the premiere on October 3, 1955, of *Captain Kangaroo*. Not even the creators of *Captain Kangaroo* could have predicted in its infancy that the program would remain on television for almost a third of a century.

The Columbia Broadcasting System (CBS) had selected the show from among five possibilities after seeing, in July, 1955, the pilot constructed by Bob Keeshan and Jack Miller, who left the show in 1958. Keeshan, a former page at the National Broadcasting Company (NBC), had played the clown Clarabelle for five years (1947-1952) on *The Howdy Doody Hour,* but he had been fired from the job. CBS was looking for a replacement for Jack Paar's morning show, and the network wanted to experiment with children's shows to try to increase the sales of television sets in general and the popularity of CBS in particular.

Eight months of unemployment must have been difficult both economically and psychologically for Keeshan, but it did not stop him from critically considering the present offerings in children's television, especially the volume of slapstick and pie throwing. As Clarabelle, he had followed directions and held steadfastly to the classic nonspeaking Clown role. He had begun experimenting with some of his ideas as Corny the Clown on *Time for Fun*, a midday children's show shown by the American Broadcasting Company (ABC). He observed his own children, and he continued his discussions with Jack Miller regarding the natural curiosity and the potential of young children.

By the time the opportunity to develop a pilot for CBS arose, Keeshan had decided that children could learn a great deal while being entertained and that appropriate analogies could be used to keep from treating children condescendingly. Keeshan and Miller themselves could not recall which one of them actually proposed using "Captain" as a label for the grandfatherly figure they envisioned featuring in the main role in the Treasure House (later called the Captain's Place). When CBS asked for pilot shows to consider as a replacement for Jack Paar's morning program, there was a limited time period to conceptualize the pilot, develop the set and costumes, rehearse, and film the program. Even the name of the Captain Kangaroo character was decided at a late date. The huge pockets (to hold various treasures) in the coat constructed for the captain prompted the decision to call the wigged and aged character Captain Kangaroo. The name served for the program as well.

Although the program evolved over the years, especially as technology developed, a guiding philosophy was obvious from the earliest days of production. Children were addressed directly and respectfully. They were encouraged to enter a fantasy land and believe in the captain, a mute but bespectacled bunny rabbit who regularly found ways to get carrots, a grandfather clock that composed poetry, a dancing bear, a talking moose, and a variety of other characters. These characters were joined by real plants and animals for the presentation of a variety of fascinating and educational material. More than two thousand species of animals appeared on the program during its existence. No topic was considered beyond the comprehension of children; topics needed only to be presented appropriately. Presentations included skits and songs; songs provided an opportunity to discuss the musical instruments used in their performance. Cartoons were used to fill time when the set had to be changed but were not a primary focus. Sometimes there were well-known guests. When the captain read a book, requests for that title increased at local libraries. Most programs (called visits) included playtime during which the construction of some item was demonstrated.

The techniques used were not unusual, but the context and the respectful orientation to children found in *Captain Kangaroo* were in marked contrast to the slapstick activities and seltzer-spraying clowns of other shows. The show was calm; children watching the show did not have their level of excitement whipped to near hysteria.

Children's television, especially at the local level in the early days of television, had low production standards. Many producers believed it unnecessary to hire professional writers or professional performers with experience in children's television. Keeshan knew the importance of writers, praising them and others behind the scenes as well as those on screen. His show thus was innovative in creating quality programming for an audience of children.

Impact of Event

Strict standards always were placed on writers and performers involved with *Captain Kangaroo*. Violence and cruel or derisive behavior had no place during the visit the captain made to children each day. Sudden loud noises were prohibited, as were deep shadows. When a suit of armor caused fear for one child, according to his mother's letter, it was enough to send the suit of armor to a dark corner of the basement. Cameras did not zoom in on subjects. A gentle approach was favored.

The overall welfare of the child was of central importance and was made apparent by a concentration on messages of safety, ethics, and health. The program refused to accept some products as sponsors of the program because these products were believed to be inconsistent with the show's philosophy.

Initially the program was aimed at six- to eight-year-olds, but the audience consisted of children aged three through nine. Frequently, mothers were as much as one-third of the audience. Attempts to cancel the show as early as 1957 revealed the power of the adult public to influence the network. Letters (as many as ten thousand in one week), phone calls, and personal visits were effective in getting the network to retain the program.

The philosophy behind *Captain Kangaroo* and the program itself encouraged a child to be imaginative. Keeshan did not understand the disillusionment some parents would heap on their children by taking them to see an uncostumed, ordinary-looking man in public and insisting to the puzzled children that that person was Captain Kangaroo. Keeshan has upon occasion denied that he is Captain Kangaroo, responding that the captain is a person in costume, much like Santa Claus, and existed in children's imaginations.

Advocates of the show claimed that it improved children's manners, as the captain encouraged the use of "please" and "thank you." He typically signed off with his reminder that it was another "Be-good-to-Mother day." When he inadvertently failed to include that statement one day, he received mail from mothers asking him not to forget.

Children apparently respected and believed in the captain. The warm relationship the captain was able to build with his young audience was confirmed by children climbing into the lap of the costumed character when he traveled. Fairly soon after the program began, the captain was taken on the road in the "Fun with Music" format. In cooperation with an orchestra, he would introduce very young children to the sounds of a symphony and have them participate in searching for a certain sound among the instruments, by riding their hobby horses, and by conducting the orchestra. Such programs were an extension of the television program's philosophy, with the added benefit of providing some feedback and a sense of satisfaction while aiding symphonies in developing future audiences.

Children did not appear on *Captain Kangaroo* as a rule. The captain wanted to emphasize that he was visiting with child viewers at home and did not want to play to (or visit with) any children on-site. Once, Keeshan's youngest daughter visited on the set and interacted with the captain. After he had removed his costume and makeup, he came out to be greeted by his daughter. She gave him a big hug and started talking about her visit with the captain.

Although the actors on screen were the visible forces on the show, Keeshan stressed that the writers and others not on screen were equally important in the attempt to set higher standards for children's television. Many of them went on to other programs after they shared their talents and had their training with *Captain Kangaroo*. David Connell began as a clerk-typist but progressed to executive producer of *Captain Kan-*

garoo before leaving to become one of the founders of Children's Television Workshop and a creator of *Sesame Street.* Kevin Clash grew up watching *Captain Kangaroo* and gained experience as a puppeteer with Jim Henson before he created puppets for *Captain Kangaroo*, acted as a puppeteer, and eventually acted on the program. Fresh ideas and personnel kept arriving while a core of regulars remained with *Captain Kangaroo.*

The need for more visible role models for males in society was given as the justification for the preponderance of male characters in the early decades of the show. Female characters were added to the cast regulars in the 1970's. Early consideration of the role of language in perpetuating gender and racial stereotypes was obvious in the way Keeshan dealt with cartoons and in the type of phrases that were not used on the program. Phrases such as "boys don't cry" and "act like a man" or other admonitions that would limit options were never acceptable.

Keeshan believed in the earliest days of *Captain Kangaroo* that there was no alternative to the use of cartoons, as time had to be made to allow changing of sets. He never hesitated, however, to speak out against the prejudice portrayed in the cartoons of the 1920's and 1930's. His director was very cooperative and would turn the camera away from an offending cartoon. Finally, Keeshan won the right to preview cartoons and splice out the offensive sections. The use of cartoons was never encouraged on the program. The cartoons of the 1950's and 1960's often included slapstick comedy or horror and other violent action. Economics, however, dictated their eventual takeover of Saturday morning network children's programming. *Captain Kangaroo* was one of the last Saturday programs featuring real people.

Some of the themes stressed in *Captain Kangaroo* are vital ones: the need for respect and knowledge of the environment, the importance of nurturing a child's self-esteem, and respect for and the need to develop each person's abilities. The emphasis on respecting the child and a soft-spoken approach are no longer unique. They have also been used by Mr. Rogers and by the Canadian Friendly Giant.

During the 1960's and 1970's, fewer local and cable television stations competed to show *Captain Kangaroo.* In spite of the desire for profits and high ratings on the part of network executives, Keeshan believed that his program was protected. That changed with the deregulation of broadcasting that occurred during Mark Fowler's tenure as chairman of the Federal Communications Commission (FCC). Fowler was appointed by President Ronald Reagan, who promoted deregulation in many industries.

Once the marketplace, rather than the FCC at license renewal time, became the regulator for television stations, there was no longer a perceived requirement that the airwaves serve the needs of special groups such as children. *Captain Kangaroo* was forced out of its 8 A.M. slot to an earlier one. Eventually it went off the air, after almost thirty years with CBS. A haven was found for a few more years with the public broadcasting stations. Keeshan's interest in children did not end with the demise of the longest-running character in television history. He founded and directed a national child-care corporation.

Bibliography

Balk, Alfred. "Captain Kangarooo's Campaign Against TV Violence." *Today's Health* 38 (August, 1960): 19-21, 62-66. Deals with the basic philosophy of the program, particularly its stance toward violence. Includes names of the principal cast members and their previous experience. Specifics on early awards, difficulties of getting sponsors, and coping with animals on stage.

Hentoff, Nat. "The Magic Mornings of Captain Kangaroo." *Reporter* 19 (October 2, 1958): 39-40. Especially useful in its description of the techniques and practices used on the program. Includes some information on Keeshan's personal life and a few anecdotes.

Keeshan, Bob. *Growing Up Happy: Captain Kangaroo Tells Yesterday's Children How to Nurture Their Own.* New York: Doubleday, 1989. A combination of autobiography and how-to book on nurturing children. Each chapter is filled with references to the television program. Excellent detail on the thinking that shaped every decision. Anecdotes from the show, excerpts from Keeshan's mail, and experiences with his children and grandchildren.

Langdon, Dolly. "Gentle Captain Kangaroo Is the Tough Skipper of a Show Now in Its 25th Year." *People Magazine* 12 (November 5, 1979): 107-108+. Mostly biographical data on Keeshan, Keeshan's family, and Allegretti, with photos from early days of the show. Refers to his lecturing and testifying as an expert witness on children's television and child rearing.

Morris, Norman S. "What's Good About Children's TV." *The Atlantic* 224 (August, 1969): 67-71. One of the few sources to view the broader field of children's television and make some judgments before *Sesame Street* made an impact. Outlines the principles of a successful children's television show and critiques cartoons. Makes reference to plans for what eventually became *Sesame Street.*

Gretta Stanger

Cross-References

Kukla, Fran, and Ollie Pioneers Children's Television Programming (1948), p. 1400; *The Flintstones* Popularizes Prime-Time Cartoons (1960), p. 1840; *Sesame Street* Revolutionizes Children's Programming (1969), p. 2185; *The Simpsons* Debuts, Anchoring the Fledgling Fox Network (1990), p. 2652.

BUCKLEY FOUNDS *NATIONAL REVIEW*

Category of event: Journalism
Time: November, 1955
Locale: New York, New York

Conservative journalist William F. Buckley, Jr., gave voice to American conservative views in his anti-Communist, antiliberal publication

Principal personages:

WILLIAM F. BUCKLEY, JR. (1925-   ), a Yale University graduate, millionaire's son, and vivid, polemical writer

WILLIAM S. SCHLAMM (1904-1978), an Austrian Jew and former Communist who joined Buckley's project in 1954

JAMES BURNHAM (1905-1987), a former Communist Party member who became an editor and regular contributor to *National Review* on foreign policy

WILLMOORE KENDALL (1909-1967), a Yale professor of political science who became a *National Review* editor and contributor

WHITTAKER CHAMBERS (1901-1961), an ex-Communist celebrity whose testimony had led to the imprisonment of former Soviet spy Alger Hiss

Summary of Event

William F. Buckley, Jr., made his reputation for conservative controversy at the age of twenty-five when he published *God and Man at Yale: The Superstitions of "Academic Freedom"* (1951), a scorching indictment of his alma mater written as soon as he was graduated. In it, he argued that Yale University had become a center of anti-Christian education and that its professors' economic outlook was dominated by collectivist, rather than capitalist, ideas. He horrified Yale's professors and administrators with his advocacy of a revolt by the university's trustees, many of them Christians and businessmen, to regain control over faculty appointments and the curriculum.

Buckley always enjoyed controversy and publicity. His father, William F. Buckley, Sr., had made a fortune in oil and had brought up his large Catholic family on a luxurious Connecticut estate. William Junior, after a precocious childhood, became an infantry officer at the end of World War II but was not shipped abroad. After demobilization, he went to college at Yale, where he edited the *Yale Daily News* and led the debating team. Following graduation and the scandal surrounding *God and Man at Yale*, he volunteered for a stint in Mexico working for the Central Intelligence Agency (CIA), but his thirst for public controversy soon brought him back to the United States. He collaborated on a second book with his brother-in-law, Brent Bozell, entitled *McCarthy and His Enemies* (1954), which argued that Senator Joseph McCarthy was, by and large, justified in his search for Communist subversives and that McCarthy's opponents were either cynical, unscrupulous, or naïve in their outlook. Buckley and Bozell made the strongest intellectual case McCarthy ever enjoyed, but the book was no great success.

Buckley believed that America had no good conservative journals and that liberals and radicals had made all the running in journalistic circles for the preceding twenty-five years or more. He contributed articles to the *American Mercury* and the *Free-man* but was dissatisfied by both, considering them airless and dry. Taking advantage of the reputation he had already made by his writing and of his father's many business contacts, he now began to travel the country seeking financial backing for a new journal; moreover, he was willing to sink much of his personal fortune into the enterprise. For help, he recruited many of the leading conservative intellectuals of his era. Several were former Communists who had recanted and become passionately anti-Communist; among them were writers who had made reputations in radical circles before their switch, including Max Eastman, John Dos Passos, James Burnham, and Whittaker Chambers.

William Schlamm, a former Communist and a Jewish exile from Austria, was particularly helpful in the preparatory stages and offered to write a regular column on the arts for Buckley's new magazine. Others among the regular contributors once the magazine had got under way included traditionalist conservatives such as Ross Hoffman and Russell Kirk (the author of the acclaimed 1953 study *The Conservative Mind, From Burke to Santayana*) and libertarians such as Frank Chodorov and Henry Hazlitt, who believed in dismantling the apparatus of government and giving free rein to laissez-faire economics. Several of Buckley's brothers and sisters helped out too, and Roman Catholics were always well represented on the magazine, often imparting to it the special concerns of their faith.

The magazine's first issue appeared in November, 1955, with a white cover edged in blue and with highlights of the contents listed in italics. Inside, it blended serious political articles with shorter news items and general cultural criticism from a conservative standpoint. Full of jokes, ironies, and scornful remarks about famous contemporary liberals including Eleanor Roosevelt (the New Deal president's widow) and Dag Hammarskjöld (secretary-general of the United Nations), the early issues of *National Review* also argued that the current Republican president, Dwight Eisenhower, was not good enough for genuine conservatives. Far from dismantling the welfare state, which had grown to sizable proportions during the long presidencies of Franklin Roosevelt (1932-1945) and Harry Truman (1945-1952), Eisenhower had come to terms with it and seemed happy to supervise countless large federal projects. Conservatives, said Buckley, had to oppose him.

National Review's foreign-policy coverage was based on James Burnham's weekly column, "The Third World War." Burnham, with Buckley's full support, argued that Eisenhower was not doing enough to attack Communism. During the election campaign of 1952, Eisenhower and his prospective secretary of state, John Foster Dulles, had promised a policy of "rollback" in Eastern Europe, freeing the nations that

Joseph Stalin's Soviet armies had seized from Nazi Germany in 1944 and 1945. In the event, however, the Eisenhower White House seemed content to coexist with the Soviet Union, to acquiesce to internal repression there, and to put up with continued Soviet puppet regimes in Eastern Europe. As the magazine approached its first anniversary in the fall of 1956, a Hungarian uprising seemed to conservatives to offer the ideal opportunity for American military intervention on behalf of anti-Soviet rebels, but Eisenhower did not move. Furious, *National Review* editorialized that conservatives should not vote for Eisenhower in the upcoming 1956 presidential election, even though the Democratic candidate, Adlai Stevenson, was precisely the type of idealistic liberal *National Review* despised.

Impact of Event

William Buckley and *National Review* stood at the center of the American conservative revival in the following decades. Buckley gradually gained national renown as a syndicated columnist, as a television personality on his long-running show *Firing Line*, and as the author of more than twenty books on topics as varied as politics and sailing; he even wrote spy fiction. Having become a friend of Ronald Reagan in the early 1960's, Buckley advised him first when Reagan was governor of California and later during Reagan's two successful presidential campaigns. In 1965, Buckley ran unsuccessfully for the office of mayor of New York City on the Conservative Party ticket; he made his defeat the basis of a seriously meant but entertaining book, *The Unmaking of a Mayor* (1966). He served President Richard Nixon as American delegate to the United Nations Human Rights Commission in the early 1970's (an experience he used as the basis of another book, 1974's *United Nations Journal: A Delegate's Odyssey*), but he turned against Nixon at the time of Watergate and was among the many voices seeking his resignation by 1974. Having seen himself in early life as a political outsider, Buckley had become by the 1980's an insider par excellence, one of the most influential political voices in New York and Washington.

Youth was a conservative constituency that Buckley cultivated with particular care. In the early days of *National Review*, both he and Russell Kirk wrote columns on academic and university affairs, believing that the forces of liberalism were strongest on America's campuses. They were especially concerned to keep alive the issues Buckley had raised in *God and Man at Yale*, and the magazine often featured stories in which college chaplains, standing up for their rights, had been rebuked, or in which professors had taught ideological liberalism and collectivism under the umbrella of academic freedom in ways Buckley and Kirk found dishonest. At the beginning of the 1960's, Buckley, at his home in Sharon, Connecticut, hosted the convention that gave birth to the Young Americans for Freedom (YAF). The YAF was to the Right what Students for a Democratic Society (SDS) was to the Left, and throughout the 1960's, SDS demonstrations against the Vietnam War would often be greeted by YAF counterdemonstrations. Buckley was the favorite speaker at YAF gatherings, and *National Review* was its members' preferred reading.

The founding of *National Review* coincided with the beginning of the Civil Rights movement. The editors, in a short, unsigned piece, defended the Montgomery Bus Boycott of 1955-1956 that made Martin Luther King, Jr., famous. It was up to the bus company, they said, to provide a better service, or else the consumers were free to withhold their patronage. In general, however, *National Review* was not a friend to African-American self-assertion in the 1950's and early 1960's. Defenders of segregation such as Georgia senator Richard Russell won a sympathetic hearing, and sit-ins, freedom rides, and civil disobedience were treated as dangerous tactics that threatened the rule of law. King was criticized for sloppy theological reasoning in his speeches and writings. James J. Kilpatrick, the editor of the *Richmond News-Leader* and a leading segregationist, was a friend of Buckley's, and his views won more space in *National Review* than the views of desegregationists. After the passage of the Civil Rights Acts of 1964 and 1965, *National Review* accepted the nondiscrimination principle, but the journal deplored the rise of affirmative action on the grounds that it undermined the individualist basis of American law in favor of group rights.

National Review itself has been and remains an influential journal, gathering together disparate voices from the political right, including libertarians, traditionalists, religious conservatives, and an array of anti-Communists. From the beginning, it paid high fees for articles and "discovered" many talented writers, including the columnist George Will, the historian and journalist Garry Wills, and the novelist Joan Didion. Appearing fortnightly, it tried to blend seriousness on politics with the sense that it was one of the defenders of Western civilization itself. In a section entitled "Books, Arts, Manners," edited for many years by another ex-Communist, Frank Meyer, book reviews ran beside articles on theater, religion, and philosophy. During the 1960's, a decade that most recall as an age of social upheaval in which the political left played a major role, *National Review*, on the right, enjoyed its heyday. It saw itself as a voice of sanity in a collapsing world and held out to isolated conservatives, especially young ones, the sense that they were not alone. Patrick Buchanan (a 1992 presidential candidate) and Peggy Noonan (a Reagan and George Bush speechwriter) both recalled in their memoirs that *National Review* had been a lifeline for them in days when they felt beleaguered by liberals and radicals.

In the 1970's, the magazine's appeal broadened to include many formerly liberal intellectuals who had turned more conservative after the storms of the 1960's. This was particularly true of several influential Jewish intellectuals, including Nathan Glazer and Irving Kristol, the magazine's "neoconservatives." More strange to many readers, Eugene Genovese, America's foremost Marxist historian and an expert on the history of the slave South, became a contributor. Like Buckley, Genovese despised what he saw as the intellectual frivolity and flaccidity of the 1960's New Left, and he appealed to the journal in the name of high intellectual standards.

From the beginning, to be sure, *National Review* had its critics. Right from the start, it suffered withering attacks from liberal journals such as *The New Republic* and *The Nation*. Dwight Macdonald, Paul Goodman, Arthur Schlesinger, Jr., Irving Howe, and other intellectual eminences of the 1950's argued that *National Review* was no more than an apology for big-business interests of the most reactionary kind and that its mix of libertarians and traditionalists was intellectually incoherent. Buckley took particular pleasure in rebutting these attacks and in debating prominent rivals. He and Schlesinger, an adviser to President John F. Kennedy, often met on the lecture circuit to exchange verbal blows. When Buckley and Gore Vidal met on television during the 1968 election, they exchanged physical blows after Vidal all but accused Buckley of fascism.

A particular antagonist of Buckley in the early years of *National Review* was the American Jesuits' magazine *America. America* criticized Buckley for playing fast and loose with papal decrees, especially in 1961, when a papal encyclical letter critical of capitalist economics, *Mater et magistra,* drew from *National Review* the flippant response "Mater Si, Magistra No!" (a parody of Fidel Castro's slogan "Cuba, Si, Yanqui No!"). Stung by the Jesuits' criticism, Buckley countered that his was not a Catholic magazine but one for all varieties of conservatives and did not need to defer to Rome. Nevertheless, he seems to have been sufficiently worried about the controversy to find Catholic scholars who backed up his more reasoned rebuttal to aspects of the encyclical. He remained a Catholic and continued to see his faith as of equal importance with his political beliefs.

Buckley and *National Review* have provided continuity in the history of American conservatism since World War II. The magazine has been a central feature of the political and journalistic landscape although, like most journals of opinion, *National Review* has rarely been commercially profitable to its owner.

Bibliography

Diggins, John. *Up from Communism: Conservative Odysseys in American Intellectual History.* New York: Harper & Row, 1975. A superbly readable and fascinating book on the many ex-Communists in the conservative movement and on the life experiences that brought them to Buckley's journal.

Judis, John. *William F. Buckley, Jr.: Patron Saint of the Conservatives.* New York: Simon & Schuster, 1988. A full-sized, illustrated biography written by a conscientious investigator who is politically well to the left of Buckley. Critical of Buckley's convictions, Judis nevertheless explains Buckley's strengths and shows how he molded post-World War II conservatism in America.

Markmann, Charles L. *The Buckleys: A Family Considered.* New York: William Morrow, 1973. Remorselessly critical and hostile to its subjects, this book should have been subtitled "a family traduced." Yet it does show what Buckley's numerous brothers and sisters did as children and in later life and how family pressures shaped William Buckley himself.

Miles, Michael. *The Odyssey of the American Right.* New York: Oxford University Press, 1980. Sober but accurate account of right-wing politics in the later twentieth century, placing Buckley's work in context.

Nash, George. *The Conservative Intellectual Movement in America, Since 1945.* New York: Basic Books, 1976. A comprehensive scholarly account that explains the intricate relationship between the various strands of conservatism and includes much detail on Buckley's work as a reconciler of factions and as a publicist. The author is himself a thoughtful conservative.

Patrick Allitt

Cross-References

The Christian Science Monitor Is Founded (1908), p. 209; Lippmann Helps to Establish *The New Republic* (1914), p. 385; Wallace Founds *Reader's Digest* (1922), p. 549; Luce Founds *Time* Magazine (1923), p. 577; Luce Launches *Life* Magazine (1936), p. 1031; Blacklisting Seriously Depletes Hollywood's Talent Pool (1947), p. 1340; *USA Today* Is Launched (1982), p. 2507.

THE "BOOM" CAPTURES WORLDWIDE ATTENTION

Category of event: Literature
Time: The late 1950's and the 1960's
Locale: Latin America

A virtual explosion of masterful novels produced within the rubric of Latin America's "new narrative" and written by authors who would gain worldwide fame catapulted the Latin-American novel to the forefront of world literature

Principal personages:
   JORGE LUIS BORGES (1899-1986), an Argentine short-story writer
   JULIO CORTÁZAR (1914-1984), an Argentine novelist
   JOSÉ DONOSO (1924-   ), a Chilean novelist
   CARLOS FUENTES (1928-   ), a Mexican novelist
   GABRIEL GARCÍA MÁRQUEZ (1928-   ), a Colombian novelist
   CLARICE LISPECTOR (1925-1977), a Brazilian novelist
   JOÃO GUIMARÃES ROSA (1908-1967), a Brazilian novelist
   JUAN RULFO (1918-1986), a Mexican novelist
   MARIO VARGAS LLOSA (1936-   ), a Peruvian novelist

Summary of Event

During the latter half of the 1950's and throughout the 1960's, Latin-American novelists produced a spate of popular and critically acclaimed novels that sent the Latin-American novel to the forefront of world literature. This period became known as the "Boom" in the Latin-American novel.

Virtually all the Boom novels were, to one degree or another, examples of the Latin-American "new novel," the novel genre's branch of Latin America's "new narrative." The new narrative had first begun to play a role in Latin-American fiction during the 1940's, when writers such as Jorge Luis Borges in Argentina and Clarice Lispector in Brazil first began to produce a brand of narrative different from that which had characterized Latin-American fiction earlier in the twentieth century. The "old" narrative had been chiefly concerned with painting a realistic and detailed picture of external Latin-American reality. Description frequently had ruled over action, environment over character, and types over the individual. Social message, also, had often been more important to the writer than narrative artistry. Presentation of story had usually been simple and direct, and the reader's role had been a passive one. The new narrative was new in that it released Latin-American fiction from its documentary nature and thus allowed fiction to be just that—fiction. The new narrative also turned its focus toward the inner workings of its fully individualized human characters, presented various interpretations of reality (expanding the conventional definition of "reality" and often incorporating magical elements—a practice often referred to as "Magical Realism"), expressed universal as well as regional and national themes, and invited (and often required) reader participation.

Works in the new style also emphasized the importance of artistic and challenging presentation of the story, particularly with respect to narrative voice, language, structure, time, and characterization (so much so that presentation of the story in some works seems more important than the story itself). The new approach began to dominate Latin-American fiction by the first half of the 1950's; during the second half of the decade and into the 1960's, the new narrative was taken up by a number of master practitioners, resulting in the Boom, one of the richest periods the novel genre has known in any literature.

A list of the principal writers of the Boom reads like a who's who of Latin-American novelists of the second half of the twentieth century. Most of these writers had begun writing in the early 1950's (and in some cases earlier), but most hit their stride during the Boom, when many produced their most famous works. One of these writers was Juan Rulfo of Mexico, whose landmark novel *Pedro Páramo* (1955), the unconventionally presented tale of a local despot, is pointed to by some, along with Brazilian João Guimarães Rosa's *Grande Sertão-Veredas* (1956; *The Devil to Pay in the Backlands*, 1963), as being the first novel of the Boom, fully exemplifying, as both novels do, the concept of the new novel. The works of Rulfo and Rosa were followed by even more famous novels by writers who would gain even more international fame. Among these was the Argentine Julio Cortázar, whose *Rayuela* (1963; *Hopscotch*, 1966) must be read twice—first from chapters 1 to 56 and then again with what the author calls "Expendable Chapters" (chapters 57 to 155) inserted between those read the first time. Also gaining fame during the Boom was the Mexican Carlos Fuentes, who produced several novels during the period, the most famous being *La muerte de Artemio Cruz* (1962; *The Death of Artemio Cruz*, 1964), the story of a Mexican opportunist told through three narrative voices from the protagonist's deathbed.

The Peruvian Mario Vargas Llosa produced three novels during the Boom as well, among them *La casa verde* (1966; *The Green House*, 1968), a technically challenging novel set both in a brothel in a northwestern Peruvian city and in the Amazonian wilderness. Four novels produced during the Boom, among them *El obsceno pájaro de la noche* (1970; *The Obscene Bird of Night*, 1973), a bizarre tale told by a schizophrenic narrator/protagonist, earned the Chilean José Donoso an international reputation. While the Boom was significantly less a factor in Brazil than in Spanish-speaking parts of Latin America, the works of Clarice Lispector earned a place alongside those of her Spanish-American counterparts, particularly her *A maçã no escuro* (1961; *The Apple in the Dark*, 1967), an ironic story of a character's quest for self-awareness. No Latin-American writer, however, earned more of a reputation during the Boom than the Colombian Gabriel García Márquez, whose *Cien años de soledad* (1967; *One Hundred Years of Solitude*, 1970), the magical story of six generations of the Buendía family, became the most famous piece of literature ever to come out of Latin America and the most highly praised and widely read Spanish-language novel since Miguel de Cervantes' *Don Quixote de la Mancha* (1612-1620). Other writers who earned their reputation in part or full during the Boom were the

Cubans Alejo Carpentier, Guillermo Cabrera Infante, and José Lezama Lima, the Argentine Manuel Puig, and the Brazilian Jorge Amado (though Amado's novels did not actually fit into the rubric of the new novel). Ironically, one of the most important names in Latin-American literature earned his international fame during the Boom as well, though he never wrote a single novel and had already produced the majority of his most famous and acclaimed works prior to the Boom. This was Jorge Luis Borges, whose short stories from the 1940's (such as those in 1944's *Ficciones*) gained an international audience in the 1960's.

Impact of Event

Though the Boom in the Latin-American novel in strictest definition concerns only the explosion in the production of new Latin-American novels, most literary historians consider as part of the Boom the various related "booms" the production of said novels inspired. These related events began to occur during the Boom period itself, and many continued long after the explosion in the production of the novels had passed. The "booms" occurred in the fields of translation (as most of the novels of the Boom were translated into various languages, especially English, soon after their publication in the original Spanish or Portuguese), sales (as the novels sold in unprecedented numbers both within Latin America and abroad), and critical attention (with literary conferences, journals, and countless articles and books dedicated to the works of the period). The Boom even helped to cause an explosion in Spanish and, to a lesser degree, Portuguese graduate programs in North American universities, as fascinated undergraduate readers of the works of the Boom pursued their interest in the period in graduate school on their way to becoming specialists and future critics in the field.

All this—the Boom itself and the related "booms" it inspired—helped to capture a worldwide audience for the Latin-American novel and its practitioners. (This was true even in the 1960's, but even more so in the 1970's and later, as translations were more widely distributed and awareness among foreign readers became more common.) Almost overnight, the new Latin-American novel moved to the forefront of world literature (it has even been suggested that it helped to rescue the ailing novel genre on a worldwide scale) and those who were responsible for its creation, such as García Márquez, Fuentes, and Vargas Llosa, became international literary celebrities. Moreover, although the Boom itself ended with the 1960's, the international audience the novels of the Boom had captured had only begun to grow. Years after the original publication, readers around the world came to know works such as *The Death of Artemio Cruz* and *One Hundred Years of Solitude*. Most of the principal writers of the novels of the Boom, most notably García Márquez, Fuentes, and Vargas Llosa, continued to write within the rubric (although an evolving one) of the new novel for years to come. Their works were now eagerly awaited by the international reading public, with translations of their latest novels reviewed in *Time* magazine, *The New York Times Book Review*, and other publications that exposed their work to audiences outside Latin America. Even Latin-American writers who had not participated in the Boom but who were practitioners, to one degree or another, of the new novel, such as the Chilean Isabel Allende, benefited from the attention the Latin-American novel had earned during the Boom. In the years that followed, an international reading public more aware of and interested in Latin-American literature readily embraced the works of the region's writers, both old and new.

The Boom in the Latin-American novel stands as the single most important period in the history of Latin-American literature, not only for its extraordinarily high number of popular and critically acclaimed works and writers but also for the attention the period won for the Latin-American new novel in particular and for Latin-American letters in general. In the case of the new novel, that attention would endure for years.

Bibliography

Books Abroad 44 (Winter, 1970): 7-50. Issue devoted to "The Latin American Novel Today." Articles both on the Latin-American novel of the Boom and on individual authors and their works largely within the context of the Boom. Articles include an introduction by Mario Vargas Llosa and "The New Latin-American Novel" by Emir Rodríguez Monegal. Most titles and quotations in English.

Brushwood, John S. *The Spanish American Novel: A Twentieth-Century Survey.* Austin: University of Texas Press, 1975. An exhaustive survey, in strict chronological order, of the Spanish-American novel from 1900 through the early 1970's. An excellent source for plot summaries and cogent, although necessarily brief, analyses of the novels of the Boom. Excellent index. Titles in Spanish; quotations in English.

Donoso, José. *The Boom in Spanish American Literature: A Personal History.* Translated by Gregory Kolovakos. New York: Columbia University Press, 1977. Fascinating first-person account of the Boom by one of its major figures. Discusses significant aspects of the Boom; also confronts, and to a large degree repudiates, several common assumptions about the period and its writers. Laced with information concerning Donoso's own personal situation within the Boom. Good index. Titles of translated works in English. Titles of other works in Spanish, with English translation.

Gallagher, D. P. "Latin American Fiction from 1940." In *Modern Latin American Literature.* New York: Oxford University Press, 1973. Seven-page discussion of the nature of Latin-American fiction since 1940, with emphasis on the type of novel produced during the Boom. Concise introduction to the subject. Very readable. Titles in Spanish.

Latin American Literary Review 15 (January-June, 1987): 7-206. Special issue entitled "The Boom in Retrospect: A Reconsideration." Article titles include "Two Views of the Boom: North and South," "The First Seven Pages of the Boom," "Translating the Boom: The Apple Theory of Translation," and "Literature and History in Contemporary Latin America." Articles are interesting for their perspective, as they were written years after the Boom. Titles and quotations in English.

McMurray, George R. *Spanish American Writing Since 1941: A Critical Survey.* New York: Frederick Ungar, 1987. Half of this book is dedicated to Spanish-American fiction writers. Brief overviews presented for each of Latin America's most important narrativists, beginning with writers of the 1940's and 1950's who sent Spanish-American narrative, as the author puts it, in "new directions." Followed by more lengthy essays on the major writers of the Boom. Fine starting point for the English-speaking reader. Titles in Spanish, with English translations.

Rodríguez Monegal, Emir. "The Contemporary Brazilian Novel." In *Fiction in Several Languages*, edited by Henri Peyre. Boston: Houghton Mifflin, 1968. Traces evolution of the twentieth century Brazilian novel, with Rosa and Lispector discussed as masters of the "post-regionalist" novel. Concluding section places the contemporary Brazilian novel within the context of Latin-American literature. Titles in Portuguese.

Schwartz, Ronald. *Nomads, Exiles, and Émigrés: The Rebirth of the Latin America Narrative, 1960-80.* Metuchen, N.J.: Scarecrow Press, 1980. Features chapters on ten novelists of the Boom (among them Cortázar, García Márquez, Vargas Llosa, Fuentes, and Donoso). Each chapter presents a brief biographical sketch, an overview of the author's works, and an analysis of one of his novels. Introduction as well as conclusion concerning the Boom. English-language bibliography and good index. Titles and quotations in English. Especially suited for reader with little or no knowledge of Latin-American fiction.

Vázquez Amaral, José. *The Contemporary Latin American Narrative.* New York: Las Américas, 1970. In-depth discussion of eleven Spanish-American novels of the twentieth century, including works by Fuentes, Vargas Llosa, García Márquez, and Cortázar. Introduction and conclusion, as well as a chapter on Latin-American fiction as a new genre, help to place the works discussed in historical, cultural, and literary context. Good index. Titles and quotations in English.

Keith H. Brower

Cross-References

Surrealism Is Born (1924), p. 604; García Lorca's *Poet in New York* Is Published (1940), p. 1179; Borges' *Ficciones* Transcends Traditional Realism (1944), p. 1268; The New Novel (*Le Nouveau Roman*) Emerges (1951), p. 1481; García Márquez's *One Hundred Years of Solitude* Is Published (1967), p. 2086.

JOFFREY FOUNDS HIS BALLET COMPANY

Category of event: Dance
Time: 1956
Locale: New York, New York

Robert Joffrey founded a touring ballet company that exhibited an American view of dance to the world

Principal personages:

ROBERT JOFFREY (ABDULLAH JAFFA ANVER BEY KHAN, 1930-1988), an American dancer who acted on his dream of creating a ballet company that would reflect the state of dance in America

GERALD ARPINO (1928-), an American choreographer whose body of works made up a large part of the Joffrey Ballet repertoire

REBEKAH HARKNESS (1915-1982), an heiress who supported Joffrey's early efforts to establish a ballet company

Summary of Event

Early one morning in October, 1956, the twenty-five-year-old Robert Joffrey waved goodbye to a company of six young, enthusiastic dancers. He was sending them in a borrowed station wagon heavily packed with costumes and a rented tape recorder on a six-week tour of the United States. These six dancers, handpicked for their versatility as performers in a wide range of choreographic styles and also for their jack-of-all-trades ability to handle backstage tasks, were the founding members of a venture that grew into a major American ballet company, the Joffrey Ballet. Among them was a young man, Gerald Arpino, destined to have almost as great a role in determining the ultimate direction of the company as Joffrey himself.

The program for this grueling tour of single-night performances consisted of four ballets, all choreographed by Joffrey. With a keen eye for what would sell in middle America, Joffrey crafted a repertoire that provided something for everyone. *Pas des déesses* was very Romantic; *Kaleidoscope*, with its Gershwin music, was very modern and jazzy; *Within Four Walls* was dramatic; and *Le Bal* offered a rousing finale, with a little humor, a lilting waltz melody, and a lot of glitter. Indeed, with such a small repertoire, every ballet had to fulfill its function.

This initial tour was so warmly welcomed that Joffrey immediately arranged another, more extended one. The number of dancers was increased by two, a stage manager was added, the station wagon was exchanged for a roomier limousine, and a *pas de deux* was added to the program. By the end of the 1956-1957 touring season, the fledgling Robert Joffrey Theatre Ballet was established as a group of young stars presenting its own brand of unpretentious ballet. In the following season, the company further expanded its numbers, its repertoire, and its touring horizons to touch on both east and west coasts.

Soon Joffrey's company evolved a pattern of lengthy tours in the hinterlands of America alternating with short periods of work in New York. While at its home base, the company added to its repertoire, presented concerts of new ballets, and earned living money by performing in productions of the New York City Opera and for the National Broadcasting Company Opera. Between opera productions, the company toured the country. By 1962, the Robert Joffrey Theatre Ballet included twenty dancers and a technical staff of ten; in its repertoire, it counted twenty-eight ballets, more than half created expressly for the company by Joffrey, Arpino, and others; and it had appeared in some five hundred cities in forty-eight states.

In the spring of 1962, the Joffrey Ballet was invited to dance at the annual summer Spoleto Festival of Two Worlds in Italy. Despite the company's great popularity, it had always been a shoestring operation, depending upon ticket revenue and Joffrey's earnings as a teacher to pay dancers' salaries and to fund new productions. To make the journey to Italy a reality, Joffrey sought outside backing for the first time. He contrived to meet wealthy Standard Oil heiress and patroness of dance Rebekah Harkness Kean, who offered to underwrite costs for the European trip through her arts foundation. Realizing the depth of this windfall, Joffrey changed his mind and requested instead a summer workshop on the Rhode Island estate of Harkness. The purpose of the workshop was to find exciting young choreographers who would create new ballets for the Joffrey repertoire. Included on the roster of choreographers that summer were Joffrey, Arpino, Donald Saddler, and Alvin Ailey. Harkness paid all the bills—salaries for dancers, choreographers, composers, and designs and costs of building sets and costumes. An amateur composer, she also wrote a score for one of the new ballets.

The prestige of sponsorship by the Rebekah Harkness Foundation prompted an invitation from the State Department for the Joffrey Ballet to represent the United States in a tour of the Near East between December, 1962, and March, 1963. This tour featured a blend of ballets from the company's standard repertoire and several of the new works just created. Everywhere the company appeared, from Portugal to India, it was received with loud applause and critical praise, enhancing the cultural reputation of the United States and adding to its own laurels.

Following a second summer workshop on Harkness' Rhode Island estate in 1963, the Joffrey Ballet embarked on its most ambitious and significant trip to that date, a nine-week tour of the Soviet Union. Every performance was sold out, and the Soviet public adored the company. Soviet critics, while taking the Joffrey Ballet to task for its less-than-perfect classical execution, admired the company for its peculiarly American qualities—its energy and its variety of style, subject, and technique.

Despite the successes of two international tours and numerous domestic tours, Joffrey found his company in trouble in early 1964. Harkness, not content with being only an underwriter, had been pressing for an increasingly active role in artistic decisions. Eventually, she proposed the creation of a new company, the Harkness Ballet, and offered Joffrey the position of artistic director. Distrusting her aesthetic judgment and unsure how much control he would have over artistic policies, Joffrey refused even to acknowledge the invitation. Harkness then withdrew all support from Joffrey, resulting in a devastating loss. In the two years of their association, Harkness, through her foundation, had acquired the rights to all the new ballets—their scores, costumes, sets, and choreography—except those by Joffrey and Arpino. Furthermore, the Harkness Foundation, not Joffrey, held the contracts of most of the dancers. Joffrey awakened one morning with virtually nothing.

Undaunted, Joffrey began rebuilding a company and a career. New dancers were sought from Joffrey's own highly reputable school. Choreographers expressed a desire to create ballets for him, and the eminent George Balanchine offered use of certain of his ballets without royalty payments. The Ford Foundation, having just recently entered the dance arena with grants to other ballet companies, made an outright donation of $35,000 to the company, following that gift early in 1965 with $120,000 in matching grant funds.

In the span of two years, Joffrey achieved his goal. Built around a nucleus of ballets from the previous repertoire, with new ballets by Arpino, Anna Sokolow, and Lotte Goslar, a new company emerged from the ashes of the old. In the summer and fall of 1965, Joffrey's young group performed at the Jacob's Pillow Dance Festival and at the Delacorte Theater in Central Park. The following spring, the company gave a short season of seven performances at the City Center for Music and Drama. The resuscitated company's impressive success in this major New York theater resulted in an invitation to become a resident company. Joffrey accepted, and the renamed City Center Joffrey Ballet embarked on a new phase of its existence.

Impact of Event

Though Joffrey very early in his career was recognized as a choreographer of novelty and freshness, his goal in creating a company was never merely to find a group of dancers that would be a vehicle for his own choreographic ideas. Joffrey's creative vision reached beyond the pattern of glorification of self through a company dedicated to one and only one artist's work. From the beginning of its existence, Joffrey enriched his troupe's repertoire with ballets by other young American choreographers such as Todd Bolender, Job Sanders, and Thomas Andrew and with the first experimental works of his principal dancer and close friend Gerald Arpino. He also sought the contributions of established choreographers such as Fernand Nault, George Balanchine, and Lew Christensen. Joffrey's objective was to develop a company that would display an American attitude, promote American talent, and develop a distinctly American dance voice.

Joffrey molded company repertoire and selected personnel with the intention of presenting a program that would reflect the company's American origins, whether performing an eighteenth century pre-Romantic ballet, a *divertissement* in the classical tradition, or a mixture of the most contemporary American movement styles. His dancers exhibited a clean, athletic line, a nonchalant virtuosity, and a look of youthful, fresh-faced wholesomeness that seemed quintessentially American. The company's ballets were picked for their contrasts in movement style, musical accompaniment, depth of emotion, and colorfulness. Both dancers and ballets demonstrated breadth and versatility, a reflection of their eclectic, heterogeneous American society. Always the emphasis was laid on the production as a whole. The "star" was the company itself, a composite of performers, choreographer, composer, and designer all speaking with one voice. Indeed, Joffrey eventually adopted the slogan "No stars, all stars" as official company policy.

Joffrey's management style, part smooth persuader and part Napoleonic martinet, and his infectious vitality attracted a small but loyal contingent. In the early days of his company, Joffrey's dedication inspired devotion from the dancers, who were expected not only to perform but also to mend costumes, set up and strike lights, sweep stage floors, and even accompany certain of the ballets on the piano. Choreographers, composers, and designers often worked without prepayment because Joffrey gave their products visibility across the country. After meeting dancers' salaries and creators' commissions, Joffrey turned all ticket sales money and a good deal of his earnings as a renowned teacher back into added repertoire, refurbishment of sets and costumes, and the acquisition of a small touring orchestra. The company's incessant touring accumulated an audience that spanned the United States and reached across the seas into Europe and the Middle East.

After eight years of pursuing his dream, Joffrey appeared to have achieved the reality by early 1964. He was artistic director of a medium-sized ballet company bearing his name, the company had a solid reputation for consistently high quality, and Harkness Foundation support had put him on apparently firm financial ground. Withdrawal of that financial base, and with it most of what the company "owned," was a potential debacle.

Joffrey's commitment to dance in, of, and about America became a rallying point. Dancers, choreographers, composers, and designers, believing that Joffrey could regenerate his dream, committed themselves wholeheartedly to his endeavors. Feverish work on the part of all produced a radically changed roster of dancers and list of ballets that became a "new and improved" Joffrey Ballet. Joffrey's ability to land catlike on his feet was rewarded with company residency at the City Center for Music and Dance. Official status as a resident company of the City Center meant a permanent New York theater in which to perform, regular semiannual New York seasons, and some financial guarantees. Joffrey willingly gave credit to the source of this solid new foundation by changing the company's name to the City Center Joffrey Ballet; he then embarked on the next stage of realizing his dream of creating an indigenous American ballet company, retaining the dance philosophy that had always guided his steps. In time, the City Center Joffrey Ballet became recognized as America's third major ballet company, after the New York City Ballet and the American Ballet Theatre.

Bibliography

Au, Susan. *Ballet and Modern Dance.* London: Thames and Hudson, 1988. A history of dance that concentrates on twentieth century developments in Europe and the United States. Analyzes the updating of ballet's image by contemporary American choreographers and company directors such as Joffrey and Arpino. Annotated bibliography.

Balanchine, George. *Balanchine's New Complete Stories of the Great Ballets.* Edited by Francis Mason. Garden City, N.Y.: Doubleday, 1968. An alphabetical report of ballets that includes production facts as well as librettos.

Brinson, Peter, and Clement Crisp. *The International Book of Ballet.* New York: Stein & Day, 1971. Chapter 7, devoted to "The Americans" and written by Don McDonagh without full credit, provides descriptions of three early Joffrey ballets. Space is also given to characterizing Arpino as a choreographer.

Coe, Robert. *Dance in America.* New York: E. P. Dutton, 1985. Presents a view of American ballet that is shaped by the Public Broadcasting System's "Dance in America" series, upon which the book is based. Describes the history and repertoire of Serge Diaghilev's Ballets Russes preparatory to a discussion of the Joffrey Ballet's faithful and meticulous reconstructions, during its middle period, of key ballets created for Diaghilev's company. Includes interviews with dancers involved in the staging process. Photographs of the company performing two Ballets Russes works.

De Mille, Agnes. *America Dances.* New York: Macmillan, 1980. A dance history with a decided American slant; synopsizes the Joffrey Ballet's early history. Contains photographs.

Doeser, Linda. *Ballet and Dance: The World's Major Companies.* New York: St. Martin's Press, 1977. Presents a history of the Joffrey Ballet, stressing the care with which Joffrey guided his company to become the third major company based in New York. Lists directors, ballet masters, dancers, and repertoire current at time of publication. Has photographs of repertoire from the late 1960's and early 1970's.

Gruen, John. *The Private World of Ballet.* New York: Viking Press, 1975. An attempt to reveal dance personalities as human beings who think and feel passionately about their art. Contains lengthy interviews with Joffrey, Arpino, and five Joffrey Ballet dancers from the second period of the company's existence. Photo portraits of each.

Percival, John. *Modern Ballet.* London: Studio Vista, 1970. Discussion of the Harkness Ballet and Joffrey Ballet. Suggests that the Joffrey Ballet built its reputation on a repertoire mixing ballet and modern-dance styles.

Unger, Craig. *Blue Blood.* New York: William Morrow, 1988. Biography of Harkness detailing the stormy period of her sponsorship of the Joffrey Ballet.

Woodward, Ian. *Ballet.* Sevenoaks, Kent, England: Hodder and Stoughton, 1977. Fixes the Joffrey Ballet squarely in the movement to democratize and popularize ballet by capitalizing on American qualities of athleticism, vitality, and youth. Describes Joffrey's alliance and breakup with Harkness.

Pegeen H. Albig

Cross-References

Balanchine and Kirstein Make New York a World Center for Ballet (1946), p. 1301; Ailey Founds His Dance Company (1958), p. 1774; The National Endowment for the Arts Is Established (1965), p. 2048; Tharp Stages *Deuce Coupe* for the Joffrey Ballet (1973), p. 2288; Multiculturalism Dominates the Dance World (Late 1980's), p. 2559.

WIESEL'S *NIGHT* RECALLS THE HOLOCAUST

Category of event: Literature
Time: 1956
Locale: Buenos Aires, Argentina; Paris, France; and New York, New York

Elie Wiesel's Night *is a powerful and widely read testimony of a Holocaust survivor and Nobel Peace Prize winner who dedicated his life to preserving the memory of the Holocaust victims*

> *Principal personages:*
> ELIE WIESEL (1928-   ), a Holocaust survivor, author, activist for human dignity, and 1986 Nobel Peace Prize winner
> SHLOMO WIESEL (1894-1945), the father of Elie Wiesel
> FRANÇOIS MAURIAC (1885-1970), a French Catholic writer and friend of Elie Wiesel

Summary of Event

In 1955, when Elie Wiesel began writing the original version of *Un di Velt hot geshvign* (1956; *Night*, 1960) in Yiddish, ten years of silence had passed since his liberation from the Buchenwald concentration camp in Germany. His silence had enabled his memories and reflections to deepen.

Wiesel was born in 1928 in Sighet, Transylvania, at that time part of Hungary. His father, Shlomo, was a shopkeeper who was always helping people, while his mother, Sarah Feig, was the pious descendant of great Hasidic rabbis and scholars. As a boy, Wiesel received a thorough Jewish education, proving to be a brilliant boy and showing great promise as a future rabbi. In 1944, Sighet was invaded by Nazi Germany, and the Hungarian fascists took power as the Nazis and their allies sought to finish the job of murdering every Jew in Europe. Wiesel, his parents, and his three sisters were put on a cattle car and taken to the Auschwitz concentration and death camp in Poland. In 1945, he and his father were marched west to the Buchenwald concentration camp in Germany. Wiesel and two sisters survived; the rest of their family perished, along with two hundred thousand other Jews from Hungary.

After the war, Wiesel sought refuge in Palestine, but because of British restrictions, he settled in Paris, where he studied at the Sorbonne and learned French, the language he chose for his novels. He became a journalist and correspondent. In 1954, he met the French Catholic writer and philosopher François Mauriac, who was so moved by Wiesel's story that he urged Wiesel to write about his experiences during the Holocaust.

In 1956, the original version of *Night* appeared. Eight hundred pages long, written in Yiddish, and published in Buenos Aires, Argentina, by an association of Polish Jews, it was entitled *Un di Velt hot geshvign* (and the world remained silent). In 1958, Wiesel condensed and translated the book into French, and with the help of Mauriac, it appeared in 1958 as *La Nuit.* After experiencing some difficulty in finding a publisher for an English-language edition of his book because of the depressing nature of his subject matter, Wiesel had the 116-page *Night* published by Hill and Wang in September of 1960. By 1986, it had gone through nine printings and had become the most widely read account of a Holocaust survivor.

Within the brief confines of its covers, *Night* encapsulates experiences of the Holocaust through the eyes of a fifteen-year-old boy. The immediacy of the episodes is conveyed superbly and could be multiplied by the millions of victims who did not survive to tell their story. Indeed, Wiesel dedicated his life to writing to memorialize the six million innocent Jewish dead. Unlike the equally popular individual account of a child's experiences during the World War II years, Anne Frank's *The Diary of a Young Girl* (1952), *Night* traces the immediate descent of a teenager into the hell of the death camps.

The story begins in 1941, when Elie is twelve years old, growing up in a typical, pious Jewish household in Eastern Europe. His mentor, Moche the Beadle, tells him that he must ask the right questions of God and that he must find the answers only within himself. This sets the stage for the spiritual struggles Elie will undergo during the Holocaust.

In 1944, the Nazis and the Hungarian fascist police descend on the village of Sighet, and some Jews are taken away, among them Moche. Moche escapes and returns with tales of horror, but the villagers do not believe him.

Soon Elie and his family are told that they must leave, that they will be "resettled." With diabolical cleverness, the Germans have concealed their murderous plan. The Wiesel family is crammed into a cattle car with the other Jews of Sighet. The unforgettable terror of the journey is conveyed in a few short pages. When they arrive at the death camp of Auschwitz, the family is separated. Elie's mother and his youngest sister are immediately sent to the gas chambers, while he and his father are spared for slave labor. Brutal guards, dogs, flames, the smell of burning flesh, and the sight of burning babies and children greet the prisoners on their first day in the camp.

The rest of the book describes Elie's unbearable physical and spiritual struggle in the camps and his constant efforts to help his father. In 1945, the two are marched west to Buchenwald. Elie's father dies of mistreatment and fever shortly before liberation. The story ends as Elie looks into the mirror after liberation: "From the depths of the mirror, a corpse gazed back at me. The look in his eyes, as they stared into mine, has never left me."

Within the pages of *Night* are myriad themes, each vital in understanding the effects of the Holocaust on the human condition. *Night* represents an education in reverse, an initiation of a pious, optimistic teenager into a scaled universe of colossal inhumanity and death. It is a story of the Exodus in reverse, a true account of the fall of humanity in modern times. Wiesel poses painful questions about the nature of evil, loss of innocence, and crises of faith, and he views himself as a living corpse at the end.

Although part of Wiesel died in Auschwitz, the look in his eyes that never leaves him is a sign of pained hope and of his recognition that he must bear witness to the horrid crimes he has seen. He commits his life henceforth to the telling of the tale.

Impact of Event

When *Night* first appeared in the United States in 1960, the accolades in scholarly, Jewish, and Christian periodicals were unanimous. It was praised for its spare, clear style, devoid of embellishment, artifice, and self-pity. Nevertheless, it was considered immensely powerful because of its compression of a variety of themes and its vivid descriptions of the camps' surrealistic conditions, the inhumanity of the perpetrators, and the humanity of many of the victims: All of this in a narrative of controlled power. Moreoever, its success and impact were also attributed to its accessible vocabulary. Reviewers immediately ranked it in importance with the *Diary of a Young Girl*. Because of the circumstances under which it was written as well as the maturity of its author, *Night* concretizes the horrifying reality of the Holocaust in a different manner from that of Frank's diary.

A few extracts must suffice to convey the amazing imagery of *Night*. In the cattle car on the way to Auschwitz, Madame Schachter prophetically screams out the fate of the Jews: "Jews, listen to me! I can see a fire! There are huge flames! It is a furnace!" Wiesel's first night in Auschwitz—during which he witnesses babies, children, and adults being burned alive—wounds his faith in human goodness, in the Western Enlightenment, and in God. "Never shall I forget that night, the first night in camp, which has turned my life into one long night. . . . Never shall I forget these things, even if I am condemned to live as long as God Himself. Never."

Wiesel encounters extremes of human behavior. Acts of great kindness and self-sacrifice exist alongside the most wanton brutality and sadism. One day, a boy accused of sabotaging the electric power station in the work camp is hung. He weighs little, so he strangles slowly. Wiesel says that God "is hanging here on this gallows" with the young boy. One night, during a lull in the death march to Buchenwald, Wiesel's friend Juliek plays a fragment of Beethoven on his violin. "I had never heard sounds so pure. In such a silence," he writes. Somehow, a broken human being was able to summon hope and beauty amid a pile of corpses.

Finally, when Wiesel's father dies on January 28, 1945, shortly before the liberation, Elie admits: "But I had no more tears. . . . I might perhaps have found something like—free at last." Such was the impact of the camp on even the closest of human relationships, and such is the unflinching honesty of Wiesel's work.

The emotionally charged passages have found their way into countless books and curricula about the Holocaust. They rank with the greatest pages in all literature. The variety of themes and literary models in the book is also astounding. The imagery of darkness, the motif of the journey, the description of hell on earth in nine chapters is suggestive of Dante Alighieri's journey through the inferno. The five defiant counts of never (to forget) as Wiesel witnesses the burning of children is reminiscent of the outcry in William Shakespeare's *King Lear* when Lear sees the body of his innocent murdered daughter, Cordelia. The confrontation with madness in the camps and the double vision in the mirror at the end are also notable.

Night is representative of the forces that helped shape Wiesel's work. They are the Jewish biblical, talmudic, and cabalistic traditions and the current of modern existentialism. Wiesel's struggles of faith are reminiscent of Job's, and the angry tone of the prophets is present, as are the chanting rhythms of the Psalmists. *Night* exemplifies the Jewish tradition of storytelling, which holds that memory is the key to conscience.

After the war, Wiesel became influenced by the new outlook and literature of French existentialism, embodied in the works of Jean-Paul Sartre and particularly Albert Camus. They stressed the modern problems of anxiety, alienation, and absurdity of life but also demanded that men and women commit themselves to defining the meaning of existence for themselves and to fighting against evil.

Wiesel fused these two traditions. In the 1970's, he became increasingly well known as *Night* was succeeded by many of his novels and essays about victims, fighters, participants, parents, and the greatness and endurance of the Jewish people—all his writings built upon *Night.*

Wiesel's commitment to human dignity parallels his writings. He has fought prejudice, genocide, and hatred, and he has defended the rights of oppressed Cambodians, Gypsies, Biafrans, Paraguayan Indians, and Black South Africans as well as the rights of persecuted Jews in the Soviet Union. In so doing, he has applied the unique catastrophe of the Jewish people to the universal concerns of all people.

In 1979, Wiesel was appointed as the first chairman of the U.S. President's Holocaust Commission. In 1985, following the example of the prophets' tradition of telling "truth to power," he gently but eloquently rebuked President Ronald Reagan in public for planning a journey to a cemetery where officers of the SS (Schutzstaffel) lay buried. In 1986, he was awarded the Nobel Peace Prize in Oslo, Norway.

Wiesel's journey from Auschwitz to Oslo was a miracle set in motion by *Night.* More than most works, it helped call attention to the experience of the Holocaust. It remains a point of entry for encountering that forbidding but vital area. As a memoir of the Holocaust, *Night* remains unsurpassed. It is used extensively in schools and colleges in a variety of disciplines. As long as memory endures in freedom, the book will remain a unique classic, a monument to memory, and a warning to the human spirit.

Bibliography

Brown, Robert McAfee. *Elie Wiesel: Messenger to All Humanity.* Notre Dame, Ind.: University of Notre Dame Press, 1983. The work of a distinguished Protestant theologian, this eloquent book stresses the impact of Wiesel's work, and particularly *Night,* on Christians. McAfee agrees with Wiesel that the Holocaust is a problem for Christians as well as for Jews. There is a fine chapter on Christian responses entitled "Birkenau and Golgotha" as well as an excellent bibliography and useful summaries of Wiesel's major works.

Estess, Ted L. *Elie Wiesel.* New York: Frederick Ungar, 1980. This excellent survey approaches Wiesel as a questioner of himself, of man, and of God. Traces Wiesel's novels that followed *Night.* Maintains (following Wiesel's own assertion) that *Night* is the foundation of all Wiesel's work.

Fine, Ellen S. *Legacy of Night: The Literary Universe of Elie Wiesel.* Albany: State University of New York Press, 1982. The best introductory survey of the work of Elie Wiesel. Contains a superb chapter on *Night* and its publication. Characterizes Wiesel as a new kind of literary figure, the "protagonist as witness." Emphasizes the father-son relationship in the novel and analyzes the ending of the book as a new beginning—writing and testimony as a reason for living.

Rittner, Carol, ed. *Elie Wiesel: Between Memory and Hope.* New York: New York University Press, 1990. Carol Rittner, a Sister of Mercy and Director of the Elie Wiesel Foundation, has assembled seventeen excellent essays in this collection, written by literary scholars, theologians, and philosophers. The theme is that Wiesel's thinking has changed over the past thirty years yet remained the same, with a focus on memory as the foundation of morality.

Wiesel, Elie. *Night.* Translated from the French by Stella Rodway. Foreword by François Mauriac. Preface for the twenty-fifth anniversary edition by Robert McAfee Brown. Toronto: Bantam Books, 1986. The most popular and accessible edition of *Night*, owing to its compact paperback format and reasonable price. Brown's eloquent preface urges that *Night* be read by all to honor the dead and to warn the living. The foreword by Mauriac must be read, for it reveals why he, as a Christian and a sensitive writer, encouraged Wiesel to break his silence.

Leon Stein

Cross-References

The Metamorphosis Anticipates Modern Feelings of Alienation (1915), p. 396; Hašek's *The Good Soldier Švejk* Reflects Postwar Disillusionment (1921), p. 523; *All Quiet on the Western Front* Stresses the Futility of War (1929), p. 767; Hitler Organizes an Exhibition Denouncing Modern Art (1937), p. 1083; The Nazis Ban Nolde's Paintings (1941), p. 1217; Sartre's *Being and Nothingness* Expresses Existential Philosophy (1943), p. 1262; *Catch-22* Illustrates Antiwar Sentiment (1961), p. 1866; Singer Wins the Nobel Prize in Literature (1978), p. 2423.

PRESLEY BECOMES A ROCK-AND-ROLL SENSATION

Category of event: Music
Time: 1956-1957
Locale: The United States

Emerging from the American South with a voice that bridged black and white musical traditions, Elvis Presley became the supreme figure in rock and roll and one of the most famous singers of all time

Principal personages:

ELVIS PRESLEY (1935-1977), a rock singer, actor, and virtual symbol of American culture in life and death

SAM PHILLIPS (1923-   ), the Memphis record producer who recognized Presley's talent, nurtured it, and then sold his contract to RCA records

COLONEL TOM PARKER (ANDREAS CORNELIUS VAN KUIJK, 1910-   ), the manager who engineered unprecedented deals for Presley—and who took an unusually large percentage for himself

Summary of Event

By the beginning of 1956, Elvis Presley had completed a musical apprenticeship that had him poised on the brink of superstardom. In 1953, the poor, white, Mississippi-born Presley had walked into Sam Phillips' Sun Records studio in Memphis, supposedly to make a vanity recording for his mother, and was noticed by secretary Marion Keisker. Keisker, in turn, brought Presley to the attention of Phillips, the producer for Johnny Cash, Jerry Lee Lewis, Roy Orbison, and other early country and rock greats. The story goes that Phillips had claimed that if he could find a white boy who could sing black music, he would make a million dollars; Elvis was that boy. Yet it had taken months of practice before the dimensions of Presley's talent became clear, and when Phillips finally sold his contract to the Radio Corporation of America (RCA), he received only forty thousand dollars (Phillips later made his million many times over by investing in a small company by the name of Holiday Inn).

Phillips decided to sell the contract because he feared—ironically—that his protégé's success would bankrupt his company. While Presley was building a large regional following making hit records for Sun in 1954 and 1955—including "That's All Right, Mama," "Good Rockin' Tonight," and "Mystery Train"—Sun lacked the credit and capacity to meet the demand for product generated by such a huge national star. RCA, like most major New York record companies, had largely ignored the groundswell of rock and roll emerging from the South and was now trying to acquire a bankable franchise. It was in this context that Presley recorded his first RCA single, "Heartbreak Hotel," which was released in early 1956. It quickly topped the pop charts and was followed in short order by "Don't Be Cruel" and "Hound Dog."

Events then moved rapidly. In January, Presley made the first of a series of appearances on national television, culminating with performances on *The Ed Sullivan Show*. Sullivan, who had sworn Presley would never appear on the program, ended up paying the then-vast sum of fifty thousand dollars for Presley's performance, though the overt sexuality of Presley's hip thrusts led censors to show him only from the waist up by the time of his last Sullivan show appearance in January of 1957.

Meanwhile, Presley began pursuing his dream of becoming a movie star. In the summer of 1956, he went to Hollywood to film *Love Me Tender*, which created a sensation when released later that year. *Jailhouse Rock*, which followed in 1957, enjoyed similar success. Ironically, the one venue where Presley failed in his early career was in Las Vegas, where a two-week engagement in April of 1956 was canceled after one week because of poor ticket sales (Las Vegas audiences in the decades to follow would prove far more enthusiastic).

By the beginning of 1957, Elvis Presley had become one of the most familiar faces in the country, adored by teenage girls, emulated by teenage boys, and viewed with much consternation by the gatekeepers of the nation's morals. Though unfailingly polite and careful to avoid political controversies later rock stars would embrace, Presley's powerful sexuality, the clear influence of African-American musical styles in his music at a time of racial segregation, and his powerful grip on a widely distrusted popular culture made him an object of scorn and fear for many middle-class white Americans. In retrospect, the draft notice Presley received in 1957 (deferred until early 1958) seems as much a covert attempt to control him as an example of the blind justice of the military system.

Meanwhile, the records kept coming: chart-topping film songs such as "Love Me Tender" and "Jailhouse Rock" as well as "All Shook Up," "Treat Me Nice," and "Loving You." Presley began 1958 with "Don't"/"I Beg of You" at number one, and he probably would have kept right on going if his induction into the Army in March had not interrupted his career. He spent most of the next two years stationed in Germany, with only one opportunity to record; a song from that session, "Big Hunk of Love," reached the top of the charts in 1959.

Presley returned home from the Army in early 1960 and quickly resumed his career. In the opinion of many critics, however, he never recovered the early brilliance of his first RCA records—or, for that matter, of his Sun recordings. For most of the 1960's, he focused on his film career, releasing a string of relatively uninteresting sound tracks to go with them. This decline was interrupted in 1968, when a television special and some exciting new recordings made in Memphis recaptured his early energy and revived his musical career. By the mid-1970's, however, Presley had once again fallen into decline, a decline all the more dramatic and painful because he was physically deteriorating as well. By the time of his fatal drug overdose in 1977, he had become a symbol of lost hope and decadence. Yet such an image could never altogether erase the profoundly powerful, even inspiring, Elvis Presley of the mid-1950's, who seemed to embody an American dream come true.

Impact of Event

In his essay "Presliad," often cited as the best piece of writing on Elvis Presley, Greil Marcus aptly summarizes what the man has come to represent for millions of Americans: "Elvis has emerged as a great *artist*, a great *rocker*, a great *purveyor of schlock*, a great *heart throb*, a great *bore*, a great *symbol of potency*, a great *ham*, a great *nice person*, and yes, a great American." With an immense influence that extends far beyond popular music, and an iconography that extends far beyond the nation's borders, Elvis Presley has come to represent the best and worst aspects of the United States' cultural dominance of the global village.

It is tempting to think that Presley entered the world stage fully formed, offering a dazzling vision of possibility in an era of unprecedented prosperity. For the many Americans chafing under the strictures of a generation gap and the stifling conformity of the 1950's, there was an irreducible reality to this view. Yet Presley was able to succeed to the extent that he did not only because he presented something new in American culture but also because he distilled some very old—and very powerful—currents in that culture.

The most central of these currents was racial. Growing up as a poor white boy in Tupelo, Mississippi, and Memphis, Tennessee, during the Great Depression, Presley was in close contact with African-American culture and evangelical religion, two forces that were to exert a powerful influence on his musical development. By the time he walked into the Sun studios as a teenager, he had developed an almost effortless ability to evoke and manipulate a wide variety of musical styles—blues, gospel, bluegrass, country and western, and others. Presley's first record for Sun was an Arthur Crudup blues tune, "That's All Right, Mama" backed with Bill Monroe's bluegrass classic "Blue Moon of Kentucky." The selection was revealing; Presley took black and white music and made them two sides of the same record, etching each with a sense of style that was wholly his own.

Contrary to the popular myth, Presley did not invent rock and roll, a term that had begun circulating in the black community as early as the late 1940's. Chuck Berry possessed far greater songwriting gifts and a penchant for integrating racial styles; Jerry Lee Lewis may have had more raw performing talent. It was Presley, however, who synthesized a variety of strains and even contradictions: technology and tradition, the sacred and the profane, poverty and wealth, and, of course, black and white. Given the racism that pervaded so many aspects of American society in the 1950's, it was virtually inevitable that great wealth and fame would be conferred on a white rock star rather than a black one. No doubt other performers deserved more recognition than they received, and Presley himself might have had a longer, happier life if he had received less.

Despite all this, Presley's signal achievement—obscured as it is amid all the hype, his mediocre acting performances, the laughable excess of his 1970's persona, and his pathetic addictions to drugs, alcohol, and other vices—remains his music. Over the course of two decades, he amassed a remarkably diverse body of work that has become a point of reference for generations of subsequent performers. He was a major inspiration to the Beatles, whose own success was measured by the yardstick Presley established. More recently, Bruce Springsteen has often named Presley as the central figure in his artistic development.

In the aftermath of his rise to national prominence in 1956 and 1957, Elvis Presley acquired an appellation that has stuck ever since: the King. There is a subtle irony in the bestowal of such a title in a nation presumably founded to resist royalty in all its forms. In any case, it is striking to consider that a poor boy with undistinguished lineage ascended to a cultural and commercial throne in the United States. Here is one more contradiction in a life full of them, and in the nation that produced him.

Bibliography

Dundy, Elaine. *Elvis and Gladys.* New York: Macmillan, 1985. Chronicles Presley's relationship with perhaps the most important person in his life—his mother. With sensitivity and solid research, Dundy explores a major inspiration to Presley, and a major source of anguish following her death in 1958.

Garulnick, Peter. "Elvis Presley." In *The Rolling Stone Illustrated History of Rock and Roll,* edited by Jim Miller. Rev. ed. New York: Rolling Stone Press, 1980. A well-written analysis of Presley's life, focused on his formative years. Garulnick clearly favors the Sun material over anything that followed. See also *Lost Highway: Journeys and Arrivals of American Musicians* (New York: Harper & Row, 1989), which includes a profile of Elvis along with other giants of early rock and roll.

Goldman, Albert. *Elvis.* New York: Avon Books, 1981. One of the best-known biographies of Elvis, and probably the worst, *Elvis* is both mean-spirited and scatological. Goldman's preoccupation with debunking Presley mythology precludes any serious engagement with his music. He later wrote *Elvis: The Last Twenty Four Hours* (New York: St. Martin's Press, 1991) as a postscript for the book.

Hopkins, Jerry. *Elvis.* New York: Simon & Schuster, 1971. Dated, but a good source of factual material. In some ways, still the standard biography of Presley; remains widely cited. See also *Elvis: The Final Years* (New York: St. Martin's Press, 1980), which supplements the original book.

Marchback, Pearce, ed. *Elvis in His Own Words.* Compiled by Mick Farren. New York: Omnibus Press, 1977. A useful collection of interviews, fan-club material, and more. Presley was not always a candid or incisive evaluator of his life and work, but read with care, this material can be revealing. Many interesting photos.

Marcus, Greil. *Dead Elvis.* New York: Anchor/Doubleday, 1991. A loose collection of pieces on Presley's lasting influence on American culture, even in death. Some critics have considered the book too fragmented and excessive, but there are keen insights throughout.

_____. "Presliad." In *Mystery Train: Images of America in Rock 'n' Roll Music.* Rev. ed. New York: Plume, 1990. A classic in the field of rock criticism. The book's final chapter on Presley, first written in 1972, remains a landmark. Especially useful for appreciating Presley's cultural significance. Includes excellent bibliographic and discographic material.

Marsh, Dave. *Elvis.* New York: Warner Books, 1982. One of the better works on Presley's life and death. More an extended essay than a biography, the book features some good analysis and evocative photographs.

Ward, Ed. "Sunrise in the South" and "Don't Lose That Kid." In *Rock of Ages: The Rolling Stone History of Rock and Roll,* by Ed Ward, Geoffrey Stokes, and Ken Tucker. New York: Rolling Stone Press, 1986. The former essay does an excellent job of placing Presley into the Memphis musical milieu; the latter chronicles the events of Presley's rise to stardom. Together, the two chapters offer perhaps the best brief narrative account of Presley's life in the years 1953-1956.

Wise, Sue. "Sexing Elvis." In *On Record: Rock, Pop, and the Written Word.* New York: Pantheon Books, 1990. A fascinating feminist reading of Presley by a lesbian critic who compellingly explores the varied ways popular cultural phenomena are apprehended and used by audiences. An unusual and important contribution to Presley literature.

Jim Cullen

Cross-References

Bill Monroe and the Blue Grass Boys Define Bluegrass Music (1939), p. 1121; Hank Williams Performs on *The Grand Ole Opry* (1949), p. 1415; Berry's "Maybellene" Popularizes Rock and Roll (1955), p. 1635; The Beatles Revolutionize Popular Music (1963), p. 1944; The Rolling Stones Release *Out of Our Heads* (1965), p. 2027; Dylan Performs with Electric Instruments (1965), p. 2038; Springsteen's *Born to Run* Reinvigorates Mainstream Rock (1975), p. 2325.

THE FRENCH NEW WAVE USHERS
IN A NEW ERA OF CINEMA

Category of event: Motion pictures
Time: 1956-1960
Locale: Paris, France

Between 1956 and 1960, a burst of fresh French films by young directors such as Roger Vadim and François Truffaut marked the debut of the internationally influential French New Wave

Principal personages:

ROGER VADIM (1928-), a noted French filmmaker whose 1956 debut, *Et Dieu créa la femme*, paved the way for other emerging New Wave directors

FRANÇOIS TRUFFAUT (1932-1984), the most successful of the New Wave directors, who formally introduced the auteur theory

JEAN-LUC GODARD (1930-), a controversial French film director who came to prominence with the New Wave after serving as a critic for *Cahiers du cinéma*

CLAUDE CHABROL (1930-), a noted New Wave film director whose earliest involvement with film was as a critic for Bazin's *Cahiers du cinéma*

ANDRÉ BAZIN (1918-1958), an important French film critic who as editor of *Cahiers du cinéma* published the early film criticism of Truffaut, Chabrol, Godard, and others

JACQUES RIVETTE (1928-), a central member of the New Wave who wrote key articles for *Cahiers du cinéma* before assuming its editorship from 1963 to 1965

ERIC ROHMER (1920-), a prominent French film director noted for his philosophical "morality tales" who championed the New Wave as editor-in-chief of *Cahiers du cinéma* from 1957 to 1963

HENRI LANGLOIS (1914-1977), the dedicated cineast who ran the Cinémathèque Française, home of the *Cahiers du cinéma* critics who in the late 1950's became the core of the New Wave

ALEXANDRE ASTRUC (1923-), a critic turned filmmaker who helped to inspire the auteur theory and the independent spirit of the New Wave

Summary of Event

The term *Nouvelle Vague*, or "New Wave," was coined in 1958 by film critic Françoise Giroud to describe a youthful group of French filmmakers who were just beginning to make themselves felt through a stunning array of debut features released during the years 1956 to 1960. It was during this period that such now-celebrated directors as Roger Vadim, Claude Chabrol, François Truffaut, Jean-Luc Godard, Eric Rohmer, and Jacques Rivette made their initial appearances as auteurs, or cinematic "authors," with highly personalized works marked by brashly audacious thematic and stylistic twists. Vadim broke the ice in 1956 with the erotic box-office blockbuster *Et Dieu créa la femme* (*And God Created Woman*). Later, the New Wave's freshness and vitality were recognized by an impressive array of festival awards, such as the Locarno Festival's prize for best direction to Chabrol for *Le Beau Serqe* (1958), the Cannes Festival's first prize for direction to Truffaut for *Les Quatre Cents Coups* (1958; *The Four Hundred Blows*), and the Berlin Festival's award for best direction to Godard for *À bout de souffle* (1960; *Breathless*). The New Wave, as epitomized by these four highly successful debut feature films, had arrived.

In part, the phenomenon of the French New Wave was a natural event. It was the coming of age of a new generation of cineasts who castigated the work of their elders as "papa's cinema." For such rebellious youth, the well-made but impersonal films of such established directors as Claude Autant-Lara, René Clément, and Henri-Georges Clouzot were marred by their calculated coolness, their literary pretensions, their emphasis on conventional narratives with too neat beginnings, middles, and ends, and their essentially artificial, theatricalized *mise en scène*, a visual style derived from the films' having been shot within a studio rather than on location.

If such barbs had been confined to café conversations along the Seine, significant changes in the French cinema undoubtedly would have been slow. During the 1950's, however, such soon-to-be New Wave directors as Vadim, Truffaut, Chabrol, and Godard vented their cinematic passions as film critics, and their broadsides and bromides were regular features of such influential film journals as *Cahiers du cinéma*.

Indeed, it was in the pages of *Cahiers du cinéma* that the tenets of the New Wave were first sketched. Under the sage and temperate editorship of renowned critic André Bazin, the "angry young men" of *Cahiers du cinéma* developed the auteur theory, which endorsed only those films in which the imprint or stamp of the director was clear. Inspired by Alexandre Astruc's seminal 1948 essay "La Caméra-Stylo" ("The Camera-Pen"), which conceptualized cinema as a mode of expression potentially as flexible and subtle as written language, the *Cahiers du cinéma* critics advocated an open-ended and personal approach to filmmaking in which the predominant "voice" was that of the director, who would "write" with the camera as the novelist wrote with words.

Though rejecting the bulk of French cinema of the late 1940's and most of the 1950's as too conservative and too "literary," the *Cahiers du cinéma* group found inspiration in the 1930's films of countryman Jean Renoir, whose naturalistic settings and antibourgeois polemics were in tune with the kind of stylistic freedom and cultural-political rebellion espoused by Truffaut, Rohmer, Chabrol, and Godard. With the aid of Henri Langlois, the head of the fabled film archive Cinémathèque Française in Paris, they also found inspiration in the films of a variety of American directors. Indeed, it was Langlois who first introduced the young cineasts to much of the work of John Ford, Howard Hawks, and Sam Fuller, among others. The eager, even obsessive critics scrutinized and argued the relative merits of such films as Ford's *She Wore a Yellow Ribbon* (1949) and Hawks's *Bringing Up Baby* (1938). Their views on these and hundreds of other American films were then formalized for publication in the pages of *Cahiers du cinéma.*

Eventually, a director such as Ford or Hawks was "certified" as an auteur after demonstrating a capacity for inscribing his personal mark—an idiosyncratic and recurring thematic or visual style—in all manner of studio films, including established genres such as the Western, the screwball comedy, the gangster film, and even the musical. Such American filmmakers were praised for their directness, their energy, and their visual style as it correlated to theme, as well as their purging of virtually anything suggesting literary or even philosophical intent. Significantly, the *Cahiers du cinéma* group was looking for a cinema untainted by the encrustations and conventions of the older arts, especially the novel and the play. The ideal cinema was to be forged from its own intrinsically unique resources, its capacity for deconstructing the continuum of actual space and time, and the reciprocal process of reconstituting its fragments into uniquely cinematic constructs.

While such theorizing was well and good, it was quite another matter to move from one's typewriter at the *Cahiers du cinéma* office to the director's chair. What was needed was an unqualified box-office success, a film that would convince the industry's money men that there was potential profit in bankrolling production costs for young and unproven directorial talent.

The breakthrough came in 1956 with Vadim's *And God Created Woman.* Starring Vadim's wife, Brigitte Bardot, the steamy and sultry tale was a box-office smash in France and abroad. The dam had burst, and a New Wave was unleashed—a tidal force that would transform the French and international film scenes.

Impact of Event

The consequences of the success of *And God Created Woman* were many. Suddenly, youth was in vogue. Also, producers were impressed that the New Wave tyros needed only a fraction of the money typically allocated to establishment directors such as Claude Autant-Lara. Combined with the gradual erosion of the French filmgoing audience as a result of competition from television, producers saw that they could underwrite eight or nine low-budget features, in expectation that at least several would generate profits, for the cost of, for example, a single Autant-Lara production.

There were also subsidies from the French government in the form of the *loi d'aide*, a prize for innovative filmmaking. On the basis of a modest grant for his short film *Les Mistons* (1958; *The Mischief Makers*), for example, François Truffaut was able to make his first feature, the celebrated *The Four Hundred Blows.*

Another auspicious factor encouraging the rapid rise of the New Wave was the postwar trend toward the development of an international youth market. During the

1950's, the worldwide ascendency of rock and roll, the quintessential musical expression of postwar teens, was paralleled by an increase in the number of youth-targeted films. It was a movement epitomized by the global success of Nicholas Ray's *Rebel Without a Cause* (1955) and the canonization of its brooding star, James Dean. In France, such developments helped to pave the way for the New Wave.

Indeed, between 1956 and 1960, more than a hundred French filmmakers made debut features. In addition to the premieres of Vadim, Chabrol, Truffaut, and Godard, there were prominent first-time efforts by other *Cahiers du cinéma* critics such as Eric Rohmer and Jacques Rivette. Along with the *Cahiers du cinéma* directors was an older cadre, the so-called Left Bank group, which included Alain Resnais, Agnès Varda, and Chris Marker. Buoyed by the success of their younger colleagues, these more politically involved and literary directors also gained new opportunities.

The French New Wave had a marked influence on American college students, who in the 1960's increasingly began dreaming of directing the next great American film rather than of writing the great American novel. Film critic Stanley Kauffmann aptly described this burgeoning group of youthful American cineasts as "the film generation." Nurtured by the auteur theory and the English edition of *Cahiers du cinéma* (expertly edited in New York by Andrew Sarris), as well as by the growth of university film programs that made the study of film an official part of the curriculum, young Americans avidly devoured the latest films of Truffaut, Godard, and Resnais in college and museum film series. The quirky freedom of such films as Truffaut's *Tirez sur le pianiste* (1960; *Shoot the Piano Player*) and Godard's *Une Femme est une femme* (1961; *A Woman Is a Woman*), as well as the formal if enigmatic brilliance of Resnais' *L'Année dernière à Marienbad* (1961; *Last Year at Marienbad*) bedazzled and inspired. Moreover, thanks to the auteur approach to criticism, Americans themselves began to take seriously the work of such directors as Ford, Hawks, and Alfred Hitchcock, and previously devalued American genres such as the Western, the musical, and the detective film were newly appreciated. The arrival of the New Wave was a watershed that at last established the motion picture as a linchpin of American culture.

The French New Wave, with its audacious use of improvisation, its breaking of technical rules such as the use of the jump cut, and its tendency to favor open-ended, unresolved narratives, was also an inspiration to filmmakers in Third World and Communist nations. In Brazil, for example, the *Cinema Novo* movement was spurred in its search for bold new aesthetic means by the deconstruction of narrative filmmaking conventions undertaken by the New Wave. Cuban directors, charged with making films that had direct political as well as aesthetic value, also increasingly looked to the New Wave for narrative and technical strategies that would cut against the grain of the bourgeois Hollywood film.

It should be remembered, however, that the French New Wave was not a cohesive stylistic or thematic movement but rather a largely fortuitous gathering of talent that was given extraordinary opportunities to express itself thanks to a propitious conglomeration of economic, social, and historical circumstances. Indeed, it is significant that many critics regard the New Wave as a phenomenon that lasted only several years. By the mid-1960's, the New Wave was a mostly self-indulgent and tepid force; the movement's reflexive preoccupations with cinema itself and its often inscrutable narratives ceased to have even novelty value. There was also a sense that youth had been served, and that the New Wave, if it were to be sustained, needed more than fresh faces and reckless detonations of traditional cinematic conventions.

The French New Wave, though, was an integral part of the cultural *Zeitgeist* of the 1960's. It was a force that helped to establish a serious-minded and worldwide "film generation." Through the agency of the auteur theory, moreover, the New Wave was a force leading to profound reevaluations of film criticism and the very history of the medium, including the cultural conditions that have supported it. Most significantly, the French New Wave gave the world a pantheon of significant directors and a canon of films that have clearly established themselves as central to any reading of film history, theory, or criticism.

Bibliography

Armes, Roy. *The Personal Style.* Vol. 2 in *French Cinema Since 1946.* 2d ed. New York: A. S. Barnes, 1970. A well-considered account of seventeen of the most important New Wave directors, including Chabrol, Truffaut, Godard, Resnais, and Vadim. A filmography and bibliography is included for each director.

Graham, Peter, comp. *The New Wave: Critical Landmarks.* Garden City, N.Y.: Doubleday, 1968. Provocative collection of seminal articles by such New Wave proponents as Astruc, Bazin, Chabrol, Godard, Truffaut, and Robert Benayoun taken from *Cahiers du cinéma* and *Positif.* Illustrated, with bibliography.

Hillier, Jim, ed. *Cahiers du Cinéma, the 1950's: Neo-Realism, Hollywood, New Wave.* Cambridge: Harvard University Press, 1985. Collection of essential essays from *Cahiers du cinéma* by Bazin, Godard, Truffaut, Rivette, Rohmer, Chabrol, and others. Hillier's comments help to contextualize the cinematic and political dynamics giving rise to the New Wave. Includes a valuable guide to *Cahiers du cinéma* articles from the 1950's that are available in English translation.

Monaco, James. *The New Wave: Truffaut, Godard, Chabrol, Rohmer, Rivette.* New York: Oxford University Press, 1976. Excellent overview of the forces that propelled the French New Wave to the summit of the international cinema. Includes useful bibliography.

Taylor, John Russell. "The New Wave: François Truffaut; Jean-Luc Godard; Alain Resnais." *In Cinema Eye, Cinema Ear: Some Key Film-Makers of the Sixties.* New York: Hill and Wang, 1964. Penetrating treatment of the early successes of Truffaut, Godard, and Resnais.

Charles Merrell Berg

Cross-References

Renoir Marks the High Point of Prewar Filmmaking (1937), p. 1073; The Italian

New Wave Gains Worldwide Acclaim (1942), p. 1228; *La Strada* Solidifies Fellini's Renown as a Brilliant Director (1954), p. 1596; Dean Becomes a Legend in *Rebel Without a Cause* (1955), p. 1640; Godard's Expressionistic *À bout de souffle* Revolutionizes Film (1960), p. 1845.

SAARINEN DESIGNS KENNEDY AIRPORT'S
TWA TERMINAL

Category of event: Architecture
Time: 1956-1962
Locale: New York, New York

Expanding his nonrectilinear sculptured architectural experiments, Eero Saarinen designed an exciting interpretation of soaring spatial liberty

Principal personages:
EERO SAARINEN (1910-1961), a distinguished Finnish-American architect
ELIEL SAARINEN (1873-1950), a noted Finnish-American architect, Eero's
father, mentor, and partner
KEVIN ROCHE (1922-   ), a brilliant associate of Eero in designing major commissions
LE CORBUSIER (CHARLES-ÉDOUARD JEANNERET, 1887-1965), an influence on Saarinen and one of the twentieth century's great architects
LUDWIG MIES VAN DER ROHE (1886-1969), a great architect who was also an early influence on Saarinen
CHARLES EAMES (1907-1978), a designer and lifelong friend of Saarinen

Summary of Event

Eero Saarinen was commissioned in 1956 by Trans World Airlines (TWA), then one of the world's leading air-passenger services, to design its prospective terminal at New York City's Idlewild (later John F. Kennedy International) Airport. Eero was the son of Eliel Saarinen, a distinguished Finnish-American architect who, after winning second prize for a design of the *Chicago Tribune* building, had brought his family to the United States in 1923. The elder Saarinen enjoyed an influential teaching career at the University of Michigan as well as at the Cranbrook School of Art and won professional praise for the execution of a number of private commissions. Notable among these were the Cranbrook School for Boys in Bloomfield Hills, Michigan; the Columbus, Indiana, Tabernacle Church of Christ; the Winnetka, Illinois, Crow Island School; the Fort Wayne, Indiana, A. C. Wermuth House, and, in collaboration with Eero, the Buffalo, New York, Kleinhans Music Hall. Both Eliel and his wife, Loja Gesellius, a gifted weaver, photographer, sculptor, and architectural modeler, had nurtured Eero's talents and seen him through Yale University's School of Architecture—and its Beaux-Arts tradition—to a place in Eliel's architectural firm in 1935. Until Eliel's death in 1950, Eero cultivated his own style within the firm of Saarinen and Saarinen, drifting from his father's Beaux-Arts eclecticism and earning personal recognition as a modernist. In 1940, he and Charles Eames won first prizes for furniture design sponsored by the Museum of Modern Art, and after three years of wartime service, Eero captured the federal competition for the design of the

Jefferson National Expansion Memorial in St. Louis, Missouri, in 1948. Completed in 1964, the memorial eventually came to be considered one of his masterworks and a national architectural landmark.

By the 1950's, architectural services of the Saarinen firm had become the most sought after in the country. Led by Eero, with a vastly expanded staff, the firm owed its prominence to Eero's conservative salesmanship coupled with exciting, novel ideas and to the prestige of having won a number of multimillion-dollar commissions. Several of these were undertaken almost simultaneously, among them the General Motors Technical Center, the Kresge Auditorium and Chapel at the Massachusetts Institute of Technology, a Bell Laboratories research complex, a research and development "campus" for International Business Machines (IBM), Yale's Ingalls Hockey Rink, the John Deere & Company Headquarters building, college buildings at Yale, the University of Chicago, the University of Pennsylvania, U.S. Embassy buildings in London and Oslo, and not least, the TWA project for Idlewild.

Amid this frenetic activity, the TWA Terminal offered Eero further opportunities to lend form and order to his own highly technologized view of civilization and to employ variations of new materials to give the most satisfying expression to each project. Thus, refinements of automotive steel and glass were used at the General Motors Technical Center, a reinforced concrete parabolic vault was developed to give lift to the Ingalls Hockey Rink, the nation's first concrete shell was built to open up the interior of Kresge Auditorium, and a massive curtain wall of glazed glass covered Bell's rectilinear research building.

From this exuberant, heuristic context, the TWA Terminal was to emerge as Saarinen's most celebrated design. The building was a clear example of Saarinen's search within each of his projects for a specifically appropriate idiom for the resolution of that work, rather than an effort to promulgate or perpetuate—like Le Corbusier or Ludwig Mies van der Rohe—a particular architectural philosophy. The terminal was intended to emphasize the drama and exhilaration of flight. Both the interior and exterior designs of the building were meant to imbue travelers with a sense of the building's constant motion. Four interlinked, slightly variegated barrel vaults supported by Y-shaped columns were joined to form the 50-foot-by-315-foot concrete shell enclosing the passenger area and defining the basic structure.

It was recognized that Saarinen's thematic inspiration owed something in a very general sense to the earlier works of others, particularly to sculptor Naum Gabo's designs and to projects previously executed by German-born Impressionist architects Erich Mendelsohn and Rudolph Steiner. Considerable experience had also accumulated to aid Saarinen (not to mention Le Corbusier and Frank Lloyd Wright) in seeking the plastic idiom of nonrectilinear structures, notably through the works of Eugene Freyssinet, Robert Maillart, and Pier Luigi Nervi. Because of the terminal's combined measure of scale, innovation, drama, and detail, however, Saarinen's design unquestionably bore his unique imprimatur. These refinements were an important result of his unprecedented reliance upon detailed model designs, which were elaborately patterned and sculpted in wire, cardboard, and other materials before being committed to paper, in order to deal with what he felt were the new architectural vocabularies required.

Saarinen conceived of the terminal, which was sited on a curving corner of Idlewild, as an emotional instrument, uplifting travelers from the sculpted entrance of massive ascending supports farther upward by convergent stairs into a central space of great flaring shells. This space yielded to huge convex windows with exhilarating panoramas of runways and sky. Entering the terminal, sensationally at least, the passenger was to be enveloped in an ambience of fluid freedom and premonitions of flight before embarking on an aircraft. Every curving detail inside—and outside, from which the structure appeared to be a bird about to soar—sought to engender this mood of expanding spatial liberty. Begun in 1956, the terminal was completed in 1962.

Impact of Event

Saarinen's TWA Terminal ranks as his most famous design, although critics are generally agreed that Dulles International Airport at Chantilly, Virginia, which was also completed in 1962, ranks as his greatest architectural achievement. Both of these accomplishments, along with the completion of eighteen other major commissions, are regarded as all the more remarkable because Saarinen worked for little more than a decade in his own right before his death in September, 1961.

Saarinen's release of his initial design studies for the TWA Terminal late in the 1950's provoked greater professional excitement and instantaneous acclaim than any other project of the period. Only plans for the Sydney Opera House solicited nearly as much attention. Accordingly, there was a breathless wait for the terminal's completion.

The gulf between conception and design and the actual construction of the terminal facility left much to be desired, though, and the finished building proved something of a disappointment to Saarinen and to critics alike. Although Saarinen had worked well with the engineering firm of Ammann & Whitney on earlier commissions, the firm's execution of his terminal design, particularly the engineering of the great concrete shells, was deemed far too conservative. Instead of appearing to rise from its site weightlessly, the structure seemed heavy. Moreover, despite the expectations generated by construction photos, the actual terminal gave the impression of being subdued and too small for its simulation of flight. Within the interior, this heaviness was accentuated by the almost perverse use of closely packed steel railings for balustrades, while the installation of glazing bars destroyed the hoped-for sense of smooth spatial flow from one part of the interior to another. Corporate cost-cutting further impaired the design's kinetic inspiration, for the moving pavements that were to have transported passengers through the terminal were abandoned, and the originally proposed interior bridgeways were supplanted by tunnels.

From critical perspectives, however, the worst blow to a full realization of Saarinen's design was the suffusion of a dominant corporate presence—and its machines—into the structure in place of the proposed ambience that was to have been devoted to the exaltation of the passenger. This loss was exacerbated by the terminal's surroundings, an aggregation of competing individual corporate headquarters, offices, and terminals that transformed Idlewild into what many felt was a vulgar modernist architectural circus. Overall, those who hoped that Saarinen's exploding genius had brought him up to date with the new technologies of jet aircraft, the incipient electronic revolution, and satellites were dismayed by the Idlewild product. To Saarinen biographer and architectural critic Allan Temko, the failure of the TWA Terminal in these respects was a consequence of the "much broader failings of our irrationally driven society." Saarinen's own assessment of the then still-unfinished terminal—perhaps too harsh a one—was that "it would make a beautiful ruin, like the baths of Caracalla."

In much more positive ways, however, the impact of the Idlewild experience both for Saarinen and architectural critics carried over into the design and construction of his masterpiece, the Dulles International Airport at Chantilly, Virginia. Design and construction of the Dulles facility—in this case, Saarinen's responsibility was not for one terminal but for an entire airport devoted exclusively to jet aircraft—began in 1958, two years after the beginning of the TWA Terminal project, and was completed at the same time, in 1962. Thus, the two undertakings proceeded almost simultaneously, with obvious interactions.

If the finished TWA Terminal might have looked more fulfilling alone atop a hill, Dulles International—appearing to hover between earth and sky, as Saarinen intended—had a profound impact upon the international architectural community, setting a world standard for jetports. As much as anyone, it was Saarinen who made TWA's Idlewild facility obsolete. Critics could concede, thereafter, that Saarinen had satisfied his quest for the identification of his works with the era's most advanced technology. More specifically, where the TWA Terminal failed to center upon the physical and aesthetic needs of the traveler, Dulles triumphed. The moving stairs that had been subtracted from TWA's construction were replaced at Dulles by newly designed, massive, mobile departure lounges that retained the kinetic feel of the passenger's movement through the great central structure—its parabolic roof a tour de force of prestressed and precast concrete—into the aircraft.

Throughout his brief yet distinguished career—the American Institute of Architects awarded him, posthumously, its Gold Medal in 1962—Saarinen, unlike his great contemporaries, eschewed formulation of a consistent philosophy. Rather, he asked why people wanted a particular structure and then considered relevant factors such as the site, the building and its functions, economics, and the users' psychological requirements. During the early years, when he came into direction of his father's firm, he adhered to a vocabulary established, in steel as it were, by Mies van der Rohe and his younger disciples. After 1956, however, Saarinen stressed an elaboration of his own vocabulary in light of his awareness of the times and the problems unique to a particular project. Through the failures of his electrifying design for the TWA Terminal to the soaring success at Dulles, critics concur that Saarinen's peculiar melding of static and mobile elements, along with an abandonment of monumentalism, may help provide one of the keys to twenty-first century architecture.

Bibliography

Carter, Peter. "Eero Saarinen, 1910-1961." *Architectural Digest* 18 (December, 1961): 45-71. An accessible journal with good summary observations on Saarinen's development. Admiring but critical.

Christ-Janer, Albert. *Eliel Saarinen.* Chicago: University of Chicago Press, 1948. Important to understanding Eero's training and development as an artist and architect. Beautifully illustrated with plans and photos. Two detailed chronologies, one personal, the other on works. Useful index.

Heyer, Paul. *Architects on Architecture: New Directions in America.* New York: Walker, 1966. Places Saarinen in context with his leading contemporaries. Informative interview of Kevin Roche on Saarinen's development and understanding of architecture. Plenty of great photos. Useful select bibliography and index. A delightful salad of professional comments and assessments.

Saarinen, Eero. *Eero Saarinen on His Work.* Edited by Aline B. Saarinen. New Haven, Conn.: Yale University Press, 1962. Editor was Eero's adoring second wife, but observations were the architect's. Saarinen was reticent about philosophizing and much less well-published than other major architects, but his musings and expositions here are important to an appreciation of him. Secure in his artistry, he had many critical observations about his work. Taken in conjunction with Heyer's interview (cited above) with Kevin Roche about Saarinen, this collection is revealing. Good photos and plans.

Spade, Rupert. *Eero Saarinen.* New York: Simon & Schuster, 1971. Excellent author's introduction provides fine context and analysis. Admiring, but objective and critical. Seventy superb photos by Yukio Futagawa, supplemented by author's excellent notes on twenty of Saarinen's major works, including the TWA Terminal. Chronological list of projects and events, select bibliography, and a useful index. A fine brief introduction to Saarinen, man and works.

Temko, Allan. *Eero Saarinen.* New York: George Braziller, 1962. Excellent reading. While Temko treats Saarinen as a cultural hero, he remains critical and objective. Fine brief treatment of the TWA project. Splendid photos and plans, a short chronology, select bibliography, and detailed index.

Clifton K. Yearley

Cross-References

Cranbrook Academy Begins a History of Design Excellence (1925), p. 610; Loewy Pioneers American Industrial Design (1929), p. 777; Wright Founds the Taliesin Fellowship (1932), p. 902; Le Corbusier Designs and Builds Chandigarh (1951), p. 1503; Fuller's First Industrial Geodesic Dome Is Erected (1953), p. 1579; The Guggenheim Museum Opens in a Building Designed by Wright (1959), p. 1806; Kahn Blends Architecture and Urban Planning in Dacca (1962), p. 1919; Expo 67 Presents Innovative Architectural Concepts (1967), p. 2081.

OSBORNE'S *LOOK BACK IN ANGER* OPENS IN LONDON

Category of event: Theater
Time: May 8, 1956
Locale: Royal Court Theatre, London, England

Raw emotions exploding, Jimmy Porter, the archetypal "Angry Young Man," defined not only his author but a whole generation of English playwrights

Principal personages:
JOHN OSBORNE (1929-   ), the author of *Look Back in Anger*
TONY RICHARDSON (1928-1991), the director of the Royal Court Theatre's production of *Look Back in Anger*
KENNETH TYNAN (1927-1980), the critic who pronounced *Look Back in Anger* "the best young play of its decade"
KENNETH HAIGH (1931-   ), the actor who played Jimmy Porter
MARY URE (1933-1975), Osborne's wife and the actress who played Alison, Jimmy's wife
ALAN BATES (1934-   ), the actor who played Cliff, a friend who lives with the Porters
HELENA HUGHES, the actress who played Helena, Alison's friend and later Jimmy's mistress
JOHN WELSH (1914-1985), the actor who played Colonel Redfern, Alison's father

Summary of Event

Emblematic of the bitter disillusionment of a whole post-World War II generation, *Look Back in Anger* is, more immediately, the story of Jimmy Porter, a highly intelligent graduate of an English "red-brick" (state-aided) university. In itself, Jimmy's educational background is a major symbol of the class division prevalent in England; despite his intelligence, he finds that the best he can do is to operate a candy store in the dreary midlands of England. According to Jimmy, the school was not, in fact, even made of red brick but, rather, white tile—a further bitter reproach on the gradations of a class system.

His sociological discontent, however, is only part of a maze of psychological and philosophical contradictions that suggest William Shakespeare's Hamlet or Molière's Alceste. An idealist, he finds himself in a world without ideals. "I suppose people of our generation aren't able to die for good causes any longer," he complains. "We had all that done for us, in the thirties and forties, when we were still kids. There aren't any good, brave causes left."

The setting of the play is reminiscent of earlier American plays, most notably Clifford Odets' *The Country Girl* (1950). Jimmy's apartment is cheaply furnished and is made even more squalid by the constant presence of Jimmy's wife, Alison, who is constantly ironing Jimmy's shirts. Jimmy's world is made up of Alison, his friend Cliff (who lives with them), Alison's friend Helena, who arrives for a short stay in the course of the play, and Alison's father, Colonel Redfern—who, as a symbol of the hated class system, is the subject of some of Jimmy's angry tirades.

The bleak monotony of things is especially pronounced on Sundays. Every Sunday, Jimmy reads the same papers, the liberal *Sunday Times* and the conservative *Observer*, which to him are the same. Even the current issues seem the same as last week's. The sameness is at the heart of Jimmy's horror; the difference between Jimmy and the other members of his household is his existential anguish. Jimmy's reaction to the pain of hopelessness and monotony is verbal violence, a fury that only intensifies with his awareness of the passivity of the others. Having no other outlet for his complex and deep-seated frustrations, he vents his anger on those nearest him. He injures those whom he loves most, Alison and Cliff, as he himself feels injured by the utter inanity of his existence. Succeeding in what has seemed to some critics to be an exercise in sadomasochism, he hurts himself more than those at whom he rails.

When his savage mockery fails to evoke a response from Alison and Cliff, the verbal attacks turn physical. There is an exhilaration in Jimmy's pain at being alive, something he accuses the others of trying to escape. The energy he invests in his anger takes on a life of its own, inhabiting every corner of his most intimate experiences.

After one of his attacks, Allison leaves to live with her upper-middle-class parents, without informing Jimmy of her pregnancy. Her actress-friend Helena, who has by now changed the *ménage à trois* into a foursome, easily slips into Alison's role not only as ironer of Jimmy's shirts but as his mistress as well. Even she, however, can finally take no more, and she leaves, as does Cliff. Eventually, Alison, having lost her baby, returns, realizing that though she cannot live with Jimmy easily, she cannot live without him at all. At the end, she and Jimmy are huddled together, exhausted, without the emotional (and sometimes physical) buffer zone provided by Cliff, Helena, or even a child who may have made a difference.

Although its explosive anger has given the play historical importance, its form is that of the prevailing realistic play, with roots in the conventions of Henrik Ibsen's social-problem drama. Osborne's malaise, like Ibsen's, is deeply rooted in the personal and societal past of the main character, and it is the function of the present to exorcise the consequences of that past.

Jimmy's complex frustrations begin with his own dysfunctional family, which is contrasted with Alison's privileged upbringing. His anger has roots in his childhood and father, whose final illness and death have left Jimmy with feelings of guilt. He is the only person who cared for his father, a maimed veteran of the Spanish Civil War, which Jimmy refers to as the "last great cause" for which idealists volunteered to fight. Jimmy speaks of having listened for hours to his father "pouring out all that was left of his life to one, lonely, bewildered little boy, who could barely understand half of what he said." As that young boy, Jimmy "learnt at an early age what it was to be angry—angry and helpless."

In addition to its Ibsen-like use of the past, *Look Back in Anger* relies on a conventional psychological theme made famous by another nineteenth century dramatist, August Strindberg. Like Strindberg, Osborne depicts the resulting violence of strong love-hate relationships, first between Jimmy and Alison and then between Jimmy and Helena. Both women are attracted to his masculinity, despite their revulsion at the form it sometimes takes. Helena, even though she despises Jimmy for his treatment of Alison, eventually subjects herself to the very same treatment. The Strindbergian forces in the play are the same as those found in the plays of Tennessee Williams and Edward Albee, in particular Williams' *A Streetcar Named Desire* (1947) and Albee's *Who's Afraid of Virginia Woolf?* (1962). Beneath the surface lives of the characters lie repressed injuries, vulnerabilities, and pain that erupt in verbal or physical violence when a breaking point is reached.

A third conventional feature of *Look Back in Anger* is its linear plot movement. Emotional tensions build and explode, causing a temporary break with Alison and permanent ones with Cliff and Helena, who leave for good—to say nothing of the loss of Jimmy and Alison's child. The powerful concluding imagery of the play—Osborne's use of a bear and squirrel huddling together in exhaustion and desolation—is a variation on the use of animal references in Ibsen's *Et dukkehjem* (1879; *A Doll's House*, 1880).

As conventional as Osborne's themes and style may have been, however, he shook the prevailing theatrical scene with the vitriolically articulate tirades of a lower-middle-class college graduate, heard for the first time on the English stage. The exhilarating freedom of such expression opened that stage to a variety of writers in two ensuing waves of drama (the first in the mid-1950's and the second in the mid-1960's). Those writers were, variously, graduates of the University of Oxford or the University of Cambridge, graduates of red-brick or white-tile universities—or, indeed, graduates of no university at all.

Impact of Event

When *Look Back in Anger* opened on May 8, 1956, at the Royal Court Theatre on London's Sloane Square, history was made, and the label "angry theater" was born. Chief among the new critics, Kenneth Tynan gave the play its only unqualified approval at a time when most critics objected to Jimmy's sadomasochistic laceration of himself and others. Conceding that the play would remain a minority taste, Tynan declared it to be the "best young play of its decade," estimating its potential minority audience "at roughly 6,733,000, which is the number of people in this country between the ages of twenty and thirty."

Although synonymous with Jimmy Porter, the term "angry young man" had already been coined as a description of many young artists of the 1950's such as film director Lindsay Anderson and novelists John Braine, Kingsley Amis, and Alan Sillitoe. In fact, as early as 1951 an Irish writer, Leslie Paul, had published an autobiographical work entitled *Angry Young Men*. Osborne's impact was to make "angry" a catchword for a variety of new social-protest plays by the early new dramatists—John

Arden, Arnold Wesker, Shelagh Delaney, Ann Jellicoe, Joan Littlewood—and, as well, for stylistic experiments by writers such as Harold Pinter and Tom Stoppard. *Look Back in Anger* directly and publicly put into sharp focus an already pervasive antiestablishment mood.

Politically, England's Suez debacle of the 1950's fed the economic and psychological malaise dramatized so intimately by Osborne in 1956. The sense of England's decline as an international power was an equivalent of the personal helplessness of Jimmy to effect any change in his own life. Osborne's anger on the stage seems a premonition of the political and cultural explosions that rocked the 1960's: the student riots in Paris, the Vietnam War protests, the political assassinations and burning of the cities in the United States, and, finally, the repeal in 1968 of the hated English stage-censorship law, which had been in effect for centuries. Rebellious Jimmy Porter is the English version of the tormented youth immortalized by American actor James Dean; antiheroes in their cultures, both are rebels without a cause.

The problems facing Jimmy were not necessarily new, but such problems had theretofore been treated obliquely, disguised in the polite, middle-class language and prevailing conventions of drawing-room problem plays. A loosely knit movement that included T. S. Eliot and Christopher Fry had made some attempts to reinvigorate the language of the theater with poetry, but neither these attempts nor anything in the prevailing drama had changed the sense of a twilight era in the English theater. It was the advent of Osborne's play that provided the needed energy, successfully realizing what the talk of poetic changes by earlier dramatists failed to do. Now Arnold Wesker (of "kitchen-sink" drama fame), Harold Pinter (with his comedy of menace), and working-class dramatists from the provinces such as David Storey and Peter Terson were part of the impetus given the English stage.

The class system had in the past been satirized in the sophisticated comedies of Oscar Wilde and George Bernard Shaw, but never had it been attacked in the self-laceratingly intimate manner to which Osborne gave expression in his antihero. Jimmy's venting of his anger on those he loves violated the famed English traditions of fair play and attention to duty, but his vulnerabilities and vitriol were real, touching a whole generation, educated and uneducated alike, with the force of emotional honesty, however brutal.

Described by George Devine as the "bomb that would blow a hole in the old theatre and leave a nice-sized gap, too big to be patched up," *Look Back in Anger* is the one event in twentieth century English drama with historical impact; it represented the public ushering-in of a new stage era. A catalyst was needed in a time ripe for change, a time when the Ibsen-influenced drama of Sean O'Casey and Shaw had run its course and the polite middle-class drawing-room plays of James Bridie, Noël Coward, W. Somerset Maugham, J. B. Priestley, and Terence Rattigan dominated theaters in the West End. The Royal Shakespeare Company was not yet established in its Barbican home, nor was the Royal National Theatre yet in its home on the south bank of the Thames.

The institutional catalyst arrived in the form of the English Stage Company, with its home in the historic Royal Court Theatre in Sloane Square and its artistic director, George Devine. Devine achieved patron-saint status as promoter of new playwrights, and the Royal Court continued in its function as encourager of new writers and stage experiments. With Tony Richardson as director of the 1956 production of *Look Back in Anger*, the fortuitous ensemble of author, director, producer, and stage home fired the first shot heard in England's stage revolution.

Look Back in Anger, however, is as much a broadly cultural event as a narrowly theatrical one; the societal conditions and the psychological and philosophical reactions to those conditions were a mid-century phenomenon. A child of its time though the play may seem, the same futility and the same anger, ironically, have continued to persist in the poor sections of the world and in the poorer sections of the richest countries.

Bibliography

Elsom, John. *Post-War British Theatre*. Rev. ed. London: Routledge & Kegan Paul, 1979. A narrative of movements, writers, and events that gives context to Osborne's plays. Includes an index.

Esslin, Martin. *The Theatre of the Absurd*. Garden City, N.Y.: Doubleday, 1961. Esslin's famous book, about European theater movements, complements Taylor's *The Angry Theatre* (see below) in its review of absurdist forces similar to those in the angry theater. Includes bibliography and index.

Hinchliffe, Arnold. *John Osborne*. Boston: Twayne, 1984. A useful chronological study of Osborne's plays. Includes chronology, index, and annotated bibliography.

Northouse, Cameron, and Thomas P. Walsh. *John Osborne: A Reference Guide*. Boston: G. K. Hall, 1974. A valuable sources list for any study of Osborne.

Taylor, John Russell. *The Angry Theatre: New British Drama*. London: Methuen, 1962. An incisive commentary that remains the most reliable guide to the major writers and general trends of the new era of drama.

_____. *"Look Back in Anger": A Casebook*. London: Macmillan, 1969. A minor encyclopedia, containing sections such as reviews of the first performance of *Look Back in Anger*, nondramatic writings of Osborne, points of view, and critical studies. Includes questions, select bibliography, and index.

Trussler, Simon. *The Plays of John Osborne: An Assessment*. London: Gollancz, 1969. Analysis of Osborne plays up to 1968, with chronology, cast lists, and bibliography.

Susan Rusinko

Cross-References

"Angry Young Men" Express Working-Class Views (1950's), p. 1454; *A Streetcar Named Desire* Brings Method Acting to the Screen (1951), p. 1487; Young Readers Embrace *The Catcher in the Rye* (1951), p. 1493; Dean Becomes a Legend in *Rebel Without a Cause* (1955), p. 1640; Behan's *The Hostage* Is Presented by the Theatre Workshop (1958), p. 1757.

LONG DAY'S JOURNEY INTO NIGHT
REVIVES O'NEILL'S REPUTATION

Category of event: Theater
Time: November 7, 1956
Locale: Helen Hayes Theatre, New York, New York

The American production of the autobiographical play considered to be the crowning achievement of Eugene O'Neill's career opened three years after the dramatist's death

Principal personages:
> EUGENE O'NEILL (1888-1953), a pioneer in modern theater and the first American dramatist to gain international recognition
> CARLOTTA MONTEREY (1888-1970), O'Neill's third wife, a stage and screen actress who married the playwright in 1929
> JOSÉ QUINTERO (1924-   ), a director noted for his productions of O'Neill's plays

Summary of Event

In 1956, the year *Long Day's Journey into Night* premiered, the reputation of America's foremost dramatist was at an all-time low. In spite of the fact that Eugene O'Neill had won the Nobel Prize in Literature in 1936, and there were stirrings of things to come with a 1956 revival of *The Iceman Cometh* in New York, most of the critics were content to think of the dramatist as an outdated, over-the-hill, third-rate thinker who had been lucky enough to write a few decent plays. When *Long Day's Journey into Night* was produced in Boston on October 16 and then three weeks later in New York, few people in the audiences were prepared for the blistering drama they witnessed. Voted the best play of the year by drama critics, *Long Day's Journey into Night* launched a complete reevaluation of O'Neill's career and won for him, posthumously, his fourth Pulitzer Prize.

In 1939, when O'Neill realized that his writing days were drawing to a close (he was suffering from a palsy that made the act of writing increasingly difficult), he set aside an ambitious cycle of plays he had been working on and took up the painful task of wrestling with the ghosts of his past. Although all O'Neill's plays are thinly veiled autobiography, none up to this point had faced the truth about his immediate family—his mother, father, brother, and himself—as directly and as pointedly as did *Long Day's Journey into Night.*

Writing the play was the most painful experience O'Neill had faced as a dramatist. Taking more than two years to complete the work, the dramatist was possessed by his vision, wrestling day and night with the terrible truths he was revealing about himself and his family. O'Neill's daily writing regimen was strict. He would rise early in the morning and, after breakfast, work steadily on the play until early after-noon. His wife, the former actress Carlotta Monterey, described him as a man "being tortured every day by his own writing. He would come out of his study at the end of a day gaunt and sometimes weeping. His eyes would be all red and he looked ten years older than when he went in in the morning."

When the play was finished in the summer of 1941, O'Neill, all but exhausted from his efforts, found the energy to complete only one more play in his life—the sequel to *Long Day's Journey into Night*, *A Moon for the Misbegotten* (1947). His inscription to his wife on the manuscript of *Long Day's Journey into Night*—dated July 22, 1941, their twelfth anniversary—read in part: "I give you the original script of this play of old sorrow, written in tears and blood. . . . I mean it as a tribute to your love and tenderness . . . that enabled me to face my dead at last and write this play—write it with deep pity and understanding for all the four haunted Tyrones."

The play, as it turned out, divulged far more about the O'Neill family than O'Neill's son Eugene O'Neill, Jr., felt comfortable with, and he asked his father to withhold the play from publication. Honoring his son's request, O'Neill carried the manu-script of the play to the offices of Random House in November of 1945, where he instructed that it be sealed with wax, stipulating in the covering document that it not be opened until twenty-five years after his death.

In light of O'Neill's stipulations against its release, the story of how the play was produced on Broadway only three years after the dramatist's death is one of the American theater's more curious episodes. After the suicide of Eugene O'Neill, Jr., in 1950, and at a time when the financial situation of O'Neill and his wife looked bleak, the dramatist referred to the play in storage as a "nest egg," explaining to Carlotta that Eugene, Jr., had requested that the play be withheld from the public. O'Neill suggested to his wife that if their situation worsened, they now could publish the play.

Nothing was done about the play, however, until two years after the dramatist's death, when Carlotta, as the executor of O'Neill's estate, requested Random House to publish the play. Thinking they were duty-bound to honor the dead playwright's wishes, Random House refused the request. At that point, O'Neill's wife retrieved the manuscript from Random House and handed it over to the Yale University Press, where it was published early in 1956. The wide success of the published version must have tickled the dead playwright, since on so many occasions he had publicly railed against the staged productions of his plays, arguing that he preferred to see them in book form so they could be judged on their own merits, without the services of actors and directors.

Shortly thereafter, Carlotta set up an appointment with Theodore Mann, Leigh Connell, and José Quintero, the people responsible for the revival of *The Iceman Cometh*, and asked them if they would be interested in bringing *Long Day's Journey into Night* to Broadway. The rest is theater history. The play was hailed as a master-piece, and O'Neill, after more than forty years on the American stage, reached a new zenith in his career as America's foremost dramatist.

Impact of Event

Eugene O'Neill's reputation as a significant force in modern American theater rests on his efforts to move the art of playwriting out of the dark ages of Victorian melodrama and into the contemporary world of serious drama. No major American dramatists wrote before O'Neill; he stands as the first American dramatist to achieve international recognition, with his plays produced around the world to critical acclaim.

Borrowing on the early twentieth century interest in the writings of Sigmund Freud and Carl Jung, O'Neill explored the psychology of the person, the play of conscious and unconscious tensions in characters as they interact with one another. Following the lead of the Norwegian dramatist Henrik Ibsen, O'Neill experimented with the confrontations of family members as they sought to discover themselves and their rightful place in the world. On more than one occasion, too, O'Neill recognized his indebtedness to the plays of August Strindberg, particularly the Swedish dramatist's attempts to delve beneath the surface features of character to discover the core of the person.

Theater, O'Neill said, should be a "source of inspiration that . . . drives us deep into the unknown within and behind ourselves. The theatre should reveal to us what we are." In fact, all O'Neill's plays have been viewed as variations on this single theme: the attempt of the protagonist to understand himself, the meaning of his relationships with others, and, by extension, the meaning of existence.

O'Neill's primary impact on twentieth century American theater was as an innovator and experimenter, both with the thematic content of his plays and his staging techniques. In fact, a whole line of American playwrights, including Arthur Miller, Tennessee Williams, Edward Albee, and David Mamet, benefited from O'Neill's earlier efforts. "My pioneering had busted the old dogmas wide open," O'Neill said, "and left them free to do anything they wanted." Sherwood Anderson, the novelist, wrote to O'Neill that "the more I see of the theatre, the more I realize what you have done for it."

Experimenting with the element of lighting, for example, O'Neill discovered he could isolate characters on the stage, create a mood, or aid with the progression of the play's atmosphere from scene to scene. *Long Day's Journey into Night*, for example, begins in bright early morning sunlight with the easy banter of the Tyrone family after breakfast and ends at night with the characters defenseless and in large measure defeated, bathed in a dim circle of light surrounded by the outer darkness. In retrospect, it is difficult to imagine the advanced lighting techniques of the modern stage without first recognizing the earlier experimental efforts of O'Neill.

Yet nowhere is the dramatist's goal of expanding theater more apparent than when he explores the depths of a character, trying to uncover the persona behind the mask. In fact, in his play *The Great God Brown* (1926), O'Neill went so far as to have the characters interchange real masks on stage to alert the audience to changes in a person. How, O'Neill questioned, can the dramatist show the differences between what characters say publicly and their private thoughts? After experimenting with traditional monologues as well as personal asides spoken directly to the audience,

O'Neill moved beyond these wooden techniques and relied directly on anger, remorse, and the need to be understood and loved to unlock a character's inner self. The efforts of O'Neill to find ways to strip away the illusions of his characters while they attempt to connect to one another set the stage for a series of electrifying moments in modern American theater—from the shattering of Blanche DuBois in Tennessee Williams' *A Streetcar Named Desire* (1947), to Biff's attempts to reach Willy Loman in Arthur Miller's *Death of a Salesman* (1949), to the battle royal between George and Martha in Edward Albee's *Who's Afraid of Virginia Woolf?* (1962), to the bitter struggle between Ruth and Nick in David Mamet's *The Woods* (1977).

Inheriting a stage limited by its puritanical sensibilities, O'Neill prided himself on his efforts to break down the barriers surrounding such topics as alcoholism, drug addiction, and sex. The broken, demented outcasts that people Tennessee Williams' plays owe much to the fledgling efforts of the earlier O'Neill to claim taboo subjects as the legitimate concerns of the theater. At one point, recognizing his debt to O'Neill, Williams said, "O'Neill gave birth to the American theatre and died for it."

Finally, Eugene O'Neill was the first American dramatist to give voice to the fashionable pessimism and despair of the twentieth century. In *Long Day's Journey into Night*, Mary Tyrone says, "None of us can help the things life has done to us. They're done before you realize it, and once they're done they make you do other things until at last everything comes between you and what you'd like to be, and you've lost your true self forever." Humans, O'Neill insisted, are fog-bound creatures, isolated, frustrated, and lost in a world of self-delusion. Occasionally the fog lifts, and one can make connections to the natural world and one's fellow human beings, but then the fog descends again, and one is thrown back into darkness.

Humans are doomed from birth, O'Neill believed, to pursue a hopeless hope for a better, more meaningful life. O'Neill was the first American dramatist to uncover the tortured soul of modern man.

Bibliography

Bloom, Harold, ed. *Eugene O'Neill's "Long Day's Journey into Night."* New York: Chelsea House, 1987. A helpful collection of scholarly articles for the reader who wants to delve more deeply into the meanings of the play. Placed in chronological order of publication, the articles define O'Neill's place in the American literary landscape and generally agree that *Long Day's Journey into Night* is his masterpiece. Chronology, bibliography, index.

Bowen, Croswell. *The Curse of the Misbegotten: A Tale of the House of O'Neill.* New York: McGraw-Hill, 1959. An early, readable biography of O'Neill, written with the assistance of O'Neill's son Shane, that explores the notion that the O'Neill family labored under a mysterious curse that worked its way out in the family's alcoholism, drug addiction, and suicides. Bowen suggests the curse that alienated and isolated the members of the O'Neill family was caused not by their inability to love but by their inability to communicate that love. Chronology of premieres of plays, index.

Floyd, Virginia. *The Plays of Eugene O'Neill: A New Assessment.* New York: Frederick Ungar, 1985. Claims that O'Neill is a pioneer of modern drama and the foremost American playwright of the twentieth century. The author, after gaining access to the extensive O'Neill collection of notebooks and manuscripts in the Beinecke Rare Book and Manuscript Library at Yale, decided a new evaluation of O'Neill's plays was in order. Floyd divides the book into four sections and provides specific biographical information to help readers understand the connections between the dramatist's plays and his life. Chronology, photographs, brief bibliography, index.

Gassner, John. *O'Neill: A Collection of Critical Essays.* Englewood Cliffs, N.J.: Prentice-Hall, 1964. Presents a range of positive and negative evaluations of O'Neill's dramatic legacy. The analyses either point to the dramatist's shortcomings as a thinker and as a writer who lacked facility with language or suggest that O'Neill was America's leading dramatist and that *Long Day's Journey into Night* was his crowning achievement. Chronology, bibliography.

Gelb, Arthur, and Barbara Gelb. *O'Neill.* Rev. ed. New York: Harper & Row, 1973. The standard, full-length biography of O'Neill, offering a wealth of details about his life and plays culled from extensive research and interviews with more than four hundred people who knew the playwright. The Gelbs recognize the autobiographical content of O'Neill's plays, suggesting that the story of his life is the key to understanding his tragic outlook in his art. Photographs, chronology of productions of published plays, extensive index.

Ralph L. Corrigan, Jr.

Cross-References

Freud Inaugurates a Fascination with the Unconscious (1899), p. 19; *The Ghost Sonata* Influences Modern Theater and Drama (1908), p. 199; Jung Publishes *Psychology of the Unconscious* (1912), p. 309; Baker Establishes the 47 Workshop at Harvard (1913), p. 343; The Group Theatre Flourishes (1931), p. 874; *Our Town* Opens on Broadway (1938), p. 1099; Kazan Brings Naturalism to the Stage and Screen (1940's), p. 1164.

BERNSTEIN JOINS SYMPHONIC AND JAZZ ELEMENTS IN *WEST SIDE STORY*

Category of event: Music
Time: 1957
Locale: New York, New York

Leonard Bernstein's West Side Story, *a musical drama based on William Shakespeare's* Romeo and Juliet, *joined symphonic techniques with Latin American and jazz elements*

Principal personages:
LEONARD BERNSTEIN (1918-1990), a conductor and composer who moved easily between the worlds of classical, show, and jazz music
STEPHEN SONDHEIM (1930-   ), a composer and lyricist who became the major force in the American musical
ARTHUR LAURENTS (1918-   ), a librettist and director who adapted Shakespeare's work to the 1950's
JEROME ROBBINS (1918-   ), a choreographer who successfully made the leap between the worlds of ballet and Broadway

Summary of Event

It is generally agreed that the original idea for *West Side Story* belonged to Jerome Robbins. It was Robbins who suggested using the *Romeo and Juliet* story in a musical with a contemporary setting. The original idea, of course, was quite different from what eventually arrived on Broadway in 1957. The first meeting of *West Side Story*'s creators took place in 1949 and involved Robbins, a noted director-choreographer, composer Leonard Bernstein, and playwright Arthur Laurents. What Robbins proposed was a musical using *Romeo and Juliet* as a foundation. Rather than Shakespeare's setting of Verona with its warring Montagues and Capulets, Robbins wanted to use the East Side neighborhoods of New York during Easter-Passover. The drama would focus on Catholic-Jewish or Irish-Jewish conflicts.

While, at one time, such a conflict was a viable issue for drama, it was decided that the original idea would not work. The world had changed too much. The East Side was not what it had been, and Bernstein felt that the recent influx of Latin Americans to the area presented a more contemporary situation. Another problem that arose at that first meeting was a problem present in most musical collaborations: Arthur Laurents made it very clear that he had no intention of creating a libretto for a "Bernstein opera." Laurents' was a perfectly understandable objection, and Bernstein and Robbins were immediately sympathetic. The tradition in opera was to recognize the composer and ignore the librettist; everyone knew that Giuseppe Verdi wrote *Aida* and *Otello*, for example, but who knew who wrote the words? The tradition continued even in musical theater; *Show Boat* was considered by many to be

"Jerome Kern's *Show Boat*," seemingly ignoring the work of Oscar Hammerstein II. It was, in fact, the advent of the songwriting teams such as Richard Rodgers and Lorenz Hart, Rodgers and Hammerstein, and Alan Lerner and Frederick Loewe that brought the librettists the attention they deserved. In some cases, admittedly, the librettists' anonymity was a chicken-and-egg problem; some books for musicals were simply forgettable. On the other hand, many first-rate playwrights understandably objected to participating in projects in which their best ideas would be turned into ballads and for which they would get little credit and would have to share any financial reward.

Bernstein and Robbins realized that, in Laurents, they had a first-rate talent. Laurents was well known for the drama *Home of the Brave*, and following *West Side Story*, he went on to write other musicals, including *Anyone Can Whistle* and the very successful *Gypsy*. Bernstein was able to convince Laurents how indispensable he would be to the process. As an accomplished playwright, Laurents understood structure and, in fact, created many scenes for musicalization. The problem was not the collaborators; it was the material. After a little work, they all agreed that an Irish-Jewish "East Side Story" was not going to work.

Work on the project did not resume until 1954; artists of such high caliber as Robbins and Bernstein were naturally drawn to other projects. In addition to his work in ballet, Robbins directed the musical *Bells Are Ringing*. It is essential to remember the mark that Robbins made in musical theater. Besides working on the physical production of his works as the director-choreographer, Robbins was often deeply involved in the writing process. In 1964, for example, Robbins was brought in to work on what would become *Fiddler on the Roof*. During the writing process, the authors (Joseph Stein, Jerry Bock, and Sheldon Harnick) told Robbins that they were writing a charming little story concerning a Russian milkman and his daughters. Robbins was not interested; day after day, he asked the authors what the show was about. One day, one of the writers responded to Robbins' badgering with the one-word reply, "Tradition." From that word, and from Robbins' pushing, *Fiddler on the Roof* went from a charming little story to a musical of universal import.

Leonard Bernstein's career was even more varied. He was, to begin with, the young conductor of the New York Philharmonic. He had also written the opera *Trouble in Tahiti* and the score and some of the lyrics for *On the Town*, and he was beginning to work on a musical version of *Candide*. At the same time, Bernstein worked on a series of "Young People's Concerts" and *Omnibus* television programs that introduced the American public to classical, jazz, and show music. His *Omnibus* lectures were later published as *The Joy of Music* (1959). As talk of the "Romeo project" began, Bernstein had envisioned himself writing the lyrics, but he realized, as the project began to take shape, that the task was too big. There were other projects, and this one had a great deal of music.

As the Robbins-Bernstein team came back together in 1954, therefore, they needed to find a lyricist; by that time, though, the idea for the project had begun to take a definite shape. While working in Hollywood on the 1954 film *On the Waterfront*,

Bernstein ran into Laurents. As they talked, they noticed a news article about increased gang violence between Latin Americans and whites. The article's subject
was topical, and it would fit into the "Romeo model." On their return to New York,
they presented the idea and the article to Robbins, who agreed that this was the
approach to take.

The search for a lyricist began and ended with Stephen Sondheim. Sondheim was
a composer and lyricist whose one score, for *Saturday Night*, had been played for
Laurents. While chatting at a party, Laurents told Sondheim about the project and
then arranged a meeting between Sondheim and Bernstein. For a young man yet to
make his mark, a meeting with Bernstein to discuss a collaboration would seem like
an answered prayer, but Sondheim was not sure he wanted to undertake the *West
Side Story* assignment. Sondheim saw himself as primarily a composer, and he did
not wish to be typed as a lyricist. (He later gained great success as both.) Sondheim
came very close to rejecting the position, but finally his mentor, Oscar Hammerstein II, discussed the matter with him. Hammerstein had known Sondheim since
Sondheim was a teenager and had encouraged the younger composer in his work. In
fact, Hammerstein had set up a curriculum for Sondheim. When Sondheim told his
teacher that he did not wish to accept the *West Side Story* job, Hammerstein convinced him it would be a wonderful learning experience and a chance to work with
real professionals.

Hammerstein was right. *West Side Story* was a chance to work with real professionals at the top of their form. The show opened in Washington, D.C., and very few
changes had to be made. On September 26, 1957, the "Romeo project," now called
West Side Story, opened in New York.

Impact of Event

West Side Story was not an instant hit. The reviews were generally good, but that
year, the New York Drama Critics Circle Award for best musical of the season went
to *The Music Man*. The show went on tour and, four years after the opening, a
highly successful film of *West Side Story* was made. At this point, the show became
a hit. The show's producers learned several lessons from this experience. Though
the show was well constructed, it was not the "happy" musical that audiences were
expecting. Of course, the source material was a tragedy, but the production team
became very aware of the education required for the audience. In subsequent revivals
and in the film, audiences were given a better idea of the story's tragic ending.
(None of the male leads are left alive, for example, and the production ends with the
funeral of the romantic lead.) Death had been used in musicals before (specifically
in the major works of Rodgers and Hammerstein), but it had rarely been used to this
degree.

The music also became an issue in audience acceptance. One of the common complaints about Bernstein's tunes was that they were not "hummable." Oddly enough,
the same complaint resurfaced in the criticism of many of Sondheim's later musicals.
There are some important similarities between Bernstein's score and Sondheim's later

work; for example, *West Side Story* did not have a conventional overture and made very little use of reprises, and it took some time for the score to get radio airplay. In his later work, Sondheim, too, used few conventional overtures and made little use of reprises, and the only Sondheim song that proved popular on the radio was "Send in the Clowns." *A Little Night Music*, which featured "Send in the Clowns," was considered Sondheim's most "hummable" score. The lesson was clear: If a song can be sung by a performer on stage, it can be hummed; what was learned from *West Side Story* was that certain criticism will be endured if the audience is not made familiar with the score. This knowledge became especially important as show music appeared less and less frequently on radio playlists.

Bernstein's music was essential to the artistic and popular success of *West Side Story*. His knowledge and use of different styles of music helped to create a score that was diverse yet correct. Latin rhythms associated with the show's Puerto Rican characters were heard in "America" and "Dance at the Gym." Show ballads were used for "Tonight" and "Maria." Jazz forms were used in "Cool," and opera stylings were used in the wonderfully complicated "Quintet."

West Side Story, though, is considered a milestone in musical theater largely because of its use of dance. Dance had been a major part of musicals since *The Black Crook* in 1866 and had been used in different ways throughout the years. *Oklahoma!* (1943), by Rodgers and Hammerstein, made important progress by integrating dance into the story through the production's "dream ballet." This device was widely copied and, in fact, was used to great effect in the "Somewhere Ballet" in *West Side Story*. Robbins and Bernstein, however, took the use of dance even further. Not only did dance help to underscore the story, but in such numbers as "Prologue," "Dance at the Gym," and "The Rumble," dance also became the story. Important plot elements were left totally to dance. Robbins had to create the choreography for this, and Bernstein had to create the music the dancers would use.

What was the final impact of *West Side Story*? After the audience caught its breath, the show became a success. The movie won eleven Academy Awards, including the best picture award for 1961. Several young talents were discovered or encouraged, including Stephen Sondheim. The producer, Harold Prince, later worked with Robbins on *Fiddler on the Roof* and was the driving force on most of the productions that earned Sondheim his reputation. For Bernstein, *West Side Story* was his Broadway masterpiece. He did earlier shows and would do later shows, but this was the musical that would be remembered. *West Side Story* would be remembered for wonderful artistry, but also it would be remembered for using music and dance to show an unapologetic, deeply moving view of contemporary America.

Bibliography

Bernstein, Leonard. *The Joy of Music.* New York: Simon & Schuster, 1959. Adapted from the music series Bernstein did for *Omnibus*, this book is highly accessible. The drawback is that some sort of sound track is required but not provided. Bernstein covers opera, jazz, classical music, and musical theater. He makes little reference to his own work, but he discusses the work that influenced him. Good for research on Bernstein and for a layman's study of music.

Engel, Lehman. *The American Musical Theater.* New York: Macmillan, 1975. One of the most useful sourcebooks for the study of musical theater. Engel looks at the genre's history, but he is more interested in the structure of the shows that he believes are successful. He writes a structural synopsis of *West Side Story* that demonstrates the strength of the libretto and compares it to other musicals.

Guernsey, Otis L., Jr., ed. *Playwrights, Lyricists, and Composers on Theater.* New York: Dodd, Mead 1974. A significant contribution to the study of musical theater by the people who made it happen. Though Bernstein is not included, there are insightful edited talks given by Sondheim and Laurents. Sondheim, in a section on "Theatre Lyrics," discusses the flaw in "I Feel Pretty"; the section shows the lyricist's mind at work. His discussion of the use of humor in "Officer Krupke" is also valuable.

Laufe, Abe. *Broadway's Greatest Musicals.* New York: Funk & Wagnalls, 1977. A standard history and one of the usual places to start. Laufe gives a good, if basic, chronological study of the growth of musical theater. The pictures are quite good, and Laufe tells his story well. An excellent foundation for further research. Includes a helpful appendix that gives vital statistics on long-running musicals.

Zadan, Craig. *Sondheim and Company.* New York: Harper & Row, 1989. A large book written and designed for popular consumption. For research on Sondheim, this is clearly the starting point. Notes on his early career, an abundance of photos, and countless interviews are all helpful. A very positive and thorough book. Zadan is especially interested in the process that gets a show to the stage.

William B. Kennedy

Cross-References

Oklahoma! Opens on Broadway (1943), p. 1256; Robbins' *Fancy Free* Premieres (1944), p. 1274; Porter Creates an Integrated Score for *Kiss Me, Kate* (1948), p. 1404; Sondheim's *Company* Is Broadway's First "Concept" Musical (1970), p. 2213; Sondheim Uses Operatic Techniques in *Sweeney Todd* (1979), p. 2433.

THE FORD FOUNDATION BEGINS TO FUND
NONPROFIT THEATERS

Category of event: Theater
Time: 1957-1962
Locale: New York, New York

The Ford Foundation initiated the first major subsidy program for nonprofit the-
aters, creating the groundwork for the establishment of professional nonprofit resi-
dent theaters across the United States

> *Principal personage:*
> W. MCNEIL LOWRY (1913-1993), a vice president of the Ford Foundation
> who, prior to his retirement in 1975, was responsible for the invest-
> ment of $280 million in the performing arts

Summary of Event

In October, 1953, W. McNeil Lowry joined the prestigious Ford Foundation as a
vice president, initially to work in its education program. Two years later, he turned
his attention to the foundation's new program for grants in the humanities, and he
subsequently convinced the foundation's officers to expand this program to include
the arts. Thus, in 1957 Lowry was appointed director of the Ford Foundation's new
Division of Humanities and the Arts. In March of that year, he began a cross-country
junket in search of a composite picture of the state of the arts in the United States.
Lowry sought information to establish Ford-supported programs in creative writing,
graphic and plastic arts, music, dance, opera, and theater.

The development of this multi-arts program, which Lowry called "organized philanthropy," was the first such private funding effort on a national scale in American
history; the foundation's program preceded the creation of its federal counterpart,
the National Endowment for the Arts, by eight years. Over the course of the next
decade, dozens of theaters across the country emerged with fledgling professional
companies. During the 1970's, their operations reached institutional status, and by
the 1980's, a network of nonprofit professional resident theaters had spread to virtually every major American city. The evolution of this phenomenon drastically altered an America that, in the late 1950's, had believed New York City was the only
home of its professional theater—and that "professional" theater meant strictly commercial theater.

Lowry's theater fieldwork during that 1957 nationwide tour included visits to community and academic theaters and winter stock companies in New York, as well as
consultations with theater professionals. Lowry's early research concluded that America's noncommercial theaters were struggling financially and needed the foundation's support to propel their efforts toward professionalism. Based on Lowry's recommendations, the Division of Humanities and the Arts sought to improve the

quality of theaters with recognized potential, and thus many of the same theaters benefited from its various programs. It was also Lowry's ultimate intention to build a national theater audience. Lowry realized that theater activity in the hinterlands differed fundamentally from that of Broadway; the hit-or-miss commercialism of Broadway created each production as a separate entity with a unique composition of creators, while the noncommercial theaters were interested in building artistic and managerial continuity. The establishment of a permanent acting company offered one possible step toward stability for such theaters. In the fall of 1957, *The New York Times* announced the first Ford Foundation grant to any theater: $130,000 to support a touring repertory company of fifteen actors during the Cleveland Play House's 1959-1960 season.

The Ford Foundation then launched several programs devised to increase communication among the country's theater professionals and to assist theaters in their quests for quality and stability. On several occasions, Lowry invited many theater professionals to New York to attend conferences; they offered Lowry their advice and expertise concerning what kinds of projects might best benefit their theaters. Following the success of its pilot program with the Cleveland Play House, in July, 1958, the foundation announced its first nationwide plan to create new plays and production opportunities by commissioning ten playwrights with growing reputations to write new scripts. To create venues for these plays, the foundation selected ten theaters outside New York, awarding them each ten thousand dollars to help with production costs. In 1959, the foundation awarded individual discretionary grants to ten directors, with the intent of encouraging the development of their talents. The honorees included Nina Vance of the Alley Theatre in Houston, Zelda Fichandler of the Arena Stage in Washington, D.C., and Angus L. Bowmer of the Oregon Shakespeare Festival. Ford's most substantial aid program to date was announced in late 1959: Four theaters (the Alley Theatre in Houston, the Actor's Workshop in San Francisco, the Arena Theatre in Washington, D.C., and the Phoenix Theatre in New York) received monies to support a company of actors for three consecutive seasons. Also in 1959, the foundation appropriated $244,000 for the creation of the Theatre Communications Group (TCG), a networking organization with the goal of improving cooperation among professional, community, and university theaters in the United States. Another program launched in 1960 encouraged new works by subsidizing year-long residencies of twenty-six of America's best novelists and poets at theaters around the nation, with the idea that their associations might inspire them to write plays. Not all of the writers produced new play scripts, but under the agreement with Ford, they were under no obligation to do so.

After the establishment of these programs, the Ford Foundation's commitment to theater took a dramatic turn. On October 10, 1962, newspaper headlines around the country announced the largest sum ever awarded to theaters by any American philanthropic institution: Nine nonprofit theaters received a total of $6.1 million for operations development. The two largest grants were specified for the construction of new buildings; the Alley Theatre in Houston was awarded $2,100,000 and the

Mummers Theatre in Oklahoma City was awarded $1,250,000 for such construction. Ford's other beneficiaries were the Actors Studio in New York, the Actor's Workshop in San Francisco, the American Shakespeare Festival and Academy in Stratford, Connecticut, the Arena Stage in Washington, D.C., the Fred Miller Theatre in Milwaukee, the Theatre Group of the University of California at Los Angeles, and the Tyrone Guthrie Theatre in Minneapolis. In the Ford Foundation's official press release, Lowry called the nonprofit professional resident theater a "significant American cultural resource." In the decades to follow, the foundation continued its support with new and innovative programs, playing a vital role in the institutionalization of this national cultural resource.

Impact of Event

By the middle of the twentieth century, professional theater in America had reached an all-time low. In cities and towns across America, the local movie house had replaced the professional theater, and the few theaters remaining were run almost exclusively by amateurs. Professional American theater meant New York theater, and New York theater meant the commercial enterprises on Broadway. The nonprofit resident theater movement, a phenomenon that began at the close of World War II, effected a decentralization of the professional American theater. New York's monopoly on professional theater was thus not only broken, but was also replaced by a truly national theater system composed of individual institutions all adhering to similar standards. Although professional theater had permeated the United States in the past, both in the form of touring companies and local establishments, the other characteristics of this post-World War II resident theater movement were decisively different.

These new theaters stood at the vanguard of a revolutionary idea of theater in the United States. The idea involved the declaration of tax-exempt status, as nonprofit organizations established these theaters, both legally and ethically, as educational institutions with an obligation to their communities. Thus, the enterprise was based on artistic goals rather than on revenue. Linked to this was the belief of many of those who ran such theaters that they should perform a variety of plays of literary merit—from the classics to contemporary Broadway plays (both successes and failures) to untried, original scripts. These theaters also extended the concept of institutionalization to indicate that they were concerned with developing a permanent audience and establishing themselves as necessary cultural resources within their communities. Finally, institutionalization meant creating continuity, with a permanent staff and a resident company of actors that would work together, usually for a minimum of one full season.

All the Ford Foundation's theater programs were designed to develop and support a kind of theater that featured these characteristics, and the venture had become known as nonprofit professional regional theater by the 1960's. By the 1980's, historians referring to the phenomenon came to replace "regional" with "resident"; as the decentralization of professional theater away from New York became reality, so had "regional" become a misnomer, as scores of theaters in New York as well as nationwide distinguished themselves from the commercial ventures of Broadway. Thus, they were not distinguishable by location; rather, "resident" emphasized their philosophy of permanence.

Without the support of the Ford Foundation's ideological and financial assistance, it is doubtful that the resident theater movement would have progressed at such an accelerated pace, if at all. Ford's conferences provided many theater artists who previously had felt as if they were conducting isolated experiments in their local communities with the opportunity to articulate their individual needs and ideals and to formulate a common philosophy. Initially, Ford's multifaceted theater program focused on personnel by subsidizing directors and other creative staff members, enabling them to visit other theaters and learn from their colleagues—further steps to eliminate isolation. In the early years, the subsidies for actors allowed directors greater leverage to lure actors away from New York and thus create productions of higher quality. Consequently, actors began to prefer the stability of the work available at resident theaters to the high risks involved with working on Broadway.

The Ford Foundation also assisted these theaters with a new strategy for building a permanent audience: Staffs were trained to initiate subscription programs in which tickets were sold for an entire season. Strategies to build a future audience were implemented through children's theater productions and youth training programs. The Ford Foundation ultimately expected the program's beneficiaries to rely on their communities for financial support, and thus it demanded that each of its institutional grants be matched with funds raised locally. The foundation offered guidance as to how to establish a relationship with the business community, and Lowry personally met with business leaders all over the country as an advocate for local theater. Through such initiatives, the Ford Foundation inspired the growth of a mutually beneficial relationship between business and the arts that has since become ingrained in American society. Respect and appreciation for the arts—as well as financial support—became standard policy for many local and national companies.

The stability resulting from the support of the business community, as well as the steady income from a subscription audience, gave artistic directors the security and flexibilty to add new plays to their repertoires. As more and more resident theaters began to seek original scripts for production and as costs began to escalate, the commercial theaters of Broadway mounted fewer and fewer original works. By the mid-1960's, plays that originated in resident theaters were frequently remounted on Broadway for healthy commercial runs. Dozens of such prizewinning plays have since premiered at resident theaters, including *Raisin* (Arena Stage; Tony Award for best musical in 1974), *Children of a Lesser God* (Mark Taper Forum in Los Angeles; Tony Award for best play in 1980), and *Crimes of the Heart* (Actors Theatre of Louisville; Pulitzer Prize in 1984). The resident theaters continue to be valuable proving grounds for original plays.

The Ford Foundation's example also inspired the beneficence of other American philanthropic organizations (such as the Rockefeller Foundation, the Andrew W.

Mellon Foundation, and the John D. and Catherine T. MacArthur Foundation) to allocate greater amounts of money to the arts. The expanded sources of private support, along with the establishment of the National Endowment for the Arts in 1965, gave impetus to the building boom of the 1960's, when almost two hundred new theater buildings and arts centers were constructed across the United States. This overwhelming visible increase of theatrical activity in America created a tangible sign of the resident theater's entrenchment in America's cultural life.

Bibliography

Baumol, William J., and William G. Bowen. *Performing Arts, the Economic Dilemma: A Study of the Problems Common to Theater, Opera, Music, and Dance.* New York: Twentieth Century Fund, 1966. A seminal study that explains the nature of the performing arts as a handcraft industry with an efficiency that cannot be dramatically improved by technology. Outlines the necessity of private funding from private patrons, foundations, and the government for the survival of the performing arts. Filled with statistics that justify the author's position.

Berkowitz, Gerald M. *New Broadways: Theatre Across America, 1950-1980.* Totowa, N.J.: Rowman & Littlefield, 1982. An excellent, readable history that places the expansion of the nonprofit resident theater in the larger contexts of both community and commercial theater developments.

Lowry, W. McNeil, ed. *The Performing Arts and American Society.* Englewood Cliffs, N.J.: Prentice-Hall, 1978. A collection of background papers for the fifty-third American Assembly held in November, 1977, at Arden House, Harriman, New York, to discuss the future of the performing arts. Includes two chapters that provide excellent summaries of the past and current status of the nonprofit resident theater: "The Past Twenty Years," by Lowry, and "The Theater," by Julius Novick.

Novick, Julius. *Beyond Broadway: The Quest for Permanent Theatres.* New York: Hill and Wang, 1968. Chronicles Novick's travels to forty-nine theaters across the United States during several months in 1966. Focuses on his personal assessment of the individual theaters visited as well as on his analysis of the general state of professional nonprofit resident theater in 1966.

Zeigler, Joseph Wesley. *Regional Theatre: The Revolutionary Stage.* Minneapolis: University of Minnesota Press, 1973. The best source for an early history of the professional nonprofit resident theater movement, this engaging work defines the movement's development through phases described by Zeigler as characterized by stability, quality, centrality, and community. Also illuminates patterns and trends shared by various theaters in the movement. Good bibliography. Photographs.

N. J. Stanley

Cross-References

The Group Theatre Flourishes (1931), p. 874; The Federal Theatre Project Pro-

BERGMAN WINS INTERNATIONAL FAME WITH
THE SEVENTH SEAL

Category of event: Motion pictures
Time: May, 1957
Locale: Cannes, France

Director Ingmar Bergman's The Seventh Seal *captured a special award at the Cannes Film Festival and brought Bergman's bleak, existential film style worldwide fame*

Principal personages:
   INGMAR BERGMAN (1918-   ), a Swedish film director known for his existential bleakness and his experimental cinematography
   CARL-ANDERS DYMLING (1898-1961), the head of Svensk Filmindustri, who accepted Bergman's unfinished script for *The Seventh Seal*
   MAX VON SYDOW (1929-   ), a Swedish actor whose portrayal of Antoninus Block, the Knight, provides an unforgettable characterization
   BENGT EKEROT (1920-1971), a Swedish actor who portrays Block's inscrutable opponent, Death
   ALBERT CAMUS (1913-1960), a French existentialist author whose work exerted a visible influence on *The Seventh Seal*
   MARCEL CARNÉ (1909-   ), a French director whose poetic realism influenced Bergman's style
   PÄR LAGERKVIST (1891-1974), a Nobel Prize-winning Swedish poet whose religious preoccupations paralleled those of Bergman
   PABLO PICASSO (1881-1973), an artist whose sad clowns helped Bergman frame his image of Death

Summary of Event

The Cannes Film Festival, the most important of the international film festivals, is known as a freewheeling marketplace attended by directors, actors, producers, publicists, writers, and others affiliated with the film industry. The first of the annual festivals at Cannes was held in 1946. (It had been planned for 1939, but it had to be postponed because of the war.) The Cannes Film Festival has been marked by controversy and political upheavals; in 1968, the festival was even closed halfway through by political demonstrations led by major directors. Despite such turmoil, however, this unruly gathering of movie people has always represented the cutting edge of the film industry. It is the event at which reputations are made, enhanced, and diminished. It was the showing of director Ingmar Bergman's *Det sjunde inseglet* (*The Seventh Seal*) at the 1957 Cannes Film Festival that gained him recognition as an international superstar.

In 1956, Bergman had a strong reputation as an up-and-coming director which had been enhanced by his winning of the prize for "Most Poetic Humor" at Cannes with his *Sommarnattens* (1955; *Smiles of a Summer Night*). At that time, he joked that Swedish directors would ordinarily go to the Cannes Film Festival only for the trip. *Smiles of a Summer Night* did not, despite the award, gain for Bergman the international acclaim for which he had hoped. The following year, he entered *The Seventh Seal*, the movie that made his reputation and gave the world the basic outlines of the popular conception of Bergman. The film did not win the Golden Palm, the film festival's major award, given to the best film of the year; that coveted prize went to William Wyler's *Friendly Persuasion* (1956). *The Seventh Seal*, however, did win a special prize. (A second special prize was awarded to polish director Andrzej Wajda's 1957 film *Kanal*.)

More important perhaps than the actual prize was the critics' enthusiastic reception of the film. Its stark black-and-white photography combined with its message of existential loneliness and alienation both startled and hypnotized; worldwide reviewers applauded. Bergman described the movie's content later as "an enormous, neurotic fear of death" that he believed he later transcended. Yet the primal anxiety about death expressed in the movie and its obscure, poetic meditation on the desire for immortality have continued to rivet audiences.

The film was based on Bergman's own play *Painting on Wood*, which was taken in part from the medieval morality play *Everyman*; elements of the works of Albert Camus and the paintings of Pablo Picasso, particularly his *Les Saltimbanques*, helped Bergman transform the one-act play into the full-length film. The film takes the returning crusader Antoninus Block and his squire Jons through a plague-ridden countryside toward home. Comedy, farce, pathos, and tragedy are mixed in the story, which involves subplots concerning rustic adultery, invasions of flagellants, and the burning of a child as a witch. The main story, however, is that of Antoninus Block, the Knight, who, confronted by Death, asks for a chess game as a delaying tactic.

While Block tries to keep Death from checkmating him, he looks for the answers to cosmic questions (none are forthcoming), and he attempts to complete one meaningful action. Thus, the plot encapsulates the existential-quest theme so popular in the 1950's (and since.) Other characters include the visionary Jof and his wife Mia (their names variants of Joseph and Mary) and their child. At the end, the Knight apparently succeeds in briefly diverting Death by upsetting the chessboard, so that Mia, Jof, and the baby escape, but of course the Knight cannot win his own game with Death. The last scene is remembered by all who see the film. Jof the seer describes seven black figures silhouetted against the gray sky as Death with his scythe leads the Knight and his friends away in a *danse macabre*: "They dance away from the dawn and it's a solemn dance toward the dark lands, while the rain washes their faces and cleans the salt of the tears from their cheeks."

The poetry and the repeated unanswered questions blend with the severe ritualized scenes, including a number of tableaux suggestive of medieval church murals, as the Knight searches for meaning. The game of chess counterpoints the chaotic actions of the other characters and the seemingly meaningless flow of events. This film was manna to a generation immersed in Camus and Søren Kierkegaard. Following *The Seventh Seal*'s exposition, the moviegoing world's attention focused on Bergman, waiting for more.

Impact of Event

The acclaim received by *The Seventh Seal* had major consequences both in Ingmar Bergman's career and in the world of film. For Bergman, it was the film that made his name known to audiences around the world, and it was his real introduction to American critics. Up until that point, he had been a promising director; now he was bracketed with Jules Dassin, Carl Dreyer, Federico Fellini, Michelangelo Antonioni, and the other greats. Bergman had also for a while found his theme and voice—the confrontation of life and death represented in a starkly simple allegorical form. His skilled manipulation of the camera and introduction of some surrealistic elements that did not, however, draw attention away from the basically linear plot added to the atmosphere of alienation and gloom. So, ironically, did his use of farce and wit as a contrast to the basic downward swing of his films. The effect of the films was also heightened by his constant use of Christian emblems and traditional formats in contexts of failed Christianity and silent divinity.

Many of Bergman's subsequent films carried further the theme of the foiled religious-existential quest, identifying Bergman clearly as the gloomy, realistic spokesman for twentieth century seekers of lost certainties. The films of this period include *Smultronstället* (1957; *Wild Strawberries*), *Ansiktet* (1958; *The Magician*), *Jungfrukällan* (1960; *The Virgin Spring*), as well as the trilogy of *Såsom i en spegel* (1961; *Through a Glass Darkly*), *Nattvardsgästerna* (1963; *Winter Light*), and *Tystnaden* (1963; *The Silence*). These films use expert photographic techniques to manipulate light and dark as symbols that define the relationship between the individual and the unknown world as a series of shades.

In the film world, Bergman's style and substance affected the new major directors who were born in the 1920's and 1930's and began their major works in the 1960's. François Truffaut and others use some of Bergman's techniques. His vision itself has been both copied and mocked: Woody Allen's 1968 play *Death Knocks*, for instance, has its main character playing gin rummy with Death—and winning both time and money. Death is made into a true clown in this parody, and a "schlep" as well:

Death: . . . Look—I'll be back tomorrow, and you'll give me a chance to win the money back. Otherwise I'm in definite trouble.
Nat: Anything you want. Double or nothing we'll play. I'm liable to win an extra week or a month. The way you play, maybe years.

Yet much of Allen's usual perspective is sheer Bergman, and he, like Bergman, has a penchant for mixing farcical with tragic elements in portraying a random, indifferent cosmos. Bergman's influence on other writers and directors cannot be overestimated, although it is not always immediately evident on the surface. The late 1950's and early 1960's saw a barrage of movies using Bergmanesque lighting and perspectives to demonstrate loneliness and alienation while reflecting on the silence of God and the indifference of the cosmos.

In the 1960's and later, Bergman's social commitments became clearer; his films beginning with *Persona* (1966) contain more direct statements about troubles in Sweden and elsewhere and attempts at solutions. These films, frequently centering on women characters, often deal with blocked communications and social alienation. In this direction, he was accompanied by many other filmmakers, as films became political statement in the 1960's and early 1970's. Yet the looming presence of death remained a constant in even Bergman's most socially purposeful films such as *Skammen* (1968; *Shame*) and *Viskningar och rop* (1973; *Cries and Whispers*). 1970's critics often rejected the earlier Bergman films as pretentious, overly abstract, or disengaged. Some found the artistic virtuosity inappropriate to the pain expressed in these movies. Later students of film, however, less ready to insist that a film articulate a particular social problem, rediscovered the power of *The Seventh Seal*.

In the years following the international reception of *The Seventh Seal*, Bergman became a regular on the Cannes Film Festival awards list, winning awards that included acknowledgment as best director in 1958 for *Nära livet* (1958; *Brink of Life*) and the International Critics Award in 1960 for *Virgin Spring*. Of course, his recognition extended worldwide; he received dozens of major film prizes, including Academy Awards. The length of Bergman's tenure as acknowledged superdirector is breathtaking. In 1992, the Golden Palm was awarded to *The Best Intentions*, made from Bergman's screenplay of his own parents' story. It was thirty-five years after his achievement had been recognized at the Cannes Film Festival with the showing of *The Seventh Seal*.

Bibliography

Braudy, Leo, and Morris Dickson, eds. *Great Film Directors*. New York: Oxford University Press, 1978. Contains an introduction to Bergman and four separate articles, "Ingmar Bergman in the 1950s," by James F. Scott; "The Seventh Seal," by Andrew Sarris; "Persona," by Stanley Kauffman; and "Persona: The Film in Depth," by Susan Sontag. Well-written essays allow comparison with other directors.

Bergom-Larsson, Maria. *Ingmar Bergman and Society*. Translated by Barrie Selman. London: Tantivy Press, 1978. Discussion of Bergman as social reporter and social critic. Discusses Bergman's view of the patriarchal structure and the artist's role in contemporary society. Abbreviated bibliography and filmography.

Cowie, Peter. *Ingmar Bergman: A Critical Biography*. New York: Charles Scribner's Sons, 1982. Weaves biographical information and critical discussion together in an easily readable study. Information about actors in and reception of Bergman's films. Critical analysis is not deep. Good notes, filmography, bibliography, list of stage productions, index. Excellent, plentiful photographs.

Gado, Frank. *The Passion of Ingmar Bergman*. Durham, N.C.: Duke University Press, 1986. Biographical criticism, precise and insightful; gives information about sources and production as well as interpretation of the films. A few photographs from the films. Exhaustive. Includes list of title translations, list of recurrent names, filmography, notes, and index.

Jones, G. William, ed. *Talking with Ingmar Bergman*. Dallas: Southern Methodist University Press, 1983. A series of five seminars given at Southern Methodist University by Bergman as recipient of the Algur H. Meadows Award. Useful as a source of personal, off-the-cuff commentary about Bergman's films. Nice photos of Bergman in a casual teaching situation. Filmography, list of stage productions, index.

Livingston, Paisley. *Ingmar Bergman and the Rituals of Art*. Ithaca, N.Y.: Cornell University Press, 1982. Critical analysis of the films, focusing on the filmmaker's major theme of the attempt to communicate. Useful discussion of *The Seventh Seal* in this context. Many photos of the films; good notes, filmography, bibliography, and index.

Petric, Vlada, ed. *Film and Dreams: An Approach to Bergman*. South Salem, N.Y.: Redgrave Publishing, 1981. Anthology of articles on Bergman's films and dreams, including one by Bergman. Worthwhile for those who wish to approach Bergman from this direction; not for the general reader. Bergman's own article, however, is particularly useful. Bibliography of articles on dream and film. Illustrations.

Thomson, David. *A Biographical Dictionary of Film*. New York: William Morrow, 1976. A useful tool for the general browser into the film world. Interesting for its 1970's perspective on Bergman and in particular on *The Seventh Seal*. Provides information about actors who appear in many Bergman films.

Janet McCann

Cross-References

Sartre and Camus Give Dramatic Voice to Existential Philosophy (1940's), p. 1174; The Italian New Wave Gains Worldwide Acclaim (1942), p. 1228; Sartre's *Being and Nothingness* Expresses Existential Philosophy (1943), p. 1262; Kurosawa's *Rashomon* Wins the Grand Prize at Venice (1951), p. 1476; *La Strada* Solidifies Fellini's Renown as a Brilliant Director (1954), p. 1596; The French New Wave Ushers in a New Era of Cinema (1956), p. 1710; Godard's Expressionistic *À bout de souffle* Revolutionizes Film (1960), p. 1845; Allen's *Annie Hall* Captures Complexities of 1970's Life (1977), p. 2381.

PASTERNAK'S *DOCTOR ZHIVAGO* IS PUBLISHED

Category of event: Literature
Time: October, 1957
Locale: Milan, Italy, and the Union of Soviet Socialist Republics

The publication of Boris Pasternak's Doctor Zhivago, *and the Soviet reaction to the Nobel Prize Pasternak was awarded in 1958, revealed the extent of Soviet repression*

> *Principal personages:*
> BORIS PASTERNAK (1890-1960), the brilliant Soviet writer whose book *Doctor Zhivago* created an international controversy
> NIKITA S. KHRUSHCHEV (1894-1971), the head of the Communist Party and Soviet government who condemned Pasternak's work
> DAVID ZASLAVSKY (1880-1965), a Soviet literary critic who screened the work of Soviet writers for the Communist Party

Summary of Event

Boris Pasternak had achieved international acclaim in literary circles well before he aroused an international sensation with the publication of his novel *Doktor Zhivago* (1957; *Doctor Zhivago*, 1958). He was known for his outstanding poetry, which he first published in 1913, and for his authoritative translations into Russian of the works of William Shakespeare and other Western writers. Even during the oppressive reign of Joseph Stalin, Pasternak, while restraining himself from political commentary, continued to produce quality writing. In 1947, he was nominated for the Nobel Prize in Literature.

Pasternak became a household name throughout the Western world when the events surrounding the publication of *Doctor Zhivago* received enormous attention in newspapers across Europe and America. Pasternak had conceived the book's story perhaps as early as the 1920's, but he actually began to write the novel in 1948. Originally, he had intended to place the story in the context of the 1905 rebellion in czarist Russia; however, he changed his mind and used the Bolshevik Revolution of 1917 for his point of departure. The basic theme of *Doctor Zhivago*, the confusion and uncertainty created for individual Russians by the revolution, was not unique. The subject already had served as the basis for Mikhail Sholokhov's *Tikhii Don* (1928-1940; *And Quiet Flows the Don*, 1934), but Pasternak couched his novel in a poignant tale of romance, some of it quite autobiographical.

Pasternak completed the manuscript of *Doctor Zhivago* in 1956 and submitted it to the editors of the journal *Novy mir*, the principal publisher of Soviet writers. The editors, after keeping the manuscript for more than a year, rejected it on the grounds that it contained views "antithetical" to those of the editors. According to journalist Murray Kempton, then of the *New York Post*, while the editors of *Novy mir* considered Pasternak's manuscript, an obscure Italian communist traveling in the Soviet Union happened to read ten of Pasternak's poems published in the Soviet magazine *Neva*. Pasternak intended to use the poems in his last chapter of *Doctor Zhivago*. The Italian, who worked as an agent for the Milanese publishing house G. Feltrinelli, told his superiors that Pasternak had finished a substantial novel and that they ought to consider acquiring the rights for an Italian translation.

A contract was sent to Pasternak, and he agreed to allow Feltrinelli to publish his work after it had appeared first in the Soviet Union. Subsequent to this arrangement, *Novy mir* turned down the manuscript, leading Feltrinelli to conclude that the clause requiring publication first in Russian was null and void. Feltrinelli therefore published Pasternak's work in October, 1957. The Union of Soviet Writers made an attempt to stop Feltrinelli from releasing the book but had no success. At the time of its release in Italy, Feltrinelli, while retaining exclusive rights, had arranged for the book to be published in Sweden, West Germany, France, and the United States.

The early success of *Doctor Zhivago* brought an immediate response from Soviet authorities. Pasternak was described as a writer consumed by egotism, decadence, and a rebellious nature. Such assaults on Pasternak's character did nothing to slow the popularity of *Doctor Zhivago*, which became an international best-seller. In 1958, the Swedish Academy of Arts selected Pasternak as the winner of the Nobel Prize in Literature. The announcement angered Soviet officials, who then began a much more intensive campaign to disparage Pasternak and the Swedish Academy of Arts. In October, 1958, a Communist Party-controlled literary magazine published an article proclaiming that "the granting of an award for an artistically feeble and malevolent work, prompted by hatred of socialism, is a hostile act against the Soviet State. *Pravda*, the Communist Party's principal newspaper, on the same day published an article by David Zaslavsky, a literary critic who worked in the Party's interest; Zaslavsky called *Doctor Zhivago* "worthless" and Pasternak a "weed" in the great socialist state. The Party further accused Pasternak of treason and stupidity. Within days of the Swedish Academy's announcement, the Union of Soviet Writers expelled Pasternak.

Behind this barrage of abuse stood the leader of the Communist Party and the head of the Soviet government, Nikita Khrushchev. Khrushchev had survived an attempt to oust him as party leader in June, 1957, and he was most unhappy about the excitement caused by *Doctor Zhivago*. He had not read the book, but Zaslavsky provided him with excerpts that indicated Pasternak's disenchantment with the consequences of the Revolution of 1917. Khrushchev was angry that the novel had first appeared in capitalist countries, and he encouraged the campaign against Pasternak.

The accusations and criticism weighed heavily upon Pasternak, who had not been in good health since a heart attack in 1953. His anguish increased when he learned that Soviet officials planned to force him to leave the country. The effort reached a crescendo by the end of October. On October 31, 1958, Pasternak wrote directly to Khrushchev pleading to remain in his homeland. He told Khrushchev that he had refused the Nobel Prize. Khrushchev then relented, and Pasternak was permitted to remain in the Soviet Union. By this time, he was a virtual recluse in his small country house near Peredelkino. He never recovered from the abuse heaped upon him, however, and he died in May, 1960.

Impact of Event

The publication of *Doctor Zhivago* and the circumstances surrounding Pasternak's Nobel Prize selection made a huge impression in Western countries. The episode also had a profound effect on writers and politicians within the Soviet Union. Of course, Cold War tensions between the Soviet Union and the capitalist West exacerbated the reaction on both sides.

The initial response in the West was that Pasternak had produced a great work of literature. *The Times* of London, in a review published on September 4, 1958, compared the book to Leo Tolstoy's *Voyna i mir* (1865-1869; *War and Peace*, 1886) for its "scale, scope, compassion, and beauty." American journalist Harrison Salisbury, writing in *Saturday Review* for September 6, 1958, argued that the novel placed Pasternak in the same category as the great nineteenth century Russian novelists. Similar critiques appeared in French, German, and Italian newspapers and journals. It was commonly agreed that Pasternak had written an epic story of romance in *Doctor Zhivago*; nearly all reviewers found little in the novel that was overtly anti-Soviet and argued that the book was really a story with a universal message. The most extensive Western review of *Doctor Zhivago* was written by Marc Slonim in *The New York Times*. In an article published on September 24, 1958, Slonim pointed out that Pasternak had produced a work that called for the "triumph of truth and human freedom."

The perspective from which the West viewed *Doctor Zhivago* made the reaction to the work in the Soviet Union all the more alarming and incomprehensible. How could any government find offense in the benign, and largely indirect, criticism of Communism contained in *Doctor Zhivago*? The bitter assault on Pasternak and on the Swedish Academy of Arts by Soviet authorities alerted the world once again to how far the Soviet Union had departed from the course intended by the architect of the 1917 revolution, Vladimir I. Lenin. Khrushchev, who had gained a reputation for reversing the oppressive policies of Socialist Realism imposed by Joseph Stalin, was now exposed as capable of Stalinesque repression. The world responded with a cascade of abuse against the Communist Party's unrelenting efforts to control individual expression. These attacks on the Party came not from the West alone but from all corners of the globe.

Newspapers in North America and Europe were joined in their condemnation of the Soviet Union by counterparts in Yugoslavia, India, Thailand, Pakistan, and various African countries. World leaders from President Dwight Eisenhower to Jawaharlal Nehru, prime minister of India, decried the attempt to limit artistic freedom. Never before had there been such an outpouring of support for the notion that governments should not interfere with individual creativity.

In a more specific way, the Pasternak affair heightened tensions between the United

States and the Soviet Union, tensions that had begun to relax somewhat since the death of Stalin in 1953. The extent to which the Communist Party would try to control the efforts of its artists in all fields was brought home again. The Pasternak controversy established a new awareness of the plight of dissidents in the Soviet Union, and it also contributed to the favorable reception in the West of Alexander Solzhenitsyn's books in the 1970's.

Within the Soviet Union itself, the attack on Pasternak continued until his death. Over and over it was said that Pasternak was a pawn used by the capitalist powers in the Cold War against communism. The First All-Union Congress of Writers, meeting in December, 1958, condemned the "pathological individualism" represented in *Doctor Zhivago.* It was not only Pasternak who suffered. Khrushchev warned all Soviet writers, sometimes by calling them to his presence, that he could tolerate no literature that departed from his vision of what was good for the Soviet people, the vision of the country put forward by the Communist Party. His watchdog, Zaslavsky, kept Khrushchev informed of any deviant writing. The result was that many imaginative writers were forced to write in secret.

The *Doctor Zhivago* affair also affected Soviet music and art. In the late 1950's, Khrushchev reiterated the Party's objection to all music and art that showed excessive individuality; hence, "modern" paintings were banned from Soviet galleries, and jazz music was strictly forbidden. These actions by Khrushchev were all too reminiscent of the 1930's repression of Stalin and his henchmen.

In one of his last letters, Pasternak wrote hopefully that, after the long suppression, "creativity and greatness" would return to Russia. In one sense, this creativity never disappeared, as he himself proved. The larger meaning of his comment became reality, at least for a time, with the 1990's collapse of the Communist Party and the Soviet system that had imposed the Party's will.

Bibliography

Davie, Donald, and Angela Livingstone. *Pasternak: Modern Judgments.* London: Macmillan, 1969. An interesting collection of articles, many translated from Russian by Angela Livingstone, which critique Pasternak's body of work. Among the insightful essays are two especially noteworthy articles by Isaac Deutscher and Irving Howe. Chronology, select bibliography, index.

Gaev, Arkady. *Boris Pasternak and Dr. Zhivago.* Munich: Institute for the Study of the USSR, 1959. A very brief, but excellent, account of the Pasternak controversy, well researched and carefully written. Gaev is particularly good in establishing the worldwide reaction to the publication of *Doctor Zhivago.* Highly recommended. Good footnotes, no index.

Hingley, Ronald. *Pasternak.* New York: Alfred A. Knopf, 1983. Provides a reasonably objective view of Pasternak by an author who knew him. This is a scholarly work, but Hingley is not afraid to put forward his opinions about Pasternak's work. A useful, well-written biography. Photographs, bibliography, index.

Hughes, Olga R. *The Poetic World of Boris Pasternak.* Princeton, N.J.: Princeton

University Press, 1974. Assesses Pasternak's view of the world as expressed in his poetry and prose. Hughes thinks Pasternak had an "affinity" with Romanticism but yet was not truly a Romantic. Especially relevant to *Doctor Zhivago* is Hughes's chapter "Time and Eternity." Very informative about Pasternak, but challenging. Chronology, bibliography, index.

Mallac, Guy de. *Boris Pasternak: His Life and Art.* Norman: University of Oklahoma Press, 1981. A thorough biography that gives considerable attention to the historical and philosophical context of Pasternak's writings. Mallac is especially strong when recounting the last three years of Pasternak's life. A highly useful work. Bibliography, notes, index.

Ronald K. Huch

Cross-References

The First Nobel Prizes Are Awarded (1901), p. 45; Socialist Realism Is Mandated in Soviet Literature (1932), p. 908; Shostakovich's *Lady Macbeth of Mtsensk* Is Condemned (1936), p. 1042; *The Gulag Archipelago* Exposes Soviet Atrocities (1973), p. 2277; Khomeini Calls for Rushdie's Death (1989), p. 2630.

WILLSON'S *THE MUSIC MAN* PRESENTS MUSICAL AMERICANA

Categories of event: Theater and music
Time: December 19, 1957
Locale: Majestic Theater, New York, New York

One of the great pieces of Americana, Meredith Willson's The Music Man *became one of the most popular musicals of the 1950's*

> *Principal personages:*
> MEREDITH WILLSON (1902-1984), an established composer of classical and popular music who wrote the libretto, lyrics, and music for *The Music Man*
> ROBERT PRESTON (ROBERT PRESTON MESERVEY, 1918-1987), an actor known for his portrayal of heavies and villains who was cast against type to create the title role of *The Music Man*
> BARBARA COOK (1927-   ), an actress who originated the role of Marian Paroo
> MORTON DA COSTA (MORTON TECOSKY, 1914-1989), the director who staged the Broadway production of *The Music Man*

Summary of Event

Meredith Willson was fifty-five years old when *The Music Man* opened in 1957. To that time, Willson's only Broadway experience had consisted of playing the flute in the Rialto Theater orchestra thirty-five years earlier. As a flutist, he had played with march king John Philip Sousa and with Arturo Toscanini in the New York Philharmonic Symphony. He had also conducted for Seattle, San Francisco, and Los Angeles symphonies and served as musical director of the National Broadcasting Company's Hollywood division. As a composer, he had written a variety of classical compositions, motion-picture scores, and several popular tunes, including the standard "May the Good Lord Bless and Keep You." Though he had not worked in musical theater, Willson drew on his extensive musical experience to create a Broadway hit that would become the quintessential American musical and alter the direction of the rest of his life.

Meredith Willson, who had also developed a reputation as a humorist, would regale his friends with reminiscences of Mason City, Iowa, the small Midwestern town where he had been born in 1902. Frank Loesser, a veteran Broadway composer, suggested that Willson write a musical about his youth as early as 1949. To his annoyance, Willson's wife, Rini, agreed and regularly reminded him of the suggestion. In 1951, Ernie Martin and Cy Feuer called to ask him to write a musical comedy for their highly successful Broadway production company. Willson still resisted, but one day he began writing notes for his Iowa play, at first entitled *The Silver Triangle*. His efforts excited Feuer, who moved to California to guide Willson while he shaped the work into a musical comedy. After six months and several drafts, an exhausted, discouraged Feuer went back to New York, releasing all claims to the work he had retitled *The Music Man.* Willson became obsessed with the project and worked on it almost exclusively for the next five years, ultimately employing Franklin Lacey to help to clarify the story and penning thirty-two separate drafts. Believing it was finally ready for production, Willson contacted Kermit Bloomgarden, who, after a midnight audition, agreed to produce the "beautiful play"—as soon as Willson fixed the problems with the book. By the time rehearsals began, Willson had written more than forty drafts and almost fifty songs that were never used in the final pro-duction. Rewriting continued until the afternoon of the Broadway opening.

Meredith Willson achieved three major accomplishments with *The Music Man.* First, he created a remarkably cohesive show; because he served as writer, composer, and lyricist, he avoided the inevitable, and often glaring, patchwork effect of the work of collaborators. Second, Willson composed a new kind of song for the Broadway theater. At the time, Broadway musicals were largely written by a small number of librettists, lyricists, and composers who shared the same background in musical com-edy. This select group had developed a distinct style for Broadway musicals. Because of Willson's different background, he created a different sound for the musical com-edy. One unique feature of his work was his lyrics, which rarely rhyme. He developed a method for writing songs in rhythms that grow out of the speech of his characters. This is most notable in Harold Hill's two soliloquies, "Trouble" and the beginning of "Seventy-Six Trombones," and in novelty numbers such as "Rock Island," in which a group of traveling salesmen create the sound of a moving train, and "Pickalittle," in which the town gossips create the sound of chickens. Another unique feature was Willson's use of the same melody for Harold Hill's march, "Seventy-Six Trombones," and for the female lead Marian's love song "Goodnight, My Someone," to show subtly that the two characters had more in common than meets the eye. Willson used contrasting songs to show differences in character in Hill's "The Sadder but Wiser Girl" and Marian's "My White Knight." Finally, he used types of music that had not before been identified with musical comedy, including the march and the barbershop quartet. In fact, *The Music Man* was the first Broadway musical to use a barbershop quartet. Ultimately, Willson successfully created an openly sentimental story about the 1912 American Midwest as seen through rose-colored glasses—the kind of story that sophisticated New Yorkers would normally hoot off the stage. Yet because of the show's honesty, its combination of love and irony, Willson delivered a valentine that was eagerly accepted by its audience.

The audience was caught up in the production from the moment the curtain rose to show the traveling salesmen creating the sound of the train as they bounced along in their railway coach, discussing the scoundrel Harold Hill. The scenery and costumes re-created the innocent America of yesterday: the Victorian parlor, the high school gymnasium, the footbridge where lovers met. By the time a handcuffed Professor Hill stood before his boys' band, leading them in the cacophonous but recognizable

"Minuet in G," the audience was cheering, crying, and applauding in unison for the show's curtain call, "Seventy-Six Trombones." Writing in *The Saturday Evening Post*, Walter Kerr described the audience response: "The rhythmic hand-clapping which greeted the finale of *The Music Man* on opening night was the only time I have ever felt a single irresistible impulse sweep over an entire audience and stir it to a demonstration that could not possibly have been inhibited."

Robert Preston's performance in the title role of Harold Hill attracted as much attention as the production. Preston had been known as a "heavy" for twenty years in the film business; he had never sung, danced, or appeared in a musical. His performance, though, was electric, winning over the audience and critics alike and earning Preston a Tony Award. He maintained the freshness and vitality of opening night through the entire Broadway run and re-created the role in the successful 1962 film version. The personal achievements of Willson and Preston overshadowed the significant contributions of Barbara Cook as Marian and Iggie Wolfington as Marcellus, who both earned Tony Awards for their supporting roles. Morton Da Costa's meticulous staging was also notable, as were Howard Bay and Raoul Pene du Bois's contributions in designing the turn-of-the-century Iowa set and the costumes of its citizens.

Meredith Willson turned his career to the musical comedy. In 1960, he collaborated with Richard Morris on the successful *The Unsinkable Molly Brown*. In 1963, he returned to Broadway as librettist, lyricist, and composer for the short-lived *Here's Love*; his final endeavor, *1491*, a 1969 musical about Christopher Columbus, closed before reaching Broadway. Nevertheless, Meredith Willson's achievements with the Broadway musical overshadowed all the other successes in his long and versatile career.

Impact of Event

The Music Man, which ran for 1,375 performances, was one of the longest-running Broadway musicals of the 1950's. Second only to *My Fair Lady* (2,717 performances beginning in 1956), it outdistanced even such notables as *The King and I* (1,246 performances beginning in 1951), *Guys and Dolls* (1,200 performances beginning in 1950), and *West Side Story* (734 performances beginning in 1957). Musical comedy and theater history textbooks barely make note of the production, mentioning only the unique success of the sentimental Midwestern story and Robert Preston's remarkable portrayal of Harold Hill. It is more often remembered as the musical that whipped *West Side Story* in every major category for every major award of the season.

Perhaps the most remarkable achievement of *The Music Man* is that it has become a picture postcard of an innocent Midwestern town, epitomizing the popular image of pre-Depression America. It is as representative as Grant Wood's 1930 painting *American Gothic*, which is created on stage in the opening of the show. At about the same time, that image was also etched in America's memory by two other Midwesterners who had been transplanted to Southern California. Walt Disney created Disneyland's "Main Street U.S.A." in 1955; Ray Bradbury's novel *Dandelion Wine*, set in 1928, evokes this same image and was published in September, 1957, three months before *The Music Man* opened. These three independent but intertwined memories, created at the height of the optimistic Eisenhower era, continue to be experienced by thousands around the world. They present a simpler America, when the "bad guy" was nothing more than a lovable rogue who could bring excitement to a monotonous summer day and when reform could be achieved through the beauty of true love and laughter.

In *The Music Man*, Meredith Willson also created a play that is accessible at a variety of levels, be it the professional, university, high school, or community theater. Its basic requirements are few: a leading man who can handle the patter songs, a leading woman who can sing, and a barbershop quartet. There are no dream ballets, no difficult harmonies. There is a plethora of roles, so entire families often take part in amateur productions. The production's dances are simple; almost anyone can march, or do a square dance, or even climb on a library table. Audiences of even the most amateurish productions respond to the bickering schoolboard that is united for the first time as a barbershop quartet, and they cry and cheer when the band muddles its way through "Minuet in G," saving Professor Hill from a mob and uniting him with Marian in love.

The appeal of the material is also evident in its acceptance outside the Broadway theater. Within one year after the play opened, at least twenty different recordings of the music were in record stores; thousands of high school bands were soon marching to "Seventy-Six Trombones." The successful 1962 film version, again starring Robert Preston as Harold Hill, re-created the look and energy of the stage production. It was the first film musical to sell to television for a million dollars, where it is frequently rebroadcast.

In 1987, when George C. White of the Eugene O'Neill Theater Center was invited to direct the first production of an American musical comedy in Beijing, China, he considered several shows for performance. *Fiddler on the Roof* (1964) and *Man of La Mancha* (1965) were turned down because of their foreign settings. *Oklahoma!* (1943), another characteristically American musical with an equally sentimental book, was rejected because of the difficulty of its dream ballet. *The Music Man* was the obvious choice as the epitome of the Broadway musical comedy because of its portrait of America and its ease of production for an inexperienced cast.

The night before the Broadway opening, a benefit performance of *The Music Man* never seemed to get off the ground. After the show, a discouraged Max Allentuck, one of producer Kermit Bloomgarden's associates, went to a restaurant and ran into some of the Broadway theater crowd, who were not encouraging about the show's prospects. One man, however, spoke up, stating that *The Music Man* was "one of the great pieces of Americana." William Saroyan was right.

Bibliography

"A Happy Oom-pah on Broadway." *Life* 44 (January 20, 1958): 103-106. The best source for several color photographs of the Broadway production of *The Music Man*. These provide a good feel for the show, but the text provides almost nothing.

Kramer, Mimi. "The Unmusical." *The New Yorker* 64 (March 21, 1988): 103. A review panning the New York City Opera's revival of *The Music Man* in 1988. Staged too much like grand opera, the show lost all the qualities that have made it a success in other productions.

"Pied Piper of Broadway." *Time* 72 (July 21, 1958): 42-46. Written six months after *The Music Man*'s successful opening, this article examines the backgrounds of the production and of Robert Preston. Offers insight on the show's success.

Willson, Meredith. *But He Doesn't Know the Territory.* New York: G. P. Putnam's Sons, 1959. Willson's folksy description of writing *The Music Man*, from the project's conception to the opening-night curtain. Provides his perception of the show's unique achievements and an informative account of the workings of Broadway theater production in the 1950's.

_____. *The Music Man.* New York: G. P. Putnam's Sons, 1958. The complete book and lyrics of *The Music Man*.

Gerald S. Argetsinger

Cross-References

Cohan's *Little Johnny Jones* Premieres (1904), p. 108; *Our Town* Opens on Broadway (1938), p. 1099; *Oklahoma!* Opens on Broadway (1943), p. 1256; Porter Creates an Integrated Score for *Kiss Me, Kate* (1948), p. 1404; Bernstein Joins Symphonic and Jazz Elements in *West Side Story* (1957), p. 1731.

BEHAN'S *THE HOSTAGE* IS PRESENTED
BY THE THEATRE WORKSHOP

Category of event: Theater
Time: 1958
Locale: Theatre Royal, Stratford, East London, England

Brendan Behan's play The Hostage, *presented by Joan Littlewood's Theatre Workshop, blended serious drama, raucous comedy, and music in unique and theatrically innovative ways*

Principal personages:
> BRENDAN BEHAN (1923-1964), an Irish playwright, wit, and autobiographer whose works draw heavily on his experiences as a youthful member of the Irish Republican Army
> JOAN LITTLEWOOD (1914-   ), the stage director who founded the Theatre Workshop, a theater company noted for its experimental and collaborative approach to drama

Summary of Event

The debut of *The Hostage* brought a new, surprising, and uniquely theatrical approach to a deadly serious subject: hostage-taking and the Irish Republican Army (IRA). The play depicts events that surround the execution of a character whom the audience never sees—an eighteen-year-old IRA member sentenced to die in a Belfast jail for having killed an Ulster policeman. As in Behan's previous play, *The Quare Fellow* (1954), this crucial event takes place offstage, but this time none of the characters is a public official or is directly involved in the death of the condemned man. The setting is a run-down brothel that is used by IRA members as the hideout—in effect, the makeshift prison—where a young British soldier, Leslie Williams, is held hostage in retaliation and eventually killed. Yet despite its grim subject, the play is full of raucous, life-affirming humor as well as Behan's most bitterly acerbic satire; its structure is more indebted to the innovations of Bertolt Brecht's Berliner Ensemble (and to the music-hall stage) than to the conventions and formulae of the "well-made play."

As the play opens, a wild Irish jig is danced by the "pimps, prostitutes, decayed gentlemen and their visiting 'friends'" in an "old house in Dublin that has seen better days." When the dance ends, an ineptly played blast from an offstage bagpipe introduces the play's more sombre theme: A "Dead March" is to be played for a young IRA member being held in the Belfast jail who is sentenced to be hanged the next day. The piper, known as Monsewer, is an ardent IRA supporter whose sentimental allegiance to the Gaelic language makes him unable to be understood by most of his hearers. Monsewer's ersatz-heroic quests are fundamentally quixotic; even his compatriot the brothel-keeper recognizes that "the I.R.A. and the War of

Independence are as dead as the Charleston." Catholicism is also a target of Behan's satire: Miss Gilchrist, a social worker from the St. Vincent de Paul Society, embodies a shallow and irrelevant piety, ready with hymns and tracts for any occasion but making ultimately no difference about the issue of the prisoner's impending death. The first act ends as the captive soldier is dragged in while the residents dance a swirling reel; surprisingly, the captive leads them in a song, "There's No Place on Earth Like the World."

The second act develops a love story between the prisoner, Leslie Williams, and Teresa, a nineteen-year-old maid who has come from a convent school to work in the house. Despite differences in their religion and nationality (he is an English Protestant), despite the inherent peril in the situation, and despite intermittent interruptions, the young couple becomes well acquainted, eventually consummating the relationship in an upstairs bedroom—a development that shocked many staid theatergoers of the late 1950's. Leslie and Teresa's, however, is in fact the only nonexploitative, noncommercial, even innocent and genuine act of love occurring among any inhabitants of the house. Subsequently, however, Leslie learns that he is to be shot, since the IRA prisoner has been executed. Nevertheless, he closes the second act with another rollicking song, following which a bugle sounds, and he sharply salutes.

As the third act opens, the house's inhabitants mourn the death of the Belfast prisoner. They become increasingly attached to—and protective of—Leslie, whose song is now the solemn hymn "Abide with Me." The fanaticism of the IRA officers and Monsewer, like the absurdity of Leslie's plight, becomes increasingly apparent. The possibility that the threat is a bluff—that he is to be questioned by intelligence officers rather than shot—is maintained, and the love interest established in the second act continues in the third. Suddenly, an explosion shakes the stage, filling it with smoke as the police attack the house. Mulleady, one of the residents, has turned informant and brought the police to the rescue; one of the house patrons, ostensibly a Russian sailor, is actually an undercover police spy. A chaotic, full-scale battle ensues onstage, replete with whistles, sirens, drums, exploding bombs, blaring bugles, and ricocheting bullets. Bodies hurtle across the stage as, absurdly, Monsewer slowly marches upright, ceremoniously blowing the bagpipe. During the fracas, Leslie makes a break for freedom but is killed in a deafening blast of gunfire, presumably from the attackers, not the defenders, of the house. After the battle, Teresa laments his death, promising never to forget him.

Such an ending—appropriately antiwar, bitterly ironic, arguably even tragic (with Leslie and Teresa a modern-day Romeo and Juliet)—would be relatively conventional. Yet, as in the preceding acts, a merry song provides the play's finale. As "a ghostly green light" glows on Leslie's body, the corpse rises and sings:

> The bells of hell
> Go ting-a-ling-a-ling
> For you but not for me.

> Oh death, where is thy sting-a-ling-a-ling
> Or grave thy victory?

This startling, controversial "resurrection" is an anti-illusionist *coup de théâtre*, effectively undercutting the audience's emotional response in essentially the manner of a Brechtian "alienation effect"—as do the characters' occasional direct addresses to the audience throughout the play (deliberately violating the "fourth-wall effect" of conventional theatrical realism, as *The Quare Fellow* did not). The entire cast then joins in with Leslie for a final chorus of the song, which, as always in Behan's work, affirms the vitality of the life force.

Impact of Event

Along with the English Stage Company, which was founded by George Devine at the Royal Court Theatre in 1956, Joan Littlewood's Theatre Workshop was at the forefront of theatrical innovation in England in the late 1950's and early 1960's. Influenced by the theories of German playwright Bertolt Brecht and the practices of his Berliner Ensemble, Littlewood's company produced a number of critically acclaimed experimental plays that were developed through unusually lengthy rehearsal periods. Littlewood viewed the theater as a collective and collaborative process during which, under the supervision of a director, authors' scripts were often radically revised by the actors and others involved in the production process. One of the company's most noted early successes was Behan's *The Quare Fellow*, a play set in the yard of an English prison before, during, and after the execution of a condemned IRA member (the title character, whom the audience never sees). Notwithstanding its grim subject and its overt ideological opposition to capital punishment, Behan's play was also filled with humor and song. Its juxtaposition of sombre events, raucous jokes, and exuberant songs—though initially disconcerting to audiences of the 1950's—characterized virtually all of Behan's writings and was even more evident two years later in *The Hostage*.

Like many of the "Angry Young Men" among the playwrights and novelists who became prominent at the time, Brendan Behan was a working-class, iconoclastic, largely self-educated writer; he was also a convicted IRA conspirator who had served time in both a reform school and an English prison. In contrast to many of the more vituperative, disaffected, but widely popular young antiheroes of the day—including Jimmy Porter in John Osborne's *Look Back in Anger* (1956), the inmate-narrator of Alan Sillitoe's novella *The Loneliness of the Long-Distance Runner* (1959), and the character played by the American actor James Dean in the film *Rebel Without a Cause* (1955)—Behan had indisputable credentials as a rebel with a cause, Irish nationalism. Yet, surprisingly, all of his writings are remarkably free of the anger and polemics that one might expect from an author who had formerly been so ideologically committed; instead, his works are filled with life-affirming vitality, raucous humor, song, and compassion for the English and Irish alike.

The Hostage was the last of Behan's major works; alcohol-related illnesses and other problems soon severely impaired his creative abilities. Originally written in Gaelic under the title *An Giall*, the play was first produced in Dublin early in 1958, but it attracted relatively little attention until the translated (and much-revised) version was produced by Littlewood's Theatre Workshop later in the year. The extent to which the final form of the play was attributable to Littlewood's improvisational, collaborative workshop methods rather than to Behan's own work remains a matter of critical debate, although Behan did publicly approve all changes that had been made. Indisputably, the production that Littlewood directed was a landmark in the elevation of the director to the status of a cocreator with the playwright.

Like the bar in Eugene O'Neill's *The Iceman Cometh* (1946) or the brothel in Jean Genet's *Le Balcon* (1956; *The Balcony*, 1957), the brothel in which *The Hostage* is set is a social microcosm. The play's action takes place in 1960, when "the days of [Ireland's] heroes are over this forty years past"—although the house's "owner isn't right in the head and thinks he's still fighting in the Troubles or one of the anti-English campaigns before that." Like their counterparts in Bertolt Brecht's *Die Dreigroschenoper* (1928; *The Threepenny Opera*, 1949), the majority of Behan's characters are unheroic, disreputable societal outcasts who, nevertheless, fundamentally and exuberantly affirm life through their raucous banter and their ostensibly "immoral" activities—offenses against traditional moralists' life-stifling propriety. As always, Behan's most scathing satire is directed against the doctrinaire supporters of traditional institutions, particularly the IRA and the Catholic church—yet his characterization of society's outcasts and even the English "enemy" is surprisingly humane. Accordingly, the captive British soldier, Leslie, is sympathetically portrayed throughout, remaining remarkably undoctrinaire about both religion and politics; in Ireland solely because he was sent there, he is uninterested in news of the royal family and the larger "Irish question" alike. Institutions and ideologies are, as always in Behan's writings, the enemies of common humanity; his most admirable characters—however socially disreputable they may be—know better than to believe in such things.

Although Littlewood's Theatre Workshop disbanded in 1973, its innovative contributions to modern theatrical style—its emphasis on directorial autonomy, its groundbreaking if disconcerting juxtaposition of seemingly disparate styles and genres—have had lasting impact. The company was in many ways a victim of its own success in the West End, which brought unremitting pressures to bear against the time-consuming, collaborative play-development process that Littlewood had pioneered; moreover, the company's status as a star attraction in its own right made it quite different from the people's theater that its founder had always envisioned. Behan, too, succumbed to the temptations of celebrity in a series of drunken, self-destructive, publicly chronicled incidents that led to his eventual fatal illnesses; his last books were compilations of anecdotes transcribed from tape recordings. Yet, with their uniquely humane perspective and then-daring theatrical juxtapositions, his plays and Littlewood's directorial genius reshaped the capabilities of the modern stage.

Bibliography

Behan, Brendan. *Borstal Boy.* London: Hutchinson, 1958. This is Behan's surprisingly comical and life-affirming autobiographical account of his experience as a teenage inmate in a borstal (reform school) and, later, in an English prison—following his conviction for participation in a planned bombing campaign of the Irish Republican Army. Includes a glossary of slang terms and prison argot.

_____. *Brendan Behan: The Complete Plays.* Introduction by Alan Simpson. London: Eyre Methuen, 1978. This collection includes *The Quare Fellow*, *The Hostage*, and *Richard's Cork Leg* (a dramatic fragment that was posthumously produced, edited with additional material by Alan Simpson) and three one-act radio plays, *Moving Out*, *A Garden Party*, and *The Big House.* Bibliography by E. H. Mikhail.

Boyle, Ted. E. *Brendan Behan.* New York: Twayne, 1969. Useful, concise overview of Behan's life and works, including a chapter on "Some Relevant Theories of Comedy." Focuses on the "peculiar juxtaposition of laughter and death" that Boyle claims is Behan's "most characteristic theme." Notes; bibliography that includes annotation of secondary sources.

Kearney, Colbert. *The Writings of Brendan Behan.* New York: St. Martin's Press, 1977. In this overview of Behan's life and works, he is seen primarily as an iconoclast who pushed broad-mindedness to its limits, both in the theater and in his personal activities.

McCann, Sean, ed. *The World of Brendan Behan.* London: New English Library, 1965. Published the year after Behan's death, this collection of twenty-four essays, recollections, and tributes provides an overview of Behan's life, although it is less comprehensive than the E. H. Mikhail volumes cited below. Affectionately anecdotal rather than critical, it also contains a list of his epigrams. Drawings by Liam C. Martin.

Mikhail, E. H., ed. *The Art of Brendan Behan.* Totowa, N.J.: Barnes & Noble, 1979. This compilation of forty-nine articles and reviews emphasizes Behan the writer rather than Behan the man. Selected reviews of each of Behan's works are arranged chronologically, following six tributes by contemporary writers.

_____. *Brendan Behan: An Annotated Bibliography of Criticism.* Totowa, N.J.: Barnes & Noble, 1980. This comprehensive bibliography of primary and secondary sources contains more than two thousand items.

_____. *Brendan Behan: Interviews and Recollections.* 2 vols. Totowa, N.J.: Barnes & Noble, 1982. Collection of extracts from published memoirs and interviews given by those who knew Behan; there are fifty-one items in volume 1 and fifty-five in volume 2. Mikhail's introduction insightfully compares Behan and Oscar Wilde.

O'Connor, Ulick. *Brendan.* London: Hamish Hamilton, 1970. Excellent, judicious biographical and critical study. Effectively captures not only Behan's charm and wit as a raconteur and celebrity but also the self-destructiveness and pain of his later life. Photographs, notes, bibliography.

Taylor, John Russell. "Brendan Behan." In *Anger and After: A Guide to the New British Drama*. London: Eyre Methuen, 1963. This quite brief account of Behan's major plays emphasizes "his roughness, his irreverence, his distaste for any establishment, even the establishment of rebellion" and deems him a product of "the new questioning spirit abroad in Britain." Particularly valuable in establishing the theatrical context of the times. Photographs, index.

William Hutchings

Cross-References

"Angry Young Men" Express Working-Class Views (1950's), p. 1454; Dean Becomes a Legend in *Rebel Without a Cause* (1955), p. 1640; Osborne's *Look Back in Anger* Opens in London (1956), p. 1721; Pinter's *The Caretaker* Opens in London (1960), p. 1861; Esslin Publishes *The Theatre of the Absurd* (1961), p. 1871.

THINGS FALL APART DEPICTS DESTRUCTION OF IBO CULTURE

Category of event: Literature
Time: 1958
Locale: London, England

Chinua Achebe's Things Fall Apart *chronicled the destruction of the culture of the Ibo tribe of Nigeria as a consequence of the incursions of the British*

Principal personages:
CHINUA ACHEBE (1930-   ), a Nigerian poet and prose writer of the Ibo (Igbo) tribe thought by many to be Africa's first and finest novelist
JOYCE CARY (1888-1957), a British administrator in Nigeria whose 1939 novel *Mister Johnson* caused Achebe to write his novel as a corrective

Summary of Event

Chinua Achebe gained immediate fame when he published his first novel, *Things Fall Apart*, in 1958. It was a novel about Africa by an African. It was composed in English, in a writing style that was both simple and effective. It contained a fascinating combination of history and fiction, anthropology and sociology. It told its important story of racial clash without anger or militancy.

Although Achebe was writing about the initial contact of British missionaries and colonial administrators with the Ibo (or Igbo) tribe of Nigeria, contact that proved immensely destructive to the extraordinary culture of his ancestors, he wrote an unimpassioned analysis of the experience. For Achebe, the Ibo culture, though ancient and ordered, was not without its cruelties and ossified superstitions; the British incursionists, though fanatical at times and callously condescending almost always, did bring to the Ibos some changes that were truly beneficial.

Achebe's central character is Okonkwo, an imposing hero by Ibo standards. He was in his teens a famous wrestler; later, he proved himself a brave warrior, killing his people's enemies in battle. Okonkwo then became a prosperous farmer, having three wives, several children, and a compound with separate huts for each wife and her children; he had taken two titles, proving his value as an Ibo man. This is the hero that the British dishonored and drove to suicide.

Surprising objectivity appears in Okonkwo's portrait. He is a troubled man, for whom hard work and success are obsessions. He fears comparisons to his father, lazy and improvident, who had died in great debt and who had been called an *agbala*, a woman, because of his worthlessness. Okonkwo beat his wives; he even shot at one of them, forcing her to scurry over the compound wall to save her life. He killed a young boy he had helped to raise when the Oracle of the Hills and the Caves demanded his death. Other warriors were ready to carry out the killing, and one advised Okonkwo not to participate; but Okonkwo was afraid of appearing weak if he did not strike the boy.

Ibo law at times punished Okonkwo severely. Okonkwo caused the death of another boy when his rifle accidentally exploded while being fired into the air during a celebration. Even though the act was inadvertent, tribal law demanded that the relatives of the dead boy burn Okonkwo's compound, kill his animals, and destroy his farm; Okonkwo himself was to be exiled for seven years. Even so, Okonkwo believed in the old Ibo ways and was willing to defend them with his life. He hated the British, with their new religion and their insistence that their laws should govern the Ibos, and he reacted violently to their presence.

Okonkwo's resistance to change was a thematic element in the novel. Some changes were appearing in Ibo culture anyway, caused simply by the relentless march of history and the different attitudes of the younger generation. One elder of the clan complained that the new generation did not value family unity sufficiently. When Okonkwo resisted British authority, killing one of the *kotma*, court messengers, the tribe's indecision allowed other *kotma* to escape. The clan no longer acted as one; the clan had fallen apart. Okonkwo hanged himself, and his death was symbolic of the death of a culture, a centuries-old way of life.

Achebe does not lament the passing of some aspects of the old Ibo ways, such as the killing of twins. Ibos thought twins evil and abandoned them in the forest. The British missionaries saved twins whenever they could find them in time.

Achebe's command of English is another factor in his success. He converts ancient Ibo proverbs into English without losing the charm and universality of the primitive originals. He is capable also of superb irony. For the Ibos, suicide was an abomination; no Ibo would touch the defiled body of Okonkwo, previously the proud defender of traditional Ibo values, as it hung from the tree on which he had died. The British that Okonkwo hated would have to take down his corpse and arrange its burial. The irony continued: For the British District Commissioner, the suicide of Okonkwo was simply another interesting item for the book he would write someday on the pacification of primitives. He thought he might get almost a whole chapter out of the day's events; then he reconsidered—maybe not a chapter, but at least a paragraph.

Achebe's next novel brought the story of Okonkwo's family into the present. *No Longer at Ease* (1960) told the story of Okonkwo's grandson, Obi, whose problems in trying to exist in the British world while still aware of the demands upon him of tribal values led him into trouble with British law. *Arrow of God* (1964) finished Achebe's trilogy. Set in the 1920's, it showed the declining authorities of Ezeulu, priest of the great god Ulu. Christian teachers undermined his power, and the Ibos eventually turned against him.

Achebe said he had lived in three Nigerias: one under British authority, one of growing nationalist tendencies, and the modern one of a self-governing state. *A Man of the People* (1966) dealt with the modern period. Its subject was political graft, corruption, and abuse of power, the inevitable results of British materialism and the destruction of traditional Ibo work ethics. In the period of African independence, the political leaders were shown as greedy and unprincipled. Chief Nanga, a candidate for president, exemplified what had happened to the old warrior class: He was not the defender of his people; he was their exploiter.

Impact of Event

Achebe illustrated that Africa at the time the British came into Nigeria was more than a continent of savagery and superstition. He set *Things Fall Apart* in a village far inland, away from the coast where slavery had already led to the debasement of Africa; in this hinterland area of the Niger, an extraordinarily viable culture had flourished for a very long time. Achebe's novel enabled Africans to feel pride in their racial past.

Before Achebe, the African novel did not really exist. Kenya, for example, had no writers who, in the strictest sense, could be called novelists. After Achebe had written of European incursions into Iboland and had argued that African writers must remain in touch with their past, a Kenyan who had been writing as James T. Ngugi began to write as Ngugi wa Thiong'o, publishing *The River Between* (1965), a novel chronicling the incursions of European missionaries into his ancestral area of Kikuyuland. Ngugi and other African novelists agreed with Achebe on several key points, one being that the African writer must stay aware of problems spawned in the new Africa. Ngugi insisted upon this, stating that the social and political problems of modern Africa were so huge that no serious writer could be forgiven if he failed to deal with them. *A Grain of Wheat* (1967) continued Ngugi's study of his country by moving to troublesome modern developments. The story began just before Kenya's celebration of independence in 1963; several characters felt great uneasiness, for they were not certain what the new Kenya would hold for them.

The impact of Achebe's success was greatest in his own country. Nigerian writers had written long prose fiction works before Achebe, but these were essentially folk tales of great adventures and supernatural powers. Many had been written in Yoruba rather than English. After Achebe showed that an African could write English effectively, one major Yoruba writer began to compose in English. Another writer who had previously written in stilted English was led by Achebe's example to discover a simpler style.

Many of the major writers of modern Africa are Nigerian; certainly a large percentage of Africa's novelists are, and Achebe's influence on their choice of subject matter has been as great as it was on their style. Their novels show how difficult it is for many Nigerians who move to the cities to do what Achebe called for, remain in touch with their cultural past. Lagos, the setting for Achebe's *No Longer at Ease*, is for many Nigerian writers a center of Nigeria's problems. It is a modernized city, and Cyprian Ekwensi contrasted its sordidness with the purity of village life in *Jagua Nana* (1961), the story of Jagua, a young village girl who became captivated by the bright lights of Lagos, especially those of the nightclubs, and fell into prostitution. Ekwensi showed the Lagos underworld, the political viciousness, the disgusting differences between the slums and a rich suburb. In *Double Yoke* (1983), Buchi Emecheta, a Nigerian, told the story of a young girl trying to find her way in the modern world while still trying to hold to traditional values.

Achebe asked Nigeria's writers to deal with the ugliest aspects of their country's life. In *Slave Girl* (1977), which was set in the 1940's, Emecheta's heroine was sold into slavery by her older brother. The military is one of the ugliest elements in Africa's modern problems. Achebe's *A Man of the People* closed with a military coup, a plot twist that soon seemed prophetic; Nigeria's first army coup followed shortly thereafter, leading to a terrible civil war in which the secessionist Ibo state of Biafra, for which Achebe worked, was destroyed. Emecheta, an Ibo, dealt with the horrors of the war in *Destination Biafra* (1982). Many of Achebe's themes reappeared in the novels of Festus Iyaye, also Nigerian. *Violence* (1979) showed greed and corruption in Nigeria. *Heroes* (1986) dealt with the Biafran war, crying out against corruption and injustice.

For some two decades, Achebe, occupied with the war and the necessity of rebuilding after it, wrote no novels. At last he produced *Anthills of the Savannah* (1987), another story of political viciousness and a rotting society. A ruthless politician who has gained power by a coup has brought to trial two childhood friends who have begun to oppose him.

Achebe has insisted that the story of Africa will have to be told by Africans. The European cannot do it. In Nigeria, several young novelists, male and female, are telling the full story—not just the attractive and pleasant parts. The young novelists are confronting the dangers and dealing with the atrocities of their troubled time.

Achebe has had an additional impact on other writers. His literary success led to fellowship awards that enabled him to travel extensively. In East Africa, he learned of the difficulty Swahili poets had in getting their works published, and he began to be involved in several publishing ventures. These provided outlets for new works by black writers, not just from Nigeria but from all over Africa.

Another travel fellowship brought Achebe to Great Britain and the United States, where *Things Fall Apart* had been published in 1959. The trip to America led to a visiting professorship from 1972 to 1975 at the University of Massachusetts in Amherst and to later appointments at other American universities, helping to make American faculty and students aware of the African experience. Achebe is revered in America and Great Britain as well as in Africa, and his reputation as a literary force is immense.

Bibliography

Carroll, David. *Chinua Achebe*. 2d ed. New York: St. Martin's Press, 1980. Very readable overview of Achebe's life and work into the late 1970's. Informative on the highly significant anthropological elements in Achebe's fiction. Discusses key stylistic elements, including the abundant use of time-honored proverbs, which are an extraordinarily rich element in the conversation of the Ibos.

Cook, David. *African Literature: A Critical View*. London: Longman, 1977. Separate chapters on *Things Fall Apart* and *No Longer at Ease*, with significant critical statements rather than plot summaries. Valuable assertions about style, structure, and irony. Discussion of Achebe in connection with broad movements in the Anglophone literature of Africa.

Innes, Catherine L. *Chinua Achebe*. Vol. 1 in *Cambridge Studies in African and Caribbean Literature*. New York: Cambridge University Press, 1990. Biographical information on Achebe and his family. Discussion of Achebe's dislike for Joyce Cary's *Mister Johnson* and analysis of the different views of the two writers. Sketch of Nigeria's modern political troubles; interesting on Achebe as critic, his involvement in politics, and his concern for justice.

Killam, G. D. *The Writings of Chinua Achebe*. Rev. ed. London: Heinemann, 1977. A revision of Killam's *The Novels of Chinua Achebe* (1969), one of the earliest and most appreciative long studies of Achebe. Discussion of Achebe's ideas and style in the novels still worthwhile; new discussions of the poems, short stories, and other works by Achebe.

Moore, Gerald. *Twelve African Writers*. Bloomington: Indiana University Press, 1980. Achebe seen in the context of African fiction. Discussion of style and organizational schemes in the early novels, with attention to poems and stories also. Comment on the way different characters' spoken English helps to characterize them as Achebe switches from pidgin to a pompous, verbose style for various figures in his stories.

Taiwo, Oladele. *Culture and the Nigerian Novel*. New York: St. Martin's Press, 1976. Relationship of Achebe to the indigenous culture of his area; discussion of how elements of the old culture are relevant to modern novelists and to the characters in their modern settings. Extraordinarily useful index pinpointing topics within Achebe's works.

Wren, Robert M. *Achebe's World: The Historical and Cultural Context of the Novels of Chinua Achebe*. Washington, D.C.: Three Continents Press, 1980. Valuable presentation of historical facts about the British presence in Nigeria, about the nature of Ibo life and customs, and about the ways in which Achebe has used these facts. Authoritative information from a scholar who knows Nigeria well.

Howard L. Ford

Cross-References

Heart of Darkness Reveals the Consequences of Imperialism (1902), p. 51; Artists Find Inspiration in African Tribal Art (1906), p. 156; The Harlem Renaissance Celebrates African-American Culture (1920's), p. 480; *Roots* Dramatizes the African-American Experience (1977), p. 2397; *"MASTER HAROLD"* . . . *and the boys* Examines Apartheid (1982), p. 2496; Soyinka Wins the Nobel Prize in Literature (1986), p. 2594.

SEVEN OF THE TOP TEN TELEVISION SERIES ARE WESTERNS

Category of event: Television and radio
Time: 1958-1959
Locale: The United States

Westerns, which were introduced to television in the mid-1950's, by the end of the decade had come to dominate the medium

Principal personages:
JAMES ARNESS (JAMES AURNESS, 1923-   ), the actor who starred as Marshal Matt Dillon in *Gunsmoke*
AMANDA BLAKE (BEVERLY LOUISE NEILL, 1929-1989), the actress who starred as saloonkeeper Miss Kitty Russell in *Gunsmoke*
WARD BOND (1903-1960), the actor who starred as wagon master Major Seth Adams in *Wagon Train*
RICHARD BOONE (1917-1981), the actor who starred as Paladin, a bounty hunter, in *Have Gun Will Travel*
CHUCK CONNORS (1921-1992), the actor who starred as homesteader Lucas McCain in *The Rifleman*
JAMES GARNER (JAMES BAUMGARNER, 1928-   ), the actor who starred as roving gambler Bret Maverick in *Maverick*
HUGH O'BRIAN (HUGH J. KRAMPE, 1925-   ), the actor who starred as lawman Wyatt Earp in *The Life and Legend of Wyatt Earp*
DALE ROBERTSON (1923-   ), the actor who starred as Special Agent Jim Hardie in *Tales of Wells Fargo*

Summary of Event

American television technology was well developed by the 1930's, but commercial television was not widely marketed until the late 1940's because World War II imposed heavy demands on production facilities. At first, all broadcasting was done by local stations. Networking presented many technical problems that were not worked out until late in 1951, when the West Coast was finally absorbed into the National Broadcasting Company's composite viewing audience.

The public was attracted to this new medium, but sales were slow because early sets were expensive, reception was only reliable in the major cities, and programming quality was inferior to what was offered by film theaters. There were no big stars on television because film stars were afraid of losing their charisma by being identified with what was considered an inferior medium, one not much different from radio. The Hollywood motion-picture studios hated and feared television, knowing it would keep people away from theaters. Filmmakers refused to sell or lease anything for television viewing except ancient cowboy films, silent comedies, and primitive animated cartoons.

Actors such as Milton Berle, a has-been film comedian who had never played anything but supporting roles in films, became television superstars. The independent stations could not afford expensive entertainment because there were not enough viewers to bring in advertising revenue to pay for it. When the Columbia Broadcasting System (CBS), the National Broadcasting Company (NBC), and the American Broadcasting Company (ABC)—known as the "Big Three"—finally established television networks that could reach the entire nation, the resulting advertising revenues and keen competition for ratings warranted greater expenditures on programming.

During most of the 1950's, the big productions featured on television were broadcast live from New York. In the mid-1950's, however, Walt Disney Studios and Warner Bros. succumbed to the lure of profits, and weekly filmed series made in Hollywood and termed "adult Westerns" began to appear. The first ones were so popular that they spawned a host of imitators. By the 1958-1959 season, Westerns had become so popular that they dominated "prime time" (the hours between 7:00 and 10:00 P.M., when audiences are largest).

What mainly distinguished adult Westerns from the old cowboy films starring such heroes as Tom Mix and Buck Jones, cranked out by the hundreds in the 1920's and 1930's, was characterization. In the old Hollywood Westerns, which were targeted at children and unsophisticated rural audiences, the hero was typically all good, and the unscrupulous villain had no redeeming virtues. There was little feminine interest; the hero was more likely to kiss his horse than to kiss the heroine. In the new television Westerns, which were strongly influenced by such innovative feature films as *High Noon* (1952) and *Shane* (1953), the hero had human foibles, and the villains were often sympathetic, or at least understandable, figures. Furthermore, there was often a strong interest in the opposite sex, and good roles existed for actresses.

For example, the hero of *Have Gun Will Travel* broke with convention by wearing all-black clothing. The show's protagonist, Paladin, was not idealistic but was instead interested in making money and living the good life. His professed occupation, as the series title suggests, was that of a hired killer, "a knight without honor in a savage land," although he seldom displayed unethical behavior.

The handsome hero of *Maverick* hated fighting, was not at all proficient with a gun, and displayed a strong interest in the opposite sex. The most popular television Western of all, *Gunsmoke*, featured a woman who ran a saloon and gambling parlor, quite possibly was earning money as a madam, and seemed to have an out-of-wedlock relationship with the show's hero, Marshal Dillon.

All the popular television Western series featured violence. Some of the heroes carried exotic weapons. Lucas McCain of *The Rifleman* killed his enemies with a trick rifle that he could fire as fast as a revolver. Steve McQueen, who played bounty hunter Josh Randall on *Wanted: Dead or Alive*, another top-ranking series, carried a sawed-off weapon that was a combination pistol and shotgun. Among the scriptwriters' biggest problems was dreaming up new ways for men to kill one another and new motives for doing so. One Hollywood writer was quoted as saying that viewers demanded three things of every Western story: a fistfight, a gunfight, and galloping horses. *Gunsmoke*, the longest-lasting Western series of all time, opened with the credits superimposed on a scene in which Marshal Dillon kills an opponent in a shoot-out on Dodge City's main street.

Audiences liked the violence, the undemanding plots, the simple morality, the escapist nature of the genre, and the handsome heroes. By the 1958-1959 season, seven of the ten top-rated series on television were Westerns: *Gunsmoke*, *Wagon Train*, *Have Gun Will Travel*, *The Rifleman*, *Maverick*, *Tales of Wells Fargo*, and *The Life and Legend of Wyatt Earp*.

Impact of Event

New York broadcasters, producers, writers, and actors had been in an excellent position to dominate the new medium of television, with its fantastic potential for making money and influencing public opinion. The East Coast controlled the lion's share of American capital. The big radio networks, the rich corporate sponsors, and the major advertising agencies were all headquartered in New York, and it would have been convenient as well as highly profitable to keep television production and broadcasting centered in the country's number-one city as well. New York was also the major center for publishing, which made it an intellectual capital. Control of programming gradually slipped through the Easterners' fingers, however, because of a variety of complex factors.

For one thing, New York writers were oriented toward the stage and radio, which meant that their productions emphasized spoken words. They did not really understand the great difference between stage plays and motion pictures; they tended to bring Broadway to the general public, perhaps thinking they were thereby elevating American tastes to their own cultural level. Furthermore, their interests were confined to the Eastern seaboard, and they had little understanding of the psychology of the rest of the country.

New Yorkers joked that, as far as they were concerned, the world ended at the Hudson River. This joke eventually backfired. New Yorkers tended to have sophisticated tastes and planned to upgrade the tastes of the rest of the country. The foremost spokesperson of this idealistic attitude was NBC president Sylvester L. Weaver, a member of Phi Beta Kappa who had graduated with highest honors from an Ivy League college. He said: "NBC must do *good*. Television must be used to upgrade humanity across a broad base." By the late 1960's, when Hollywood had come to dominate the medium, the distinguished journalist Edward P. Morgan stated: "Once upon a time television was supposed to operate in the public interest, but lo and behold, it has captured the public and made it a product—a packaged audience, so to speak, which it sells to advertisers."

It was impossible for people with high artistic standards to turn out the amount of cheap programming that the new medium demanded. Some television stations in major cities were already broadcasting around the clock and creating a demand for material that was beginning to make television seem like an insatiable monster. It was probably inevitable that the Hollywood studios would inherit the bulk of program production.

Hollywood studio heads had never tried to upgrade public taste; their philosophy had always been to give the public what it wanted. What the majority of the public wanted was escapist entertainment that required no mental effort to follow. Hollywood writers understood that people go to *see* films but that they *watch* television: The visual aspect of the medium is far more important than the dialogue. This relationship was even more true of television than of motion pictures because, in order to adjust to the small television screen, the cameras had to feature close-ups and "tight shots." This requirement meant not only that more information was conveyed by subtle changes of characters' expressions but that the viewer had to stay "glued to the tube" to understand the story as well.

The explosion of Westerns that occurred on television in the late 1950's signaled the beginning of a new era for the medium. The Hollywood studios proved their long-established expertise in turning out cheap entertainment for mass audiences. The film medium was by far the most practical, if not the most elevating or edifying, means of producing television entertainment. Once the shows were on film, they could be shown over and over again and could be exported overseas to earn additional revenue. Westerns were a very practical commodity, since the genre has always proved popular with viewers all over the world. Furthermore, Westerns are a form of costume drama, they do not become dated with changes in clothing or hairstyles.

The Hollywood studios might have been content to continue making Westerns forever if the public had not become satiated with shoot-outs, barroom brawls, poker games, cattle drives, Indian attacks, and the other limited features of the genre. Violence in drama tends to escalate because it acts like a drug, requiring larger and larger doses to create the same effect. Educators, church officials, and other civic leaders began to protest against the orgy of violence on American television screens. Most of the scriptwriters knew nothing about the Old West and quickly ran out of inspiration. Westerns were superseded on television by a plethora of crime dramas featuring private detectives and police officers. The formula remained essentially the same, however, with the same hero facing a new villain each week, with cars replacing horses and automatics replacing six-shooters.

Television started out as a New York medium featuring "legitimate" drama, vaudeville acts, musicals, and comedies. The demands for mass-produced entertainment that would appeal to a mass audience, one that included children, inexorably changed television into a Hollywood medium the staple product of which was filmed series. Many people deplored the degradation of this great invention. Contemporary educators often blame television for the decline in learning achievement, while others blame television's emphasis on violence for increases in crime.

Bibliography

"The American Morality Play: TV's Western Heroes." *Time* 73 (March 30, 1959):

52-60. An article about the top-rated television Westerns of 1959 featured as the cover story in the nation's leading newsmagazine. Especially interesting because it gives a contemporary version of the enormous impact that television Westerns were having on the American public.

Balio, Tino, ed. *Hollywood in the Age of Television.* Boston: Unwin Hyman, 1990. A collection of essays on the business aspects of Hollywood film production and television network competition, written by various authorities, mostly academicians. Each essay is heavily documented with endnotes and also provides a list of valuable suggestions for further reading.

Barnouw, Erik. *Tube of Plenty: The Evolution of American Television.* 2d rev. ed. New York: Oxford University Press, 1990. The history of television from its earliest beginnings, stressing its emergence as a dominant factor in American life and in American influence throughout the world. Contains a chronological log highlighting important events in television history. An excellent annotated bibliography and an index are provided.

Lackmann, Ron. *Remember Television.* New York: G. P. Putnam's Sons, 1971. This richly illustrated book covers the history of television programming from 1947 through 1958. It gives an excellent overview of what television was like before the onslaught of the mass-produced Hollywood made-for-television Westerns in the late 1950's. Important news events are headlined at the beginning of each chapter to orient the reader to what was going on in the world at the time.

MacDonald, J. Fred. *One Nation Under Television: The Rise and Decline of Network TV.* New York: Pantheon Books, 1990. Covers the history of television for four decades, from the earliest beginnings of network television up to the end of the 1980's. Heavily documented with endnotes; contains an exceptionally thorough bibliography.

_____. *Who Shot the Sheriff? The Rise and Fall of the Television Western.* New York: Praeger, 1987. MacDonald, author of several other books on mass media, analyzes the development of Western characters and themes on television as a mirror of American values, beliefs, and ideals. He states that Westerns lost their popularity because they could not express contemporary ideology.

West, Richard. *Television Westerns: Major and Minor Series, 1946-1978.* Jefferson, N.C.: McFarland, 1987. Describes all Western series appearing on television from 1946 to 1978, including biographical information on the principal actors. Contains photographs of the more prominent ones. Appendices contain comprehensive information on casting, Emmy Award winners, popularity ratings, title changes for syndication, and air times. Informative introduction and thorough index.

Bill Delaney

Cross-References

Grey's *Riders of the Purple Sage* Launches the Western Genre (1912), p. 304; Ford

Defines the Western in *Stagecoach* (1939), p. 1115; Westerns Dominate Postwar American Film (1946), p. 1313; *Gunsmoke* Debuts, Launching a Popular Television Genre (1955), p. 1668; *Bonanza* Becomes an American Television Classic (1959), p. 1800; Leone Renovates the Western Genre (1964), p. 1984.

AILEY FOUNDS HIS DANCE COMPANY

Category of event: Dance
Time: March 30, 1958
Locale: New York, New York

Alvin Ailey presented his first modern dance concert, strengthening the cultural diversity of American modern dance and integrating ballet, jazz, and modern dance forms

Principal personages:

ALVIN AILEY (1931-1989), an African-American modern dancer and choreographer who introduced multicultural themes to mainstream modern dance

LESTER HORTON (1906-1953), the West Coast choreographer who served as Ailey's teacher and mentor

TALLEY BEATTY (1923-   ), an African-American modern dancer and choreographer who performed as guest artist at Ailey's premiere concert

CARMEN DE LAVALLADE (1931-   ), an original member of the Horton Dance Theater who frequently danced with Ailey

JUDITH JAMISON (1944-   ), a soloist with the Ailey dance company who succeeded Ailey as artistic director

Summary of Event

Billed simply as "Alvin Ailey and Company," an ensemble of six black dancers that included Charles Moore, Claude Thompson, Jacqueline Walcott, Clarence Cooper, Nancy Reddy, and Alvin Ailey were joined by guest artist Talley Beatty at the Ninety-second street Young Men's Hebrew Association (YMHA) in New York City. This premiere concert performance by the Ailey dance company, on March 30, 1958, broadened the scope of American dance through the debut of works that reflected multicultural influences. As would be the case in future performances, the Ailey company's debut included pieces that purveyed aspects of the African-American experience.

In addition to the development of multicultural thematic material, Ailey's personal movement style burgeoned in his first concert appearance. Ailey had teamed up with Ernest Parham to recruit dancers from the cast of the Broadway show *Jamaica* (1957) in order to present the concert. *Dance Magazine* critic Doris Hering commented on the energy, technical prowess, and versatility of the dancers, with particular mention of guest artist Talley Beatty.

Alvin Ailey, Jr., was born and reared in Rogers, Texas. His parents separated when he was very young, and in 1942 Ailey moved with his mother to Los Angeles. Although Ailey previously had studied tap dance and some ethnic forms, he began professional dance training in 1949 with West Coast choreographer Lester Horton.

By 1953, Ailey was performing with the Horton company and made his debut in a revue titled *Bal Caribe.*

Horton died in 1953, and soon thereafter Ailey took over much of the responsibility of company direction. Original members of the Lester Horton Dance Theatre who later danced with the Ailey company include Carmen de Lavallade, Joyce Trisler, and James Truitte. Ailey's most famous work, *Revelations,* premiered on January 31, 1960, at the Ninety-second Street YMHA. This signature piece of the Alvin Ailey American Dance Theater, which many maintain is a masterpiece of modern dance, premiered scarcely two years after the Ailey company's concert debut.

Dance critic Selma Jeanne Cohen reviewed the work favorably in *Dance Magazine* and specifically noted the vivid theatrical characterizations created by Ailey. On November 27, 1960, the Ailey company performed *Revelations* at the Clark Center of the West Side Young Women's Christian Association (YWCA) in New York City. In her review, Cohen noted the enthusiastic audience response.

According to the program notes, *Revelations* explores the "motivations and emotions of American Negro religious music." The suite is set to a series of American spirituals and reflects universal themes of deliverance and joy. *Revelations* contains images that depict much of the Southern life of the nineteenth century. The dance can be viewed as Ailey's interpretation of American spirituals. *Revelations* quickly became a signature piece for the Ailey company and it was included in nearly every concert for many years. James Haskins noted that in December, 1988, the dance continued to elicit rave reviews from critics, twenty-nine years after its premiere.

During the fall of 1960, several months after the premiere of *Revelations,* Ailey based his company at the Clark Center. During this period, Ailey augmented the company's repertory with the works of other choreographers. It was unusual at this time for a choreographer to include other artists' dances in a company repertoire, but Ailey viewed the Alvin Ailey American Dance Theater as a purveyor of all types and styles of modern dance, including works that represented a broad spectrum of cultural differences.

It is interesting to note that Ailey integrated his dance company at a time when black nationalism and separatism were becoming popular. Ailey kept his company integrated even though he received some negative criticism. By maintaining integration within the Alvin Ailey American Dance Theater, Ailey helped to eliminate stereotypes; he showed that dance movement is culturally based rather than racially intrinsic. Within Ailey's dance theater, white dancers perform the blues, black dancers perform classical ballet, and Asian dancers execute jazz combinations.

Six years after the premiere of *Revelations,* Ailey's vision was to maintain a company of twelve to sixteen dancers who would perform a varied repertory of modern dance works. He also envisioned a school in which to train dancers. By the beginning of the next decade, he would find those visions fulfilled: In 1971, the choreographer established the Alvin Ailey American Dance Center. Twenty years after it was founded, the company school enrolled more than twenty-five hundred students each year and sponsored a junior company, the Alvin Ailey Repertory Ensemble.

Impact of Event

Perhaps the greatest impact Ailey had on the field of modern dance was his propensity to bring black traditions and black artists into the mainstream of American dance. Since its inception, the Alvin Ailey American Dance Theater has served as a means to present works by black choreographers. In addition to several of Talley Beatty's dances, the company presented pieces by modern dance pioneers Katherine Dunham and Pearl Primus. Also included on the company roster have been works by Ulysses Dove, George Faison, Louis Johnson, Bill T. Jones, Donald McKayle, and Billy Wilson.

Ailey also created one of the first successful modern dance repertory companies to perform the works of many different choreographers. The dance movement originally created by Ailey has become part of the vocabulary of contemporary dance; the images he choreographed have become an irrevocable part of American culture.

Ailey's choreography maintains universal appeal and developed from many sources. The African-American experience served as source material for many of Ailey's works, including *Revelations*; however, scholars and critics agree that his choreography cannot be simplistically categorized. Rather than only representing black dance, the works exist as part of the total multicultural American experience. Just as American culture is syncretistic, the repertory of the Alvin Ailey American Dance Theater represents a spectrum of diversity.

Like the pioneering efforts of Katherine Dunham, who fused concert dance forms with Caribbean movements and steps, Ailey's style was a fusion of modern dance, ballet, and black dance forms. Ailey's choreography has enjoyed much popularity, and many of his signature movements have become standard dance vocabulary. The Ailey style is inextricably woven into the fabric of modern dance. Ailey has commented that his particular fusion of dance genres includes aspects of ballet, modern, folk, jazz, music visualization, and both Oriental and Spanish forms.

Dance scholar Brenda Dixon states that only certain sections of specific Ailey dances can be classified as black dance. She further emphasizes that it is important to view certain Ailey works within an appropriate frame of reference. Dances by Ailey that do reflect certain black aesthetic and cultural principles should be viewed within the appropriate cultural context. For example, *Love Songs*, choreographed in 1972, is a solo song cycle based in the tradition of the vocalized black ballad. *Love Songs* illustrates the black tradition of song-as-survival.

In 1962, Ailey decided to integrate his company, expanding the cultural roster of his dancers as he had expanded the troupe's repertory with the inclusion of many styles of modern dance. The company began to represent not only black dance but also the entire field of modern dance, which included much cultural diversity.

Just as his choreography and style were distinctly American, Ailey added the word "American" to the name of his company, and the troupe became known officially as the Alvin Ailey American Dance Theater in the mid-1960's. The company continued to represent the United States on many national and international tours. In 1964, the troupe embarked on its first European tour and received enthusiastic responses, especially in Hamburg, Germany, where one performance elicited sixty-one curtain calls. After that tour, Ailey retired from dancing and focused his energy on choreography and artistic direction of the company.

From 1969 until 1971, the Alvin Ailey American Dance Theater was based at the Brooklyn Academy of Music. During this time, Ailey created no less than ten new works, including *Mary Lou's Mass* and his famous tribute to the African-American woman, *Cry.* This solo was created for company member Judith Jamison, who later would direct the Alvin Ailey American Dance Theater after Ailey's death in 1989. *Cry* was representative of the black woman's life in white society. Moreover, the dance was representative of the oppressed everywhere. Jamison became renowned for her performance of the solo, and the piece maintains universal appeal.

The City Center in Manhattan became the home for the company in 1971. Around this time, Ailey began to revive modern dance classics for inclusion in the company repertory. Dances by prominent black choreographers such as Donald McKayle, Katherine Dunham, Pearl Primus, and Talley Beatty appeared on concert programs. Ailey's intent was to maintain older works for future generations rather than lose classics of modern dance. These pieces also reflected the roots of the African-American experience and significant contributions of black choreographers and dancers. In addition, Ailey presented choreography by Mexican-born José Limon and modern dance pioneer Ted Shawn.

The Alvin Ailey American Dance Theater left City Center as its permanent home during the 1980's. Although annual performances continued to occur there, the company also appeared at Lincoln Center, the Metropolitan Opera House, and a variety of other theaters. A 1984 performance at the Metropolitan Opera House marked only the second time a modern dance company had appeared there.

In the late 1980's, the Ailey company sponsored a revival of much of Katherine Dunham's choreography, which was originally created in the 1930's and 1940's. Funded with foundation grants, the Ailey company performed and filmed Dunham's major works, many of which never had been recorded. Dunham served as consultant to the project, which included choreography such as *Choros* and *L'Ag'Ya.* The revival project also included the restoration of original costumes and set designs created by Dunham's husband, John Pratt.

The 1988-1989 season was Ailey's last full season with the company. Despite a battle with a rare blood disease, Ailey managed to premiere four new works in New York. The company performed a new work by Ailey titled *Opus* as well as revivals of his *Streams* and *Masakela Language.* Other choreographers represented on the season's program were Donald Byrd, Kelvin Rotardier, and Rovan Deon. In 1988, Ailey's company performed at the National Black Arts Festival in Atlanta, Georgia, where the integrated dance troupe represented the art form of dance.

Ailey's influence extends beyond those with whom he directly worked. An entire generation of modern dancers who did not necessarily work with Ailey were nevertheless influenced by him. Kevin Jeff is one such individual. In 1981, Jeff formed Jeff's Jubilation! Dance Company, an all-black modern dance company in Brooklyn,

New York. The Black Pearl Dance Company of the Bronx, New York, is another black modern dance company indirectly influenced by Ailey. Founder Maria Mitchell established the company in order to preserve and present black literature via dance theater. The six-member ensemble is often joined by children and guest artists in performance. Other multicultural groups exist across the country: Philadanco, directed by Joan Myers Brown in Philadelphia, and the Dallas Black Dance Theatre are two such examples of companies that share the legacy of Ailey's work.

The Alvin Ailey American Dance Center in New York City is managed by the Alvin Ailey Dance Theater Foundation, which also administers the junior resident company. During a span of thirty-five years, the Alvin Ailey American Dance Theater evolved from an ensemble of six members to a company of twenty-eight dancers who by 1993 had performed for more than fifteen million spectators in forty-five countries. The Alvin Ailey American Dance Theater's performance of the "Rocka My Soul" section from *Revelations* proved to be as galvanizing as ever when the ensemble performed at President Bill Clinton's preinauguration gala held in Hanover, Maryland, on January 19, 1993.

Two years before his death, Ailey received the Scripps Dance Award at the American Dance Festival. Upon receipt of the award, Ailey reaffirmed his role as a conduit for American modern dance. He stated, "I am part of Isadora Duncan. I am part of Martha Graham. I am part of Doris Humphrey. I am part of Asadata Dafora. And I am part of Lester Horton, who made a boy, an eighteen-year-old athlete in sweat pants, feel important."

Bibliography

Cook, Susan. *The Alvin Ailey American Dance Theater.* New York: William Morrow, 1978. A wonderfully visual book with many excellent photographs of Ailey's dances. The text mainly addresses Ailey's more popular works. Excellent section on *Revelations.* Includes a chronology of Ailey's work through 1976.

Emery, Lynne Fauley. *Black Dance from 1619 to Today.* 2d rev. ed. Princeton, N.J.: Princeton Book Company, 1988. A definitive book on black concert and vernacular dance forms. A valuable resource for the student of history and dance. Emery presents a comprehensive history of black dance within historical, social, and cultural contexts. Excellent notes, bibliography, and index. Limited black-and-white photographs.

Haskins, James. *Black Dance in America.* New York: Thomas Y. Crowell, 1990. Although categorized as juvenile literature, Haskins' text presents a thorough survey of black dance in America. Included are brief biographies of prominent dancers, choreographers, and companies. An annotated videography provides excellent film resources. Select bibliography and index. Photographs.

Kraus, Richard, Sarah Hilsendager, and Brenda Dixon. *History of the Dance in Art and Education.* 3d ed. Englewood Cliffs, N.J.: Prentice-Hall, 1991. Offers a comprehensive view of all major dance forms through historical and cultural perspectives. A brief biography of Ailey is included, and a chapter on black dance in

America is informative and detailed. Endnotes for each chapter are included. Bibliography, index, and photographs.

Thorpe, Edward. *Black Dance.* New York: Overlook Press, 1990. Though not a thorough compilation of black history and dance, the book contains some interesting chapters. Chapters on Asadata, Dafora, black ballet, and black dance in Britain contain information not found in other sources. An overview of Ailey's career is included that focuses on his choreography and company. Excellent illustrations. Index.

John R. Crawford

Cross-References

Baker Dances in *La Revue nègre* (1925), p. 665; Taylor Establishes His Own Dance Company (1954), p. 1602; Joffrey Founds His Ballet Company (1956), p. 1694; Mitchell Founds thc Dancc Theater of Harlem (1968), p. 2110; Festivals Mark a Peak in the Dance Created by Black Artists (1983), p. 2521; Multiculturalism Dominates the Dance World (Late 1980's), p. 2559.

GRASS PUBLISHES *THE TIN DRUM*

Category of event: Literature
Time: 1959
Locale: West Germany

Günter Grass's novel, greeted with both critical praise and public outrage, forced Germans to reexamine their own complicity in bringing about the nightmare that was the Third Reich

Principal personage:
GÜNTER GRASS (1927-   ), a multitalented artist, a former member of the Hitler youth and wounded German war veteran who refused to bury his Nazi past

Summary of Event

Beginning in the early 1950's, West Germany experienced what is often called the *Wirtschaftswunder*, a miraculous economic recovery after the devastation of the country during World War II. The mounting tensions of the then-raging Cold War made a rearmed Germany strategically useful to the U.S.-led Western Bloc nations. The U.S. government began the economic and military rehabilitation of its former enemy to establish a front line of defense against a possible Soviet Bloc invasion of Western Europe. A rising prosperity among the West German population accompanied the military buildup. By the end of the decade, West Germany had recovered from much of the devastation caused by the bombing and the battles of World War II.

West Germany's economic and military partnership with the Western Bloc engendered an attempt on the part of many Germans to disassociate themselves from their country's Nazi past. Many German teachers, historians, writers, and government officials argued that Adolf Hitler and his movement represented a historical anomaly, not the logical development of German history. Hitler came to power, these apologists maintained, because of a special set of circumstances: the German defeat in World War I and the ensuing Treaty of Versailles (universally despised among all social classes in Germany); the economic dislocations in Germany during the Weimar Republic (especially the Great Depression), and middle-class fear of a Communist takeover. The German nation as a whole, they concluded, should not be forced to bear the guilt for atrocities committed by a group of madmen who illegally seized control of their government.

During the period between 1945 and 1959, a whole body of literature emerged in Germany and elsewhere underscoring the thesis that most Germans had deplored Hitler and the Nazis. Accounts of various German resistance groups that had actively sought to overthrow Hitler appeared alongside stories of individual Germans who had helped to rescue numerous Jews from deportation to concentration camps.

German artists, writers, and scientists pointed out that many of their number emigrated shortly after Hitler came to power. Most of those who remained insisted that they had been part of the "inner emigration," that though they had remained in Germany they had never cooperated with the regime and had worked in subtle ways to thwart Hitler's purposes.

Günter Grass's iconoclastic novel *Die Blechtrommel* (1959; *The Tin Drum*, 1961) shattered the moral complacency of German intellectuals and the German people, forcing them to acknowledge their own responsibility for the triumph of Nazism. Born in the free city of Danzig (which had been forcibly separated from Germany by the Treaty of Versailles) in 1927 to a grocer and his wife, Grass grew up during the Nazi era. Like most German children, he was a member of the Hitler Youth and thus was subjected to Nazi indoctrination throughout his childhood. Drafted into the army in 1944, he was wounded and finally captured by soldiers of the U.S. Army. Released from a prisoner-of-war camp in 1946, he worked at various jobs in a nearly destroyed Germany that was occupied and administered by the victors of the war.

In 1951, Grass resumed educational pursuits interrupted by the war, enrolling in the Fine Arts Academy at Düsseldorf. He married another student at Düsseldorf, traveled with her to Paris, and while she continued her studies, began writing poetry and plays and pursuing his interest in sculpture and graphic arts. Moving to West Berlin in 1954, Grass published a book of poetry that won him an invitation to join Group 47, an organization of German writers. The members of Group 47 were determined to rejuvenate their country's literary tradition, which had been virtually destroyed by the intellectual repression of the Third Reich.

Grass had won minor acclaim for his poetry prior to *The Tin Drum*, but in 1958, Group 47 awarded him its prepublication cash prize for his novel. When the novel appeared the next year, it caused the greatest uproar in the history of German literature. Translated into most major languages over the next few years, the novel won international critical acclaim, often accompanied by public condemnation. Grass himself instantly became the best-known and most controversial figure of postwar German literature.

Impact of Event

In addition to the prepublication prize of Group 47, *The Tin Drum* won three major international literary awards during the years following its publication. In 1965, while Grass was accepting the coveted Georg Buchner Prize, members of a youth organization in Düsseldorf publicly burned copies of his novel. Despite critical acclaim and many awards, Grass and *The Tin Drum* became the target of more than forty lawsuits and innumerable denunciations in the letters-to-the-editor columns of virtually every publication in Germany. People from all social strata in Germany accused Grass of pornography, blasphemy, sacrilege, slander, defamation, and many other heinous crimes.

Despite the various reasons given by Grass's many detractors for their denunciation of him and his novel, the furor over *The Tin Drum* arose from one central theme: Grass refused to exculpate himself or any other German from the guilt of the Nazi regime. Using as his storyteller a deranged dwarf named Oscar Matzerath (who willed himself to stop growing at the age of three to gain protection from the insane society of the interwar period and who had magical powers imparted by a succession of tin drums), Grass identified Nazi affinities in most of the people and all of the institutions of German society.

Critics have called Oscar's account of the Nazi era wildly satirical, wickedly humorous, and often morally chilling. Oscar presents a German religious institution only too willing to accommodate itself to Hitler's regime. Some of his most damning barbs are directed at Grass's own Catholicism, but Protestants are not spared their share of guilt. The picture of the world-acclaimed German educational institution presented by Oscar suggests that its discipline and regimentation accommodated Hitler's purposes admirably. The German political tradition of authoritarianism and antiliberalism almost invited a Hitler to take power. The Nazis capitalized on and institutionalized a widespread view of women that relegated them to a subordinate status in family relationships and the workforce. All economic classes willingly sacrificed their personal freedom to gain the economic prosperity that Hitler promised and delivered. In short, Hitler was no accident but the logical development of German history. Therefore, all the evil of the Nazi era was the direct responsibility of all living Germans. Still more disquieting was the implicit suggestion that the same forces that had brought Hitler to power were still operating in contemporary German society.

Oscar portrayed those Germans who had engaged in active resistance to Hitler's regime as having been opposed only to Hitler himself and not to the substance of Nazism. He also dismissed those German intellectuals engaged in the "inner emigration" as being nothing more than court jesters for Nazi Propaganda Minister Joseph Goebbels. Taken in total, the novel condemned all Germans and insisted that they acknowledge the moral and spiritual shortcomings of their institutions; little wonder that almost every German reader found something offensive in *The Tin Drum*.

Despite the controversy surrounding Grass and the widespread condemnation of *The Tin Drum*, the novel was widely read (more than half a million copies sold in Germany during the five years following its publication) and discussed, especially by young people. The West German government began insisting that students be taught the history of the Nazi era, which had been until then neglected in the postwar schools. In the succeeding decades, *The Tin Drum* and Grass's subsequent novels and poetry became the foci for the people, the intellectuals, and the artists of a whole nation reinterpreting their own past and reexamining the moral foundations of their institutions.

When Ralph Mannheim's translation of *The Tin Drum* appeared in the United States in 1961, Grass immediately won acclaim from many critics as Germany's greatest living writer. Literary critics in France, Denmark, and many other countries went so far as to acknowledge Grass as the world's greatest living novelist and praised his courage in raising such controversial issues in his own country. A few critics were perceptive enough to point out that the elements of German society that Grass satirized so scathingly and that led directly to the triumph of Nazism could be found in every industrialized nation. Although Grass directed his message to Germans, many of his admirers argued that all humankind must learn from his pages or suffer a resurgence of the tyranny that nearly engulfed the world before 1945.

Bibliography

Hänicke, Diether H. "Literature Since 1933." In *The Challenge of German Literature*, edited by Horst S. Dämmrich and Diether H. Hänicke. Detroit: Wayne State University Press, 1971. Hänicke's article is a broad account of German literature since the advent of Hitler. It is valuable in understanding the context of *The Tin Drum* (which it discusses in some depth) and in showing how Grass's novel was both a culmination of previous German literature and, at the same time, a harbinger of a new German literary tradition.

Hatfield, Henry. "Günter Grass: The Artist as Satirist." In *The Contemporary Novel in German: A Symposium*, edited by Robert R. Heitner. Austin: University of Texas Press, 1967. Hatfield's article is virtually a paean of praise to Grass and *The Tin Drum*. Its major value is in its explanation of the satirical intent of many passages in the novel that are obscure to readers not intimately familiar with German history and the German language.

Hollington, Michael. *Günter Grass: The Writer in a Pluralist Society*. London: Marion Boyars, 1980. Although Hollington devotes only one chapter to *The Tin Drum*, references to the novel permeate his entire book. Hollington credits Grass with forcing Germans to look candidly at the Nazi era and with inspiring a younger generation to fight diligently against the complacency of their elders.

Maurer, Robert. "The End of Innocence: Günter Grass's *The Tin Drum*." In *Critical Essays on Günter Grass*, edited by Patrick O'Neill. Boston: G. K. Hall, 1987. Maurer presents a long interpolation of Grass's novel complete with several questionable conclusions. The major value of the article is in showing the many literary influences manifest in *The Tin Drum*, ranging from Voltaire to Thomas Mann. O'Neill's book contains several reviews of Grass's first novel and a number of articles that will help the reader understand Grass himself and the controversy that still surrounds him.

Miles, Keith. *Günter Grass*. New York: Barnes & Noble Books, 1975. Although only chapter 2 of Miles's book deals exclusively with *The Tin Drum*, readers will learn much about the novel and about its impact in the introduction and in the other seven chapters. Miles considers Grass to be Germany's and perhaps the world's greatest living novelist. His interpretations of and insights into *The Tin Drum* are perceptive and very useful to the reader trying to understand Grass's often cryptic prose.

Tank, Kurt Lothar. *Günter Grass*. Translated by John Conway. New York: Frederick Ungar, 1969. Contains a short biography of Grass and considerable analysis of Grass's early works, most especially *The Tin Drum*. The analysis will be difficult for those not steeped in German literature and fortified with the argot of literary criticism.

Willson, A. Leslie, ed. *A Günter Grass Symposium*. Austin: University of Texas Press, 1971. The seven articles in this slender volume discuss various aspects of Grass's prose and poetry. The articles will aid more advanced students of Grass's work in understanding the complexities of *The Tin Drum*.

Paul Madden

Cross-References

Hitler Organizes an Exhibition Denouncing Modern Art (1937), p. 1083; The Nazis Ban Nolde's Paintings (1941), p. 1217; German Writers Form Group 47 (1947), p. 1357; Brecht Founds the Berliner Ensemble (1949), p. 1410; Wiesel's *Night* Recalls the Holocaust (1956), p. 1700.

THE FIRST SUCCESSFUL SYNTHESIZER IS COMPLETED

Category of event: Music
Time: January, 1959
Locale: New York, New York

Music was forever changed when the RCA Mark II synthesiser was delivered to the Columbia-Princeton Electronic Music Center, giving composers a wider variety of sounds to choose from for their compositions

Principal personages:
HARRY F. OLSON (1902-   ), a scientist working for the Radio Corporation of America (RCA) and co-inventor of the RCA Mark II
HERBERT BELAR, a scientist and co-inventor of the RCA Mark II
VLADIMIR USSACHEVSKY (1911-1990), a well-known composer and music instructor at Columbia University who helped to found the Columbia-Princeton Electronic Music Center
OTTO LUENING (1900-1991), a composer and Columbia instructor who also helped to found the Columbia-Princeton Center
MILTON BABBITT (1916-   ), a serialist composer and one of the most significant figures in American music, who also helped to found the Columbia-Princeton Center
ROBERT MOOG (1934-   ), a physicist and inventor of voltage-controlled devices who created the Moog synthesizer

Summary of Event

Fascination with music and experimentation with its various forms resonates throughout the whole of human history. From at least as early as the ancient Greek civilization, humankind has explored the creation of music through mechanical means. Three hundred years before the birth of Christ, the Greeks invented the *hydraulos*, a reed organ operated by water pressure. Music's history is filled with innovators as well as innovations. From Wolfgang Amadeus Mozart to John Cage, music has benefited from those individuals who strove to push the barriers of conventional thought. It was in this long tradition of musical exploration that the first synthesizer was created. Like many inventions that came before, the RCA Electronic Music Synthesizer Mark II would change the face of music.

Although the development of the RCA Mark II was important to many types of music, it was within the field of electronic music that the new synthesizer had its greatest effects. The RCA Mark II's completion and installation in the newly formed Columbia-Princeton Electronic Music Center in early 1959 radically changed electronic music composers' control over their medium. The new synthesizer was designed and built by Harry Olson and Herbert Belar, two men working for the Radio Corporation of America (RCA) in the David Sarnoff Laboratories in Princeton, New

Jersey. The origins of their work in the field can be traced back to the late 1940's, when they became interested in possible applications of technology to the composition and production of music and human speech patterns. RCA, which had long been interested in the electronic production of music, quickly decided to fund their research.

After several years, Olson and Belar developed a machine for musical composition that was founded on a system of random probability. They tried to transform some of the creative principles of composition into programmable electromechanical functions. This attempt, unfortunately, was doomed to failure, as they had misunderstood the inherent need for a composer's intuitive faculties rather than a statistically based analysis of that same intuition. Learning from their mistakes, Olson and Belar spent most of the 1950's developing their next two machines, the RCA Mark I and the RCA Mark II. These two machines were the first to deserve the name "synthesizer." Thomas B. Holmes's *Electronic and Experimental Music* (1985) defines a synthesizer as "a self-contained instrument designed for the generation, modification, amplification, mixing, and presentation of electronic sounds." These synthesizers were able to take "raw" sound in the form of electric current and manipulate it into a composer's desired composition by selecting and modifying the four basic components of sound: volume, pitch, duration, and timbre. Olson and Belar's modular construction meant that each component of the entire synthesizer was linked so that the electronic signal could undergo all of its modifications and then be broadcast or recorded in one process. This interlinking was a revolutionary idea at the time, as was the remarkable type of control a composer could exert on the process. Although some of the components still had to be adjusted by hand, the RCA synthesizers included a punched-tape control system. This punched tape was programmed by a composer using a keyboard similar to a typewriter's keyboard and was then fed into the synthesizer, thereby controlling the various manipulations that the synthesizer went through to shape the composer's work. This technique drastically reduced the time it took to produce music in the electronic studio, even though the inspiration of the work was still up to the composers.

Although the inspiration was still the province of the composers, the RCA Mark II had finally provided them with the means to explore that inspiration. Electronic music can be thought of as a legacy of Alexander Graham Bell's 1876 discovery that sound could be translated into electrical signals and vice versa. This discovery had resulted in a succession of electro-acoustic machines before the invention of the RCA Mark II. Unfortunately, technology still lagged far behind the dreams of composers. During the first half of the twentieth century, composers began to dream of creating mechanical means to express every sound that the mind could imagine. Avant-garde composers such as Edgard Varèse and Ferruccio Busoni were frustrated by the limitations of the conventional orchestra. They wanted to explore imagined vistas of music that contained new sounds that simply were not available. Nearly fifty years later, other avant-garde composers were to find much of their answer in the RCA Mark II.

The potential of the RCA Mark II came to public attention through the efforts of three composers, Vladimir Ussachevsky, Otto Luening, and Milton Babbitt. After completing studies of electronic music in Europe and the United States, Ussachevsky and Luening teamed up with Babbitt to work with a new synthesizer they heard had been developed at RCA. After receiving a grant of $175,000 from the Rockefeller Foundation, they set up the Columbia-Princeton Center in New York City. This new studio would have all the latest technology, including the brand new RCA Mark II, on permanent loan from RCA. The event would change forever the composition and production of electronic music.

Impact of Event

When the RCA Mark II was installed in the Columbia-Princeton center, it generated enormous publicity and controversy. The center quickly became the focal point for electronic music composition in the United States. The publicity engendered by the RCA Mark II was its primary impact on music; many people reacted antagonistically. They feared electronic music was only robot music for robot people. They imagined a long, monotonous drone punctuated by hisses and metallic sounds that would quickly dehumanize music and those people who listened to it. Many musicians, as well, were not pleased with this latest development. Musicians' unions strongly objected to the RCA Mark II and the Columbia-Princeton Center, fearing that they would make musicians obsolete. All this opposition began to subside as fears eased and were replaced by wonder at the many possibilities the synthesizer held.

Soon after becoming operational, the Columbia-Princeton Center invited several internationally known composers to come to New York to work with the new synthesizer. In the first two years, the center sponsored the work not only of Babbitt, Ussachevsky, and Luening but also of Mario Davidovsky, Halim El-Dabh, Charles Wuorinen, and Bülent Arel. Several of the works produced in this period were presented to the public in the center's inaugural concerts on May 9 and 10, 1961, in the McMillin Theater of Columbia University. These concerts sparked even further interest in the medium of electronic music. Spanning the widest spectrum of stylistic possibilities, these compositions helped to dispel the image that this music was simplistic and robotic. The primary impact of the RCA Mark II lay not in its revolutionary technology but in the enormous amount of research that went into electronic music technology as a result of the publicity it received.

Although the RCA Mark II brought composers' dreams much nearer to reality, there were still several drawbacks. One of these drawbacks was its enormous expense. Another was its use of vacuum-tube technology, which made it large enough to fill a studio wall. These two facts made it impossible for the RCA Mark II to be disseminated to other composers. While the RCA synthesizer did give composers much easier control over the manipulation of the music than anything previously developed, it still required a lengthy process to "tune" many components and to enter the programming on the punched tape. Fortunately, the research sparked by the

RCA Mark II soon created the technology to surmount these obstacles.

As technology overcame these problems, the modern age of electronic music began. Electronic music composition was further spurred by the development of a new device by a young physicist by the name of Robert Moog. Interested in music, he collaborated with the composer Herbert Deutsch to construct a transistorized voltage-controlled oscillator and amplifier. Moog's innovations allowed composers to modify the components of sound by use of a keyboard, enabling them to program their voltage-controlled synthesizers in real time as they were playing. In addition, the new Moog synthesizer, finished in 1966, also benefited from technological advances in solid-state circuitry, rendering it much smaller and more affordable. The Moog synthesizer, less expensive, more portable, easier to operate, and with greater facility to control operations than the RCA Mark II, opened the doors for electronic music to permeate the marketplace.

In 1968, an album by Wendy Carlos entitled *Switched-On Bach* featuring music of Johann Sebastian Bach played on a Moog synthesizer became a best-seller and made the synthesizer a household word. At the same time, rock musicians were beginning to explore the possibilities presented by the synthesizer and by electronic music in general. Artists such as the Beatles, Keith Emerson, Pink Floyd, and Brian Eno were among the first rock performers to use the techniques of electronic music and synthesizers to create sometimes energy-laden, sometimes surreal musical landscapes. No longer was electronic music only the province of classical composers. Through public awareness, lower costs, and easier operations, synthesizers became an indelible part of the cultural landscape.

In many ways, it probably would have been difficult for those early pioneers of the RCA Mark II to imagine the extent of their work's influence. Electronic music has been featured in scores of hit movies, including *Star Wars* (1977), *A Clockwork Orange* (1971) and *Batman* (1989). Much music for television shows and commercials also owes a debt to early work done on the synthesizer. Classical composers such as John Cage, Terry Riley, Isao Tomita, and Philip Glass have continued to stretch the boundaries of theoretical work and human ears with their compositions utilizing synthesizers and electronic music. The development of digital technology and personal computers further enhanced the performance of synthesizers and created still more possibilities for electronic music.

Although the technology of the RCA Mark II was a landmark step in the search for the mechanical means to meet the demands of composer's imaginations, it was the climate the RCA synthesizer created that was its greatest achievement. Something inherent in the idea of the synthesizer and the Columbia-Princeton Center seemed to spark humankind's curiosity enough to spur musical technology onward; perhaps one day it will reach the state prophesied by John Cage in 1937, when he said, "I believe that the use of noise to make music will continue and increase until we reach a music produced through the aid of electrical instruments which will make available for musical purposes any and all sounds that can be heard."

Bibliography

Darter, Tom, ed. *The Art of Electronic Music.* New York: William Morrow, 1984. Edited from material published in *Keyboard* magazine. Value of the book lies in its articles and interviews with some of the leading electronic music artists. Contains an interview carried out at the Columbia-Princeton Center with Babbitt, Ussachevsky, Luening, Davidovsky, and Carlos, among others. Includes photographs.

Deutsch, Herbert A. *Synthesis: An Introduction to the History, Theory, and Practice of Electronic Music.* Rev. ed. Sherman Oaks, Calif.: Alfred Publishing, 1985. Deutsch was the composer who worked with Robert Moog to build the first voltage-controlled synthesizer. His book is more theory than history and is helpful for understanding how the musical currents of the past affected the course of electronic music. He also suggests studio experiments for readers to try.

Holmes, Thomas B. *Electronic and Experimental Music.* New York: Charles Scribner's Sons, 1985. An excellent book, containing an informative section giving descriptions of the basics of sound, music, and electronic music technology. Holmes dwells at length on the early electroacoustic instruments. He also includes an excellent electronic music record guide as well as an informative glossary.

Mackay, Andy. *Electronic Music.* Minneapolis, Minn.: Control Data Publishing, 1981. Contains an excellent selection of color pictures. Mackay's book also carries an informative section on the lives and work of various composers associated with electronic music. The text is sometimes rambling but conveys a basic sense of the fundamentals of electronic music.

Manning, Peter. *Electronic and Computer Music.* Oxford, England: Oxford University Press, 1985. An in-depth, comprehensive history of electronic music. Manning is particularly focused on the technological aspect (including charts and graphs) of each phase in electronic music. While technically oriented, Manning's work manages to flesh out the history with abundant quotations. Contains the best description of how the RCA Mark II works.

Schwartz, Elliot. *Electronic Music.* New York: Praeger, 1973. Outdated, but contains insightful passages on the development of compositional theory. Includes an interesting section on further listening and suggested reading and a selected discography and bibliography. Also contains an intriguing section of observations by composers.

Charles R. Caldwell

Cross-References

Busoni's *Sketch for a New Aesthetic of Music* Is Published (1907), p. 166; Varèse Premieres *Déserts* (1954), p. 1629; Riley Completes *In C* (1964), p. 1979; Hendrix Releases *Are You Experienced?* (1967), p. 2092; The Beatles Release *Sgt. Pepper's Lonely Hearts Club Band* (1967), p. 2098; Laurie Anderson's *United States* Popularizes Performance Art (1983), p. 2517.

GORDY FOUNDS MOTOWN RECORDS

Category of event: Music
Time: January, 1959
Locale: Detroit, Michigan

Motown Records produced hundreds of recordings that crossed over from rhythm and blues to pop and came to define urban popular music

Principal personages:

BERRY GORDY, JR. (1929-   ), the Detroit native who founded Motown Records and helped to change the landscape of popular music

EDDIE HOLLAND (1939-   ),

LAMONT DOZIER (1941-   ), and

BRIAN HOLLAND (1941-   ), a songwriting and producing team who were among the premier creative forces at Motown in the 1960's

NORMAN WHITFIELD (1943-   ), a songwriter and producer who was a key figure in the recordings of Marvin Gaye and the Temptations

SMOKEY ROBINSON (1940-   ), the lead singer of the Miracles, a major songwriter at Motown

DIANA ROSS (1944-   ), the star of Motown's most famous group, the Supremes

MARVIN GAYE (1939-1984), one of Motown's most successful crossover stars

STEVIE WONDER (STEVELAND JUDKINS or STEVELAND MORRIS, 1950-   ), a 1960's Motown child star who became an adult superstar in the 1970's

MICHAEL JACKSON (1958-   ), the lead singer for the Jackson Five, who became a superstar as a solo performer

Summary of Event

After years of writing songs for such singers as Detroit's Jackie Wilson and dabbling in record production for others, Berry Gordy, Jr., decided in early 1959 to open his own company. Born in Detroit into a stable, determined, and ambitious family, Gordy had tried boxing and work on an automobile assembly line before he found his true vocation as the builder of the largest and most successful black-owned independent record company in American history.

After leasing his recordings to major labels for pressing and distribution, Gordy decided to set up his own labels (Tamla, Motown, and Gordy) and soon scored with hits on the rhythm-and-blues and pop charts. One of the keys to his success was his knowledge of the local Detroit music scene, which was rich in amateur singing groups in the doo-wop and rhythm-and-blues vein and in jazz musicians. By using the talent of Detroit's black ghettos and housing projects, Gordy had the dream of making such music palatable to young white people as well as to black youth. It was from the start a crossover dream, and it succeeded beyond Gordy's greatest expectations.

From 1961 into the 1970's, the carefully trained artists and neatly crafted and produced records from Motown would be the biggest sellers in rhythm and blues and would cross over to the mainstream market as black music had never done before. Gordy nurtured a stable of in-house songwriters, musicians, and producers who redefined black popular music and then went on to change mainstream music-making permanently. The soul music of Motown, Atlantic Records in New York City, and Stax Records in Memphis met the British Invasion head-on and offered a native challenge.

Gordy initially worked closely with his friend Smokey Robinson in writing and producing. Robinson became one of the most creative songwriters and singers with Motown, first as lead singer with the Miracles and then as a superstar solo singer. The Motown labels focused on romantic love ballads and uptempo dance numbers that were aimed at a young audience and a crossover pop market. A song such as the Miracles' "Shop Around" of 1960 (the company's first big pop hit) was typical of the kind of material Gordy wanted: an upbeat, lighthearted song about a young man and his search for a girlfriend. The Miracles continued to make both the rhythm-and-blues and pop charts with similar songs and slow ballads featuring Robinson's delicate high tenor. Groups such as the Four Tops, the Temptations, the Marvelettes, Martha and the Vandellas, and Gladys Knight and the Pips helped Motown to turn out hits throughout the 1960's and beyond.

Some acts were already experienced when they signed with Gordy; others, such as the Supremes, Stevie Wonder, and later the Jacksons, had to be carefully trained and directed. Motown was a comprehensive enterprise that dealt with every aspect of making and selling music, including songwriting, recording, manufacturing, distribution, touring, publishing, and grooming.

In the studio, Gordy made sure his teams of songwriters, musicians, singers, and producers worked together to craft songs that would attract both blacks and whites. Older rhythm-and-blues styles, with their raw energy, were smoothed over and polished with the use of the new technology of multitrack recording and overdubbing. Gordy demanded quality control and each week organized executive sessions to preview intended releases. His in-house production system reminded some of the Detroit automobile companies' production-line method, but it worked wonderfully for a decade and more. Songwriters and producers Eddie Holland, Lamont Dozier, and Brian Holland were originally at Motown's center and became known simply as "H-D-H." Later, Norman Whitfield effectively took the team's place as a force in the studio.

Gordy was determined that his acts could play any venue, from the older "chitlin' circuit" houses such as New York's Apollo or Chicago's Regal to supper clubs, the best concert halls and auditoriums, and television. For this purpose, he had an artists' development department that functioned as a sort of finishing school for singers who had to learn stage deportment and dancing. Choreographer Cholly Atkins trained dozens of performers relentlessly. Again, the system worked: Motown's singing acts built upon traditions of black dance to produce some of the finest and most dynamic routines of the time.

Many of Gordy's artists later complained about his tough standards, and many eventually left Motown for better financial terms and more creative freedom on other labels. Most admitted at least grudgingly, however, that Gordy got them on their feet and prepared them for survival in the harsh world of the music business.

Impact of Event

By 1966, 75 percent of Motown's single releases reached the pop charts. *Billboard* magazine, the leading music trade journal, even dropped its separate rhythm-and-blues chart between November, 1963, and January, 1965, because there seemed no difference at the time between black popular music and mainstream pop. By late 1968, *Billboard* had changed the name of its black music chart to "Soul." Along with the British rock groups, Motown acts dominated the market. The Supremes (with Diana Ross), the Miracles (with Smokey Robinson), the Temptations, the Four Tops, Stevie Wonder, and Marvin Gaye were leading the roster with hit after hit. By the start of the 1970's, the Jackson Five (with Michael Jackson as lead) had begun a second generation of Motown headliners.

The "Motown Sound" shows its roots in gospel, featuring tambourines, hand-clapping, and call-and-response vocals. The groups did not feature group harmonies but rather lead vocals over backing voices. With responses and interjections by other group members and sometimes extra voices added to enrich the sound, Diana Ross, Levi Stubbs with the Four Tops, and David Ruffin and Eddie Kendricks (often as dual leads, one medium, one higher into falsetto) with the Temptations were the outstanding voices to emerge from the Detroit scene.

The studio musicians, carefully nurtured by Gordy, varied in number and changed over two decades, but there was a solid core group in the 1960's that helped to define the sound. A group led by pianist Eddie Van Dyke and featuring drummer Benny Benjamin and bassist James Jamerson formed the core of the studio band. Jamerson, in particular, became famous for his busy and percolating bass figures and riffs, which gave Motown its distinctive "bottom" sound. His inventive playing used jazz-influenced syncopated phrases in eighth- and sixteenth-note configurations with frequent harmonic changes. Benjamin's thudding and kicking drumming pulse and the chopping and staccato rhythm chords of electric guitars combined with Jamerson's bass to create the rhythmic base upon which other musicians, with the guidance of producers such as H-D-H and Whitfield, garnished the songs. Members of the Detroit Symphony added swirling strings; flutes and vibes softened the harsher tones, and ethereal backing voices often finished the mix. Varieties of this formula applied to nearly all recordings. Funk was sweetened and decorated, saxes and horns mellow. The hits flowed.

In spite of the sense of a production-line mentality, diversity flourished at Motown. At the same time that there was plenty of mellow crooning that would sit well in intimate club settings or on television, there was still the harder-edged tradition of rhythm-and-blues shouting and rasping vocals. Lightweight teen love songs and lyrically sparse uptempo dance pieces alternated with more mature songs that reflected pain and loss.

Singer Marvin Gaye epitomized the conflicting directions Motown's music took. Always aspiring to be a pop singer of slow ballads, he was directed by Berry Gordy to work on harsher vocal styles and more hard-driving songs reflective of black roots. He recorded both with consummate artistry. In 1971, he recorded *What's Goin' On*, an album of mostly his own songs focused on social issues. Such songs as "What's Going On," "Mercy Mercy Me," and "Inner City Blues" were in the line of message songs Motown artists started to write and record in the late 1960's and early 1970's. For a time, the real world of black poverty was reflected directly in Motown's music. Smokey Robinson, on the other hand, always sang with a high tenor that easily soared into a falsetto. As a central songwriter at Motown and as first a member of the Miracles and then a solo singer, Robinson favored romantic love songs with an almost ethereal quality. Similarly, Diana Ross while with the Supremes had a light, sweet voice with a slight breathiness that worked well for crossing over into mainstream pop. Later, as a solo artist, she broadened her repertoire; her voice deepened and grew stronger, allowing her to handle songs of mature love and almost any sort of popular music. Stevie Wonder grew from a novelty instrumental act into a strong singer with a versatile repertoire made up largely of his own searching compositions, many of them in a socially conscious vein.

In 1971, Gordy moved the center of Motown's operation to Los Angeles and became more deeply involved in the solo career of Diana Ross, who soon became a film actress. By this time, many of the pioneer artists and producers had departed Motown, so Gordy focused more on a second generation of acts, notably the Jacksons. From 1971 through 1975, they had innumerable hits, both as the Jackson Five and with Michael Jackson as a solo performer.

The 1983 twenty-fifth anniversary television show that celebrated Motown's dominance of popular music demonstrated that even after many acts had left the company, the skills they had learned there had made them stars in mainstream pop music, black and white. Worldwide record sellers and international stars, they had taken the sound of Detroit and forever altered American music. The Jacksons, reunited for that show, were the highlight; they sang a medley of their old hits and let Michael, now twenty-five and recording for another label, reveal how great a dancer and performer he had become. Berry Gordy's dream had come true.

Bibliography

Davis, Sharon. *I Heard It Through the Grapevine: Marvin Gaye, the Biography.* Edinburgh: Mainstream Publishing, 1991. A thorough study of Gaye's troubled life. Davis has a command of facts about the music business that makes this study more than just a celebrity biography. Illustrated and indexed, with a discography.
_____. *Motown: The History.* Enfield, England: Guiness Publishing, 1988.

The most thorough history of the company. Davis covers everything; her interviews with Motown artists are invaluable and quite frank. Fully illustrated and indexed, with complete listing of releases. Also informative about the international popularity of Motown.

George, Nelson. *Where Did Our Love Go?: The Rise and Fall of the Motown Sound.* New York: St. Martin's Press, 1985. George offers more insight into the relation of Motown to earlier black music than Davis does. Critical yet appreciative. Illustrated, with a discography by artist. Indexed.

Haskins, Jim, with Kathleen Benson. *The Stevie Wonder Scrapbook.* New York: Grosset & Dunlap, 1978. A useful look at the rise of the musical genius of Wonder. Amply illustrated. Brief bibliography, no discography or index.

Hirshey, Gerri. *Nowhere to Run: The Story of Soul Music.* New York: Times Books, 1984. Hirshey devotes individual chapters to important soul singers and groups, using interviews and commentary to reflect back on the 1960's. Motown artists receive ample coverage. Illustrated, indexed.

Ritz, David. *Divided Soul: The Life of Marvin Gaye.* Rev. ed. New York: Da Capo Press, 1991. Ritz wrote the lyrics for Gaye's hit "Sexual Healing" and knows his man. Illustrated, discography, indexed.

Robinson, Smokey, with David Ritz. *Smokey: Inside My Life.* New York: McGraw-Hill, 1989. An engaging autobiography. Quite frank about tensions and issues within Motown. Illustrated, with discography and index.

Shaw, Arnold. *The World of Soul: Black America's Contribution to the Pop Music Scene.* New York: Cowles, 1970. One cannot go wrong with any of Shaw's studies of black music. Although less concerned with details, business matters, and specific chronologies than others, he fills in the broad pre-Motown era of soul music and its roots in earlier forms. Illustrated, general discography, index.

Taraborrelli, J. Randy. *Call Her Miss Ross: The Unauthorized Biography of Diana Ross.* Secaucus, N.J.: Carol Publishing Group, 1989. A celebrity biography that can enrich an understanding of the problems of superstardom. Notes and sources, discography, index.

_____. *Michael Jackson: The Magic and the Madness.* New York: Carol Publishing Group, 1991. Another celebrity biography with the limitations of the type: conflicting sources, gossip, and so forth. Taraborrelli, though, knows the music scene. Source notes, bibliography, index. No discography.

Frederick E. Danker

Cross-References

Berry's "Maybellene" Popularizes Rock and Roll (1955), p. 1635; Presley Becomes a Rock-and-Roll Sensation (1956), p. 1705; The Beatles Revolutionize Popular Music (1963), p. 1944; Brown Wins a Grammy for "Papa's Got a Brand New Bag" (1966), p. 2059; Wonder Releases *Innervisions* (1973), p. 2294; *Thriller* Marks Michael Jackson's Musical Coming-of-Age (1982), p. 2512.

HANSBERRY'S *A RAISIN IN THE SUN* DEBUTS ON BROADWAY

Category of event: Theater
Time: March 11, 1959
Locale: Ethel Barrymore Theatre, New York, New York

Lorraine Hansberry's A Raisin in the Sun *became one of the first plays written by an African-American woman to achieve artistic and commercial success*

Principal personages:

LORRAINE HANSBERRY (1930-1965), the first black playwright writer to win the New York Drama Critics Circle Award

LLOYD RICHARDS (1922-   ), a black director who directed the first production of *A Raisin in the Sun*

ROBERT NEMIROFF, a writer and songwriter, Hansberry's husband and literary executor

SIDNEY POITIER (1924-   ), an actor who starred as Walter Lee in the play's first production

CLAUDIA MCNEIL (1917-   ), an actress who played the role of Lena in the original production

RUBY DEE (RUBY ANN WALLACE, 1924-   ), an actress who played the role of Ruth

DIANA SANDS (1934-1973), an actress who earned an Outer Circle Critics Award as best supporting actress for her role in the original production

Summary of Event

On March 11, 1959, after playing in Chicago, Philadelphia, and New Haven, Connecticut, Lorraine Hansberry's *A Raisin in the Sun* opened at the Ethel Barrymore Theatre in New York City. The play instantly met with rave reviews from both black and white critics and became a quick financial success. It ran for 530 performances, setting a new record for the longest-running Broadway play written by a black American. It was also the first play written by a black woman to be performed on Broadway.

A Raisin in the Sun won the prestigious New York Drama Critics Circle Award for the year's best play over Tennessee Williams' *Sweet Bird of Youth*, Eugene O'Neill's *A Touch of the Poet*, and Archibald MacLeish's *J. B.* At age twenty-eight, Hansberry was the youngest playwright to receive the award. *A Raisin in the Sun* was also instrumental in furthering the careers of the play's actors and its director, Lloyd Richards. Moreover, the play's commercial success enabled other black playwrights to get their work produced and gave Hansberry a visibility that made her an important voice in the theater. She spoke and wrote prolifically about theater and the arts, society and politics, and equal rights for blacks, women, and homosexuals.

A 'living-room drama," the play focuses on the financial and emotional struggles of three generations of a black family in late 1950's Chicago. The play's central conflict begins when Lena Younger receives a ten thousand dollar check from her deceased husband's insurance company. Walter Lee, her son, who works as a chauffeur, wants to use the money to finance a liquor store, while Beneatha, Lena's daughter, wants to go to medical school. After Lena takes some of the money and puts a down payment on a house in an all-white neighborhood—an emotional and economic decision, not a political one—she gives the rest to Walter, entrusting him to deposit half of it in the bank for Beneatha's education and to use the rest for his business. Walter, though, gives the money to a con artist, who absconds with it. Meanwhile, a white representative from Clybourne Park, the neighborhood where the family's new house is located, attempts to bribe the family not to move there through the rhetoric of good-neighborliness and thinly veiled threats. In the play's final scene, as Walter understands the significance of his family's pride, he refuses the white man's offer, and the family prepares to move.

Critics in 1959 discussed a number of reasons for the success of *A Raisin in the Sun*. Many praised the believability of the characters, and some even suggested that they were universal and not necessarily specifically African American. Some critics saw the play as supporting assimilation, and others noted its focus on Africa and its complex and sympathetic portrayal of Pan-Africanism. Certainly, the critics agreed on the play's emotional impact and on the significance of a Broadway theater filled with racially mixed audiences.

In addition to providing a concrete example of the Broadway success of an African-American drama, Hansberry's play articulates many significant political issues. Her representations of African Americans are complex and varied. In terms of class, for example, she portrays George, an upper-middle-class black man who will inherit his father's business and who thinks that school is merely a means to an end; Beneatha, a young woman who wants to go to medical school to save people but who is also exploring her identity through various artistic expressions; Lena, the matriarch, who is concerned with providing a home for her family; and Walter Lee, the son who wants to make quick money and who harbors romantic dreams of success.

The various characters also have different relationships to their racial identity. George is portrayed as supporting assimilation, while Asagai, Beneatha's Nigerian beau, finds black Americans apolitical. Asagai's clothing and values are foreign to Lena, who identifies with black American culture. Never before had such a range of black characters been portrayed on the American stage.

While much of the plot of *A Raisin in the Sun* revolves around Walter Lee and his growth, Hansberry's female characters are strong and complex and do not merely function as sexual objects. Rather, George, Asagai, and Walter Lee are overt chauvinists. In this way, *A Raisin in the Sun* is an excellent example of the complicated intersections of oppressions of gender, race, and class.

Hansberry grew up in Chicago, the daughter of a prominent real-estate broker and the niece of a Harvard University professor of African history. Her parents were intellectuals and activists, and her father won an antisegregation case before the

Illinois Supreme Court, upon which the events in the play were loosely based. Although her family was middle class, she attended segregated schools. She went to the University of Wisconsin for two years, then moved to New York in 1950. She met and married Robert Nemiroff, an aspiring writer, in 1953.

Several years later, Hansberry showed a draft of *A Raisin in the Sun* to Nemiroff, who suggested that she read it to a producer friend of his, Philip Rose. Rose wanted to produce the play and immediately started to raise money. Because it seemed like a risky proposition to many New York producers, though, *A Raisin in the Sun* opened out of town, without a New York booking.

Hansberry completed one other play, *The Sign in Sidney Brustein's Window* (1964), a philosophical play about a white man in Greenwich Village. It opened before her death from cancer at age thirty-five but was neither a financial nor critical success. Later critics commented that the play was misunderstood.

Nemiroff continued Hansberry's legacy by compiling various letters and notes, which he edited and published as *To Be Young, Gifted and Black: A Portrait of Lorraine Hansberry in Her Own Words* (1969). He also arranged for the television production of *The Drinking Gourd* (1972), completed Hansberry's unfinished manuscript of *Les Blancs* (1970), and published another play, *What Use Are Flowers?* (1972).

Impact of Event

Since its first production in 1959, *A Raisin in the Sun* has served as an artistic, literary, and political touchstone for African-American theater. The play influenced the black theater movement of the 1960's by showing black artists that success on Broadway was attainable, and it opened a place for black realism as a dramatic genre. The play's visibility positioned Hansberry as a spokesperson for issues about race, gender, politics, and the arts.

The play effectively launched the careers of many of the people involved. *A Raisin in the Sun* was the first Broadway directing job for director Lloyd Richards, who had worked previously as an actor and a director; he was the first black man to direct on Broadway. Richards went on to direct many plays on and off Broadway, including many of the plays of Pulitzer Prize-winning dramatist August Wilson. He has also served as the director for the prestigious O'Neill Playwrights' Center, as the dean of the Yale School of Drama, and as the artistic director of the Yale Repertory Theatre.

Before the opening of *A Raisin in the Sun*, only Sidney Poitier and Claudia McNeil were well known among the play's cast. Poitier began acting with the American Negro Theatre in 1945, and McNeil worked as a nightclub and vaudeville singer before performing on Broadway in Arthur Miller's *The Crucible* in 1953. Poitier subsequently acted in many plays, films, and television shows, and he won an Oscar for his performance in 1963's *Lilies of the Field*. Ruby Dee, who worked with the American Negro Theatre in Harlem before *A Raisin in the Sun*, went on to establish herself on the stage, in films, and on television. Other well-known African-American actors who performed in *A Raisin in the Sun* include Lonne Elder III, Glynn Turman, and Diana Sands, who died of cancer at age thirty-nine.

Numerous African-American black playwrights, actors, directors, and producers have cited *A Raisin in the Sun* as having influenced their work and their ambitions. Hansberry preceded the Black Arts movement and affected Amiri Bakara, James Baldwin, and Charles Fuller. August Wilson's plays, each of which, in realist form, focuses on an African-American family, are probably the best illustration of Hansberry's artistic legacy. Hansberry's work has also been important to the work of black women playwrights, including Adrienne Kennedy and Ntozake Shange.

There have been many critical debates about the meaning and significance of *A Raisin in the Sun*. Particularly during the Black Arts movement of the 1960's, many African-American artists objected to the realist form of Hansberry's play, which they saw as artistically conservative. They also saw success on Broadway as a political compromise. Some thought Hansberry sacrificed her integrity to make her message palatable to a white audience. Similarly, many critics have argued over the play's meaning and about whether or not the play is assimilationist. Some have criticized the fact that many white audiences seem to have been able to identify with the characters, disregarding their own racism.

Some critics have quoted Hansberry as saying that *A Raisin in the Sun* is a play about people who happen to be black, but Nemiroff has commented on this frequent misquotation, which does imply that the play has an assimilationist meaning. In actuality, Hansberry said that *A Raisin in the Sun*, is, first and foremost, a black play.

In *A Raisin in the Sun*, Hansberry anticipated many aspects of the Civil Rights and women's movements. For example, Beneatha wears an Afro hairstyle, which was uncommon in 1959 but which emerged a few years later as a significant political statement of black pride; Beneatha, who clearly represents Hansberry in the play, also discusses the political implications of her choice of hairstyle. Ruth struggles over whether or not to have an abortion, and, of course, the central issue of the play is whether or not the family should move to a white neighborhood.

Since 1959, there have been countless productions of *A Raisin in the Sun* in both professional and nonprofessional theaters. A film version was made in 1961, and a revival was produced for television's *American Playhouse* in 1989.

The script has also undergone a number of revisions. Scholar Margaret Wilkerson has traced the changes in the play's script, citing the different meanings that emerge from the addition of two scenes. The first addition focuses on a neighbor, Mrs. Johnson, who, though black, does not support the family's move and who describes the real physical dangers that the family may face by moving to Clybourne Park. The second addition is a scene with Walter Lee and Travis, his son, in which the father confesses his hopes and dreams.

In 1973, Nemiroff and Charlotte Zaltzberg adapted the play as a musical, *Raisin*. The production received excellent reviews, ran on Broadway for 847 performances, and won the Tony Award for best musical; Virginia Capers, as Lena, won the Tony for best actress in a musical. *Raisin* was revived in 1981, when Claudia McNeil, who had played Lena in the original 1959 production, re-created the role in the musical adaptation.

Bibliography

Brown-Guillory, Elizabeth. *Their Place on the Stage: Black Women Playwrights in America.* Westport, Conn.: Greenwood Press, 1988. A study of the lives and plays of Lorraine Hansberry, Alice Childress, and Ntozake Shange. Places each of the playwrights in historical context by tracing issues in black playwriting. Discusses each playwright's work in relation to form, images, symbols, and themes. Excellent bibliography.

Carter, Steven R. *Hansberry's Drama: Commitment amid Complexity.* Urbana: University of Illinois Press, 1991. A study of all of Hansberry's work and many of her unpublished pieces and letters. Separate chapter on *A Raisin in the Sun* analyzes the play, the 1959 production, the film, the musical, and subsequent productions. Excellent and extensive bibliographic sources. Photographs.

Cheney, Anne. *Lorraine Hansberry.* Boston: Twayne, 1984. The first full-length biography of Hansberry. One chapter focuses on the written playscript of *A Raisin in the Sun*; information about the original production is included in an earlier chapter. Excellent bibliography.

Freedomways 19, no. 4 (1979). Special issue of the journal dedicated to Hansberry, who worked for *Freedomways* in the 1950's. Includes articles by Woodie King, Jr., Douglas Turner Ward, Jean Carey Bond, and others. Many of the writers discuss their personal relationships with Hansberry. Bibliography.

Hansberry, Lorraine. *"A Raisin in the Sun"; and, "The Sign in Sidney Brustein's Window."* New York: New American Library, 1987. Edited by Robert Nemiroff. Complete playtext and comments by Frank Rich, Amiri Baraka, and Nemiroff

Keyssar, Helene. *The Curtain and the Veil: Strategies in Black Drama.* New York: Burt Franklin, 1981. An astute critical, chronological survey of black dramatists. Pays attention to the relationship between the theater and its audiences. One chapter on *A Raisin in the Sun.*

Wilkerson, Margaret B. *"A Raisin in the Sun*: Anniversary of an American Classic." In *Performing Feminisms: Feminist Critical Theory and Theatre*, edited by Sue-Ellen Case. Baltimore: Johns Hopkins University Press, 1990. Hansberry's biographer describes the changes made between the original 1959 production and later productions.

Stacy Wolf

Cross-References

Hallelujah Is the First Important Black Musical (1929), p. 772; *Stormy Weather* Offers New Film Roles to African Americans (1940's), p. 1159; Poitier Emerges as a Film Star in *The Blackboard Jungle* (1955), p. 1650; Baraka's *Dutchman* Dramatizes Racial Hatred (1964), p. 2000; *The Wiz* Brings African-American Talent to Broadway (1975), p. 2334; *The Jeffersons* Signals Success of Black Situation Comedies (1975), p. 2339; Shange's *for colored girls* . . . Is a Landmark (1976), p. 2370.

BONANZA BECOMES AN AMERICAN
TELEVISION CLASSIC

Category of event: Television and radio
Time: September 12, 1959-January 16, 1973
Locale: The United States

An American classic of the television Western genre, Bonanza, *has been ranked among the most highly rated shows of all time*

> *Principal personages:*
> LORNE GREENE (1915-1987), an Ottawa-born broadcaster and actor who starred on *Bonanza* as widower Ben Cartwright
> MICHAEL LANDON (EUGENE MAURICE OROWITZ, 1936-1991), supporting actor, writer, and director for *Bonanza*
> DAN BLOCKER (1929-1972), a Texas native who played a supporting role as Ben Cartwright's middle son
> PERNELL ROBERTS (1930-   ), a *Bonanza* costar who left the program because he disagreed with its style and theme

Summary of Event

The showpiece of the prime-time schedule of the National Broadcasting Company (NBC), *Bonanza*, American television's first family-oriented Western series, ran for fourteen years. The series premiered on September 12, 1959, opposite *Perry Mason*, a tough contender, and did not become a smash hit until the fall of 1961, when it moved to Sunday night at 9:00 P.M. as a replacement for *The Dinah Shore Chevy Show*. A long-lived success, *Bonanza* survived viewer ennui and serious plot and casting problems following the departure of Pernell Roberts in 1965 and the unexpected death of Dan Blocker in 1972.

The series formula, simple and unassuming in its appeal, lured fans with the familiarity of a cohesive television family. The show opened with a rousing Western theme composed by veteran songwriters Jay Livingston and Ray Evans. The title screen displayed a parchment map of the setting. As a flame burned away the center, the characters, in period costume and mounted on horseback, appeared in its place. The show, which some critics denigrated as a Western melodrama, starred four notable talents. Lorne Greene was Ben Cartwright, a kindly, authoritative widower and owner of the thousand-acre Ponderosa Ranch who set the moral tone for his family and read the Bible to set an example for his sons, each of whom was born to a different wife. Pernell Roberts was the eldest son Adam, the somber, smooth-talking thinker of the family who chose words over fists when tempers flared. Dan Blocker was the middle son, Hoss, the clowning muscleman and foil for his stern father. Michael Landon was Little Joe, the winsome, mischievous youngest son who was the most likely to get into trouble, requiring intervention by the other three family members.

Secondary characters proved equally popular with fans. Victor Sen Yung appeared in the appealing role of Hop Sing, the family cook and housekeeper who often intervened as comic relief and choric commentator during serious emotional situations. Other supporting regulars who beefed up the program's later years included David Canary as Candy, an itinerant ranch worker who hired on at the Ponderosa; Mitch Vogel as Jamie Hunter, a homeless, emotionally ill-at-ease teenage son of a deceased rainmaker; Lou Frizzell as Dusty Rhoades, a middle-aged character and friend of Ben; and Tim Matheson as Griff King. In addition to these supporting roles, the producer stressed quality acting by importing a series of guest stars for cameo roles.

Set in the mid-1860's on the Cartwrights' sizable ranch on the outer edge of Virginia City, Nevada, *Bonanza* reflected the boom-town atmosphere that permeated the mining complex east of San Francisco. Following Henry T. P. Comstock's 1859 discovery of the Comstock Lode, a gold-threaded vein of silver, the fabulously rich strike lured a stream of miners, netting more than $300 million in precious metals before its demise around 1882. The mushrooming city, named for Comstock's associate, James "Old Virginny" Fennimore, suffered a series of fluctuations of fortune and notoriety, culminating in 1873 in the discovery of the Big Bonanza, America's richest strike. The city at its height reached a population of thirty thousand, a blend of privileged, moneyed landowners, imported laborers, mining consultants, financiers, support personnel, easy women, and drifters.

Capitalizing on the variety of plots and characters clustering around Virginia City's historic past, *Bonanza*, only peripherally associated with the silver and gold industry, was anchored in a timber and cattle-ranching economy. As a natural outgrowth of their entrepreneurial responsibilities, Ben Cartwright and his three sons, inexplicably unencumbered by ranch work, presided over the comings and goings of strangers, invited guests, Indians, animals, hired hands, outlaws, and city dwellers. Much of the story line involved protection of the family's vast land holdings and water rights as well as measured responses to threats, both to the characters themselves and to innocent bystanders, particularly pretty, vulnerable women.

The controlled, empathetic patriarch, Ben Cartwright—affectionately known as "Pa"—was played by Lorne Greene. His intuitive fathering on the show offset his three motherless sons' lack of wisdom, experience, and patience. Styling his performance after Daniel, his own father, a Jewish cobbler and boot maker who immigrated to Canada from Russia, Greene, a native of Ottawa, achieved a quiet dignity by emulating his father's masterful presence.

Greene abandoned his university study of chemical engineering in favor of French, German, and drama. After he completed postgraduate study at New York's Neighborhood Playhouse School of Theater and the Martha Graham School of Contemporary Dance, his commanding baritone was molded by years as an award-winning radio newscaster and pitchman for the Canadian Broadcasting Corporation. So riveting was his delivery of wartime commentary and sales pitches for war bonds that he earned the nickname "The Voice of Canada."

Following brief service in the Canadian army, Greene opened the Academy of

Radio Arts, where he taught more than four hundred students the basics of broadcasting and helped to establish the Jupiter Theatre. He moved to New York in 1953 to appear on *Studio One* productions. Later roles cast him as Captain Ahab in a radio broadcast of *Moby Dick*, in various Broadway roles, and in leading and supporting roles in Stratford Shakespeare Festival productions. He left Shakespeare for parts in a series of films including *Peyton Place* (1957), *Autumn Leaves* (1956), *The Gift of Love* (1958), and *The Trap* (1959). Even though *Peyton Place* had popular and financial success, none of his cinema efforts brought much return for his considerable acting talent.

At this point in Greene's career, television, an even better financial bet than theater or film, proved more promising. He received contracts for quality productions including *The Elgin TV Hour, Producers' Showcase, Omnibus, Alfred Hitchcock Presents, You Are There*, and *Playhouse 90.* Although he lacked experience with horseback riding and Westerns, after a single appearance on *Wagon Train* he was cast as the lead on *Bonanza.* The producer, impressed with Greene's burly good looks, self-confidence, masculine vocal delivery, and decisive stage presence, tailored the character of Ben to fit the star's age and demeanor.

As the youngest son and impish, curly-haired enticement to teenage female viewers, Michael Landon, portraying the family hothead who often chose to settle disputes with fists rather than diplomacy, played the foil for his older brother Adam, the cool, level-headed, contemplative man. Landon had abandoned college, which failed to satisfy his theatrical needs, and developed his versatile talent in television drama, including *Studio One, Playhouse 90, General Electric Theater*, and *Schlitz Playhouse of Stars.* Although he lacked maturity at *Bonanza*'s inception, he grew into the part of Little Joe, building a sizable audience following. In 1964, he won a Silver Spurs Award as most popular actor in a television Western.

The other two sons presented the greatest contrast in the Cartwright quartet. They were not as blessed by success and satisfaction as Landon. Pernell Roberts, stymied as Adam, the oldest and most academic of the three sons and probable heir to the Ponderosa, wearied of his role and quit the series in disgust in 1965. He had worked a variety of odd jobs and served with the Marines before initiating his dramatic career. An award-winning professional who began in summer stock, he acted on Washington's Arena Stage and in Off-Broadway roles before joining the *Bonanza* cast.

In the role of the middle son, Dan Blocker, the ingenuous, gap-toothed mountain strongman provided an important diplomatic balance against the taciturnity of Ben, the cerebral self-assurance of Adam, and the naïve, roguish impetuosity of Little Joe. Blocker's most poignant performances called for tender, doomed love scenes that revealed the depth of his sensitivity. His death left a serious gap in the Cartwright household and caused an immediate dip in ratings.

Impact of Event

Produced from a soundstage in Hollywood, *Bonanza*, the first television Western to be filmed in color, was conceived for two purposes: to foster America's father-son relationships and as a ploy to sell color sets manufactured by Radio Corporation of America (RCA), NBC's parent company. The series took hold slowly and received heavy criticism for its lush sentimentality, which reviewers compared to that of soap operas. Later public response, indicating a stronger viewer identification with the characters, bolstered sponsor confidence. Bankrolled by Chevrolet and produced by former scriptwriter David Dortort, the series, touted as a revival of family values and a classic of the television Western genre, featured a blend of comedy and realism along with social themes such as race prejudice, greed, alienation among families, and political corruption. Critics gave the program high marks for its story lines, many of which featured reconciliation and acceptance as major themes.

A demographic triumph of *Bonanza* was the nationwide pattern of regular viewers who followed the program week to week. Viewed by tens of millions of American fans in addition to audiences in dozens of other countries, *Bonanza* peaked from 1964 to 1967, when it ranked first in popularity for three successive years. It finished second only to *Gunsmoke* as the public's favorite television Western of all time. Even Queen Elizabeth II confided to the show's cast that she and her three children were faithful *Bonanza* viewers. *Bonanza* thus became one of television's first long-lived series and set a pattern of regular viewing habits.

Bonanza, basically a pacifist Western, had a tremendous impact on television pro duction. Less involved with assault, robbery, murder, rustling, prejudice against Indians, and the flagrant bloodshed associated with stereotypical Westerns, *Bonanza* stressed the Cartwrights' relationships with a rapidly expanding territory, where law by necessity was augmented by reason. This emphasis helped to shift later broadcast efforts to a more humanistic plane, particularly those programs set in the American West.

Because of its quality production and emotional appeal, the series outlived and outearned some two dozen carnage-ridden series such as *Wagon Train, Broken Arrow, Tombstone Territory, Have Gun Will Travel, Rawhide,* and *Sugarfoot.* In its final years, *Bonanza* returned in reruns and as a revamped series entitled *Ponderosa.* The series also brought personal and commercial success to its cast; rerun rights were sold in 1970 for a handsome but undisclosed sum.

His initial salary of $20,000 per episode, at thirty-four episodes per year, quickly turned Lorne Greene, the highest-paid cast member, into a millionaire. As an added enhancement, he received poignant, flattering fan mail from young men wishing for fathers like Ben Cartwright and developed a strong identity with the role, which bore a significant likeness to his own personality. He extended his tie with the series by serving as backstage mentor and financial adviser to Michael Landon and Dan Blocker, achieving comfortable profits for each of them. So taken was Greene with his role that he supervised the construction of a duplicate Ponderosa on his own property. To keep in touch with his fans, he made frequent personal appearances, often at rodeos, state fairs, Salvation Army benefits, and Boy Scout assemblies.

Pernell Roberts, whose departure was colored by an undercurrent of discontent, derided the show's sentimentality and lack of challenge. After he was depicted as departing to the East to study, the other costars appeared at more frequent intervals, and new characters were written into later scripts to cover his absence. He heeded idealistic urges that eased emotional stress by going back to theater but he returned to television and achieved fame in *Trapper John, M.D.*, a television series that aired from 1979 to 1986 and cast him in the role of a modern doctor based loosely on a character from the *M*A*S*H* series.

Michael Landon, who submerged himself in his role as Little Joe, used the part as a learning experience. After ten years' service as the youngest Cartwright, he ranged outward to direct twelve *Bonanza* episodes and write scripts for thirty more. The shift in point of view brought him into conflict with producer Dortort, who was forced to intercede in bitter squabbles with writers and directors who resented Landon's interference. The experience, however, became the seed for his future directing and writing.

At the expiration of *Bonanza*, substantial numbers of opportunities awaited Landon, some of which, such as hosting the Junior Miss pageant, seemed too banal for his talents. His decision to star in *Little House on the Prairie*, which aired from 1974 to 1983, proved advantageous for his career. At the time of his death from pancreatic cancer in 1991, critics were still lauding his roles on *Bonanza*, *Little House on the Prairie*, and *Highway to Heaven* (1984-1989), all family-centered television fare that earned him the regard of religious and educational leaders.

A measure of Landon's success in family roles lies in the public outpouring of love and support during his fight with terminal illness. Fans, reviving their love affair with the Cartwright family, recounted nostalgic stories of Little Joe and the Ponderosa and of Charles Ingalls, head of the family on *Little House on the Prairie*. The lasting devotion of audiences who continued watching both programs in reruns is a tribute to the staying power of traditional mores.

Bibliography

Brooks, Tim, and Earle Marsh. *The Complete Directory to Prime Time Network TV Shows: 1946-Present.* 4th ed. New York: Ballantine Books, 1988. A thorough overview of television shows and series, including major and minor characters, casts, broadcast histories, theme songs, and formats.

Brown, Les. *Les Brown's Encyclopedia of Television.* New York: New York Zoetrope, 1982. A spotty overview of programs, series, and isolated topics. Dotted with candid shots, the text gives snippets of information, including dates, critical response, stars, format, changes in casting, sponsor, network, and production information.

MacDonald, J. Fred. *Who Shot the Sheriff? The Rise and Fall of the Television Western.* New York: Praeger, 1987. Analyzes the development of Western characters and themes on television, viewing them as mirrors of American values, beliefs, and ideals. Offers the opinion that Westerns lost their popularity because they no longer expressed contemporary ideology.

Poppy, John. "Bonanza." *Look* 28 (December 1, 1964): 80-91. Written at the height of *Bonanza*'s popularity. The text, interspersed with photos, delves into crucial questions about television's shortcomings, particularly its banality. Poppy emphasizes the contrast in perspectives, particularly those of Lorne Greene and Pernell Roberts.

West, Richard. *Television Westerns: Major and Minor Series, 1946-1978.* Jefferson, N.C.: McFarland, 1987. Describes all Western series appearing on television between 1946 and 1978. Includes biographical data on principal actors, with some photographs. Informative introduction. Appendices contain information on casting, Emmy Awards, ratings, title changes, and air times. Thorough index.

Young, Pamela. "Death of a TV Patriarch." *Maclean's* 100 (September 21, 1987): 42-43. An obituary of Lorne Greene that describes his early years and the success of *Bonanza.* Contains a portrait shot and a closeup of the four series stars on horseback.

Mary Ellen Snodgrass

Cross-References

Grey's *Riders of the Purple Sage* Launches the Western Genre (1912), p. 304; Ford Defines the Western in *Stagecoach* (1939), p. 1115; Westerns Dominate Postwar American Film (1946), p. 1313; *Gunsmoke* Debuts, Launching a Popular Television Genre (1955), p. 1668; Seven of the Top Ten Television Series Are Westerns (1958), p. 1768; Leone Renovates the Western Genre (1964), p. 1984.

THE GUGGENHEIM MUSEUM OPENS IN A BUILDING DESIGNED BY WRIGHT

Category of event: Architecture
Time: October 21, 1959
Locale: New York, New York

Frank Lloyd Wright's controversial spiral design for the Guggenheim Museum changed the historic relationship between museum form and function and made architects and architecture newsworthy

Principal personages:

FRANK LLOYD WRIGHT (1867-1959), a pioneer American architect interested in natural forms who designed more than six hundred buildings

SOLOMON R. GUGGENHEIM (1861-1949), a mining magnate and millionaire whose collection of avant-garde European paintings formed the core of his namesake museum's holdings

HILLA REBAY (BARONESS HILDEGARD REBAY VON EHRENWIESEN, 1890-1967), the Guggenheim's prime mover and founding curator whose commitment to nonobjective painting shaped the museum's identity

JAMES JOHNSON SWEENEY (1900-1986), the director of the Guggenheim from 1952 to 1960, who imposed upon Wright design changes necessary for the museum's functioning

Summary of Event

In the 1930's, Solomon R. Guggenheim stopped buying the old master paintings popular with his fellow millionaires. Inspired by the German artist and curator Hilla Rebay, he began to collect contemporary art. Guggenheim and Rebay focused on nonrepresentational painting and sculpture by avant-garde Europeans such as Wassily Kandinsky and Piet Mondrian, whose work was fueled by utopian beliefs. Spurred by Rebay's conviction that abstract art and art education could change the world, Guggenheim decided to found a museum. In 1939, Rebay installed much of Guggenheim's collection in a temporary space on East Fifty-fourth Street in New York City called the Museum of Non-Objective Art. In 1943, Guggenheim signed a contract with Frank Lloyd Wright to design a permanent home for the museum.

Wright was then America's premier architect, known as much for his flamboyant private life as for his revolutionary house and office designs. Rebay chose him over European practitioners of the International Style (for which Wright's early work had been important), among them Marcel Breuer, Le Corbusier, and Walter Gropius. Wright's "organic" architecture used natural forms and aimed for unity of all parts; Rebay thought it the architectural analogue to Guggenheim's collection. Wright's comparative inexperience with urban building and museum design mattered less to Rebay than his spirituality. The Guggenheim, sixteen years in the making, was

Wright's first major New York commission, and his only museum.

The Solomon R. Guggenheim Museum opened on October 21, 1959, at 1071 Fifth Avenue, across from Central Park. Public and critics were primed. City newspapers had followed Wright's battles with civic authorities over building codes and with Rebay, her successor as director, James Johnson Sweeney, and the Guggenheim trustees over museum matters. (Guggenheim had died in 1949.) There had been difficulties, too, with financing and with finding a site. Wright died in April, 1959, six months before the museum's completion. At the opening, debate about the building and its architect overshadowed discussion of Guggenheim and his landmark collection.

No one had seen any buildings, let alone any museums, remotely like Wright's giant cast-concrete spiral set on a low, horizontal base. While praising Wright's genius, observers and critics groped for comparisons. The Guggenheim was likened to natural forms, to machine-made objects, to food: a monstrous mushroom, a snail-shell, a just-landed spaceship, a corkscrew, a washing machine, an ice-cream freezer, an overturned cereal bowl. One critic suggested that the building was intended as a monument to the architect's ego. Much commentary centered on the Guggenheim's essential character and on its relationship to its site. It was an insult, some said, to its decorous neighbors on the upper East Side's Museum Mile and to Central Park across the street. It was vital, modern, fast, American, others asserted, like an automobile or a Jackson Pollock painting.

The inaugural exhibition showed the cream of the Guggenheim collection, much expanded during Sweeney's tenure. (Rebay had been forced to retire in 1952.) In addition to paintings by Kandinsky and Mondrian, there were works by important early modernists including Paul Cézanne and Georges Seurat and by newcomers such as Pollock and Willem de Kooning. Critics acknowledged the collection's scope, but it was Wright's interior that fascinated them.

The visitor, fresh from the experience of the great spiral outside, entered the museum through a low-ceilinged space and looked up into a vast central core (Wright called it a "seedpod"). There were no conventional galleries hung with pictures. Instead, a cantilevered ramp enclosed the core and wound for a quarter of a mile and up ninety-two feet to a skylit dome. The paintings were displayed on the ramp itself.

Unique in appearance, the Guggenheim was typically Wrightian in its theme and architectural elements. Unity, key for Wright, was provided by the central light well, by interpenetrating forms, and by the interior's mirroring of the spiral exterior. The continuous ramp ensured that visitors experienced architecture and art simultaneously while walking along as they might have on a mountain trail. Wright had meant to prop the paintings against the ramp walls, as if on a gigantic easel. This "natural" solution was rejected by Sweeney, who suspended the paintings on nearly invisible bars, so that they were given a measure of protection while seeming to float in space. The circular forms, the wish to "break the box" of traditional architecture, the ascending ramp, and the exterior massing of forms all had precedents in earlier and nearly contemporary works by Wright. Notable among these were the Larkin Building in Buffalo (1904-1906), the Johnson Wax Building in Wisconsin (1936-1939), the

V. C. Morris Gift Shop in San Francisco (1946-1948), and the David Wright house in Phoenix (1948-1950).

Many contemporary reviews, even those well disposed to the Guggenheim's unusual exterior, criticized the interior for its functional failures. Wright's egotism (another signature theme, it was said) led him to ignore the needs of museum staff and artists, to favor form over function. Such criticism had preceded the museum's opening. In 1957, a number of prominent artists, alarmed by newspaper reports of Wright's intentions for the exhibition spaces, had presented a petition to the Guggenheim trustees asking that the building's design be changed to serve works of art better. Among the signers were Milton Avery, Willem de Kooning, and Robert Motherwell. Particularly objectionable was the curved spiral ramp, which was seen as the wrong "frame" for rectangular paintings and as an instance of Wright's contempt for artists. (Wright had gone on record as saying that the Guggenheim interior itself was the perfect frame.) The ramp was also seen by some critics as a show of contempt for museum visitors, who, one writer claimed, were deprived of their freedom of choice, rushed up the one path and through the museum, and then spit out. Even observers who found Wright's interior deficient as an exhibition space, however, seemed struck by its beauty and its force. Critics used adjectives such as "Shakespearean," "glorious," and "majestic" to describe the space. Some noted its otherworldly qualities, finding them appropriate to the museum's spiritually charged collection. (Wright, surely not by accident, had labeled an early drawing for the museum "ziggurat," in allusion to ancient Near Eastern temples with squared, skyward paths.)

The Guggenheim is a bold statement of Wright's philosophy of organic architecture. The abstract composition in three dimensions looks Wrightian, but as built, it was not the Guggenheim Wright designed. Rebay persuaded Wright to compromise on display, Guggenheim refused to finance the lush marble exterior Wright had envisaged (they settled on the use of painted concrete), and Sweeney and the trustees imposed many other changes in lighting, color, and design, largely against Wright's will. Objects of controversy during the sixteen years of planning and construction, the Guggenheim and its architect became yet more famous and controversial upon the museum's official opening.

Impact of Event

On June 28, 1992, the Guggenheim Museum reopened after a two-year closure for renovation, restoration, and addition. New York newspapers were filled with reports on and reviews of the changes. Much of the work involved repairing damage to the building's fabric and removing or minimizing changes imposed by Sweeney and his successors. The cracked and peeled façade was repaired and repainted. Wright's skylight was stripped of paint, and the core was flooded with natural light, as Wright had intended. Intersecting galleries added in 1968 by architects of the Taliesin Fellowship, Wright's foundation, were altered so that they interfered less with Wright's great central space. The roof was converted into a sculpture garden, as the original plan had dictated.

Another major change involved expansion of the museum's office and gallery space. Architects Charles Gwathmey and Robert Siegel erected a ten-story tower behind and above Wright's Guggenheim. According to the museum and the architects, the new tower was built on Wrightian foundations and accorded with Wright's intentions. (An intermediate office building added after the museum's opening and before the renovation was torn down.) A new inaugural exhibition was mounted to show off the collection's range and depth.

All these changes, said Thomas Krens, the Guggenheim's director, related to the expansion of the Guggenheim's collection and the broadening of its educational mission. They were part of an ambitious plan of global expansion. Not only was Wright's Fifth Avenue Guggenheim involved, but so were a series of other Guggenheims already existing and to come. First, the SoHo Guggenheim, located in a nineteenth century building on the corner of Broadway and Prince Street renovated by the Japanese architect Arata Isozaki, was to open in the summer of 1992. It would provide 31,000 square feet of exhibition space to be used to show contemporary work too large or too difficult for the "old" Guggenheim. The Peggy Guggenheim Foundation in Venice, Italy, was to be enlarged. A major project was underway in the northwestern corner of Massachusetts to convert abandoned nineteenth century factory buildings into a contemporary art showcase under the Guggenheim's aegis. Additionally, mini-Guggenheims were scheduled to open in Salzburg, Austria, and Bilbao, Spain, within the decade.

As it had in 1959 at the Guggenheim's opening, comment on the building took precedence over analysis of the new inaugural exhibition. As before, controversy erupted; opinion was once again divided. While the restoration and renovation met with almost universal approval, the new addition did not. On the one hand, it was said to dwarf Wright's spiral and to attempt to civilize the rough character of the original building. On the other hand, it was described as deferring too much to the Guggenheim and for failing to assert a strong enough personality of its own.

Critics in 1959 thought that Wright's building spoke more to the future than it had to the past. The Guggenheim represented a radical departure from architectural norms in its use of materials, in its form, and in its effect on the public. The use of reinforced concrete on such a scale, and with such daring, had some precedents in the United States, none of which took technology to quite the point Wright did in the Guggenheim, and none of which had the Guggenheim's effect. (Two nearly contemporary examples, both by foreign architects, would be Eero Saarinen's Kresge Auditorium at the Massachusetts Institute of Technology and Minoru Yamasaki's Lambert Terminal for the St. Louis airport.) Most major American cities now boast cubic acres of reinforced-concrete buildings, many boldly cantilevered and heavily massed like the Guggenheim. Similar massing and cantilevering characterizes Marcel Breuer's Whitney Museum. Clad in gray granite rather than concrete, the Whitney achieves effects very like the Guggenheim's and clearly alludes to it.

The Guggenheim sums up many of Wright's theories and architectural trademarks, particularly in its treatment of interior space. Its location in New York, its visibility, and its history of controversy have generated a vast literature and kept interest in Wright and his philosophies high. Richard Meier's High Museum of Art in Atlanta (1983), with its light-filled central core and its winding ramp, pays direct homage to Wright and the Guggenheim. (Meier had worked on the intermediate addition to the Guggenheim.) Commercial structures such as John Portman's Hyatt hotels, with their signature atriums, are less copies of Wright than responses to him and to the architectural vocabulary of the Guggenheim.

The Guggenheim was among the first museums to rate front-page coverage, but it is now one of many. Controversy has attended plans by Michael Graves to enlarge Marcel Breuer's Whitney Museum of 1966. Similar attention has been given to, and similar controversy stirred by, among others, I. M. Pei's glass pyramid for the Louvre, James Stirling's Clore Gallery at the Tate Gallery in London, and Robert Venturi and Denise Scott Brown's extension to the National Gallery in London. With the Guggenheim came new ideas about what a museum was and what it meant. No longer simply conventional structures built to house and protect treasures, museums became stars, as did their architects.

In only a few decades, the Guggenheim was transformed from a monster into a sacred monster, a much-loved building. Front-page news from its inception, it is among America's best-known museums. Its very name conjures up the image not of a collection or its namesake but of the museum structure itself and its builder. Frank Lloyd Wright's Guggenheim Museum brought architecture and architects into the public eye and public consciousness, where they—and the Guggenheim and its builder—remain.

Bibliography

Blake, Peter. "The Guggenheim: Museum or Monument?" *Architectural Forum* 111 (December, 1959): 86-93. Critical analysis of the museum, illustrated with many black-and-white photographs, and including as appendix a selection of critical comments from the New York press. Fair-minded, straightforward, and ultimately quite positive.

Gill, Brendan. *Many Masks: A Life of Frank Lloyd Wright.* New York: G. P. Putnam's Sons, 1987. Popular biography by an architecture critic and writer for *The New Yorker.* Tries to account for Wright's contradictions and his appeal. Chapter on Guggenheim saga. Footnotes, index, many photographs of people and buildings.

Jordy, William H. *The Impact of European Modernism in the Mid-Twentieth Century.* Vol. 3 in *American Buildings and Their Architects.* New York: Oxford University Press, 1972. Thorough, evenhanded, scholarly case studies of landmark buildings by an eminent architectural historian. Long chapter on Guggenheim. Well-illustrated with plans and photographs; excellent bibliography.

Wright, Frank Lloyd. *An Autobiography.* Rev. ed. New York: Horizon Press, 1977. Wright's own account of his life and works. Photographs, index.

_____. *Frank Lloyd Wright: The Guggenheim Correspondence.* Edited by Bruce Brooks Pfeiffer. Carbondale: Southern Illinois University Press, 1986. Wright's letters give his view of the Guggenheim story. Useful commentary by Wright specialist. Models, plans, photographs of construction, personages.

Susan Benforado Bakewell

Cross-References

Kandinsky Publishes His Views on Abstraction in Art (1912), p. 320; *De Stijl* Advocates Mondrian's Neoplasticism (1917), p. 429; The Whitney Museum Is Inaugurated in New York (1931), p. 885; Wright Founds the Taliesin Fellowship (1932), p. 902; Peggy Guggenheim's Gallery Promotes New American Art (1942), p. 1239; Breuer Designs a Building for the Whitney Museum (1966), p. 2064.

IONESCO'S *RHINOCEROS* RECEIVES A RESOUNDING WORLDWIDE RECEPTION

Category of event: Theater
Time: October 31, 1959
Locale: Düsseldorf, West Germany

Eugène Ionesco vividly confronted his audiences with absurdities of social and political conformity in light of the senselessness and irrationality of life

Principal personages:
EUGÈNE IONESCO (1912-   ), a playwright and a major absurdist author
GUILLAUME APOLLINAIRE (GUILLAUME ALBERT WLADIMIR ALEXANDRE APOLLINAIRE DE KOSTROWITZKY, 1880-1918), a poet and playwright influenced by cubism's goal of making art larger than life
ANTONIN ARTAUD (1896-1948), a Surrealist actor, director, poet, and designer who developed the Theater of Cruelty concept
ALBERT CAMUS (1913-1960), a writer and philosopher who wrote about the feeling of absurdity
MARTIN ESSLIN (1918-   ), a writer and theorist, first to label many plays of the 1950's and 1960's as absurdist
JEAN-PAUL SARTRE (1905-1980), an essayist, novelist, playwright, and existential philosopher whose works challenged people to be politically engaged in their situations
ALFRED JARRY (1873-1907), a playwright who wrote the first absurdist play, *Ubu roi*, performed December 10, 1896, in Paris

Summary of Event

In order to understand the work of Eugène Ionesco, it is necessary to examine several factors that heavily influenced the theater prior to his writing *Rhinocéros* (1959; *Rhinoceros*, 1959). When Alfred Jarry wrote *Ubu roi* (1896), it represented the earliest example of expressionism in the theater. August Strindberg followed in 1902 with *A Dream Play*. After World War I, there was a distinctive movement against realism. The movement was labeled expressionism because it did not imitate reality but instead sought to have audiences become emotionally involved with the dramatic action of a production. The expressionist playwrights assumed that people's problems were a result of society. Bertolt Brecht, the perfecter of "epic theater," embraced expressionism for a period of time before moving on to his work with epic drama through the Berliner Ensemble.

Surrealism was a vital force in the theater during the 1920's and 1930's. The Surrealists were convinced that reality could be grasped only at an unconscious level and through irrationality. Representative playwrights of this movement include Guillaume Apollinaire (*The Breasts of Tiresias*, 1917) and Jean Cocteau (*Orpheus*, 1926).

There were three important developments outside the theater that influenced Ionesco. First, the scientific work of Charles Darwin convinced Ionesco that the world was constantly changing and people were part of the evolutionary process in the animal kingdom. Second, the economic philosophy of Karl Marx proved to Ionesco that the rich and powerful received more power and the poor simply got nothing. The third development was Sigmund Freud's "psychic" determinism, which led Ionesco to believe that people act as a result of irrational and unconscious fears and motives.

Two existential philosophers and playwrights provided the ideological foundations for the work of Ionesco. Albert Camus wrote that people's lives are separated from themselves, resulting in a feeling of absurdity. Camus illustrated this great divorce in his allegorical work *The Myth of Sisyphus* (1942). Jean-Paul Sartre, not unlike Camus, found that the world was filled with chaos. Sartre's *No Exit* (1946) is a play in which the characters search for meaning in their lives through meaningless relationships. In his book *The Theatre of the Absurd* (1961), Martin Esslin identified the antirealism movement he called absurdism. The movement's major writers include Ionesco, Samuel Beckett, Jean Genet, and Harold Pinter.

Ionesco's play *La Cantatrice chauve* (*The Bald Soprano*) was written in 1948 and first performed in 1950. This play epitomizes Ionesco's work during the 1950's. The play is a parody of the absurdism found in the existing society. Ionesco uses clichés of language and thought to underscore the absurdity of human irrationality.

Ionesco attacked people's tendency to conform to sociopolitical pressures in the bizarre and hilarious play *Rhinoceros*. Throughout the play, people turn into rhinoceroses. Through the dramatic action of the play, the character Bérenger discovers how difficult it is to resist the pressure to conform to the social structures in his life. Ionesco does not try to provide a rational basis for Bérenger to resist the social pressures to conform; he only shows a character in the process of discovery and rediscovery, searching for meaning in the events occurring around him.

Later works by Ionesco are parabolic plays dealing with human evil. In these later plays, he examines the need people seem to have for power. In these works, Ionesco writes about the inevitability of death for each person.

Probably one of the most influential people affecting Ionesco was Antonin Artaud. Artaud was a Surrealist. He worked as an actor, director, poet, designer, and playwright. In 1938 he published *Le Théatre et son double* (*The Theatre and Its Double*), which established his concept of the Theater of Cruelty.

There are a number of themes present throughout the works of Ionesco. Ionesco uses fantasy to force his audience from the security induced by reason. His plays challenge people to recognize the illusion of the world and all its strangeness. He writes about the loneliness people experience in a universe without God. His characters reveal an inability to communicate with each other, and mass communication is the instrument used to dehumanize people. In light of loneliness and dehumanization, individuals find that they are impotent and at the mercy of powerful people in society. Ionesco deals with the idea that ultimately all a person has to look forward to is death. There is no way to escape it. In essence, Ionesco hoped that through his work the audience would accept that reality is absurd, irrational, illogical, and senselessly futile. Ionesco writes about a world with highly developed social institutions filled with madness.

Certainly *Rhinoceros*, with its nonhuman characters, is a part of the avant-garde movement in the theater. The play is a wildly extravagant tragic farce. The world premiere of the play was in Düsseldorf, Germany, on October 31, 1959. Ionesco's *Rhinoceros* is a complex picture of "reality," showing multiple levels of reality. The challenge is to consider a variety of realities without the playwright giving the audience the "final" meaning.

The play is likely a comment on the Nazi movement. Characters turn into rhinoceroses; Ionesco uses this device to suggest that the Nazi Party was trying to force people to conform to its standards of what was morally correct. A rhinoceros was a metaphor for a moral pachyderm or, in other words, a Nazi. The absurdist theme of isolation is evident in that Bérenger is the only human in a town full of rhinoceroses.

The play, however, works on another dimension. It is quite possible to view the play as a relational statement about the characters Jean and Bérenger. Throughout the action there is an ongoing struggle to establish what the characters mean to each other. They try to communicate with each other, yet the language is stale and filled with clichés. Jean promises to stay with Bérenger, but she gives in to the urges she is feeling. In her conformity, she becomes a rhinoceros and abandons Bérenger. He is left isolated and lonely, waiting for the end to come.

Ionesco confronted spectators with a philosophical paradox to solve. *Rhinoceros* is a bizarre play with a tragicomic spirit. Ionesco did not believe that this fantastic situation had a solution. He seemed to want his audience to recognize the absurdity of life, thereby being freed from the obsessions they carried with them daily. People, thus confronted, are able to laugh and enjoy the drama. When so challenged, they will be able to be free from the bonds that hold them.

Impact of Event

Rhinoceros was received with enthusiasm. After its world premiere in Germany, it was produced by Jean-Louis Barrault at the Odéon-Théâtre de France in Paris on January 22, 1960. It next opened in London, England, at the Royal Court Theatre in April, 1960, under the direction of Orson Welles.

The play makes a somewhat positive statement, as Bérenger does resist the temptation to conform. This is not to overlook the strong absurdist philosophy contained in the play, which is representative of Ionesco's complete works. All of his plays acknowledge the uselessness of clichés in communication; ideologies of all types, including those found in religion, politics, and society; and the prevailing sense of materialism intended to bring people happiness.

Rhinoceros served as an example to other playwrights that audiences were concerned with similar themes in their individual lives. Ionesco posits two lines of thought: In their relationships with others, people feel loneliness and isolation; and people are bothered by a materialistic bourgeois society. The playwright develops these themes through situations showing that life's endeavors are illogical and that language is inadequate in providing a resolution. People's only refuge from the absurdity surrounding them in a world without the certainty that God will provide a rational escape is to be found in laughter: at themselves, at others, and at society.

Ionesco has shown in *Rhinoceros* that "pure" theater can exist outside and separated from a framework based on an accepted conceptual rationality. The characters reflect the existential view that people create "selves" by the choices they make in a given situation. To heighten the absurdity of the plot, Ionesco uses the avant-garde technique of having nonhuman characters in the play.

Rhinoceros resembles expressionism and epic theater. The use of Brecht's principle of alienation is evident in the play. Ionesco wants the audience to be confronted with the impossibility of the human condition. Emotional empathy is denied to the spectator, since it is impossible to identify with and understand the motives of the characters. As viewers watch the absurd event of people turning into rhinoceroses, they are brought face to face with the irrational side of life. *Rhinoceros* enables the audience to remain detached and to evaluate critically the message of the play. This was something Brecht's epic theater was not able to achieve, even though it was a primary goal of the movement.

Rhinoceros had an immediate and a long-term impact on the theater, because it countered both verbal and logical solutions to the absurdity in life. It represented a revolt. Throughout the decade of the 1960's, *Rhinoceros* was in the advance guard of a movement that continued to have major influences on contemporary theater.

Ionesco showed that people must resist conformity. Each person must learn to cope in a manner uniquely his or her own. The individual must continue on in life despite the fact that death and a void wait at the end. As Ionesco did in his works, playwrights continue to grapple with existential themes such as how language prevents people from really thinking, how people displace what is really valuable in life with material things, and how, in a world of weapons of mass destruction and high technology, people often find themselves dehumanized. Ionesco has left an existential heritage for other playwrights.

Ionesco, in *Rhinoceros*, created a sense of crushing despair that can be brought on by life's absurdity. He developed characters not fully aware of their own rootlessness in life and struck at the elusiveness of life's reality. Certainly the play has meaning. That meaning, however, often must be found in the subtext of the plot. He even allowed directors to end the play with their own interpretations.

Ionesco's *Rhinoceros* serves the theater as an example of the chaotic, formless inanities people must face each day of their existence. The playwright recognized a common bond among people, in that each person shares with others a common memory, regrets, fear of nothingness, and death. He is aware that people are likely to comfort themselves by accumulating material possessions and through rigid religious, sociopolitical, and philosophical ideologies. This is the world Ionesco left to other playwrights, to grapple with and to write plays about. *Rhinoceros* is the epito-mizing example of the avant-garde of absurdist theater.

Bibliography

Artaud, Antonin. *The Theater and Its Double.* Translated by Mary C. Richards. New York: Grove Press, 1958. Artaud provides his initial thinking on the Theater of Cruelty, which intends to force the audience to confront itself.

Barnet, Sylvan, Morton Berman, and William Burto. *Types of Drama: Plays and Essays.* Boston: Little, Brown, 1972. The sections on the nature of drama, the language of drama, and tragicomedy are useful to the student of absurdism in understanding the movement.

Barranger, Milly S. *Understanding Plays.* Boston: Allyn & Bacon, 1990. An intro-duction to various genres of plays. Barranger provides a brief yet excellent discus-sion of absurdism.

Boyce, Sandra N. *Welcome to the Theatre.* Chicago: Nelson-Hall, 1987. A good in-troductory work, providing information concerning theater conventions, play pro-duction, and discussions of major movements throughout theater history.

Brockett, Oscar G. *History of the Theatre.* 6th ed. Boston: Allyn & Bacon, 1991. This comprehensive study of the theater is highly recommended for the serious student of the theater. Brockett provides a thorough look at trends and movements affecting the evolution of the absurdist movement in theater.

Hall, James B., and Barry Ulanov. *Modern Culture and the Arts.* New York: McGraw-Hill, 1967. A confrontation with cultural heritage that is stimulating and enlight-ening. A good source of information on which to build a foundational knowledge of the arts.

Hartnoll, Phyllis. *The Concise History of Theatre.* New York: Harry N. Abrams, 1968. Gives a synoptic view of major movements in the theater.

Robinson, Paul R. *The Freudian Left: Wilhelm Reich, Geza Roheim, Herbert Mar-cuse.* New York: Harper & Row, 1969. Provides an interesting discussion of psy-choanalysis for those interested in understanding how it influenced absurdism in the theater.

Roose-Evans, James. *Experimental Theatre: From Stanislavsky to Today.* New York: Universe Books, 1970. Roose-Evans provides a clear and concise development of major movements in the theater, beginning with Stanislavsky and running through the experimental work done in the United States up to 1970. A unified view of what led to much of contemporary practice in modern theater.

Wilson, Edwin. *The Theater Experience.* 4th ed. New York: McGraw-Hill, 1988. Examines numerous aspects of the theater in a discussion that highlights various developments in staging, acting, directing, and playwriting. The book contains an excellent set of five appendices, including "Major Theatrical Forms and Move-ments" and "Historical Outline."

Willis M. Watt

Cross-References

Sartre and Camus Give Dramatic Voice to Existential Philosophy (1940's), p. 1174; Sartre's *Being and Nothingness* Expresses Existential Philosophy (1943), p. 1262; Brecht Founds the Berliner Ensemble (1949), p. 1410; *Waiting for Godot* Expresses the Existential Theme of Absurdity (1953), p. 1573; Esslin Publishes *The Theatre of the Absurd* (1961), p. 1871; Tawfiq al-Hakim Introduces Absurdism to the Arab Stage (1961), p. 1893; *The American Dream* Establishes Albee as the Voice of Pessimism (1961), p. 1903.

VILLA-LOBOS' DEATH MARKS THE END
OF A BRILLIANT MUSICAL CAREER

Category of event: Music
Time: November 17, 1959
Locale: Rio de Janeiro, Brazil

Heitor Villa-Lobos, one of the twentieth century's foremost Latin-American com-posers, wrote his works in a style deeply influenced by Brazilian folk music as well as European composers

Principal personages:
HEITOR VILLA-LOBOS (1887-1959), a Brazilian composer and conductor, the most famous of all Latin-American musicians
ARTHUR RUBINSTEIN (1887-1982), a renowned pianist who promoted Villa-Lobos' work by playing it for audiences worldwide
JOHANN SEBASTIAN BACH (1685-1750), a Viennese composer whose work inspired Villa-Lobos and whom Villa-Lobos considered a "universal source" of music
LUCILIA GUIMARÃES VILLA-LOBOS (1886-?), a pianist who married Villa-Lobos in 1913, enthusiastically interpreted his works, and helped to support him

Summary of Event

Heitor Villa-Lobos was born on March 5, 1887, in a section of Rio de Janeiro, Brazil, called Laranjeiros. His father was a functionary at the National Library, a politically conservative man with great intellectual curiosity. He wrote books on many subjects, sketched portraits, and skillfully played the cello. When he became aware that Heitor had precocious musical talent, he began to instruct him in ear training and on the cello.

Raul Villa-Lobos died of smallpox in 1899, leaving his son and his widow with little money to live on. Villa-Lobos' mother began to work to support the two of them. Villa-Lobos had begun to study the clarinet and guitar just before his father died. He had developed skill on the cello and written his first composition, "Os Se-dutores," that same year. During this difficult period, he sought the friendship of popular musicians who played *choros*.

The Choro is an improvised, melancholy kind of music performed at *serestas*, or serenades. The term is related to the Portuguese verb *chorar* ("to weep") and was also used for the groups performing this sad, amorous music. Although "serenade" suggests a vocalist, the *chorões*, or instrumentalists, were rarely accompanied. They produced beautiful harmonies in a spontaneous original ensemble, improvising mel-odies and variations. A cultish devotion to their music was ascribed to the players, who would assemble for weddings or parties but then continue to play in the streets, often urged on by followers throughout the night. Young Villa-Lobos played the guitar in a *choros* group whose other members went on to become well known. The influence of these times surfaces especially in his *Bachianas Brasileiras, No. 1,* in its fugue composed in the style of another popular player of the time.

The young musician's interest in the *choro* groups grew to the point of devotion. He began to stay out all night with them, to the detriment of his schoolwork and to the distress of his mother. At the age of sixteen, he left home to live with his Aunt Zizinha and escape his mother's reprimands. Zizinha was more tolerant of his love for *choros* and the popular musicians.

In Rio de Janeiro, he played in nightclubs, hotels, movie theaters, and bars with *choro* groups. At the same time, he was a cellist in the orchestra of Recreio Theater, the most popular theater in Rio de Janeiro, where operas and operettas were performed. He was also composing waltzes, schottisches, military marches, and polkas. He met many well-known artists whose styles he absorbed and analyzed well enough that echoes of their playing appeared later—and authentically—in his work.

At the age of eighteen, Villa-Lobos left Rio de Janeiro obsessed with a desire to travel and see the world. To finance his travels, he sold several books from a rare collection his father had left to him. He visited the northern Brazilian states of Espírito Santo, Bahia, and Pernambuco, then went further into the northeastern hinterland, where he studied the music of popular singers, their styles of interpretation, and their primitive instruments. In a shorthand he devised himself, he recorded calls, chants, *desafios* (improvisational musical duels between two singers), and music of dramatic dances and plays. His deep interest in popular music later evoked strong national feelings in his classical works.

Villa-Lobos' bohemian life-style lasted for several years. Except for brief periods of time, he was absent from his home in Rio de Janeiro during the years 1905 to 1911. In 1907, he became a student at the National Institute of Music for a few months. He then decided that formal classes were not as interesting as the folk music he had heard on his travels. He traveled in northeastern Brazil again as well as in the western areas of the country. In Bahia, he heard some compositions by Claude Debussy for the first time and was not much impressed, although Debussy's music was to influence a later period of his works.

Despite almost constant traveling and his refusal of formal training, Villa-Lobos wrote at least forty-three compositions between 1899 and 1911. Most were short songs and pieces for guitar, his favorite popular instrument, along with some pieces for piano, chamber groups, and band or chorus. The most significant of the period were *Suite Populaire Brésilienne* (1908-1912), a five-movement suite for guitar; and *Trio No. 1* for piano, violin, and cello.

Back in Rio de Janeiro in 1912 (after his mother, believing him dead, had ordered a mass to be said in his name), the nonconformist musician continued to compose a variety of works, including one-act operas and religious choruses. He was briefly fascinated with Richard Wagner and Giacomo Puccini. On November 12, 1913, he married Lucilia Guimarães, a pianist who had been graduated from the National Institute of Music. His wife became an enthusiastic promoter and interpreter of his piano works.

In 1915, he began to establish his reputation through public performances of his works. The first major performance in Rio de Janeiro was on November 13, 1915. Reviews were favorable. Villa-Lobos had written more than one hundred works but was still relatively unknown, although critics recognized his talent. His works indicated a great desire for harmonic innovation, as in the experiments of Igor Stravinsky, whose music he had not yet heard.

Meeting Arthur Rubinstein in 1918 helped Villa-Lobos get established. He still had no regular income, except his wife's salary and fees for music lessons, in addition to a small income from performing in cinemas and restaurants. The famous pianist Rubinstein was able to convince a number of wealthy Brazilians that Villa-Lobos deserved support. He included many of Villa-Lobos' works in his concert tours, gaining worldwide attention for the composer. All this time, Villa-Lobos was continuing to experiment with typical Brazilian subjects and popular themes in his work, including the tunes of children's songs in his piano pieces.

In 1923, he was sent by the Brazilian government to Paris to introduce his work, but not until a second trip in 1927 did he make his mark. His Paris apartment became a popular meeting place for artists and musicians. A Villa-Lobos festival held in Paris in October, 1927, had great success. During the 1920's, he crowned his success by completing his *Chôros* series, considered along with the *Bachianas Brasileiras* (1930-1944) to be his best contribution to modern music. He also finished his piano masterpieces based on children's tunes, the *Cirandas* (1926), and *Rudepoema* (1926), which was dedicated to Rubinstein.

The last twenty-seven years of his life were dominated by the *Bachianas*, as well as seven more symphonies and thirteen string quartets. He explained that the *Bachianas* were inspired by Johann Sebastian Bach's work, which he called a universal source of music. With a sort of mystic devotion, he adapted Bach's baroque contrapuntal style and applied it to Brazilian folk music.

Villa-Lobos spent the 1930's composing and promoting music education. In 1932, he took charge of musical education throughout Brazil and established musical instruction programs for public schools. He directed a school he helped to found for the education of music teachers. It was a time of incredible activity for the composer. He founded the Brazilian Academy of Music in 1945.

In 1948, Villa-Lobos was diagnosed with cancer of the bladder. The bladder was removed, and he continued with his active life as a conductor and composer. In 1944, he had begun yearly trips to the United States to conduct orchestras, fulfill commissions, and speak to organizations. He never stopped composing. His incredibly demanding schedule, which would have taxed a healthy man, required him to follow a carefully supervised medical regimen.

On his seventieth birthday, in 1957, the city of New York paid Heitor Villa-Lobos special tribute and published an editorial in his honor in *The New York Times.* The

Ministry of Education and Culture in Brazil declared 1957 "Villa-Lobos Year." The following year, he composed *Magnificat Alleluia* at the request of the Vatican. He died in Rio de Janeiro on November 17, 1959.

Impact of Event

"My music is Brazil but international!" Villa-Lobos once exclaimed. He said his *Bachianas Brasileiras* were "Bach placed in Brazil." His genius, inventiveness, and creative vitality—and the flagrant lack of convention in his music—led followers and critics in his own time to call him the undisputed avant-garde musician of Latin America. No other Western composer had thrived so intensely on his own country's indigenous music and transformed it so strikingly in classical compositions. He loved taking his inspiration from the streets, from the language and rhythms of the Brazilian populace. On the other hand, he knew the work of European composers very well and was keenly aware of his indebtedness. Once, during an orchestral rehearsal of his *Magdalena*, he was asked why he kept popping up to tip his hat to the music. "I pay my respects to Debussy, Strauss, Beethoven, Villa-Lobos, as they pass by," he said. The composer had a gift for comedy as well as for music.

Although his instinctive and revolutionary approach to classical composition led some critics to oppose the self-taught musician and composer, many have considered him to be the greatest musical talent to emerge in modern times from the Western hemisphere. Others maintain that his importance in the history of Western music is questionable—or rather, not yet understood. Musically, he was a rebel who scorned academic learning. His defiance of scholarship and his love for melodies from children's songs and popular music both delighted and perplexed his audiences. The ongoing disputes over the extent of his genius at the very least confirm Villa-Lobos' uniqueness. Although they may not agree on the measure of his greatness, scholars accept his importance and the need to demonstrate and further define his place in twentieth century music.

His position in the history of Brazilian music is fundamental; naturally his music influences every contemporary Brazilian composer. It is likely that much "primitive" and popular Brazilian music would have been lost without his devotion to it. He denied the notion that his music reflected Brazilian nationalism and that the soul of Brazil resided in everything he wrote. He was against blind nationalism in art and believed that every country contributed its culture to world music, because "music is for itself." He maintained that great music had commonality, or universal appeal.

Besides helping to reveal Brazil's great treasury of folk and popular music, Villa-Lobos left Brazil with a valuable legacy: a means to learn to appreciate the joy of music. He almost single-handedly reformed the system of public-school music instruction in Brazil. He spent much of the 1930's and early 1940's trying to reorganize the system nationwide. In order to arouse public concern over the issue of arts education, he organized demonstrations in which enormous choral groups performed in carefully planned and organized events. These "canto orfeônico" concerts had upwards of thirty thousand performers singing and using body gestures to enhance the effect of the music. To lead the group, which included one thousand instrumentalists, Villa-Lobos used an individualized system of hand signals and several choral assistants. The numbers were chosen for their civic and patriotic effect. The performances of these gigantic choral groups have not been duplicated anywhere.

The music of Villa-Lobos is generally accepted as the embodiment of the soul of Brazil, but its spirit has touched lovers of music all over the world. Its dazzling combination of wild exuberance and haunting melancholy may provide some listeners with a musical metaphor for the clash of cultures between the Old World and the New World. The tension between the primitive and the sophisticated is often a theme: the mechanistic culture of the city rising from a jungle, perhaps to overtake it; the energy and fertility of the jungle and virgin frontier eclipsing the decayed and crumbling ruins of old "civilization."

Heitor Villa-Lobos was one of the most prolific composers of the twentieth century. He is said to have lost count of the pieces he wrote; about two thousand works are credited to him. His influence on the music of Latin America was enormous, and his death left a distinct vacancy in the world of modern music. In 1987, centennial celebrations of his birth took place in many nations.

Bibliography

Appleby, David P. *Heitor Villa-Lobos: A Bio-Bibliography.* Bio-Bibliographies in Music 9. New York: Greenwood Press, 1988. A short informal biography is followed by a complete listing of the composer's works and performances, including dates of composition and first performances. The discography section lists all major recordings and recently available recordings. Includes a selected bibliography, two appendices, and index.

Gustaphson, Ralph. "Villa-Lobos and the Man-Eating Flower: A Memoir." *Music Quarterly* 75 (Spring, 1991): 1-11. This remembrance of Villa-Lobos by one of his friends describes the composer during a visit to the United States in 1948 and provides insights as to the composer's opinions on music, including his own music. Entertaining, thoughtful sketch.

Mariz, Vasco. *Heitor Villa-Lobos: Brazilian Composer.* Gainesville: University of Florida Press, 1963. A biography of Villa-Lobos and study of his works by a Brazilian musicologist. Mariz offers a chapter on each genre of music the composer wrote: the *Bachianas*, the *Chôros*, the chamber music, the piano compositions, the symphonies, the vocal music, and the ballets. Originally published in Portuguese in 1949.

Peppercorn, Lisa M. *Villa-Lobos, the Music: An Analysis of His Style.* London: Kahn and Averill, 1991. Peppercorn discusses selected works by Villa-Lobos and likes to point out what he borrowed from other composers, such as Claude Debussy and Peter Ilich Tchaikovsky. She does not demonstrate satisfactorily why Villa-Lobos is a great composer.

Wright, Simon. *Villa-Lobos.* Oxford Studies of Composers. New York: Oxford University Press, 1992. This study of Villa-Lobos' music is useful and concise. Includes bibliographical references and an index.

JoAnn Balingit

Cross-References

Bartók and Kodály Begin to Collect Hungarian Folk Songs (1904), p. 102; Schoenberg Breaks with Tonality (1908), p. 193; Schoenberg Develops His Twelve-Tone System (1921), p. 528; Stravinsky Completes His Wind Octet (1923), p. 561; Guthrie's Populist Songs Reflect the Depression-Era United States (1930's), p. 810.

QUANT INTRODUCES THE MINISKIRT

Category of event: Fashion and design
Time: The early 1960's
Locale: London, England

Mary Quant's effective marketing of the miniskirt started a fashion revolution that glorified youthful sexuality and freed a generation of designers from constraints of the hemline

Principal personages:
MARY QUANT (1934-   ), the onetime art student whose bold sense of style popularized the miniskirt
ALEXANDER PLUNKET GREENE (1933-1990), a fellow art student who married Quant and guided her clothing business
ANDRÉ COURRÈGES (1923-   ), a French designer whose space-age *mini-jupe* dress was a model for Quant's miniskirts
CRISTOBAL BALENCIAGA (1895-1972), the Spanish-born fashion designer who inspired Quant's use of brightly patterned tights with miniskirts
ARCHIE MCNAIR (1919-   ), a close friend of Quant and Plunket Greene whose management skill got the first Bazaar clothing store off the ground

Summary of Event

Mary Quant began raising the hemlines of her own skirts a decade before the miniskirt defined 1960's fashion, simply because she hated the long skirts fashionable in postwar London, where she was an art student at Goldsmith's College of Art. Quant never let convention stand in her way. She knew what she liked, and she did not hesitate, as she moved steadily upward in the fashion world, to use the ideas and resources of others.

She readily acknowledged that the idea of a short, short skirt—a miniskirt—came from a "whole group of designers." Her husband and business partner, Alexander Plunket Greene, once said, "We started shortening skirts in 1955 and finally Courrèges made it respectable." Quant was called the mother of "mod" fashion and the creator of the "Chelsea Look"; she shied from claiming sole credit for either.

It was at art school that she met Plunket Greene. The two quickly formed a deep and lasting bond, and they made a striking impression together: he a tall English aristocrat, she a petite schoolteachers' daughter. They determined early to go into the fashion business. When Plunket Greene turned twenty-one (Quant had been working for a few years in millinery design), he inherited five thousand pounds, and they used the money to open a boutique. They had another investor, Archie McNair, a former lawyer and an astute businessman.

The trio acquired a building in Chelsea, a London neighborhood bubbling with antiestablishment creativity. Young artists, writers, musicians, and actors flocked to Chelsea to explore a new world of expression that challenged what they considered the staid and restrictive ways of their elders. Quant and other young commercial designers burst onto this scene with a colorful exuberance that perfectly reflected the mood of the mid-1950's. Soon, thousands of teenagers, the first wave of the baby boomers born after World War II, were leaving school at an early age and earning good money in a growing economy. The juxtaposition of youthful earning power and a new fashion sense contributed to the immediate success of Quant's shop, Bazaar, which opened in 1955. It "went z-o-o-m from the start," she said.

Quant knew the types of clothing and accessories she wanted to carry at Bazaar— but in most cases, no one was designing or manufacturing them. If she found something she liked, she was often shunned by wholesalers who did not care for her eccentric appearance. She thus set about making her own fashions to sell. At first, she worked in her room, making each day's supply of stock at night after paying retail prices for fabric from department stores. Soon, she hired part-time assistants to work in her room, then full-time employees, before moving to larger quarters.

The business end of the operation was also handled in a hurried and sometimes careless way. Bazaar took in thousands of pounds a week, far more than the partners had anticipated, and often it was deposited in a dresser drawer. Unpaid bills piled up because there was no filing system at first. Because Quant, Plunket Greene, and McNair misunderstood retail pricing in the beginning, they alienated other fashion merchandisers and nearly lost the wholesalers they did have.

Yet the customers found Bazaar—and Quant's daring miniskirt designs— irresistible. Plunket Greene explained the philosophy: "The young are terrified of salespeople. Our selling people must never sell. They must be in sympathy with the young and show them things always aiming toward self-service but never to pressure them. Fashion is part entertainment and should be fun."

Quant used sex and technology as fashion tools; the birth-control pill and leggy models helped to give Quant's miniskirts a potent appeal. A textile breakthrough, the invention of Lycra in 1959, meant new possibilities. "I am trying to find a modern way to be feminine," she explained.

Quant's fashion business flourished in this culture of change. By 1964, the original Bazaar was making a million pounds a year; two more of the shops opened in London, and Quant's fashions sold in hundreds of stores in Europe, North America, Africa, and Australia. She was discovered by the fashion press, and in the early 1960's, American clothing-store chains (J. C. Penney, for one) and a home-sewing pattern firm (Butterick) asked Quant to design their sportswear collections. Not only did she tour North America to promote the miniskirt, but the international fashion establishment also rushed to London to see and buy the ever-smaller minis.

In 1965, the designer André Courrèges elevated the miniskirt to the level of haute couture by including it in his Paris collection. Although some French and American commentators decried the miniskirt for its lack of modesty and predicted its quick demise, the pages of popular magazines mirrored its growing popularity.

Miniskirts would remain fashionable into the 1990's. Quant, too, continued to turn out quirky, colorful miniskirt designs and added lines of brights tights and shoes, jewelry, cosmetics, makeup, and even bed linens and wallpaper.

Impact of Event

Mary Quant's successful marketing of the miniskirt put her at the epicenter of a "youthquake" that still rumbles through society. The miniskirt has endured as a symbol of liberated sexuality; it changed the face of fashion through the second half of the twentieth century and affected the fashion trade worldwide.

When Queen Elizabeth II awarded the Order of the British Empire to Quant in 1966, the honor was in recognition of the enormous boost that the miniskirt gave to British exports. During one short buying spree in 1965, American retailers made nearly $1 million in orders for the new London styles; twenty-five years later, fashion was the fourth-largest industry in Great Britain.

Tourism grew, too, with beautiful Chelsea girls in their provocative miniskirts acting as a magnet for visitors. ("Sex appeal has absolutely Number One priority," Quant said.) The image of a stuffy Great Britain exporting such intangibles as government and finance changed and Quant's miniskirts were a major part of the new image of "swinging London."

Quant's fashion empire expanded steadily, with sales in the millions of dollars (two more Bazaar stores opened in London in the 1960's and became tourist attractions on their own; by 1990, Quant had 150 stores in Japan alone).

With commissions for the design of scores of sportswear collections in the 1960's, Quant churned out new ideas, and Plunket Greene evaluated them for marketing potential. By the late 1960's, nearly twenty manufacturing firms worldwide held licenses to produce her clothing. Her work, though, went beyond clothing to include the development of new products: waterproof makeup, crazily textured and patterned tights, eyewear, jewelry, men's ties, and carpets. All this buoyed domestic consumption (postwar researchers found that young workers preferred spending money on clothes over any other item).

When Quant "split the fashion atom" with her uninhibited youth-oriented styles, Paris lost its place as the center of the fashion universe. London, New York, Florence, Dublin, Tokyo, Madrid—all developed as fashion centers, often with their own specialties in fabrication.

"High society had disintegrated incredibly," wrote Diana Vreeland, editor-in-chief of *Vogue* in the 1960's. "Meanwhile, the young did things their way, without regard to the old world. And anyone who wasn't with them made no difference at all."

Youth was the new engine of fashion. The miniskirt was meant to be worn on a lean body. The principal erogenous zone, long the bosom, became the leg, the thigh; then the whole body, sheathed in Lycra and highlighted with colorful plastic baubles, became an erogenous zone. Vreeland wrote that "the idea of beauty was changing. If you had a big nose it made no difference, so long as you had a marvelous body and a good carriage. You held your head high, then you were a beauty. The throat was long, the wrist slim, the legs long."

The treatment of legs at the dawn of the miniskirt era changed lingerie forever. New textiles allowed the development of tights to replace stockings held up with garter belts (and bras had to become streamlined under tight sweaters). In this respect, the miniskirt was a tease, for just as the tender inner thigh looked set to be exposed by the miniskirt, it was covered by tights.

This "erotic defusing" was part of the powerful and long-lasting women's liberation movement that was born in the 1960's. The long skirts of the past, according to the new thinking, hobbled women, immobilized them, and bound them into dependency. Miniskirts, in contrast, allowed total freedom of movement and ushered women into an age of equality.

Despite the hopeful predictions of some fashion writers that the miniskirt would not last, it grew in popularity through the 1960's. In 1969, the maxiskirt was introduced, followed by the midiskirt, but they died a quick death, rejected by women who were not ready to return to their former state of modesty (or immobility). Pants became the 1970's way for women to express fashion independence. Still, the miniskirt survived; indeed, its durability illustrates how Quant helped women break free from the dictates of fashion designers. In the 1980's, one critic noted, London designers showed "torn, misaligned clothes which show a savage rejection of polite society"—just what Quant had done twenty years earlier.

Ultimately, the miniskirt's message was that youth, British youth at first, had broken away from constraints of sexual modesty and tradition to embrace styles of great originality. In rejecting traditional English style, with its careful tailoring and slow changes, Quant and others reflected the times they lived in; they wished to reject the pessimism and hardship of the recent World War II era and longed to embrace optimism, newness, and prosperity—in short, the future.

Bibliography

Bender, Marylin. *The Beautiful People.* New York: Coward-McCann, 1967. A former fashion reporter for *The New York Times* wrote this fast-paced book, making good use of quotes and other detail to illustrate the 1960's fashion scene. Thirty-two pages of illustrations range from the model Veruschka in body paint to prominent patrons of design salons.

Ewing, Elizabeth. *Dress and Undress.* New York: Drama Book Specialists, 1978. A history of women's underwear. Shows how technology (including the development of Lycra in 1959) played a part in the miniskirt revolution. Separate bibliographies for American and British libraries.

_____. *History of Twentieth Century Fashion.* Totowa, N.J.: Barnes & Noble, 1986. A careful narrative history of fashion from 1900 to the mid-1980's. Touches on war, economics, technology, employment patterns, and designers. Nearly three hundred black-and-white illustrations, with bibliography and index.

Glynn, Prudence. *Skin to Skin: Eroticism in Dress.* New York: Oxford University Press, 1982. A tantalizing and richly illustrated guide to the erotic symbolism of dress. Humorous but thorough. Photos of the smallest miniskirts and fashion oddities such as the plastic corset.

Laver, James. *Modesty in Dress.* Boston: Houghton Mifflin, 1969. A history of modesty from earliest times. Illustrates extreme cases of fashion fetishism. Strident tone dates back to 1960's; lack of index is a weakness. Does, however, contain comprehensive bibliography for fashion and society.

McDowell, Colin. *McDowell's Directory of Twentieth Century Fashion.* Englewood Cliffs, N.J.: Prentice-Hall, 1985. A copiously illustrated, essential guide to fashion designers of the twentieth century, with cross-references to show their influences upon one another and over time. Glossary, listing of fashion awards, bibliography of autobiographies, guide to fashion education and fashion organizations.

Quant, Mary. *Quant by Quant.* New York: Random House, 1966. Freewheeling firsthand account of the life and times of the famous designer.

Steele, Valerie. *Fashion and Eroticism.* New York: Oxford University Press, 1985. Good historical overlay for *The Beautiful People* and good source for the origins of historical fashion illustrations.

Nan K. Chase

Cross-References

Poiret's "Hobble Skirts" Become the Rage (1910), p. 263; Chanel Defines Modern Women's Fashion (1920's), p. 474; Jantzen Popularizes the One-Piece Bathing Suit (1920), p. 491; The Bikini Swimsuit Is Introduced (1946), p. 1324; Dior's "New Look" Sweeps Europe and America (1947), p. 1346; Warhol's *The Chelsea Girls* Becomes a Commercial Success (1966), p. 2053; Punk's Antifashion Style First Appears (1974), p. 2299; Madonna Revolutionizes Popular Fashion, p. 2449.

SOCIAL PHILOSOPHERS REDISCOVER
THE WORKS OF HESSE

Category of event: Literature
Time: The 1960's
Locale: Germany and the United States

The themes of Hermann Hesse's fiction, widely read by American college students during the 1960's, reflect many of the issues and concerns of this turbulent era in American history

Principal personages:
HERMANN HESSE (1877-1962), a modern German writer who was awarded the Nobel Prize in Literature in 1946
FRIEDRICH WILHELM NIETZSCHE (1844-1900), a German philosopher whose work influenced Hesse
CARL JUNG (1875-1961), the founder of analytic psychology

Summary of Event

During the 1960's, students, philosophers, and members of the hippie movement in the United States rediscovered the works of Hermann Hesse, a German writer of the early twentieth century. His novels expressed rebelliousness and disillusionment with material culture, along with a search for spiritual meaning. Young people looked to Hesse and his works during the 1960's as they performed their own self-evaluations, rediscovering in his relatively obscure works Hesse's philosophies of life.

Any discussion of Hesse's American reception during the 1960's should be prefaced by a brief discussion of the life and major works of the author himself. Hesse was born on July 2, 1877, in Calw, Germany, to missionary parents. A rebellious, solitary, and highly sensitive child, he was a burden to his parents and a horror to school authorities. After years of academic failure, he returned home, and in 1895 he became an apprentice in a Tübingen bookstore. Hesse had been interested in literature since childhood, and his true vocation began to emerge during this time. His early poetry and fiction remained, for the most part, largely derivative of the themes and style of an earlier literary epoch; they were, in essence, the diffused and romantic musings of an estranged and poetic soul. Gradually, however, he began to develop a more realistic narrative style that gave his work a mature tone. Hesse moved to Basel, Switzerland, in 1899 and married in 1904.

In the autobiographical school novel *Unterm Rad* (1906; *The Prodigy,* 1957; *Beneath the Wheel,* 1968), Hesse gave expression to some of the more painful experiences of his tormented adolescent years. The characters of Giebenrath, an introspective and docile student who eventually commits suicide, and Heilner, a rebellious individualist and malcontent, represent aspects of Hesse's own personality conflicts at the time. Despite the births of two sons, Hesse's marriage began to fall apart. In 1911, he traveled to several Asian countries. In 1912, he and his family moved to Bern. His unhappy married life, the death of his father in 1916, and the outbreak of World War I cast Hesse into a deep depression. He subsequently underwent psychoanalysis with a doctor who had been a student of the famous Carl Jung, later undergoing therapy with Jung himself.

Like many of his contemporaries at this time, Hesse came under the influence of the ideas of the German philosopher Friedrich Wilhelm Nietzsche. His experiences with Nietzsche and with Jungian psychoanalysis found expression in the novel *Demian* (1919; *Demian*, 1923). He used the same technique employed in *Beneath the Wheel*, that of having two separate characters express dimensions of his own personality. *Demian* is the story of Emil Sinclair's adolescence. Sinclair, a sensitive and introspective youngster reared in a clean and well-ordered bourgeois home, first encounters evil in the world when he is blackmailed by a fellow student named Franz Kromer and becomes entangled in a web of lies, thefts, despair, and guilt. He is eventually aided by a new student, Max Demian, who becomes his mentor and idealized alter ego (what Jung had termed the imago). From Demian, Sinclair receives the Nietzschean lesson that the truth of reality lies beyond traditional bourgeois-Christian notions of good and evil; he must learn to accept both the light and the dark dimensions of the world and of his own spirit.

During 1920, Hesse wrote most of what would become one of his most popular novels, *Siddhartha* (1922; *Siddhartha*, 1951). This text gives expression to his longstanding interest in Eastern religion and philosophy and also expresses his central theme of the duality of the intellectual and spiritual versus the physical and sensual. Set in India, it is the story of a man's quest to attain enlightenment. At first Siddhartha pursues an ascetic life of contemplation with his friend Govinda, but he realizes that this path will not give him the release he seeks. He then moves to the city, where he discovers sensuality with the prostitute Kamala (with whom he has a son) and wealth and worldly power with the businessman Kamaswami. The pursuit of sensuality and material goods also proves to be a false path, and he returns to a simple life with the ferryman Vasudeva, who teaches him to listen to the constantly changing flow of the river. After he is rejected by his son, an experience that causes him to make a final complete surrender, Siddhartha finally gains self-transcendence. Hesse again took up the Eastern motif in the story *Die Morgenlandfahrt* (1932; *The Journey to the East*, 1956).

Hesse's wife became psychotic in 1918 and was hospitalized; they were divorced in 1923. When a second, short-lived marriage ended, he became even more depressed and spent most of his time frequenting the bars and jazz clubs of Zurich. These bitter years served as the basis for one of his most famous novels, *Der Steppenwolf* (1927; *Steppenwolf*, 1929), the sometimes surreal tale of the alcoholic and intellectual idealist Harry Haller, whose initials are those of Hesse himself. Isolated from bourgeois society, the estranged Haller contemplates suicide. One night, he meets the beautiful prostitute Hermine, who informs him that he will fall in love with her and that later she will ask him to murder her. She tells him that he must learn to relax and laugh at the imperfections of life; she then proceeds to teach him to dance and to make love with her friend Maria. Her friend Pablo, a jazz musician, invites him to a drug party, where he hallucinates the Magic Theater, in which he realizes that his perception of himself as a lone wolf is an illusion, that his true self consists of many, at times conflicting, wishes and desires. When he awakes, he sees Pablo and Hermine together, and in a jealous rage, he stabs her. Since she really represents the feminine part of Harry himself—the Jungian notion of the anima— she vanishes, and Harry again learns that he must affirm all aspects of life and his own self.

By 1927, Hesse's life had become more stable, and in 1931 he remarried. This marriage succeeded. He spent the remainder of his years in Switzerland in relative peace and comfort, devoting his time to writing, painting, and gardening. His last novel, *Das Glasperlenspiel* (1943; *Magister Ludi*, 1949), tells the life story of Josef Knecht in the futuristic realm of Castalia. Knecht is a master of the Glass Bead Game, a complex game in which all elements of human knowledge and experience are synthesized. As are most of Hesse's characters, Knecht is torn between the contemplative, spiritual life and the life of action and secular commitment. He eventually leaves Castalia and becomes the tutor of his friend's son. Hesse won the Nobel Prize in Literature in 1946, largely on the basis of this last ambitious novel. He died on August 9, 1962, of leukemia.

Impact of Event

The American publication of several Hesse texts during the first part of the twentieth century met a rather lukewarm response from critics. Even after he won the Nobel Prize in Literature in 1946, only nine of his novels were available in English translation. Publishers were unprepared for the sudden surge of interest in this obscure German writer during the mid-1960's, when his works became enormously popular on American university campuses and throughout various segments of the public at large. The reasons behind Hesse's phenomenal popularity during this period have as much to do with the state of American society as they do with the works of the writer himself.

During the early 1960's, the first members of the postwar "baby boom" generation began to come of age. Unlike their parents, most of whom had experienced the Great Depression and World War II, these children had been reared in the relative security and prosperity of the 1950's. They were healthy, well educated, and largely critical of the spirit of conformity and materialism, the "keep up with the Joneses" mentality that had so dominated their parents' suburban neighborhoods, filled with neatly trimmed lawns and sterile shopping malls. They were ready to explore other visions of life. Given the themes of Hesse's works, it is easy to see how he became their spiritual companion and guide.

These young people became members of the "do your own thing" era, a time of intense individualism in which personal self-expression and even eccentricity were valued. Long hair and bright clothes became the fashion as the "hippies" appeared in countless cities and towns across the United States. The individualist themes in the works of writers such as Jack Kerouac and Allen Ginsberg and in the songs of Bob Dylan seemed to echo the sentiments voiced by Hesse decades earlier through fictional characters such as Giebenrath from *Beneath the Wheel*, Sinclair from *Demian*, and Haller from *Steppenwolf*. These figures were all loners and rebels, and they gave a disaffected young generation of Americans the sense that there were kindred souls in the universe.

The 1960's were, in part, a time of Dionysian revelry; this was, after all, the era of "sex, drugs, and rock and roll." Timothy Leary urged people to "tune in, turn on, and drop out." The puritanical spirit of the 1950's gave way to the sexual license of "free love." Harry Haller's sexual liaison with Maria in *Steppenwolf*, Siddhartha's relationship with the courtesan Kamala, and the many love affairs of Goldmund in Hesse's medieval novel *Narziss und Goldmund* (1930; *Death and the Lover*, 1932; *Narcissus and Goldmund*, 1968) all seemed to echo the feelings of a generation. Experimentation with drugs such as marijuana and LSD by many young people furthered this turn to sensuality. They found this reflected in Harry Haller's drug-induced hallucinations. Music, above all, captured the spirit of the age. The psychedelic drug-inspired music of such performers as Jimi Hendrix and the Beatles proved to be the proverbial drummer to which many seemed to march. Mass concerts such as Woodstock in 1969 were truly Dionysian events in which the individual became immersed in the masses. The founding of the popular rock group *Steppenwolf* in 1968 as well as a film version of the novel in 1974 indicated how much Hesse had captured the spirit of the era.

Along with the popularity of music and the alternative experiences afforded by psychedelic drugs, the 1960's also saw an increase in interest in spirituality, especially in Eastern religions and philosophies. Many people came to reject traditional Christianity and Judaism and turned to various forms of Buddhism, especially Zen. The Beatles' short-lived flirtation with the transcendental meditation techniques of the Indian Maharishi Mahesh Yogi gave expression to what had become a major interest in the lives of numerous members of the American public. The chanting of mantras and the burning of incense were common in the typical hippie household. Again, many found similar themes in Hesse's writings. Both Hesse's father and his grandfather had been missionaries in India, and he had grown up steeped in the ideas of the East. Novels such as *Siddhartha*—which was filmed in 1973—and *The Journey to the East* seemed to reflect the trends of American society. The spiritual or existential quest that was so prominent in virtually all of Hesse's writings captivated the minds of many who believed themselves to be on similar inner journeys.

The 1960's were also a highly political time. The American military presence in Vietnam, which had begun to increase in the early 1960's under the administrations of Dwight Eisenhower and John F. Kennedy, elicited widespread protest. The ensuing controversy split the nation apart. Hesse was himself an ardent pacifist and internationalist. During World War I, he had taken a strongly antiwar position and had written numerous pieces denouncing the carnage. He was often attacked in the press for his stance by those who favored militarism. This experience is reflected in *Steppenwolf*, when Harry Haller is ostracized for his pacifist sentiments. Those who opposed the Vietnam War again found a spiritual companion in Hesse.

Protest was not confined to the Vietnam War demonstrations. There was a widespread sense of social criticism that was largely directed at the political and economic supremacy of the male-dominated, white middle class. The early 1960's saw the beginning of the Civil Rights movement, as both African Americans and whites demonstrated on behalf of equal education and equal access to public facilities for all Americans. The struggle for social equality represented only one dimension of the social criticism of the era. There was also a strong sense of antimaterialism as well as a rejection of modern technology, a "back to nature" mentality. Many of the privileged sons and daughters of middle-class families gave up their comfortable life-styles and went to live in communal groups under relatively primitive conditions. Many of Hesse's novels, especially *Steppenwolf* and *Demian*, are strongly critical of the bourgeois world, with its regimentation and materialism, as well as of the modern age. In the Magic Theater section of the former text, there is a scene in which Harry joins a rebellion against the machines of the modern world.

Above all, the 1960's were a time of youthful idealism and faith in the bringing forth of a new kind of world. Kennedy's Peace Corps and Volunteers in Service to America (VISTA) attracted thousands of people, both young and old, to altruistic service. Although most of Hesse's characters go through great personal despair and suffering, there is always a sense that change for the better is possible, that there is an ultimate spiritual meaning to existence. This last message appealed to thousands of Americans who, during this turbulent era, sought affirmation of their own lives. They read Hermann Hesse, and he spoke to them.

Bibliography

Boulby, Mark. *Hermann Hesse: His Mind and Art.* Ithaca, N.Y.: Cornell University Press, 1967. A perceptive discussion by a respected scholar that explores Hesse's thematic and aesthetic concerns. Contains notes and bibliography.

Casebeer, Edwin F. *Hermann Hesse.* New York: Crowell, 1972. A somewhat cursory but acceptable study for the beginning student. Contains notes and bibliography.

Rose, Ernst. *Faith from the Abyss: Hermann Hesse's Way from Romanticism to Modernity.* New York: New York University Press, 1965. A good scholarly commentary on the modernist existential themes in Hesse's major works. Contains notes and bibliography.

Ziolkowski, Theodore. *The Novels of Hermann Hesse: A Study in Theme and Structure.* Princeton, N.J.: Princeton University Press, 1965. One of the best scholarly works in English on Hesse's major texts. Recommended to the advanced student who seeks detailed and perceptive discussions. Contains notes and bibliography.

——————, comp. *Hesse: A Collection of Critical Essays.* Englewood Cliffs, N.J.: Prentice-Hall, 1973. A first-rate English-language collection of essays by both

American and European critics, edited by a leading Hesse scholar. Contains chronology, notes, and bibliography.

Thomas F. Barry

Cross-References

Jung Publishes *Psychology of the Unconscious* (1912), p. 309; *The Metamorphosis* Anticipates Modern Feelings of Alienation (1915), p. 396; Eliot Publishes *The Waste Land* (1922), p. 539; Mann's *The Magic Mountain* Reflects European Crisis (1924), p. 588; *Catch-22* Illustrates Antiwar Sentiment (1961), p. 1866; Vonnegut's *Cat's Cradle* Expresses 1960's Alienation (1963), p. 1939; Hendrix Releases *Are You Experienced?* (1967), p. 2092; The Beatles Release *Sgt. Pepper's Lonely Hearts Club Band* (1967), p. 2098; The Woodstock Music Festival Marks the Climax of the 1960's (1969), p. 2180.

SITUATION COMEDIES DOMINATE TELEVISION PROGRAMMING

Category of event: Television and radio
Time: The 1960's
Locale: The United States

Situation comedies featuring ridiculous premises, gimmicky situations, bizarre characters, and slapstick silliness became popular on American television

Principal personages:
JAMES AUBREY (1918-   ), the CBS president who guided that network to ratings leadership with situation comedies
PAUL HENNING (1911-   ), the creator of *The Beverly Hillbillies*, the highest-rated 1960's situation comedy
NEWTON MINOW (1926-   ), a Federal Communications Commission chairman and critic of 1960's programming

Summary of Event

By the early 1960's, a number of factors resulted in the proliferation of youth-oriented situation comedies and other escapist fare on American television. The baby-boom generation had grown up with the medium and by that time constituted a viable market. Concurrently, escapist situation comedies were becoming the most popular programs among corporate sponsors. Advertisers reasoned that such comedies rarely dealt with conflict and that audiences did not become as emotionally involved with such shows as they did with dramatic programs. Consequently, it was believed, viewers were not irritated when a commercial interruption occurred. Additionally, situation comedies were establishing themselves as the highest-rated programs by the early 1960's. Humorous programming also satisfied those who wished to decrease the amount of violence presented on television. The era was marked by programmers' reliance upon farfetched premises, gimmicks, vaudeville and slapstick humor, and characters who ranged from corny to campy to literally otherworldly.

With the coming of a new decade, all three networks and their major sponsors saw the profitability of escapist programming. Five genres of escapist shows soon developed. Shows that centered around the humor of growing up were the first to emerge. There were the rural, folksy shows that became the staple of the Columbia Broadcasting System (CBS) and the prime-time cartoon shows that became identified with the American Broadcasting Company (ABC). The other genres were dispersed throughout the networks. These include farcical comedies and gimmick programs. Although most of the programs would fall into a particular category, elements of other genres were often seen in all programs.

The humorous trials and tribulations of youth were included in a number of situation comedies during the 1950's. *Leave It to Beaver* and *The Adventures of Ozzie and Harriet* are but two examples. The "traditional family" was still the focus of these programs, and for the most part, the situations that occurred were common to families across the United States. Most also presented a moral along with the humor. Two programs that debuted in the 1959-1960 season, though, broke from this format and became harbingers of new trends. In *Dennis the Menace*, Jay North starred as the high-spirited comic-strip character. He was forever involving the hapless Mr. Wilson in humorous incidents that sometimes bordered on the absurd. *The Many Loves of Dobie Gillis*, featuring Dwayne Hickman and Bob Denver, dealt with late adolescence in an offbeat and witty manner. In both programs, the focus was on humor, not the teaching of a lesson. Later lighthearted youth comedies included *Gidget*, starring Sally Field as a coastal California teenager, and *The Patty Duke Show*, which chronicled the lives of two lookalike but personally dissimilar cousins.

The rural, folksy genre was established by CBS in 1960 with the premiere of *The Andy Griffith Show* and was nurtured by network president James Aubrey. Griffith was featured as the easygoing sheriff in the fictitious town of Mayberry, North Carolina. He was supported by a cast consisting of characters steeped in local color. While primarily escapist comedy, the show did have its serious and sentimental moments. Although it viewed rural residents in a humorous manner, it generally did not portray them negatively. The success of the show's folksy theme led to the creation of a number of rurally set comedies that made no pretense of seriousness. Included in this group was the Griffith spinoff *Gomer Pyle, U.S.M.C.*, starring Jim Nabors as an incompetent but likable Marine. The mainstay of the CBS rural lineup, and indeed one of the most popular shows in television history, was *The Beverly Hillbillies*. Created by Paul Henning and starring veteran actor Buddy Ebsen, the program centered on the misadventures of the Clampetts, a newly rich Ozark mountain family who had moved to a mansion in Beverly Hills. The show was disdained by critics but loved by the public; although eight of the series' episodes were among the fifteen highest-rated single programs of the 1960's, critics complained about the absurdity of the show's premise and the manner in which rural people were portrayed. *The Beverly Hillbillies* spawned two spinoff series, *Petticoat Junction* and *Green Acres*.

The prime-time cartoon genre was established on ABC during the 1960 season. *The Flintstones*, created by the Hanna-Barbera production team and advertised as an adult cartoon series, received the bulk of the advance publicity. Essentially a Stone Age version of *The Honeymooners*, *The Flintstones* showed some imagination in its adaptation of prehistoric animals and artifacts into the lives of a suburban family, but the show suffered from predictable plots and mediocre animation. Other Hanna-Barbera cartoons included *Top Cat* (an attempt at a feline *Sergeant Bilko*) and the space-age *The Jetsons*, which was essentially *The Flintstones* in reverse. Perhaps the most adult-oriented prime-time cartoon was *The Bugs Bunny Show*, which relied upon old Warner Bros. movie-theater shorts. As a result, it had higher-quality animation and greater plot sophistication than the other prime-time cartoons.

Although farce had previously been used in such programs as *I Love Lucy* and *The Honeymooners*, there was a wider range of format and quality of this style during the 1960's. In the early part of the decade, *Car 54, Where Are You?*, *McHale's Navy*, and *I'm Dickens—He's Fenster* were featured, along with one of the most critically despised programs in television history, *Gilligan's Island*. The latter show, which dealt with the absurd adventures of the marooned passengers of a small cruise ship, has often been referred to as a prime example of banality in television. Later in the decade, the World War II prison-camp comedy *Hogan's Heroes* and the spy spoof *Get Smart* continued the tradition of farce in situation comedies. Although some questioned the choice of a prison camp as a setting for comedy, Bob Crane did lead a cast of solid comic actors. In *Get Smart*, Don Adams received critical praise for his deadpan portrayal of the incompetent spy Maxwell Smart. Another show of note was *The Monkees*. This half-hour situation comedy with musical interludes had some innovative features, although it was primarily a promotion vehicle for a made-for-television rock band. Farce and vaudeville also made their way into variety programs and were used in topical and innovative style in the top-rated *Rowan and Martin's Laugh-In* and the controversial *The Smothers Brothers Comedy Hour*.

Gimmick programs, ranging from absurd nonsense to witty, clever chicanery, were another genre. The style was launched in 1961 when *Mr. Ed* became a surprise hit in syndication. Later that year, CBS began to carry the series, which featured Alan Young as the owner of a talking horse. The gimmick of young men having an unusual conversation companion continued with *My Favorite Martian* and *My Mother the Car*. Supernatural and bizarre premises were also utilized. *The Addams Family*, created by cartoonist Charles Addams and starring John Astin and Carolyn Jones, was a clever spoof on a wealthy but strange family. *The Munsters* depicted a family of horror-film lookalikes in a middle-class household. *Bewitched* and *I Dream of Jeannie* starred Elizabeth Montgomery and Barbara Eden as characters with magical powers, while *The Flying Nun* featured Sally Field as an airborne nun. Although not a situation comedy, *Batman*, starring Adam West, was such a campy comic-book takeoff that it actually was quite humorous. One of the worst series in this genre was *The Hathaways*, a short-lived show about a family raising chimpanzees in a middle-class American household.

By the early 1970's, the tumultuous nature of the American political and social scene caused a shift in situation comedies. Beginning with *All in the Family*, relevancy became the focus of many shows. As a result, the lighthearted youth-oriented genre became outmoded. By the middle of the decade, after the American withdrawal from Vietnam and the Watergate crisis, escapist comedies made a mild comeback and continued to have some success in later decades. The style, however, was never to regain the overwhelming popularity it enjoyed during the 1960's.

Impact of Event

The popularity of the 1960's youth-oriented situation comedies brought forth a debate that became a central focus in television history. From the offices of the network and corporate sponsor executives to the living rooms of viewers, a recurring question has been asked—is it the quality of a program or the quantity of its audience that is the true measure of a program's success? The debate revolves around the fact that most American television has been controlled by private enterprise; the profit motive has thus been a critically important factor in many programming decisions.

Disillusionment with television grew soon after the escapist programming began in the 1960's. Although critics were quick to find fault with weak shows during the 1950's, they could take heart in the high-quality drama, variety, and comedy that was presented in the medium's "golden age." With more escapist fare making its way to the airwaves, however, serious questioning of television's future was under way. On May 9, 1961, newly appointed Federal Communications Commissioner (FCC) chairman Newton Minow launched the critical barrage at the annual National Association of Broadcasters convention in Washington, D.C. In the past, most speakers at the convention had offered praise and mild suggestions for improvement, but Minow, a former law partner of Adlai Stevenson, shocked the major television executives with scathing remarks about the medium. He referred to television as a "vast wasteland" consisting of "very, very few" enjoyable programs. He then implied that much of television programming was terrible because the network executives lacked creativity and settled for mediocrity.

The reaction to Minow's critique was mixed. "Vast wasteland" became the chosen phrase used to describe the lack of quality in television programming for years to come. The cry for more thoughtful and intelligent series was taken up annually by television critics. Network executives promised to make reforms and took some steps in the direction of more news and dramas. Yet the public's desire for escapist television continued. Since the major goal of television was network and sponsor profit, executives continued to schedule simplistic series that people would watch.

The debate spurred by the 1960's escapist situation comedies was not a simple case of good versus bad. The role of the networks and the public was complex. Since Americans were watching these shows, it could be argued that the networks merely reflected the nation's taste. According to some, it would have been presumptuous and financially disastrous for television executives to impose the preferences of critics and the intelligentsia upon the whole viewing audience. This argument was countered by the claim that, if given enough exposure to high-quality shows, the American public would eventually come to prefer such programs. In this scenario, the networks could serve in the capacity of teachers to their viewers. Some also argued that nothing was wrong with using television simply as a recreational activity. After a hard day of work, a few hours of escapist fare could be a pleasant diversion. Moreover, some of these youth-oriented situation comedies were actually quite witty and clever. Opponents countered by claiming that television should offer more alternatives to such simplistic shows. It was also noted that a constant diet of escapism could be detrimental to certain viewers, especially children.

Throughout the 1960's, 1970's, and 1980's, the debate over quality in television continued. The decline of network domination within the industry reduced the controversy to some extent, since by the mid-1980's most viewers in the United States had gained access to high-quality programming on cable or public television. Still, the criticisms regarding the merits of network programming continued. Such issues seemed likely to be debated as long as people have different perceptions of what television should accomplish. In effect, the dubious quality of many of the 1960's youth-oriented situation comedies was the beginning of a greater public and critical input into the nature of television programming.

Bibliography

Brooks, Tim, and Earle Marsh. *The Complete Directory to Prime Time Network TV Shows, 1946-Present.* 4th ed. New York: Ballantine Books, 1988. Lists cast members, dates of broadcast, and other useful information about thousands of shows. Also provides summaries of program premises and discusses broadcast histories.

Castleman, Harry, and Walter J. Prodrazik. *Watching TV: Four Decades of American Television.* New York: McGraw-Hill, 1982. Gives an excellent description of the 1960's situation comedies and discusses their critical and popular merits. A valuable source in understanding the development of television.

Fireman, Judy, ed. *TV Book: The Ultimate Television Book.* New York: Workman, 1977. Brief articles on numerous facets of television history. Some references to the 1960's situation comedies are made. Information regarding ratings and programming is included.

Gitlin, Todd. *Inside Prime Time.* New York: Pantheon Books, 1983. Deals with a wide variety of program formats. The focus is on the decision-making process of program selection; provides a good insight into the reasons why the 1960's situation comedies were aired.

Marc, David. *Comic Visions: Television Comedy and American Culture.* Boston: Unwin Hyman, 1989. An excellent chronicle of the relationship of situation comedies and public viewership. Although all venues of television comedy are discussed, there is a great deal of information relevant to the 1960's situation comedies. The style is scholarly, but the book can be recommended to a general readership.

Paul J. Zbiek

Cross-References

THE FLINTSTONES POPULARIZES
PRIME-TIME CARTOONS

Category of event: Television and radio
Time: 1960
Locale: The United States

Cartoons took on new significance as The Flintstones, *a satirical look at modern-day life, aired during peak adult viewing hours*

> *Principal personages:*
> WILLIAM HANNA (1910-   ), a cofounder of Hanna-Barbera and the pioneer of *The Flintstones*
> JOSEPH BARBERA (1911-   ), a cofounder and executive producer of Hanna-Barbera and the man who developed *The Flintstones*

Summary of Event

By scheduling *The Flintstones* during prime-time hours, the American Broadcasting Company (ABC) showed initiative. No other major television network had considered airing a cartoon during peak adult viewing time. Produced originally by Hanna-Barbera Productions, *The Flintstones* did not exhibit any outstanding cartoon merit, yet the program aired for six full seasons. As a programming decision, ABC's choice was inspired; *The Flintstones* became the most popular cartoon of all time. Decades after its cancellation, *The Flintstones* remained widely seen through syndication. More than three hundred million people in eighty countries have watched *The Flintstones* in dozens of languages.

The Flintstones centers on Fred Flintstone, who lives in the town of Bedrock. Fred and his family live in suburbia with a twist—the setting is Stone Age suburbia. Fred is married to Wilma, who acts as a devoted and very tolerant wife. While Fred is a kind and considerate husband, he believes a wife's place is in the home.

Living in a split-level cave next door are the Flintstone's neighbors, Barney and Betty Rubble. There is nothing that Barney would not do for his friend and mentor Fred. Barney is not bright, and he usually ends up having to explain to Wilma and Betty why his latest escapade with Fred has gone seriously wrong. Most of the time, Wilma and Betty can only laugh and commiserate with each other at the way Fred has managed to get Barney involved in his schemes. The Stone Age housewives simply describe their unpredictable husbands as "the boys." No matter what happens to Fred and Barney, their wives always accept them back with laughs and hugs.

The Flintstones was based on the very successful 1950's live-action situation comedy *The Honeymooners.* Like *The Flintstones, The Honeymooners* satirizes the American life-style. Jackie Gleason played the bombastic husband Ralph Kramden; Art Carney played Ralph's ever-present sidekick Ed Norton. When Mel Blanc auditioned to play the part of the voice of Barney Rubble, he was asked by Hanna-Barbera to imitate the voice of Art Carney. Blanc told the studio that he did not imitate other people, at which point Blanc gave a rendition of what became the famous voice of Barney Rubble.

The Honeymooners is more biting and satirical than *The Flintstones*. Ralph Kramden is much more cynical about life than Fred is, and he treats his wife with far less respect than Fred does Wilma. *The Flintstones* manages to lose much of the biting edge of *The Honeymooners* and replaces the earlier show's dark comedy with slapstick. Neolithic Bedrock provides numerous opportunities to enhance the simple stories with time-appropriate solutions. Whereas the Brooklyn apartment of the Kramdens is quite sparse, the Flintstone residence has every convenience.

Wilma vacuums the floor with the long trunk of a friendly baby mastodon. A needle-billed bird plays the family's records. When Fred sits down at the piano to play for his family, the instrument of choice is of course the "Stoneway." Before going to work in the morning at the Rock Heap and Quarry Construction Company, Fred uses his automatic razor, a clam shell with a bee flying around inside. A hungry buzzard acts as a garbage-disposal unit, and a wide-billed pelican is used as a waste receptacle. Wilma dusts her house with a long-necked plumed bird, giving special attention to the turtle lampshade. Out in the yard, Fred can be seen cutting the lawn with a sharp-toothed dinosaur strapped to a stone-wheeled cart. Denizens of the Bedrock community have drive-through restaurants, a bowling alley, and a Y.C.M.A. (Young Cave Men's Association). For the Flintstones, Bedrock proves to be the perfect middle-class suburb.

By the end of *The Flintstones'* first season, the show had become part of American viewing habits. To open the show's second season, the cartoon featured a much-publicized appearance by songwriter Hoagy Carmichael. The episode marked the first time a celebrity portrayed an animated character in a cartoon. Such innovation only enhanced the show's ratings. For the episode, Carmichael wrote and performed his own music; to fit the occasion, the music was written in "rocks-trot time." Introducing celebrities further established *The Flintstones* as the forerunner of the new animation. Other guest appearances were made by Tony Curtis, who played "Stony Curtis," and Cary Grant, who played the matinee idol "Cary Granite." The cartoon appealed as much to adults as to children, and its ratings soared when actress Ann-Margret played herself and sang in the episode entitled "Ann Margrock Presents."

Executive producers William Hanna and Joseph Barbera had discovered in the making of the cartoon *Huckleberry Hound* that adding satirical humor attracted an adult audience. Building on this success, the writers of *The Flintstones* incorporated as much satire as was possible. This in turn encouraged a strong adult viewership and caused Fred's "yabba-dabba-doo" cry to become a symbol of the new American cartoon. For thirty minutes each week, families could gather around the television and enjoy the Flintstones and the Rubbles living the American Dream in Bedrock, the seat of Cobblestone County.

Impact of Event

Television entertainment, like its motion-picture counterpart, demands continual change and innovation. Up until the late 1950's, cartoons had been very expensive to produce. Television continued to have a voracious appetite for programming that in many ways obliged the makers of cartoons to become more cost-effective. Hanna-Barbera was at the time producing two very successful cartoons, *Yogi Bear* and *Huckleberry Hound*, which were the prototypes for *The Flintstones.*

A new method of creating cartoons had been developed at Hanna-Barbera. By maintaining a stationary background and limiting characters' facial expressions to only six movements, the cost of making a cartoon was vastly reduced. For some, this new method suggested a step backward in the field of animation. On a strictly economic basis, however, television could now successfully air cartoons more regularly as a result of reduced production costs. The number of drawings required to make a thirty-minute show was reduced in some instances by nearly ninety-seven percent.

Previously, such studios as Walt Disney, Metro-Goldwyn-Mayer, and Warner Bros. had placed great emphasis on the quality of their animation. Disney led the way in this respect and had become the industry standard; any full-length Disney animated film was assured success at the box-office. More basic cartoons still appealed to audiences, who were interested as much in character and story as in breadth of animation technique. *The Flintstones* managed to bring these two dimensions together.

Situation comedies and soap operas had become the staples of television by the late 1950's. Television operated on the basis of providing entertainment that offered an escape from everyday responsibilities. With *The Flintstones*, that escape also provided a humorous look at modern America. At a time when new inventions were continually making housework less laborious, *The Flintstones* managed to mimic this new trend in technology.

Social commentary is always best received when approached indirectly. *The Flintstones*, unlike *The Honeymooners*, took a mellow approach to living in a progressive society. Bedrock had all the conveniences that a modern twentieth century city had, yet life seemed easier and simpler. The message that *The Flintstones* presented in its half-hour broadcasts was that technology served man, and not the other way around.

Fred Flintstone in many ways typified the early 1960's American male. Fred was a simple man at heart whose first priority was his family. A strong believer in the work ethic, he exemplified middle-class America. Politics, religion, and sex were subjects that did not seem to exist in prehistoric Bedrock. What did matter to the Flintstones was getting the lawn mowed on the weekend and perhaps going and watching a film at the drive-in theater or listening to Fred play on the Stoneway. The most difficult part of Fred's life was dealing with his boss, Mr. Slate, at the gravel pits where Fred worked. *The Flintstones*, unlike many other animated cartoons, managed to appeal to the adult community through stories that had much relevance to everyday life. In many ways, *The Flintstones* represented real people with whom audiences could identify. In turn, the show's real-life basis assured its popularity. The Flintstones and Rubbles, along with their families, became more than mere cartoon characters—

they became part of the decade's cultural fabric.

The birth of Fred and Wilma's daughter Pebbles was a major television event. Never before in television or theater cartoons had there been such anticipation of the arrival of a child. The birth of Pebbles on February 22, 1963, was the highest-rated television birth since Lucille Ball, playing the character of Lucy in *I Love Lucy*, gave birth to her television son. With the adoption of a son by the Rubbles later in the season, both families on *The Flintstones* could boast special offspring, making the television families' lives even more like the lives of the baby-boom families that were the show's audience.

Taking the formula that had been developed with *The Flintstones*, Hanna-Barbera launched *The Jetsons* in September of 1962. *The Jetsons*, too, was family-based, with episodes revolving around George Jetson, his wife Jane, and their children, Judy and Elroy. *The Jetsons* was a fast-paced show that portrayed a future in which machines perform many of life's daily tasks. Though designed to appeal to the same audience as *The Flintstones*, the show did not do as well as expected and was soon canceled. In 1985, forty-one new episodes were made, and this time *The Jetsons* became popular.

The Flintstones have managed to remain timeless. Successive generations have been able to identify with the cartoon family, and the program attained lasting success in syndication. While the show was never intended as anything more than mere entertainment, somehow *The Flintstones* managed to represent an America that was hardworking and enjoyed the fruits of a technological society.

Bibliography

Lenburg, Jeff. *The Encyclopedia of Animated Cartoon Series*. Westport, Conn.: Arlington House, 1981. One of the most comprehensive and complete guides to cartoons produced up until 1980. Every Flintstone episode is listed along with the season in which it first aired. A valuable reference for any cartoon aficionado, as the book cites all the major cartoons made for theatrical and television distribution.

Sennett, Ted. *The Art of Hanna-Barbera: Fifty Years of Creativity*. New York: Viking Studio Books, 1989. A lavishly produced book; the introduction gives a brief history of the founders of Hanna-Barbera. Every cartoon series Hanna-Barbera produced is discussed. *The Flintstones* is discussed in considerable detail.

Solomon, Charles. *Enchanted Drawings: The History of Animation*. New York: Alfred A. Knopf, 1989. Follows animation from the first known commercial cartoons to the 1980's. The approach is historical, although the emphasis is to show that cartoons play an important role in modern culture. Solomon's contention is that the cartoon has a legitimate place in entertainment programming.

Woolery, George W. *Animated TV Specials: The Complete Directory to the First Twenty-Five Years, 1962-1987*. Metuchen, N.J.: Scarecrow Press, 1989. More than just a reference book, this volume gives a brief synopsis of some of the many special episodes of *The Flintstones* that aired after the original series. Each synopsis outlines the main plot of an episode and explains the outcome; these specials tried to recreate the Flintstones in their heyday.

_____. *Children's Television: The First Thirty-Five Years, 1946-1981.* Metuchen, N.J.: Scarecrow Press, 1983. Another comprehensive title from Woolery. Gives a complete list of all principal characters and voices of *The Flintstones*. Also has an extensive article outlining the origins of the cartoon and a complete index to all the spin-offs from the original work. An invaluable guide for those who want to compare *The Flintstones* with other cartoons of the period.

Richard G. Cormack

Cross-References

Disney Releases *Snow White and the Seven Dwarfs* (1937), p. 1053; Disney's *Fantasia* Premieres and Redefines the Boundaries of Animation (1940), p. 1195; ABC Makes a Landmark Deal with Disney (1954), p. 1612; *The Honeymooners* Enchants Audiences of All Ages (1955), p. 1673; *Captain Kangaroo* Debuts (1955), p. 1678; *Sesame Street* Revolutionizes Children's Programming (1969), p. 2185; *The Simpsons* Debuts, Anchoring the Fledgling Fox Network (1990), p. 2652.

GODARD'S EXPRESSIONISTIC À *BOUT DE SOUFFLE* REVOLUTIONIZES FILM

Category of event: Motion pictures
Time: 1960
Locale: France

Jean-Luc Godard, the most innovative of the French New Wave directors, applied expressionistic concepts of modern art to filmmaking and changed the medium forever

Principal personages:
> JEAN-LUC GODARD (1930-   ), the iconoclastic genius who has indelibly influenced filmmakers worldwide
> JEAN-PAUL BELMONDO (1933-   ), the actor who played the antihero of *À bout de souffle* and went on to become an international star
> JEAN SEBERG (1938-1979), a beautiful American actress whose performance in *À bout de souffle* gained worldwide attention
> CLAUDE CHABROL (1930-   ), a leading member of the French New Wave movement who served as production supervisor of *À bout de souffle*
> FRANÇOIS TRUFFAUT (1932-1984), another leading New Wave director whose story treatment was used for *À bout de souffle*

Summary of Event

Jean-Luc Godard's *À bout de souffle*, released in English-speaking countries under the title *Breathless* in 1961, received widespread critical acclaim when it appeared. The story moves at a "breathless" pace from start to finish. The hero, Michel Poiccard, played by the homely but charismatic Jean-Paul Belmondo, is a small-time hoodlum who seems to specialize in stealing cars and fencing them to crooked dealers. "Seems" is an indispensable word to use in describing any Godard film, because this director has never gone to any great trouble to explain plot points to his audience.

Almost immediately, Michel steals a flashy Oldsmobile convertible. His passion for American cars is symbolic of the onslaught of American materialism and consumer culture that Godard believed was destroying French culture. Instead of keeping a low profile, Michel passes every car on the road and soon attracts the attention of highway patrolmen. He kills one of the motorcycle officers with a pistol that he happens to find in the car. Godard started a trend by photographing the murder in slow motion and with diffused lighting, as if it were a subject of aesthetic interest.

Abandoning the stolen car, Michel flees on foot across the fields. He soon learns from the newspapers that the police have identified him and are hot on his trail. Oddly enough, Michel does not seem frightened. Godard shows him admiring a large photograph of Humphrey Bogart in front of a theater, and the viewer understands that Michel is trying his best to emulate his tough, worldly American film hero. Like Bogart, Michel is constantly smoking cigarettes and letting them hang from the corner of his mouth as "Bogie" did in some of his most famous films, such as *The Maltese Falcon* (1941) and *The Big Sleep* (1946).

Instead of going into hiding, Michel begins courting an American woman named Patricia Franchini, who is played by Jean Seberg. Patricia aspires to be a journalist but is making a living by doing a little modeling and selling copies of the European edition of the *New York Herald Tribune* out on the boulevards. She speaks French with a strong American accent; here again, Godard evidently wishes to emphasize Michel's fatal attraction to things American.

Michel has no car and no money, but this does not seem to bother him. In a restaurant toilet, he casually knocks a patron unconscious and robs him of his wallet in order to pay for his meal. Evidently, Godard's antihero is completely devoid of a moral conscience; he is a true citizen of the godless modern world. He has acquired his values from watching American films, which emphasize materialism and are produced only for the purpose of making money.

Michel's name and photograph begin appearing in Paris newspapers. He seems to enjoy his notoriety and does not react with appropriate concern to the fact that he is facing execution or a lifetime in prison. When Patricia finds out from the police that Michel is wanted for murder, this information only seems to whet her interest in him. Soon she is helping him to elude the police and riding around with him in yet another stolen American car while he tries to raise money.

The relationship between these modern young lovers is almost the antithesis of that between such classic lovers as Romeo and Juliet. Michel and Patricia are incapable of communicating. Both are selfish individuals lost in their private fantasy worlds. When Patricia becomes either bored or disenchanted, she casually turns Michel in to the police, and he dies on a Paris street with a bullet in his back. With his dying breath, he calls her a bitch. Ironically, her French is so rudimentary that she does not even understand the insult. Patricia seems to symbolize the attractiveness and shallowness of American culture, and Michel's last words are a double entendre, expressing Godard's and Truffaut's love-hate attitude toward the United States.

In *À bout de souffle*, Godard took the hackneyed gangster story that had been told repeatedly in American films and showed how it could be used for social commentary. The film naturally showed the impact that American art forms and American values were making on the rest of the world in the second half of the twentieth century. American art had generally been regarded by Europeans as a second-rate imitation of European art, but that was true only of the older art forms such as literature and painting. In the new art forms such as film, the Americans were the innovators, even though Europeans might object to the purely commercial spirit that was often so evident in Hollywood productions. Godard caught the spirit of American films while rejecting their capitalistic profit motive.

À bout de souffle was highly successful at the box office and received enthusiastic reviews in Europe. When it was released in the United States under the title *Breathless*, it excited great interest and controversy there as well. Roger Angell, writing in *The New Yorker*, stated that the film was "far and away the most brilliant, most intelligent, and most exciting movie I have encountered this season." Pauline Kael called it "the most important New Wave film which has reached the United States."

Impact of Event

Many essays have been written about Godard's technique, philosophy, and politics, often leading the reader into a morass of Hegelian and Marxist terminology and failing to explain the simple fact that audiences flock to attend retrospectives of his films. Throughout his career, Godard has done with the film story what painters such as Pablo Picasso were doing with the subjects that they painted: Godard has been using the motion picture as a vehicle for expressing his own feelings. Often the story seems bizarre and confusing, just as a Picasso painting often seems grotesque to anyone who does not understand that the great Spanish artist's purpose was to express his feelings and not to produce an accurate copy of reality.

This artistic expressionism had been the dominant trend in modern art throughout the twentieth century, but it was only with the French New Wave that filmmakers demonstrated how it could be applied to film. With Godard as leader, the New Wave movement introduced the concept of the director as *auteur* (that is, author). The director was no longer a hired hand who faithfully rendered a script onto film but a creative artist who used the script as a vehicle for self-expression.

In *À bout de souffle*, Godard took the camera outside the studio. His films have always expressed a passion for the outdoors, and he understood that this freedom to move about in the world was one of the great advantages of motion pictures over stage dramas. While outside, Godard's camera revels in the wealth of things to be seen in a fascinating city such as Paris or in the beautiful scenery of France.

It is typical of Godard to pay as much attention to the background as to the foreground of a shot, as much attention to the faces of passersby as to those of the characters in his story. For the American viewer, watching a Godard film is like taking a trip to France and being admitted into even the most secret places. This approach to filmmaking naturally places the viewer in a different position vis-à-vis the plot. The viewer is made to feel like a voyeur who has somehow become interested in a certain set of people but who might lose them in the crowd at any moment. When a Godard character disappears to steal a car or make a telephone call, the viewer has no guarantee that that character is ever coming back.

Often the viewer does not even know the characters' names or anything about their past history. A New Wave director such as Godard does not bother to introduce his characters to the audience, any more than he would bother to introduce himself or his film crew. This approach is meant to reflect the alienation of modern life. While audiences may not understand such philosophical or political concepts, they do respond to the feelings conveyed by Godard's films. They know what it is like to be surrounded by strangers, to go through days on end without ever seeing a familiar face, without understanding what is happening around them. They see strange events, such as car crashes or violent confrontations, and are never able to find out what happened or why.

When viewers leave the theater after seeing a typical Hollywood production, they go back into the real world; when viewers leave the theater after seeing a Godard film, they find that they are *still* in a Godard film. This reflection of reality is what viewers like about Godard and what has made him so influential. He has shown how to paint the fast-moving, complex, incomprehensible, and often frightening modern world in pictures that move and talk.

In addition to American films, animated cartoons, and comic strips, another American innovation that has captivated Godard is jazz. He frequently uses this genre as background music in his films, but the improvisational spirit of jazz is obvious in his entire approach to filmmaking. The difference between a conventional dramatic film and one by Godard is like the difference between a conventional rendition of a popular tune and one played by saxophonist Charlie Parker.

The artistic influence of Godard and the New Wave movement has been so pervasive that there is hardly a director who does not subscribe to the *auteur* theory. Godard's influence can be seen in the works of such virtuoso directors as Woody Allen, Robert Altman, John Cassavetes, Rainer Werner Fassbinder, Roman Polanski, Tony Richardson, John Schlesinger, Andy Warhol, Lina Wertmüller, Wim Wenders, and many others.

The *auteur* theory has had unfortunate results as well as brilliant ones. It has led some directors to think that they can make a good film out of any story, or even with no recognizable story at all. This fallacy has led to the production of many bad films the box-office and critical receptions of which have tended to dampen the *auteur* mania. Some considered one of the worst offenders to be writer/director Michael Cimino's production of *Heaven's Gate* (1980), which had the dubious distinction of being the biggest box-office failure in Hollywood history.

Perhaps Godard's most important influence has been in showing aspiring young filmmakers all over the world that they can produce significant works of art using simple equipment and taking advantage of natural settings. It has been argued that the most important advances in the art of cinema are made by young filmmakers using rented equipment, inexperienced crews, and unknown actors.

Bibliography

Andrew, Dudley, ed. *Breathless.* Rutgers Films. Print 9. New Brunswick, N.J.: Rutgers University Press, 1987. A collection of materials relating to the production of Godard's *À bout de souffle*, including an annotated continuity script, selections from critics' reviews, commentaries, interviews, and a filmography. The editor's intention was to suggest the aesthetic density involved in Godard's film.

Angell, Roger. "All Homage." *The New Yorker* 36 (February 11, 1961): 102-104. This enthusiastic review of *Breathless* is an example of the reception accorded Godard's film in the United States. Angell states that Godard had almost immediately become the most discussed and sought-after director in Europe.

Cameron, Ian, ed. *The Films of Jean-Luc Godard.* New York: Frederick A. Praeger, 1969. A collection of essays about Godard and his films, written by sixteen authors representing many different countries. Contains many direct quotations in which Godard discusses his technique and philosophy. Copiously illustrated with black-and-white photographs. Contains a complete filmography up to 1968 and some valuable references.

Kael, Pauline. *I Lost It at the Movies.* Boston: Little, Brown, 1965. A collection of reviews and essays by this popular and highly influential American film critic. Her book contains a discussion of *Breathless*, along with reviews of films by François Truffaut and a penetrating examination of the *auteur* theory of filmmaking in an essay entitled "Circles and Squares."

Lesage, Julia. *Jean-Luc Godard: A Guide to References and Resources.* Boston: G. K. Hall, 1979. An outstanding reference source containing biographical information, criticism, detailed descriptions of Godard's films, a film title index, an author index, a comprehensive bibliography, and a wealth of other information.

Lloyd, Ann. *The Illustrated History of the Cinema.* New York: Macmillan, 1986. This 455-page book is beautifully illustrated with both black-and-white and color photographs. Covers the evolution of filmmaking on an international scale, devoting close attention to Godard and the New Wave movement in France. The index lists hundreds of films and individuals.

Monaco, James. *The New Wave: Truffaut, Godard, Chabrol, Rohmer, Rivette.* New York: Oxford University Press, 1976. Defines the New Wave, discusses the careers of the five most prominent French directors in the movement, and examines their works in detail. Amply illustrated with black-and-white photographs to highlight the distinctive characteristics of the New Wave genre. Excellent bibliography is provided.

Roud, Richard. *Jean-Luc Godard.* Garden City, N.Y.: Doubleday, 1968. A detailed discussion of the films of Godard up to 1967 by an author regarded as an authority on his subject. Deals with Godard's complex philosophical, political, artistic, and technical theories without overly complex language. Contains many black-and-white photographs from Godard's films to illustrate the author's points.

Bill Delaney

Cross-References

Little Caesar, Public Enemy, and *Scarface* Launch the Gangster-Film Genre (1930), p. 839; Hitchcock Becomes England's Foremost Director (1934), p. 946; Welles's *Citizen Kane* Breaks with Traditional Filmmaking (1941), p. 1200; *The Maltese Falcon* Establishes a New Style for Crime Films (1941), p. 1223; The Italian New Wave Gains Worldwide Acclaim (1942), p. 1228; The French New Wave Ushers in a New Era of Cinema (1956), p. 1710.

PLATH'S *THE COLOSSUS* VOICES WOMEN'S EXPERIENCE

Category of event: Literature
Time: 1960
Locale: England

Sylvia Plath's The Colossus *fused personal pain and women's issues in revealing poems that would help to popularize "confessional" poetry*

Principal personages:
SYLVIA PLATH (1932-1963), a suicidal poet whose work gave confessional poetry a much wider audience
TED HUGHES (1930-   ), a well-known British poet, Plath's husband
THEODORE ROETHKE (1908-1963), an American poet whose autobiographical poetry of the 1940's and 1950's helped Plath find her own confessional "voice"

Summary of Event

Although Sylvia Plath's reputation as a poet was growing in the late 1950's, she had a hard time publishing her first book-length collection. After some dickering and delay, *The Colossus* was first published by Methuen Press in England in the fall of 1960. Plath herself was living in England, where she had gone to live with her British husband after her college graduation and her first literary success. There her startlingly revealing, but tightly crafted, poems were received favorably but quietly. Reviewers for *The Manchester Guardian*, *Time and Tide*, *Punch*, and other journals praised her craft and precision while in some cases criticizing the elements of gloom and negativity that dominated the collection. Plath's earlier losses, depressions, and flirtations with death are present in the poems, but they are concealed and controlled by patterns that range from sonnets to syllable-counting forms. British readers and critics basically liked her approach.

Plath, however, would not feel that she had fully arrived as a poet until she had had an American publisher issue her book and an American audience receive it. Her personal life was in turmoil during the two years between her English and American publications, and her poetic style was changing, veering more toward acutely painful revelation and away from the forms that controlled the earlier emotional outpourings and the masks that disguised them. Her husband, the poet Ted Hughes, was achieving rapid success, but her own life seemed to be on hold. Her baby took up most of her time, and she suffered a miscarriage, underwent an appendectomy, and then conceived the couple's second child. Financial pressures were an ever-present worry. Nevertheless, while she attempted to keep her life together and while she continued to write poems in her developing new style, Plath was also trying to find an American outlet for those earlier poems that she knew to be successful.

Finally, on the recommendation of Stanley Kunitz, the book was accepted by

Alfred A. Knopf for publication in 1962. (Kunitz had suggested that one or two of the poems in the British edition be deleted because they were too obviously like those of Theodore Roethke, a poet Plath much admired for his ability to weld craft to personal revelation in poems that were both moving and intelligent.) Plath returned home from the hospital after her appendectomy in March, 1961, to the good news that Knopf had bought her book. The editors finally chose to delete a number of poems, finding the collection too long, but Plath was so ecstatic upon achieving her goal of receiving a contract from a major American publisher that she did not care.

The Colossus was published on May 14, 1962. At that time, Plath's newer poems were appearing in *The New Yorker, Harper's, Poetry,* and elsewhere; her professional accomplishments were at a peak. By then, however, her personal life was deteriorating drastically. Her husband was unfaithful, and the couple separated, leaving Plath to rear two children alone and without money. Partly because of this financial need and partly because she had sold her autobiographical novel, *The Bell Jar* (1963), to Heinemann in England, Plath began to entertain the possibility of supporting herself through commercial fiction. Knopf, though, rejected *The Bell Jar*—Plath's own editor criticized its point of view as unbelievable—and she received rejections of other work as well. Her career appeared to have gone into a sudden downswing to match that of her personal life. First reviews of the American version of *The Colossus* were warm but sparse. Her frustration and desperation grew as she dealt with the difficulties of planning a divorce, taking care of the children, and trying to find time to write.

Plath's letters, poems, and notes from the period of May, 1962, until her death show that the optimism and high spirits engendered by the publication of *The Colossus* faded very quickly in the face of personal disaster and apparent professional rejection. She seemed unable to decide on a course of action and follow it. She needed to find a place to live, and she decided to remain in England, perhaps because it seemed to her that England was more hospitable to her work. Money continued to be a pressing problem. She decided to move from the country area to London; more services were available to her there, and she believed that she would have more stimulating company, but she could not find an affordable London apartment. As her last personal triumph, however, she found a flat in London in the building that had once housed William Butler Yeats and promptly moved into it, believing that Yeats's spirit would inspire her.

The winter that followed this move, however, proved to be the last straw for Plath. She found herself physically isolated with her children, cold most of the time, and sick with the flu and other illnesses. She was now writing poetry of sheer, unadulterated pain, and she was seeing doctors and psychiatrists to seek remedies for her multiple problems. Her unresolved feelings about the death of her father in her childhood merged with her rage and pain at her husband's rejection into a cloud of depression. She rose early each morning before the children and wrote agonized, death-dominated poems until her children's needs claimed her. "The blood jet is poetry," she claimed in one of her last pieces. "There is no stopping it." Yet she found a way to stop it. On the night of February 11, 1963, she left mugs of milk and plates of bread for the children, sealed the kitchen door with towels to prevent the escape of gas, turned on the taps of the gas oven, and put her head in the oven. Her suicide came less than a year after the triumph of the American publication of *The Colossus* and, ironically, was the cause of her book's later success.

Impact of Event

The publication of *The Colossus* by itself did not, as the number and extent of reviews testify, rock the literary world. Upon its appearance, the book received only a few brief notices. Ironically, the most enthusiastic first reviews of the book were written immediately but did not appear until after the poet's death; these included responses by Richard Howard and Mark Linenthal. A brief, ambivalent review appeared in the *Times Literary Supplement* in August of 1961; that and a review by an old friend, E. Lucas Myers, which offered qualified praise, may have been all the published responses available to Plath by the time of her death.

It was the suicide of the poet and the resultant attention to the problem of the troubled artist that made the name Sylvia Plath a household word and made her one of the leading figures of the confessionalist school of poetry. In fact, of course, Robert Lowell's *Life Studies* (1959) was a major influence on Plath's later poems, and Lowell and Theodore Roethke both preceded her in this subgenre. Critics of the 1970's, during which many believe the confessional mode dominated poetry, linked Plath's name with those of Roethke, Lowell, Anne Sexton, and John Berryman in a list of major confessionalist poets whose work has outlasted the trend.

A group of Plath's late poems appeared in *Encounter* five months after her death, sparking discussions of the connection between art and pathology and initiating research into Plath's work. The *Encounter* group includes two of her most intensely painful outcries, "Daddy" and "Lady Lazarus," poems dealing directly with her suicide attempts and her frantic need to cut loose from her father's ghost and her husband's memory. Interest in these poems led to increased sales of *The Colossus* and to the publication of her posthumous book *Ariel* (1965). Critics enjoyed comparing the violent and explosive poems of *Ariel* to the more formalized passions of *The Colossus*, usually to the detriment of one or the other.

A major effect of Plath's suicide was to widen the audience for poetry to those who did not usually read contemporary poetry. Many of these readers were women who found in Plath's description of her paralysis and fear in the male-dominated social machinery a mirror of their own preoccupations. *Ariel* and *The Colossus* both sold well, and Plath's work began to appear in anthologies worldwide and to leave her traces on creative writing programs, where Plathlike revelation became commonplace. Biographer Edward Butscher commented, "Her suicide seemed to have confirmed her pathological art and instigated the kind of cult worship Sylvia herself would have loved."

The suicide itself was imitated by sister poet Anne Sexton ten years later, after

Sexton had written in a poem about her envy of Plath's suicide. The two had apparently talked about methods and means of killing oneself years before. Other American poets in the 1960's and 1970's committed or attempted to commit suicide; no one can estimate what effect Plath's act had as an influence on these poets. One can only say that there was a tendency in the 1960's and 1970's, a tendency observable in the lives and works of Randall Jarrell (1914-1965), John Berryman (1914-1972), Sexton herself (1928-1974), and others, to write about nervous breakdowns and suicide attempts, and then ultimately to commit suicide. Plath was the first of this group to follow this pattern.

As the 1970's drew to a close, however, the whole phenomenon of confessional poetry diminished, and newer poetry tended to diverge in two directions. Writers such as the Language Poets composed work that was increasingly abstract and obscure; other poets, such as Carolyn Forché and Adrienne Rich, moved toward direct political statement. Critics tended to decry confessional poetry as self-indulgent and sensationalistic.

The true and lasting value of Plath's contribution to American literature, ironically, was not much noted until after the cults died down. Then it could be seen not only that Plath articulated a new female myth but also that her diction and rhythms are very finely attuned to the varying content of her work. Critics of the later periods focus on her gift for mythologizing and the consistency of her myths as well as on her skilled use of poetic conventions to contain and sustain emotion in *The Colossus.* She is also praised for representing the repression of women of her time with a level of realism few others achieved.

Bibliography

Anderson, Paul. *Rough Magic: A Biography of Sylvia Plath.* New York: Viking Penguin, 1991. Readable biography pinpointing sources of many Plath themes and images.

Bassnett, Susan. *Sylvia Plath.* Totowa, N.J.: Barnes & Noble Books, 1987. Part of the *Women Writers* series; basic critical introduction. Discusses major images and themes and introduces some of the major critics. Describes formative events in Plath's life. Easy to read, this book is a good first stop for students. Brief bibliography, index.

Butscher, Edward. *Sylvia Plath: Method and Madness.* New York: Seabury Press, 1976. A well-written biography featuring an impressive group of photographs. Detailed but readable; uses the poetry and novel to support inferences about Plath's psyche. Good endnotes; useful bibliographical notes. Index.

_____, ed. *Sylvia Plath: The Woman and the Work.* New York: Dodd, Mead, 1977. A collection of essays including reminiscences about Plath herself and interpretations of her work. Very useful for a general introduction to Plath. These essays are not heavy-duty scholarship but easy-to-read memoirs and impressionistic analyses.

Hayman, Ronald. *The Death and Life of Sylvia Plath.* New York: Carol Publishing

Group, 1991. Biography that emphasizes the suicide and what led up to it. Clear and fascinating, good writing style. No critical analysis. Good photographs. Chronology, notes, brief bibliography, index.

Kroll, Judith. *Chapters in a Mythology: The Poetry of Sylvia Plath.* New York: Harper & Row, 1976. Focuses on the mythological content of Plath's poems and traces these mythic figures and events. Well written and persuasive; of particular use to those interested in archetypal criticism or in myth generally.

Stevenson, Anne. *Bitter Fame.* Boston: Houghton Mifflin, 1989. Readable biography; good source for early Plath. Last part is blurred and dubious. Contains appendix of Dido Merwin's memories of Plath. Index.

Wagner, Linda W., ed. *Sylvia Plath: The Critical Heritage.* London: Routledge & Kegan Paul, 1988. Gives the reviews and other critical receptions of the individual Plath works. Allows the reader to see how attitudes toward Plath developed. Useful bibliography; index.

Wagner-Martin, Linda. *Sylvia Plath: A Biography.* New York: Simon & Schuster, 1987. Excellent, thoroughly researched biography. Includes unusually well-chosen photographs that capture the time period as well as sidelights of Plath's life. Very useful bibliographies, especially of primary sources. Index.

Janet McCann

Cross-References

Eliot Publishes *The Waste Land* (1922), p. 539; Woolf's *Mrs. Dalloway* Explores Women's Consciousness (1925), p. 637; Beauvoir's *The Second Sex* Anticipates the Women's Movement (1949), p. 1449; The Beat Movement Rejects Mainstream Values (1950's), p. 1460; Young Readers Embrace *The Catcher in the Rye* (1951), p. 1493; Dean Becomes a Legend in *Rebel Without a Cause* (1955), p. 1640; Shange's *for colored girls* . . . Is a Landmark (1976), p. 2370.

PSYCHO BECOMES HITCHCOCK'S MOST FAMOUS FILM

Category of event: Motion pictures
Time: 1960
Locale: The United States

Filmmaker Alfred Hitchcock defied Hollywood thinking and anticipated industry trends by making the low-budget shocker Psycho, *the film that became his most popular*

Principal personages:

ALFRED HITCHCOCK (1899-1980), a filmmaker, for whom *Psycho* would be his forty-seventh film and a departure from his previous work in its emphasis on shock and violence

JOSEPH STEFANO (1921-   ), the writer of the film script in collaboration with Hitchcock

ROBERT BLOCH (1917-   ), the author of the 1959 novel *Psycho,* from which the film's story line was drawn

BERNARD HERRMANN (1911-1975), the composer of the music for the film, a score that uses only string instruments

ANTHONY PERKINS (1932-1992), the actor who played Norman Bates, a character with a split personality loosely based on a reclusive, real-life murderer

JANET LEIGH (JEANETTE HELEN MORRISON, 1927-   ), the actress who played Marion Crane, who is murdered at the Bates Motel

VERA MILES (VERA RALSTON, 1929-   ), the actress who played Lila, Marion's sister, who undertakes the investigation of her sister's disappearance

JOHN GAVIN (JACK GOLENOR, 1928-   ), the actor who played Sam Loomis, Marion's lover

SAUL BASS (1920-   ), the designer of the opening titles and a contributor to the film's key scenes

Summary of Event

The popularity of *North by Northwest* (1959) affords a good example of Alfred Hitchcock's remark "style is self-plagiarism." A big money-maker, *North by Northwest* also conforms to a Hitchcock formula that goes back to his British thriller *The Thirty-Nine Steps* (1935): the innocent-man story structured with a double-chase plot. Hitchcock had Americanized the formula of the falsely accused protagonist pursuing the real culprit while being chased by the police in *Saboteur* (1942), though *Foreign Correspondent* (1940) and *To Catch a Thief* (1955) also employ aspects of the same design. Viewers can instantly recognize these films as Hitchcockian, but the works are also, as the director himself knew, self-imitative.

Hitchcock's search for new ideas was motivated by the box office as well as by the need for originality. As shrewd a businessman as an artist, Hitchcock still remembered the disappointment of *Vertigo* (1958), a daring psychological film that deemphasized plot and became a commercial failure. While ticket buyers enjoyed Hitchcock's return to familiar material in *North by Northwest*, the director sought something new but not too risky.

He had also noticed the recent, surprising success of some low-budget horror films. Hammer Film Productions released one of the first of these, Terence Fisher's *The Curse of Frankenstein* (1957), a technicolor retelling of Mary Shelley's novel starring Peter Cushing and Christopher Lee. Working for Allied Artists and Columbia, director William Castle combined shoestring budgets with publicity gimmicks to bring in audiences. In promoting *The House on Haunted Hill* (1958), for example, Castle requested that exhibitors run a skeleton on wires over the audience's heads (a process he called "Emergo"); for Castle's *Macabre* (1958), ushers handed out policies insuring the audience in the event of death by fright; and for *The Tingler* (1959), selected seats in the theater were wired to administer added jolts to viewers. More respectable, Henri-Georges Clouzot's *Diabolique* (1955), a black-and-white French thriller about a husband who is murdered by his wife and mistress, played to big audiences in America and won acclaim for its frightening murder-in-a-bathtub scene.

Hitchcock knew of these trends when his assistant Peggy Robertson called his attention to a review of Robert Bloch's novel *Psycho* (1959). Bloch's book fictionalized the ghastly murders committed by a real-life Wisconsin recluse named Ed Gein. In the novel, fortyish, alcoholic Norman Bates runs a seedy motel and quarrels with his hectoring, possessive mother. By funneling much of the action through Norman's consciousness, Bloch misdirects the reader and sets up a surprise ending: The brutal murders that appeared to be the work of Norman's mother (such as the shower stabbing of motel guest Mary Crane) have really been committed by Norman, who has preserved his dead mother's body for years and who has psychologically merged with her personality. Attracted by the element of Gothic horror and by the surprise murder of the heroine early in the narrative, Hitchcock purchased the film rights to Bloch's novel for nine thousand dollars.

The development of the property into a workable film treatment encountered obstacles. Paramount Pictures, the studio at which Hitchcock had most of his success in the 1950's, did not want to finance a film about necrophilia. Hitchcock decided to underwrite the film himself, to shoot it on the Universal-International lot using the crew from his television program *Alfred Hitchcock Presents*, and to have Paramount publicize and distribute the film. Hitchcock retained sixty percent ownership of the picture, a move that earned him $2.5 million in only the first four months after the film's opening on June 16, 1960. His financing of the film cost him only $800,000.

A first screenplay by writer James Cavanagh struck the wrong note by developing a love story between Mary Crane's sister and Mary's boyfriend as they investigate Mary's disappearance. Joseph Stefano met with Hitchcock in numerous story conferences to block out a narrative structure and to write a second screenplay. Stefano's idea was to begin the film with Marion (her name was changed from Mary) and her lover Sam. The opening scene of two partly clad lovers in a rented room would immediately announce the film's audaciousness. Hitchcock wanted Anthony Perkins to play Norman Bates, a casting choice that made the character more boyish and vulnerable. Stefano worked on the dialogue, while Hitchcock concentrated on the technical challenges posed by the visual set pieces of the shower murder and the killing of the detective Arbogast.

As filming neared, Hitchcock's personal financing made him unwilling to use expensive "name" stars. Janet Leigh, the most famous performer in the film, agreed to play Marion. John Gavin (Sam Loomis), Vera Miles (Lila), and Martin Balsam (Arbogast) completed the principal cast. The shooting of the film proceeded from November 11, 1959, until February 1, 1960. Oddly, the censors asked for only slight alterations. Arguing that the knife used in the shower murder is never shown to touch the victim's body (and, of course, declining to point out that the scene actually creates its violence through the staccato editing and shriek of violins), Hitchcock slipped the entire scene past the censors. Hitchcock decided on most of the deletions himself to tighten the running time of the film, which finally came to 109 minutes. He made cuts in dialogue and shortened a later scene that showed Sam's sense of loss for Marion. Joseph Stefano objected strongly to such changes and blamed the negative reaction that *Vertigo* had received for making Hitchcock reluctant to explore character deeply.

To publicize the film, Hitchcock may have reverted to the gimmicks of William Castle. He stipulated that no preview showings would be held, a decision intended to protect the secrecy of the surprise ending. The move angered many critics, however, who had to watch the film with regular audiences and who gave the film mixed or negative reviews. In another attempt to keep word of mouth from revealing the ending, Hitchcock concluded the preview trailer for *Psycho* with the warning that no one would be seated after the film had started. The publicity kit for theater owners even suggested ways to enforce this policy: the use of Pinkerton detectives, large lobby clocks, and audio speakers playing a tape of Hitchcock consoling impatient ticket buyers in line.

Impact of Event

The growth of film as a field of casual and classroom study in many ways accompanied the increased attention Alfred Hitchcock received as his career progressed. The first book about Hitchcock's films was written by Eric Rohmer and Claude Chabrol in 1957; it gave serious attention to technique and theme, in particular the theme of the transfer of guilt. The popularity of *Psycho* boosted Hitchcock's already considerable fame and fueled more critical attention. French filmmaker François Truffaut asked Hitchcock in 1962 if he would answer some five hundred questions about his career; a transcription of those fifty hours of conversation was published in 1966. Added critical scrutiny of Hitchcock and of film in general indirectly gave rise to film programs at universities. Cause and effect become tangled, but as a generalization it may be said that, just as nineteenth century university courses in William Shakespeare developed into the field of literary studies, critical attention to the films of Hitchcock did much to create film studies as a discipline.

Other influences of *Psycho* were less felicitous. Though William Castle's early films had shown Hitchcock the way, Castle and others now followed the trail of *Psycho*'s popularity. Castle's first *Psycho* imitation was *Homicidal* (1961), a black-and-white film based on a real-life case and featuring an old house, transvestitism, and a gimmick (a "fright break" just before the resolution to permit frightened viewers to leave the theater). More films followed by Castle and others: Robert Aldrich's *What Ever Happened to Baby Jane?* (1962), Castle's *Straight-Jacket* (1964), which was made from a script by Robert Bloch, Silvio Narizzano's British production *Die! Die! My Darling!* (1965), and Aldrich's *Hush . . . Hush, Sweet Charlotte* (1965). During this period Hitchcock, again trying to avoid repetition, struck out in a new direction and made *The Birds* (1963), the first of a genre that would be called "disaster movies." The string of exploitation films also continued (with series such as the *Friday the Thirteenth* and *Nightmare on Elm Street* films), creating a profitable if dubious genre known as "splatter movies."

The rise of more explicit horror and violence in films also had an effect on eroding the production code that had been the industry's self-censoring system since the 1930's. The popularity of *Psycho* illustrates well how filmmakers were beginning to realize that the film-going public actually consisted of a number of smaller audiences with different tastes. Films from the classical period of the 1930's and 1940's traditionally targeted a mass audience, but motion pictures such as *A Streetcar Named Desire* (1951), *On the Waterfront* (1954), and *Baby Doll* (1956), all directed by Elia Kazan, clearly sought out a more select audience of adult viewers. The films' mature subjects and naturalistic style in time loosened other restraints. More sexual permissiveness appeared in *Lolita* (1962), *The Pawnbroker* (1965), and *The Graduate* (1967). In 1968, the motion-picture industry abandoned the production code entirely in favor of a rating system that classified films according to their content.

Practically all of these influences were unintentional on the part of the filmmaker, who was using his talent to craft a cinematic style that would arouse emotion. Hitchcock's comments on *Psycho* emphasize his concern with style and can almost be taken as a credo for formalist filmmakers: "I feel it's tremendously satisfying for us to be able to use the cinematic art to achieve something of a mass emotion. And with *Psycho* we most definitely achieved this. It wasn't a message that stirred the audiences, nor was it a great performance or their enjoyment of the novel. They were aroused by pure film."

Bibliography

Anobile, Richard J., ed. *Alfred Hitchcock's "Psycho."* New York: Avon Books, 1974. Presents a photographic reproduction of the film in more than 1,300 frame enlargements, with the complete dialogue printed below the accompanying shots.

Although the book does not indicate camera pans, voice inflections, and the presence of music, it is useful for examining the visual design and editing of the film.

Bloch, Robert. *Psycho.* New York: Simon & Schuster, 1959. Hitchcock has sometimes been wrongly credited for material from Bloch's original novel: the early killing of the heroine, the shower murder, Norman's voyeurism, the mirror imagery. Even details such as the indentation in "mother's" bed and the final line, "She wouldn't even harm a fly," come from Bloch.

Deutelbaum, Marshall, and Leland Poague, eds. *A Hitchcock Reader.* Ames: Iowa State University Press, 1986. Designed as a text for college courses on Hitchcock, this collection of essays is intended for film devotees as well as for students. Each topical grouping has its own introduction; the fifth unit, "A *Psycho* Dossier," collects three essays and includes a bibliography.

Kendrick, Walter. *The Thrill of Fear: 250 Years of Scary Entertainment.* New York: Grove Weidenfeld, 1991. A lively survey of the history of horror as entertainment. Kendrick theorizes that the more society attempts to distance death, the more prominently horror appears in popular culture. His final two chapters are devoted to film horror, *Psycho*, and its formative influence on "splatter" films.

Naremore, James. *Filmguide to "Psycho."* Bloomington: Indiana University Press, 1973. Short (eighty-seven-page) but thoughtful companion to the film. Chapter of analysis provides a running commentary on the film, with many worthwhile insights on Hitchcock's visual artistry and skill at story construction.

Rebello, Stephen. *Alfred Hitchcock and the Making of "Psycho."* New York: Dembner Books, 1990. Drawing on interviews with Hitchcock and others as well as on the director's private papers, this is the most thorough and authoritative book on the creation of the film. Especially informative and useful on the two screenplays for the project and on the filming of the murder scenes.

Rothman, William. *Hitchcock: The Murderous Gaze.* Cambridge, Mass.: Harvard University Press, 1982. A detailed, scene-by-scene (sometimes shot-by-shot) analysis of five Hitchcock films, *The Lodger* (1927), *Murder!* (1930), *The Thirty-Nine Steps, Shadow of a Doubt* (1943), and *Psycho*, with hundreds of frame enlargements. Rothman's discerning insights, free from academic jargon, may be appreciated by general readers, film students, and scholars.

Spoto, Donald. *The Art of Alfred Hitchcock.* 2d ed. New York: Doubleday, 1992. Valuable for the breadth of its film-by-film approach. Virtually a complete rewrite of the 1976 edition, with revised judgments based on Spoto's experience teaching the films and the research for his controversial 1983 Hitchcock biography.

Truffaut, François. *Hitchcock.* Rev. ed. New York: Simon & Schuster, 1984. A transcript of fifty hours of conversation with Hitchcock on his films through *Torn Curtain* (1966). Truffaut updated the book with comments about various tributes and honors for Hitchcock from 1966 to 1979. Includes some interviews not in the first edition.

Glenn Hopp

Cross-References

Kuleshov and Pudovkin Introduce Montage to Filmmaking (1927), p. 701; Hitchcock Becomes England's Foremost Director (1934), p. 946; Welles's *Citizen Kane* Breaks with Traditional Filmmaking (1941), p. 1200; *A Streetcar Named Desire* Brings Method Acting to the Screen (1951), p. 1487; The French New Wave Ushers in a New Era of Cinema (1956), p. 1710.

PINTER'S *THE CARETAKER* OPENS IN LONDON

Category of event: Theater
Time: April 27, 1960
Locale: Arts Theatre, London, England

The Caretaker, *Harold Pinter's first widely acclaimed drama, established the career of one of the century's leading playwrights*

> *Principal personages:*
> HAROLD PINTER (1930-   ), an English dramatist whose strange plays, often imbued with a sense of menace, proved widely influential
> ALAN BATES (1934-   ), the actor who inaugurated the role of Mick in *The Caretaker*
> DONALD PLEASENCE (1919-   ), the actor who inaugurated the role of Davies
> PETER WOODTHORPE (1931-   ), the actor who inaugurated the role of Aston
> DONALD McWHINNIE (1920-1987), the play's director

Summary of Event

In early 1960, Harold Pinter was a young English playwright whose dramas *The Room* (1957), *The Birthday Party* (1958), and *The Dumb Waiter* (1959) had met with mixed receptions. Although *Sunday Times* drama critic Harold Hobson had championed Pinter's works, other reviewers had been hostile; *The Birthday Party* had lasted only one week on the London stage. Pinter's dramas, set in shabby, working-class surroundings and marked by long pauses between often terse and hesitant dialogue, reflected the influence of both absurdist literature and the "Angry Young Men" movement of 1950's Britain. Observers remarked on the distinctive aura of menace that seemed to envelop the plays despite their banal settings, but neither critics nor audiences were especially enthusiastic.

The Caretaker would change all that. Pinter's inspiration for the drama came from a conversation the author had shared with a British panhandler. The man and his milieu became the nucleus of the drama, a curious *ménage à trois* that relates to psychological and physical acts of violence that permeate humankind's impulses for power and dominance. Pinter was quick to affirm that he followed no prescriptive ideology in writing his drama and that he was not a political theorist in any way. The characters presented, however, proclaim a disengagement that renders them ineffectual as they relate to the common occurrences of life. Brilliantly, Pinter projects T. S. Eliot's image of modern people "Like a patient etherized upon a table."

Aston, one of the three major characters of the play, is a former mental patient whose paranoia caused his incarceration in a mental institution; he has received shock treatments that have left him generally ineffective. He is the caretaker of a flat owned by his brother, Mick. Aston serves as a symbol of the sterility imposed by psychological victimization. The angst imposed by two world wars manifests itself significantly in Aston, whose life is played out among objects indicative of depersonalization and displacement: a leaking roof, a gas stove that does not work, a pond without fish, an electrical plug that needs mending, a vase of screws, paint buckets that stand idle, a statue of Buddha that Aston has acquired from a shopkeeper. He is constantly in the act of fixing or repairing something. The plug, on which he works incessantly, perhaps symbolizes his inadequacies and his inability to connect himself to life's situations. He is isolated and remote, occupying a flat of which only one room is habitable.

Davies, the second character, is a bum whom Aston saves from a beating at a local pub and brings home. Davies has two identities, his true one, Mac Davies, and an assumed one, Bernard Jenkins. Davies cannot remember where he was born, and his identity is suffused with shadows of unreality. He is plagued by shoes that do not fit, and he repeatedly speaks of his need to visit Sidcup, a suburb of London with an army pay office where, Davies claims, he has left important papers. He makes vague references to the war as his point of demarcation from what society considers usual. He is full of bigotry and prejudice, referring pejoratively to blacks, Poles, Indians, and Greeks. Ironically, he calls them "aliens," further heightening his own sense of alienation. He remarks that he left his wife because he found a pile of her unwashed underclothing in the vegetable pan. He is fired from his job of cleaning a pub because he refuses to take a bucket of rubbish out back, a chore he believes to be outside his job description. He is quite discriminating; he asserts that he can drink his beer only from a thin glass, not the thick mug in which it is served. He complains about the heat, the noise, and the other conditions in the apartment, even though he is freeloading. He is, nevertheless, asked by both Aston and Mick to be caretaker of the building.

Mick, Aston's brother, is the owner of a van, the flat, and his own business. Mick is aggressive; he forces Davies to the floor upon their first meeting. Mick's interaction is the total projection of crass commercialism. He speaks to Davies of renting the flat to him, and his language is filled with the terminology of business. He speaks incessantly of insurance, shares, benefit schemes, banks, and so forth. Mick's actions culminate when he smashes Aston's Buddha (representing enlightenment). He is concerned only with building his business and protecting, increasing, and projecting his interests.

Impact of Event

The Caretaker, which opened at London's Arts Theatre on April 27, 1960, brought Pinter the success that had hitherto eluded him. After receiving broadly favorable reviews, the production was moved to the Duchess Theatre in London's West End in late May. The *Evening Standard* chose the play as the best London production of 1960; some critics went so far as to call *The Caretaker* the most important British drama since World War II. An American production opened in New York City in

October of 1961 and also earned praise; a 1963 film version (retitled *The Guest* for American release) won prizes at film festivals in Berlin and Edinburgh.

The Caretaker inspired numerous interpretations from drama critics and academicians. The play was seen as an allegory of the relationship between humanity (Davies), God (Aston), and Satan (Mick); as a symbolic dramatization of Oedipal conflict; as a condemnation of twentieth century imperialism; and in numerous other ways. Puzzled critics attempted to classify the work as an experiment in such familiar avant-garde genres as the Theater of the Absurd and the Theater of Cruelty; some used the term "comedy of menace" to describe Pinter's drama. At a loss for clearly appropriate labels for such a work, however, many commentators simply chose to refer to the author's style as "Pinteresque." Pinter steadfastly refused to comment on the many attempts to find meaning in the play, but some general truths are clear. Whatever its deeper meaning, *The Caretaker* presents twentieth century victims who have been rendered mentally, psychologically, and emotionally impotent by such dehumanizing processes as military activity, crass commercialism, and scientific experimentation.

The play's title speaks to the nature of the relationships in the drama, literally and symbolically. Aston asks Davies to be caretaker of the flat, as does Mick. Mick has also been Aston's caretaker since Aston's experience with psychological evaluation and treatment. All these characters, therefore, are victims who, in turn, try to victimize one another. Davies' point of demarcation is his military service. He has become disoriented and fragmented as a result of this activity. His constant allusions to Sidcup, an army pay station where he says his papers and references are, reflect his purported desire to ascertain his identity; however, he finds excuses not to make his way there.

Aston reflects the plight of the individual who is denuded of identity through psychological evaluation and scientific experimentation. The sources of his victimization are others' cruelties; his mother gave consent to the doctors at the psychiatric hospital for the treatment that has rendered him vague and dispossessed. His paranoia has its origins in some sort of persecution that is not specified, and he is reduced to listless wandering, even picking up and bringing home bums. The objects of the flat heighten and symbolize his emotional and physical sterility, painfully reflecting the plight of those displaced through labeling and archaic and primitive treatment. Thus, he is made caretaker of a flat filled with meaningless objects that symbolize modern humanity's attempt to find meaning after scientific experimentation has displaced ingenuity and skill. The secondhand Buddha, a symbol of enlightenment and Aston's single hope, is smashed by Mick. This icon, perhaps representative of regenerative impulses, perishes, as have humanity's hopes for spirituality.

Mick embodies crass commercialism, the impulse to satisfy one's sense of self through capital gain. He constantly refers to business, and his language reflects the primary emphasis of his thoughts and interests. His continual references to "rateable value," insurance, interest, deposits, payments, bonus schemes, shares, benefits, compensation, comprehensive indemnity, and banking profoundly detail his obsession.

His aggressive neuroses manifest themselves in interesting ways and contribute to his role not only as caretaker but also as one who seeks the comfort of a caretaker.

The Caretaker does reflect many of the characteristics of the Theater of the Absurd in its distortion of the characters, whose environments displace them even further because of the lack of attendant value judgments and meaningful interactions. More important, however, the play is a projection of modern humankind's disintegration in the face of the increasing violence, both physical and psychological, of the modern world.

Pinter's characters are prototypical in their interactions and their attempts to place themselves in a society that long ago relegated them to these acts of meaninglessness and futility. They cower, dispossessed, invested by powers outside themselves, reaping the interest of disassociation, displacement, and futility—a twentieth century pietà. Just as they are the perfect victims, so, too, do they become victimizers. Mick attempts to victimize Davies, who attempts to victimize Aston with threats of further shock treatments; Davies even threatens Aston with a knife. Thus, each character also illustrates the dysfunctional sterility of aggression.

The Caretaker secured Pinter's reputation. Such subsequent successes as *The Homecoming* (1965) and *Old Times* (1971) confirmed him as the leading British dramatist of his time, and he was soon in demand as a writer of radio, television, and film scripts. In 1966, he was made a Commander of the Order of the British Empire; in 1967, a New York production of *The Homecoming* earned him both a Tony Award and a New York Drama Critics Circle Award.

Beginning with *Landscape* (1968), Pinter abandoned the often squalid settings of his early plays to explore the lives of the middle and upper classes, but his work retained its characteristic pauses, naturalistic dialogue, and explorations of psychology. His effect on contemporary British drama has been considerable; the works of such younger playwrights as Tom Stoppard, John Orton, and Simon Gray contain unmistakable "Pinteresque" touches. Although Pinter's influence stemmed largely from his early plays, he continued to produce acclaimed drama, a fact testified to by his 1980 receipt of a second New York Drama Critics Circle Award for *Betrayal* (1978).

Bibliography

Burkman, Katherine H. *The Dramatic World of Harold Pinter: Its Basis in Ritual.* Columbus: Ohio State University Press, 1971. Interesting assessment of Pinter's plays from the standpoint of myth and ritual. Burkman asserts that a scapegoat of ancient ritual or tragedy is the center of action of most Pinter plays. Provocative chapter on "Pinter in Production" that discusses technical aspects of the plays from the standpoint of producers and actors.

Esslin, Martin. *The Peopled Wound: The Work of Harold Pinter.* Garden City, N.Y.: Doubleday, 1970. Biographical data of significance are presented in Esslin's psychoanalytical approach to the subject matter and themes of Pinter's plays. Good coverage of the plays, with interesting references to playwrights usually associated with the Theater of the Absurd. The weakness of the study is its almost over-zealous attempt to find historical perspective.

Gabbard, Lucina Paquet. *The Dream Structure of Pinter's Plays.* Rutherford, N.J.: Fairleigh Dickinson University Press, 1976. Fascinating explication of Pinter's plays from the standpoint of Sigmund Freud's work on dreams. Discusses plays in groups. The first group centers on fear and guilt, the second on the desire to kill, the third on the Oedipal wish, and a fourth on the fulfillment of the Oedipal fantasy.

Gale, Steven H. *Butter's Going Up: A Critical Analysis of Harold Pinter's Plays.* Durham, N.C.: Duke University Press, 1977. Sees Pinter's childhood as a Jew in London during World War II and the fear generated by the situation as cause for the development of the plays, the key concept of which is menace or threat. Themes are love, loneliness, menace, communication, and verification. Strong chapter on technique, with emphasis on language and revision. Section on production data of the plays. Extensive bibliography.

Hinchliffe, Arnold P. *Harold Pinter.* Boston: Twayne, 1981. Normal Twayne bill of fare, with overview of criticism and detailed plot summary of dramas. Uses clichés employed by earlier critics for categorization and explication—comedies of menace and comedies of manners. Good detail on Pinter as actor, director, and adapter. Cursory look at material of and about Pinter. Good for a quick overview.

Merritt, Susan Hollis. *Pinter in Play.* Durham, N.C.: Duke University Press, 1990. Brilliant assessment of Pinter criticism, with superb chapter on the bases for literary criticism. Definitive examination of material about Pinter, with provocative material on gender. The bibliography is extensive and comprehensive. Traces the shifting emphasis of Pinter critics with perceptive insight. Best scholarly approach to the playwright.

Quigley, Austin E. *The Pinter Problem.* Princeton, N.J.: Princeton University Press, 1975. Linguistic analysis of Pinter's plays. Explores the origin of Pinter's use of language in his menacing childhood experiences; sees his dialogue as the result of threats to identity.

Dinford Gray Maness

Cross-References

Sartre and Camus Give Dramatic Voice to Existential Philosophy (1940's), p. 1174; "Angry Young Men" Express Working-Class Views (1950's), p. 1454; *Waiting for Godot* Expresses the Existential Theme of Absurdity (1953), p. 1573; Behan's *The Hostage* Is Presented by the Theatre Workshop (1958), p. 1757; Ionesco's *Rhinoceros* Receives a Resounding Worldwide Reception (1959), p. 1812; Esslin Publishes *The Theatre of the Absurd* (1961), p. 1871; Tawfiq al-Hakim Introduces Absurdism to the Arab Stage (1961), p. 1893; *The American Dream* Establishes Albee as the Voice of Pessimism (1961), p. 1903.

CATCH-22 ILLUSTRATES ANTIWAR SENTIMENT

Category of event: Literature
Time: 1961
Locale: New York, New York

This novel's strong antiwar stance and absurdist view of life struck a chord with many readers, especially as U.S. involvement in Vietnam began to deepen

> *Principal personage:*
> JOSEPH HELLER (1923-   ), the author, who achieved instant cult status with this, his first novel

Summary of Event

Catch-22 is set on the imaginary island of Pianosa during World War II and focuses on Captain John Yossarian and his attempts to circumvent the illogic of his bomber squadron's commanders and thus earn the privilege of going home. As the death toll rises, the quota of bombing missions required for home-leave is increased repeatedly. By pleading insanity, Yossarian hopes to find a way out. The military doctor quotes the infamous Catch-22, which can be summarized as follows: Flying missions is crazy. To get out of flying them, one must plead insanity; however, since wanting to get out of flying them is proof of sanity, pleading insanity to get out of flying invalidates the claim of being insane.

Although Yossarian does not want to fight, he is not a coward. He is often called an antihero because he was on the wrong side in a popular war, but in reality he has all the attributes that make up the idealized hero. He loves life, culture, travel, and adventure, but because he is sensitive to injustice, irrationality, and inhumanity, he finds himself constantly at odds with his superiors. Once he realizes the full implications of his predicament, he has the courage to take action.

In his opposition, Yossarian comes up against two immovable forces: the Establishment and the System. He finds it impossible to live within the Establishment, or even to reform it, because he believes that it treats human beings as mechanisms, values conformity above creativity, regards people's files as more important than the people themselves, and encourages official lying as a matter of policy. As for the System, it tends to use war not so much to fight a national enemy as to regulate its own people. It fosters power struggles that victimize the fighting man in wartime and the creative person in peacetime. On every level, the System needs scapegoats and always finds them. The Establishment formulates humanitarian policies not for its own practice but for use in measuring the enemy, for propaganda purposes. Corruption runs rampant in all professions and institutions because private greed is sanctified.

Yossarian possesses traits that set him apart from those who are content to conform to authority, one of them being his ability to question assumptions and to think for himself. He prides himself on his individuality, and he values individuality and freedom more than status or official recognition. To him, money and machinery are means, not ends.

Yossarian is more interested in humanity than in organizations, and when the Organization turns against human values, Yossarian has the courage to assert that there is a higher law than the state and that there are times in history when the state is the villain, when what is needed is a new kind of hero. Yossarian is this new kind of hero, and the notorious Catch-22 is his *bête noire*. In every law, it is the loophole that empowers authorities to revoke rights whenever it suits them. Because of Catch-22, justice is mocked, the innocent are victimized, and Yossarian's squadron is forced to fly more than double the number of missions prescribed by Air Force code.

Hovering always in the background of the novel is the haunting, mysterious presence of the anonymous "soldier in white," bandaged from head to foot and kept alive by an endless rotation of body fluids. What begins as a grotesque joke—whatever is excreted at one end is what is ingested at the other—becomes a grim symbol of the mechanical regulation of human life: facelessness, self-containment, the withdrawal and isolation of the patient who is thoroughly dehumanized yet kept alive because it has become possible to do so. There is even doubt about whether someone actually exists beneath the bandages of the soldier in white. Even if someone does exist, can he hear what is going on around him? Can he think? Can he feel? These monstrous possibilities go far in expressing the novel's image of the madness of war.

This madness is demonstrated in a similarly bizarre scene in which a character named Dobbs suggests to Yossarian that they assassinate Colonel Cathcart because of his illegal treatment of his men. Dobbs is carried away by the idea and soon envisions a bloodbath. Although his desire to punish a guilty commander is understandable, it is clear that Dobbs would soon exceed even Cathcart's brutality in his thirst for revenge.

Dobbs's misguided fanaticism is symptomatic of the larger fanaticism that informs the entire narrative of *Catch-22*. A democracy has declared war on the fascist powers because they are aggressively antidemocratic, inhumane, and uncivilized, but the American military establishment is revealed repeatedly as itself being antidemocratic and quasifascist. Clevinger, for example, believes that Scheisskopf is sincere in asking for suggestions, and he responds accordingly with several sensible proposals. As a result, he is punished for his presumption, even framed and then humiliated in a travesty of justice worthy of the most heinous of Nazi court trials. Colonel Cathcart's contempt for enlisted men, General Dreedle's flaunting of his privileges, the way Korn insists that disagreement with him is tantamount to disloyalty to the flag, and the sadistic Star Chamber tactics of the men from the Criminal Investigation Department all demonstrate that the military is not defending democracy but undermining it.

The novel challenges many sacred assumptions on the side of the victors of World War II and raises the suspicion of hypocrisy at every turn. How, for example, can the army Yossarian is serving be called antifascist when Captain Black considers a certain corporal to be un-American because he disapproves of Hitler? What is one to make of the Texan Yossarian meets in the hospital and of Cathcart, both of whom feel free to express racist attitudes? Does not the tribal history of the Native American White Halfboat make it clear that the American people are themselves guilty of genocide?

Scene after scene in *Catch-22* postulates the likelihood that war brings out the worst in men, and that it can turn humanitarians into butchers. War triggers the release of sadistic impulses and creates a climate favorable only to cynical people such as Korn and General Peckem, exploitative people such as Lieutenant Milo Minderbinder, and manipulative people such as Private First Class Wintergreen. War allows military police to commit an arbitrary, illegal act simply because there is no way to stop them. In the name of efficiency, armies convert people into mechanisms, as typified by the activities of Scheisskopf and the fate of the soldier in white. The ultimate antihumanitarian aspect of even a "good war" is shown in the decision to bomb an unwarned civilian population in an undefended village purely for military purposes. An act of this sort makes it impossible for the as-yet-uncorrupted to see any difference between the enemy and themselves.

Impact of Event

Catch-22 is a satire on the bureaucratic madness of the military and on the logical inanity of the military mind. In a curious twist of fate, this peculiar antiwar novel managed to attract two otherwise incompatible audiences. To veterans of World War II, it was a hilarious reminder of the chaos and disorder that seemed always to hover just beneath the structured surface of military life. To them it was the way things were, and if it poked fun at the military, it was simply stating the obvious, not grinding an ax. To others, however, especially as the decade of the 1960's progressed and the war in Vietnam escalated, it was the ultimate pacifist tract, the best reasoning yet presented for turning one's back on war of any kind and lighting out for neutral ground. The very catch in military logic that it ridiculed—the infamous "Catch-22"—was also their way out: "Be crazy, it's all crazy anyway." As disenchantment with American foreign policy abroad and domestic oppression at home mounted, "Catch-22" became the rationale for opposition, desertion, draft dodging, dropping out, whatever it took to lodge a passive protest against what many considered to be an unjust war.

Readers had no trouble applying the message of *Catch-22* to events in their own lives. A police officer might make an illegal arrest in order to break up a demonstration, but the demonstrators must submit to arrest or else they would be guilty of disobeying the police. By the time the courts assert the law and free the demonstrators, the police have accomplished their purpose.

Treating *Catch-22* as merely another antiwar novel does not account for its phenomenal impact. What does account for it is the book's premise that military methods make a mockery of political goals. Because of the very nature of war, even a "good war" will become an evil, extremist enterprise. World War II may have begun as an idealistic war, with justifiable, humanitarian aims, but it quickly degenerated—as all wars do—into a self-negating, militaristic crusade. No matter how noble the ends, the means become identical with the enemy's. This was the message that most appealed to the young readers of the 1960's, and it is this message that continued for a long time to influence those who opposed all military action, no matter how justifiable it seemed on the surface.

Young readers who took this book to heart as an antiwar novel saw the scale of evil tilted toward their fathers who, they believed, had excused their wartime misdeeds with the blood of Auschwitz, pretending to have waged a holy war when in reality they found out about the Holocaust only after they got back home. Heller wrote the novel during the Korean War, but it appeared at the dawn of the Vietnam War and found its greatest popularity during the time that war was escalating. The time was right, then, for an assault against the rationalization of what Dwight D. Eisenhower had called the "Crusade in Europe" and for a blanket denunciation of war for any reason and against any enemy. In this respect, it goes far beyond being a major war novel to become the definitive statement of the modern antiwar position.

Catch-22 also provided readers with not only a rationale for evading military duty but also a destination. "I'm not running *away* from my responsibilities," says Yossarian as, at the end of the novel, he takes off for Sweden, a favorite place of exile for those avoiding Vietnam. "I'm running *to* them." To war protesters, of course, Yossarian's decision pointed the way for their own escape from an immoral obligation. They found running away to be much braver than going off to fight a war in which they did not believe. As far as they were concerned, personal refusal was the only heroism left, and Yossarian was the hero who would lead them to "a new morality."

Although the term "Catch-22" has become a permanent part of the English language and the novel continues to attract new readers, by and large its day has passed and its message has no more impact than that of the antiwar novels it tried to surpass. Perhaps the ultimate "Catch-22" is to be found in the fact that war's very absurdity is at bottom its most irresistible attraction and that antiwar novels, like all warnings, whet an appetite for the thing they warn against.

Bibliography

Kam, Rose. *Joseph Heller's "Catch-22."* Woodbury, N.Y.: Barron's Educational Series, 1985. A good, serviceable introduction to this complex work. Contains all the standard critical responses plus excellent character sketches and a fair chronology of events. Good material on background and reception of the book.

Kiley, Frederick, and Walter McDonald, eds. *A "Catch-22" Casebook.* New York: Crowell, 1973. The first and still the most wide-ranging collection of materials on the first decade of *Catch-22.* Includes several reviews, critical essays, a pair of interviews, and informal articles on the book and on the film.

Merrill, Robert. *Joseph Heller.* Boston: Twayne, 1987. Critical studies of all of Heller's novels and plays. The section on *Catch-22* discusses the novel's generic classification as well as the relationship of structure and meaning.

Nagel, James, ed. *Critical Essays on "Catch-22."* Encino, Calif.: Dickenson, 1974. Essays, including some solicited just for this volume, on all of Heller's major works, with a useful introductory essay by Nagel on the history of Heller scholarship.

Potts, Stephen W. *"Catch-22": Antiheroic Novel.* Boston: Twayne, 1989. A lively, thorough look at Heller's major novel. Fresh, original, and provocative. Contains excellent reference tools, including a comprehensive bibliography and an excellent and very useful chronology of the novel's events.

_____. *From Here to Absurdity: The Moral Battlefields of Joseph Heller.* New York: Borgo Press, 1982. An earlier version of the author's challenging insights into this phenomenal book. Mature, reasoned, and thoroughly readable.

Ramsey, Vance. "From Here to Absurdity: Heller's *Catch-22.*" In *Seven Contemporary Authors*, edited by Thomas B. Whitbread. Austin: University of Texas Press, 1968. An early essay relating the issues of sanity, absurdity, and antiheroism.

Richter, David H. "The Achievement of Shape in the Twentieth Century Fable: Joseph Heller's *Catch-22.*" In *Fable's End: Completeness and Closure in Rhetorical Fiction.* Chicago: University of Chicago Press, 1974. An analysis of Heller's method as representing a modern breakthrough in fabulist literature.

Seed, David. *The Fiction of Joseph Heller: Against the Grain.* New York: St. Martin's Press, 1989. *Catch-22* as seen within the context of Heller's other, less successful books. Throws new light on the phenomenal success of *Catch-22* compared to the indifferent reception to Heller's other works.

Thomas Whissen

Cross-References

Hašek's *The Good Soldier Švejk* Reflects Postwar Disillusionment (1921), p. 523; *All Quiet on the Western Front* Stresses the Futility of War (1929), p. 767; Mailer Publishes *The Naked and the Dead* (1948), p. 1373; Heinlein Publishes *Stranger in a Strange Land* (1961), p. 1883; Vonnegut's *Cat's Cradle* Expresses 1960's Alienation (1963), p. 1939; *M*A*S*H* Reflects 1970's Sentiments (1972), p. 2271.

ESSLIN PUBLISHES *THE THEATRE OF THE ABSURD*

Categories of event: Theater and literature
Time: 1961
Locale: The United States

Martin Esslin's classic study of Samuel Beckett, Arthur Adamov, Eugène Ionesco, Jean Genet, and other avant-garde playwrights helped to define one of the major trends in modern drama

Principal personages:
MARTIN ESSLIN (1918-   ), a renowned scholar of drama who wrote *The Theatre of the Absurd*
ARTHUR ADAMOV (1908-1970), a Surrealist dramatist who became the philosophical guru of the absurdist movement
SAMUEL BECKETT (1906-1989), an absurdist writer famous for both his novels and dramas
JEAN GENET (1910-1986), a Parisian criminal who, while in prison, wrote important absurdist plays
EUGÈNE IONESCO (1912-   ), a Romanian-born Parisian playwright
HAROLD PINTER (1930-   ), an English playwright noted for such absurdist plays as *The Birthday Party* (1958)

Summary of Event

The 1950's produced an avant-garde theater movement in Europe that in its technique and content left many of its audiences bewildered—even, at times, exasperated and angry. Although the various playwrights involved did not belong to a self-conscious artistic clique, they seemed to share a post-World War II disillusionment with humankind and a fervid rejection of ideals, including belief in God and the purposefulness of human existence. In its bleakness and morbid humor, the new drama seemed to have risen from the charnel houses of Europe.

Commentators during the 1950's often noted the kinship of some of these playwrights, largely on the basis of their presumed nihilism and their general break with realistic theater in mood and method. Remarking on influences apart from socio-political events, perceptive critics tied the avant-garde drama to various artistic and philosophical strains, including the existential philosophy then in vogue, Surrealism, the early experimental work of Alfred Jarry, and the antitheater preachments of Antonin Artaud, whose *Le Théâtre et son double* (1938; *The Theater and Its Double*, 1958) provided a new, widely disseminated artistic credo.

Still, there was no single study that penetrated to the common marrow of the avant-garde playwrights. Their works were very different from the typical Broadway and West End fare seen in New York and London, and for many they were simply baffling. Unlike Jean-Paul Sartre and Albert Camus, whose plays espoused their existential philosophy in traditional form and method, Samuel Beckett, Arthur Adamov, Jean Genet, and Eugène Ionesco wrote plays that violated virtually all the conventions of the commercial stage. The problem was that each writer did this in his own way, and to most observers, these playwrights seemed as different from one another as they did from those of more conventional dramatists.

Perplexed and even threatened by the avant-garde movement's penchant for devaluing language and its rejection of a time-honored dramaturgy, some critics assaulted the movement's works as nonsense, mere charlatanism, or, even worse, seditious blasphemy hopelessly negative in perspective. The resistance to the movement's influence culminated in a celebrated 1958 exchange of views in *The Observer* between Kenneth Tynan, one of England's foremost drama critics, and Ionesco, who by that time had achieved considerable success on London's more experimental stages.

In 1961, with the publication of *The Theatre of the Absurd*, Martin Esslin singlehandedly put much of the controversy to rest. A scholarly study of diverse avantgarde playwrights, the book brilliantly finds in the concept of absurdity a common link among his subject playwrights. In its epiphanic insight, it also reveals that a good deal of sense can be made of their works. Further, in his chapter entitled "The Significance of the Absurd," Esslin vigorously and convincingly defends the absurdist playwrights as visionaries devoted to making modern man shake off a narcosis induced by false dreams and illusions and face life honestly, or, in existential terms, authentically.

Although earlier he had written an important, critically acclaimed study of Bertolt Brecht, *Brecht: A Choice of Evils* (1959), when Esslin published *The Theatre of the Absurd*, he had not yet achieved significant standing as a theater historian or scholar. At the time, he was working for the British Broadcasting Corporation (BBC) as a broadcaster, writer, and producer. He was, however, fascinated with the new theater of Europe, and he had an affinity with some of the dramatists because, like many of them, he had been uprooted by the sociopolitical events leading up to World War II. Cut adrift from his own roots and having to cope with the vagaries of an adopted language, he had, for example, a special empathy for Ionesco, who was prompted to write *La Cantatrice chauve* (1950; *The Bald Soprano*, 1956), his first play, as a result of trying to learn English by aping the fatuous phraseology of a language primer.

Despite having no academic credentials as a scholar, Esslin reveals remarkable thoroughness and care in his study. Tracing the confluence of the absurdist movement to various sources both in and out of theater, he probes more deeply and widely than any earlier commentator on the avant-garde movement. Among other things, he points out the relationship of absurdist plays to other works by the playwrights themselves and to such diverse influences as mime, clowning, the silent-film comedy of Charles Chaplin, Buster Keaton, W. C. Fields, the Marx Brothers, and others, Surrealism, the Dada movement, cubism and abstract painting, the nonsense verse and prose of such writers as Lewis Carroll and Edward Lear, the fiction of Franz Kafka and James Joyce, and, in theater directly, the *commedia dell'arte* and the works of diverse playwrights, including William Shakespeare, Georg Büchner, Jarry, August Strindberg, Guillaume Apollinaire, Yvan Goll, and Brecht.

The first edition of *The Theatre of the Absurd* focuses on Adamov, Beckett, Genet, and Ionesco, treating each of them at length; others more briefly discussed in a chapter entitled "Parallels and Proselytes" include such new-wave playwrights as Harold Pinter, Arthur Kopit, Slawomir Mroszek, Vàclav Havel, Günter Grass, Edward Albee, and Fernando Arrabal. In naming these and other playwrights as the movement's neophytes, Esslin showed remarkable prescience; within the next several years, most of them would validate his insights.

In discussing the works of those writers together under the rubric "theatre of the absurd," Esslin opened a path to an intelligent approach and appraisal of the works of his subject playwrights. Further, as a clarifier of what Beckett, Ionesco, and the rest were attempting to achieve, Esslin had no obvious mentor and certainly no peer. His work was thus almost immediately recognized as an extremely important, seminal study, one of those rare works of scholarship that breaks through the branches to find not just a tree but a whole forest to which it gives a fortuitous and highly suggestive name.

Impact of Event

The influence of Esslin's *The Theatre of the Absurd* can hardly be overstated. During the 1960's, the work was widely read on college campuses, and the author's coined term for the theater of Beckett, Ionesco, and the rest became a familiar catchphrase. Inevitably, the term was also bandied about by some who never read a word of what Esslin had written, contributing to some dangerously facile interpretations of Esslin's meaning—a fact he lamented in the preface to the Pelican edition of his study, published in 1968.

For Esslin, the phrase "theatre of the absurd" was a "working hypothesis" designed to open up to discussion and understanding avant-garde works by a consideration of what they had in common, nothing more and nothing less. It irritated him that some contemporaries glibly surmised that such diverse writers as Pinter and Genet shared a confidential and sympathetic understanding of each other's work and ideas by virtue of belonging, consciously, to the same movement. Esslin had never meant to suggest that his subject writers had knowingly formed something like a fraternal order of absurdist playwrights.

Despite his disclaimer, however, Esslin had virtually defined a new dramatic genre, in which, partly as a result of his study, a whole generation of playwrights would, quite consciously, try to write. For example, through the 1960's and into the 1970's, hundreds of new plays in the absurdist mode were staged in the avant-garde Off-Off-Broadway and Fringe theaters of New York and London, alongside repeated productions of the "classic" works of Beckett, Ionesco, Adamov, Genet, and many of Esslin's "proselytes" such as Pinter, Albee, and Norman Frederick Simpson. If some of the new writers seemed to equate the absurd with mere nonsense, others produced works of lasting merit, giving the experimental stages a vitality that would gradually influence everything from amateur and university theaters to regional theaters and even, at times, the large, urban commercial houses, that, in New York at least, too often pandered only to popular taste.

In that same preface to the second edition of his study, Esslin also noted that, in 1964, Beckett's *En attendant Godot* (1952; *Waiting for Godot*, 1954) was staged at the Royal Court Theatre in London to favorable reviews. The only fault found with the production was the obviousness of both the symbolism and meaning of this major absurdist drama. Beckett's play, which a decade earlier had confounded and perplexed its audiences, had become old hat, or in kinder code words, a venerable classic of the modern stage. Esslin found the rapidity with which a seemingly opaque avant-garde work had been transformed into a readily and too easily penetrated classic astonishing.

Although he was too unassuming to claim responsibility for such a spectacular and rapid transformation, Esslin must be given some of the credit for it. His study became a primer, making dramatists such as Beckett and Ionesco palatable and comprehensible, not only to the intelligentsia but to the average theatergoer as well.

Although erudite, *The Theatre of the Absurd* is very lucid and commonsensical, easily within reach of any interested and moderately intelligent reader. It has also been a widely disseminated book, and by 1980 had already been through three editions and several reprints. Yet, despite its pervasive influence, not all critics and scholars have adopted Esslin's title phrase as the definitive classification for the dramatists he studied. French critics prefer the term *nouveau théâtre*, which suggests nothing about the nature of the plays except newness. Less neutral is the familiar "the theater of cruelty," which, reflecting the influence of Artaud, was used by Peter Brook and Charles Marowitz in England. Although it refers more to methods of directing and staging a play, that label has been loosely applied to some of the same playwrights that Esslin studied, thanks, in part, to Brook's fascination with Artaud and Genet.

The Theatre of the Absurd is largely descriptive, never prescriptive, which explains why it has had considerable sticking power. Because of the great diversity among the various avant-garde playwrights, Esslin advances no single play as even typical, much less as an ideal model, and he thereby avoids simple formulas for either interpreting or creating such a play. He wrote the study when the avant-garde movement was in a state of flux, uncertain of its own direction or even its purpose. As a result, Esslin was circumspect, never strident; he was suggestive, not imperious. He opened a window of understanding on a difficult phenomenon, and that window has remained open ever since.

Bibliography

Cohn, Ruby. *From Desire to Godot: Pocket Theater of Postwar Paris.* Berkeley: University of California Press, 1987. An excellent critical study with chapters on Artaud, Sartre, Ionesco, Beckett, Genet, and Adamov. Carefully documented work recommended for advanced students.

Esslin, Martin. *The Theatre of the Absurd.* 3d ed. London: Penguin, 1980. The last
   version of the original study, which supplements, rather than supersedes the first.
   A chapter is devoted to Pinter, whom Esslin promotes to the front rank with
   Beckett, Ionesco, Adamov, and Genet. Adds discussion of newer works and up-
   dates the bibliography, making it the preferred version for study.
Gaensbauer, Deborah B. *The French Theater of the Absurd.* Boston: Twayne, 1991.
   Studies the absurdist movement in Paris between 1948 and 1968, with a principal
   focus on Adamov, Ionesco, Genet, Fernando Arrabal, and Beckett. Also assesses
   the formative roles played by Artaud, Jarry, and Apollinaire. Obviously influenced
   by Esslin. Very helpful select bibliography.
Grossvogel, David I. *Four Playwrights and a Postscript.* Reprint. Westport, Conn.:
   Greenwood Press, 1975. Originally published in 1962. Compares four strident "blas-
   phemers"—Brecht, Ionesco, Beckett, and Genet. Useful as a companion study
   for Esslin's works, but not updated and lacking a bibliography.
Hassan, Ihab. *The Dismemberment of Orpheus.* Madison: University of Wisconsin
   Press, 1982. An important study of the relationship between existentialism and the
   theater of the absurd. Excellent chapters on Genet and Beckett. Strongly recommended for advanced students.
Hayman, Ronald. *Artaud and After.* Oxford: Oxford University Press, 1977. Offers a
   thorough analysis of Artaud's work and his influence on the avant-garde theater of
   Beckett, Ionesco, and their followers. Includes an expansive chronology and ex-
   tensive bibliography.
_____. *Theatre and Anti-Theatre: New Movements Since Beckett.* New York:
   Oxford University Press, 1979. Important for its focus on the "anti" elements
   in the plays of Beckett and his avant-garde successors. Has helpful chapters on
   Beckett, Ionesco, Peter Handke, Pinter, Tom Stoppard, Albee, Sam Shepard, and
   Artaud and also discusses antitheater directors Peter Brook, Jerzy Grotowski,
   and Joseph Chaikin. Includes a select bibliography and chronology of performances.
Killinger, John. *World in Collapse: The Vision of Absurd Drama.* New York: Dell,
   1971. An excellent, in-depth study focusing on metaphysical emptiness as the thematic springboard for many absurdist plays. Killinger, a theologian, finds entropy,
   anarchy, and collapse as themes emerging from what he terms the death of tran-
   scendence. Highly recommended for college students. Has a select bibliography.

John W. Fiero

Cross-References

The Ghost Sonata Influences Modern Theater and Drama (1908), p. 199; Sartre
and Camus Give Dramatic Voice to Existential Philosophy (1940's), p. 1174; *Waiting
for Godot* Expresses the Existential Theme of Absurdity (1953), p. 1573; Ionesco's
Rhinoceros Receives a Resounding Worldwide Reception (1959), p. 1812; Pinter's
The Caretaker Opens in London (1960), p. 1861; Tawfiq al-Hakim Introduces Ab-

surdism to the Arab Stage (1961), p. 1893; *The American Dream* Establishes Albee as the Voice of Pessimism (1961), p. 1903; Havel's *The Garden Party* Satirizes Life Under Communism (1963), p. 1967; Weiss's Absurdist Drama *Marat/Sade* Is Produced (1964), p. 2005.

FOUCAULT'S *MADNESS AND CIVILIZATION* IS PUBLISHED

Category of event: Literature
Time: 1961
Locale: Paris, France

Michel Foucault analyzed how attitudes toward madness changed in Western Europe from the sixteenth to the nineteenth centuries

Principal personages:

MICHEL FOUCAULT (1926-1984), a French historian and moral philosopher who wrote extensively on madness and the history of psychiatric asylums

PHILIPPE PINEL (1745-1826), an influential French psychiatrist who implemented humane and scientific methods for the treatment of the mentally ill

SAMUEL TUKE (1784-1857), an English writer and social reformer who, with his brother William Tuke, established asylums where the mentally ill received effective medical care

JEAN-ÉTIENNE-DOMINIQUE ESQUIROL (1772-1840), a French psychiatrist whose 1817 book *Les Maladies mentales* was the first clinical study of mental illness

Summary of Event

In 1960, Michel Foucault defended his doctoral dissertation on the evolution of attitudes toward mental illness in Western Europe between the early sixteenth century and the middle of the nineteenth century. In 1961, his dissertation was published under the title *Folie et déraison: Histoire de la folie à l'âge classique.* Three years later, Foucault abridged his dissertation. This revised version, which included a less extensive historical documentation, served as the basis for Richard Howard's 1965 English translation *Madness and Civilization: A History of Insanity in the Age of Reason.*

Foucault showed that in the late fifteenth century and during the early decades of the sixteenth century, the two illnesses most feared by Europeans were leprosy and the plague. Leper colonies and leprosariums had been established throughout Europe in order to segregate lepers from the general community. This fear of leprosy (or Hansen's disease, as it is now called) is understandable because Hansen's disease is highly contagious and had no cure until the 1940's. Europeans were terrified of Hansen's disease for two major reasons. First, it was then absolutely impossible for a leper to avoid both disfigurement and death. Second, those diagnosed as suffering from Hansen's disease were forcibly separated from their families, and they could not leave the leper colonies to which they were assigned. Bubonic plague, which had killed so many people during the Middle Ages, continued to inspire profound terror throughout Europe.

Mental illness, on the other hand, was considered to be a medical condition that society had to learn to accept. In his *Moriæ Encomium* (1511; *The Praise of Folly*, 1549), Desiderius Erasmus argued persuasively that mentally healthy individuals could learn much from those who seemed insane to certain members of the community. Madness was a relative concept during the Renaissance. Erasmus drew attention to the concept of "Christian folly." In his two letters to the Corinthians, St. Paul argued that Christians are fools who have rejected the ephemeral values of this world, which respects above all wealth and high social standing, in order to accept the revealed wisdom of "Christian folly," which is essential for eternal salvation. Erasmus reminded readers that Christian folly could be very useful for his fellow believers because "we are fools for Christ's sake," as St. Paul wrote in 1 Corinthians 4:10. Erasmus believed that wisdom and folly could be interchangeable. For sound theological reasons, Europeans were tolerant of madness during the better part of the sixteenth century. Foucault showed, however, that this tolerant attitude toward the mentally ill was replaced in the early seventeenth century by the belief that society no longer needed to accept forms of behavior that offended its sensitivities or value systems.

A basic thesis in Foucault's *Madness and Civilization* is that the ruling classes in England, Germany, and France during the seventeenth and eighteenth centuries decided quite deliberately to exclude from society those who failed to act in a logical or rational manner or whose actions made life uncomfortable for their families. Foucault showed that there was then no systematic attempt to distinguish between true mental illness and voluntary or involuntary actions that struck the political elite as odd or abnormal. Among those imprisoned as insane were epileptics, mildly depressed people, spendthrift or sexually active unmarried adolescents, men and women who had contracted venereal diseases, and even priests who had mistresses. A priest who chose not to respect his vow of chastity was subject to imprisonment for reason of insanity simply because his behavior might scandalize his parishioners. Epileptics whose involuntary seizures scared ignorant people were systematically removed from society and incarcerated.

With an impressive amount of historical documentation, drawn largely from France and England but also from Germany, Foucault showed that no effort was made to cure or treat the mentally ill or to separate them from the general prison population. Prison directors and even some clergymen whose ministry dealt with prisoners affirmed that the insane were more like animals than like human beings possessing feelings and immortal souls. This extraordinary arrogance on the part of the ruling class and its administrators enabled generations of the English and the French in the seventeenth and eighteenth centuries to deceive themselves into believing that it was permissible and even praiseworthy to imprison the insane so that society would not be bothered by their presence.

Foucault demonstrated that this deplorable situation in France and England did not change until the 1790's, when enlightened social reformers and psychiatrists established asylums in which the mentally ill received humane treatment from medical doctors who tried their best to cure them and to help them resume normal lives in society. Until the 1790's, people imprisoned in France and England for reason of insanity received no regular psychiatric treatment from medical doctors. Although Foucault questioned the effectiveness of some of the psychiatric treatments implemented by the French psychiatrists Jean-Étienne-Dominique Esquirol and Philippe Pinel and by the English social reformers Samuel and William Tuke in the late eighteenth century and in the early years of the nineteenth, one should not underestimate the importance of their contributions to the history of psychiatry. Esquirol, Pinel, and the Tukes were the first major reformers to establish asylums in which the mentally ill received the best medical care then available.

Impact of Event

While Foucault was writing his doctoral dissertation in the 1950's, he was unable to obtain a teaching position at a French university. Between 1954 and 1960, he taught French courses at universities in Sweden, Poland, and Germany. His dissertation was received so favorably by his colleagues that he was offered not only a professorship but also the position of head of the department of philosophy at the University of Clermond-Ferrand in central France. This was quite an unusual honor for a scholar who had just received his doctorate. Why was *Madness and Civilization* considered to be such an important book?

Since its publication in 1961, critics of *Madness and Civilization* have pointed out that this is an important work for many different fields, including social history, political science, ethics, the history of ideas, and the history of psychiatry. Many scholars have asked whether Foucault was more a historian or a philosopher. This opposition between history and philosophy assumes that the objective analysis of social history is somehow incompatible with theoretical and philosophical reflections on the history of ideas. Foucault believed, however, that such a distinction between history and philosophy was artificial because historical research based on extensive analysis of primary sources can lead to an understanding of how people perceived ethical, social, or religious problems in earlier centuries or in foreign cultures. This approach, which combined rigorous historical research with a study of the history of ideas, represented the method developed by the eminent French historians Marc Bloch and Lucien Febvre in the 1930's and 1940's in order to study what they called "the history of mentalities." Foucault wanted modern readers to understand the basic assumptions and popular beliefs or misconceptions that led generations of Europeans to conclude that it was perfectly acceptable to imprison the insane and to deny medical doctors access to the mentally ill.

Foucault argued persuasively that the justification for this egregious mistreatment of the mentally ill was the specious assumption that those whose behavior, opinions, or even religious beliefs did not conform to socially accepted norms were unreasonable and therefore should not be allowed to remain free. Freedom was then considered a privilege and not a right. Until the French Revolution, a person in France could be imprisoned for insanity without a judicial hearing if the king signed a *lettre de cachet* (a letter bearing the royal seal) ordering that the individual be imprisoned until the king decided otherwise. This use (or abuse) of power was absolute, and people imprisoned for insanity were not permitted to challenge such royal decisions in a court of law. Foucault showed that many people were then imprisoned for insanity at the request of their parents. A father could request that his profligate adolescent son or daughter be imprisoned for insanity so that the offspring's unacceptable behavior could no longer cause embarrassment to parents and siblings. Such requests were granted routinely, especially to politically influential fathers, and no efforts were made to verify the validity of the charges brought against those who had been accused of insanity. Foucault pointed out that this use of *lettres de cachet* was an overt form of political repression designed to discourage all types of resistance to the ruling class. Anyone who did not conform to specific socially accepted norms could be imprisoned without a judicial hearing.

Foucault argued that the arbitrary incarceration of those considered to be insane did not change in France until the 1790's, when the revolutionary government decreed that henceforth a French citizen could not lose his or her freedom because of insanity without a court hearing and unless a medical doctor certified that the person was, in fact, insane and could well cause harm to others. At the urging of the eminent French psychiatrists Esquirol and Pinel, the French government ordered that people imprisoned for insanity before the French Revolution be freed unless a court concluded that such people were both insane and a danger to society. The French government further ordered that people judged to be insane henceforth would be sent not to prisons but rather to psychiatric asylums where they would be under the care of medical doctors. Similar changes occurred in England in the 1790's, when the Quakers founded the York Retreat with financial support from the Tuke family. The York Retreat was the first English psychiatric asylum in which mentally ill patients received humane and effective medical treatment. The reforms proposed by Esquirol, Pinel, and the Tukes would soon spread well beyond the borders of England and France. Their influence in the field of psychiatry was both profound and long-lasting.

Between the publication in 1961 of *Madness and Civilization* and his death on June 24, 1984, Foucault wrote extensively on a wide variety of topics including prison reform, the treatment of the mentally ill, the history of psychiatry, linguistics, and sexuality. It is ironic that Foucault died in the neurological hospital of La Salpetrière in Paris. Until the French Revolution, La Salpetrière had been one of the major prisons in which large numbers of people were incarcerated because of insanity; it was later transformed into a hospital for the treatment of neurological disorders. In *Madness and Civilization*, Foucault had written extensively about the terrible mistreatment in La Salpetrière of the mentally ill before the French Revolution.

Although there was considerable diversity in Foucault's writings, a major focus in his books was the analysis of the diverse techniques that societies have used over the centuries in order to control those whose behavior does not conform to specific norms. In his works published in the 1960's, he analyzed extensively the mistreatment of the mentally ill. In his three-volume *Histoire de la sexualité* (1976-1984; *The History of Sexuality*, 1978-1987), Foucault described the many techniques of repression directed against women, from ancient Greece to the modern era. Throughout his works, Foucault consistently affirmed the necessity for societies to recognize and to respect the dignity of each individual and diversity of all kinds. His many books and articles revealed his extraordinary ability to combine solid historical research with thoughtful reflections on important philosophical and ethical problems.

Foucault's writings probably influenced, at least indirectly, reforms that occurred from the 1960's onward in mental health treatment, though critics have been reluctant to posit such links. Abuses of power by Soviet officials, who claimed that dissidents were mentally ill and hospitalized them as a poorly concealed means of incarceration, were exposed and gradually eliminated. Even in the United States, treatment of the mentally ill came under closer examination. Foucault's influence is more noticeable in the humanities. His use of historical materials as a means of examining the values of society has been emulated by later scholars.

Bibliography

Arac, Jonathan, ed. *After Foucault: Humanistic Knowledge, Postmodern Challenges.* New Brunswick, N.J.: Rutgers University Press, 1988. Contains insightful essays by nine scholars who examine Foucault's writings on social history, feminism, politics, linguistics, and literary theory.

Burns, Eric. "Michel Foucault." In *Twentieth-Century Authors*, edited by George Stade. New York: Charles Scribner's Sons, 1990. Explains clearly the significance of Foucault's contributions to the history of ideas. Contains a short but excellent bibliography on Foucault.

O'Farrell, Clare. *Foucault: Historian or Philosopher?* Basingstoke, England: Macmillan, 1989. Examines whether it is more appropriate to consider Foucault as a social historian or as a moral philosopher. O'Farrell concludes that the approaches are equally valid and complement each other very nicely. Contains an extensive bibliography on Foucault.

Scott, Charles E. "Ethics Is the Question: The Fragmented Subject in Foucault's Genealogy." In *The Question of Ethics: Nietzsche, Foucault, Heidegger.* Bloomington: Indiana University Press, 1990. Examines Foucault's reflections on ethical problems and discusses the profound influence of the German philosophers Friedrich Nietzsche and Martin Heidegger on Foucault.

Shumway, David R. *Michel Foucault.* Boston: Twayne, 1989. Presents an excellent general introduction to the philosophical and ethical dimensions in Foucault's works. Describes very well Foucault's importance in modern French philosophy. Contains an annotated bibliography on Foucault.

Smart, Barry. *Michel Foucault.* Chichester, England: Tavistock, 1985. Presents a sociological interpretation of Foucault's writings on the use and abuse of political power to limit personal freedom. Describes well the unity of Foucault's social philosophy.

Edmund J. Campion

Cross-References

Freud Inaugurates a Fascination with the Unconscious (1899), p. 19; Jung Publishes *Psychology of the Unconscious* (1912), p. 309; Beauvoir's *The Second Sex* Anticipates the Women's Movement (1949), p. 1449; Lévi-Strauss Explores Myth as a Key to Enlightenment (1964), p. 1995; Weiss's Absurdist Drama *Marat/Sade* Is Produced (1964), p. 2005; Derrida Enunciates the Principles of Deconstruction (1967), p. 2075; *The Gulag Archipelago* Exposes Soviet Atrocities (1973), p. 2277; Forman Adapts *One Flew Over the Cuckoo's Nest* for Film (1975), p. 2320.

HEINLEIN PUBLISHES *STRANGER IN A STRANGE LAND*

Category of event: Literature
Time: 1961
Locale: New York, New York

This subversive and irreverent science-fiction classic gained a cult following, especially among students, even though Heinlein was in many ways dissimilar to his counterculture admirers

Principal personages:
ROBERT A. HEINLEIN (1907-1988), a science-fiction writer who explored new themes and expanded the readership of the genre
JOHN W. CAMPBELL, JR. (1910-1971), a science-fiction writer and long-time editor of *Astounding Science Fiction*
CHARLES MANSON (1934-   ), a mass murderer who read *Stranger in a Strange Land* during the 1960's and organized his "family" according to his interpretation of Heinlein's Martian model

Summary of Event

By 1961, Robert A. Heinlein was considered the dean of American science fiction. An Annapolis graduate, his first career was as a naval officer. After retiring for medical reasons in 1934, he did graduate work in physics and mathematics at the University of California at Los Angeles. His writing career began when *Astounding Science Fiction* published his first story, "Life-Line," in 1939.

At that time, science fiction was a minor literary form read mainly by dedicated fans. Much of it was "space opera," adventure stories that involved spaceships and alien monsters. Some writers and editors attempted to popularize science and technology through fiction. Among them was Hugo Gernsback, who founded *Amazing Stories* magazine in 1926 to popularize what he called "scientifiction."

Joseph Campbell, a science-fiction writer himself, had assumed the editorship of *Astounding Science Fiction* in 1938 and continued in that role until 1950. He is credited, as an editor, with moving science fiction toward its modern form. Under Campbell's influence, science-fiction writers grounded their stories in scientific concepts but then speculated about how technology might affect the lives of ordinary people and society in general. Heinlein's fiction fit into this more sociological mode.

From 1947 to 1959, Heinlein produced sixteen novels, winning Hugo Awards for *Double Star* (1956) and *Starship Troopers* (1959). Many were written for juvenile readers. His early novels emphasized adventure. In many ways, Heinlein was a conservative, and conservative views often were apparent in his work. In *Starship Troopers*, he preached the value of law and order and the need for military force. He also set forth the idea that some people, in this case the military, constitute a natural elite. In this vision of the future, only military veterans could vote or hold political office. As in his other early books, there were almost no female characters.

The audience for science fiction was growing, perhaps because of real scientific advances and the space program, but the genre still was being read mainly by a select group of fans. In 1961, after Heinlein had edited some sixty thousand words from his original text, Putnam published *Stranger in a Strange Land*. At 408 pages, it was his longest book so far. Released in paperback in 1968, it became the most successful science-fiction novel ever published and the first to appear on the best-seller list of *The New York Times Book Review*. A new, 525-page edition with all the deleted passages restored was published by G. P. Putnam's Sons in 1991.

Heinlein did win a third Hugo Award for *Stranger in a Strange Land*, but this book differed dramatically from his other work. It received strong critical reaction, both positive and negative. In his earlier fiction, Heinlein seemed unsure of whether to emphasize adventure or propaganda; *Stranger in a Strange Land* definitely emphasizes propaganda, satirizing American sexual mores and religion. Some critics saw the sexual content as cheap eroticism.

The "stranger" is Valentine Michael Smith, child of two members of the first expedition to Mars. He was reared by Martians in their culture after all the humans on Mars died. When he is twenty-five years old, a second Mars expedition discovers him and brings him back to Earth. Mike is young, naïve, and an outsider. Although he is physically human, Earth's culture is strange to him. Saved from manipulative politicians by a young nurse, Jill, he is sheltered and educated by Jubal Harshaw, an old doctor, lawyer, and successful writer. Harshaw's open mind is not limited by the culture in which he lives, and critics agree that his voice is Heinlein's voice.

Mike's Martian training has given him paranormal powers including telepathy, psychokinesis, and the ability to make any human or object cease to exist. Because everything is alien, however, he seems helpless at first. As he learns English, he grows more human. He reads copiously from Harshaw's library and is socialized by Harshaw, Jill, and Harshaw's young employees. He matures when he discovers sex. Martians are different from humans in that all adults are males and all children are females. Sex is solely for the propagation of the species, with no other interaction. Adult Martians grow closer through mental telepathy and sharing water, a precious resource on Mars. Mike realizes that sex is a way for humans to grow closer. Because human males and females are polar opposites, theirs is a dynamic relationship and therefore superior to that of Martians.

In the second half of the book, Mike starts a new religion based on Martian philosophy. Only certain humans are selected for this elite fellowship, and they must struggle to learn the Martian language so they can understand the Martian view of the universe. With proper discipline and instruction, Mike's male and female disciples, called "water brothers," begin to develop the same abilities that he has. The water brothers share everything, including bed partners. Since sex is a way of growing closer, it is a good thing and logically is shared among water brothers freely and without jealousy.

Because of the sexual content, *Stranger in a Strange Land* seems a radical departure from Heinlein's earlier works. His basic philosophy, however, still comes through. Heinlein believed that a free society would allow a natural elite to rise in a sort of social Darwinism. Mike's water brothers are a select group, better than the rest of humanity. The elite may use force for the good of society, illustrated by Mike using his powers to weed out people in whom he senses wrongness.

Two later Heinlein novels explore sexual themes: *I Will Fear No Evil* (1970) and *Time Enough for Love* (1973). The first is about Johann Smith, an elderly white male who, when he dies, has his brain transplanted into the body of Eunice, his beautiful young black secretary, whose consciousness is somehow preserved. A dual male-female consciousness in a female body presents interesting problems of sexual identity. To further complicate matters, Johann has this body impregnated with his frozen sperm. Both consciousnesses die when giving birth. *Time Enough for Love* recounts the life of Lazarus Long, who lives sometime in the future, when medical science has made humans virtually immortal. Long has many sexual adventures, but all the major characters turn out to be some form of himself. Long has himself cloned into female twins and then has sex with them, an act which is not so much incest as masturbation. He also travels back in time, falling in love with and having sex with his own mother.

George Edgar Slusser, a noted science-fiction critic, describes *I Will Fear No Evil* as one of the worst things Heinlein ever wrote. *Time Enough for Love* was not well received either. *Stranger in a Strange Land* was Heinlein's best attempt at philosophical fiction and by far the most widely read.

Impact of Event

Read at first almost entirely by science-fiction fans, *Stranger in a Strange Land* eventually found a wider audience, especially after the paperback version was released in 1968. It has been popular among college students and other young adults ever since.

Stranger in a Strange Land has been described as a book that readers can interpret as they wish. It appeals to young people, who may identify with Mike because he is different from other people and seemingly helpless at the beginning of the book but possessing special powers. They may wish for the type of friends that Mike has in his water brothers, people who care about and accept one another totally.

During the late 1960's and early 1970's, many readers considered the book a blueprint for a whole new way of living. Although Heinlein claimed that he was not giving answers, merely posing questions and challenging his readers' preconceptions, many of the ideas espoused by Valentine Michael Smith seemed to dramatize the values of the counterculture that emerged in the 1960's.

One example is the sexual revolution. Mike perceives that sex is a way for people to grow closer and that it should be shared without jealousy. Monogamy and the confines of traditional sexual mores do not apply. This matched closely the "free love" philosophy that spread in the 1960's.

Valentine Michael Smith's new religion seemed to incorporate aspects of the changing attitudes toward religion. Unlike the Fosterites, the largest religious group in the book, Mike and his followers do not value material success. Mike himself is a modern Christ figure, rebelling against established authority. Some elements of the Martian religion appear to stem from Zen Buddhism. For Mike, God is not a separate being but is present in all creatures—himself, his followers, the police, the cat, even the rose bushes. When Mike sends into nonexistence a human who is threatening his group, he is merely sending that individual back to the starting line to try again, in a sort of reincarnation. Like the Zen Buddhists, Mike and his followers meditate to reach insights and deepen their understanding.

Mike's superhuman abilities appealed to the counterculture's interest in parapsychology. His psychokinetic and telepathic talents, his ability to make something happen by wishing it, and his willingness to teach other humans attracted those who rejected the avowed objectivity of conventional scientists.

The strangest and most grotesque influence of the book was on Charles Manson, whose "family" murdered actress Sharon Tate and six other people in 1969. From 1961 to 1967, Manson was incarcerated in McNeil Island Penitentiary, where he read heavily. He was influenced greatly by Scientology, a religion that believes in reincarnation and was founded by L. Ron Hubbard, another author who wrote for Campbell's *Astounding Science Fiction*. Manson read *Stranger in a Strange Land* and identified with Valentine Michael Smith.

When he started his "family" in Berkeley, San Francisco, and Los Angeles, Manson borrowed some of the terminology and ceremonies from the book. It is reported that his followers held water-sharing ceremonies as well as group sex orgies. He referred to his parole officer as "Roger Smith Jubal," after Jubal Harshaw, Mike's mentor. When Mary Theresa Brunner, one of Manson's followers, gave birth to a baby boy in 1968, Manson named the child Valentine Michael Manson.

In the book, Smith uses his paranormal powers to eliminate people and things that he senses are wrong. Manson apparently felt qualified to make similar judgments and to eliminate those that he thought deserved nonexistence. It is ironic that Heinlein, who in *Starship Troopers* promoted the value of law and order, including such punishments as public floggings for drunk driving, should have created the model for a psychotic mass murderer.

Stranger in a Strange Land became a cult book for members of the counterculture, even though Heinlein himself was essentially conservative. It has outlasted that period. It was the first science-fiction book to find a wide audience outside the community of science-fiction fans, and it helped usher in an era in which other science-fiction books as well as television programs and movies would be accepted by the general public.

Bibliography

Budrys, Algis. "An Essay on Robert A. Heinlein (1907-1988)." *Fantasy and Science Fiction* 75 (September, 1988): 26-32. Written shortly after Heinlein's death, this essay discusses Heinlein's life, his work, and his place in the science-fiction genre.

The influences of others in the field, especially Joseph Campbell, are mentioned.
"Contact." *The New Yorker* 50 (July 1, 1974): 17-18. Reports on a talk Heinlein gave on the writing of science fiction.

Franklin, H. Bruce. *Robert A. Heinlein: America as Science Fiction.* Oxford, England: Oxford University Press, 1980. A critical discussion of Heinlein's work. Includes helpful biographical and bibliographical information. The author divides Heinlein's work into five periods: early fiction, new frontiers (1947-1959), a voice of the 1960's, the private worlds of the 1970's, and the last years.

Gunn, James. *Alternate Worlds: The Illustrated History of Science Fiction.* Englewood Cliffs, N.J.: Prentice-Hall, 1975. Traces the development of science fiction from the ancient Greeks to Kurt Vonnegut, Jr., and Ursula K. Le Guin. Very readable, with numerous illustrations.

"A Martian Model." *Time* 95 (January 19, 1970): 44-45. Reports the discovery that Manson tried to emulate the life-style of Heinlein's man from Mars.

Nicholls, Richard E. "The Biggest, Fattest Sacred Cows." *The New York Times Book Review* (December 9, 1990): 13. A brief background of the writing of *Stranger in a Strange Land* and the effect the book had.

Olander, Joseph D., and Martin Harry Greenburg, eds. *Robert A. Heinlein.* New York: Taplinger, 1978. A collection of critical essays on Heinlein's work. Each essayist focuses on a different theme, ranging from Heinlein's juvenile novels to the social Darwinism evident in his work.

Sanders, Ed. *The Family: The Story of Charles Manson's Dune Buggy Attack Battalion.* New York: E. P. Dutton, 1971. Tells the story of Charles Manson, including how he was influenced by *Stranger in a Strange Land.*

Slusser, George Edgar. *Robert A. Heinlein: Stranger in His Own Land.* San Bernardino, Calif.: Borgo Press, 1976. A critical discussion of *Stranger in a Strange Land* and other later works. The author shows how these books, although different from Heinlein's previous works, are consistent with his general philosophy.

Vonnegut, Kurt, Jr. "Heinlein Gets the Last Word." *The New York Times Book Review* (December 9, 1990): 13. A review of the unabridged version of *Stranger in a Strange Land.* The author also discusses the importance of the work.

Eunice Pedersen Johnston

Cross-References

American Science Fiction Enjoys Its Golden Age (1938), p. 1094; The Beat Movement Rejects Mainstream Values (1950's), p. 1460; Tolkien Publishes *The Lord of the Rings* (1954), p. 1607; Syndication Turns *Star Trek* into a Cult Classic (1972), p. 2260; The *Star Wars* Trilogy Redefines Special Effects (1977), p. 2391; Scott's *Blade Runner* Is a Visual Masterpiece (1982), p. 2486; *E.T.: The Extraterrestrial* Breaks Box-Office Records (1982), p. 2491.

THE ROYAL SHAKESPEARE COMPANY ADOPTS
A NEW NAME AND FOCUS

Category of event: Theater
Time: 1961
Locale: Stratford-on-Avon and London, England

The professional acting company operating out of Stratford-on-Avon, William Shakespeare's birthplace and hometown, changed its name as part of a sweeping change of focus under the leadership of new managing director Peter Hall

Principal personages:
PETER HALL (1930-   ), a visionary artistic director appointed to manage the operations of the Royal Shakespeare Company in 1959
FORDHAM FLOWER (1904-1966), the chairman of the executive council of the Shakespeare Memorial Theatre from 1945 to 1966
PETER BROOK (1925-   ), one of the three resident directors of the Royal Shakespeare Company in the early 1960's

Summary of Event

The redesignation of the Shakespeare Memorial Theatre Company as the Royal Shakespeare Company in 1961 was both a culmination and a beginning. The theater troupe that took the name had in fact been working at the Shakespeare Memorial Theatre in Stratford-on-Avon for more than four decades. They were themselves the inheritors of a stage that had been used by touring companies for almost half a century; these groups had been coming to the village on the banks of the Avon every year to participate in a festival honoring the city's most famous son on the occasion of his birthday. Productions had been carefully controlled and were under the supervision of the theater's executive committee, which had been ruled by members of the Flower family ever since Charles Flower, a prominent Stratford citizen, had spearheaded a tribute to William Shakespeare in the mid-nineteenth century. The memorial company had provided opportunities for serious young actors to work in repertory on numerous Shakespeare productions during seasons that had extended well beyond the original birthday festival period.

The appointment of Peter Hall as managing director of the company upon the resignation of Byam Shaw signaled a new direction for operations of the group. Hall, appointed in November, 1958, assumed his duties on January 1, 1960. He followed Shaw, Anthony Quayle, and Barry Jackson in the line of fine directors who had worked to reestablish the Shakespeare Memorial Theatre Company's reputation from the low point it had reached during World War II. Assuming his duties in what has been described as "the frenetic expansionist spirit of the age," Hall capitalized on the company's long-standing royal patronage to change the image of the group. The Shakespeare Memorial Theatre Company had been granted a royal charter in 1925; by 1960, however, little had been done to capitalize on that association, although

Queen Elizabeth II was urging the group to adopt a new name to indicate its status. Hall was quick to seize the chance afforded him. In one of his first moves after assuming directorship of the organization, he moved to rename the building in Stratford the Royal Shakespeare Theatre, and he changed the name of the permanent company playing there to the Royal Shakespeare Company.

Hall saw the name change as significant for two reasons. First, it allowed him to "jettison the somewhat funereal Victorian associations of 'Memorial' "; second, he believed the change would be seen by the public as a signal that the company was indeed taking off in a new direction. Such a move was necessary, since the Stratford operation was not highly thought of in London, the center of English (and world) theater at the time. Though many big-name stars had played at Stratford with the regular members of the company for years, most theater fans still thought of the Shakespeare Memorial Theatre as a countrified operation not worthy of sophisticated Londoners' time. Though the prudent fiscal management of the Flower family had helped keep the theater and its acting company in the black for most of the years it had operated, there was still a stigma attached to the entire organization. The best young actors from the company often left to take roles in London or, by the end of the 1950's, in films. Rising stars such as Peter O'Toole and Richard Burton (soon to be followed by others such as Diana Rigg and Glenda Jackson) departed after a season or two for more lucrative offers in locations more cosmopolitan than the sleepy banks of the Avon.

Hall had far-reaching ideas for expansion of the company's operations, and even before he was named managing director, he had secured the approval of Fordham Flower to strike out in new directions. The most significant change he wished to make, concurrent with the adoption of a new name, was the establishment of a London center at which the company could perform regularly. Hall saw this as a way of getting his actors before larger audiences and allowing them to perform in modern dramas, thereby affording them variety outside the confines of Elizabethan theater (at Stratford, productions were almost exclusively limited to works of Shakespeare and his contemporaries). Hall also used this opportunity to commission modern works from aspiring young playwrights, among them Robert Bolt and Peter Shaffer, who subsequently established themselves as premier dramatists in England.

Hall was concerned, too, as his predecessors had been, that moves to start a national theater company in London would have a serious negative effect on the Stratford operation. He wanted to be certain that his company was considered national in scope, and not simply a local house operating to commemorate a native son on his home turf. Hall may well have envisioned that, if a national theater were formed, he would be asked to serve as its director—if he could establish his reputation as an executive-level manager with the Royal Shakespeare Company and its theater.

Impact of Event

The direct impact of Hall's renaming the company may not have been immediately apparent to anyone inside the organization or out. Nevertheless, this shrewd move positioned the "new" Royal Shakespeare Company favorably in the eyes of both the general public and, especially, the political establishment immediately before the government embarked on a radically new venture in public funding: subsidy for theater in Great Britain.

The idea that the country should have a national theater had been percolating in both theater and government circles for decades before Hall's move to change his company's title. A National Theatre Act had been passed in 1949, and from that date efforts had been going on, in a somewhat desultory fashion, to select a site on which to build a theater and to draw up plans for a permanent company to act there. In 1951, the Duchess of York (the wife of King George VI and mother of Queen Elizabeth II) had laid a cornerstone for a national theater at a site on the south bank of the Thames River in London, near the former site of Shakespeare's Globe Theatre. Nothing was done toward construction of an edifice, but the notion that some action would be taken eventually was, from that moment, on the minds of everyone involved in the English theater.

Of course, all plans called for such an operation to be based in London. The Stratford company had perhaps seen itself as a kind of national theater, especially since the centerpiece of its operations had always been the works of England's and the world's greatest dramatist. Since the possibility that it would be named the national company was remote, a number of members of the company's executive committee (especially Fordham Flower) and artistic directors before Hall had worked to assure the Stratford group's inclusion in any plans—if for no other reason than to guard against the new national theater's eclipsing and perhaps bankrupting the Stratford company.

Concurrent with the redesignation of their organization, Hall and Flower took a second bold step, securing the use of the Aldwych Theatre in London so that members of the Royal Shakespeare Company could perform modern plays there. Though the Aldwych operation was never a financial success, the men who ran the Royal Shakespeare Company were acting from political as well as artistic motives: They wanted to be sure that their company was already operating in London as well as in the provinces when the committee working toward the establishment of a national theater presented its proposals for government subsidy to Parliament. The ploy worked, for as the national theater project moved from concept to reality, the Stratford troupe's leaders were able to become important figures in negotiations regarding the location of the facility, the organization of the board for the theater, and most important, the allocation of subsidies.

The project, however, was not without its pitfalls. Fordham Flower and Peter Hall were promised substantial financial help from members of Prime Minister Harold Macmillan's cabinet, but they found that their requests were cut substantially. Theater moguls hostile to the Royal Shakespeare Company's tenure at the Aldwych Theatre convinced politicians that only one company should be designated as "national"— and that the Stratford organization did not merit that designation. Nevertheless, the reputation the company had developed in the early years of Hall's governance (in part as a result of several brilliant productions directed by Peter Brook) was so impressive that the Royal Shakespeare Company became one of only a handful of agencies to be designated for permanent subsidy by the government. Of course, the government money alone would not have been sufficient to keep the company afloat without private help, and Hall spent considerable time working with the executive committee to continue seeking outside funding for his various projects. Ultimately, he left the Royal Shakespeare Company to take control of its new rival, the National Theatre Company.

The decades following receipt of government subsidies were not without difficulties, and on occasion, the company found itself struggling to recover from financial deficit despite the money it received. Nevertheless, Hall's successors, notably Trevor Nunn, who followed him as managing director, were able to build on the successes enjoyed by the company in the early 1960's, and the Royal Shakespeare Company became recognized as fully deserving of the support of the government. The British theater-going public, moreover, continued to travel to Stratford-on-Avon to see the Bard's work performed by a group of professionals dedicated to keeping alive the works of Shakespeare and the traditions of the Elizabethan stage.

The significance of the Royal Shakespeare Company in the history of the British theater has been aptly summarized by Sally Beauman, the author of a study of the company: "All the major changes that have affected the macrocosm of British theatre over the past hundred years," she notes, "can be seen in microcosm in the development of Stratford and its companies"; not the least of these changes, she notes, has been "the restitution of Shakespeare to the centre of the classical repertoire." Hall's strategy of renaming his group the "Royal Shakespeare Company" immediately gave the organization the national stamp it needed to continue its work amid increasing competition in a healthy theater environment.

Bibliography

Addenbrooke, David. *The Royal Shakespeare Company: The Peter Hall Years.* London: William Kimber, 1974. Detailed analysis of Peter Hall's efforts to reshape the image of the Royal Shakespeare Company and of his ongoing battle to gain subsidies from the British government for the company's operations. Includes information from numerous interviews with company members and Hall himself. Illustrated with photographs from company productions.

Beauman, Sally. *The Royal Shakespeare Company: A History of Ten Decades.* New York: Oxford University Press, 1982. Comprehensive study of the company from its founding to its inclusion in the nationally subsidized theater consortium in Great Britain during the later years of the twentieth century. Focuses on the personages who shaped the organization and the tensions between the business and artistic aspects of mounting productions. Photographs of several memorable actors, actresses, and productions.

Chambers, Colin. *Other Spaces: New Theatre and the Royal Shakespeare Company.*

London: Methuen, 1980. Outlines the Royal Shakespeare Company's venture into alternative theater under the leadership of feminist radical Buzz Goodbody. Includes an introductory chapter on the company's struggles during the years immediately after its receipt of government subsidies. Examines several Shakespearean and modern productions presented in alternative formats.

Coveny, Michael. "The NT and the RSC." *Drama* 150 (Winter, 1983): 4-8. Examines the history of the rival companies that fought over government subsidy during the early 1960's. Helpful for understanding why both the National Theatre Company and the Royal Shakespeare Company believed themselves to have been treated less than favorably by each other and by the government. Traces the development of both companies into the early 1980's.

David, Richard. *Shakespeare in the Theatre.* Cambridge, England: Cambridge University Press, 1978. Overview of important productions of Shakespearean dramas during the years 1949 to 1976. Includes significant discussions of Royal Shakespeare Company performances and good comparisons to the offerings of other companies. Richly illustrated with photographs.

Goodwin, John, ed. *Royal Shakespeare Theatre Company, 1960-1963.* New York: Theatre Arts Books, 1964. Photographic summary of major productions of the Royal Shakespeare Company during the first four years under Peter Hall's management. Shows some of the innovations introduced by Hall and those he hired. Includes essays on the theater and on acting by Hall and Robert Bolt; reprints selections from reviews and editorials concerning the productions.

Hall, Peter. *Peter Hall's Diaries: The Story of a Dramatic Battle.* Edited by John Goodwin. New York: Harper & Row, 1984. Selections from Hall's private diaries kept during the years 1972 to 1980, after he left the Royal Shakespeare Company for the National Theatre Company. Useful for tracing the influences of Hall's experiences at Stratford on his work and for understanding the relationship between the National Theatre Company and the Royal Shakespeare Company.

Laurence W. Mazzeno

Cross-References

Olivier's *Hamlet* Is Released to Acclaim and Controversy (1948), p. 1378; Osborne's *Look Back in Anger* Opens in London (1956), p. 1721; Great Britain Establishes the Royal National Theatre (1962), p. 1924; Weiss's Absurdist Drama *Marat/Sade* Is Produced (1964), p. 2005; The Theatres Act Ends Censorship of English Drama (1968), p. 2131.

TAWFIQ AL-HAKIM INTRODUCES
ABSURDISM TO THE ARAB STAGE

Category of event: Theater
Time: 1961
Locale: Tawfiq al-Hakim Theater, Cairo, Egypt

Tawfiq al-Hakim, Egypt's most distinguished modern author, was known for his experimentation with different dramatic styles, but he surprised the Arab world with his absurdist play The Tree Climber, *which was extremely contrary to Islamic thinking*

Principal personage:
> TAWFIQ AL-HAKIM (1898-1987), a novelist, essayist, and playwright considered the father of modern Egyptian theater who introduced several European dramatic styles to Arab literature

Summary of Event

By 1961, Tawfiq al-Hakim had secured for himself the leading position in Egyptian letters. Although he had written several novels and important essays and incidental pieces, al-Hakim's reputation rested principally on his work in drama. This circumstance would not be unusual in Western countries, where drama has always been considered a branch of literature; in the Middle East, however, there is no long tradition of writing for the theater. Indeed, in such great cities as Cairo, ancient capital of an ancient civilization, no theaters existed until the Napoleonic invasion (1798-1801), and the playhouse erected at that time was intended to provide entertainment for the invading troops. For most of the nineteenth century, the plays performed in Cairo were translations or adaptations of European dramas. In rural areas, several performance traditions had developed since medieval times. These included certain types of shadow puppet plays as well as singing, dancing, and comic skits. All these plays or dance plays were in the vernacular and were thus not considered worthy to be called literature.

During the first two decades of the twentieth century, theater emerged as a feature of Cairo's urban life, with plays written and performed in classical Arabic as well as the vernacular. In 1935, the Egyptian government established the National Theater Troupe, and al-Hakim's play *Ahl al-Kahf* (1933; *The People of the Cave*, 1955-1957) was selected for its debut. Thus, in a sense, Egyptian theater and al-Hakim sprang up together, and some consider *The People of the Cave* to be the first Arabic work that may properly be called drama.

There were theatrical movements at work through the twentieth century that would prepare the Egyptian public for al-Hakim's *Ya tali. al-shajarah* (1962; *The Tree Climber*, 1966). The Institute for Theater Arts, established at approximately the same time as the National Theater Troupe in order to train theater artists, had graduated a large number of accomplished actors, directors, designers, and writers by the 1950's, and several of these graduates established the Free Theater, an alternate to the National Theater Troupe. Within a decade, another alternative group, the Pocket Theater, had been formed. Most of the work presented in the alternative theaters, and to a great extent by the National Theater Troupe as well, was realistic and naturalistic, but modern issues of alienation, lack of communication, and human despair in the face of uncontrollable social and economic forces were all explored. This exploration doubtless presaged the inevitable introduction of existential themes.

Al-Hakim himself had been steadily supplying this "adolescent" theater of Egypt with quite producible and often compelling and powerful plays. He was strongly influenced by Western theater, for his career as a dramatist actually began in France, where on an extended visit from 1925 to 1928, he claimed that he was able to drink from real culture and to discover that, in Europe at least, literature and the theater were considered one entity. He especially fell under the influence of Henrik Ibsen, George Bernard Shaw, Luigi Pirandello, and Maurice Maeterlinck. Ibsen's and Shaw's works tutored al-Hakim in the presentation of social and economic issues; Pirandello's and Maeterlinck's revealed the power of symbolism and nonrealistic structures.

Throughout his prolific career as a playwright, al-Hakim experimented with all types of theater, classical, romantic, realistic, and surrealistic, and thus it is no surprise that, after a second visit to France in 1959 and 1960, he turned his hand to experimenting with France's new absurdist style. Introducing absurdism to the Arabic world was not, however, merely an issue of a new style. Basically, there is no compatibility between the tenants of absurdism and those of Islam, for the Islamic faith is rooted in the view of a harmonious world created by God with a wise purpose. On the other hand, the Theater of the Absurd grew out of the existential view that the universe is illogical and that the only order is that which man creates for himself. Despite the success of the premiere production of *The Tree Climber*, Egypt's two leading critics, Taha Husayn and al-Aqqad, had very negative reactions; al-Aqqad argued that it was not yet time to give up on rationality, and he urged a general rejection of the Theater of the Absurd.

Without question, al-Hakim's play is unremittingly absurdist and irrational. Structural devices and thematic issues common to the Theater of the Absurd shape *The Tree Climber*. Like Samuel Beckett's *Waiting for Godot* (1952), al-Hakim's play calls for a stage that is bare enough to represent everywhere or nowhere. At times the audience sees the home of the lead characters. At other times, though without change of scenery or special production effect, the audience sees a garden or the interior of a train. Moreover, time is as fluid and irrational as space. The playwright has "the present" on one area of the stage, while in another area scenes from "the past" occur, so that the same actor plays the past and present character simultaneously on different parts of the stage. Thus, the Husband, a man of sixty, speaks with the Detective in the present, while, simultaneously, a conversation between the young Husband and the young Wife is taking place in the past.

To the disordering of past and present, the dramatist adds an irrational plot. A man, known only as the Husband, is accused of murdering his wife. He is closely questioned by the Detective, but the questions and answers—seemingly so rational when taken individually—lead only to continuing confusion. In exasperation, the Detective asks if there is any way of getting to the point. The Husband replies that he does not know the way.

The circuitous questioning of the Husband and the Housemaid is intercut with scenes from the past, scenes in which viewers discover that the Wife has continuously vanished and reappeared. At the end of act 1, the Husband is taken to prison for more questioning, while the police dig under a mysterious tree in the garden searching for the Wife's corpse.

Act 2 begins with the appearance of the Wife. Since there is no murder, the Husband is returned from jail. He attempts to discover where the Wife has been, but his constant inquiries result only in the same baffling irresolution as the act 1 questioning. Maddened by a world without rationality, the Husband now murders the Wife.

Or does he? Is this a real world or a tissue of intangibles, of fantasy in which the murdered Wife will continue to reappear and the accused Husband continue to be jailed? Al-Hakim poses his question: Is not all of life an absurdity, an irrational ritual? His answer may be found in an exchange between the Detective and the Husband in which the Detective angrily accuses the Husband of twisting words to suit himself. The Husband replies that such is not the case at all, because the words become twisted to suit themselves.

Impact of Event

The Tree Climber was published in 1962, almost immediately after its premiere production. Because it was written in classical Arabic, the play enjoyed wide circulation in the Arab world and was, and continues to be, read by many who live in places where theaters never existed. For Arabic culture, al-Hakim's accomplishment is in joining modern Western existentialism to ancient Islamic attitudes. There followed in 1963 another absurdist play from al-Hakim, *al-Ta'am li-kull fam* (*Food for the Millions*, 1964), and in 1964 two more absurdist works. Indeed, after 1961, al-Hakim employed absurdist themes and devices even in his stylistically realistic and renowned work *Masir Sursar* (1966; *The Fate of a Cockroach*, 1973). His embracing of certain aspects of the Theater of the Absurd and his ability to interweave these very Western techniques and ideas with the Islamic belief in a fundamental order in the universe influenced a new generation of Arabic playwrights, including Numan Ashur, Yusef Idris, Alfred Farag, and Ali Salim. These writers have become aware of new trends in Europe and America and have learned the value of importing dramaturgic ideas even as they create a new, Islamic theater. Were it not for al-Hakim's bold move in *The Tree Climber*, Egyptian theater may well have stalled in realism.

For it is difficult for Islamic fundamentalists, even in the contemporary world, to accept the irrational. Al-Hakim had always considered in his works the contradictions in human existence: the contradiction between things of the mind and things of the heart; the contradiction between life's tangibles and mysterious, abstract forces; the contradiction between the desire to know and the inability to communicate. These contrary forces can sometimes get out of balance. Conflict ensues, and conflict is the essence of drama. Consequently, al-Hakim used drama to study the clash of contradictions. In plays such as *The Tree Climber*, al-Hakim does not attempt to solve the conflict but merely tries to suggest a balance. The lives of the humans in the play are pointless, and their search for logic in their affairs proves futile. Powerful emotions such as the Husband's love for the Wife cannot be made concrete, nor can they be made knowable. Hence the Wife is associated with a green lizard, which is always present in the garden whenever the Wife appears. The audience knows only that the lizard is attractive and mysterious, much as the Wife, and is left to accept the mystery. On the other hand, the Husband is associated with the marvelous tree in the garden, which grows out of a corpse and under which the Detective believes the murdered wife to be buried. The tree seems to promise some special knowledge, but the Husband cannot decipher its secret. Thus, the conflict between the desire to know and the impossibility of realizing that desire remains unresolved.

Finally, there is the character of the Dervish, who has puzzled analysts of *The Tree Climber*. He seems the personification of all that is abstract, ineffable. Yet he is there, promising at any minute to reveal a special secret about life. Even with his mysterious qualities, perhaps especially because of them, the Dervish remains attractive.

The lizard, the marvelous tree, and the Dervish are all drawn from the well of Eastern symbolism, as is the play's title, which is taken from an Egyptian children's song. These symbols suggest that though the intellect sees the absurd, the heart might sense a way to a greater order, that accepting present absurdities also allows one to gain a balance with the more abstract, more irrational forces in the universe. This is what the Wife does, while the Husband, seeking to resolve the conflict, only loses the precious balance, falls into violence, and solves nothing. Thus it was that al-Hakim wed the modern Theater of the Absurd to the traditions of Islam and offered a challenge for a new generation of Arabic dramatists.

Yet al-Hakim was not merely an importer and adapter of Western ideas to the Arab world. He exported his work as well. Within four years of its first production, *The Tree Climber* had been translated into English and produced in London and America. His ties with France have always been important, and *The Tree Climber* was well received in that country. After the first production of *The Tree Climber*, international interest in his works intensified. More than seventy of his plays, novels, stories, and essays have been published in various translations, including translations of forty-one pieces into English. Productions of his works, especially *The Tree Climber* and *The Fate of a Cockroach*, are frequent internationally. His memory is revered in Egypt, where a major theater in Cairo bears his name. In the West, al-Hakim has taught anew the route out of Western intellectualist dilemmas through Eastern mysticism.

Bibliography

Allen, Roger, ed. *Modern Arabic Literature*. New York: Frederick Ungar, 1987. A useful general discussion for background and for placing al-Hakim in the context of modern Arabic writers. Philosophic and theological issues of Islam discussed as these matters influence Arabic literature of the twentieth century.

Badawi, Muhammed Mustafa. *Early Arabic Drama.* Cambridge, England: Cambridge University Press, 1988. Forerunners of al-Hakim and his contemporaries. Sources of their tradition and what they often revolted against. Excellent review of various folk drama and festival performances and traditions.

_____. *Modern Arabic Drama in Egypt.* New York: Cambridge University Press, 1987. Badawi discusses nineteen Egyptian playwrights, with consideration given to thematic issues and to each writer's place in modern Egypt's life and thought. For al-Hakim specifically, the discussion ranges from minor works written before *The People of the Cave* to the absurdist plays.

Hakim, Tawfiq. *Plays, Prefaces and Postscripts of Tawfiq al-Hakim.* Translated by W. M. Hutchins. 2 vols. Washington, D.C.: Three Continents Press, 1984. A relatively complete collection of al-Hakim's dramatic works and his essays that were first published with each play. Includes other commentary and postscripts that al-Hakim later added concerning the plays.

_____. *The Tree Climber.* Translated by Denys Johnson-Davies. London: Oxford University Press, 1966. Probably the best English translation of this influential play.

Long, Richard. *Tawfiq al-Hakim: Playwright of Egypt.* London: Ithaca Press, 1979. Chronological description of al-Hakim's life and works. First part is a biography; second part provides synopses and general comments on thirty-two plays. Plays are arranged thematically, with discussions of similarities and differences between various plays dealing with the same issues.

Starkey, Paul. *From the Ivory Tower: A Critical Analysis of Tawfiq al-Hakim.* London: Ithaca Press, 1988. A study of the themes and issues in al-Hakim's novels, plays, and essays, with particular emphasis on contradictions that developed in the author's thinking throughout his long career. Also offers a discussion of language, form, and structure. Particular attention is given to what the author perceives as structural shortcomings in the dramas.

August W. Staub

Cross-References

The Ghost Sonata Influences Modern Theater and Drama (1908), p. 199; Sartre and Camus Give Dramatic Voice to Existential Philosophy (1940's), p. 1174; *Waiting for Godot* Expresses the Existential Theme of Absurdity (1953), p. 1573; Ionesco's *Rhinoceros* Receives a Resounding Worldwide Reception (1959), p. 1812; Esslin Publishes *The Theatre of the Absurd* (1961), p. 1871; *The American Dream* Establishes Albee as the Voice of Pessimism (1961), p. 1903; Mahfouz Wins the Nobel Prize in Literature (1988), p. 2625.

WEBSTER'S THIRD NEW INTERNATIONAL DICTIONARY SPARKS LINGUISTIC CONTROVERSY

Category of event: Literature
Time: 1961
Locale: Springfield, Massachusetts

Publication of this new dictionary was received with protests from purists who thought that the Merriam-Webster Company had betrayed standards by recording the actual speech of Americans

Principal personages:

PHILIP B. GOVE (1902-1972), the chief editor of *Webster's Third New International Dictionary*

DWIGHT MACDONALD (1906-1982), a prominent journalist who attacked the dictionary in *The New Yorker*

WILSON FOLLETT (1887-1963), a scholar and journalist whose severe judgment appeared in *The Atlantic Monthly*

JAMES SLEDD (1914-   ), a professor at Northwestern University who strongly supported the new work

MARIO A. PEI (1901-1978), a professor at Columbia University who wrote a balanced appraisal of the new dictionary

PATRICK E. KILBURN (1922-1974), a professor at Union College who supported Gove and his work

Summary of Event

In October, 1961, the G. & C. Merriam Company published its *Webster's Third New International Dictionary*, a direct descendant of Noah Webster's famous *An American Dictionary of the English Language* of 1828. Production of *Webster's Third* cost more than $3,500,000, about three times the amount of its predecessor, *Webster's New International Dictionary of the English Language* (1934); it was based on more than ten million citations, and it included among its more than 450,000 main entries 100,000 words or new meanings not found in previous editions. Other features included 200,000 usage examples, three thousand black-and-white illustrations, one thousand synonym articles clarifying five thousand often-confused words, rich etymologies, careful distinctions in pronunciation by region and by level of formality, fifty tables of special information, and sections explaining punctuation conventions and forms of address. Yet it also contained 150,000 fewer entries than a 1959 revision of the 1934 work had and took up nearly five hundred fewer pages. *Webster's Third* weighed in at thirteen and a half pounds and cost $47.50.

Such a detailed and comprehensive work of scholarship would probably strike most people as exemplary, but writers and editors screamed their outrage at once. *The New York Times*, the *Chicago Tribune*, *Life* magazine, and many other magazines and newspapers condemned the new dictionary and indignantly proclaimed their allegiance to its predecessor, in which they thought more rigorous standards still guided the serious dictionary user.

The reasons for this mass protest from the American press lie in human psychology and can be traced to popular conceptions (or *mis*conceptions) of the nature of language and to the expectations people nurture of dictionaries. As far back as the seventeenth century, English men of letters such as John Dryden had hoped to arrest change in the English language. In the eighteenth century, Joseph Addison and Jonathan Swift had envisioned an English academy as the proper institution to slow corruption of the language. Samuel Johnson sympathized with this conservative viewpoint but opposed the idea of an academy, and as he worked on his *A Dictionary of the English Language* (1755), he came to realize that the ideal of stability in a language was unrealistic. Even so, Johnson hoped that his dictionary would work against the eventual decay of the tongue, and he thus became a powerful force behind the philosophy that saw the lexicographer as an arbiter of standards in usage and spelling.

In America, John Adams, the second president of the United States, proposed an American academy in 1780, a goal taken up by Noah Webster and others in 1788 when they formed a philological society in New York. The proposal was criticized by, among others, the dramatist Royall Tyler, and the society soon expired. The urge to regularize lived on, but it became entangled with nationalistic spirit. Whereas some Anglophiles (the philologist John Pickering, for example) wanted to fix American English in the forms of cultivated British speech, Webster identified language usage with patriotism, and his view soon dominated practice.

Although Webster had originally considered recent changes in the language to be a falling off from Elizabethan perfection, he soon realized that it was too late to preserve the language of a bygone age. He thus aimed for a distinctly American speech that would offer a national standard and unify its peoples. In spelling, for example, he wanted words such as *favour* and *colour* to lose their *u*'s, *theatre* and *centre* to become *theater* and *center*, and *musick* and *publick* to drop their *k*'s. Other innovations, strictly phonetic, such as *thum* for *thumb* and *lether* for *leather*, failed to stick.

Webster's great *An American Dictionary of the English Language* was the most important work in lexicography since Johnson's dictionary seventy-three years earlier, and he hoped it would help guide the language back to correctness. The whole issue of authoritarianism in language broke out anew, however, in mid-century with the 1830 publication by Joseph E. Worcester of his *Comprehensive Pronouncing and Explanatory Dictionary of the English Language.* Worcester was closer to British forms, and his work attracted support from Anglophiles and Boston Brahmins who had never been fully won by Webster's American spirit. With the publication of a revised, clearly superior edition of Webster's work in 1864, though, the dispute faded into history.

A long history thus lay behind the uproar caused by *Webster's Third*, which had a genealogy extending back to Noah Webster himself. The G. & C. Merriam Company had bought the rights to Webster's dictionary when he died in 1843 and had produced more than a century of revisions. When it was published in 1961, therefore, *Webster's Third* was merely the latest battle in a long campaign fought between linguistic prescriptivists and descriptivists.

Impact of Event

Serious, detailed criticism of the new work began with Wilson Follett's attack in *The Atlantic Monthly* in January, 1962. According to Follett, *Webster's Third* was "a very great calamity," a hodgepodge of "the questionable, the perverse, the unworthy, and the downright outrageous." In addition to lamenting that such facts as the names of the apostles were not to be found in *Webster's Third*, Follett inveighed against "the extreme tolerance of crude neologisms and of shabby diction generally" and protested the book's condoning of such usages as *due to* as an adverb, *center around*, *different than*, and other solecisms. Follett's peroration envisioned a domino effect of uninformed language use leading to "the really enormous disaster that can and will be wrought by the lexicographer's abandonment of his responsibility."

Dwight Macdonald's long, well-reasoned, and well-written piece in *The New Yorker* of March 10, 1962, was much more perceptive and difficult to defend against. Macdonald shared the common suspicion of *Webster's Third*'s attitude toward usage questions, but he mounted a far subtler attack on what he considered the philosophical underpinnings of the work. Macdonald referred specifically to the school of language study known as structural linguistics and pointed to its basic precepts as outlined by Philip Gove, the chief editor of *Webster's Third*: Language changes constantly; change is normal; spoken language is the language; correctness rests on usage; and all usage is relative. Such a vision of the nature of language, Macdonald argued, had engendered Gove's mistaken conception of a dictionary as "a recording instrument rather than as an authority." Macdonald viewed Gove's scholarship as part of the barren enterprise of modern science.

With this fundamental critique established, Macdonald revealed that he had spent considerable time reading *Webster's Third*. Although much of his discussion offered only the good reviewer's informative account of his subject, he also pointed out embarrassing inconsistencies (in the adjectival forms of proper names, for example) and absurdities in the tedious listing of words beginning with *non-* and *un-*. Macdonald's essay was a stimulating exploration of the issues, but its main criticism was the same as Follett's: that civilization was threatened by the barbarisms of the mob.

Among the more temperate reviewers, Mario Pei in *The New York Times Book Review* discovered some inconsistencies in *Webster's Third* but commented that the book was "the closest we can get, in America, to the Voice of Authority." The prestigious British science journal *Nature* was very pleased with *Webster's Third*, but its American counterpart, *Science*, bemoaned an inadequate distinction between illiterate and literate usage. The *American Bar Association Journal* entitled its review "Logomachy—Debased Verbal Currency," while the *Law Times* proclaimed that Gove's confidence in the new work was "well founded."

One of the best defenses of *Webster's Third* came from Patrick Kilburn. Writing in the *Union College Symposium*, Kilburn described Follett's purism as no longer respectable and charged Macdonald with "linguistic arrogance." Kilburn was convincing because his homework was excellent; for example, by comparing the usage judgments of six prominent dictionaries, he revealed a complete lack of consensus on the meanings and status of twenty-five questionable words. Kilburn accused *Webster's Third*'s critics of not following their own preachments, and he struck a telling blow by quoting Ambrose Bierce's definition of a *dictionary* as "a malevolent literary device for cramping the growth of a language and making it hard and inelastic."

When James Sledd and Wilma Ebbitt edited *Dictionaries and* That *Dictionary* (1962), Sledd invited Macdonald to respond to Kilburn's defense of *Webster's Third*. Macdonald then raised three questions: Can a dictionary be nonprescriptive? What is the nature of change in language? and What kind of authority, if any, should attempt to direct and control change? Macdonald elaborated at length on his third question, and Kilburn and Sledd answered his questions in separate essays. Sledd seethed with a sense of having been personally attacked, and his defense was feisty; he called Macdonald's review "portentously bad" and "disgraced by just that sort of ignorance and unfairness which cheap journalism in a mass culture would substitute for scholarship." After setting this personal tone, Sledd charged Macdonald with sloppiness with facts, ignorance of the nature of linguistic change, and a confused sense of what constitutes good English. Sledd closed with a spirited proposal: "The constructive critic of the *Third International* will be the man who shows how its descriptions can be improved."

The great usage debate eventually subsided, and *Webster's Third* earned a secure spot in many libraries, public and private. For the ordinary user, the most practical result of the controversy was perhaps the innovations it produced in subsequent dictionaries; *The American Heritage Dictionary of the English Language*, for example, now explains after its entry on *infer* that ninety-two percent of its judges do not accept *infer* as a synonym for *imply*. The reasonableness of such a solution seems inevitable. Although the universal hunger for a priori truths will no doubt keep the debate of usage questions alive, nothing will arrest change in a living language.

Bibliography

Gove, Philip Babcock, ed. *The Role of the Dictionary*. Indianapolis, Ind.: Bobbs-Merrill, 1967. Designed for classroom use with questions and exercises, this collection of thirteen short essays generally supports Gove and the principles of *Webster's Third*. The contributors include well-known language scholars such as Bergen Evans and Albert H. Marckwardt as well as Kurt Vonnegut, Jr., who writes entertainingly—and sensibly—on "The Latest Word."

Gray, Jack C., ed. *Words, Words, and Words About Dictionaries*. San Francisco: Chandler, 1963. A collection of twenty pieces discussing such topics as "Words and Meaning" and "Words over *Webster's Third New International Dictionary*." A good collection with well-designed materials for classroom use.

Hulbert, James Root. *Dictionaries: British and American.* London: Andre Deutsch, 1955. Although he sketches the history of English dictionaries, what Hulbert does best is spell out the steps involved in making a dictionary—from deciding on its scope to choosing such nonlexicographical features as tables of money and pronouncing gazetteers. He also describes *The Oxford English Dictionary* and others like it.

Kraske, Robert. *The Story of the Dictionary.* New York: Harcourt Brace Jovanovich, 1975. A short and very readable account for young people. Chapters on the first dictionary makers, on Samuel Johnson and Noah Webster and their dictionaries, on *The Oxford English Dictionary*, on the sources of the words in dictionaries, on the making of a modern dictionary, on dictionaries for young people, and on the living English language. Illustrations.

Lodwig, Richard R., and Eugene F. Barrett. *The Dictionary and the Language.* New York: Hayden, 1967. An excellent survey. Separate chapters treat early dictionaries, the variety of modern dictionaries, the making of dictionaries (including "The W3 Controversy"), dictionary usage, the history of English, the processes of word creation, word meanings, and word changes. Exercises for classroom use.

Sledd, James H., and Wilma R. Ebbitt, eds. *Dictionaries and* That *Dictionary: A Casebook on the Aims of Lexicographers and the Targets of Reviewers.* Chicago: Scott, Foresman, 1962. The best source for students of the *Webster's Third* controversy. Seven lexicographers speak for themselves in the first section. Part 2 is a rich collection of reviews, favorable and unfavorable, and responses. The book's postscript includes a lively debate between Dwight Macdonald and Patrick Kilburn and James Sledd. Excellent teaching materials.

Wells, Ronald A. *Dictionaries and the Authoritarian Tradition: A Study in English Usage and Lexicography.* The Hague: Mouton, 1973. Scholarly but completely readable history of the prescriptive, as opposed to descriptive, view of dictionary editing. Informative chapters on the origins of English lexicography, the authoritarian tradition in both England and America, the war over *Webster's Third*, and dictionaries and usage. Long and indispensable bibliography.

Frank Day

Cross-References

The Book-of-the-Month Club and the Literary Guild Are Founded (1926), p. 686; The New Criticism Holds Sway (1940's), p. 1169; The Great Books Foundation Is Established (1947), p. 1351; McLuhan Probes the Impact of Mass Media on Society (1964), p. 1973; Derrida Enunciates the Principles of Deconstruction (1967), p. 2075.

THE AMERICAN DREAM ESTABLISHES ALBEE AS THE VOICE OF PESSIMISM

Category of event: Theater
Time: January 24, 1961
Locale: York Playhouse, New York, New York

An American play in the absurdist tradition, The American Dream *was a caustic and hilarious examination of U.S. society*

Principal personages:
EDWARD ALBEE (1928-), a playwright considered by many to be the best American writer of the 1960's
SAMUEL BECKETT (1906-1989), an avant-garde playwright of international fame
EUGÈNE IONESCO (1912-), a playwright who focused on the futility of life and the inadequacies of language

Summary of Event

Born on March 12, 1928, Edward Albee was abandoned by his birth parents. He was adopted by Reed and Frances Albee. His adoptive grandfather was Edward F. Albee, who made a fortune on the vaudeville stage. At the age of nineteen, the younger Edward moved to Greenwich Village. As a result of his unsettled beginnings, Albee was an unstable and undisciplined youth. His life was filled with rebellion; his time was spent dropping in and out of schools. During the early period of his life, he held many odd jobs.

In this book *The Theatre of the Absurd* (1961), Martin Esslin identified an anti-realism movement that he labeled absurdism. The movement's major international writers included Eugène Ionesco, Samuel Beckett, Jean Genet, and Harold Pinter. These writers told of the absurdity of life. It was their central belief that the world was full of evil, a malevolent condition that could not be explained by traditional standards of morality. Without a supreme being in control of the universe, people are confronted with lives filled with pain and despair. Since there can be no certainty that God exists, individuals find themselves forced to live without hope in a chaotic world filled with irrationality and certain death. Albee wrote his plays in this context.

Albee had four absurdist plays produced Off-Broadway in the late 1950's and early 1960's: *The Zoo Story* (1959), *The Sandbox* (1960), *The Death of Bessie Smith* (1960), and *The American Dream* (1961). Each of these plays followed in the absurdist tradition that had developed during the 1950's in Europe. These Off-Broadway productions established Albee as the leading American playwright of the period.

The Zoo Story, his first published play, was written shortly before he turned thirty. The play shows Albee's rebellion against a world filled with conformity. It reflects a protest of disillusioned cynicism. The play comments directly on material comfort, hypocrisy, relational inadequacies, and the optimism that pervaded culture in the United States during the 1950's.

The playwright had begun work on *The American Dream* prior to receiving a commission to write *The Sandbox*. The plays reflect similar themes and characters: American family life is portrayed as complacent and cruel. Both plays look at and attack the lack of true family values.

The American Dream begins with Mommy and Daddy angrily waiting for a visitor. Their small talk is filled with clichés. When Grandma enters, she talks about being old and useless. It is Mommy's and Daddy's intention to send her to an extended care facility. Grandma reproaches her daughter for the daughter's scheming plans to do away with her. Grandma reminds Daddy of her warning not to marry "this monster" (Mommy). Suddenly, Mrs. Barker arrives. She is confused, and no one seems to know why she has come to the apartment.

When Mommy and Daddy have left the room, Mrs. Barker learns the reason for her visit, as perceived by Grandma. Apparently, twenty years earlier Mrs. Barker had helped Mommy and Daddy adopt a baby boy. It seems the boy was punished for misbehaving. Its eyes were poked out, its hands were cut off, its tongue was cut out, and finally it was castrated. The baby died. Mommy and Daddy want satisfaction for their loss. When the doorbell rings again, a Young Man, the American Dream, is standing there, asking for work. The Young Man reveals to Grandma information about his long-lost twin. The Young Man also tells Grandma about his "infirmity"—his progressive deterioration of spirit and body. His physical mutilations are like those suffered by the boy adopted by Mommy and Daddy. The Young Man finds himself unable to express or experience feelings and love. Grandma and Mrs. Barker arrange to have Mommy and Daddy adopt the Young Man. The play ends abruptly, with Grandma telling the audience that this is a good place to end the show, with everyone happy and thinking they got what they desired. The play serves as an absurd comment on the sanctity of the American family and its values.

This and other early plays made Albee the leading absurdist in the United States. The plays focused on existential issues. His characters struggled with moral issues and had to learn the lesson that truth is what a person thinks it is. The tension between morality and "truth" creates his characters' struggles.

By 1962, Albee had moved into the theatrical mainstream. His play *Who's Afraid of Virginia Woolf?* (1962) offered an examination of a bitter, alienated, and bored society. The play links him with realist playwrights such as Tennessee Williams and August Strindberg. Albee attacks the vulgarity of a society that will not accept the value and importance of life. This play depicts an older generation that has struggled to order and structure the chaos of human existence. A younger generation is unwilling to recognize the need to order the chaos and will not accept the validity of traditions. *Who's Afraid of Virginia Woolf?* is, in part, an examination of generational conflict set in a world of confusion and chaos. The conflict leaves neither group untouched.

Albee's later works primarily deal with values. The dramatic action seems to center around the characters' attempts to give rational explanations of why it is they have been "picked on" in life. The characters seem to have martyr complexes. They do not see themselves as responsible for their situations and instead blame others.

Impact of Event

The philosophical foundation of *The American Dream* can be found in the work of existentialists Albert Camus and Jean-Paul Sartre. Their works presented a world view filled with absurdity. They saw sociopolitical structures of the world as façades constructed by those with power and money. Camus and Sartre questioned the established moral standards and the existence of universal or absolute moral truths. They claimed that morality was an individual matter.

The American Dream combines the French avant-garde and the American theater tradition. It is a nightmarish comedy. The action and dialogue of the play reveal characters overcome with their life situations in a nihilistic and immoral world. The family is an empty façade. Albee condemns the complacency and cruelty found in American family relationships. The relational dimension is without content and form. Words pass mechanically among the characters without any real meaning. They are caught living lives filled with worry about trivial and mundane issues, such as whether the color of the hat purchased by Mommy is beige, wheat, or cream. Albee shows the family as it really is when confronted with empty relationships, old age, and death.

The American Dream's theme springs from the burden of Albee's personal rejection by his natural parents as an infant. His attack on maternal instinct and the stereotypical view of the American family reveals his resentment. This one-act satirical farce unveils the anguish of a man whose ideal has been destroyed. *The American Dream* is Albee's voice of pain. In the style of Eugène Ionesco, Samuel Beckett, and Jean Genet, the playwright assimilates the techniques of French absurdism in order to produce a play of American absurdism.

Albee was convinced that a playwright's drama should create awareness while challenging an audience to examine societal diversity and complexity. He has said, "Creative artists are encouraged to put people into a sleep of the mind—when the true function of the arts, of course, is to make us more aware." A world of chaos is what surrounds people. The daily existence of people is hopeless and worthless. The absurdity of it all is heightened by the reality that, with the weapons of mass destruction that exist, the world could come to an end at any given moment in time.

In Albee's *The American Dream*, however, there is a sense of ordered absurdity. The dramatic structure follows the realistic form. This serves to highlight the actual absurdity of the relationships in the play. Unlike the work of many of the European absurdist playwrights, *The American Dream* makes use of realistic scenery, lighting, costumes, and makeup.

The recognition gained by the Off-Broadway production of *The American Dream* propelled Albee to worldwide acclaim as one of the best absurdist playwrights. In fact, the play was his first to gain immediate acclaim in the United States. The hostile publicity surrounding the play helped to focus attention on the playwright and on *The American Dream*. This particular play has been identified as one of the best dealing with familial relationships.

The language contained in *The American Dream* accentuates the relational absurdity in the characters' lives. Mommy attempts to attribute the desire to put Grandma into a nursing home to Daddy, when in fact the plan is hers. Her rationale is that she cannot stand to see Grandma cooking, doing housework, and moving furniture—all seemingly actions of someone fully prepared and able to continue to lead a non-institutionalized life. It is clear that Albee is expressing the absurdity of the good life in the United States. The contradictions of relationships, the feelings of frustration, and the futility of life are evident in what the characters say to each other. Realistic dialogue is structured in elliptical events revealing a certain absurd logic of social confusion.

Styled in the absurdist theater tradition, *The American Dream* brought a European flavor to the American stage. The play makes a caustic attack on American values and morals. Participants find the play to be hilariously funny. Albee uses wild exaggeration, not to imitate but to mock the prevailing societal values of the late 1950's and early 1960's. A domineering wife and henpecked husband make a statement about the façade of American values. The play rattles the observer, who must pause to examine and to consider the true meanings of values and relationships.

Albee's ability to capture the absurdity in American culture was not limited to *The American Dream*. *The Zoo Story*, *The Death of Bessie Smith*, and *The Sandbox* consolidated the strength of his position as the leading absurdist playwright in the United States. In *Who's Afraid of Virginia Woolf?*, some have seen a move away from his absurdist writings. If, however, one considers the bitter language, the sense of alienation, and the boredom of the characters, it is easy to recognize continued absurdist tendencies.

The effect of *The American Dream* on Albee's writing can be seen throughout his work in the 1960's and into the 1970's. Such works as *Tiny Alice* (1964), *A Delicate Balance* (1966), and *All Over* (1971) extended Albee's influence as a writer focusing on people's alienation. *Seascape* (1975) continued to reflect absurdist influences. Along with the short plays produced Off-Broadway in the 1960-1961 season, Albee's later plays strongly influenced the work of many other dramatists. Albee's success Off-Broadway opened the door of opportunity for other American playwrights.

American culture and society felt the impact of Albee's message. Thoughtful individuals raised questions about the validity of the moral standards of society. Questions concerning how to function as members of a family, obligations to other family members, and the plight of the elderly challenged audiences to examine the prevailing sense of optimism in the United States.

Bibliography
Archer, Stephen M. *How Theatre Happens*. New York: Macmillan, 1978. Covers topics including architecture, directing, acting, designing, and playwriting. Also

includes a theoretical discussion of what theater is.

Boyce, Sandra N. *Welcome to the Theatre.* Chicago: Nelson-Hall, 1987. A good introduction providing information on theater conventions, play production, and major movements throughout theater history.

Brockett, Oscar G. *History of the Theatre.* 6th ed. Boston: Allyn & Bacon, 1991. This comprehensive study of the theater is recommended reading for serious students of the theater. Brockett provides a thorough look at trends and movements affecting the evolution of the American theater.

_____. *The Theatre: An Introduction.* 4th ed. New York: Holt, Rinehart and Winston, 1979. In chapters 11 through 13, Brockett offers an excellent overview of historical trends in modern theater from 1915 through 1975.

Debusscher, Gilbert. *Edward Albee: Tradition and Renewal.* Translated by Anne D. Williams. Brussels, Belgium: Center for American Studies, 1969. Provides invaluable information about *The American Dream* and its influence on 1960's theater in the United States in one short section.

Hartnoll, Phyllis. *The Concise History of Theatre.* New York: Harry N. Abrams, 1968. Gives a synoptic view of major movements in the theater.

Wilson, Edwin. *The Theater Experience.* 4th ed. New York: McGraw-Hill, 1988. Examines numerous aspects of the theater in a discussion that highlights various developments in staging, acting, directing, and playwriting. The book contains an excellent set of five appendices, including "Major Theatrical Forms and Movements" and "Historical Outline."

Woods, Porter. *Experiencing Theatre.* Englewood Cliffs, N.J.: Prentice-Hall, 1984. Along with a brief history of the theater, Woods provides information about various aspects of the theater, including actors, playwrights, designers, and directors.

Willis M. Watt

Cross-References

The Ghost Sonata Influences Modern Theater and Drama (1908), p. 199; Pirandello's *Six Characters in Search of an Author* Premieres (1921), p. 534; Sartre and Camus Give Dramatic Voice to Existential Philosophy (1940's), p. 1174; *Waiting for Godot* Expresses the Existential Theme of Absurdity (1953), p. 1573; Ionesco's *Rhinoceros* Receives a Resounding Worldwide Reception (1959), p. 1812; Pinter's *The Caretaker* Opens in London (1960), p. 1861; Esslin Publishes *The Theatre of the Absurd* (1961), p. 1871.

THE DICK VAN DYKE SHOW POPULARIZES SITUATION COMEDY

Category of event: Television and radio
Time: October 3, 1961-September 7, 1966
Locale: The United States

The Dick Van Dyke Show *helped to mature the situation comedy through its strong scripts, believable characters, a realistic approach to light comedy, and good ensemble performing*

Principal personages:

CARL REINER (1922-   ), the creator of the series, who wrote many of the show's scripts and played the egotistical television star Alan Brady

SHELDON LEONARD (1907-   ), the producer of the series, who made important casting changes and saved the program after its first-season cancellation

DICK VAN DYKE (1925-   ), the actor who played Rob Petrie, the head writer of the fictional variety program *The Alan Brady Show*

MARY TYLER MOORE (1937-   ), the actress who played Laura Petrie, Rob's wife

JERRY PARIS (1925-1986), the actor-director who directed many episodes of the series and who played Jerry Helper, the Petries' next-door neighbor

BILL PERSKY (1931-   ) and

SAM DENOFF (1928-   ), a writing team that contributed many scripts for the third, fourth, and fifth seasons of the show

MOREY AMSTERDAM (1914-   ), the actor who played Buddy Sorrell, one of Rob's writing staff on *The Alan Brady Show*

ROSE-MARIE (ROSE-MARIE MAZZATTA, 1925-   ), the actress who played Sally Rogers, one of Rob's writing staff on *The Alan Brady Show*

RICHARD DEACON (1922-1984), the actor who played Mel Cooley, Alan Brady's brother-in-law and the producer of *The Alan Brady Show*

ANN MORGAN GUILBERT (1928-   ), the actress who played Millie Helper, the Petries' friend and next-door neighbor

Summary of Event

To Carl Reiner, the writers' room of *Your Show of Shows*, the popular comedy-variety television show starring Sid Caesar, was "the most interesting room I'd ever been in." Reiner wrote and performed on *Your Show of Shows*, but in 1959, when he was considering offers for a new television project, he was disappointed by the quality of the material he read.

Deciding that a situation comedy would be a better vehicle for him than the older format of the variety show, Reiner began searching for a premise. He fell back on the first rule for writers: "Write about what you know." Reiner later recalled that he asked himself, "What ground do I stand on that no one else stands on? I thought, I am an actor and writer who worked on the Sid Caesar shows. That's a different milieu: the home life of a television show writer." From that concept came *The Dick Van Dyke Show.*

The program was to be called *Head of the Family*, and Reiner would play Robert Petrie, whose work life and home life the show would explore. Until then, television had often focused on one or the other. Mel Brooks, another writer from *Your Show of Shows*, has said that every memorable television show is about a house and a family; Reiner's new comedy would explore two family situations—one at home, one at work. Reiner wrote thirteen scripts for the prospective series before a pilot was filmed.

Although the sponsors later rejected the pilot episode (at the time, Westerns were the most popular shows on television), producer Sheldon Leonard saw potential in Reiner's idea. Leonard read Reiner's other twelve scripts and told him that he wanted to "rewrap the package" by recasting the lead and tailoring the show to the studio-audience, three-camera format pioneered by *I Love Lucy*. Reiner agreed, and they began redesigning the show. Leonard and Reiner saw Dick Van Dyke on Broadway and chose him over Johnny Carson for the part of comedy writer Rob Petrie. Leonard completed the rest of the cast, choosing Mary Tyler Moore to play Rob's wife Laura, Morey Amsterdam and Rose-Marie to play his writing partners Buddy Sorrell and Sally Rogers, Jerry Paris and Ann Morgan Guilbert to play the best friends next door, and Richard Deacon to play the producer of the fictional program *The Alan Brady Show*, for which Rob and his staff would work.

The program debuted on the Columbia Broadcasting System (CBS) network on October 3, 1961, but did not develop a loyal following until its second season. Sheldon Leonard (who remarked that "the more realistic the show, the more honest the characters, the longer it takes to become part of your lifestyle") talked the sponsor, Procter & Gamble, into reversing the network's decision to cancel the show after the first season. When the series began its third year, the writing team of Bill Persky and Sam Denoff, attracted to the show by its quality, contributed a number of scripts and eased the writing duties of Carl Reiner. Eventually, the series ran five years (158 episodes), until June 1, 1966. The last first-run episode, "The Last Chapter," brought the show full circle by having Alan Brady buy Rob's autobiography for a television project to be written by Rob, Buddy, and Sally. Dick Van Dyke and Carl Reiner both agree that the crew had decided when the show first became popular to quit after five years to safeguard quality. By that time, many cast members wanted to pursue new projects. When the show left the air, it had received fifteen Emmy Awards, two Golden Globe Awards, and three Writers Guild of America Awards.

A good one-word description of the Van Dyke series can be found in Sheldon Leonard's remark: honest. Reiner stressed to prospective writers for the show that they should never have Rob Petrie do anything that they themselves would not do.

This honesty permitted the show to narrow the distance between life as shown on television and as experienced by everyday people. Norman Lear has praised the program as being "the first situational comedy to deal with authentic human behavior in the context of a real marriage." Moreover, Reiner's background in 1950's television extended the authenticity into Rob's workplace, giving *The Dick Van Dyke Show* a genuine behind-the-scenes show-business flavor.

Viewers often saw the writers working on script ideas. In one episode from the first season ("The Curious Thing About Women"), the two settings of home and work blend perfectly. Rob politely chides Laura at breakfast for opening his mail. Later at work, he tells Buddy and Sally about the incident, inspiring a frantic writing session in which the mild disagreement from that morning becomes an exaggerated sketch about a wife who cannot resist opening a mysterious package addressed to her husband. After the skit airs, Laura's patience is tested when her neighbors assume that the zany wife on the show is really her. The strength of the episode—and of many in the series—lies in the distance between the false television reality of what plays on *The Alan Brady Show* and the "real" reality of Rob and Laura's world. With a touch of superiority, Laura points out the difference between her behavior and that of the woman caricatured on television. The episode concludes with a large package arriving that Laura finds she cannot help but open—the "life" of the Petries imitating the "art" Rob had written for Alan Brady.

Impact of Event

In the earlier days of television, a number of arbitrary distinctions existed between comedy and drama. Many dramatic genre shows featured characters—policemen, lawyers, doctors—whose private lives were barely suggested. Did Joe Friday date? What did Perry Mason's home look like? The implication was that viewers who asked such personal questions were expecting the wrong things from the shows. On the other hand, audiences could regularly watch home-based situation comedies such as *Father Knows Best* and *My Three Sons* and not know that Jim Anderson (Robert Young) made his living selling insurance or that Steve Douglas (Fred MacMurray) worked as a consulting engineer at an aviation plant. *The Dick Van Dyke Show* presented a believable picture of both environments and deepened the genre by showing its protagonist equally convincing and comfortable at home and at work. Quality shows now had to measure up to a new level of excellence. Over the years, the greater viewing expectations of audiences added to the plausibility of new shows, so that it became less likely that a series would virtually ignore half the star's life. The quality of *The Dick Van Dyke Show* in part helped to accomplish this.

More important, however, by not stooping to the easy laugh and thereby violating the integrity of the characters, the series also fostered a more realistic approach to light comedy. This influence can be seen best in shows that featured the later work of some of the Van Dyke crew, such as *That Girl* (created and produced by the writing team of Bill Persky and Sam Denoff), *My World and Welcome to It* (produced by Sheldon Leonard), *The Mary Tyler Moore Show* and its many spinoffs, and

Kate & Allie (coproduced and sometimes directed by Bill Persky). In these series, the depiction of character usually supersedes comic situations and jokes. The opposite end of the comedy spectrum, where everything is subordinated to the jokes, would include the early years of *M*A*S*H* (in the show's later years, the characters became more rounded, the writing less anchored on the quip), *Barney Miller, Taxi, Cheers* and its clone *Wings*, and *Murphy Brown*. The history of the genre has become rich enough to contain a number of good examples of both types of shows.

The idea of a comedy series featuring an ensemble cast in which the star is not always the source of the humor also became more prevalent in later situation comedies. To some extent, Jack Benny's radio and television programs established this practice. Benny, though a famous comedian, would often play the straight man to announcer Don Wilson, singer Dennis Day, costar Mary Livingstone, bandleader Phil Harris, or one of the many voice characterizations of Mel Blanc, his sound-effects man. The fun came from hearing or watching Benny's growing exasperation as he was confronted with situations out of his control. In a less caricatured way, *The Dick Van Dyke Show* also explored the acting abilities of its ensemble by building episodes around each member of its talented players; by so doing, the show influenced the practices of other ensemble series (Mary Tyler Moore's later show is a good example).

Although the three-camera technique of filming each episode before a live audience was not new when the Van Dyke series aired, neither was it common (as it later became for situation comedies). Sheldon Leonard and Carl Reiner's work on the series helped to popularize and perfect this style. One of the requirements for such a method is a good script. If the reactions of the live audience lack enthusiasm, then the sound track has to be "sweetened," that is, electronically enhanced with "canned" laughter. Van Dyke claimed that his show never resorted to such artificiality. Another necessity for a successful three-camera approach is a skilled cast. Good performers draw energy from both the other actors and the live responses of the audience. Reiner's script from the fourth season "Never Bathe on Saturday," for example, confines Laura offstage behind a locked bathroom door, her big toe caught in a bathtub faucet. This idea elicits more laughs because, as in a filmed play, the camera records only Rob's comic efforts in the outer room to unlock the door, and the audience must imagine trapped and frustrated Laura inside. Mary Tyler Moore used the same three-camera technique for her own later situation comedy, as did many other series. She described the method as partaking of the best of film and the best of theater.

Another legacy of the show that elevated the quality of television comedy was the careful editing of the series' scripts. Not only did Reiner insist that writers for the show avoid slang and contemporary references that would date the program in syndication, but each script was also collectively scrutinized and edited by the entire cast during the weekly read-throughs. Since the actors knew their characters so well (most admitted to essentially playing themselves), they could make productive suggestions about what would sound real for their roles. Sometimes lines written for one character were reassigned to another; a wisecrack that would make Rob sound cruel would be witty coming from Buddy. Reiner pushed in the direction of the new and experimental (as in some of the dream episodes he wrote), while Leonard trusted proven situations. Together, they formed a good mix. Script supervisor Marge Mullen made note of good but discarded jokes that would fit better in some future episode. In short, everyone understood the type of quality the show sought and worked to realize it.

Bibliography

Hamamoto, Darrell Y. *Nervous Laughter: Television Situation Comedy and Liberal Democratic Ideology.* New York: Praeger, 1989. Part of the "Media and Society Series," Hamamoto's work makes scattered references to *The Dick Van Dyke Show* but is convincing about the way television explains American society to itself.

Jones, Gerard. *Honey, I'm Home! Sitcoms: Selling the American Dream.* New York: Grove Weidenfeld, 1992. A lively, always interesting account of the way situation comedies from the beginning of television to the 1990's have mirrored society. Jones notes that the sitcom has been a "primer," a "mirror," a "daydream," a "teacher," and, of course, a corporate entertainment product.

Marc, David. *Comic Visions.* Boston: Unwin Hyman, 1989. Good comments on *The Dick Van Dyke Show* and on the situation comedy in general. Marc shows how Carl Reiner's work on his series and Norman Lear's on *All in the Family* had some interesting parallels.

Reiner, Carl. *Enter Laughing.* New York: Simon & Schuster, 1958. Reiner's autobiographical novel, written in the hiatus between his work with Sid Caesar and the start of *The Dick Van Dyke Show.* In 1967, Reiner directed a film version of his book starring Shelley Winters, Jose Ferrer, and Elaine May.

Weissman, Ginny, and Coyne Steven Sanders. *The Dick Van Dyke Show: Anatomy of a Classic.* New York: St. Martin's Press, 1983. Includes an essay on the inception and development of the show, a complete episode guide, a script of one show, numerous photographs, a list of awards won by the show, and a foreword by Carl Reiner. A good book-length study of the program.

Glenn Hopp

Cross-References

Television Family Comedy Becomes Extremely Popular (1950's), p. 1470; *I Love Lucy* Dominates Television Comedy (1951), p. 1525; *The Honeymooners* Enchants Audiences of All Ages (1955), p. 1673; Situation Comedies Dominate Television Programming (1960's), p. 1835; *The Mary Tyler Moore Show* Examines Women's Roles (1970), p. 2218; *All in the Family* Introduces a New Style of Television Comedy (1971), p. 2234; *The Jeffersons* Signals Success of Black Situation Comedies (1975), p. 2339; *The Cosby Show* Makes Television History (1984), p. 2532.

DR. NO LAUNCHES THE HUGELY POPULAR JAMES BOND SERIES

Category of event: Motion pictures
Time: 1962
Locale: Great Britain and the United States

Dr. No *began a long series of adventure films about British secret agent James Bond and touched off an international craze for spy stories and films*

Principal personages:
IAN FLEMING (1908-1964), the author who originated and developed the James Bond character in a number of highly successful spy novels
ALBERT R. BROCCOLI (1909-   ), the producer and prime architect of the Bond film series
HARRY SALTZMAN (1915-   ), the coproducer of nine Bond films with Broccoli
SEAN CONNERY (1930-   ), the actor who first brought Bond to life on movie screens around the world
TERENCE YOUNG (1915-   ), the director who stamped the series with his personal vision of Bond
RICHARD MAIBAUM (1909-1991), an author who wrote or cowrote the screenplays for most of the Broccoli-produced Bond films
JOHN BARRY (1933-   ), the composer who wrote the theme music for the film series

Summary of Event

The release of *Dr. No* in 1962 marked the first film appearance of Ian Fleming's superagent James Bond. Produced by Eon Productions for United Artists, the film was seen as a risky venture (in fact, "Eon" stood for "everything or nothing"). The box-office success of spy movies had not been proven, and *Dr. No* was unlike any previous adventure movie. Sean Connery, the picture's star, was a relative unknown, and the movie had a budget of only one million dollars, a modest amount in light of the ambitiousness of the script. As it turned out, *Dr. No* was highly successful, earning double its production cost in Great Britain alone and doing even better in the United States. The film was successful enough to be followed by a 1963 sequel, *From Russia with Love*, which was superior to *Dr. No* both artistically and at the box office. With this second triumph, the James Bond series was well on its way to a memorable run, spanning three decades and, with the benefit of bigger and bigger operating budgets, generating huge profits.

The ingredients of this success were many, beginning with the raw materials provided by Fleming's novels. Fleming, a journalist and former Navy intelligence officer, produced his first Bond novel, *Casino Royale*, in 1953. Eleven more novels and two short story collections would follow during the next decade and a half. What distinguished the books was their mixture of adult fantasy (featuring large doses of sex and violence and a superspy outwitting menacing supervillains) with grim realism about espionage and covert operations, politics, human nature, and moral values. After all, Bond's "double-0" rating, 007, signified that he was licensed to kill, a circumstance the books presented as a necessity to the triumph of good over evil. This mixture, together with Fleming's storytelling ability, made the series successful, particularly in Great Britain.

The translation of the Bond series into the medium of motion pictures was the brainchild of Albert (Cubby) Broccoli. Broccoli, a longtime veteran of the film business, had missed out on a deal to buy film rights to most of the Bond stories in 1958, when his partner in the deal backed out. In 1961, another opportunity to bring Bond to the screen fell into his lap when an assistant to Harry Saltzman, who had bought the rights to most of the stories, asked for Broccoli's help in arranging a film deal with a major studio. Broccoli went into partnership with Saltzman and struck a deal with United Artists to make *Dr. No* and five more Bond films (provided the first was profitable). It was Broccoli who put together the crew and cast of *Dr. No* and who remained the most important constant in the Eon-produced Bond series. (*Casino Royale*, 1967, and *Never Say Never Again*, 1983, were produced by other companies.) Actors, directors, and other personnel came and went. Gate receipts and the Cold War ebbed and flowed. Saltzman sold his shares of Eon to United Artists in 1975, but Broccoli continued to work on the Bond films, bringing a modicum of consistency and continuity to the series.

The young man Broccoli selected to direct *Dr. No* was Terence Young. Though he directed only two more Bond films, Young is generally given credit for establishing the overall tenor, pace, and high quality of the series. He did so with important contributions from film editor Peter Hunt, production designer Ken Adam, and main title designer Maurice Binder. Young also is credited with preparing Sean Connery for what was a rather unfamiliar role.

The man most responsible for translating the Bond stories into workable screenplays was Richard Maibaum, who wrote or cowrote most of the Eon-produced Bond scripts. Maibaum's most conspicuous contribution was the addition of humor to the Bond equation. While Fleming's novels are deadly serious, Maibaum included occasional comic relief without jeopardizing the urgency or drama of Fleming's stories. These changes of pace kept the series from becoming pretentious or grim, but the series never descended into pure camp, though the humor became more pronounced after Roger Moore took over the role of Bond.

Musical scores have also played a significant role in making the Bond films work. John Barry wrote the scores for eleven of the films, including *From Russia with Love*, *Goldfinger* (1964), *You Only Live Twice* (1967), and *The Living Daylights* (1987), all of which are as lovely to listen to as they are exciting to watch. Barry is also variously given credit for composing or arranging the catchy "James Bond Theme" that introduces all the Eon productions. Barry's ability to capture the mood of the moment in music has played a key role in preserving the series' balance between humor and drama.

Sean Connery, the man first selected to play Bond, had never played a similar role. Nevertheless, Connery managed to bring a credibility and depth to the Bond character without which the film series might never have survived. While Young helped him to affect Bond's somewhat aristocratic bearing, Connery brought substantial natural talent to his role, including an ability to portray both Bond's violent and comic sides credibly.

When Connery grew unhappy with his work as Bond after five films, he was replaced by George Lazenby, a move that turned out to be one of Broccoli's mistakes. Lazenby was a model, not an actor. *On Her Majesty's Secret Service* (1969), Lazenby's only Bond film, was relatively unsuccessful, and Lazenby, having spurned a long-term contract, was let go. Connery returned for *Diamonds Are Forever* (1971) before departing the role a second time. Broccoli and company replaced him with Roger Moore, a veteran actor, for 1973's *Live and Let Die*, and Moore went on to star as Bond in seven films. Though marred by occasionally indifferent scripts, the Moore films continued the Bond tradition quite ably. Moore played a more humorous Bond, but he proved capable of handling the series' more serious moments. By the time Moore left the series, he had successfully escaped Connery's shadow, though he had certainly not eclipsed him. Timothy Dalton, who replaced Moore in the series beginning with *The Living Daylights*, returned to a more Connery-like balance of humor and seriousness, and his performances were critically acclaimed by most observers.

Supporting actors important to the series have included Bernard Lee as "M" (Bond's boss for the first half of the series), Lois Maxwell as Miss Moneypenny ("M"'s secretary), and Desmond Llewelyn as "Q" (the dispenser of clever Bond gadgets and weapons). Throughout the series' run, numerous stars have appeared in the roles of guest villains and female leads.

Impact of Event

The most immediately apparent impact of the Bond series was the creation of an international legion of fans devoted to the adventures of 007. As a result, even the less successful Bond movies brought in a sizable financial return. In addition to creating this lucrative Bond industry, the series also launched Sean Connery's career. Along with fame came opportunities for Connery to act in a broad range of feature films, an indication of the considerable ability he brought to the Bond role—an ability so expansive that Connery escaped being typecast.

The Bond series also created a worldwide mania for spy films and helped to inspire a new generation of fantastic adventure films. Following *Dr. No*, spy movies of varying quality and seriousness were made in the dozens all over the world. Notable among the many Bond takeoffs were the non-Broccoli production of *Casino Royale*; *The Liquidator* (1966), starring Rod Taylor as a reluctant Bond-like agent; the *Flint* series starring James Coburn; the *Matt Helm* series, featuring a rather sleepy-looking Dean Martin; and even Woody Allen's spoof *What's Up, Tiger Lily?* (1966). Such espionage-oriented television series as *I Spy*, *Get Smart*, *The Man from U.N.C.L.E.*, and *The Girl from U.N.C.L.E.* all were spawned by the success of 007, as were more serious films such as *The Spy Who Came in from the Cold* (1965), *The Quiller Memorandum* (1966), and *The Russia House* (1990)—the last of which marked a return by Connery to the spy genre in a role very different from that of James Bond.

The Bond series also helped to inspire numerous popular adventure films involving fantastic heroes, futuristic technology, memorable stunts and special effects, the characteristic Bond mixture of danger and humor, creative editing, and huge budgets. Both the *Indiana Jones* series, the third installment of which included a key role for Connery, and the *Star Wars* series were in many respects heirs to the Bond legacy.

Sales of Fleming's books jumped dramatically in the wake of the Bond films' success; after Fleming died in 1964, first Kingsley Amis and then John Gardner took over the series, producing numerous Bond novels that continued to be vigorous sellers. In addition, other spy series flourished, and related books such as Tom Clancy's techno-thrillers attracted millions of readers. (Fittingly enough, when the film version of Clancy's *Hunt for Red October* was released in 1990, it, too, starred Connery.)

The Bond series has also been alleged to have had an impact on the values of its fans and of society at large; whether this impact has been positive or not has been the subject of vigorous debate. Critics of the Bond character have contended that he is a violent, sexist, and snobbish role model who has contributed to increased permissiveness in sexual conduct. Supporters argue that, in displaying commitment to duty and to convictions, Bond is a symbol of active engagement in a world that all too often breeds apathy.

Even such controversy testifies to the success of the Bond films, which, despite occasional misfires, have managed to keep fans coming back for more. In light of the decades-long span of the series and the high number of films it contains, this maintenance of popular and critical appeal stands as a significant achievement.

Bibliography

Amis, Kingsley. *The James Bond Dossier.* New York: New American Library, 1965. Amis, a well-known British humorist and man of letters, wrote this book in order to defend the Bond character as depicted in the Fleming novels. Fleming's Bond is not the snob, sexist, or sadist his critics make him out to be, according to Amis. Concludes with a handy reference guide to Fleming's Bond novels. (After Fleming's death, Amis wrote 1968's *Colonel Sun: A James Bond Adventure*, a moderately successful Bond novel.)

Boyd, Ann S. *The Devil with James Bond!* Richmond, Va.: John Knox Press, 1967. Boyd interprets the Bond character as a modern-day knight slaying contemporary dragons, argues that Fleming meant his character to be a symbol of action in opposition to apathy, and likens Bond to clergyman Dietrich Bonhoeffer, who was martyred for openly opposing the Nazi regime during World War II.

Hibbin, Sally. *The Official James Bond 007 Movie Book.* Foreword by Albert Broccoli. New York: Crown, 1987. A treasury of facts and photographs (many in color) for Bond fans. Hibbin summarizes each of the Eon-produced Bond films, closing with complete cast lists and a brief index.

Pearson, John. *The Life of Ian Fleming.* London: Jonathan Cape, 1966. An authoritative biography that remains the standard work for Fleming scholars. Pearson's research is augmented by his personal acquaintance with Fleming. Informative and well written.

Pfeiffer, Lee, and Philip Lisa. *The Incredible World of 007.* Introduction by Albert Broccoli. New York: Citadel Press, 1992. A fan's delight, full of excellent illustrations (many in color) and interesting gossip. Also includes a section on Bond bloopers.

Rosenberg, Bruce A., and Ann Harleman Stewart. *Ian Fleming.* Boston: Twayne, 1989. A scholarly analysis of Fleming's life and work by two Brown University professors. Draws interesting links between Fleming's often harsh youth, his adult quirks, and the Bond series. Includes a helpful bibliography.

Rubin, Steven Jay. *The Complete James Bond Movie Encyclopedia.* Chicago: Contemporary Books, 1990. Rubin, who also wrote *The James Bond Films: A Behind-the-Scenes History* (1981), has collected as many pertinent facts about the Bond film series as one could possibly hope to find in one place. Highly readable, gossipy, and easy to use, with occasional photographs. Includes discussion of the non-Eon productions.

Sauerberg, Lars Ole. *Secret Agents in Fiction.* London: Macmillan, 1984. Focusing on the work of Fleming, John le Carré, and Len Deighton, Sauerberg distinguishes the essential elements of formula spy fiction. According to Sauerberg, Fleming had the least literary talent of the three but had a very sure grasp of the formula, which explains his ability to draw millions of readers.

Starkey, Lycurgus Monroe. *James Bond's World of Values.* Nashville: Abingdon Press, 1966. A Methodist minister and professor of church history, Starkey offers a vigorous critique of the Bond character's womanizing, violence, snobbery, hedonism, and elevation of patriotism to the level of an absolute. The book serves as an interesting counterpoint to those by Amis and Boyd cited above.

Van Dover, J. Kenneth. *Murder in the Millions.* New York: Frederick Ungar, 1984. With something less than reverence, Van Dover looks at the popular appeal of Fleming, Erle Stanley Gardner (the creator of Perry Mason), and Mickey Spillane (the creator of Mike Hammer). Van Dover also sees knight-like qualities in Bond, but he argues that such qualities are largely irrelevant in real life.

Ira Smolensky
Marjorie Smolensky

Cross-References

Little Caesar, Public Enemy, and *Scarface* Launch the Gangster-Film Genre (1930), p. 839; Hitchcock Becomes England's Foremost Director (1934), p. 946; The Sherlock Holmes Film Series Begins (1939), p. 1131; *The Maltese Falcon* Establishes a New Style for Crime Films (1941), p. 1223; Le Carré Rejects the Fantasy World of Secret Agents (1963), p. 1934; *I Spy* Debuts to Controversy (1965), p. 2044; The *Star Wars* Trilogy Redefines Special Effects (1977), p. 2391.

KAHN BLENDS ARCHITECTURE AND
URBAN PLANNING IN DACCA

Category of event: Architecture
Time: 1962-1974
Locale: Dacca, Pakistan

*Dacca afforded Louis I. Kahn unique opportunities to express his architectural
spirituality, through the master planning of a new urban complex*

Principal personages:
LOUIS I. KAHN (1901-1974), a distinguished Philadelphia architect and
master designer of Dacca
MOHAMMAD AYUB KHAN (1907-1974), the Pakistani president who com-
missioned the building of Dacca
PAUL PHILIPPE CRET (1876-1945), one of Kahn's influential teachers
LE CORBUSIER (CHARLES-ÉDOUARD JEANNERET, 1887-1965), an important
modernist influence on Kahn and one of the most significant archi-
tects of the twentieth century
OSCAR STONOROV (1905-1970), an architect who made Kahn aware of the
modern movement
WALTER GROPIUS (1883-1969), a founder of the Bauhaus school and an
influence on Kahn
GEORGE HOWE (1886-1955), a close friend and architectural associate of
Kahn

Summary of Event

Created under provisions of the India Independence Act of 1947, Pakistan was
geographically separated by Indian territory into East and West Pakistan. Although
East Pakistan would itself gain recognition as the new state of Bangladesh in 1974,
the problems preventing the development of unified national sentiments and coherent rule were evident in the intervening twenty-seven years. To ameliorate such
difficulties, Pakistani president Mohammad Ayub Khan decided during a June 12-13,
1959, governor's conference at Nathiagali that, in addition to Pakistan's western capital, Islamabad, the construction of a second capital for the eastern provinces at Dacca
was essential. A Pakistani committee initially selected a two-hundred-acre capital
site; as a result of discussions over the next two years and the urgings of the plan's
architect, however, the land to be made available for the capital enclave in Dacca was
extended to one thousand acres to afford greater architectural freedom of expression.

The master plan for Dacca's capital complex was entrusted by the Pakistani government to Philadelphian Louis I. Kahn, an architect whose work had only recently
begun bringing him broad recognition. After years of artistic and spiritual evolution,
Kahn had progressed from being a follower of Beaux-Arts traditions toward producing his own interpretations of the modern movement, or International Style. Born

on a Russian Baltic island in 1901, Kahn emigrated to Philadelphia with his father, a stained-glass craftsman, and his mother, a harpist, in 1905. His parents were educated Orthodox Jews, and as a youngster Louis excelled in painting and music. Although Kahn intended to pursue art, a high school course in architecture effectively determined his life's work.

Early recognized for exceptional abilities, Kahn nevertheless had an unexceptional career until he was middle-aged. Initially, he studied architecture at the University of Pennsylvania, where the tradition was Beaux-Arts, an appreciative, eclectic attitude toward architects and buildings of the past. The particular influence upon him was one of Beaux-Arts' principal exponents, Paul Philippe Cret, in whose office a few years later Kahn would work on drawings for the Chicago Centennial of 1933 and for a design of Washington's Folger Shakespeare Library. Meanwhile, upon his graduation Kahn was employed by Philadelphia's city architect to design the city's 1926 Sesquicentennial Exhibition, architecturally a conventional baroque exercise. Over the next fifteen years, Kahn was exposed to new currents in architecture, first through a trip to Europe, then through association with Oscar Stonorov, an exponent of the modern movement inspired by Le Corbusier and Walter Gropius, and through additional involvement in designing early federal public-housing projects. The latter task encouraged him to reflect comprehensively on the role of architecture on the whole human environment. As his writings indicate, by the close of the 1940's, Kahn was convinced that what his generation notoriously lacked were its own grand architectural statements in behalf of the human spirit.

Considered more a thinker and teacher than a practitioner—although he had executed notable commissions in association with George Howe and Stonorov—Kahn also enjoyed several professorial and consultative posts after 1947: professorships at Yale University, the Massachusetts Institute of Technology, the American Academy in Rome, and more permanently at the University of Pennsylvania, and consultant positions with the Israeli and Japanese governments and with the city of Philadelphia. In time, tributes were accorded him as a leading professional architect, among them several prestigious prizes and fellowships, publications about his works, and national and international lectures. The Dacca project and Kahn's own artistic and architectural maturation coincided to produce his finest opportunities, for the existence of an entire city waited upon the application of his imagination and skill.

The Dacca project called for design and construction of an entire government complex: a national assembly hall, a supreme court building, a diplomatic enclave, hostels and lounges for visitors and lobbyists, schools, a stadium, living quarters, a market, roads, and a viable traffic pattern. Lying between branches of the Yamuna and the Bramaputra rivers, the Dacca designs also had to take account of tropical heat, seasonal floodings, and tornadic storms. Both symbolically and spiritually, Kahn was challenged, not only by terrain but also by the siting of the capital's central institutions amid artificial lakes, ponds, walkways, and parks.

His inspired perception was that the design and grouping of Dacca's central institutions should express the transcendent nature of their human functions. To this end, Kahn's arrangement of the national assembly and the supreme court buildings was made palatable to Pakistani officials by the design of a mosque joining, but also insulating, these two institutions. The overall design of these and other related structures was characterized by bold geometric simplicity and, in accord with Kahn's philosophy, by close attention to "form," that is, the essence of the relationships of elements in a whole. Although much of Kahn's Dacca was completed, construction was delayed between 1971 and 1973 by civil war, while economic problems, floods, and governmental inanition left some projects incomplete—the national assembly building, in fact, was not used until 1982. Nevertheless, Dacca represented a monumental architectural achievement.

Impact of Event

Architects, engineers, public officials, and perceptive laypersons around the world have almost unanimously pronounced Kahn's Dacca capital complex one of the monumental artistic and architectural achievements of the twentieth century. This remains true despite the city's incompletion at Kahn's death in 1974 and despite shortcomings in some of the design's executions: the lack of craftsmanship in some of the details, failures of poorly prepared concrete, and, not least, economic problems caused by Pakistan-Bangladesh's impoverishment and by Kahn's own business inefficiencies.

Modeled after the Roman baths of Caracalla but lying amid a carpet of grass and reflecting ponds, the complex's geometric, essentially futuristic concrete structures, with their sensitive positioning, produced an ethereal impression upon observers. Such sensations were heightened by contrast with the traditional, premodern lifestyles, dress, habitations, and street markets of Dacca's generally poor indigenous population, as well as by the absence of urban motor traffic. Kahn's response to the contrast, characteristically, was that the architect's desire or inspiration in turn produced the world's need for it.

Embodied in his conceptualization of the whole project was a synthesis of his artistic and philosophical convictions about architecture. Three values in particular, he believed, should be manifest in his designs: "commodity," or social utility, firmness of the logic of a structure, and delight or beauty. Inseparable from these values were his deep, poetic concerns—about which he had frequently written and lectured—over insuring a proper balancing of silence and light within his structures. "Silence," artistically, meant darkness and the creation of things, while "light" implied life and beauty. Translated into the construction of his buildings, for example, such a philosophy meant that the choice of series of columns was a choice in light; when columns were huge and hollow, as Kahn liked to form them, their walls became makers of light, and their interior voids, therefore, became rooms.

To Kahn a room (or an assembly of rooms) had special character as a basic concept in architecture, for only man could make a room and take into it the other rooms in his mind. Moreover, thoughts exchanged in one room were unlike those exchanged in another. In Kahn's sense, a street divided by its intersections also was a "room," and so too was a community an assemblage of rooms. In reference to these concepts Dacca represented an effort to halt urban decentralization and to recrystallize the institutional integrity, as Kahn perceived it, of the center city. Much of the impact that Dacca had upon observers resulted not only from the intrinsic appreciation of Dacca's buildings but also stemmed from the recognition of the embodiment of Kahn's artistic philosophy.

Remarkable in its own right, Kahn's Dacca design, in broad context, was part of a renewed global interest in urban reconfiguration and urban planning during the 1960's. In microcosm, Kahn's career, like that of many professional architects, had begun with the designing of specific houses and structures and had progressed to the redesigning of larger sections of old communities. London, for example, was busily refiguring areas laid waste by the bombings of World War II, as were most major cities in West Germany. Extensive replanning and rebuilding were also underway in Paris. Throughout Asia, urban-renewal committees and commissions were equally hard at work.

New urban sectors, in addition, were being projected in older countries to relieve longstanding housing problems and facilitate slum clearance. Elsewhere, as in Brazil, the Soviet Union, Pakistan, and India (among many others), national economic programs and the exigencies of national defense and political geography opened opportunities for the ground-up development of wholly new cities.

American architects were involved in the same general process. Urban renewal, particularly metropolitan revitalization, attained urgent priority under the aegis of President Lyndon Johnson's Great Society, and accelerating suburbanization laid fresh emphasis on larger and larger planning projects: large residential complexes, shopping malls, theme parks, waterfront redevelopment, and industrial parks. Grand social changes, in essence, were giving experienced architects of vision and imagination, like Kahn, an increasingly broad ambit for the play of their talents.

Indeed, Kahn's success at Dacca soon brought additional commissions. Both he and Le Corbusier (in a combination of two of the greatest architects of the twentieth century) designed a structure for the Indian Institute of Management at Ahmadabad in 1963, and Kahn received an independent commission from the Indian government to draft the master plan for the town of Gandhinagar in 1963 and 1964, though the plan could not be executed. More important, leading architecture critics and observers (Mitchell Rouda, among others) had already described Kahn as an inspired genius who had risen above the acknowledged banality of most of his profession to become a legend. Kahn was credited with effecting at Dacca and elsewhere the most monumental changes witnessed since the emergence of modern architecture in the 1920's. What he had accomplished uniquely through his works was to reinvest the role of architecture with the humanity, inspiration, and spiritual values required by its users.

Bibliography

Kahn, Louis I. *Louis I. Kahn: Writings, Lectures, Interviews.* Edited by Alessandra

Latour. New York: Rizzoli, 1991. Readable enough, but poorly edited, with too much repetition of Kahn's views. Lay readers, though, can still absorb the flavor of Kahn's sometimes obscure, oblique, or poetic thoughts. Good photos of Kahn, along with some of his doodles. Unlike most architecture books, contains no plans or site photos of projects. Good chronologized select bibliography covering 1931 to 1974. A perfunctory index makes referencing awkward.

_____. *What Will Be Has Always Been: The Words of Louis I. Kahn.* Edited by Richard Saul Wurman. New York: Access Press, 1986. Authoritative, insightful, clear, and easy to read. The main title is drawn from one of Kahn's favorite (and often repeated) statements. Kahn's written and spoken words have to be mined to be understood. They often appear vague and general and are sometimes poetically obscure. Yet extensive readings do turn up important specific meanings and convey Kahn's feelings, spirit, and inspiration. He is hardly culpable for such difficulty, for he, after all, chose to express himself through his plans and structures. Contains a useful bibliography.

Lobell, John. *Between Silence and Light: Spirit in the Architecture of Louis I. Kahn.* Boston: Shambhala, 1985. An excellent survey of Kahn's life as well as a keen look at concepts central to the architect's visions. While there are excellent photos, this is essentially a philosophical analysis. Easy to read, easy to use.

Ronner, Heinz, and Sharad Jhaveri. *Louis I. Kahn: Complete Work, 1935-1974.* 2d rev. ed. Boston: Birkhauser Verlag, 1987. Authoritative and masterful. Hundreds of beautiful plans and photos. Informative annotated notes attend all plans and site photos, including those of Dacca. Chronologized cross-references make this massive work easy to use. It is a compendium so well thought out that Kahn's genius and inspiration shine forth in it far better than they do in his spoken or written works. The authors have provided the public—and Kahn's memory—with unmistakable evidence of the architect's greatness.

Tyng, Alexandra. *Beginnings: Louis I. Kahn's Philosophy of Architecture.* New York: John Wiley & Sons, 1984. An easy, interesting read, with valuable insights into Kahn's personality and perspectives that perhaps only the author (Kahn's daughter) could reveal. Ample materials on Dacca. Some photos and illustrations. Informative and usable.

Clifton K. Yearley

Cross-References

Le Corbusier Designs and Builds Chandigarh (1951), p. 1503; Fuller's First Industrial Geodesic Dome Is Erected (1953), p. 1579; Saarinen Designs Kennedy Airport's TWA Terminal (1956), p. 1716; The Guggenheim Museum Opens in a Building Designed by Wright (1959), p. 1806; Breuer Designs a Building for the Whitney Museum (1966), p. 2064; Expo 67 Presents Innovative Architectural Concepts (1967), p. 2081; The Pompidou Center Opens in Paris (1977), p. 2402.

GREAT BRITAIN ESTABLISHES
THE ROYAL NATIONAL THEATRE

Category of event: Theater
Time: August 9, 1962
Locale: Chichester and London, England

After a struggle of more than one. hundred years, Great Britain finally established a national theater, but the development met with mixed reaction from critics

Principal personages:
> SIR LAURENCE OLIVIER (1907-1989), a celebrated actor who served as the Royal National Theatre's first director
> KENNETH PEACOCK TYNAN (1927-1980), a theater critic who became Olivier's dramaturge and who helped to shape the National Theatre's repertoire
> LORD OLIVER SYLVAIN BALIOL ESHER (1881-1963), the chairman of the Joint Council of the National Theatre
> LORD CHANDOS (OLIVER LYTTELTON, 1893-1972), a Stratford governor and chairman of the National Theatre

Summary of Event

On Tuesday, July 5, 1962, the British press reported that Sir Laurence Olivier was to be the first director of Great Britain's Royal National Theatre. Olivier had been sounded out about the directorship by Lord Chandos, a former Conservative cabinet minister, in 1957. Widely regarded as the greatest actor of his time, Olivier had already been an actor-manager at London's famous Old Vic from 1944 to 1949. Summarily dismissed by the theater's board of governors, a deeply hurt Olivier formed Laurence Olivier Productions (which boasted Alexander Korda as a shareholder and board member) and, on November 14, 1949, took a four-year lease on the St. James, a plush Victorian theater once famous as 1890's dominion of actor-manager Sir George Alexander. The company's biggest success with critics and audiences alike was the 1951 pairing of George Bernard Shaw's *Caesar and Cleopatra* and William Shakespeare's *Antony and Cleopatra*, with Olivier and his second wife, Vivien Leigh, playing the title roles.

Olivier's name had long been linked with the dream of a national theater. In 1949, after the National Theatre Bill had been passed by Parliament, he had served on a committee advising on the selection of a suitable building to house the theater. Although a foundation stone was laid on the south bank of the Thames in 1951, nothing further occurred in the matter until Olivier directed the 1962 Chichester Festival, which was widely regarded in the press as a trial run for the National Theatre.

The lukewarm reviews for the Chichester Festival's two opening productions, *The Chances* and *The Broken Heart* (both directed by Olivier), were fortunately transcended by unanimous accolades for a production of Anton Chekhov's *Uncle Vanya*, also directed by Olivier (who played Astrov), which came as close to Chekhovian perfection as is possible in English. Olivier turned his repertoire into a preview of what was to come at the National Theatre—a wide spectrum of plays done in distinctive styles.

Olivier's official appointment came on August 9, when it was determined that the Old Vic Company's last season as such would end in June, 1963. Olivier wanted George Devine, the founder and manager of the English Stage Company at the Royal Court, to be his second-in-command, but Devine did not want that subsidiary role, though he agreed to direct a production in the National Theatre's first season. Devine also allowed Olivier to recruit John Dexter and William Gaskill from the Royal Court, both of whom (along with Tony Richardson) had helped to bring Devine's company enormous prestige.

Olivier's first press conference as head of the National Theatre was held on August 6, when he announced his desire to present a spectrum of world drama and to develop the best company in the world. He was assisted in his phrasing by Kenneth Tynan, a brilliantly acerbic critic for the *Spectator*, the *Observer*, and other sources, who was engaged as dramaturge.

Olivier redesigned the Old Vic with the assistance of Sean Kenny, who served as designer for the National Theatre's opening production, an uncut version of *Hamlet*. In his zeal to make over the Old Vic, though, Olivier extended the forestage at a grave cost to acoustics. As rehearsals for *Hamlet* proceeded amid bedlam and mess, it seemed that the Royal National Theatre was royal only in name and intent.

The National Theatre did not get its own home until 1976, three years after Olivier's reign had ended. His successor, Sir Peter Hall (his former chief rival as head of the Royal Shakespeare Company), had the signal honor of ushering in a new era in Denys Lasdun's new building on the south bank of the Thames. Though Olivier was no longer associated with the company, the larger of the National Theatre's two auditoriums was named after him.

Impact of Event

Olivier's inaugural production at the National Theatre did not fare well. Hamlet was played by Peter O'Toole (hair dyed blonde), who lacked technique and discipline for the role, and Olivier was unable either to inspire him or to curb his pranks both on stage and off. Sean Kenny's large new revolving stage was unpredictable, jamming without warning (it was nicknamed the "revolt"), and his trapdoor, crucial to the graveyard scene, stayed shut on opening night. Though the critics were generally diplomatic in their complaints, this *Hamlet* was hardly an auspicious beginning for Great Britain's most prestigious theater, and the production's failings led to subsequent grumblings about Olivier's contributions as director and administrator.

In general, critics contended that the National Theatre was trendy and eclectic and lacked a distinctive ensemble style. Kenneth Tynan was assailed for a sometimes perverse selection of plays and for interfering in casting and production matters, and Olivier was reviled for being dependent on him. The breadth of repertoire was considered mainly conservative and not especially welcoming to modern English playwrights. Critics suggested that Olivier should stick to acting—where his greatness was secure—and leave the other businesses to people more temperamentally suited to them.

Even when it came to acting, however, Olivier was not immune to carping comments. He played thumping Shakespearean roles such as Othello and Shylock in addition to essaying smaller parts in plays by Anton Chekhov, Somerset Maugham, William Congreve, and George Farquhar. His starring roles confirmed his greatness, but even some of his smaller parts turned miniatures into superbly wrought showpieces, thereby illustrating his passion for acting. Yet he was criticized for this; his critics contended that the National Theatre should not be a showcase for stars but a testing ground for ensemble distinction. On the one hand, he was criticized for not acting enough (he took on only five leading roles in ten years); on the other hand, he was attacked for not giving other heavyweight actors a starring opportunity. He was widely taken to task for not acting alongside John Gielgud or Paul Scofield and for not inviting Ralph Richardson or Alec Guinness into the company. Olivier, though, refused to turn his productions into acting contests.

Olivier's company consolidated the reputations of Joan Plowright, Maggie Smith, Rosemary Harris, Colin Blakely, Anthony Hopkins, and Billie Whitelaw, while developing a new generation of actors such as Derek Jacobi, Lynn Redgrave, Frank Finlay, Tom Courtenay, Robert Stephens, and Michael Gambon. Olivier's company proved that it could perform in almost any style required by a text, and although it was impossible to pinpoint with any accuracy a distinctive National Theatre style—in contrast, say, to the very identifiable Comédie Française or Royal Shakespeare Company house styles—the level of achievement was enviably high, a fact borne out by three triumphant international tours (to Moscow and Berlin in 1965, to Canada in 1967 and to Los Angeles in 1970).

Foreign directors of the stature of Ingmar Bergman, Jacques Charon, and Franco Zeffirelli were successfully wooed to work at the National Theatre, with some outstanding results, and foreign designers such as Josef Svoboda and René Allio contributed their genius to production standards.

Olivier, however, was vulnerable to charges that by relying excessively on Tynan's literary taste, he was leaving himself open to his dramaturge's power politics. Certainly, Olivier was publicly embarrassed by controversies over productions of Rolf Hochhuth's *Soldiers* in 1967 (which held Winston Churchill responsible for the bombing of Dresden), Seneca's *Oedipus* in 1968 (for which Peter Brook insisted on sensational phallic symbolism), and Fernando Arrabal's *The Architect and the Emperor of Assyria* in 1971 (directed by Victor Garcia to emphasize the play's nudity and cannibalism).

Such controversies did not bode well for the head of Great Britain's most prestigious theater, and in March, 1972, Sir Max Rayne, the new chairman of the National Theatre's board after Lord Chandos' death the same year, gave Olivier a six-month formal termination notice. Olivier formally resigned in 1973.

Bibliography

Beauman, Sally. *The Royal Shakespeare Company: A History of Ten Decades.* Oxford, England: Oxford University Press, 1982. In telling the story of one of the world's most famous acting companies—and especially the postwar renaissance of the theater's work under Barry Jackson, Anthony Quayle, Peter Brook, Peter Hall, and Trevor Nunn—this book has an interesting account of negotiations between Olivier and Peter Hall over the formation of the National Theatre. Good sketch of theater power politics.

Cook, Judith. *The National Theatre.* London: Harrap, 1976. Part history, part collection of profiles of various theatrical figures, this slim volume is useful for historical background and as a quick reference about some key players.

Cottrell, John. *Laurence Olivier.* Englewood Cliffs, N.J.: Prentice-Hall, 1975. Well-researched biography that concentrates on Olivier's greatness as an actor and on his Englishness rather than on nagging details of his reign at the National Theatre. Handsomely illustrated.

Fairweather, Virginia. *Olivier: An Informal Portrait.* New York: Coward, McCann, 1969. A chatty memoir by a personal friend of Olivier and his press representative at the National Theatre. Contains interesting anecdotes about the creation of the Chichester Festival, the inception of the National Theatre, and the problems of the National Theatre Company's first triumphal overseas tour. Illustrated.

Gourlay, Logan, ed. *Olivier.* London: Weidenfeld & Nicolson, 1973. A collection of interviews with leading actors, directors, and playwrights. Some remarkably candid and provocative assessments of Olivier's achievements as actor, director, and administrator. Of particular interest are interviews with John Osborne, Tony Richardson, and William Gaskill. Illustrated, with a sampler of reviews.

Holden, Anthony. *Olivier.* London: Weidenfeld & Nicolson, 1988. A book by a well-known journalist and biographer of Prince Charles. Treats Olivier very much as a royal institution. Much of the material is a reprocessing of information already familiar from earlier studies, but the twist is a depiction of a great man's shrivelling up. Illustrated.

Olivier, Laurence. *Confessions of an Actor.* London: Weidenfeld & Nicolson, 1982. Pleasingly illustrated, this autobiography irritated many of Olivier's critics for its arch-modest tone and calculated omissions about personal and professional relationships. Contains documents by Olivier, Tynan, and Lord Chandos about the Hochhuth controversy and also includes Olivier's maiden speech in the House of Lords on July 20, 1971.

Spoto, Donald. *Laurence Olivier.* New York: HarperCollins, 1992. A psychosexual portrait that provides glimpses of Olivier's relationship with Tynan at the National Theatre. Perversely tendentious about Olivier's private life, but contains some new material about his career at the National Theatre. Illustrated.

Keith Garebian

Cross-References

Stanislavsky Helps to Establish the Moscow Art Theater (1897), p. 1; Reinhardt Becomes Director of the Deutsches Theater (1905), p. 145; The Group Theatre Flourishes (1931), p. 874; Olivier's *Hamlet* Is Released to Acclaim and Controversy (1948), p. 1378; Brecht Founds the Berliner Ensemble (1949), p. 1410; Osborne's *Look Back in Anger* Opens in London (1956), p. 1721; The Royal Shakespeare Company Adopts a New Name and Focus (1961), p. 1888.

BALDWIN VOICES BLACK RAGE IN *THE FIRE NEXT TIME*

Category of event: Literature
Time: 1963
Locale: New York, New York

*Reflecting on his youth and the growing popularity of the Black Muslim move-
ment, James Baldwin wrote a thoughtful, prophetic statement on race in America*

Principal personages:
JAMES BALDWIN (1924-1987), a writer and black activist
ELIJAH MUHAMMAD (1897-1975), the leader of the Black Muslims
MALCOLM X (MALCOLM LITTLE, 1925-1965), Elijah Muhammad's chosen
successor, assassinated after he parted ways with Muhammad
NORMAN PODHORETZ (1930-   ), editor of *Commentary* magazine
ROBERT F. KENNEDY (1925-1968), the attorney general of the United States

Summary of Event

James Baldwin's *The Fire Next Time* created a stir even before the book was published. By 1962, Baldwin had delayed for three years writing an article on Africa
that *The New Yorker*, perhaps the most influential popular literary magazine in the
United States, had commissioned. Baldwin received an advance from the magazine
and did in fact travel to Africa, but he never finished the series of articles that he had
promised. He did, however, finish an article suggested by Norman Podhoretz, then
the new editor of *Commentary*, called "Down at the Cross," based on Baldwin's
meeting with Elijah Muhammad, leader of the Black Muslims. With William Shawn,
the editor of *The New Yorker*, growing impatient to receive a finished article, Baldwin sent him the article that had originally been intended for *Commentary* but that
had grown in scope well beyond its original conception. Undismayed that the article
Baldwin was submitting was quite unlike the article *The New Yorker* had commissioned, William Shawn retitled the essay "Letter from a Region of My Mind" and
published it in the November 17, 1962, issue of *The New Yorker*. The essay caused an
immediate stir and formed the bulk of *The Fire Next Time*, which was published in
1963.

The Fire Next Time actually begins with a short piece entitled "My Dungeon
Shook: Letter to My Nephew on the One Hundredth Anniversary of the Emancipation," written to Baldwin's fourteen-year-old namesake, his brother's son, whom
Baldwin at one point refers to affectionately as "Big James." The piece was originally published in *The Progressive* in December, 1962; in *The Fire Next Time*, it
serves largely as a prologue to the themes that the longer essay treats in greater
length. As an essay, "My Dungeon Shook" suffers from some of the cumbersome
demands of the form of the public epistle, particularly the need to focus on an audience of one while addressing a much larger audience. Thus, when Baldwin tells his

nephew that he—"Big James"—was born in conditions similar to those of Charles Dickens' London, he interrupts himself to say, a bit too coyly, "I hear the chorus . . . screaming, 'No! This is not true!' . . . —but I am writing this letter to *you.*" Clearly, Baldwin is not, in fact, writing this letter to his nephew. The essay, however, is not without the characteristic insight and rhetorical zest of much of Baldwin's work. Such lines from the essay's final paragraph as "You know, and I know, that the country is celebrating one hundred years of freedom one hundred years too soon. We cannot be free until they are free" neatly introduce some of the major ideas discussed in his longer essay: that freedom has not been achieved for either blacks or whites and that, for people of one race to live free, people of all races must live free.

It is the longer piece, later restored to Baldwin's original title, "Down at the Cross" (with *The New Yorker*'s title for the essay retained as a subtitle), that constitutes the bulk of *The Fire Next Time.* The essay begins with Baldwin's recollection of a religious crisis of his own that began when he was fourteen, when he began to be afraid of the world of Harlem around him because it seemed that he himself could conceivably become one of the "whores and pimps and racketeers on the avenue." He sought refuge in the safety of church, becoming a preacher while still a teenager. It was not long, however, before he found himself disappointed by the hypocrisy of the church. The command to love everybody, he found, was supposed to apply "only to those who believed as we did, and it did not apply to white people at all"—and it certainly did not apply to such people as Baldwin's Jewish school friends. These autobiographical reflections constitute the first third of the essay and are compelling in their own right. In addition, they provide the basis for Baldwin's understanding of both the attractions and limitations of a religion, such as that of the Black Muslims, that preaches racial separation, the main topic of the second section.

The middle third of the essay describes a meeting Baldwin had in Chicago with Elijah Muhammad, the head of the Nation of Islam (or Black Muslims), a black separatist religion that maintains that God—or Allah—is black, that blacks are the chosen people of Allah, and that a separate Black Muslim country must be founded on American soil if American blacks are to control their own destiny. Further, the Nation of Islam movement sanctions violence when necessary as a legitimate means not only of self-defense but also of self-assertion. Baldwin found himself in the position of being attracted to Elijah Muhammad and defending many of the positions taken by the Nation of Islam while disagreeing sharply with the racially separatist perspective held by Muhammad and his followers. Nevertheless, Baldwin and Muhammad parted on friendly terms, and Muhammad and his followers seemed to accept Baldwin as a likely future convert to their cause.

The third part of the essay is an intellectual and rhetorical tour de force that uses ideas—without acknowledgment—from sources as diverse as the French existentialist Jean-Paul Sartre and the American civil rights leader Martin Luther King, Jr. On a very deep level, Baldwin says, Americans refuse to accept the inevitability of death and the essentially tragic nature of the human condition. As a result, there is something immature within the American psyche. Mature consideration would show that black and white Americans need each other—a separate black nation would be doomed to economic failure—and need to accept one another as fully equal partners whose identities inevitably depend upon one another. The only option left is for Americans, black and white, to love one another—not with what Baldwin calls the "infantile" type of love that demands its own gratification, but in a tougher sense of the word that demands that one be willing to grow to be worthy of love. Baldwin concedes that what he is asking may be impossible, but surely, "the impossible is the least that one can demand." Baldwin ends his essay by warning that if blacks and whites fail in the task of re-creating America, a prophecy from the Bible, re-created in a slave song, would be fulfilled: "God gave Noah the rainbow sign, No more water, the fire next time."

Though many aspects of Baldwin's essay actively condemn the roles that organized religions have played in the history of American race relations, and though he invites his reader to dispense with a belief in God if necessary, the end and the title of the book both seem to place the essay into a Christian context. Baldwin's message is not essentially religious, however; rather, his essay uses a religious context to add a sense of urgency to his prophecy. The reference to fire surely is a warning that the racial violence and rioting that have marked American society will destroy it if the deep underlying causes are not treated.

Impact of Event

The immediate impact of the publication of "Letter from a Region of My Mind" in *The New Yorker* and republication by Dial Press of the same essay under the title "Down at the Cross" in *The Fire Next Time* was that James Baldwin found himself a leading spokesman for American Negroes (Baldwin's preferred term for African Americans). The situation was somewhat ironic, since Baldwin had for most of his career resisted being labeled a "Negro writer," preferring to consider himself simply a writer. Nevertheless, during the civil rights struggles of the 1960's, Baldwin was aware that he had an important voice to add to the ongoing national dialogue.

By the time *The Fire Next Time* was published in 1963, Baldwin had already established himself as an important novelist, having published *Go Tell It on the Mountain* (1953), *Giovanni's Room* (1956), and *Another Country* (1962). After *The Fire Next Time*, however, he was often treated by the press as a celebrity intellectual. For example, in its January 4, 1963, issue, *Time* magazine ran a short article about the importance of Baldwin's *The New Yorker* piece as a news story under the headline "Races," rather than reviewing the essay as a literary event. Similarly, for its May 17, 1963, issue, shortly after the release of *The Fire Next Time*, *Time* used Baldwin's face on its cover; again, though, the magazine discussed the publication of his most recent book as a political event rather than a literary one. Similarly, the May 24, 1963, issue of *Life* magazine ran a feature on Baldwin that treated him as a celebrity and proclaimed that "in today's literary circles it is a sign of considerable chic to know James Baldwin well enough to refer to him as Jimmy."

Baldwin tried his best to use his newfound celebrity to promote the cause of racial integration. He traveled the South, meeting James Meredith, the first black student to be enrolled at the University of Mississippi, and Medgar Evers, the chief legal counsel for the NAACP in Mississippi, among other civil rights leaders. He also set up a series of meetings with Robert Kennedy, then the attorney general of the United States, to discuss the problems of racial segregation in the urban North.

By most accounts, the meetings with Robert Kennedy ended disastrously. Baldwin had assembled a group of friends, including playwright Lorraine Hansberry, singer and actress Lena Horne, singer Harry Belafonte, and many others. Robert Kennedy arrived apparently expecting a businesslike discussion of proposals and priorities to ease the racial unrest brewing in America's cities. What Baldwin wanted to offer was a crash course in understanding what it felt like to be black in America. The two camps quickly grew impatient with each other, and the meeting ended in frustration and exhaustion, leaving Baldwin feeling bitter toward both Robert Kennedy and his brother, President John F. Kennedy. This bitterness lasted even beyond President Kennedy's assassination and was recorded in Federal Bureau of Investigation (FBI) files, as Baldwin was now suspected of being a revolutionary.

If Baldwin's emotional relationship to ideas compromised his ability to be a cool political leader, his relatively moderate integrationist views, as well as his homosexuality, made him a favorite target of younger, more revolutionary blacks such as Eldridge Cleaver, who attacked Baldwin in *Soul on Ice* (1968). Though personally wounded by such attacks, Baldwin refused to engage in tabloid squabbling. In fact, he remained something of an apologist for black revolutionaries, even those who had attacked him in public. Seven years after the publication of *The Fire Next Time*, in an open letter to Angela Davis printed in the *Manchester Guardian* on December 12, 1970, he seemed on the verge of despairing that white America would ever come to the awakening that in *The Fire Next Time* he had insisted was necessary.

The long-term impact of *The Fire Next Time* on Baldwin's literary reputation was to convince many readers and reviewers that Baldwin's foremost gift as a writer was his talent as an essayist. Baldwin found this perception frustrating, but he unwillingly contributed to it during the 1960's by publishing works of fiction that many readers found disappointing while at the same time continuing to publish much top-quality nonfiction. This is not to suggest that *The Fire Next Time* was universally well received, either; F. W. Dupee, for example, though applauding the autobiographical section of "Down at the Cross," wondered why Baldwin had not done more research into the Black Muslim movement before publishing. Hannah Arendt, in a letter to Baldwin, wondered if love could ever serve as a panacea for society's ills. The consensus that has emerged over the course of time, however, is that Baldwin's nonfiction certainly demands a permanent place in American literature, and that *The Fire Next Time* is one of his most powerfully written and most comprehensive statements on race in America.

Bibliography

Baldwin, James. *Go Tell It on the Mountain.* New York: Alfred A. Knopf, 1953. James Baldwin's first published novel, which treats fictionally some of the same experiences with religion and race that are dealt with nonfictionally in *The Fire Next Time.*

—————. *The Price of the Ticket: Collected Non-Fiction, 1948-1985.* New York: St. Martin's/Marek, 1985. Reprints all of *The Fire Next Time* and many other of Baldwin's essays, including "Stranger in the Village" and "No Name in the Street." Allows the reader to trace Baldwin's changing views on race and identity.

Bloom, Harold, ed. *James Baldwin.* New York: Chelsea House, 1986. A collection of critical essays assembled prior to Baldwin's death in 1987. Harold Bloom's introduction, as well as the essays focusing on Baldwin's nonfiction by F. W. Dupee, Marcus Klein, and James A. Snead, will be of particular interest to readers of *The Fire Next Time.* Contains a chronology of Baldwin's life, a bibliography of secondary sources, and an index.

Campbell, James. *Talking at the Gates: A Life of James Baldwin.* New York: Viking Press, 1991. A well-written, critically distant but intellectually engaged biography of James Baldwin. Of particular interest to readers of *The Fire Next Time* will be the section "A Severe Cross." Includes a bibliography of writings by Baldwin and an index.

Porter, Horace A. *Stealing the Fire: The Art and Protest of James Baldwin.* Middletown, Conn.: Wesleyan University Press, 1989. A full-length study of Baldwin's writing that emphasizes the importance of Baldwin's nonfiction. A chapter entitled "This Web of Lust and Fury" analyzes the importance of Harriet Beecher Stowe's *Uncle Tom's Cabin, Or, Life Among the Lowly* (1851) to Baldwin's *The Fire Next Time.* Includes chronology, bibliography, and index.

Weatherby, W. J. *James Baldwin: Artist on Fire.* New York: Dell Books, 1989. A biography written by a friend of Baldwin. Occasionally suffers from a lack of critical distance, but benefits from the author's close knowledge of his subject. Includes a chapter on *The Fire Next Time.* Index and bibliography.

Thomas J. Cassidy

Cross-References

Wright's *Native Son* Depicts Racism in America (1940), p. 1185; Ellison's *Invisible Man* Is Published (1952), p. 1541; Gordy Founds Motown Records (1959), p. 1790; Baraka's *Dutchman* Dramatizes Racial Hatred (1964), p. 2000; *The Autobiography of Malcolm X* Is Published (1965), p. 2022; *Do the Right Thing* Establishes Lee as a World-Class Director (1989), p. 2641.

LE CARRÉ REJECTS THE FANTASY WORLD
OF SECRET AGENTS

Category of event: Literature
Time: 1963
Locale: Great Britain and the United States

At a time when Ian Fleming's James Bond was riding high, John le Carré rejected the fantasy world of super agents, offering instead a powerful antiheroic character study

Principal personage:

JOHN LE CARRÉ (DAVID JOHN MOORE CORNWALL, 1931-   ), a onetime British Foreign Service agent whose novels paint an unpleasant picture of the world of espionage

Summary of Event

The Spy Who Came in from the Cold is a novel of and about the Cold War. The main character, Alec Leamas, a British spy, is a Cold Warrior who has seen his spy network in East Berlin disintegrate under relentless pressure from the other side. His failures have made it certain that he will have to "come in from the cold," that is, he will have to retire from the field to a desk job. Yet he would still like to destroy Hans-Dieter Mundt, his cruel and dreaded counterpart in the Abteilung (the East German intelligence agency) and the man who has destroyed Leamas' networks. Leamas accepts one last assignment in the belief that he can bring his opponent down. In the denouement, Leamas realizes that there is little difference between the two sides.

The story opens with Leamas waiting at a checkpoint, an official gateway through the Berlin Wall. He is waiting for Karl Riemeck, his last significant agent in East Berlin, to escape the disaster that has befallen Leamas' Berlin network. Riemeck is shot before he can escape, yet another victim of Mundt's remorseless destruction of all for which Leamas has worked. Leamas returns home to London, sure that his failure means his own exit from active spying, for as he notes, "intelligence work has one moral law—it is justified by results."

When he arrives in London, he meets with Control, the head of the Circus, the espionage branch of the British Intelligence Service. Control commiserates with Leamas over the tragedy, then offers Leamas a chance to destroy Mundt. Control's plan is for Leamas to debase himself to where he might be considered as a possible intelligence source for the Abteilung. If he is then contacted, by carefully mixing truth with fiction, Leamas might be able to convince the Abteilung that Mundt is actually a traitor working for the British. Leamas agrees to the plan.

To begin the process, Leamas is first degraded for his Berlin failures. He is posted to the banking section, where he performs poorly and drinks incessantly. He is finally dismissed from the Circus for financial impropriety. He takes on odd jobs, but his drinking and personal habits are so offensive that he cannot maintain one. At one of the jobs, however, he meets Liz Gold, who falls in love with him. Ever aware of his job, he leaves her, telling her to forget him. He then assaults a grocer and goes to jail. Leamas has hit bottom.

Upon his release from prison, Leamas is contacted by East German agents. Leamas is then taken to Holland, where he is further interrogated. To build his credibility, he willingly details his Berlin operations. He then offers the information regarding "Operation Rolling Stone," which had involved the payment of money to a highly placed East German, the name of whom only Control had known. Leamas denies that he had ever known about the agent before being transferred to the Banking Section. Only there, and only because Leamas had been responsible for making certain payments, had he deduced that there had been a top-level agent in British pay in the Abteilung.

Leamas' story is convincing enough for him to be taken to Berlin, where he is turned over to Jens Fiedler, chief of East German counterintelligence. Fiedler has long suspected Mundt of being a British agent, but he has not found any concrete evidence to support that belief. Leamas' information regarding "Operation Rolling Stone" apparently offers the proof he needs. Fiedler and Leamas are able to verify that the payment monies that had been deposited in various banks had been withdrawn when Mundt was on a business trip for the Abteilung in the city where the banks were located. This and other evidence is enough to convince Fiedler that he can bring charges of treason against Mundt.

At the trial, Fiedler presents his case, with Leamas as his star witness. Mundt is accused of having been turned by British intelligence, of having accepted the payments for his services, and of having used Riemeck as his conduit for sending information to British intelligence via Leamas. Riemeck's death is explained as a ploy to deflect Fiedler's suspicions from Mundt. Mundt's defense, however, is stunning. Fiedler is countercharged with treason; as proof, Liz Gold, who had been lured to East Germany, is produced as a witness. She simply tells the truth: She had loved Leamas, but he had told her he was leaving; when he was gone, British intelligence had taken care of her needs. Her testimony reveals Leamas' role as a fabricator; and Fiedler is doomed.

After the trial, Mundt arranges for the escape of Leamas and Liz. What Leamas has come to suspect has finally become clear. Mundt was exactly what the fabricated "Operation Rolling Stone" had supposedly proved he was—a spy for British intelligence. All the information that Fiedler had collected had been absolutely correct. Yet Fiedler, by all accounts a decent man, was to be executed, and Mundt, a man whom Leamas despises, has been saved. As he tells Liz, "Fiedler lost and Mundt won. London won—that's the point. It was a foul, foul operation. But it's paid off, and that's the only rule." At the Berlin Wall, when they are almost free, Liz is killed. Leamas, knowing that she was shot in order to ensure her silence, refuses to jump to safety. He chooses instead to remain by her body, opting to die rather than to come in from the cold and return to such a foul, foul business.

Impact of Event

To understand the significance of *The Spy Who Came in from the Cold*, the novel must first be placed in perspective. World War II, a war against totalitarianism, had ended; but the Cold War, an ideological battle, had immediately followed. Two sides—the Soviet Union and its allies against the United States and its allies— confronted each other throughout the world. Crisis occurred with alarming frequency. Each side resorted to elaborate propaganda campaigns, painting itself in the most favorable light and the other side in the worst possible light.

With the entire world a battleground, and with each side portraying itself as absolutely right, humanity was perpetually in fear of a nuclear Armageddon. The Cuban Missile Crisis of 1962 appeared to be merely a portent of crises yet to come. Europe itself was especially plagued by crises, with Berlin, because of its location, being a frequent hot spot. It was along the Iron Curtain in Germany that the two sides were most visibly poised to fight, and it was there that the weapons buildup was greatest. Thus, the spy business was most essential in Germany; it was there that the most information was needed.

It was in this environment that David Cornwall came of age. Born in 1931 and educated at British public schools and on the Continent, Cornwall was an ideal candidate for the Foreign Service. Temperamentally, however, he was not an ideal candidate for the deviousness of such work. Cornwall's moral values were revulsed by the espionage of the era and by the amorality exhibited by both sides. To Cornwall, it was not a world in which good was combating evil; from his viewpoint, he saw both sides using the same tactics and following the same rules. It was not a matter of black or white; all was gray.

When he became a writer, Cornwall took the nom de plume John le Carré; while *The Spy Who Came in from the Cold* was actually his third novel, it is the work that best exemplifies his interpretation of the Cold War. It was also the work that allowed him to retire from the Foreign Service to devote himself full-time to his writing. Le Carré dismisses as absurd Ian Fleming's James Bond type of spy. For le Carré, the prototypical master spy was George Smiley, a shy, reserved, physically unattractive yet brilliant agent. Yet Smiley, too, is an integral part in the deception that ultimately results in the death of Fiedler, of Liz, and of Leamas, his own agent.

The Spy Who Came in from the Cold is much more than a good spy story. It is also a good novel. Le Carré uses the spy-thriller genre to educate his audience and to elucidate the themes of the Cold War for his readers. He continually harps upon the themes of amorality, of the difficulty of telling good from bad or right from wrong, and of the nature of spying. In this regard, le Carré could be grouped with Joseph Conrad, Jaroslav Hašek, Erich Maria Remarque, or Aleksandr Solzhenitsyn, for all are interested not in the glorification of nationalistic conflict, but in the dehumanizing behaviors that result from such conflict. For a cruel and devious man such as Mundt to win is immoral; in the world of the Cold War, however, it is amorality that triumphs. There is room only for success, whatever the cost. There are no heroes, only victims and victors.

A film version of *The Spy Who Came in from the Cold* was released in 1965. Filmed in austere black and white and starring Richard Burton, the motion picture was true to the novel. In the tradition of Jean Renoir and Stanley Kubrick (whose black comedy *Dr. Strangelove: Or, How I Learned to Stop Worrying and Love the Bomb* was released in 1964), *The Spy Who Came in from the Cold* pulled no punches in its portrayal of the inhumanity of man. Yet each antihero, despite individual flaws, manifested a basic goodness at some point in the story. Leamas, the penultimate frontline Cold Warrior, was a flawed but good person. As the story unfolds, Leamas discovers the part of his psyche that he had deliberately submerged while he worked as a spy. At the end of the story, knowing better who he truly is, he refuses to leave the one good person in his life. He chooses to die with her rather than to return to the world he knew. It is an end little different from that met by Paul Bäumer, the hero of Remarque's *All Quiet on the Western Front*, who dies before he can return to a world from which he is permanently alienated.

Bibliography

Bloom, Clive, ed. *Spy Thrillers: From Buchan to le Carré.* New York: St. Martin's Press, 1990. A collection of thirteen essays that survey the development of the spy novel genre from the late nineteenth century to the present. Useful for understanding the range of styles within the genre.

Bloom, Harold, ed. *John le Carré: Modern Critical Views.* New York. Chelsea House, 1987. Eleven essays on the craft of le Carré. Articles range from analyses of le Carré's fiction to studies of le Carré's role in the Cold War.

Homberger, Eric. *John le Carré.* New York: Methuen, 1986. A biography of le Carré that analyzes not only the fiction of le Carré but also the person who is the author. Particularly useful for understanding the interrelationship between the author and his writing.

Lewis, Peter. *John le Carré.* New York: Frederick Ungar, 1985. A biography of John le Carré that focuses primarily on his writing. Lewis sketches the life history of the author, then devotes succeeding chapters to each novel in succession. Excellent analysis of *The Spy Who Came in from the Cold.*

Monaghan, David. *The Novels of John le Carré: The Art of Survival.* New York: Basil Blackwell, 1985. A collection of five essays that seek to explain the craft of le Carré within the context of the author's worldview. Monaghan is particularly interested in le Carré's use of spying as a metaphor for modern society.

_____. *Smiley's Circus.* London: Orbis, 1986. A collection of biographies, chronologies, glossaries, and explanations that detail and elucidate le Carré's spy world. Particularly useful for understanding the myriad deceptions that frequent le Carré's work.

Sauerberg, Lars Ole. *Secret Agents in Fiction: Ian Fleming, John le Carré, Len Deighton.* London: Macmillan, 1984. Important study of the spy-thriller genre. Of significance is the comparison of the work of the three best British spy novelists of the Cold War era, each of whom interpreted his spies differently.

Wolfe, Peter, *Corridors of Deceit: The World of John le Carré.* Bowling Green: Bowling Green State University Popular Press, 1987. An analysis of le Carré's work as well as a study of the psychological processes and moral values it expresses.

William S. Brockington, Jr.

Cross-References

Heart of Darkness Reveals the Consequences of Imperialism (1902), p. 51; Hašek's *The Good Soldier Švejk* Reflects Postwar Disillusionment (1921), p. 523; *All Quiet on the Western Front* Stresses the Futility of War (1929), p. 767; Renoir Marks the High Point of Prewar Filmmaking (1937), p. 1073; *Dr. No* Launches the Hugely Popular James Bond Series (1962), p. 1913.

VONNEGUT'S *CAT'S CRADLE* EXPRESSES
1960'S ALIENATION

Category of event: Literature
Time: 1963
Locale: New York, New York

Cat's Cradle, *one of Kurt Vonnegut's four powerful 1960's novels, reflected the fear of atomic annihilation and the rejection of establishment values but also showcased the author's trademark satirical wit and cast of eccentric characters*

> *Principal personages:*
> KURT VONNEGUT, JR. (1922-   ), an author of experimental fiction whose central theme is the search for human purpose in an incomprehensible universe
> J. ROBERT OPPENHEIMER (1904-1967), an American physicist who served as the prototype for *Cat's Cradle's* Felix Hoenikker

Summary of Event

By 1963, Kurt Vonnegut had already published two science-fiction novels and many short stories; he was established but not widely popular as a writer. He was becoming increasingly afraid of being associated permanently with the pulp-fiction world, where so much short science fiction was represented; in 1962, *Mother Night* signaled his move into experimental fiction.

Vonnegut worked after World War II as a publicist with the industrial giant General Electric, but he quickly became disillusioned with the thrust of the corporation's research and its involvement with the U.S. military complex. What he viewed as the too-cozy relationship between industry and the military became central to his vision of what science should be and what it actually was. After leaving General Electric, he had stints as a teacher and a businessman.

The end of the 1950's was turbulent for Vonnegut; his own family of three children was suddenly augmented by three of his sister Alice's sons after she and her husband died almost simultaneously. This catastrophe particularly affected Vonnegut, as Alice had been his favorite sibling. W. R. Allen, in his 1991 study *Understanding Kurt Vonnegut*, points to critical agreement that Vonnegut's almost exclusive choice of first-person narrative in much of his fiction was based on a personal belief that a narrator's voice should address itself to an intimate. In Vonnegut's case, he himself has said, that intimate was his sister Alice.

Scholars have also noted Vonnegut's stated belief that "the writer's function in society . . . is to respond to life." Personal sadness appears to have exacerbated Vonnegut's general pessimism about life in the post-World War II era, a pessimism that had begun in a childhood and young adulthood marked directly by other significant world events. His father's success as one of Indianapolis' leading architects and his mother's position as heiress of a successful brewer had meant a wealthy start to life, but the family's economic and social prominence was so shattered by the 1929 stock market crash and the ensuing Depression that Vonnegut's father never recovered his confidence, and his mother endured crushing depressions that ended only with her suicide in 1944. As a prisoner of war in Dresden, Vonnegut survived, witnessed, and was compelled to clean up after Dresden's devastation in the Allied bombings of February 13, 1945; on August 6 of that same year, the war was brought to a rapid close with the American destruction of Hiroshima (and Nagasaki three days later) with the atomic bomb. Vonnegut considered this latter event indeed as "the day the world ended"; it has since shaped his fictional themes.

Both Vonnegut's moral vision and his style in his best writing are shaped not only by the experiential but also by the academic track of his life since youth. His father's profession as an architect must at least partly explain the familiarity with design and structure so strongly present in Vonnegut's fictional worlds. Architectural design may also have shaped the experimental styles and structures of his writing, which have earned both critical praise and scorn. As a high school and university student, Vonnegut wrote for his school newspapers, practicing and honing the factual and stylistic straightforwardness, brevity, and simplicity that also mark his writing. In college, he majored in chemistry as an undergraduate and in anthropology as a postwar graduate student—which perhaps explains his interest in the perceived moral problems inherent in the subjugation of "pure" science to technological wizardry. In a 1992 television interview, Vonnegut reiterated his belief that science and its implications for humankind remain among the twentieth century's most pressing moral issues.

During the time Vonnegut was preparing to burst on the mass literary consciousness in the mid-1960's, world events were occurring that probably did nothing to allay his pessimism. Yet some may also have served to affirm his enduring underlying faith in the joyous genius of humankind, a faith that saves his work from nihilism. After World War II, causes for both despair and exhilaration coexisted in unfolding world events. Throughout the 1950's, the escalation of the Cold War precipitated a worldwide buildup of armaments, especially nuclear arms; Cold War escalation culminated in the 1961 erection of the Berlin Wall and the frightening Cuban Missile Crisis of 1962, when global atomic war was barely averted. Also in 1962, the antinausea "wonder drug" thalidomide, dispensed to pregnant women, was found to have caused the severe deformity of thousands of children and was withdrawn from the market. The Civil Rights movement was gaining momentum, largely as a result of many ugly racial confrontations precipitated by 1954's *Brown v. Board of Education* Supreme Court decision ruling segregation of public schools unconstitutional. In late 1963, just after *Cat's Cradle*'s publication, President John F. Kennedy was assassinated. At the same time, though, science and the imagination could cheer the global advances in space that began with 1957's successful flight of the Soviet satellite Sputnik I and continued in 1962 with the American launching of Telstar, the satellite that allowed the first transmission of intercontinental television signals. The sordidness of Great Britain's Profumo Scandal was counterbalanced by Martin Luther King, Jr.'s "I Have a Dream" speech, which galvanized the huge March on Washington in 1963 and provided lasting inspiration. Thus, *Cat's Cradle*'s informing irony has a solid basis in social reality.

Impact of Event

Cat's Cradle was not immediately popular, but its publication provoked much lasting contradictory critical opinion about both its themes and its style. The novel is an iconoclastic, satirical treatment of issues that profoundly affect twentieth century humankind: the loss of religious faith; science as a false god; humankind's deceptive rationale for creativity ("No damn cat, and no damn cradle," one character observes of the intricate, ancient child's string game that gives the novel its title and is symbolic of science's smoke-and-mirrors aspect); the unattractiveness of modern reality; a missing sense of human purpose; but finally, affirmation of humanity's will to survive in a meaningful way.

All these are explored through narrator Jonah's fatal involvement with the Hoenikker family when he begins research for his intended book *The Day the World Ended*, which is meant to discover "what important Americans had done on the day when the first atomic bomb was dropped on Hiroshima, Japan." Clearly, Jonah had planned a stance of moral condemnation, as his work was to be "a Christian book" written by a man not yet converted to Bokononism, the informing antireligion of *Cat's Cradle*. Instead, like his biblical counterpart, Jonah bears witness to apocalyptic events and heralds an unredemptive messiah.

In the novel, Felix Hoenikker, developer of the atom bomb, Nobel Prize winner, now dead, is kept vividly alive through the reminiscences of his three freakish offspring. Out of their memories, Hoenikker emerges not (as some critics allege) as a monster but more as a giant infant, limitlessly curious and inventive but totally incapable of forming reciprocal, loving human relationships or of comprehending morality or religious faith. "What is sin?" he asked a fellow scientist anguishing over the destructiveness of the atomic bomb; "What is God? What is love?" he inquired of a conventionally devout employee.

The three peculiar Hoenikker children, despite their physical and personality differences, are early united in their grief for their neglected, dead mother, their reverential horror of their father, and now by their shared, secret possession of crystals of "ice-nine," the last of their father's inventions. Now they, Jonah, and an assorted collection of outcasts, adventurers, and eccentrics, mostly American, are gathered on the rectangular Caribbean island of San Lorenzo, a travesty of a republic presided over by dying dictator "Papa" Monzano. The island is also inhabited by the elusive Bokonon, an adventurer and soldier of fortune whose banned religion nevertheless pervades and shapes life on the island and transforms Jonah.

On San Lorenzo, Jonah's planned book becomes an after-the-fact narration of a descent to near-annihilation. The absurd events leading up to the magnificently described cataclysm of destruction by ice-nine exemplifies Vonnegut's talent at juxtaposing the trivial and the grand, the absurd and the significant, the comic and the terrible that is his (and Bokonon's) view of human existence. Ice-nine, the vehicle of man's destruction by instant freezing, is kept in three picnic-sized flasks guarded by the Hoenikker siblings, who, for all their pathetic personal inadequacies, are thus the arbiters of human existence.

The novel ends when Jonah finally encounters Bokonon, now a mild-mannered old man surviving this holocaust with detached aplomb. He is preparing the conclusion of *The Books of Bokonon*, his antireligion's testament. He dreams, he says, of destroying himself with ice-nine and of becoming frozen on his alluring San Lorenzo mountain peak into a position of rudely thumbing his nose at "You Know Who." So humankind, Vonnegut implies, should spit bravely into the wind of the twentieth century, asserting his will to survive over his impulse to self-destruction. It is perhaps Bokonon's outlook that most offended some of *Cat's Cradle*'s critics; certainly, Jonah creates a conundrum by founding his artistic odyssey, the novel itself, on Bokononism's paradoxical basic premise: "All of the true things I am about to tell you are shameless lies." Such a statement has provoked critical charges of Vonnegut's flippancy and superficiality. Others commend the satirical wit that successfully enlivens the novel's serious themes.

Cat's Cradle's style provoked as much critical discussion as its themes did. Critic James Mellard lists Vonnegut, along with literary contemporaries such as Jack Kerouac, Donald Barthelme, John Barth, and Richard Brautigan, as one of the prime creators of the "exploded" novel form. Such a fragmented style reflects the twentieth century's anxious preoccupation with alienation, disintegration, even impending annihilation.

The novel has 127 chapters, many as brief as a page. The short, rapid bursts of narrative, delivered mostly in straightforward, unadorned prose, suit the tone taken by narrator Jonah: wry, often self-mocking, masking an underlying depth of seriousness. The narrative frequently reads like notes toward a journalistic piece. In vignette after vignette, place, character, event, or mood is strongly evoked; dialogue, often choppy, is lent significance and overtone, even if the dialogue is trivial in subject; and cliff-hangers or implied logical conclusions tantalize at each chapter's end. Thus, Jonah's sense of urgency and mission is emphasized; after all, he is writing after the destruction of the known world by ice-nine. He feels even more the need to record, to set down, especially as this is his designated job within the little surviving group gaily referred to by one member as "the Swiss Family Robinson." Jonah's resulting work—*Cat's Cradle*—ultimately achieves an overall coherence and a compelling energy that makes it readable and probably does much to explain the novel's eventual popular appeal. The younger reading generation, responding in the 1950's to Cold War politics, accelerating materialism, and the more pessimistic premises of existentialism, was turning by 1963 to the burgeoning Civil Rights movement. If at *Cat's Cradle*'s publication there was only a small readership for the book, by the mid-1960's and the acceleration of the anti-Vietnam War movement the audience was growing and enthusiastic, receptive to Vonnegut's blend of despair and the comic and to his sense of both the absurdity and sublimity of human existence. Above all, Vonnegut celebrates man's creativity, not so much in the science as in the artistry of life.

Bibliography

Allen, William Rodney. *Understanding Kurt Vonnegut.* Columbia: University of South Carolina Press, 1991. An indispensable study, written in clear, accessible style. The book's seven chapters consider Vonnegut's major fiction chronologically; the exhaustive bibliography and index are probably the most inclusive in print.

Giannone, Richard. *Vonnegut: A Preface to His Novels.* Port Washington, N.Y.: Kennikat Press, 1977. A short but solid introduction to Vonnegut's themes and art as a novelist, with illuminating analysis of *Cat's Cradle.* Includes chronology, bibliography, and index.

Klinkowitz, Jerome. *Kurt Vonnegut.* New York: Methuen, 1982. An elegant short discourse on Vonnegut the novelist by the foremost Vonnegut expert.

Klinkowitz, Jerome, and Donald L. Lawler, eds. *Vonnegut in America: An Introduction to the Life and Work of Kurt Vonnegut.* New York: Delacorte Press, 1977. An omnibus work, essential to the serious student of Vonnegut. Presents a variety of scholarly essays on Vonnegut's life and works. Includes a thorough bibliography and photographs.

Mustazza, Leonard. *Forever Pursuing Genesis: The Myth of Eden in the Novels of Kurt Vonnegut.* Lewisburg, Pa.: Bucknell University Press, 1990. Chapter 5 in this thorough thematic study treats *Cat's Cradle.* Also included are endnotes on each chapter and an index.

Schatt, Stanley. *Kurt Vonnegut, Jr.* Boston: Twayne, 1976. A meticulous study of Vonnegut's major novels, with separate chapters on his short fiction, drama, and essays. Contains thorough notes, bibliography, and index.

Jill Rollins

Cross-References

The Metamorphosis Anticipates Modern Feelings of Alienation (1915), p. 396; Huxley's *Brave New World* Reflects Fears About the Future (1932), p. 896; American Science Fiction Enjoys Its Golden Age (1938), p. 1094; *Nineteen Eighty-Four* Portrays Totalitarianism and Mind Control (1949), p. 1421; Heinlein Publishes *Stranger in a Strange Land* (1961), p. 1883.

THE BEATLES REVOLUTIONIZE POPULAR MUSIC

Category of event: Music
Time: 1963-1965
Locale: Great Britain and the United States

After generating hysteria in their native England, the Beatles, four youths from Liverpool, visited the United States and revolutionized rock music, becoming among the most influential cultural figures of the 1960's

Principal personages:
JOHN LENNON (1940-1980), the guitarist, vocalist and songwriter usually seen as the most intellectually innovative member of the group
PAUL MCCARTNEY (1942-   ), the bassist, vocalist, and songwriter who collaborated with Lennon and is widely recognized for his melodic gifts
GEORGE HARRISON (1943-   ), the guitarist, vocalist, and songwriter who contributed an Indian influence to the band's music
RINGO STARR (RICHARD STARKEY, JR., 1940-   ), the drummer and vocalist considered the most affable member of the group

Summary of Event

At the beginning of 1963, the Beatles had evolved from a ragtag group of working-class men into a unique amalgam of personalities and talents on the brink of stardom. In 1957, sixteen-year-old John Lennon had met fourteen-year-old Paul McCartney while the two were performing with different groups at a church event in a suburb of Liverpool, England. The two would form the nucleus of a band that would include McCartney's young friend George Harrison, Lennon's art-school colleague Stu Sutcliffe, and Pete Best, a drummer with a following on the Liverpool music scene. Moving gradually from small local clubs to relatively high-paying gigs in Hamburg, Germany, the group—variously calling itself the Moondogs, the Moonshiners, and the Silver Beatles, among other names—refined its repertoire of American rock and roll and began composing original material. By the summer of 1962, Sutcliffe had died of a cerebral hemorrhage, Best had been replaced by Ringo Starr, and the group, now known as the Beatles, had attracted the attention of Brian Epstein, a record-store manager who saw potential in the group. Epstein landed the band a record contract, and the band released its first single, "Love Me Do," in August, 1962. It became a minor hit that fall.

In January of 1963, the Beatles recorded "Please Please Me," which became their first number-one single in Britain, followed in turn by "From Me to You," "Twist and Shout," "She Loves You," and "I Want to Hold Your Hand." By the spring of that year, screaming from the audience began accompanying their performances; by the fall, the riotous welcomes greeting the band at airports had been dubbed "Beatlemania." In the early 1960's, though, England and Europe were still popular music backwaters, and it remained to be seen whether the group could succeed in the vast American cultural and commercial market.

The early signs were not auspicious. "I Want to Hold Your Hand," leased to a small independent label in the United States, appeared at the bottom of the American pop charts in late 1963 and went virtually unnoticed. After Capitol Records invested $50,000 to promote the group, however, their records began to sell. On February 7, 1964, the Beatles arrived in New York to mass hysteria, with thousands of screaming teenage girls following their every move, entrepreneurs hawking licensed products (for which the Beatles received shockingly little), and their music flooding the airwaves and record stores. The first of their three appearances on *The Ed Sullivan Show* drew seventy million viewers, and a brief tour that followed received national press coverage, largely focusing on the band members' long hair, their sense of humor, and the silliness of the furor surrounding them.

In their wake, other British rock groups (among them Gerry and the Pacemakers, the Dave Clark Five, and, of course, the Rolling Stones) also enjoyed success in the United States, a phenomenon observers dubbed the "British Invasion." Yet the Beatles remained the preeminent figures in this movement. In April of 1964, Beatles songs simultaneously occupied the top five positions on *Billboard* magazine's pop chart—a feat that has never been equaled. That summer, the group's first movie, *A Hard Day's Night*, was released to wide acclaim and was followed the next year by *Help!* A series of tours in between 1964 and 1966 made John, Paul, George, and Ringo household names around the world (fifty-five thousand fans saw the group at New York's Shea Stadium in 1965, the largest concert audience ever at the time). In recognition for their achievements, Queen Elizabeth made the four Members of the Order of the British Empire. Some members of this august group, appalled that a rock band would be so honored, turned in their medals. (Lennon himself would do the same in 1969 to protest Great Britain's role in the Vietnam War.)

Young adults worshiped the Beatles with an intensity reminiscent of the hysteria provoked by the early Frank Sinatra or Elvis Presley. Cynical adults tended to look at Beatlemania as a cheap commercial rip-off, while more sociologically minded observers offered grief over the recent death of John Kennedy or the sublimated sexuality of girls as explanations for the hoopla. In any case, as the weeks turned into months and months into years, it become increasingly clear that the Beatles were not simply a passing fad.

Meanwhile, the band continued making records, and its music showed increasing lyrical and musical sophistication. McCartney's elegiac "Yesterday," complete with a string arrangement, became one of the most-recorded songs of all time, while Lennon's "Help!," one of the biggest hits of 1965, showed an uncommonly mature sense of vulnerability. By this time, the group was being directly influenced by the work of Bob Dylan, who himself had just become a convert to rock and roll; together, the two acts would profoundly influence the course of popular music in the next five years, injecting new levels of complexity, diversity, and social protest into what had previously been considered a limited musical form.

Impact of Event

Following the consolidation of their talents in 1963 and their conquest of the United States in 1964, the Beatles emerged as one of the most influential forces in the development of modern popular music. In synthesizing a number of strands in Anglo-American musicology, in stylistic innovations and the path-breaking use of studio technology, in relying on their own songwriting as the cornerstone of their recordings, and in articulating the social and political possibilities of cultural celebrity, the group blazed a path followed by many others. These achievements were not altogether evident in the early 1960's, and in the decades to follow, it was the Beatles of the late 1960's who were remembered as cultural pioneers. Yet it is also clear that, whatever the group went on to achieve, the creative burst of 1963 to 1965 represents one of the great flowerings in rock and roll history.

In order to understand just how striking the Beatles sounded in those early years, it is worth recalling the enervated state of popular music in the years prior to the group's arrival in the United States. By 1962, the early excitement generated by Elvis Presley had ebbed, and Presley's two-year stint in the Army seemed to have taken the edge off his work. Buddy Holly was dead, Chuck Berry was in jail, and Jerry Lee Lewis had disappeared from the scene in disgrace after marrying an adolescent cousin. Insipid, highly commercialized crooners such as Pat Boone sang heavily diluted versions of songs that had far more vitality in their original (often African American) versions. While some interesting records continued to be made—notably those of the Beach Boys, the Drifters, and the Ronettes—there was a widespread perception that rock and roll's fortunes were not as high as they had been five years before.

The Beatles, meanwhile, had been avid fans of American popular music, especially black music, and performed it regularly. Growing up in England, however, the group was relatively isolated from the most current stateside trends, and they overlaid such influences with native accents (this is particularly true of Paul McCartney, whose work bears the unmistakable stamp of English dance-hall music). In an odd way, the Beatles' attempts to mimic American music failed, and in so failing the band created something new. Listeners who compare, for example, Junior Walker's version of "Money" to the Beatles' rendition of the same tune can hear two different songs: The former is a good-natured, even warm, lament; the latter—distinguished by Lennon's snarling vocal—becomes a fierce affirmation of crass materialism.

Yet the overall mood of the Beatles' early records was buoyant. Songs such as "I Want to Hold Your Hand," "She Loves You," "All My Loving," and "Can't Buy Me Love" are marked by a joyous energy that transcends the simple pieties of the lyrics. These are strongly collaborative records, not only in the songwriting between Lennon and McCartney, but in the exuberant blend of voices and instruments that sounds unlike anything produced in the United States at the time.

While many observers considered the Beatles a fad, more acute listeners recognized the potential for something more lasting. Perhaps the group's most important fan was Bob Dylan. "They were doing things nobody was doing. Their chords were outrageous, just outrageous, and their harmonies made it all valid," he recalled. "It seemed to me a definite line was being drawn. This was something that never happened before."

As Dylan's music became more complex under the Beatles' influence, the Beatles' lyrics became more complex under Dylan's influence. Songs such as "You've Got to Hide Your Love Away," "Paperback Writer," "In My Life," and "Nowhere Man" convey an emotional richness and ambiguity far more complex than that of "I Want to Hold Your Hand." The Beatles' palette would range still wider in years to come, especially after the use of hallucinogenic drugs led the group to write surrealistic songs about their experiences.

Meanwhile, the band was experimenting musically as well. Nowhere is this spirit more evident than in the 1965 album *Rubber Soul*. On "In My Life," for example, a tape of a piano is speeded up to sound like a harpsichord, while Lennon's elliptical "Norwegian Wood (This Bird Has Flown)" shows an Eastern influence that would later become a staple of George Harrison's songwriting. *Sgt. Pepper's Lonely Hearts Club Band*, released in 1967, is generally assumed to be the group's greatest achievement, but many critics consider *Rubber Soul*, with its unique balance of simplicity and complexity, to be the Beatles' true masterpiece.

Indeed, one could argue that the years following 1965 marked a long, slow decline for the Beatles as a group. After that date, Lennon and McCartney collaborated less frequently, and a series of centrifugal forces—the death of manager Brian Epstein in 1967, Lennon's divorce and his increasing involvement with Yoko Ono, Harrison's growing restlessness under Lennon and McCartney's tutelage—would eventually lead to the group's breakup. While it would be a mistake to consider the period between 1965 and 1970 as nothing more than the prelude to the band's unraveling, for much remarkable music was made during that period, such an angle on the group's history does allow one to appreciate just what the Beatles did achieve in their early years.

Even if it ultimately precipitated their undoing as a group, the Beatles' greatest achievement was a capacity for growth and change. The band almost singlehandedly made it possible to imagine rock and roll as a vehicle for artistic expression over the course of a lifetime (even if, in the case of John Lennon, that lifetime was tragically short). Moreover, the Beatles endowed rock with a sense of cultural legitimacy that other performers ranging from Joni Mitchell to Michael Jackson could follow. As such, their legacy extends far beyond a body of work that shows no sign of fading from popular memory.

Bibliography

Harrison, George. *I Me Mine*. New York: Simon & Schuster, 1981. Harrison is the only Beatle to write his own memoir, but this book is less an autobiography than a published scrapbook of memorabilia, including song lyrics, photos, and reminiscences.

Marcus, Greil. "The Beatles." In *The Rolling Stone Illustrated History of Rock and Roll*, edited by Jim Miller. Rev. ed. New York: Rolling Stone Press, 1980. A brief but evocative essay that suggests the breadth and depth of the Beatles' achievements. Marcus is particularly strong in analyzing the larger cultural resonance of the band.

Norman, Philip. *Shout! The Beatles and Their Generation.* New York: Simon & Schuster, 1981. Perhaps the best general account of the Beatles' history. Norman, who has also written distinguished biographies of the Rolling Stones and Elton John, is particularly strong on the financial aspects of the Beatle empire and its collapse.

Schaffner, Nicholas. *The Beatles Forever.* New York: Cameron House, 1977. In a market flooded with books on the band, this one ranks among the finest—solid writing, interesting photographs, and extensive discographies and charts. An excellent reference source. The book was reprinted by McGraw-Hill in 1978.

Sheff, David. *The Playboy Interviews with John Lennon and Yoko Ono.* Edited by G. Barry Golson. New York: Playboy Press, 1981. The book is a mess, poorly organized and full of less-than-interesting questions, but the interviews—conducted shortly before Lennon's death—are an important historical document for his recollections on the making of dozens of songs.

Stokes, Geoffrey. "Roll Over, Frankie Avalon" and "Brits Rule." In *Rock of Ages: The Rolling Stone History of Rock and Roll*, by Ed Ward, Geoffrey Stokes, and Ken Tucker. New York: Rolling Stone Press, 1986. These two chapters do a good job of placing the Beatles in the larger context of British and American music of the early 1960's.

Wenner, Jann. "The Rolling Stone Interview: John Lennon." In *The Rolling Stone Interviews, 1967-1980*, edited by Peter Herbst. New York: St. Martin's Press, 1981. This discussion, conducted in 1971 in the immediate aftermath of the Beatles' breakup, is a classic in the magazine's history of distinguished interviews. A must for anyone interested in the band's history.

Jim Cullen

Cross-References

Berry's "Maybellene" Popularizes Rock and Roll (1955), p. 1635; Presley Becomes a Rock-and-Roll Sensation (1956), p. 1705; The Rolling Stones Release *Out of Our Heads* (1965), p. 2027; Dylan Performs with Electric Instruments (1965), p. 2038; Hendrix Releases *Are You Experienced?* (1967), p. 2092; The Beatles Release *Sgt. Pepper's Lonely Hearts Club Band* (1967), p. 2098; The Sex Pistols Spark Punk Rock's Musical Insurrection (1975), p. 2360.

MINIMALISM EMPHASIZES OBJECTS AS ART

Category of event: Art
Time: 1963-1968
Locale: New York, New York

Minimalist art focused on the direct visual perception of objects rather than on the symbolic interpretation of them

> *Principal personages:*
> FRANK STELLA (1936-   ), an American painter whose work inaugurated the period of minimalism
> MICHAEL HEIZER (1944-   ), an American sculptor whose work signaled the demise of the Minimalist period
> ROBERT MORRIS (1931-   ), an American sculptor whose work continued to exhibit elements of minimalist style long after the 1960's
> ANNE TRUITT (1921-   ), an American sculptor who had the first identifiably minimalist show in 1963
> DONALD JUDD (1928-   ), an American sculptor who consistently worked the margins of minimalist art

Summary of Event

The term "minimalist art" describes abstract, geometric painting and sculpture executed in the United States during the 1960's. Its basic organizing principles include the right angle, the square, and the cube, rendered with a minimum of compositional manipulation. Historically a reaction to what young artists saw as the autobiographical gestures of abstract expressionism (a broad movement in art characterized by a lack of representation and by an emotional approach to concept and execution), minimalist art also encompassed the formal innovations of abstract expressionism, particularly as articulated by the paintings of Jackson Pollock and Barnett Newman. Although minimalism shared with pop art ("popular" art) anonymous design, deadpan flatness, and natural or industrial color and was even described as "Imageless Pop" in 1966, the minimalists avoided any form of comment, representation, or reference in their work. Minimalism and pop art also shared a philosophical commitment to the abstract, material object.

Frank Stella's "Black Paintings," which were shown as early as 1959 in the Museum of Modern Art's "Sixteen Americans" exhibit, inaugurated the period, while Robert Morris' process-oriented work and Michael Heizer's earthworks of the late 1960's signaled minimalism's decline. Although minimalist art continued to be produced into the 1980's, it flourished from 1963 to 1968.

Anne Truitt's exhibition of sculpture in February of 1963 at André Emmerich's gallery is generally regarded as the first identifiably minimalist show. The first minimalist exhibition to attract significant critical attention, however, was Robert Morris' show at the Green Gallery. During the fall of 1963, the gallery was occupied by Morris' two distinct types of art objects. Smaller neo-Dada works were interspersed among huge gray plywood constructions. The future of minimalism was decisively announced by the sculptor Donald Judd's first solo exhibition of red wooden reliefs and floor structures at the Green Gallery in December.

The most sensational New York exhibition of minimalist art was called "Primary Structures," which consisted of sculpture of clean order and high finish, with referential connections to manufactured objects, organized by Kynaston McShine at the Jewish Museum in 1966. Forty-two British and American sculptors were represented. The originality of the show seemed to predict a future trend—minimalist art as a unique retrospective glance at the 1960's. By 1968, however, much of this art had become mainstream. Minimalist art lay dormant through the 1970's, rejected, by the end of that decade, as authoritarian modernism by younger artists. It came to symbolize the final stage of the linear progress and reduction associated with the avant-garde and was sometimes referred to as "the last of the modernist styles."

The term "minimalist art" cannot be credited to any particular individual. In the late 1920's, John Graham named a movement "minimalism"; however, he used the term to designate the presence of a minimum of operating means. Donald Judd used the adjective "minimal" as early as 1960 in a review and later to describe Robert Morris' constructions. Although there continued to be a reaction to such a seemingly pejorative term, several critics used it without hesitation in reviews of "Primary Structures." The artists of this period, however, never considered themselves as part of any group or movement.

Aside from being labeled "minimalist art," the work of this period was also referred to as "primary structures," "cool art," "literalist art," "ABC art," and even "*Dragnet* art" (alluding to the popular television show's catchphrase "just the facts"). It was described as nonrelational, nonhierarchical, reductive, serial, literal, unitary, and specific. Terms such as "presence," "gestalt," "nonanthropomorphic," and "environmental" abounded. Minimalist objects were described as more "real" than previous art, although no one attempted to define what they meant by "reality."

Two things distinguish minimalism from previous modernist art. First, the spectator is given a new role as contributor of meaning. As with pop and op ("optical") art, the "meaning" of a minimalist work is considered to exist outside the work itself. It is part of the nature of these works to act as triggers for thought and emotion preexisting in the viewer, as opposed to the more traditional concept of the work of art as the source of meaning.

One of the reasons for the external orientation of minimalism and subsequent emphasis on the spectator is the requirement that the work be literally and metaphorically empty; the work is a hollow object. The lack of expressive content then induces the outer-directedness of the object, forcing the spectator to locate the meaning of the work within the experiencing self rather than within the object.

Materiality—an unparalleled commitment to matter—was an essential goal of minimalist art. Literal, nonreferential "objecthood" took priority over any form of reference, representation, or illusionism. Yet while theories such as objecthood and all that it implies necessarily exist outside the work of art, they are dependent on the work for their justification. Minimalist art, although austere, is essentially visual. It stimulates perceptually and kinesthetically as well as conceptually. Since much of its impact results from experiential factors such as presence and scale, face-to-face confrontation with the physical object is essential. Since its objects lack what were traditionally necessary conditions for being considered works of art, minimalist art appeared to many observers not to be art at all.

Impact of Event

Minimalism represents one of those periodic movements of revolt against the "vulgar prosperity" that resulted from the collision of democratic politics and capitalist ambition. Minimalism embodies the frustrated American ideal of simplicity, refracted through the formal idioms of modern art; it exerted a powerful influence on the complex patterns of American culture.

The minimalist moment of stylistic clarity, simplicity, and critical purpose in art was a brief one, partly because no stable community existed to sustain it. Its social basis was the art world—a competitive, sometimes fickle subculture the economy of which depends on a constant renewal of novelty both in art and in opinion about it.

The demise of minimalism is the story of how its critical stance was neutralized by the art business and by the general backlash in American society against the liberal spirit of the 1960's; a kind of self-righteous greed began to supplant its iconoclasm.

By the mid 1970's, minimalist art had become the currency of lucrative careers for a number of artists, despite the contradiction inherent in the conversion of works of critical import into marketable commodities. The political intensity associated briefly with minimalism reemerged in the late 1960's in conceptual art, which reached the conclusion implicit in minimalist sculpture that elimination of the artwork-as-commodity was the only logically consistent basis on which artists could criticize the culture from within. The conceptual artists' basic strategy was to eliminate the art object completely, offering only written or spoken ideas or enigmatic performances as works, leaving little or no artistic remnants except documentation. Since documentation can be converted into marketable goods, not even conceptual art could circumnavigate the art market. Yet certain conceptual art activities that were never documented—and so eluded the commodity system—continued to live in people's memories as a kind of artistic folklore.

Minimalism was a compelling and important episode in American art because it clarified the fact that artists, despite their ambitions, can only play at superseding the values by which society's ruling groups legitimize their power. At its best, minimalist art was a plea for commitment to values—such as a clear, contemplative vision, the recognition of illusions for what they are, and a love of physical reality for its own sake—that are not, and probably could not be, widely shared in a highly techological, economically unstable mass society, no matter what its form or content.

The artistic backlash against minimalism was slow in coming, but by the late 1970's it hit powerfully. A desire for "forbidden" content and emotional surprise coincided with the need to stimulate a cooling contemporary art market and gave rise to a number of works in new media. "Pluralism" became the catchword for the new forms and for the resurgence of painting marked by decoration, narrative, fantasy, and pastiche. Some works in new media reflected social struggles; many others merely registered career ambitions with a new shamelessness characteristic of the time.

Because minimalism was not considered an "art style" by some critics, they believed that it would be little more than a mere passing phenomenon in art history. Its objects were industrially produced in rigid materials without any trace of the artist's hand. Its forms were those of an idealistically conceived geometry rather than of intuitive self-expression. Since its dominant period (1963-1968), however, critics have used the word "minimalist" to categorize any painting or sculpture that is nonfigurative, nonreferential, and nonnarrative or that is even remotely geometric.

What made minimalist art unique was not so much its materials or methods as its philosophical underpinnings. Minimalist art expresses beliefs about the self and the self's perception of the world that are based on material—objecthood—and space as occupied by that material and the artist/viewer's body. It is the condition of objecthood that elevates the work of art, theoretically, from the status of mere physical things.

Minimalist art influenced and was superseded by conceptual art, which can be seen as one more step in the reductive process, or what has been called the "dematerialization" of the object. Conceptual art can also be viewed as a reaction to minimalism's materialistic commitment to the object, for which conceptualists substituted photographic and typescript documentation. Unlike minimalist art, conceptualism placed no premium whatsoever on the object. Both minimalist and conceptual art, however, shared a commitment to straightforward simplicity and austerity through a denial of figurative or formal elaboration. It was exacting art that placed strong demands on the spectator. These demands were anathema to the neoexpressionists, who returned to the hand-painted figure, apparently replete with emotive expression. Art in the late 1980's revived geometry and industrial production but put them at the service of political, rather than aesthetic, content.

By the end of the 1960's, a decade that viewed the future optimistically, it was clear that minimalist abstraction had been challenged by a new set of formal and moral values, imperatives tempered by despair over the conduct of American politics (Vietnam, Watergate) and energized by the insurgency and success of the women's movement. "Postminimalism" was a term coined to denote the shift in sensibility away from the frozen and hierarchical American abstract painting and sculpture of the 1960's and to characterize the radical nature of new efforts. These attempts embrace open and unstable modes, forms beautiful in themselves despite their unfamiliarity—beautiful on the level of unmediated sensation—as well as forms that called into question the stabilized appearance of the day's abstraction.

Younger artists, excluded from a circle of elect painters and sculptors, were repulsed by the agenda based in modernist self-referentiality. Abstraction thus became the adversary, and postminimalism emerged.

Bibliography

Baker, Kenneth. *Minimalism: Art of Circumstance.* New York: Abbeville Press, 1988. In this insightful volume written for the general reader as well as the specialist, the author is concerned not with minimalism as a style but as a historical moment. Contains numerous illustrations and statements by many artists themselves.

Battock, Gregory, ed. *Minimal Art: A Critical Anthology.* New York: E. P. Dutton, 1968. A collection of twenty-eight enlightening essays by both critics and artists analyzing all aspects of "Minimal art" in American painting and sculpture. More than 170 photographs showing important minimalist works are included.

Colpit, Frances. *Minimal Art: The Critical Perspective.* Ann Arbor, Mich.: UMI Research Press, 1990. In this excellent documentary history, Colpit chronicles the minimalist art movement of the 1960's. Drawing upon the critical writings of the artists themselves and on interviews by herself and others, Colpit sets forth issues and arguments and identifies key concepts that are crucial to an understanding of minimalist art. In addition, an appendix listing major exhibitions and reviews influencing the growth of the movement, numerous illustrations, and an extensive bibliography are included.

Fried, Michael. "Shape as Form: Frank Stella's New Paintings." *Artforum* 5 (November, 1966): 25-27. Fried's criticisms of sculpture with respect to surface were first aired in this article. The author's argument is intricate; he claims that opticality cannot be achieved in sculpture because of the medium's emphasis on surface. According to Fried, sculpture does not partake of spatial illusionism because it is without a picture plane.

Pincus-Witten, Robert. *Postminimalism into Maximalism: American Art, 1966-1986.* Ann Arbor, Mich.: UMI Research Press, 1987. This scholarly collection of essays traces the history of avant-garde American art over two decades. Aside from the rejection of formalist values and the emphasis on autobiography, the artistic persona and psyche stripped bare, the essays reveal an essential constancy of modern art—the uniqueness of the personality. Contains numerous illustrations.

Sandler, Irving. *American Art of the 1960's.* New York: Harper & Row, 1988. In this well-written and well-researched survey of American art of the 1960's, Sandler discusses minimalism in its historical context. He examines the political, social, and economic—as well as artistic—reasons for its emergence and decline. Numerous plates and a bibliography are included.

Seitz, William C. *Art in the Age of Aquarius, 1955-1970.* Washington, D.C.: Smithsonian Institution Press, 1992. Presents a survey of art from 1955 to 1970 and includes a discussion of minimalism. Serves as a time capsule of the 1960's, providing an interesting angle of vision on the culture of the decade. Contains illustrations, chronology.

Genevieve Slomski

Cross-References

Duchamp's "Readymades" Challenge Concepts of Art (1913), p. 349; The Dada Movement Emerges at the Cabaret Voltaire (1916), p. 419; Henry Moore Is Inspired by Shapes in Subway Shelters (1940), p. 1190; Rosenberg Defines "Action Painting" (1952), p. 1557; Laurie Anderson's *United States* Popularizes Performance Art (1983), p. 2517; Christo Wraps the Pont Neuf (1985), p. 2548.

NAM JUNE PAIK EXHIBITS VIDEO
AND TELEVISION AS ART

Category of event: Art
Time: March 11-20, 1963
Locale: Galerie Parnass, Wuppertal, West Germany

Using concepts inspired by Dadaist artists, avant-garde musicians, and communication philosophy, Nam June Paik turned his attention to television and video, creating works that questioned the one-sidedness of broadcasting

Principal personages:

NAM JUNE PAIK (1932-   ), a musician and performer closely affiliated with the Fluxus movement who became the key figure in the emergence of video art

JOHN CAGE (1912-1992), an avant-garde composer who redefined music by integrating everyday noises into his compositions in an attempt to blur the distinction between art and life

GEORGE MACIUNAS (1931-1978), the leader of the international Fluxus movement in art

CHARLOTTE MOORMAN (1933-   ), a cellist and interpreter of avant-garde music who collaborated with Nam June Paik on his performance pieces

Summary of Event

On March 11, 1963, Nam June Paik opened his first one-man exhibition, entitled "Exposition of Music-Electronic Television," at the Galerie Parnass, a three-storied space in Wuppertal, Germany. He exhibited three different types of work: "Objets Sonores," four "prepared" and decorated pianos; "Instruments for Zen Exercises," a combination of found objects that could make noise; and "Electronic Televisions," thirteen manipulated or broken television sets that altered broadcasted images. After this exhibition, Paik devoted more of his creative energy to demystifying and deconstructing the medium of television, removing it from its role as bland entertainer. In the process, he sought to change viewers' perceptions of their role in the transmission/ reception process. It is important to note that although he is a major visual artist, Paik was trained as a performing musician and composer, gaining considerable recognition for this work. Many of his concerns in the visual arts are influenced by his musical performance experiences and ideas of the radical Fluxus art movement of the 1960's.

Nam June Paik was born in Seoul, Korea, where he studied piano and composition. He and his family were forced to move to Japan during the Korean War. While in Japan, he enrolled in the University of Tokyo to study twentieth century music, including electronic techniques. He was graduated in 1956 with a degree in aesthetics, having written his thesis on the influential twentieth century German composer Arnold Schoenberg, whose atonal and twelve-tone techniques replaced traditional concepts of harmony and tonality. In the 1950's, Germany was the center for electronic and avant-garde music, and Paik was drawn to that country to continue his studies at the University of Munich and at the Freiburg Conservatory, where he focused on art history and philosophy in addition to music.

In 1958, Paik enrolled in the International Summer Course for New Music in Darmstadt, Germany. There he met the famous American musician John Cage, who was to become a major influence on Paik's life and art. Cage had been a student of Arnold Schoenberg in the 1930's, and he continued Schoenberg's innovations by confronting established musical traditions. In addition, Cage was an acquaintance of Marcel Duchamp, the famous French artist and Dadaist philosopher. Duchamp proved to be an inspiration to many artists of the 1950's and 1960's, acting as a link for them with prior artistic thoughts. Cage also was influenced by Japanese Zen master Daisetz T. Suzuki, who lectured at Columbia University from 1949 to 1951. Cage combined Duchamp's philosophies of the "readymade" and concern with technology with the Zen Buddhist's philosophy of the importance of truly living in the now, attempting to apply these ideas to music.

Cage is credited with many innovations and experiments in modern music. For example, in 1938, early in his career, Cage dared to insert various objects between or on top of the strings of a piano. His "prepared piano" created sounds different from those that could be made by the instrument alone. Cage continued to stretch and explore the possibility of music. In some of his compositions, he included the noises of everyday life. Noting that audiences often were bored during a concert, having little to see and nothing to do, Cage also developed the idea of musical indeterminancy, in which the elements of the musical composition are left undecided by the composer and are chosen instead by the musician who performs it, thus imbuing musical performance with the unexpected quality of theater. He also is credited with having developed the first "happening," or multimedia audience participatory event, in 1952 at Black Mountain College in North Carolina. These ideas inspired George Maciunas to become leader of the Fluxus group, which continued Dadaist traditions by writing manifestos, publishing journals, and encouraging artists to perform as ways to challenge the current forms of high culture. This loosely knit international group of artists, writers, composers, filmmakers, and performers had enormous effects on the development of visual and performance art.

In the fall of 1958, Germany held its first show of Dadaist work since such art had been banned by Adolf Hitler. Paik was able to study work by Marcel Duchamp at first hand. He also was impressed with ideas of artist Kurt Schwitters, who included nontraditional materials in his collages in an attempt to fuse art and life. That fusion was an important part of Cage's ideas as well. Schwitters developed the concept of "Merz," which meant an art that was free from all constraints and bonds, and then took this one step further by developing the idea of "total theater," which he called "Merzbuhne." These ideas meshed closely with ideas of John Cage and the Fluxus artists. Inspired by all these ideas, Paik began to investigate the techniques of collage, action performance, and ideas of Zen in his own electronic work.

After the summer institute, Paik studied at the University of Cologne, where he did experimental work in the Studio for Electronic Music of Radio Cologne. While working at the radio station, he came in contact with people working in television. As he became more adept at electronics, he started to see the relationship his work in electronic music might have with the medium of television. Paik wrote to Cage about his artistic interest in the use of television as early as 1959. He began to perform his compositions, acquiring a reputation with what he called his "action music" at the Galerie 22 in Düsseldorf and at Mary Bauermeister's Atelier in Cologne, an important outlet for young composers. His original intent was to perform actions that would complement his collaged musical creations of live and taped sounds, but early on, his music took a back seat as his actions demanded more and more attention. In "Hommage à John Cage," Paik cut the strings of a piano and later pushed the instrument over on its side. In the Cologne performance of this piece, Paik included a motorcycle engine as one of his instruments. He left the scene without leaving instructions to have anyone turn the engine off. The space where the audience still watched and waited filled with carbon monoxide gas. This added an element of fear and physical danger to music, a notion that appealed to the critics of the time. In his piece entitled "Etude for Pianoforte," Paik ran into the audience with a large pair of scissors and cut off part of Cage's shirt and tie. Paik continued the performance by lathering Cage's hair with shampoo, eventually running out of the performance area and telephoning back to let the audience know that the piece was ended—making him perhaps the first person to use the telephone as an artistic medium.

Some of the inspiration for these performances came from ideas of Zen Buddhism, part of the Korean culture and Paik's heritage even if not his religion. In Zen, it is not uncommon for a master to act in a bizarre manner in order to shock the senses of his students, forcing them to arrive at some awareness. No one could be certain of what Paik would do next—perhaps not even Paik. There was no way of writing notation for his kind of "music," and he had at one time considered the use of video to record his performances, eventually using these tapes as a musical "score." He ultimately rejected this plan in fear that his pieces would be reproduced mechanically. The variability and uncertainty was what made the performances intense. Paik had incorporated and made his own the Fluxus idea that the artist's job was to oppose accepted norms in order to come up with the unexpected.

George Maciunas invited Paik to perform at Fluxus events and to write for Fluxus publications in the early 1960's. In his piece "One for Violin Solo," Paik destroyed a violin by smashing it to pieces on a table. This destruction was more violent than original Fluxus philosophy yet fit in with the Fluxus ideas of destroying the boundaries between the artwork and the viewer. In "Sonata Quasi una Fantasia," Paik played parts of Ludwig van Beethoven's "Moonlight Sonata" while stripping off pieces of his clothing. More and more he became aware of sex, or lack of sex, in modern music, and he wanted to investigate that idea. He wrote descriptions of work, or "scores," for his pieces such as "Young Penis Symphony," in which young men would stick their penises out through holes cut into large sheets of white paper. In "Chronicle of a Beautiful Paintress," he advised staining flags of different countries with menstrual blood and exhibiting them in a "beautiful gallery." These scores, or ideas for performances or artwork, were among the first conceptual pieces. The shocking themes of sex and destruction, combined with audience participation, are recurring ones in the artist's work.

While Paik performed his compositions and wrote for Fluxus publications, he also began creating a series of sculptures or assemblages of found objects that would eventually lead to his one-person showing in the Galerie Parnass. Inspired by German painter Karl Otto Goetz and his idea of creating abstract images on a television screen, Paik became more interested in electronics and in television. He rented a small studio and worked with hired engineers to alter thirteen old television sets. Electronically, Paik was able to stretch the horizontal and to turn the picture into its negative, turning black to white and white to black. He also had engineers create an interactive device with which the viewer could manipulate the broadcasted image by moving a dial, making the viewing of television an active rather than passive occupation. In one case, Paik discovered that the television was broken, so that the only image to appear was a horizontal line. The artist turned this set on its side, making the horizontal line into a vertical one. By this action, he showed total disregard for the sanctity of a machine that, since the 1930's and especially during the 1950's, had alarmingly invaded households worldwide. Paik was the first person to recognize the potential of television as an art form and was the first artist actually to transform the electronic mechanisms of the television set to enhance or distort the viewed pictures.

Impact of Event

Although his television sets did not make a large impression on art critics at this time, Paik realized the importance of what he had done. Cage also realized that someone would be bound to turn television into art. Paik shared that belief but did not think initially that he would be that person. After the exhibition, however, he wrote that "by no previous work was I so happy working as in these TV experiments." Soon after this time, he left Germany for Japan so that he could work with color television, which was not then available in Europe. He began a collaboration with Shuya Abe, an electronics engineer who helped Paik realize many of his ideas, including his family of robots series and his video synthesizer for color television. Paik had the idea that video would be the new technological painting of the future and that whichever artist owned the first videotape recorder would become the best painter of his times.

Paik and his working robot, K-456, visited New York City to participate in Fluxus events. George Maciunas had returned from Europe in 1964 and was encouraging artists of the Fluxus group to occupy loft spaces in the SoHo area of Manhattan, making this area an exciting one for the new avant-garde. Maciunas convinced fellow Lithuanian Jonas Mekas to move his Filmmakers' Cinematheque to the basement of his loft, adding the energy of the underground filmmakers to the avant-garde movement. Some of those to experiment with film would also become video artists themselves. SoHo was located near Canal Street, where electronic parts and gadgets were placed in bins on the open sidewalk to be sold cheaply to passersby. Paik found himself to be in the right place at the right time, and what was planned as a temporary visit turned out to be a permanent living arrangement for him.

Paik continued his exploration of avant-garde performance, collaborating with cellist and avant-garde interpreter Charlotte Moorman in an effort to add sex, in the form of nudity, to music. In this, they were rebelling against the conservative dress of the classical musician. Paik was an active participant in the New York avant-garde festivals Moorman organized. Her performance of Paik's "Opera Sextronique" at the Filmmakers' Cinematheque gained them much notoriety by landing them in jail with an arrest for indecent exposure. Their defense ultimately contributed to a change in New York State law, allowing nudity for artistic or performance purposes.

More and more, Paik turned to television and video as his means of expression. In 1965, he held his first exhibition in the United States at the New School for Social Research, to which Cage had connections. Here, Paik exhibited the completed experiments he and Abe had worked on in Japan, interrupting normal broadcast images by means of feedback signals from an audiotape recorder. He also had powerful magnets available to allow viewers themselves to distort the television images.

That same year, Paik bought one of the first commercially available Sony video recording systems, becoming the first artist to exhibit work created on videotape. In a cab on the way home from picking up this equipment, he was stuck in traffic caused by Pope Paul's visit. Paik taped the traffic jam and exhibited this work that same evening at SoHo's "Cafe à Go Go" for the Fluxus-sponsored "Monday Night Letters" series. It was here that he made his bold prediction that "someday artists will work with capacitors, resistors, and semi-conductors as they work today with brushes, violins, and junk."

His career moved quickly from this point in time. Mary Baumeister, an acquaintance from Cologne, introduced him to Fernanda Bonino, who gave him a series of exhibitions in her Galeria Bonino in New York. There he exhibited his "Demagnetizer," a circular electromagnet that created abstract patterns on the television screen, and what he called his "dancing pattern," created by feeding audio signals into color television sets. At his second show in the Galeria Bonino, Paik exhibited his video installation, *TV Cross*, for the first time in the United States. This piece consisted of eight television sets mounted in the shape of a cross. He was recognized as being an important artist and was invited to produce work for shows at the Wise Gallery in New York, the Institute of Contemporary Arts in London, the Corcoran Gallery in Washington, D.C., and the Los Angeles County Museum of Art, becoming identified as the founder of the emerging field of video art. He received various grants and became artist-in-residence at the State University of New York at Stony Brook. He also was resident artist at public television station WGBH in Boston (where his videotapes were the first ones produced by an artist ever to be broadcast) and then at WNET in New York City, where he produced the live four-hour broadcast *Video Commune*.

Paik had a love/hate relationship with the television set reminiscent of his relationship with the piano and the violin. His innovations in the use of the medium set him apart from other underground video artists, who often used the standard video format to explore unconventional themes. Aside from creating videotapes, he uses the television set itself as a sculptural material, making a bra, a pair of glasses, a penis, a bed, a cello, and numerous other images out of television sets. In these works, his videotaped images become a part, but not all, of his total video installation. He has decorated or gutted the television set and replaced the electronic insides with a fish bowl and with a candle. He has placed the machine on the ceiling for his piece *Fish Flies on Sky*, among plants for his work *TV Garden*, and face up on the floor for his work *TV Sea*. Just as he was disturbed by the passivity of the concertgoer, he was equally disturbed by the passivity of the television viewer, declaring that "TV has attacked us all our lives; now we're hitting back!" He became determined to free and make accessible this commercial and very inaccessible medium of bland, narrative communication. Paik continued to assault television and its viewers, inserting the hand of the artist to break the illusion that television projects. In his broadcast piece *Electronic Opera No. 1*, he instructed the viewer first to close one eye, then to close both eyes, and eventually to turn the television set off.

Paik also loved the medium, acknowledging that no one once taped could ever truly die. He envisioned his synthesizer, a special-effects generator created with Abe, being adapted for home use, allowing viewers to alter their television images at will, turning a colored television set into an electronic canvas with which viewers could become active creators of art. Influenced by Marshall McLuhan's concept of the "global village," Paik dreamed of a "global art" based on television technology. He created his interactive piece *Good Morning, Mr. Orwell*, which was broadcast by satellite to an estimated twenty-five million people on January 1, 1984, the year in which George Orwell set his famous book about a terrifying future in which media are invasive and the populace is helplessly at their mercy. Paik continually shows that technology is not so holy that it cannot be mocked and, ultimately, tamed.

Bibliography

Hanhardt, John G. *Nam June Paik*. New York: W. W. Norton, 1982. Issued in connection with a show at the Whitney Museum. A collection of essays on the artist's work from the perspective of museum personnel, who must first investigate their own reactions as they confront the Fluxus artist. There is heavy reporting on objects and performances but also some interesting information on what led to the creation of particular works.

Hayward Gallery. *Nam June Paik, Video Works 1963-88*. London: Author, 1988. Catalog of Paik's show. Short but concise, giving the history of the artist as leading to the development of his work. Text is accompanied by photographs from videos, of video sculptures, and of video installations as well as of his performances with Charlotte Moorman.

Kang, Taehi. *Nam June Paik: Early Years (1958-1973)*. Gainesville: Florida State University School of Visual Arts, 1988. This Ph.D. dissertation is the most comprehensive investigation of the artist and his work.

Paik, Nam June. *Art for Twenty-five Million People: Bon jour, Monsieur Orwell.* Berlin: Daadgalerie, 1984. An anthology of information concerning Paik's satellite-transmitted piece of the same name. This live, interactive program was produced by WNET in New York and by FR3 in Paris and simultaneously broadcast via satellite on January 1, 1984, to an estimated twenty-five million viewers. Not all the text is in English.

Rosebush, Judson, ed. *Nam June Paik: Videa 'n' Videology, 1959-1973.* Syracuse, N.Y.: Everson Museum of Art, 1974. A scrapbook of articles, essays, reviews, letters and other documents describing the artist's work and ideas, with Paik's own notes and explanations written in the margins.

D. Tulla Lightfoot

Cross-References

Duchamp's "Readymades" Challenge Concepts of Art (1913), p. 349; The Dada Movement Emerges at the Cabaret Voltaire (1916), p. 419; Cage's *4' 33"* Premieres (1952), p. 1546; Minimalism Emphasizes Objects as Art (1963), p. 1949; McLuhan Probes the Impact of Mass Media on Society (1964), p. 1973; Warhol's *The Chelsea Girls* Becomes a Commercial Success (1966), p. 2053; MTV Changes the Look of American Popular Culture (1981), p. 2475; Christo Wraps the Pont Neuf (1985), p. 2554.

NUREYEV AND FONTEYN DEBUT ASHTON'S
MARGUERITE AND ARMAND

Category of event: Dance
Time: March 12, 1963
Locale: London, England

Frederick Ashton took advantage of Rudolf Nureyev's extraordinary partnership with Margot Fonteyn to choreograph Marguerite and Armand, *one of the first works in which the male lead was of equal dramatic weight to the female*

Principal personages:

RUDOLF NUREYEV (1938-1993), the first male dancer since Vaslav Nijinsky to transcend the usual function of the male dancer as little more than a support for the ballerina

DAME MARGOT FONTEYN (1919-1991), the Royal Ballet prima ballerina assoluta whose partnership with Nureyev after his defection extended an already great career and inaugurated a new era in the ballet

SIR FREDERICK ASHTON (1904-1988), the choreographer considered by many critics to be the founder of British classical style

MIKHAIL BARYSHNIKOV (1948-), the male principal dancer whose defection from the Soviet Union in 1974 seemed like a repetition of Nureyev's, and who ranks with Nijinsky and Nureyev as one of the three great male dancers of the twentieth century

Summary of Event

Rudolf Nureyev's dazzling defection from the Soviet Union and the Kirov Ballet in Paris in 1961 brought a male dancer to the attention of the world whose like had not been seen since Vaslav Nijinsky danced for Sergei Diaghilev's Ballets Russes in the 1910's and 1920's. Teaming up with Margot Fonteyn, the cool and serenely elegant dancer who was the epitome of the English style, Nureyev brought a new vitality to the ballet, became a multimedia megastar in the process, and gave this once limited-appeal art form a passion that translated into vastly increased popular involvement.

Frederick Ashton's *Marguerite and Armand*, choreographed expressly for Nureyev and Fonteyn and the Royal Ballet, was among the first major works to take advantage of Nureyev's extraordinary stage presence and skills by giving the male lead a dramatic weight equal to that of the ballerina. Cecil Beaton designed the set and costumes, and Humphrey Searle arranged the orchestral score. The ballet premiered at Covent Garden on March 12, 1963. The event was a Royal Gala performance held in the presence of Queen Elizabeth II, whose favorite choreographer was Frederick Ashton. Thousands of white carnations decorated the old theater as a fitting tribute to the ballet's tragic heroine.

The ballet is based on Alexandre Dumas' play *La Dame aux camélias* (1852; *Camille*, 1856), which was in turn based on the true story of an ill-starred courtesan who had counted among her lovers the pianist and composer Franz Liszt. Using Liszt's own B-minor Piano Sonata for his score, Ashton compressed the action into six short, highly dramatic scenes: the lovers' first meeting, their escape to the countryside, Armand's father's confrontation with Marguerite, Marguerite's consequent renunciation of her beloved, her return to Paris, and Armand's return to attend at Marguerite's deathbed.

Ashton set the ballet as a fevered dream in which Marguerite, from her sickbed, looks back on the great romance of her short life. The entire work contains no ensemble numbers and is effectively (with the exception of the scene between Marguerite and Armand's father) one extended *pas-de-deux* between the two principals. *Marguerite and Armand* was thus a very special vehicle for Nureyev and Fonteyn. Richard Buckle described it later as "less a ballet than a series of psychological closeups." The leonine stage presence of Nureyev together with the delicate elegance of Fonteyn brought a tremendous chemistry to the stage.

The Observer in London recalled its former ballet critic Peter Brooks to cover the gala premiere. He wrote: "The work is simple, beautiful and satisfying. . . . Ashton can even permit himself the audacity of stillness—the breath is caught, the gestures suspended in pauses which . . . are as lyrical as any steps." Of Nureyev and Fonteyn's performance, he wrote: "In this ballet Nureyev and Fonteyn play as actors; extraordinary actors who bring to each moment and each movement that quality of death which makes the most artificial of forms seem human and simple. All great art eventually is realistic; the art of these two dancers leads them continually to moments of truth."

Despite Brooks' enthusiasm, the ballet was a mixed critical success. The *Daily Mail* critic said that it "revealed no new aspects of the dancers." *The Guardian* called the whole work "a glaring example of trespass on other media, literary and operatic." The *Daily Telegraph* thought the ballet worked only because of "a prodigious outburst of mutually inspired and totally extrovert dancing." *The Scotsman* conceded that it involved virtuosity of a high order but reported that it brought in return "no emotional response." Nevertheless, the public loved *Marguerite and Armand* and came in droves to see the fabled chemistry between Nureyev and Fonteyn at work.

Fonteyn had danced for Ashton many times before she premiered as Marguerite, one of her triumphs being in his masterpiece *Symphonic Variations* (1946), in which the ballerina must deliberately play down her personality—not an easy task for a prima ballerina assoluta—and become one of a group. "I can think of no other dancer of such stature who could accomplish this," critic Arnold Haskell has noted. This humility and pliability of her character would stand her in good stead when she came to dance with Nureyev.

Fonteyn was almost twenty years older than Nureyev and until his defection had been on the point of retiring after a long and illustrious career. Fonteyn had recently suffered a bout of hepatitis that she thought had weakened her system, but Nureyev personally requested the opportunity to dance with her on his arrival in the West. She accepted with reservations. Their first joint performance was in *Giselle* in February, 1962, followed by *Swan Lake* in July and *Le Corsaire* in November.

Over the course of their first years together, Nureyev showed Fonteyn a different way to work, strengthening her technical gifts and thus allowing her to bring a raw passion to her dancing that had not been seen before. Fonteyn went into a second flowering, this time as an even stronger and finer ballerina in her forties than she had been in the glorious days of her youth. It was an unprecedented "second wind," as most ballerinas retire in their forties. Fonteyn continued dancing with Nureyev for more than fifteen years.

In October of 1964 at the Vienna State Opera, Fonteyn and Nureyev received an unprecedented eighty-nine curtain calls after a performance of *Swan Lake*. Theirs was an inspired and inspiring partnership, of which Nureyev once said, "It's not her, it's not me, it is the sameness of the goal. She convinces me." It was the dramatic quality of her work, her emotional expressiveness rather than mere technique, that made their collaborations so powerful.

Fonteyn retired at last in her sixties. She lived on her husband's cattle ranch in Panama until her death in 1991. Nureyev, plagued in his later years by complications of acquired immune deficiency syndrome (AIDS) that he bore with great fortitude, continued to work as director and choreographer with the Paris Opera Ballet until shortly before his death in 1993.

Marguerite and Armand was choreographed as, and frankly intended to be, a star vehicle—a vehicle for the unique partnership of Nureyev and Fonteyn. It closed after a single season and has seldom been revived. This is no doubt because, as Richard Buckle suggests, "its choreography is not important enough to make it worthwhile giving without these two powerful personalities." One 1968 revival, at about the time that critic Kenneth Tynan declared ballet a dying art, brought forth this apt riposte from Richard Buckle: "I don't know whether an art can be dying and excessively popular, but I can only say that if all the applause in all the London theatres where drama is being performed was played end to end it would not add up to half of what greets Fonteyn and Nureyev [as Marguerite and Armand] after one of their evenings at the Garden."

Impact of Event

Marguerite and Armand as a work of choreography had little impact: It was the presence in it of Nureyev and Fonteyn that captured the imagination of audiences. Fonteyn and Nureyev were at the pinnacles of their respective careers, and this ballet was their showcase. Together they would set the standard by which all future leading partnerships in ballet would be measured.

Their partnership was exemplary in several ways. Physically, they were well matched—both small, her slender femininity contrasting with his muscular frame, her delicate oval face with his wild Slavic features. Their partnership had a chemistry that was undeniable. It combined two very different styles of dance: the calm and ordered simplicity of Fonteyn with the fiery, impulsive passion of Nureyev, his pyrotechnics with her cool restraint.

Their partnership brought something more, something dynamic, to the stage. As Alexander Bland noted, their conception of partnering "in which—as in opera—a duet involves equal contributions from both, was something new." It was largely a question, then, of Nureyev's ability to transform the male role from that of an accomplice to that of an equal. "Sometimes," Bland continued, "part of the man's role is to show off the ballerina; but Nureyev never became a passive 'porter' in the old manner, just as Fonteyn never lost touch with him to make an effect with the audience. They seemed aware of each other even when their backs were turned. When their eyes met, a message passed."

Fonteyn wrote later: "It was paradoxical, that the young boy everyone thought so wild and spontaneous in his dancing, cared desperately about technique, whereas I, the cool English ballerina, was so much more interested in the emotional aspect of the performance." This mutual spontaneity meant that they could vary their interpretations of a role from night to night. If the mood struck, they were so much in harmony with each other as characters on the stage that she might initiate a new emphasis in a role, and he would respond instantly. It gave their performances a constant freshness, and their audiences experienced a unique blend of confidence and expectation, coming to the theater with the sense that any night might be like no other.

These qualities were the ones against which the partnership of Gelsey Kirkland and Mikhail Baryshnikov would be judged after his 1974 defection. They too were physically well matched, and they had undoubted chemistry. They brought two very different styles to their partnership, his classical Russian training, hers in the neoclassical tradition of George Balanchine. The young Baryshnikov, like Nureyev, was concerned with learning a new technique, while Kirkland, like Fonteyn, was looking for greater emotional depth.

By this time, there were a number of male dancers, such as Ivan Nagy, Anthony Dowell, Christopher Gable, Edward Villella, and Valery Panov, who had taken Nureyev's lead. The male principal's role was no longer that of support, even in Balanchine's own New York City Ballet company and despite Balanchine's oft-repeated remark, "ballet is woman." The astonishing transformation in the austere and tradition-bound world of the ballet would not have been possible without Nureyev's extraordinary technical facility, supported by the willingness of choreographers such as Ashton to shape it and give it direction. The ballet had changed from a ballerina vehicle to a vehicle for dancers in partnership.

A resetting of Sergei Prokofiev's *Romeo and Juliet* with Nureyev and Fonteyn themselves (later danced by Dowell and Kirkland), Twyla Tharp's eccentric and brilliant *Push Comes to Shove* (with Baryshnikov), and Ashton's own *A Midsummer Night's Dream* (Dowell) were among the many ballets that followed, choreographed to give the new brand of male principals an equal role with their ballerinas. Nureyev had shown what was possible. The world had followed.

It is not Nureyev alone who deserves the credit, but rather the marvelous partnership of Nureyev and Fonteyn. After watching that gala first performance of *Marguerite and Armand*, Peter Brook wrote, "When Fonteyn curtseyed before the curtain . . . when she and Nureyev stood together, tired and tender, a truly moving quality was experienced; they manifested to that audience a relationship graver, paler and less flesh-bound than those of everyday life." In the words of Alexander Bland, theirs was a partnership "that would change the course of ballet history."

Bibliography

Barnes, Clive. *Nureyev*. New York: Helene Obolensky Enterprises, 1982. *The New York Times'* dance and drama critic's comprehensive account of Nureyev's career in the West, insightful and well illustrated.

Bland, Alexander. *Fonteyn and Nureyev: The Story of a Partnership*. New York: Times Books, 1979. Lavishly illustrated account of twenty-six roles danced together by Nureyev and Fonteyn, including a commentary by Bland citing the responses of a wide variety of critics. The standard work on their collaboration. Illustrated in black and white, no index.

_____. *The Nureyev Image*. New York: Quadrangle, 1976. Photographic study of Nureyev, including a section on *Marguerite and Armand*. Brief biography; sections on Nureyev the man, the dancer, the choreographer, and the interpreter; appendix of roles, companies, productions, and films.

Fonteyn, Margot. *Autobiography*. London: W. H. Allen and Company, 1975. Fonteyn's lively and heartfelt account of her training and life as a ballerina, including her long partnership with Nureyev. With photo section. Amusing and anecdotal reading.

Robertson, Allen, and Donald Hutera. *The Dance Handbook*. Essex, England: Longman, 1988. A practical guide with entries on influential works, choreographers, dancers, and companies. Includes critiques. Glossary, index, and sources.

Anne Atwell-Zoll

Cross-References

Pavlova First Performs Her Legendary Solo *The Dying Swan* (1907), p. 187; Diaghilev's Ballets Russes Astounds Paris (1909), p. 241; *L'Après-midi d'un faune* Causes an Uproar (1912), p. 332; Baryshnikov Becomes Artistic Director of American Ballet Theatre (1980), p. 2459; Baryshnikov's White Oak Dance Project Debuts (1990), p. 2663.

HAVEL'S *THE GARDEN PARTY* SATIRIZES
LIFE UNDER COMMUNISM

Category of event: Theater
Time: December 3, 1963
Locale: Prague, Czechoslovakia

Václav Havel aimed the weapons of satire against Communism in The Garden Party *and other plays of the 1960's, helping to keep alive the spirit of resistance to the Communist regime*

Principal personages:
VÁCLAV HAVEL (1936-   ), a Czech playwright and political activist who would be elected president of Czechoslovakia in 1989
JAN GROSSMAN (1925-   ), the director of Prague's Theater on the Balustrade from 1962 to 1968
GUSTÁV HUSÁK (1913-1991), the Communist dictator of Czechoslovakia from 1969 to 1989
JOSEPH PAPP (YOSL PAPIROFSKY, 1921-1991), a New York City theatrical impresario who arranged for the performance of some of Havel's plays in the United States
ALEXANDER DUBČEK (1921-   ), a reformist Czechoslovak Communist who led the "Prague Spring" liberalization movement of 1968
ANTONÍN NOVOTNÝ (1904-1975), the Communist dictator of Czechoslovakia from 1953 to 1968
MILAN KUNDERA (1929-   ), a Czech novelist of the 1960's who went into exile
MILOŠ FORMAN (1932-   ), a Czech filmmaker of the 1960's who went into exile
TOM STOPPARD (TOMAS STRAUSSLER, 1937-   ), a Czechoslovakian-born British playwright and friend of Havel

Summary of Event

When the four-act play *Zahradní slavnost* (*The Garden Party*, 1969), written by a twenty-seven-year-old Czech playwright named Václav Havel, was performed for the first time at the Theater on the Balustrade in Prague on December 3, 1963, few could recognize that this was the first step toward the peaceful overthrow of Communism in Czechoslovakia. Havel, denied access to higher education by the Communist state because of his upper-middle-class family background, had begun his career as a stagehand. By 1963, he had become literary manager of the Theater on the Balustrade, a small, independent, experimental theater with an innovative director, Jan Grossman, who would introduce Western European absurdist plays to the Czech stage. *The Garden Party* was the first play that Havel wrote alone; he had coauthored a play in 1961.

In *The Garden Party*, Hugo Pludek, an initially inarticulate youth, gains fluency by listening to his father's proverbial middle-class wisdom and by repeating the clichés of officialdom. Using his new glibness to climb the bureaucratic career ladder, Hugo meets a knotty problem when he is placed in charge of both the Office of Liquidation and the Office of Inauguration. The latter is supposed to dissolve the former, but officials of the Office of Liquidation argue that only the Office of Liquidation can liquidate itself, which is a logical impossibility. A new bureaucratic behemoth is formed, the Office of Liquidation and Inauguration. Pludek's rise in the world causes him to lose touch with his initial identity; at the end of the play, he undertakes a visit to his former self.

In thus treating the problem of man's alienation, Havel implies that this malaise is, contrary to Marxist-Leninist orthodoxy, found in both Communist societies and capitalist ones. He suggests that the new Communist elite embodies much of the philistinism and status-hungry opportunism often ascribed to the capitalist bourgeoisie. Havel, a master of wordplay, also shows that language can be used to veil reality as well as to reveal it; proverbs and slogans, mindlessly repeated, are seen as especially likely to lead one astray. Often his characters make statements that, while grammatically correct, are utter nonsense.

The emphasis on the absurd in *The Garden Party*, an emphasis found in all of Havel's plays, has led some critics to compare him to the Western European dramatists of the absurd Samuel Beckett and Eugène Ionesco. Yet there is often an element of moral protest against specific evils present in Havel's drama that is absent from the Western European drama of the absurd, a moral protest no less real for being expressed through gallows humor rather than indignant jeremiads. Havel's comic streak has been compared to that of turn-of-the-century Czech antimilitarist satirist Jaroslav Hašek; his somber streak, to that of the Prague German-Jewish novelist Franz Kafka.

It is remarkable that such a play as *The Garden Party* could be performed at all in a Communist country such as Czechoslovakia. The Communist takeover of 1948 had been followed by purges and by the regimentation of intellectuals. After Soviet dictator Joseph Stalin's death in 1953 and Soviet Communist Party chief Nikita Khrushchev's denunciation of Stalin's crimes in 1956, Czechoslovak Communist Party leader Antonín Novotný, uncertain about just how much repression Moscow wanted, loosened the reins on the arts somewhat. The pairing of an Office of Liquidation and an Office of Inauguration in *The Garden Party* can be seen as Havel's metaphor for the contradictory tendencies to repression and tolerance within the Novotný regime. The period from the early 1960's up through the Prague Spring of 1968 witnesses an extraordinary flowering of Czech cinema and literature as well as drama.

The year 1965 saw the performance of Havel's *Vyrozumění* (*The Memorandum*, 1967), also at the Theater on the Balustrade. This play treats the problems faced by Josef Gross, the director of an office, when the use of an artificial language, Ptydepe, is mandated by his new bosses. Frustrated when told that a petition to get a memorandum in Ptydepe translated must itself be written in Ptydepe, Gross is demoted for his lack of enthusiasm for the new language. His fortunes recover only when he persuades a secretary to make an unauthorized translation of the memorandum, which turns out to be a criticism of the new language. Later, when yet another artificial language is introduced, Gross goes along, cravenly refusing to help the secretary to get her old job back. This play satirizes both bureaucratic timidity and the pitfalls of a rigidly ideological view of the world; like *The Garden Party*, it can be seen as an allegory of the vacillation between Stalinism and de-Stalinization under the Novotný regime.

In January, 1968, the Prague Spring began when liberal Alexander Dubček succeeded Novotný as the Czech Communist Party's first secretary. In April, 1968, Havel's play *Ztížená možnost soustředění* (*The Increased Difficulty of Concentration*, 1969) was performed at the Theater on the Balustrade. This play is about a scholar, Edouard Huml, torn between the demands of his wife and his mistress and hounded by a research team's inquisitive computer; it deals with the problems of any modern society; communist or noncommunist. It was the last of Havel's dramas to be legally performed in Czechoslovakia. In August, 1968, the Soviet Union invaded Czechoslovakia; in April, 1969, Gustáv Husák became Communist party first secretary, and the repression of dissident intellectuals was resumed.

Impact of Event

Any discussion of the impact of Havel's plays inevitably turns to the question of how a playwright could become the symbol of hope for freedom-loving Czechoslovaks and the leader of a successful anti-Communist revolution. Of course, *The Garden Party* and *The Memorandum* both made a far deeper impression on Czech theatergoers than any play would make on American theatergoers. In Novotný-era Czechoslovakia, with its tightly controlled press, audiences were starved for information and debate; hence, they responded enthusiastically to plays containing criticism of the existing order that was just sufficiently disguised to get past the censors. Yet as late as the Prague Spring of 1968, Havel remained merely one of a number of daring Czech artists and intellectuals. These included the novelist and playwright Milan Kundera, whose novel *Žert* (1967; *The Joke*, 1969) was widely viewed as a subtle criticism of Czechoslovak Communism, and the filmmaker Miloš Forman, whose film *The Firemen's Ball* (1967) acquired a similar reputation.

One thing that elevated Havel's stature among his own people was his decision, after the Soviet invasion of August, 1968, to stay in Czechoslovakia and carry on the struggle for intellectual freedom there, rather than either conform or go into exile. In 1975, Havel wrote an open letter of protest to Husák. In early 1977, Havel joined with other brave Czech intellectuals in signing the Charter 77 manifesto, protesting the regime's failure to respect human rights; he was one of the charter's three chief elected spokesmen. A wave of arrests followed, and from 1979 to 1983, Havel himself was imprisoned for his political activities.

Miloš Forman, by contrast, went to the United States in 1969 and there rebuilt his career as a filmmaker. Milan Kundera took a teaching post in France in 1975. Many intellectuals who remained in Czechoslovakia, even if liberal in their views, kept quiet once the Husák crackdown got under way for fear of losing their jobs.

Havel himself lost the right to practice his profession or to have any of his plays performed in Czechoslovakia; for a while, he toiled as a stacker in a brewery. Yet he continued to write plays, though in Czechoslovakia they could be performed only clandestinely. Among the plays written under the Husák regime were *Audience* (1976; *Audience*, 1976), *Vernisáž* (1976; *Private View*, 1977), and *Protest* (1978; *Protest*, 1980). In *Audience*, which is semiautobiographical, a dissident intellectual working in a brewery is asked by his boss to inform on himself so that the boss can convince the authorities that antiregime activities are being closely monitored. *Protest* concerns a dissident intellectual's vain attempt to persuade a collaborationist intellectual to sign a petition for someone else's freedom.

Another factor that aided Havel's rise to leadership, and even his very physical survival, was his favorable reputation in the non-Communist world. In the late 1960's, his first two plays were translated into English by Vera Blackwell, a Czech émigré living in Great Britain; translations into German were also made. Tom Stoppard, the Czech-born British dramatist, discovered Havel's work in 1967; the two would later become good friends. In the spring of 1968, Havel visited New York City, where *The Memorandum* was produced by theatrical impresario Joseph Papp's Public Theatre. The production received an Obie Award and won raves from New York City critics.

The ties of respect thus forged withstood the test of post-1968 repression; Havel's resistance to that repression enhanced his reputation abroad. Some of the plays produced after 1968, once their texts had been smuggled out of Czechoslovakia, were performed in Vienna, New York City, or London. It was Joseph Papp once more who brought about the performance of three Havel plays, *Private View*, *Audience*, and *Protest*, at the Public Theatre in New York City in the 1983-1984 season; these three plays were also performed in London. In 1978, Stoppard dedicated a television play to Havel. In 1983, the strong sympathy for Havel among intellectuals in the non-Communist world, expressed in the form of a letter to the Czech government, helped to win Havel's release from prison, where he had become ill from his treatment.

Havel's rise to leadership was also favored by sheer good luck. In 1985, the more liberal Mikhail Gorbachev came to power in the Soviet Union. In November, 1989, when it became clear that Gorbachev would not intervene militarily to support hard-line Czechoslovak Communists, Havel, the man who had struggled for Czechoslovak freedom for so long and under such hard conditions, found leadership of the anti-Communist revolution (the Civic Forum movement) almost thrust upon him. He became the first president of post-Communist Czechoslovakia.

Václav Havel was a model not only of the creative artist but also of the nonviolent revolutionary. He fought against Communism not with bombs or bullets but by aiming at that ideology, and its bureaucratic servants, the sharp arrows of ridicule. *The Garden Party* was the first such arrow in his quiver. Unlike Soviet dissident Aleksandr Solzhenitsyn, whose anti-Communist writings bristle with righteous anger, Havel kept his sense of humor. He avoided the extremes of amoral opportunism on the one hand and fanaticism on the other. No Havel school of playwrights arose; yet it was Havel's combination of high principles and genuine humility, not merely the quality of his plays, that endeared him to both Western intellectuals and the Czech people.

Bibliography

Baranczak, Stanislaw. "All the President's Plays." *The New Republic* 203 (July 23, 1990): 27-30. *The Garden Party* is not discussed; *The Memorandum* and several of the more recent plays, as well as Havel's autobiography, are. The author, a Polish émigré teaching in the United States, sees Havel's plays as expressing Havel's attitude toward politics: moralistic without being dogmatically self-righteous.

Echikson, William. *Lighting the Night: Revolution in Eastern Europe.* New York: William Morrow, 1990. By a young Yale-educated journalist. Treats Havel's plays only in the sketchiest fashion; covers fully the 1989 revolution. Helps readers compare Havel the dissident intellectual with similar figures in other Eastern European countries. Critical bibliography, photographs (including one of Havel), index. For the general reader.

Esslin, Martin. "A Czech Absurdist: Václav Havel." In *Reflections: Essays on Modern Theatre.* Garden City, N.Y.: Doubleday, 1969. Esslin, an expert on Western European absurdist drama, saw Havel's plays performed in Prague, and he discusses *The Garden Party* and *The Memorandum.* Esslin compares Havel to Franz Kafka, whose fiction probes existential anguish, and to Jaroslav Hašek, whose *The Good Soldier Švejk* (1921-1923) mocked military idiocy. One of the earliest Western commentaries on Havel.

French, Alfred. *Czech Writers and Politics, 1945-1969.* New York: Columbia University Press, 1982. Written before the 1989 revolution; helps readers to place Havel's career within the context of the post-World War II Czechoslovak journey from repression of intellectuals to liberalization and then back to repression. Cites particularly amusing bits of dialogue from *The Garden Party.* Endnotes, select bibliography, index. For scholars.

Goetz-Stankiewicz, Markéta. "Václav Havel." In *The Silenced Theatre: Czech Playwrights Without a Stage.* Toronto: University of Toronto Press, 1979. An illuminating discussion of Havel's plays, including *The Garden Party.* Compares Havel with other Czech playwrights and with Western absurdist dramatists; stresses differences between Havel and the latter. Sees Havel as a critic of modern society, not merely Communist society. For lower-level undergraduates. Photographs, endnotes, list of playwrights and plays, index.

Havel, Václav. *Disturbing the Peace: A Conversation with Karel Hvizdala.* Translated and with an introduction by Paul Wilson. New York: Alfred A. Knopf, 1990. Havel provides information about his childhood and adolescence, his theatrical career; his life as a dissident, and the meaning of *The Garden Party* and other plays. Question-and-answer format makes for somewhat difficult reading. For the general reader. Notes on interviewer and translator, glossary, index.

Schamschula, Walter. "Havel." In *Fiction and Drama in Eastern and Southeastern Europe*, edited by Henrik Birnbaum and Thomas Eekman. Columbus, Ohio: Slavica Publishers, 1980. Analyzing nine plays (including *The Garden Party*), Schamschula lists various techniques Havel uses to create a sense of the absurd and gives examples of each. Points out subtle changes in plays after 1968. Sees Havel's plays as speaking to audiences in free as well as Communist countries. For scholarly readers. Notes.

Schiff, Stephen. "Havel's Choice." *Vanity Fair* 54 (August, 1991): 124-128. Based on a journalist's interviews with Havel and Havel's acquaintances. Provides a useful biographical sketch of Havel's life from his birth to his rise to the presidency of Czechoslovakia. Argues that what appeals to people about Havel's plays is not the plays themselves but the admirable qualities of the man who wrote them. For the general reader. Photographs.

Trensky, Paul I. "The Drama of the Absurd." In *Czech Drama Since World War II*. White Plains, N.Y.: M. E. Sharpe, 1978. Compares Czech absurdist drama with Western European absurdist drama and compares three Havel plays (*The Garden Party*, *The Memorandum*, and *The Increasing Difficulty of Concentration*) with one another. Three lesser-known Czech absurdist playwrights are also discussed. Selected bibliography (mostly Czech-language sources), list of playwrights and plays. For scholarly readers. Endnotes, index.

Paul D. Mageli

Cross-References

Hašek's *The Good Soldier Švejk* Reflects Postwar Disillusionment (1921), p. 523; *The Bedbug* and *The Bathhouse* Exemplify Revolutionary Theater (1929), p. 787; Socialist Realism Is Mandated in Soviet Literature (1932), p. 908; *Waiting for Godot* Expresses the Existential Theme of Absurdity (1953), p. 1573; Pasternak's *Doctor Zhivago* Is Published (1957), p. 1747; Ionesco's *Rhinoceros* Receives a Resounding Worldwide Reception (1959), p. 1812; Esslin Publishes *The Theatre of the Absurd* (1961), p. 1871; *The Gulag Archipelago* Exposes Soviet Atrocities (1973), p. 2277; Forman Adapts *One Flew Over the Cuckoo's Nest* for Film (1975), p. 2320.

McLUHAN PROBES THE IMPACT OF MASS MEDIA ON SOCIETY

Categories of event: Television and radio; literature; journalism
Time: 1964
Locale: Toronto, Canada, and New York, New York

Marshall McLuhan explored the ways electronic media were transforming the values, life-styles, and institutions of Western civilization

Principal personages:
> MARSHALL MCLUHAN (1911-1980), a professor of English who wrote about the rise and fall of literacy
> WALTER J. ONG (1912-   ) a colleague who helped McLuhan to formulate theories about rhetoric, media, and history
> HOWARD LUCK GOSSAGE (1917-1969), a San Francisco advertising man who introduced McLuhan to top executives and popularized his ideas

Summary of Event

In his 1964 book *Understanding Media: The Extensions of Man*, Marshall McLuhan stunned the world with a radical analysis of social change. "The medium is the message," he wrote, meaning that society is shaped as well as reflected by communications media and that media's effects are the result of form more than of content. His commentary on various forms of print and electronic media amounted to a comprehensive explanation of society, past and future.

Media can be viewed as extensions of human faculties: radio an extension of the tongue, the book of the eye, electronic circuitry of the nervous system. Extending a sense alters the others accordingly. For example, before the invention of writing, information was exchanged by speech, so the ear was the dominant organ of sensory and social orientation. With the invention of the alphabet, humans learned to speak to the eye, which gained ascendancy over the ear. Writing changed ways of thinking and acting, for sounds are not like letters, which are arbitrary visual symbols with a meaning that depends upon their lineal sequence. The tribal world of the ear—primordial, intuitive, directionless, and emotional—was overthrown by the literate eye, with its fixed point of view, perspective, linear precision, and sequential logic. The mighty pen produced roads, architecture, bureaucracies, and standing armies, though it corroded memory and oral tradition.

When writing was all done in manuscript, few were literate. The invention of the printing press, however, put books into the hands of a broad public. Many were dominated by the literate eye, which, isolated from other senses and used in private on the printed page, confers upon the mind a precision, toleration, disengagement, and perspective foreign to the ear. It reformed emotions and ways of perceiving. As detached observers, literate people gained a private, noninvolved, fixed point of view. The human mind craved categorization, fragmentation, specialization, individualism, sequence, and repetition as never before.

The invention of the telegraph, telephone, and radio reestablished the importance of sound in communication, and humanity was once again enveloped in the auditory web of the preliterate tribe. Instantaneous electronic communication erased barriers of time and space. Detachment, fixed points of view, and the step-by-step techniques of literate, mechanical humanity were drowned in a sea of flowing consciousness, social awareness, and in-depth involvement.

Television activates the senses as no other medium can. Unlike print, which isolates the visual sense, television excites the visual and auditory senses simultaneously. Television demands participation and involvement of the whole being.

McLuhan described media as "hot" or "cool" according to the degree of participation needed to extract meaning. For example, the telephone is "hotter" than the telegraph, since the telephone presents words ready-made for the hearing, whereas the telegraph's code of blips must be deciphered. Generally, hot media impart more information and generate a more private, intense response than cool media, which convey less detail and foster more sympathetic social interaction. Television is the "coolest" medium, for its picture must be assembled in the viewer's head; the television picture is an optical illusion built up by the brain as an electrical "dot" scans the screen.

Unlike print, television calls forth a flowing, empathetic, unified consciousness. War stories in newspapers provoke angry, patriotic reactions; the same stories on television, however, leave viewers siding with victims, feeling the pain as their own. By unifying feeling with thought, television softens individualism and encourages collective social involvement.

McLuhan's views on the vast social changes wrought by electronic media were ambivalent. He scorned moralizing as an obstacle to the exploration of social phenomena. Steeped in the study of literature, he was wary of cataclysmic cultural upheaval; yet he thought the isolation of the literate eye was neurotic, and he disapproved of the selfish greed and violent nationalism such isolation spawned. McLuhan welcomed the new consciousness and sensibility of what he called the "global village," where people could be peaceful, involved, and free. He viewed the individualistic liberty of literate man as a fragmentation of a social unity that television would restore. His enthusiasm for the young and his zest for the new at times amounted to a euphoria for the new possibilities of postliterate civilization.

His writings in the 1930's and 1940's were largely academic works on English language and literature, especially that of Renaissance dramatist Thomas Nashe and modern novelist James Joyce. Studying the changeover from Middle English to Modern English, he noticed how poetry had been reformed to appeal to the eye instead of the ear. From early insights grew his more elaborate theories about media and culture. In *The Gutenberg Galaxy: The Making of Typographic Man* (1962), he documented his analysis of the printing press. *Understanding Media* focused on the electronic media, as did *The Medium Is the Massage* (1967), *War and Peace in the Global Village* (1968), and *Through the Vanishing Point: Space and Poetry in Painting* (1968). Controversial though it was—the book was snubbed by academic specialists and New York literary elite whom McLuhan criticized—*Understanding Media* remains McLuhan's masterpiece, the most incisive and readable exposition of his philosophy of the mass media. It made America media-conscious.

Impact of Event

Understanding Media was published during an era of youthful rebellion, when Americans were divided by a "generation gap." McLuhan considered this gap a turning point in history, as significant as the transition from the Middle Ages to the European Renaissance. As Johann Gutenberg's printing press had inaugurated an age of enlightenment, so the electronic media were supplanting literate culture and ushering in a postindustrial, postmodern epoch. Youngsters who grew up with television would not share the values and cultural assumptions of their parents, whose worldview was shaped by typography.

So radical and shocking was his analysis that, for a time, McLuhan was recognized as a celebrity, a guru with an esoteric philosophy grasped by an intellectual cult. Woody Allen gave him a cameo role in the 1977 motion picture *Annie Hall*. Some of McLuhan's catchy phrases, such as "cool media," "the global village," and "the medium is the message," passed into the vernacular.

In vogue for a while, McLuhan was misunderstood or ignored by many academics and literati. Yet he was heard by many artists, businessmen, network executives, and the young. His impact was felt in advertising, management, sociology, psychology, history, fashion design, the media, and the arts. The perceptive powers of artists and thinkers were stimulated by his bold idea that media alter the balance of the five senses. A world fashioned after the linear eye was giving way to sound and the sense of touch newly extended by television. For reasons he explained, music got a lot louder. As McLuhan predicted, young people demanded new styles: sculptured haircuts, layered clothing of varied textures, round collars, and small cars. Straight lines, which please the eye, receded in fashion, architecture, and automobile design and were replaced by wraparound designs. The tribal life-styles of the hippies were not the first manifestation of McLuhan's global village, nor the last.

Continuity and sequence are properties of space and time as conceived by the literate eye, but an artist's sensorium dominated by the sense of touch or of hearing produces unexpected effects. Continuity and sequence were handled with the irascible, nervy abruptness of the tribal era by McLuhan's early followers, among them musician John Cage, painter Larry Rivers, and filmmaker Stanley Vander Beeck.

Businessmen watched as McLuhan's predictions came true: The automobile industry faltered, films were packaged and sold like books on videotape, broadcasting networks lost their monopoly over television, newspapers minimized print and line in favor of color and picture before going out of business in droves. Managements downsized products and executive hierarchies, streamlining management around systems design and systems analysis. McLuhan urged educators to forge a transition from the fragmented, visual realm of print, which thrives on the indoctrination of texts, and to rebuild education around discovery rather than instruction. With computers, audiovisual aids, and holistic approaches, educational reformers did indeed desegment curricula to make learning more associative and participatory.

The political ramifications of McLuhan's ideas surfaced in the decades that followed *Understanding Media*. His analysis of the 1960 presidential debates has guided political campaign strategies ever since. McLuhan noted that people who heard the debates on radio (a "hot" medium) thought Richard Nixon the winner, but those who watched on television (a "cool" medium) thought John Kennedy came across better. From that moment, the art of politics in America became very largely a matter of manipulating images of candidates in the media.

Politically and economically, the world became smaller and smaller, increasingly like the global village McLuhan envisioned. Businesses became more interdependent on foreign markets and labor. Political crisis in faraway places became big issues in the local politics of distant nations. Tribal animosities flared, and national unities crumbled, as McLuhan predicted. *Understanding Media* explained to historians how Rome fell when the supply of papyrus failed. Without being able to give orders in writing from the central government, military leaders could not secure distant borders on the margins of the empire. Since the political unity of empires and nations depends upon a command structure rooted in literacy, the decline of literacy loosens the hold of distant capitols. Having explained how political unity dissolves in less-literate societies than America, McLuhan did not live to see the disintegration of the Warsaw Pact and the Soviet Union.

Most people have viewed the late twentieth century as a period of cultural upheaval; McLuhan, though, was one of the few thinkers and artists who understood the dynamics of a culture radically transforming itself. He was a prophet of the postindustrial West's being Easternized by a postliterate sensibility. He was a literary and philosophical exponent of the postmodern consciousness shared by Pablo Picasso, Ludwig Wittgenstein, Buckminster Fuller, André Breton, Jean-Luc Godard, and Samuel Beckett.

A century earlier, Matthew Arnold had remarked that culture was based on art, which he considered a vehicle for moral, social, and political ideas. For McLuhan, art was an extension of life, with the active power to alter the modes of consciousness and perception that constitute culture. Thus, media are more than tools to use to transfer ideas; media make the culture in their own image, becoming the content as well as the conveyance. McLuhan's continual emphasis upon process rather than product, context over text, form over content, and relation rather than entity prefigured advances in phenomenalist philosophy, deconstructivist criticism, and avant-garde art.

Bibliography

Kuhns, William. "The Sage of Aquarius: Marshall McLuhan." In *The Post-Industrial*

Prophets: Interpretations of Technology. New York: Weybright and Talley, 1971. A balanced assessment of McLuhan's theories. Kuhns finds McLuhan's ideas stimulating and explanatory, though unproven and at odds with common sense. The chapter includes a glossary of McLuhan's terminology. An index and bibliography show his relation to the postmodern tradition.

McCormack, Thelma. "Innocent Eye on Mass Society." In *Mass Media and Society*, edited by Alan Wells. Palo Alto, Calif.: National Press Books, 1972. A negative review of *Understanding Media* typical of the misunderstanding McLuhan encountered among academics. Trying to force McLuhan into a category along with depth psychologists, McCormack finds him lacking a theory of motivation and other baggage of the trade. To her, he is no prophet but an idealogue misguided by "irrationalism, determinism, and folk romanticism."

McLuhan, Marshall. *The Gutenberg Galaxy: The Making of Typographic Man.* Toronto: University of Toronto Press, 1962. The forerunner to *Understanding Media*, indispensable to serious students of McLuhan. This erudite, exhaustive survey of ancient and modern learning that tends to support McLuhan's theories concentrates primarily on the printing press with movable type developed by Johann Gutenberg in the late fifteenth century.

Rosenberg, Harold. "Philosophy in a Pop Key." In *McLuhan: Hot and Cool*, edited by Gerald Emanuel Stearn. New York: Dial Press, 1967. The first serious review of *Understanding Media* in America, this essay, first published in *The New Yorker* in February, 1965, introduced McLuhan to a wide audience. Rosenberg is an observer of popular culture and an expert on modern art. His sensible and cogent essay is still a useful introduction to McLuhan's philosophy.

Sontag, Susan. "One Culture and the New Sensibility." In *Against Interpretation.* New York: Farrar, Straus & Giroux, 1966. Sontag locates McLuhan squarely within the artistic and intellectual tradition of postmodernism. Against McCormack and other critics, she insists that McLuhan and the postmodern philosophers and artists are not amoral anti-intellectuals conniving at the demise of art and culture. Rather, she defends them as bold, original thinkers transforming the function of art.

Wolfe, Tom. "The New Life Out There." In *McLuhan: Hot and Cool*, edited by Gerald Emanuel Stearn. New York: Dial Press, 1967. On a jocular romp through the mind and times of Marshall McLuhan, Wolfe imparts a feeling for the 1960's milieu of the guru-celebrity. Wolfe challenges businesspersons, professionals, and artists to rise to the level of McLuhan's understanding of their walks of life, posing the question: "Suppose he is what he sounds like, the most important thinker since Newton, Darwin, Freud, Einstein . . . what if he is right?"

John L. McLean

Cross-References

Surrealism Is Born (1924), p. 604; Radio Programming Dominates Home Leisure (1930's), p. 828; Television Enters Its Golden Age (1950's), p. 1465 ; Nam June Paik

Exhibits Video and Television as Art (1963), p. 1955; Derrida Enunciates the Principles of Deconstruction (1967), p. 2075; *60 Minutes* Becomes the First Televised Newsmagazine (1968), p. 2136; The Decline of the Big Three Networks Becomes a Fall (Late 1980's), p. 2554.

RILEY COMPLETES *IN C*

Category of event: Music
Time: 1964
Locale: San Francisco, California

A *minimalist and largely improvised work,* In C *reflected composer Terry Riley's background as a performer*

Principal personages:
TERRY RILEY (1935-   ), a noted American composer and performer whose minimalist works, including *In C,* often use repetitive motifs, a basic pulse, and improvisation
JOHN CAGE (1912-1992), a fabled avant-garde composer who established the experimental context in which later minimalist composers such as Riley have worked
PHILIP GLASS (1937-   ), a critically and commercially successful practitioner of minimalist compositional strategies and a frequent participant in varied multimedia projects
STEVE REICH (1936-   ), a well-known American composer of experimental music, an exponent of minimalist approaches to composition, and one of Riley's collaborators
LA MONTE YOUNG (1935-   ), an important American composer of experimental music who influenced Riley's development as a minimalist and who became one of his most important collaborators

Summary of Event

Terry Riley's *In C* was a watershed in the evolution of American experimental music. In large part, its significance derived from its status as a work conceived by a performer who happened to compose, rather than a composer who happened to perform. Although it is structured upon a pulse, or drone, and a sequence of fifty-three notated but extremely short motifs, *In C*'s distinguishing characteristic is the collaborative role assigned to its performers. The piece begins with the pulse, a piano part not included in the score, which consists of notes played steadily on the top two C's of the keyboard (hence the title of the work) throughout the performance. Each player is then free to determine when to enter, how many times to repeat each motif, and how to fit each motif into the composition's overall flow and texture.

From a compositional standpoint, *In C* marked a culmination of Riley's interest in notated repetition. Repetition has always been one of music's basic organizing principles, but for Riley—and fellow minimalists La Monte Young, Steve Reich, and Philip Glass—repetition had taken on a significance far greater than it typically had in folk, popular, or classical music. Indeed, during the 1960's repetition was Riley's primary means of permutating and structuring a restricted number of highly abbreviated melodic motifs.

For Riley, the fascination with repetition was heightened during a 1962-1964 stay in Europe, where he had access to the recording facilities of the state-supported French broadcasting system. Riley used tape loops and overdubbing to explore the effects of lengthy repetitions of short melodic cells set against steady metronomic pulses, a process permitting the building of superimposed layers of recorded sound. One such piece, *Mescalin Mix* (1963), evoked dreamlike sensations apparently stimulated by the overlapping of slowly evolving melodic, rhythmic, and harmonic patterns. The piece's effect stemmed from an emotional-cognitive process that also produced a perception of gradual shifts in the stress points of the repeated phases. Indeed, one of Riley's main interests in repetition has been as a psychological-physiological means of arousing "emotional vibrations" in the listener.

In 1964, Riley transferred his preoccupation with repetition from studio-constructed tape pieces to live performances. In *Keyboard Studies No. 2* (1964), Riley employed a sequence of fifteen modal figures, or cells, indicated with traditional Western notation. The first cell is repeated throughout the performance, thereby functioning as a pulse against which the other figures are played. The overall length of the performance is not predetermined, and the length of the separate notes may be long or short, at the discretion of the player, provided that they are of equal duration. Variations in dynamics and articulation are not permitted, and each melodic cell is to be played loudly. For Riley, *Keyboard Studies No. 2*, and similar piano pieces in the series that were never notated, served as études, daily improvisational exercises used by Riley to limber up for his solo keyboard concerts.

Later in 1964, Riley composed *In C*, now regarded as the archetypal pulse piece. Based on principles first explored in *Mescalin Mix* and *Keyboard Studies No. 2*, *In C* was conceived as an exclusively ensemble undertaking. Instead of the fifteen melodic cells of *Keyboard Studies No. 2*, *In C* featured fifty-three repetitive motifs. The number and kinds of instruments to be used are not specified, except for the requirement that they be capable of negotiating the octave-and-a-half range notated in Riley's score. *In C*'s gravitational center, the reference point regulating the tempo of the individual parts, is a rapidly and continuously pulsing C, doubled at the octave on the piano's two high C's; the pulse, incidentally, is not scored like the other parts but instead indicated by Riley's written instructions.

Each of *In C*'s parts is of equal significance, since there is no real foreground, background, or leading melody. The performers, except for the pianist generating the pulse, play from copies of the same brief, one-page score. Each player is granted the liberty of determining when to start, and since the number of repetitions of each motif is also left to the performers' discretion, each player will take a different length of time to complete the cycle of fifty-three melodic cells.

Since so much of the decision making in the execution of *In C* rests with the players, each performance is a unique event. Riley's considerable trust, though, is not without limits. One stricture specifies that no player should function as a soloist. Indeed, each musician is urged to relate his individual part to the aggregate effort of his colleagues. The overall unreeling of the piece is similarly governed by a concern for the ensemble's interpersonal dynamics. Composer-musicologist Michael Nyman has observed that the performers "should not wander too far ahead or lag behind the ensemble" in order to guarantee that "the basic textural density and structure is maintained." Nevertheless, performance times for *In C* have ranged from half an hour to three hours.

In C was premiered at the San Francisco Tape Music Center in the fall of 1964, and the event set off ripples among avant-gardists, musicians as well as partisans of painting, film, and the other arts. Yet it was not until the 1968 release of an inspired recording of *In C* by members of the Center for Creative and Performing Arts at Buffalo's State University of New York—a recording that featured the composer himself on soprano saxophone—that the general public began to understand and even to accept Riley's experimental minimalism.

Impact of Event

Predictably, *In C*, like so many other experimental artworks that appeared in the 1960's, was met by wildly divergent responses. For musical traditionalists, the self-styled keepers of the European classical flame, *In C* was dismissed for its lack of substance and form. Naysayers also pointed out that since a "composition" such as *In C* could be successfully performed by amateurs, it in no way qualified for consideration as "serious" music.

In C, however, arrived at a perfect moment in America's social-cultural history. In a sense, the 1960's was a gigantic laboratory in which old assumptions about race, sex, politics, and the arts were challenged and tested by countless alternative and experimental probings. As a result, *In C* found a large and sympathetic group of supporters. The fact that the recording of Riley's *In C* was produced and distributed by the prestigious Columbia Masterworks label amplified the impact of Riley's minimalist masterpiece.

The minimalist impulse was an important part of the 1960's *Zeitgeist*. In sculpture, there was Tony Smith's six-foot steel cube called *Die* (1962). In painting, there were bold, geometric arrangements of primary colors such as Ellsworth Kelly's *Red, Orange, White, Green, Blue* (1968). In film, there were experiments such as Tony Conrad's *The Flicker* (1966), a stroboscopic progression of flashing light. In each medium, conventional content had been virtually erased; as in *In C*, traditional content of a mimetic, narrative, or emotional nature had been reduced—or "minimized"—so as to focus on other, often more formal and basic, elements having to do with the very natures of the various media.

In the evolution of twentieth century music, the tonal system codified by Johann Sebastian Bach and the European classicists had been challenged by the introduction of the twelve-tone serial procedures of Arnold Schoenberg. Since Schoenberg and other serialists reduced composition to a stipulated set of procedures and a specified twelve-tone row, musicologists such as Wim Mertens have suggested that serialism can be regarded as having been in the vanguard of twentieth century minimalism, a quest in large part motivated by the epistemological search for each art form's fundamental functions, materials, and working methods.

In the post-World War II world of American music, the decks were cleared to ground zero when experimentalist John Cage brought forth *4' 33"* (1952). In effect, by sitting a "musician" at a piano for four minutes and thirty-three seconds of silence, Cage was posing the question, "What is music?"

For Riley and fellow minimalists Young, Reich, and Glass, the work of Cage and the serialists provoked great curiosity about the nature of music and, indeed, acoustic phenomena in general. This curiosity, in turn, led to an array of experiments by the minimalists, a curiosity that was directed to various but specific aspects of the musical event. For Riley, at least during the mid-1960's, such experiments focused on the intertwining of repetition and improvisation, the hallmarks of *Keyboard Studies No. 2* and the seminal *In C*.

In C became the cornerstone of a compositional approach that, in addition to acquiring the designation "minimalist," has also been called "trance music," "meditative music," and "pattern music." In particular, the repetitive echoes of *In C* can be discerned in the highly successful and widely disseminated works of Glass and Reich. Moreover, because *In C* can be regarded as a template for collective improvisation, the work has also provoked interest among jazz musicians seeking to explore territories beyond the bounds of mainstream jazz.

The repetitively pulsing qualities of *In C* that seem to evoke sensations of both stasis and movement have been taken up in the experimental rock music of Soft Machine, Brain Eno, John Cale, and Kraftwerk as well as in the work of such European composers of repetitive music as Michael Nyman in England, Peter Michael Hamel in Germany, and the group Urban Sax in France.

Riley and the minimalists also helped to pave the way for the "new age" music phenomenon of the 1980's. Although most new age music is greatly simplified in comparison to a work as nuanced as *In C*, its meditative nature is based largely on the use of repetition to create soothing, pulse-like mantras.

In 1989, the silver anniversary of *In C* was celebrated with performances around the world. A performance in the People's Republic of China was recorded for release by the Celestial Harmonies label.

Musicologist Edward Strickland has laid stress on the "wildly imaginative" nature of much of Riley's work, which, Strickland has noted, demonstrates "an abiding sense of wonder." These, indeed, are the qualities that have helped to make *In C* a continuing source of inspiration, and Riley a figure of enduring fascination.

Bibliography

Berg, Charles Merrell. "Philip Glass on Composing for Film and Other Forms: The Case of *Koyaanisqatsi." Journal of Dramatic Theory and Criticism* (Fall, 1990): 301-322. Glass talks about the application of his minimalist compositional techniques to his collaborations with film director Godfrey Reggio, for whom he scored *Koyaanisqatsi* (1982).

Mertens, Wim. "Terry Riley." In *American Minimal Music: La Monte Young, Terry Riley, Steven Reich, Philip Glass.* Translated by J. Hauteklet. New York: Alexander Broude, 1983. Mertens offers particularly keen analyses of *Keyboard Studies No. 2* and *In C.* Includes Michael Nyman's preface, an incisive overview of the minimalist approach, and Merten's chapter on the movement's historical background, with emphasis on serial composers Arnold Schoenberg, Anton von Webern, and Karlheinz Stockhausen and the avant-garde advocate of indeterminacy, John Cage. Bibliography.

Nyman, Michael. *Experimental Music: Cage and Beyond.* New York: Schirmer Books, 1974. Nyman's chapter on "Minimal Music, Determinancy and the New Tonality" contains an excellent discussion of Riley's working methods and compositions, including *In C.* Includes a highly useful bibliography.

Parsons, Michael. "Terry Riley." In *The New Grove Dictionary of Music and Musicians*, edited by Stanley Sadie. Vol. 16. Washington, D.C.: Grove's Dictionaries of Music, 1980. A concise yet insightful overview of Riley's career.

Riley, Terry. "Terry Riley: Doctor of Improvised Surgery." Interview by Robert Palmer. *Down Beat* 42 (November 20, 1975): 17-18, 41. An illuminating interview with Riley that also includes Palmer's thoughtful discussion of *In C.*

Strickland, Edward. *American Composers: Dialogues on Contemporary Music.* Bloomington: Indiana University Press, 1991. Music critic Strickland's volume includes a probing 1987 interview that examines Riley's career with frequent references to *In C.* Includes equally fascinating interviews with Riley collaborators La Monte Young and Steve Reich and fellow minimalist Philip Glass.

Charles Merrell Berg

Cross-References

Schoenberg Breaks with Tonality (1908), p. 193; Webern's *Six Pieces for Large Orchestra* Premieres in Vienna (1913), p. 367; Schoenberg Develops His Twelve-Tone System (1921), p. 528; Cage's *4' 33"* Premieres (1952), p. 1546 ; *Einstein on the Beach* Is a Triumph of Minimalism (1976), p. 2375; Adams' *Nixon in China* Premieres (1987), p. 2599.

LEONE RENOVATES THE WESTERN GENRE

Category of event: Motion pictures
Time: 1964-1969
Locale: Italy and the United States

Italian director Sergio Leone made four increasingly popular "spaghetti Westerns" that renovated the Western genre, introduced a wide-screen style, and launched or revived several film careers

Principal personages:

SERGIO LEONE (1929-1989), an Italian director-writer who made "sword-and-sandal" epics in the 1950's

CLINT EASTWOOD (1930-   ), an American actor whose work in Leone's films catapulted him to prominence

ENNIO MORRICONE (1928-   ), an Italian composer whose music and sound effects became integral to Leone's films

LEE VAN CLEEF (1925-   ), an American character actor with whom Eastwood shared the lead in the second and third of Leone's Westerns

ELI WALLACH (1915-   ), an American actor who portrayed the comic "ugly" against Eastwood's "good" and Van Cleef's "bad" in the *The Good, the Bad, and the Ugly* (1968)

HENRY FONDA (1905-1982), a distinguished American actor who played the murderous hired gun in *Once Upon a Time in the West* (1969)

CHARLES BRONSON (CHARLES BUCHINSKY, 1922-   ), a versatile American actor who played the lead in *Once Upon a Time in the West*

KLAUS KINSKI (NIKOLAUS NAKSZNSKI, 1926-1991), an intense German actor who became one of Leone's most memorable villains

GIAN MARIA VOLONTÉ (1933-   ), an Italian star who played Eastwood's main opponent in Leone's first two Westerns

JASON ROBARDS (1922-   ), an American actor who played a likable outlaw in *Once Upon a Time in the West*

Summary of Event

In 1967, American filmgoers were treated to two Italian-made Westerns featuring a little-known American actor, Clint Eastwood, playing a fast gun who never gives his name. *A Fistful of Dollars* and *For a Few Dollars More* had already made Eastwood and director Sergio Leone celebrities in Europe since their releases there in 1965 and 1966, respectively. American reviewers did not react positively to the films' grubby, unheroic protagonists, the "minimalist acting" of Eastwood, the unglamorous towns, the graphic violence, the massive body count, the intrusive camerawork, and the films' display of cynicism toward society. The fact that Europeans peopled this Western (Spanish-Yugoslav) landscape, their lips not always synchronized with the dubbed English dialogue, the fact that the films were self-consciously based on B-Westerns, with some almost cartoon-like sequences, and finally, the fact that the films broke such time-honored Western conventions as allowing the villains to draw first blood all operated against a sympathetic critical reception. The films were derisively called "spaghetti Westerns," but young Americans flocked to them.

Before 1964 and *A Fistful of Dollars*, Sergio Leone's major film credits included work with Italian neorealist director Vittorio De Sica and on "sword-and-sandal" epics, such as *The Last Days of Pompeii* (1960) and *The Colossus of Rhodes* (1961). Through these films, he learned how to stage spectacles, how to use the full width of the CinemaScope frame, and how to renovate a Hollywood genre.

Leone, with several other scenarists, wrote the screenplay for *A Fistful of Dollars*, basing it upon Akira Kurosawa's *Yojimbo* (1961), the story of an unattached samurai who plays two gang-families against each other, decimating their numbers to the point that he can single-handedly finish the job. Leone may have been inspired too by *The Magnificent Seven* (1960), a popular Western by John Sturges that had adapted the plot of an earlier Kurosawa film, *The Seven Samurai* (1954). Reputedly, legal problems arising from the adaptation created the three-year delay between the Italian and American release.

For his first Western, Leone called upon student-friend Ennio Morricone to compose the score, beginning a relationship that was to last to the end of Leone's career. The resulting sound track defined the Morricone style, which was unlike anything Western fans had heard before: "Nonmusical" whipcracks, whistles, bells, and gunshots were incorporated into familiar guitar and male-chorus tracks; unfamiliar flute motifs or mariachi band arrangements, with lead horns carrying bullfight-style melodies for dramatic moments, punctuated the films. At other points, seemingly under Morricone's influence, the natural sounds of hoofbeats, the wind, a creaking door, and insects were "played" against the silence of many scenes. Morricone gradually managed to make his sound tracks more integral, sometimes substituting a chorus' chants for natural sounds or musical flourishes for dialogue. Most memorable in the latter category is the flute motif that accompanies Eastwood's twitch of a cigar; the music makes a nervous gesture into a kind of comment. Morricone worked so well with Leone that the director is reputed to have planned some scenes only after Morricone had written the music for them. Although he has done distinguished sound tracks for Gillo Pontecorvo's *Battle of Algiers* (1965), Bernardo Bertolucci's *1900* (1977), Brian DePalma's *The Untouchables* (1987), and Roland Joffe's *The Mission* (1986), Morricone's considerable reputation rests largely on his work with Leone.

After having starred for five years on television's *Rawhide*, Eastwood was not excited about working on another Western, but he was attracted by the unusual plot, recognizing immediately the outline of *Yojimbo*. He brought with him to Europe the main accoutrements of the "man with no name": the woolen serape, the black jeans, the ever-present cigars. He also cut down the dialogue of his character, creating the cool, often ironic terseness that became an Eastwood trademark.

Lee Van Cleef joined Eastwood in *For a Few Dollars More* as Colonel Mortimer, a bounty hunter who helps Eastwood take on a gang. Van Cleef brought a mature and premeditated presence to balance Eastwood's youthful assurance. In *The Good, the Bad, and the Ugly*, Leone enlarged his American leads to three, using Eli Wallach to embody a comic emotionality that played well against Eastwood's steadiness and Van Cleef's calculating ruthlessness.

A Fistful of Dollars and *For a Few Dollars More* were released in European markets from 1964 to 1966 and were enormous hits, but they were not released in American until the summer of 1967. Neither broke into the top twenty moneymakers for that year, but, as of 1971, they had earned a respectable $8.5 million. Released in the United States a year after the first two had paved the way, *The Good, the Bad, and the Ugly*, featuring three American leads, with $6 million in American receipts, was Leone's biggest success in the United States, though it ranked second to *For a Few Dollars More* in worldwide receipts. In 1969, *Once Upon a Time in the West*, with a different set of lead actors—Charles Bronson, Henry Fonda, Jason Robards, and Claudia Cardinale—earned more respectful critical notices, but its languid, operatic style did not draw action fans as well.

Impact of Event

Eastwood's own career underwent a two-stage take-off, first in Europe, then in America. When the first two of Leone's Westerns hit in America in 1967, United Artists attempted to capitalize with an all-American spaghetti-style Western, *Hang 'Em High*, directed by Ted Post, which was among the top twenty box-office films of 1968, outstripping the third of Leone's trilogy. Eastwood became a top-ten box office star in 1968, a position he retained through the 1970's and 1980's; his success was fueled largely by the "Dirty Harry" series of films, in which he played a sort of "cowboy" policeman willing to dispense instant justice. Eastwood continued to make spaghetti-style Westerns, including *Pale Rider* (1985) and *Unforgiven* (1992), action pictures such as *The Eiger Sanction* (1975), and a series of action comedies in which he explored the "cowboy individualist" as performer—in professional fistfights (*Every Which Way But Loose*, 1978, and *Any Which Way You Can*, 1980) and in Wild West or musical shows (*Bronco Billy* and *Honkytonk Man*, 1980 and 1982). After 1971, Eastwood increasingly chose to control his films by directing and, in the 1980's, by producing them.

The spaghetti Westerns arrived in time to appeal to two Western-literate audiences, at a time when the genre had passed its classical stage and when Hollywood was struggling to meet the challenge of television. The younger viewers had grown up in the heyday of television Westerns; their parents had lived during the late 1930's and the 1940's, when the likes of John Wayne, Gary Cooper, Henry Fonda, and Joel McCrea defined the classic Western and the matinee Westerns of Roy Rogers and Hopalong Cassidy flourished. In the late 1950's and early 1960's, only a handful of Westerns found major box-office success; those that did tended to be expensive spectacles (such as 1960's *The Alamo* and 1962's *How the West Was Won*) or adult-themed films such as *The Left-Handed Gun* (1958) and *One-Eyed Jacks* (1961). The Western had entered an ironic or skeptical phase with *High Noon* (1952), *Shane* (1953), and *Johnny Guitar* (1954); the theme of the vanishing West and the isolated hero was strong in such early 1960's films as *The Misfits* (1961), *Ride the High Country* (1962), and *Lonely Are the Brave* (1962). When the first two of Leone's Westerns were released in 1967, American fans had recently been exposed to a series of releases that openly questioned the conventions of the classical Western: the comic *Cat Ballou* (1965), the mercenary *The Professionals* (1966), the grimly allegorical *Welcome to Hard Times* (1967) and the anti-idealistic *Hombre* (1967).

The time was right for renewal, even if temporary: Critics worried that the familiar heroes were aging and that the Westerns themselves had, like their television competition, turned to the less expensive sound stage for too many scenes. With the lower costs of on-location filming in Europe and an established studio to support him, Leone had more freedom to make his kind of Western. After the success of the trilogy, he was lured to America to make the epic end-of-the-West film *Once Upon a Time in the West*, filmed in "John Ford country," Monument Valley, and featuring such icons as Jason Robards, Woody Strode, Jack Elam, and, most memorably, Henry Fonda. As a result, 1969 became perhaps the last great year of the Western: Paul Newman and Robert Redford's *Butch Cassidy and the Sundance Kid*, John Wayne's self-reflective *True Grit*, and Sam Peckinpah's bloody *The Wild Bunch* joined Leone's film in commemorating the passing of the cowboy hero. (*Easy Rider* might even bid for inclusion on such a list because of the film's open comparison of its doomed motorcyclists to cowboys of yesteryear.)

For all their anti-Western cynicism about community values, and for all their grotesque violence so criticized by reviewers, Leone's films arrived in an America that was seeing more violence in its films, an America growing accustomed to linking violence with a breakdown of national unity. The assassinations of public figures, racial disturbances, and the divisions fostered by the Vietnam War created a ready market for the rough justice meted out by James Bond, for cynical or darkly humorous war films such as *The Dirty Dozen* (1967), *The Blue Max* (1966), and *Dr. Strangelove* (1964), and for a variety of successful pictures that called into question the moral stability of society. A culture in such conflict readily "read" the new anti-Westerns as explorations of the present. The politicized young, in particular, were ready to accept Leone's depiction of impotent, absent, or corrupt public officials, vengeful shootouts, fine lines dividing the good from the bad, senseless deaths, and the brutality of corporate capitalism as both good revisionist history and as a reflection of where "the establishment" had led America in the late 1960's. Leone's subsequent films, *Duck, You Sucker!* (1972) and *Once Upon a Time in America* (1984) continued to explore these themes through American history up to 1968.

Of course, the first result of Leone's success was more of the same by other European directors. Most of these 300-plus productions were never screened in U.S. theaters, although cable television and video rentals have made many available. Lee Van Cleef became a B-Western star in his own right, but none of his vehicles achieved the popularity of his Leone Westerns. The broadly comic Trinity series, directed by Enzo

Barboni and starring Terence Hill, achieved American box-office success in the 1970's. Whether American productions directly reflected the spaghetti Western "look," as did Eastwood's *High Plains Drifter* (1973), there was no looking back to the simple heroism of the classical Western except in such self-consciously mythic or patchwork productions as *The Legend of the Lone Ranger* (1981) and *Silverado* (1985). Nor could violence that was cleansed of impact sounds and exit gore be deemed realistic after the spaghetti Westerns, as evidenced by Sam Peckinpah's films made after 1965 and by the *Godfather* films of the 1970's. The few Westerns that achieved popularity after 1970 tended to feature antiheroic, often outlaw, protagonists and often involved the revision of Western history, especially with regard to the treatment of Native Americans in such films as *Soldier Blue* (1970), *Little Big Man* (1971) and *Dances with Wolves* (1990). More broadly, the spaghetti Western motifs of the righteous avenger or the antihero operating outside and sometimes against the law have surfaced in countless action pictures.

Bibliography

Cumbow, Robert C. *Once Upon a Time: The Films of Sergio Leone.* Metuchen, N.J.: Scarecrow Press, 1987. The best general guide to Leone's films, with chapters on each film, on Leone's moral themes, typical images, actors, and production company, and on Morricone.

Frayling, Christopher. *Spaghetti Westerns: Cowboys and Europeans from Karl May to Sergio Leone.* London: Routledge & Kegan Paul, 1981. The best resource on the Italian film industry and on the ideology and style of important German-Italian Westerns.

Johnston, Iain. *The Man with No Name: The Biography of Clint Eastwood.* London: Plexus, 1981. A brief, illustrated recounting of Eastwood's life and career through the 1970's.

Kaminsky, Stuart. "The Samurai Film and the Western." In *American Film Genres: Approaches to a Critical Theory.* New York: Dell, 1974. Explores the connection between Leone's *A Fistful of Dollars* and Kurosawa's *Yojimbo.*

Ryder, Jeffrey. *Clint Eastwood.* New York: Dell, 1987. Very readable and sound study of Eastwood's film career up to *Heartbreak Ridge* (1986).

William M. Hagen

Cross-References

Grey's *Riders of the Purple Sage* Launches the Western Genre (1912), p. 304; Ford Defines the Western in *Stagecoach* (1939), p. 1115; Westerns Dominate Postwar American Film (1946), p. 1313; *Gunsmoke* Debuts, Launching a Popular Television Genre (1955), p. 1668; Seven of the Top Ten Television Series are Westerns (1958), p. 1758; *Bonanza* Becomes an American Television Classic (1959), p. 1800.

KUBRICK BECOMES A FILM-INDUSTRY LEADER

Category of event: Motion pictures
Time: 1964-1971
Locale: Great Britain and the United States

A remarkable series of three artistically stunning and financially successful films established Stanley Kubrick as a director of nearly unlimited capabilities

Principal personages:
> STANLEY KUBRICK (1928-   ), a perfectionist director of technically innovative and highly influential films who exerted great control over all aspects of his productions
> PETER SELLERS (1925-1980), a protean British comic actor who performed three key roles in *Dr. Strangelove*
> DOUGLAS TRUMBULL (1942-   ), a special-effects artist whose career was launched by *2001: A Space Odyssey*
> MALCOLM MCDOWELL (1943-   ), a British actor who gave *A Clockwork Orange* its chilling lead
> STERLING HAYDEN (JOHN HAMILTON, 1916-1986),
> GEORGE C. SCOTT (1927-   ),
> and SLIM PICKENS (1919-1983), the three leading American actors of *Dr. Strangelove*, all cast to represent facets of the "ugly American"

Summary of Event

When Stanley Kubrick's black comedy about the accidental start of World War III, *Dr. Strangelove: Or, How I Learned to Stop Worrying and Love the Bomb*, was released to a general audience on January 30, 1964, the film was more thoroughly the creation of its director than was usual for a major production of the time. Yet from his first short sports documentary, *Day of the Fight* (1950), Kubrick had kept tight artistic control over his films; in turn, he insisted on a costly level of perfection that, fortunately, paid off at the box office. The product neither of a film school nor of a studio's careful grooming, Kubrick was a self-taught still photographer and avid film-watcher whose work promised to combine artistic and financial success.

The filming of *Lolita* (1962), Vladimir Nabokov's risqué story of a man's obsession with a pubescent girl, had introduced Kubrick to actor Peter Sellers and to the experience of directing a comedy. These two developments proved crucial to *Dr. Strangelove*, Kubrick's film adaptation of Peter George's thriller *Red Alert* (1958). Struck by the absurdity that he saw beneath supposedly rational military and political thinking about thermonuclear warfare, Kubrick quickly abandoned his plans for a serious movie.

Because of *Dr. Strangelove*'s satirical nature, Kubrick had to rely entirely on his imagination and nonclassified material to build the film's main sets: a lone B-52 bomber, the American president's "war room," and Burpleson Air Force Base. From the latter, deranged General Jack D. Ripper (Sterling Hayden) orders a first strike against the Soviet Union to prevent Communist pollution of America's "precious bodily fluids." Aghast at this insubordination, President Muffley (Peter Sellers) warns the Soviets and orders an assault on the base, where British Group Captain Mandrake (played by Sellers in a second role) finally deciphers the secret recall code for the strike force of bombers minutes after Ripper's suicide. One B-52 cannot be recalled, however, because a Soviet missile has destroyed its radio; manually opening the damaged bomb doors, the plane's bomb-busting cowboy, Major Kong (Slim Pickens), personally rides the nuclear warhead to its target.

Kubrick brings home the film's ultimate message that it is dangerous to abrogate moral responsibility to a machine when he reveals that the Soviets have automated retaliation through a "Doomsday Machine," which sets off a chain reaction of nuclear explosions. The ex-Nazi scientist Dr. Strangelove (also played by Sellers) then explains that a select few will survive in deep mine shafts—and fight over these shelters in the next war.

While directing *Dr. Strangelove*, Kubrick involved himself in hands-on supervision of the film's trendsetting, precision-crafted sets and models. For his next movie, he urged his specialists to still further frontiers in special effects. The results of his insistence on precision and innovation paid off with his landmark science-fiction film *2001: A Space Odyssey* (1968).

Epic in narrative design, *2001* tells how an alien race brings intelligence to humanity's ape-shaped ancestors, who in turn develop a space-age civilization that finally searches for the aliens. A gigantic spacecraft is built and, rather like the Doomsday Machine, is placed under the control of an all-powerful computer, which later malfunctions and has to be disconnected by the spaceship's sole surviving astronaut, Dave (Keir Dullea). After a journey across a series of bizarre false-color landscapes full of flashing lights, Dave reaches his goal and is reborn, even though the film does not show what awaits him at the end of this mission. What captured the imagination of *2001*'s huge international audience was less the story than Kubrick's brilliant cinematography. The film's 205 special-effects sequences, which Kubrick personally supervised, earned *2001* an Academy Award.

With *A Clockwork Orange* (1971), Kubrick moved to the more immediate future, applying his craftsmanship to compose sets that depicted psychological, social, and political horrors with the same technical edge he had brought to the presentation of outer space. Based on Anthony Burgess' 1962 novel, *A Clockwork Orange* follows the crime spree of the juvenile delinquent Alex (Malcolm McDowell). Along the road to its antihero's eventual imprisonment, the film travels through near-surrealist sets that externalize the mental depravity of a morally bankrupt society: The Korova milk bar, for example, has bar tables made of naked female mannequins. Released from prison after he undergoes aversion therapy that disables his violent instincts, Alex is helpless to defend himself against torment meted out by his former victims.

After enduring extraordinary punishment, he is restored to his original, violent self by a frightened government.

While *2001* entranced with its futuristic technology, *A Clockwork Orange* stunned Kubrick's audience with its carefully choreographed acts of violence. To carry further this juxtaposition of technical brilliance and horrifying subject matter, Kubrick, who had used Viennese waltzes to accompany the elegant movement of his spaceships in *2001*, employed classical music to accompany Alex's crimes: While Alex races from assault to rape, the music of Gioacchino Rossini fills the ears of the audience.

After *A Clockwork Orange*, Kubrick's films lost some of their magnetic appeal. *Barry Lyndon* (1975), a brilliantly photographed period film, left audiences indifferent to the protagonist. Critical response to the supernaturalistic thriller *The Shining* (1979) was mixed, despite a star performance by Jack Nicholson as the film's demoniacal killer. *Full Metal Jacket* (1987), Kubrick's response to the Vietnam War, is often judged to fall just short of being a masterpiece.

Altogether, however, Stanley Kubrick's work has been of unusually high quality. The combined artistic and financial success of his three technically perfect and thematically innovative films earned him an international artistic reputation and a position of leadership in the film industry.

Impact of Event

Stanley Kubrick's almost unprecedented ability to preserve his artistic independence and to exert great control over all aspects of the production of his films even when working on major projects earned him the respect and admiration of many younger American filmmakers such as Francis Ford Coppola, who looked to him as an alternative to obeying the dictates of the still-powerful Hollywood studios. Indeed, even with *Dr. Strangelove*, which cost a substantial $1,500,000 in 1964, Kubrick reserved for himself the right to decide on the final shape of the film; such power was not usually granted to an American director. Extensive creative control was more commonly possible for young European directors such as Federico Fellini and François Truffaut, who evoked some envy in young Americans for their ability to film, and release, works that were truly their own.

Unlike fellow American director Roger Corman, who escaped from Hollywood by concentrating on low-budget films (and was rewarded for his act of defiance by the discipleship of such future major American filmmakers as Coppola and Martin Scorsese and actors such as Robert De Niro and Jack Nicholson), Kubrick never compromised on quality. Working with large budgets, Kubrick contained costs through meticulous preproduction planning and thus freed resources to fulfill his goal of technical perfection. This strategy quickly endeared him to the film industry. His analysis of three years' worth of architectural magazines to find the best-looking locations for *A Clockwork Orange*, for example, meant that he had to build only one set from scratch. His planning also allowed Kubrick to keep unusually tight shooting schedules, which reduced his costs further and thus ensured him even greater artistic freedom.

Like Corman, Kubrick was one of the first American directors to move production abroad. Beginning with his first major film, *Paths of Glory* (1957), Kubrick shot all his films but *The Shining* exclusively in Europe, mostly in British film studios. Using the relatively inexpensive expertise of brilliant British film technicians, Kubrick set new standards for precision and craftsmanship. The success of *Dr. Strangelove, 2001*, and *A Clockwork Orange* led to a substantial widening of Anglo-American cooperation in the film industry. Characteristically, this relationship continued to operate along Kubrick's principles: American star actors provided international appeal, and British star craftsmanship set the films apart technically.

Kubrick's independence enabled him to choose projects beyond the traditional genre limitations within which Hollywood directors had traditionally built their fame. Again, aspiring American filmmakers looked to Kubrick for inspiration; George Lucas, for example, achieved prominence in science fiction films after a period of genre-hopping in the wake of his character study *American Graffiti* (1973).

Ironically, Kubrick's thematic choices reveal an uncanny instinct for topicality documented by the near-simultaneous release of competing films with similar subjects. During his most influential period, Kubrick's films regularly trounced the competition. After the Cuban Missile Crisis of October, 1962, had raised popular concerns about nuclear war to a new pitch, *Dr. Strangelove* handily outperformed *Fail Safe* (1964), Sidney Lumet's deadly serious treatment of the subject. When the 1960's brought a general interest in science fiction, *2001* set a standard for audience appeal not paralleled until George Lucas' *Star Wars* (1977) opened the floodgates for lavishly produced space operas. The gorilla suits worn by the actors in "The Dawn of Man" opening sequences of *2001* easily outshone their counterparts in Franklin Schaffner's contemporaneous *Planet of the Apes* (1968).

The competition, however, gradually increased and improved. Oliver Stone's Vietnam War film *Platoon* (1986), for example, won over American audiences with its hyperrealistic depiction of the common soldier's experience of jungle warfare. Released only months later, *Full Metal Jacket* did not steal the show as the most memorable example of its genre, as Kubrick's best films had done.

Those best works, however, continue their hold on the imagination. In Europe, for example, *Dr. Strangelove*'s portrayal of three ugly Americans for a long time personified the Old World's misgivings about the nuclear arms race. Not accidentally, Kubrick's theme was taken up again in *WarGames* (1983) during another era of widespread Western European discontent with American nuclear policy. In *WarGames*, however, the catastrophe triggered by a teenage computer hacker's penetration of a Pentagon computer is averted.

Rarely has a film dominated a genre for as long as did Kubrick's *2001*. Even when the late 1970's saw the emergence of the next generation of special-effects-driven science-fiction films, *2001* was still considered a shaping influence. This connection is personally underlined by the work of special-effects artist Douglas Trumbull, who learned so much working for Kubrick that he himself became one of the field's masters a decade later. Trumbull provided the special effects for Steven Spielberg's

Close Encounters of the Third Kind (1977) and Ridley Scott's *Blade Runner* (1982) and even directed the first *Star Trek* (1979) film.

Some of Kubrick's work, however, has met with increasing criticism. Commentators have never been comfortable with Kubrick's choreography of violence in *A Clockwork Orange*, and fears that the film might promote what it said it condemned soon proved accurate in Great Britain. There, hooligans dressed up in antihero Alex's elaborate costume and sought to ape his violence. Distraught, Kubrick withdrew the film from distribution in Great Britain in 1973, but the damage had been done. Feminist critics, with some justification, took exception to what they charged was the film's reveling in violent rape scenes, in which masterful cinematography and a powerful sound track apparently conspire to celebrate the event.

As critics and audiences continue to discuss and view Kubrick's films and eagerly await each new release, the director's influence within the film industry remains substantial. A successful model for many aspiring filmmakers, Stanley Kubrick has also given cinema a legacy that continues to grow.

Bibliography

Agel, Jerome. *The Making of Kubrick's "2001."* New York: New American Library, 1970. Best description of the creation of *2001*, with detailed references to special-effects techniques, which are analyzed for effect and innovation. Includes critical essays, reprints of film reviews, and a *Playboy* interview with Kubrick. Offers many photographs of Kubrick directing. Trumbull's contributions are highlighted as well.

Ciment, Michel. *Kubrick.* Translated by Gilbert Adair. New York: Holt, Rinehart and Winston, 1983. In-depth thematic study of Kubrick's artistic development up to *The Shining*. Ciment pays special attention to Kubrick's recurrent themes, innovative filmic techniques, and cinematographic accomplishments. Analytical in tone, yet clearly written. Numerous illustrations (some color) include film frame enlargements. Three interviews with Kubrick, four with key colleagues. Filmography, bibliography.

Coyle, Wallace. *Stanley Kubrick.* Boston: G. K. Hall, 1980. Comprehensive look at Kubrick's work complements a detailed bibliography, the book's primary focus. Secondary strengths are synopses of and full credits for every Kubrick film up to *The Shining*. Brief biography, index, helpful information about individual films. Ideal overview.

Kagan, Norman. *The Cinema of Stanley Kubrick.* New York: Holt, Rinehart and Winston, 1972. Sympathetic account of Kubrick's work that often quotes the director. Production, narrative shape, and critical reception are discussed in separate chapters for each film from *Paths of Glory* to *A Clockwork Orange*. Identifies major themes and offers a full filmography for the works presented. Valuable also for its many still photographs.

Philips, Gene D. *Stanley Kubrick: A Film Odyssey.* New York: Popular Library, 1977. Perceptive, analytical discussion of all Kubrick's films up to *Barry Lyndon*. Generally highly sympathetic, but not groveling. Philips' interview with Kubrick in England is a valuable addition. Extensive bibliography and full filmography for all works presented; many well-chosen photographs.

Walker, Alexander. *Stanley Kubrick Directs.* Rev. ed. New York: Harcourt Brace Jovanovich, 1972. Expanded version of the first major book on Kubrick's career. Very good on the earlier works; seeks to identify general themes throughout. Includes an extended interview; complete filmography with full credits up to *A Clockwork Orange.* Many still photographs are used to show Kubrick's development of plot and themes.

R. C. Lutz

Cross-References

Syndication Turns *Star Trek* into a Cult Classic (1972), p. 2260; The *Star Wars* Trilogy Redefines Special Effects (1977), p. 2391; Scott's *Blade Runner* Is a Visual Masterpiece (1982), p. 2486; *E.T.: The Extraterrestrial* Breaks Box-Office Records (1982), p. 2491; *Platoon* Explores the Vietnam Experience (1986), p. 2576.

LÉVI-STRAUSS EXPLORES MYTH AS A KEY TO ENLIGHTENMENT

Category of event: Literature
Time: 1964-1971
Locale: Paris, France

Claude Lévi-Strauss examined the myths of North, Central, and South America, finding in them an underlying structure of thought that he saw as fundamental to an understanding of the world

Principal personages:
CLAUDE LÉVI-STRAUSS (1908-), the major figure in the structuralist school of anthropology
EDMUND LEACH (1910-1989), a University of Cambridge anthropologist who criticized Lévi-Strauss' anthropology
OCTAVIO PAZ (1914-), a Mexican diplomat and poet whose interpretation of Lévi-Strauss illuminates the latter's place as a voice in the ongoing dialogue between the arts of poetry, music, dance, and myth

Summary of Event

Claude Lévi-Strauss is the premier anthropologist of a school known as structuralism. In 1964, he published *Le cru et le cuit*, the first volume of his masterpiece, *Mythologiques* (1964-1971; *Introduction to a Science of Mythology*, 1969-1981). It appeared in English as *The Raw and the Cooked* in 1969 and was followed quickly by three more volumes.

Lévi-Strauss connected the definition of structuralism, a highly theoretical issue, with the question of why racism and sexism exist. There is a connection between these two topics, and understanding that connection aids in understanding the kind of thinking that Lévi-Strauss explores in all of his major works as well as in understanding why this seemingly very abstract style of thought is considered to be so important by those who have made it through the dense, almost impenetrable thickets of his magnum opus, *Introduction to a Science of Mythology*.

From the moment of birth, well before the acquisition of language, people experience opposites—there is day, and there is night. Life experience enforces this opposition. The day is the time for being awake and getting things done. The night is the time for rest and recuperation. Day and night are not absolute phenomena, however: There are passages called twilight and dawn, when no one is quite sure whether it is day or night. In this sense, the division between day and night is both practical (easily perceived and understood) and somewhat arbitrary. It is also universal.

Language creates a structure. It divides time into days and nights, and people understand them—dimly at first—as opposites. By extension, that division can be made more abstract, so that one can speak of "light" and "darkness" in other circumstances than day and night—light and dark within a room—and can be abstracted again, making "white" and "black" opposites as well. The opposition of day and night becomes the basis for many other opposites. In the daytime, one is able to see clearly; by night, there is less visual information available. Night, then, is like ignorance, and day is like knowledge, understanding, and enlightenment. Night is the opposite of day, and ignorance is the opposite of understanding.

The sun is in the sky by day, the moon is in the sky by night. Both are disks that subtend the same angle to the eye, and they illuminate, respectively, the day and the night. Sunlight, however, is warm to the skin, and moonlight confers no heat. "Hot" and "cold" therefore can be mapped onto the same primary division of day and night. The sun is always round and full; the moon waxes and wanes, disappearing altogether for three nights every month. The sun is thus unchanging and dependable, the moon inconstant and unpredictable. Children are afraid of the dark. It, too, is unpredictable and hence dangerous.

A variety of opposites can be mapped onto the primary opposition between day and night: sun and moon, waking and sleeping, activity and inactivity, industriousness and laziness, warmth and cold, knowledge and ignorance, and safety and danger. The map of opposites begins to take on a moral tone. One can sense that inactivity, cold, ignorance, and danger are "not so good," while activity, warmth, knowledge, and safety are better. It is not far from this to the propositions that light is good and dark is bad, or that white is good and black is bad. It is a small jump by this line of thought to the idea that people whose skins are black are probably also lazy, unpredictable, and ignorant. This is the threshold of racism.

Women have a monthly menstrual cycle, tied to the moon's phases. They are "lunar" beings and can be presumed to partake in the lunar attributes. The line of reasoning above leads to a conclusion that they can be expected to be inconstant, fickle, ignorant, and dangerous. This is the threshold of sexism. The step from day and night, then, via the logic of opposition, to racism and sexism is much shorter than it might at first appear.

Structuralism is the study of this kind of thinking, this kind of logic. Because it is a logic that people learn very early, it is something that is carried unconsciously. It is the logic of dreams, rituals, and myths. Like technology, it works for good and ill, informing both the greatest poetry and the deepest fears of humanity.

Lévi-Strauss' purpose, then, like that of the Welsh poet Robert Graves, is to discover the logic that underlies mythological thinking. Graves entitled one book *The White Goddess: A Historical Grammar of Poetic Myth* (1948); Lévi-Strauss' title for his masterpiece, *Mythologiques*, suggests much the same kind of endeavor. Lévi-Strauss seeks a universal logic in the ways people divide and classify the perceived world and in the ways people use fundamental divisions by mapping them onto other areas of experience.

As the title of the first volume of *Mythologiques* suggests, it is the distinction between raw food and food that has been cooked that Lévi-Strauss uses as an aid in untangling the complexities of structure and association that underpin a wide variety of myths from Central and South America. Raw corresponds to "natural" and cooked to "social" in a mapping that corresponds roughly to the nature/nurture of sociobiological debate, which also includes the distinction between concepts such as organic and man-made.

In the first volume, he begins by comparing a Bororo myth about the origin of water with a Ge myth about the origin of fire. By the conclusion of the fourth volume, Lévi-Strauss' net has taken in the mythologies of the North American native peoples and added 284 new myths and their variants to 529 already discussed in the first three volumes.

By the end, Lévi-Strauss (if not his reader) is ready to assert that his first myth "contains the whole system in embryo." It is a system that, as he unravels it, has encompassed fire and water, foods raw and cooked, honey and tobacco, hollow trees and canoes, marriage and incest, stars, flagellation, and much more. Taken as a whole, it comprises "a symbolic gesture holding in balance the most profoundly meaningful oppositions that it is given to the mind of man to conceive: between the sky and the earth on the level of the physical world, between man and woman on the level of the natural world, and between relations by marriage on the level of the social world." There is all of this—and still, to quote the title of the final volume's penultimate chapter, it is "One Myth Only" that Lévi-Strauss has explored throughout.

Impact of Event

By the time that *The Raw and the Cooked* appeared in English in 1969, the next two volumes had appeared in French: *Du miel aux cendres* (1967; *From Honey to Ashes*, 1973) and *L'Origine des manières de table* (1968; *The Origin of Table Manners*, 1978). The fourth and final volume in the series, *L'Homme nu*, appeared in 1971 (translated as *The Naked Man*, 1981). For Lévi-Strauss, the task was over. For his readers, the task had just begun.

The argument of *Mythologiques* is dense. To follow it, one must be able to hold whole groups of myths from many cultures simultaneously in mind, along with a variety of correspondences, oppositions, and inversions. The form of Lévi-Strauss' entire work is consciously and appropriately modeled on musical form (*The Raw and the Cooked* is dedicated "to Music," and Lévi-Strauss is himself an accomplished musician), with sections titled "Overture," "Theme and Variations," "Fugue of the Five Senses," and "Opossum's Sonata." The style (in French) is filled with puns and plays on words. Poet Octavio Paz, a sensitive reader of Lévi-Strauss, has compared his writing to that of Marcel Proust.

Most anthropologists are specialists in the tradition of Bronisław Malinowsky: They study a handful of societies at most and usually can speak the native languages concerned. Others, in a tradition that can be traced back to Sir James Frazer and his classic *The Golden Bough* (1890-1915), make broad generalizations about all cultures and all human thought, based on their readings of many specialist anthropologists working with many different cultures.

The specialists in particular cultures tend to believe that Lévi-Strauss' theories are often based on inaccurate readings of local details, but this kind of charge can almost always be leveled by specialists against even the most brilliant of generalists. Some among them also find Lévi-Strauss' view fascinating, even compelling, in its grand sweep.

Anthropologist Edmund Leach of King's College, Cambridge, published a critique and appreciation of Lévi-Strauss. He noted that Lévi-Strauss "can never have stayed in one place for more than a few weeks at a time" in the course of his Brazilian travels, and that he "was never able to converse easily with any of his native informants in their native language." Further, he suggested that Lévi-Strauss was willing to cite "any evidence, however dubious" that suited his purpose, while either bypassing or ridiculing other evidence that did not fit in with his overall scheme.

Despite this, Leach clearly admired *Mythologiques*. He declared that Lévi-Strauss was in some sense a poet. His object of exploring the mysterious interconnections between myth-logics and other logics, Leach wrote, "is poet's country, and those who get impatient with the tortuous gymnastics of Lévi-Straussian argument—as most of us do—need to remember that he shares with Freud a most remarkable capacity for leading us all unawares into the innermost recesses of our secret emotions."

If anthropologists, then, find Lévi-Strauss to be a poor fieldworker but an insightful "poetic" theorist, it is not surprising that one of the readers most drawn to Lévi-Strauss' work should be the Mexican poet and Nobel laureate Octavio Paz. Paz's comments on Lévi-Strauss are to be found in his slim volume *Claude Lévi-Strauss, O, el nuevo festín de Esopo* (1967; *Claude Lévi-Strauss: An Introduction*, 1970). Paz suffered "intellectual vertigo" while reading *The Raw and the Cooked* for pleasure. He found himself elated, enlightened, and annoyed by turns. "The reading of Lévi-Strauss revealed so much to me and awakened so many questions in me that, almost without realizing it, I made some notes." These notes became his book.

Paz, like Leach, finds Lévi-Strauss "brilliant, although not always convincing." He notes that Lévi-Strauss claims to have been influenced by three currents of thought—geology, Marxism, and psychoanalysis—and that of the three, geology was his first love. Geology, the coming together in one place of distinct places and times by natural process, informs the reading of a structure implicit in the invisible strata buried beneath the contemporary landscape. With this in mind, Paz observes, Marxism can be seen as a geology of society and psychoanalysis as a geology of the psyche.

What do these disciplines have in common? "Marx, Freud and geology taught [Lévi-Strauss] to explain the visible by the hidden; that is, to search out the relationships between the sensible and the rational." Lévi-Strauss' search is not, Paz concludes, for "a dissolution of reason in the unconscious, but a search for the rationality of the unconscious." It is an attempt to understand the reasons of the heart, as in Blaise Pascal's well-known remark that "the heart has its reasons which reason knows nothing of." "Like all of science's great hypotheses," Paz writes—and, he might have added, particularly those hypotheses that treat this hidden reason of the heart—Lévi-Strauss' ideas "are destined to change our image of the world and of man."

The impact of Lévi-Strauss' work, then, has naturally been felt less within his own chosen field of anthropology than in a wider context: the developing understanding of unconscious processes. *Mythologiques* is a work to set beside Frazer's *The Golden Bough*, Graves's *The White Goddess*, Sigmund Freud's *The Interpretation of Dreams* (1900), or Carl Jung's *Psychology of the Unconscious* (1912). It is, perhaps, not so much an exploration of the varied cultures it pretends to address as it is an exploration of a single brilliant mind, that of Lévi-Strauss himself.

Bibliography

Leach, Edmund. *Claude Lévi-Strauss.* New York: Viking Press, 1970. The classic anthropological introduction to Lévi-Strauss' work explains structuralism, faults Lévi-Strauss on many points of detail, and welcomes his overall vision as a contribution to rank with that of Freud. Short bibliography and index.

Lévi-Strauss, Claude. *Introduction to a Science of Mythology.* 4 vols. New York: Harper & Row, 1969-1981. Lévi-Strauss' masterwork, in which he ties more than eight hundred myths from South, Central, and North American tribal cultures into an almost persuasive explanation of almost everything. With extensive bibliographies, indexes of myths, and general indexes.

_____. *The Savage Mind.* Chicago: University of Chicago Press, 1966. Another major work by Lévi-Strauss, this one dealing largely with totemism.

_____. *Structural Anthropology.* New York: Basic Books, 1963. A collection of key essays by Lévi-Strauss that can serve as an introduction to his thought. See especially "Structural Analysis in Linguistics and Anthropology" and "The Structural Study of Myth."

Paz, Octavio. *Claude Lévi-Strauss: An Introduction.* Ithaca, N.Y.: Cornell University Press, 1970. The Mexican poet's notes on reading Lévi-Strauss themselves make for enjoyable reading, as Paz emphasizes and explores the analogies Lévi-Strauss sees between poetry, music, dance, and myth. With bibliographic notes and index.

Charles Cameron

Cross-References

Freud Inaugurates a Fascination with the Unconscious (1899), p. 19; Jung Publishes *Psychology of the Unconscious* (1912), p. 309; Wittgenstein Emerges as an Important Philosopher (1921), p. 518; Sartre's *Being and Nothingness* Expresses Existential Philosophy (1943), p. 1262; Derrida Enunciates the Principles of Deconstruction (1967), p. 2075.

BARAKA'S *DUTCHMAN* DRAMATIZES RACIAL HATRED

Category of event: Theater
Time: March 24, 1964
Locale: The Village South Theatre, New York, New York

Audiences were shocked by the language and ideas of Dutchman, a venomous play filled with the emotions of contempt, anger, and hatred and ending in emasculation and murder

Principal personages:
> AMIRI BARAKA (LEROI JONES, 1934-   ), a playwright, director, poet, novelist, essayist, and teacher who earned renown as an uncompromising black militant
> LANGSTON HUGHES (1902-1967), a poet and playwright whose black-centered work influenced Baraka
> LORRAINE HANSBERRY (1930-1965), a successful black playwright whose 1958 success with *A Raisin in the Sun* opened doors for other black dramatists

Summary of Event

LeRoi Jones emerged as a leading American playwright in 1964, when his striking drama *Dutchman* was produced Off-Broadway at New York's Village South Theatre. The play, which was widely acclaimed as one of the year's best, catapulted Jones into the front ranks of African-American writers, and he soon became known as an uncompromising black militant. In the wake of his newfound prominence, he severed many of his ties with white American culture; in 1966, he renounced the name "Jones" and became known as Imamu Amiri Baraka (he later dropped the name "Imamu").

Baraka became the leading writer of militant black theater. He articulated the black condition. To support his work as a theater revolutionary, he founded the Black Arts Theatre and School in Harlem. Much of the subject matter of Baraka's works was designed to attack the "white establishment." The objective Baraka sought through his drama was not integration but the separation of whites and blacks by the driving of a wedge between them.

Throughout his career, Baraka has continued to write drama that denounces whites and has continued to express his militant philosophy espousing the need for blacks to force whites to redress the injustices of the past and present. He has strongly advocated the creation of a separatist society for blacks in the United States. These themes have remained evident in his activities and playwriting.

Dutchman makes use of the techniques of Antonin Artaud's "Theater of Cruelty." The play's major characters, Clay and Lula, force the audience to examine their prejudices through the violence of the dramatic action. Baraka makes the audience face and confront the violent reality of the subconscious hatred buried in its psyche. He clearly challenges the audience to recognize that it makes the moral standards by which it chooses to live. Certainly, Baraka wants his viewers to see Clay and Lula as real people; at the same time, however, these characters must be understood to be character types.

Dutchman is set in a New York City subway car in which Clay and Lula are riding beneath the city. The action of the play thus takes place in the heart, the very infrastructure, of the city; the setting thus seems emblematic of the sociopolitical structure of the United States. As the dramatic action evolves, it is possible to see the "true" feelings of the characters as demonstrated by their language and gestures. It seems obvious the action is intended to represent the class struggle going on in society. Clay wants to be a man, but Lula hatefully attacks his attempts toward manhood; she asks him, accusingly, "What right do you have to be wearing a three-button suit and striped tie? Your grandfather was a slave, he didn't go to Harvard." Racial stereotypes are revealed in the play's dialogue; Lula, for example, remarks on the black male's supposed sexual ability.

The title is clearly metaphorical. The word "Dutchman" does not appear in the dialogue of the play. It could be a reference to the myth of the *Flying Dutchman*, the phantom ship forever doomed to sail the seas. The title may also allude to the Dutch ship that brought the first African slaves to America. Whichever interpretation one prefers, the play is clearly a study of the black-white experience. Clay represents American blacks who are trying to live and survive in a white-controlled society; Lula stands for white efforts to prevent blacks from achieving equal status in the United States.

The play is a blend of realism, expressionism, and absurdism. Baraka successfully brought together realism in the play's structure and characters, expressionism in the juxtaposition of the emasculation and the emancipation of Clay, and absurdism in the play's dialogue. Moreover, Baraka successfully pulled together emotions that represent frightening savagery. Baraka's anger toward, contempt for, and hatred of white culture is forcefully portrayed in raw, ugly, and repelling dramatic action.

Dutchman is powerful and compelling in its statement. Ritualistic violence underscores the conflict between blacks and whites. Baraka forces the audience's attention on a variety of cultural and racial differences between blacks and whites, creating a startling portrayal of white brutality and black accommodation in the United States.

In the tradition of the absurdist writings of the period, Baraka has created a world of black Clays and white Lulas. From Baraka's point of view, Clay is as much to be despised as Lula is to be hated. Clay represents "Uncle Tom" blacks, accommodationists who have surrendered their heritage in an effort to conform to the demands of white society. Baraka seems to have nothing but cold hatred for the Clays of black society; he sees them as emasculated, on a road leading to death.

Baraka also expresses the same cold hatred for the white Lula. She is the play's great contradiction; she seems to offer Clay the opportunity to be a free person, but she actually denies him any true hope. Freedom appears at hand, but in reality it is only domination that Clay receives from Lula. At the play's conclusion, the ultimate domination occurs when Lula stabs Clay to death. The allegorical point of the drama is played out in Clay's execution by Lula.

Dutchman gained positive critical acclaim. Despite the violent nature of the play, it was enthusiastically received by audiences. The play earned an Obie Award as the best Off-Broadway play of 1964.

The major themes of venomous hate and intense violence expressed in *Dutchman* were carried through in many of Baraka's other contemporary works, including *The Baptism* (1964), *The Toilet* (1964), and *The Slave* (1964), which revealed a similar disdain for white liberals and black conformists. Baraka's plays viciously attacked American religious, social, and sexual life. The attacks, moreover, were not limited to his plays; in his short stories, poems, and novels, he has expressed many of the same ideas.

Impact of Event

The 1960's were a time of social unrest in which the United States experienced severe political, social, and racial turmoil. The theater created by citizens of color reflected this upheaval. *Dutchman* proved to be an important element in the black drama of the 1960's, both mirroring and fostering the black militancy of the time.

Although *Dutchman* was successful, both it and other works by Baraka were often criticized as being too blatantly antiwhite. Even some African-American critics were not always pleased by his plays, which were sometimes seen as attempts by Baraka to set himself up as "blacker than thou."

The success of Lorraine Hansberry's *A Raisin in the Sun* in 1958 had showed black drama to be a vital part of the United States theater scene. White audiences were challenged by such plays to examine their prejudices toward those seeking to escape the ghetto. Yet the work of Baraka and many others in the 1960's reflected an unrestricted commitment to the cause of the black American. Black revolutionary theater brought to the United States a new aesthetic. This movement saw the creation of groups such as the Black Arts Theatre and School in Harlem; by the end of the decade, more than forty groups devoted to the production of African-American drama had been created.

Dutchman was also, in part, responsible for the growth of a genre of black literature known as the Black Arts movement. Younger black writers, including Don L. Lee (Haki Madhubuti), Ed Bullins, Sonia Sanchez, Marvin X, and Larry Neal, soon produced a torrent of black-themed work that sought to establish the artistic validity of African-American cultural idioms and that was often openly antiwhite. *Dutchman* was the opening shot in this volley of militant 1960's works. With *Dutchman*, Baraka opened the doors for black American writers to deal with a broad range of political, racial, and social themes. These works included examinations of the lives and times of black historical figures, of race relations in the United States, and of the black bourgeoisie. The black American plays of the 1960's included black militant dramas, comedies, allegories, ritual dramas, and even musicals.

Amiri Baraka's influence on the drama of the period made him one of the black cultural and spiritual leaders of the era. His leadership was best demonstrated by his revolutionary theater. Such prominent later black playwrights as Ed Bullins, August Wilson, and Charles Fuller seemed to receive an impetus to excel as a result of the force Baraka brought to the ethnic theater. Moreover, Baraka's revolutionary theater was a major factor in the appearance and success of agitprop street plays in the 1960's and 1970's. In recognition of his success as a playwright, director, poet, novelist, and activist, Baraka in 1972 received an honorary doctorate from Malcolm X College in Chicago, Illinois.

Bibliography

Allison, Alexander W., Arthur J. Carr, and Arthur M. Eastman, eds. *Masterpieces of the Drama.* 5th ed. New York: Macmillan, 1986. The editors provide an excellent dramatic analysis of Baraka's *Dutchman.*

Barnet, Sylvan, Morton Berman, and William Burto, eds. *Types of Drama: Plays and Essays.* Boston: Little, Brown, 1972. The editors discuss Baraka's *Home: Social Essays* (1966), in which he explains the goal of revolutionary theater, and provide an interesting analysis of *Dutchman.*

Branch, William B., ed. *Black Thunder: An Anthology of Contemporary African-American Drama.* New York: Mentor, 1992. A collection of plays examining the racial fabric of contemporary life in the United States. Each of the plays was written between 1975 and 1990. Branch provides an informative historical introduction to the collection and biographical sketches of each of the playwrights.

Brockett, Oscar G. *The Theatre: An Introduction.* 4th ed. New York: Holt, Rinehart and Winston, 1979. Surveys the historical development of African-American drama. Discusses the significant role Baraka has played through his work as a playwright, director, and leader in forming associations to promote black theater.

Brockett, Oscar G., and Mark Pape, comps. *World Drama.* New York: Holt, Rinehart and Winston, 1984. Includes Baraka's *Slave Ship: A Historical Pageant* (1967), a symbol for the entrapment, brutalization, and violently inhumane treatment common in the black American experience. The book offers interesting historical information about the development of black drama in the United States.

Brown, Lloyd Wellesley. *Amiri Baraka.* Boston: Twayne, 1980. A useful critical introduction to Baraka's work. Includes bibliography and index.

Hudson, Theodore. *From LeRoi Jones to Amiri Baraka: The Literary Works.* Durham, N.C.: Duke University Press, 1973. Includes a chapter of biography based on interviews with Baraka and his parents. Analyzes Baraka's philosophy as well as his essays, fiction, poetry, and drama of the 1960's and early 1970's. Notes, index, bibliography.

Jones, LeRoi. *"Dutchman" and "The Slave": Two Plays.* New York: William Morrow, 1964. The original text of the play that brought Baraka (then known as Jones) to the forefront of African-American drama. Both plays included focus on black-white conflict.

_____. *Tales.* New York: Grove Press, 1967. Baraka wrote numerous essays, short stories, and poems expressing his view of the oppressiveness of the white culture in which he and other blacks were forced to survive. His militant attacks on "whitey" and "Uncle Tom" liberals may put off some readers, yet they will be challenged to examine Baraka's themes.

Lacey, Henry C. *To Raise, Destroy, and Create: The Poetry, Drama, and Fiction of Imamu Amiri Baraka (LeRoi Jones).* Troy, N.Y.: Whitston, 1981. A wide-ranging survey of Baraka's literary achievement. Index.

Willis M. Watt

Cross-References

Wright's *Native Son* Depicts Racism in America (1940), p. 1185; Brecht Founds the Berliner Ensemble (1949), p. 1410; Osborne's *Look Back in Anger* Opens in London (1956), p. 1721; Hansberry's *A Raisin in the Sun* Debuts on Broadway (1959), p. 1795; Baldwin Voices Black Rage in *The Fire Next Time* (1963), p. 1929; *The Autobiography of Malcolm X* Is Published (1965), p. 2022; Shange's *for colored girls . . .* Is a Landmark (1976), p. 2370; *"MASTER HAROLD" . . . and the boys* Examines Apartheid (1982), p. 2496; Innovative Black Filmmakers Achieve Success (Late 1980's), p. 2565; *Do the Right Thing* Establishes Lee as a World-Class Director (1989), p. 2641.

WEISS'S ABSURDIST DRAMA *MARAT/SADE* IS PRODUCED

Category of event: Theater
Time: April 29, 1964
Locale: West Berlin, West Germany

Peter Weiss delivered a Marxist viewpoint in an absurdist documentary drama that established him as a leading dramatist of the 1960's

> *Principal personages:*
> PETER WEISS (1916-1982), a painter, film director, novelist, and playwright who brought his special concept of absurdist theater to the international stage
> BERTOLT BRECHT (1898-1956), a theorist and playwright who used "epic drama" to promote Marxist theory through "alienation" of the audience during performances
> ANTONIN ARTAUD (1896-1948), a film actor, director, and playwright who revolutionized theater with his theories about the Theater of Cruelty
> PETER BROOK (1925-   ), a director who produced Weiss's play as part of a program entitled "Theater of Cruelty"

Summary of Event

Playwright Peter Weiss vaulted to international fame with the 1964 production of his *Der Verfolgung und Ermordung Jean-Paul Marats, dargestellt durch die Schauspielgruppe des Hospizes zu Charenton unter Anleitung des Herrn de Sade* (*The Persecution and Assassination of Jean-Paul Marat as Performed by the Inmates of the Asylum of Charenton Under the Direction of the Marquis de Sade*, 1965, known as *Marat/Sade*). The work is a play within a play dealing with historical events of the French Revolution. In *Marat/Sade*, Roux, a priest, serves as the mouthpiece to express several philosophical positions held by Weiss. Roux advocates the value of communal living and ownership. He also suggests that churches should be converted into schools, so that the masses can be educated and overcome their social situation. Roux also calls for an end to all wars. The play ends with Roux confronting the audience with two questions asked by many dramatists in the twentieth century: When will you learn to see? and When will you learn to take sides?

Weiss's methods of moral, social, and political commentary were deeply embedded in the theatrical techniques and style of Antonin Artaud's Theater of Cruelty. Weiss used the Brechtian structure of short scenes, with each one having a separate title, to develop his plot. Through the plot and characters of *Marat/Sade*, Weiss argued that nature is indifferent to humankind. He also pointed to the belief that the strong overrun weaker people in society. Weiss considered individuals to be basically selfish. His contention was that it is worthless to espouse idealistic solutions to situations in people's lives.

Several movements in the theater and events outside the theater influenced Weiss. Inside the theater, from about 1870 until the early 1900's, naturalism sought to put a "slice of life" on the stage for the spectators. Not unlike realism, this movement believed that "reality" was contained in the existing materialistic society. Realism became the dominant form from 1900 through 1950. As a movement, it sought to create an art form that systematically presented the human condition. It was thought possible to portray people as they lived while providing them with answers to the difficulties in their lives.

By 1910, the theater began to embrace a countermovement to realism and naturalism. This movement was labeled expressionism. Expressionists were convinced that fundamental truth for individuals could be found only through the human spirit and its desires and visions. A similar reaction to realism was futurism. This movement rejected the past and its materialism. The answer to people's problems was believed to exist in the future, as individuals were transformed into machinelike perfection.

Not every movement in the theater was hopeful that society could overcome its problems. Dadaism was one such movement. Dadaists were skeptical. Adherents to this movement were disturbed by the madness of World War I. Their works replaced rationality with madness and absurdity. The effects of Dadaism were felt strongly in the 1960's.

The Surrealists thought that the only way for people to find solutions to the world's problems was through understanding the human psyche. Surrealists focused on the subconscious mind as the artist's source for significant ideas. Absurdists adopted a similar philosophy.

After 1950, a full-fledged movement appeared that was labeled by Martin Esslin as absurdism. Playwrights such as Samuel Beckett, Eugène Ionesco, Harold Pinter, and Jean Genet were caught up in a genre that revealed to the world a universe gone mad. Absurdists saw life as senseless and irrational. Their plays challenged conventional ideas of plot, action, character, and language. For these dramatists, productions themselves were creative acts, not just portrayals of play scripts on a stage. New production techniques involving adaptation of the physical space, music, dance, painting, kinetic art, mime, gesture, chanting, and lighting were employed along with the deemphasis on the value of traditional language and play structure.

Outside the theater, three movements had a significant impact on the work of Weiss. First, Charles Darwin's theories on evolution and the origin of species suggested the ever-changing nature of the world. Second, Sigmund Freud's psychic determinism established the notion that people's actions were actually motivated by unconscious, hidden fears and motives. Finally, Karl Marx's writings on economic determinism convinced Weiss that society was the domain of the rich and powerful.

Weiss was influenced by the writings of Albert Camus, Jean-Paul Sartre, and Antonin Artaud. The existentialist Camus believed that the universe was in chaos. Morality was a fabrication designed to keep the average person in line. Camus believed that the ultimate truth was that life is filled with chaos, contradictions, and everyday inanities. Sartre, also an existentialist, believed that the world was neutral.

People and societies assigned meanings to facts and events, rather than those facts and events having inherent meanings. Further, Sartre believed that "truth" was a lack of logic, order, and certainty. Holding to similar beliefs, Artaud developed the Theater of Cruelty. This was an attempt to have drama reach unconscious, buried human impulses. He thought it was necessary to subvert the conscious mind and confront the spectator through the psychic in order to bring about personal and social change. Artaud attempted to establish direct communication between the audience and the theatrical event as well as between the characters and the action on the stage.

Perhaps the most influential person affecting Weiss was Bertolt Brecht. Brecht developed the "epic" theater. It was Brecht's work with the Berliner Ensemble that perfected many of the theatrical techniques used by Weiss. Brecht worked with themes dealing with humanitarian causes and progressive social reforms. In his theater, he used dialogue to comment on sociopolitical, religious, and economic conditions. Brecht used such devices as a relatively bare stage with set pieces instead of full sets, lack of a front curtain and the usual imaginary "fourth wall" between the actor and the spectator, projections, placards, musicians on the stage, episodic scenes, and lighting in full view of the audience to achieve his purposes. He used these devices to alienate the audience, to distance them from the dramatic action so that they would have to confront, think about, and respond to the need for change in society. Weiss used Brecht's "historification." In the plot structure of *Marat/Sade*, Weiss draws attention to the "pastness" of the events shown to illustrate that change can occur. He wanted his viewers to accept the idea that they can bring about change in the world. In *Marat/Sade*, it is possible to see the eclectic assimilation of these various influences.

Impact of Event

Marat/Sade represents the epitomizing example of a truly twentieth century dramatic technique. The play established the use of documentary drama as a practice in the theater. Although the play was not entirely based on historical fact, it did present Weiss's ideas in a historical context and used real-life characters including the Marquis de Sade and Jean-Paul Marat. The use of documentary drama spread from the theater into the film and television industries. As the line between documentary works and entertainment blurred, both film and television often failed to draw a clear distinction between the art form and real life.

The impact of *Marat/Sade* on the theater is best realized when it is understood that the play represents the best theatrical elements drawn from Brecht, didacticism, absurdism, and the Theater of Cruelty. Weiss used alienation, historification, songs, a play within a play, a herald making announcements (Greek chorus), action set in an asylum (representing the irrationality of an absurd world), frequent interruptions, interpolations, discussions that transcend the immediate action of the plot, vast amount of spectacle, and one-dimensional characters (character types).

Weiss brought together a variety of dramatic elements that have influenced modern theater. Inclusion of Vsevolod Meyerhold's "living newspaper" is evident in Weiss's dramatic creation. *Marat/Sade* contains several characters telling many brief stories. As noted above, the play is constructed as a play within a play, with several subplots developed simultaneously. Another element of the play is its exemplification of the Theater of Cruelty. It is filled with the sights and sounds of an asylum. Movements, cries, and noises give as much, if not more, meaning to the dramatic action as do the scripted words. Surrealism is yet another element of drama perfected in the play. The juxtaposition of "realities" can be found in the dramatic action. The "reality" of the various characters is commented upon by themselves and others. At various times during the drama, the plot line is interrupted by one or more of the characters. The characters make comments that challenge the audience to consider alternate views of "reality."

In effect, *Marat/Sade* rejects the concept of the well-made play by incorporating the irrational, dreamlike realities of the insane to comment on historical events. Weiss seems to have developed a dramaturgical form that focuses on the subjective reality of his characters while suggesting that the external world beyond the asylum was empty and meaningless.

Marat/Sade has helped to revolutionize modern theater. It has allowed modern practitioners to reject conventions of dialogue. Weiss showed that in place of a standard script it is possible to use fragmented and nonsensical dialogue and that it was possible to use episodic action in place of the traditional dramatic structure. Through *Marat/Sade*, he demonstrated that sequential logic was not necessary. Elaborate sets and scenery were no longer needed. Weiss thrust the audience into the action of the play, as a part of it rather than casual observers of it. Weiss demonstrated that it was possible to deal with the relativity of the human experience from a historical perspective in an entertaining manner. He challenged the audience to look at history, learn from it, and avoid the mistakes of the past.

The modern theater has learned that it can abandon rationality and logic. Using a historical setting, Weiss showed that it is possible to deal effectively with human paradoxes and with their illogical behaviors. *Marat/Sade* used a historical setting to reveal a degenerate society and depraved humankind. Contemporary artists have learned to recognize that it is possible to understand reality by confronting human situations that deal with the absurd human condition.

Peter Brook's production of *Marat/Sade* in London, England, and later in New York City was part of a series of plays billed as "Theater of Cruelty." Brook included *Marat/Sade* because the activity of the characters along with the multiple acting areas represented the Artaudian mode of theater. The Theater of Cruelty was a rejection of traditional use of texts and language. Brook's production used constant activity, heightened by sights and sounds, and incorporated the use of nudity and sex. Further, Brook used physical violence directed toward the audience to create a theater of cruelty, exactly as Artaud had urged. *Marat/Sade* has become recognized as the masterpiece of the Theater of Cruelty.

The success of *Marat/Sade* led Weiss to write another documentary drama entitled *Die Ermittlung* (1965; *The Investigation*, 1966). Other works of his include *Trotski im Exil* (1970; *Trotsky in Exile*, 1972) and *Hölderlin* (1971). These focus on broad universal issues rather than examinations of specific historical events or facts.

Other playwrights capitalized on the success of *Marat/Sade*. A movement known as "theater of fact" evolved. Plays representing this movement include *Der Stellvertreter* (1963; *The Deputy*, 1963) by Rolf Hochhuth and *In der sache J. Robert Oppenheimer* (1964; *Oppenheimer*, 1967) by Heinar Kipphardt. The influence of this type of avant-garde theater seemed to decline in the 1970's. Commercial demands in the contemporary theater took their toll on the production of works similar to *Marat/Sade*.

Weiss's *Marat/Sade* represented "total" theater. In this play, all elements of the theater worked together. *Marat/Sade*, and other plays of this type, have continued to be produced. The play has remained a part of theater workshops and summer stock companies; college and university theaters have continued to produce the play. As the epitomizing example of the Theater of Cruelty, *Marat/Sade*, with its use of all the dramatic elements, has had an ongoing impact in the theater.

Bibliography

Brockett, Oscar G. *The Essential Theatre.* 5th ed. Forth Worth, Tex.: Holt, Rinehart and Winston, 1992. Brockett discusses the nature of theater along with providing an excellent overview of the continuing absurdist tradition in modern theater.

_____. *History of the Theater.* 6th ed. Boston: Allyn & Bacon, 1991. This comprehensive study is required reading for the serious student of the theater. Brockett provides a thorough look at trends and movements affecting the evolution of absurdist drama.

Gillespie, Patti P., and Kenneth M. Cameron. *Western Theatre: Revolution and Revival.* New York: Macmillan, 1984. The authors offer a short discussion of Peter Weiss and Peter Brook's production of Weiss's *Marat/Sade*.

Roose-Evans, James. *Experimental Theatre: From Stanislavsky to Today.* New York: Universe Books, 1970. Roose-Evans provides a clear and concise discussion of major movements in the theater. This book gives the reader a unified view of what has led to much of the contemporary practice in modern theater.

Wilson, Edwin. *The Theater Experience.* 4th ed. New York: McGraw-Hill, 1988. The author examines numerous aspects of the theater in a discussion that highlights various developments in staging, acting, directing, and play writing. Contains an excellent set of five appendices including "Major Theatrical Forms and Movements" and "Historical Outline."

Willis M. Watt

Cross-References

The Ghost Sonata Influences Modern Theater and Drama (1908), p. 199; Sartre and Camus Give Dramatic Voice to Existential Philosophy (1940's), p. 1174; Brecht

Founds the Berliner Ensemble (1949), p. 1410; *Waiting for Godot* Expresses the Existential Theme of Absurdity (1953), p. 1573; Ionesco's *Rhinoceros* Receives a Resounding Worldwide Reception (1959), p. 1812; Pinter's *The Caretaker* Opens in London (1960), p. 1861; Esslin Publishes *The Theatre of the Absurd* (1961), p. 1871.

CUNNINGHAM STAGES HIS FIRST DANCE "EVENT"

Category of event: Dance
Time: June 24, 1964
Locale: Vienna, Austria

Modern-dance choreographer Merce Cunningham broke with tradition by presenting sections of dance repertory in diverse performance spaces such as museums, gymnasiums, and public squares

Principal personages:

MERCE CUNNINGHAM (1919-   ), a dancer and choreographer who expanded perceptions of modern dance through innovative compositional techniques

JOHN CAGE (1912-1992), the musical director of the Merce Cunningham Dance Company and a leading exponent of experimental music

ROBERT RAUSCHENBERG (1925-   ), an experimental visual artist who collaborated with Cunningham and provided a set piece for the first "Event" in Austria

Summary of Event

In June, 1964, the Merce Cunningham Dance Company embarked on an extensive tour that included performances in Asia and Europe. While traveling through Austria during the first month of the tour, the company was asked by the people of Vienna to present an unscheduled concert. Since the only space available for the performance was the city's Twentieth Century Museum, citizens provided a platform for the dance company in front of a large glass wall that formed the back of the building. As there were no wing spaces, stage lights, or curtains, choreographer Merce Cunningham realized he could not present a traditional concert of repertory pieces and instead opted for a nontraditional performance. He called the ninety-minute performance a "Museum Event" and included sections of pieces and parts of repertory, sometimes presenting two dances on stage at the same time. Visual artist Robert Rauschenberg created a set piece specifically for the "Event," and composer John Cage supplied the musical score, which was performed by a quartet of players. This "Museum Event" unfolded continuously, without an intermission.

Later during the 1964 tour, the Cunningham company was asked to perform in the Modern Museum of Stockholm, Sweden. The company offered two separate evenings of dance that included a collage of dance movement from Cunningham repertory pieces. The two performances in Stockholm and the one in Vienna were the first "Events" that Cunningham staged.

From the latter part of the 1960's through the 1980's, Cunningham presented more than two hundred Events in the United States and on international tours. The company performed Events in instances where a stage was too small or circumstances elicited a nontraditional performance. Cunningham has stated the Events were principally meant to advocate the use of alternative spaces for dance performances and to present the company members with intriguing opportunities to solve problems and to adjust to different performance environments. For example, in Venice, Italy, at the Piazza San Marco, Cunningham and dancers designed an Event in which the audience followed the performers from one place to another. Dressed in sneakers and sweat pants, the dancers filed out to the square carrying chairs and brooms. After selecting a performance area, the dancers sat on the chairs in a tightly knit group. Each performer then proceeded to sweep the ground and push the chairs out, thus enlarging the dance area. Next, the company performed sections of repertory until a single dancer picked up a chair and cued the others to do likewise. Followed by the audience, the group carried the chairs and brooms to a new location and repeated the entire procedure. After five repetitions of this sequence, the Event ended.

Cunningham presented six Museum Events between 1964 and 1968. In 1968, the choreographer expanded his Event sites to include gymnasiums, and in 1969, the company performed Events in theater spaces as well. In the early 1970's, Cunningham began staging Events in the United States on a regular basis. Similar to the previous Events, these performances did not take place in traditional proscenium theaters but in alternative performance spaces such as museums, gymnasiums, sports arenas, or Cunningham's own dance studio. Cunningham also staged Events in churches, parks, and shopping plazas. Events were generally assembled only a few days prior to performance, and each individual Event was considered unique. Cunningham has stated that one intention of the Events was to reveal to the audience the experience of dancing rather than to offer an evening of traditional dance performance. As an experimental choreographer, Cunningham challenged the viewer to perceive each dance performance as a unique phenomenon.

In March, 1973, the Merce Cunningham Dance Company presented four performances at the Brooklyn Academy of Music in New York City as Events. Each Event was a ninety-minute mosaic of dance sequences, sections of dances, and entire pieces performed in random order, with no intermission. The audience reaction was bewilderment, confusion, and even contempt. Members of the crowd shouted and jeered. Some adolescents even ran disruptively through the balcony of the theater. After this upheaval at the Brooklyn Academy of Music, Cunningham decided to stage the Events in his studio at the Westbeth artists' cooperative in Greenwich Village, New York. The Events were offered on the weekends at the Westbeth studio and gradually attracted a growing audience. By 1977, Cunningham had presented more than 140 Events, each of which the choreographer had numbered. By 1985, Cunningham abandoned the practice of numbering the Events when the total exceeded two hundred.

Impact of Event

The field of avant-garde dance and choreographic experimentation is Cunningham's progeny. In conventional approaches to choreography, the dance movement, music, costumes, set design, and lighting all adhere to a central idea or theme. In Cunningham's approach, the dance, music, and visual elements remain independent and autonomous, although the viewer still perceives them simultaneously as part of the dance performance. In this way, the individual art forms do not illustrate a single theme expressed in the dance but comprise a tripartite performance event. For example, an eighty-minute Event held at the Cunningham dance studio during the mid-1980's originated in a typical manner from the juxtaposition of several Cunningham dances. Excerpts from *Fielding Sixes* (choreographed in 1980), *Scramble* (1967), *Winterbranch* (1964), and *Changing Steps* (1975) were grafted to parts of Cunningham's 1964 work *Cross Currents* and a duet from the 1977 dance *Fractions*. As in the majority of Cunningham's work, the accompanying musical score was composed independently of the dance. The dancers heard the sound score for the first time during the actual performance. Cunningham has worked with experimental visual artists and composers in this way throughout his career and was the first modern dance choreographer to do so. Elements of set design, costume, and music were created separately and assembled for the first time during the performance. To Cunningham, this seemingly aleatoric method of composition is symbolic of the world's complexity; he has stated that "You can hear the sound, say, of a boat and see a bird flying at the same time, and the two become a single energized moment."

The 1964 tour that saw the inception of Cunningham's Events also marked the first extensive press coverage given to the company. The increased media attention manifested itself back in the United States in the form of expanded audiences. The Events, however, created a furor among dance audiences. Cunningham's unorthodox approach to choreography was elusive to many viewers, and controversy over the Events increased. Some audience members walked out when the four Events premiered at the Brooklyn Academy of Music. Others became avid supporters of the new approach to choreography.

Undaunted by occasional negative audience response, Cunningham continued to experiment with innovative ideas. On July 23, 1965, shortly after the 1964 world tour, Cunningham created *Variations V* for a Franco-American festival. This multimedia performance included dance, television, and film and featured music composed by John Cage. Dancers moved among a grid of poles that supported numerous antennae. As the performers moved past the antennae, they triggered music that responded to the movement. Simultaneously, films were projected on stage.

Cunningham cultivated an enduring association with visual artists and musicians. He has collaborated with visual artists such as Robert Rauschenberg, Jasper Johns, and Andy Warhol. In 1944, Cunningham began a long-term collaboration with musician and composer John Cage, who served as the musical director for the Cunningham dance company. Videographers and poets have accompanied Cunningham's Events as well.

Cunningham's choreography has supplied a vital force within the field of dance and has constantly challenged viewers to question, renew, and adjust conceptions about the art form. Perhaps the greatest contribution Cunningham's work has made to the dance world is his use of chance elements, of serendipity, to structure a work. *Suite by Chance* (1952) was the first Cunningham piece in which the element of chance dictated the resultant choreography; for the piece, Cunningham created a series of charts that notated body movements, spatial directions, and duration of movements. The dancers followed the instructions on the charts in order to perform the piece. In 1975, Cunningham choreographed *Torse*, which is also representative of his experimentation with chance operations. Cunningham has tossed coins and thrown dice in order to determine movement sequences.

The juxtaposition of pedestrian or vernacular movement with more stylized dance sequences is also characteristic of Cunningham's choreography. The content of each dance often resides in the actual physical nature of the movement rather than in overt storytelling. In Cunningham's dances, many different things happen at once. No central focus exists, which suggests that no one event is of more importance than another. The discontinuity of music and dance results from the autonomic creation of sound score and choreography. The theatrical elements of music, dance, lighting, costume, and set design are created independently and only assembled in actual performance. The process of making the dance, rather than the production of a specific piece, is emphasized. As typified by the Events, Cunningham has consistently placed more importance on the procedure rather than the result.

Cunningham's Events changed the way the dance world viewed choreography. Dance was no longer viewed as an event that took place only in a proscenium theater. Dance could take place in myriad environments and could be perceived from a number of vantage points. The Events had a major impact on the "happenings" of the late 1960's and early 1970's. Audiences came to view dance as capable of occurring anywhere: in sports arenas, churches, and city streets. In the late 1960's, Ann Halprin and the Dancers' Workshop of San Francisco experimented with dance in nontraditional spaces. In the late 1970's, choreographers such as Twyla Tharp and Meredith Monk sought out diverse environmental settings for many of their dances.

The advent of Merce Cunningham's Events in the mid-1960's expanded the audience's viewpoint of dance to include more than just the proscenium stage. In addition, Cunningham challenged the viewer to consider dance as a random collage of movement, often assembled by chance. Within the field of experimental dance, Cunningham stands as an instigator and pioneer.

Bibliography

Coe, Robert. "The Moderns and Beyond." In *Dance in America*. New York: E. P. Dutton, 1985. Provides a thorough overview of Cunningham's work, including detailed descriptions of several Events. Extensive videography of modern dance is included that offers complete information on a 1977 Event for television presented by the Merce Cunningham Dance Company. Bibliography and index. Black-and-white photographs that illustrate the range of Cunningham's work.

Cunningham, Merce, and Jacqueline Lesschaeve. *The Dancer and the Dance*. New

York: Marion Boyars, 1985. A definitive work on Cunningham and his choreographic process. Format of the book is an extensive interview with Cunningham. Includes detailed information on the Events. Chronology of choreography performed by the Merce Cunningham Dance Company is included; a list of films and videos featuring Cunningham is also provided. Photographs and index. An interesting feature is the inclusion of some of Cunningham's handwritten choreography scores.

Emily Lowe Gallery. *Diaghilev/Cunningham.* Text by David Vaughan. Hempstead, N.Y.: Author, 1974. A compilation of a gallery showing at the Emily Lowe Gallery at Hofstra University. Includes excellent photographs of the Cunningham dance company. Several photographs illustrate the company performing in nontraditional spaces. Photographs of dance posters and Cunningham's handwritten choreographic scores supplement the limited text. Includes a chronology of choreography from 1942 to 1974. No bibliography or index is provided.

Highwater, Jamake. "Notes on Twelve Contemporary Rites." In *Dance: Rituals of Experience.* Pennington, N.J.: Princeton Book Company, 1992. A look at Cunningham's contributions to the dance field through a critical analysis of his choreography. Includes an extensive description of Cunningham's work *Rainforest* (1968). Photographs, index, and limited bibliography. Highwater employs an interesting historical and cultural perspective throughout the book, although information on Cunningham's Events is limited.

McDonagh, Don. "Freedom and New Formalism." In *Complete Guide to Modern Dance.* New York: Doubleday, 1976. Encapsulation of Cunningham's work from 1942 to 1975. Includes complete descriptions of twelve of the choreographer's dances. Chronology of Cunningham's work is also included. McDonagh features a chronology of significant dates and events in modern dance development. Includes an annotated bibliography and an index.

Mazo, Joseph H. "Merce Cunningham." In *Prime Movers: The Makers of Modern Dance in America.* New York: William Morrow, 1977. An extensive chapter on Cunningham's choreographic process, including descriptive information on the Events. Mazo provides many quotes from Cunningham in his essay and also offers comments on Cunningham's work from other sources. Includes extensive annotated bibliography on modern dance, index.

Siegel, Marcia. "Crystallization II." In *The Shapes of Change.* Boston: Houghton Mifflin, 1979. A chronology of modern dance presented via the description of actual dances. Siegel includes extensive accounts of Cunningham's dances *Summerspace* (1958) and *Winterbranch*, which were used as material for some of the Events. The author provides discussion of Cunningham's use of chance operations. Photographs are limited, but the book includes a chronology of significant modern dance premieres, extensive notes, bibliography, and index.

_____. "Human Events." In *Watching the Dance Go By.* Boston: Houghton Mifflin, 1977. A definitive chapter that specifically addresses Cunningham's Events. Siegel includes vivid descriptions of two Events as performed at the Westbeth

Cunningham dance studio and the Brooklyn Academy of Music. Photographs and index.

John R. Crawford

Cross-References

Taylor Establishes His Own Dance Company (1954), p. 1602; Ailey Founds His Dance Company (1958), p. 1774; Tharp Stages *Deuce Coupe* for the Joffrey Ballet (1973), p. 2288; The New Dance U.S.A. Festival Celebrates Contemporary Dance (1981), p. 2480; Multiculturalism Dominates the Dance World (Late 1980's), p. 2559; Baryshnikov's White Oak Dance Project Debuts (1990), p. 2663.

PEYTON PLACE BRINGS SERIAL DRAMA TO NIGHTTIME TELEVISION

Category of event: Television and radio
Time: September 15, 1964-June 2, 1969
Locale: The United States

Peyton Place, *based on a best-selling novel of the same name, gained a large audience as the first hit television serial as it explored sex and personal intrigue in a New England town*

Principal personages:
MIA FARROW (1945-   ), the actress who played Allison Mackenzie on *Peyton Place*
RYAN O'NEAL (1941-   ), the actor who played Rodney Harrington on *Peyton Place* and who later became a leading man in Hollywood
DOROTHY MALONE (DOROTHY MALONEY, 1925-   ), the actress who played the mother of Allison Mackenzie
ADRIAN SAMISH (1920-   ), the director of *Peyton Place*, who defended the series against those who criticized both the artistic and the moral content of the show
PAUL MONASH (1921-   ), the executive producer of *Peyton Place*, who argued that the show was a production of high moral worth
GRACE METALIOUS (1924-1964), the author of the novel *Peyton Place*

Summary of Event

The television series *Peyton Place* was based on the 1956 Grace Metalious novel of the same name and was set in the New England town of Peyton Place. Eighteen years prior to the events portrayed on the television program, series character Constance Mackenzie, now owner of the Peyton Place Bookstore, had engaged in premarital sex. Allison Mackenzie was the child produced by that affair. Constance had always kept from Allison the truth about her conception but, in the series, Allison always appeared to be on the verge of discovering it. To complicate matters, the father turned up in Peyton Place after spending the last eighteen years in prison and, at about the same time, so did Dr. Michael Rossi, who witnessed the birth of Allison while still a medical student. Also in town was Rodney Harrington, son of a wealthy industrialist, who was tricked into marrying his supposedly pregnant girlfriend, Betty, even though he had already fallen in love with Allison. The cast included a number of other characters at any given time, and in any half-hour episode a dozen characters might appear in separate scenes.

The production crew of *Peyton Place* took pains to produce a lifelike, authentic set because they believed that the content of the show was lifelike. They often referred to Peyton Place as "a town of the mind." Although many critics called the series a soap opera, the production crew preferred the term "TV novel" because the characters grew as the episodes accumulated.

The show certainly was not realistic, even if individual elements were lifelike. The town of Peyton Place, as *The New York Times* observed, had "no Jews, no Negroes, no bigotry, no religious or political division." The problems in Peyton Place revolved around murder, adultery, premarital sex, dating, social status, and illegitimacy. These circumstances occurred in everyday life but not to the extent that they did in the lives of the characters on *Peyton Place.* Although it avoided many controversies, the show challenged accepted conventions. Sexual activity frequently was implied, and double entendre was used regularly. The action on the show was viewed by many people in the context of the popular novel from which the show took its name. The novel had been much more explicit in its sexuality. On the other hand, many conventions were respected. Villains were always punished, justice was always done, character was improved by adversity, and steady progress seemed to be made toward solving most problems.

Peyton Place used a serial format. At first broadcast twice a week, it moved to three nights a week beginning in June, 1965, before dropping back to two nights a week in September, 1966. This series format allowed the show to achieve realistic effects as the audience got to know the characters over a long period of time. The audience could gain an intimate connection with the characters via a shared history.

One of the most appealing characters was Allison Mackenzie, played by Mia Farrow, only nineteen years old when the show went on the air in 1964. Mia viewed her character as typifying a vulnerable part of every person. She played Allison as something of a wallflower.

Mia came to performing naturally. Her father, John, was a writer and film director, and her mother was Maureen O'Sullivan, an actress. Although Mia once considered becoming a nun, she gave up the idea when she secured her mother's aid in getting a part in an Off-Broadway production of *The Importance of Being Earnest.* She was with the touring company of that production when asked to take the role of Allison Mackenzie.

Variety magazine commented on her performance in the role by calling attention to her "pensive, soft quality," while director Adrian Samish called her "a female Billy Budd." Soon known to millions of viewers for her long, loose blonde hair as well as her acting skill, Mia became thoroughly identified with her character. Allison Mackenzie, however, was written out of the show by August, 1966.

Ryan O'Neal played the character of Rodney Harrington, son of a wealthy, lecherous industrialist. O'Neal's real-life family had moved around the United States, the Caribbean, and Europe, following the film industry. While Ryan was in high school, his family was in Germany. Rather than attend the rather strict U.S. Army School, Ryan wangled a job from Kirk Douglas Productions, which was making a series for German television. After returning to Hollywood, O'Neal got several bit parts on various television series and finally got his big chance when he was recommended for a role on *Empire* by Richard Egan, who starred in that Western series. As a result of his exposure on *Empire*, O'Neal was offered his *Peyton Place* role.

As Rodney Harrington, O'Neal was popular with the fans of the show. To satisfy their demands, he appeared in almost all of the 514 episodes filmed. This very demanding schedule was not appealing to O'Neal, who said, "the key to success on *Peyton Place* was to learn your lines quickly. We worked five days a week grinding out ninety minutes of TV each week."

Dorothy Malone received top billing on the show and proved to be popular with the public in her role as Constance Mackenzie. Malone was an experienced Hollywood actress who had won an Oscar as Best Supporting Actress in *Written on the Wind* (1956).

The continuing saga of Peyton Place and its citizens became regular multiweekly fare for up to sixty million viewers. In February, 1969, the show began airing only once a week, and the last episode was broadcast on June 2, 1969. The show was revived as a daytime serial from 1972 to 1974.

Impact of Event

Peyton Place made a distinct impact on the television industry. It claims the distinction of introducing the soap opera, or continuing melodramatic serial, to nighttime television. Although there had been other shows that revolved around a continuing cast of characters, this was the first to have a continuing story line that dealt with adult situations. The format caught on quickly with the viewing public.

During the 1964-1965 television season, *Peyton Place* was broadcast twice a week. The episodes always rated in the top twenty shows for popularity on their respective nights. When the show was broadcast three times a week, beginning in June, 1965, it met with equal success. The ability of the show to make such an impact was enhanced by the popularity of the novel on which it was based. The novel had also been made into a successful film in 1957.

Despite this preparation, some executives at the American Broadcasting Company (ABC) feared that the traditional soap-opera genre, though it had been a staple of radio and daytime television, would not translate well to nighttime television. The scriptwriters for *Peyton Place* took care to see that it succeeded. Although it brought to prime time all the twists of plot and steamy romance previously played out on daytime soap operas, the action was speeded up. Unlike the older soap operas, in which nothing ever happened quickly, *Peyton Place* had subplots that developed rapidly. This approach attracted an average of sixty million viewers to each episode, according to the Nielsen ratings.

With ABC making a success of *Peyton Place*, the Columbia Broadcasting System (CBS) and the National Broadcasting Company (NBC) were quick to follow suit. CBS planned to bring a spin-off from its successful daytime soap opera *As the World Turns* to a nighttime slot. NBC converted its popular *Dr. Kildare* show, which went on the air on September 28, 1961, to a serial format. Not resting on its laurels, ABC planned *The Girl from Peyton Place* as a spin-off to fill yet more evenings but later dropped the plans.

Members of the ABC production crew all agreed that *Peyton Place* was a radical departure for television. As to whether that departure was desirable, there was disagreement. The National Association for Better Radio and Television said, "*Peyton Place* is an obvious exploitation of the sordid and tasteless elements of Grace Metalious' novel, and a monument to ABC's search for ratings, regardless of the social impact of unrelieved sex and sin." At any rate, *Peyton Place* ran for five seasons and left the air only to return as a daytime soap opera that ran for two and one-half years on NBC. During the last two years of its daytime run, *Peyton Place* had a difficult time maintaining an audience.

Peyton Place also had an impact on some of its performers. Whether on radio or daytime television, soap operas have provided a good showcase for talent. Relative newcomers introduced to television by *Peyton Place* included Mia Farrow, Ryan O'Neal, Christopher Conelly, Barbara Parkins, and Mariette Hartley. Mia Farrow progressed to a film career, featuring most prominently in films by Woody Allen including *Another Woman* (1988), *Broadway Danny Rose* (1984), *Hannah and Her Sisters* (1986), *Radio Days* (1987), and *The Purple Rose of Cairo* (1985). She also starred in *Rosemary's Baby* (1968) and *Secret Ceremony* (1968). Ryan O'Neal became a leading man, starring in *Love Story* (1970) and its sequel *Oliver's Story* (1978), *Paper Moon* (1973), and *What's Up, Doc?* (1972), among many others.

Perhaps the most important impact of *Peyton Place* was on the content of television shows generally. ABC had been on the bottom in ratings when it began implementing a strategy of including greater sexual content in its shows. Critics called *Peyton Place* "a sex comic strip" and "a happy combination of sex, sin, and soap." The producers of *Peyton Place* believed the show to be maligned by these characterizations. Instead of sex, they thought the show portrayed realism, truthfulness, and moral enlightenment. Executive producer Paul Monash said *Peyton Place* was "a cautionary tale with a high moral intention." Director Adrian Samish commented, "We are in the business of gathering the largest audience we can. We don't seek the freedom of drama. . . . I feel we have all the freedom I want."

Without a doubt, the novel *Peyton Place* used the greater freedom usually accorded to print, as compared with television, to be much more graphic in its sexual content, though it was relatively mild by the standards of later decades. By the standards of the 1970's and 1980's, *Peyton Place* was far from a "sex comic strip."

Paul Monash, who also wrote novels and teleplays, evaluated the difference between the television show and the novel this way: "The novel is a negativistic attack on the town written by someone who knew it well and hated it. The TV series is a love affair with the town." He went on to say that *Peyton Place* was a moral show, although the moral guidelines were self-imposed. Monash saw the success of the program not in titillating the viewer but in offering a cast that the audience basically liked as people.

This may have been true, but the show did break new ground in program content. Prior to *Peyton Place*, there were few even veiled hints about sex and sexuality on television. Married couples were shown in twin beds and, even then, men's pajamas were buttoned at the neck. Teenage and premarital sex most often progressed no further than a good-night kiss at the front door with the porch light on. The public was already reading descriptions of sexuality that were much more graphic, and the theater was much more open about the subject. It was only a question of time until the changing public taste and demand created a television show that reflected these changes. *Peyton Place* was the show that opened the gate for this change. By the 1980's, such nighttime dramas as *Dallas* and *Dynasty* were on the air with far more scandalous subject matter.

Bibliography

Buckman, Peter. *All for Love: A Study in Soap Opera.* Salem, N.H.: Salem House, 1984. Soap opera is the most popular of all television genres, yet it is often derided by critics, so some fans feel ashamed of enjoying it. This book tells what is right about soap opera.

Cassata, Mary, and Thomas Skill. *Life on Daytime Television: Tuning-in American Serial Drama.* Norwood, N.J.: Ablex Publishing, 1983. Although the title mentions daytime programming, the material in the book applies to all serial dramas on television. There is a good discussion of how serial dramas set and maintain a mood.

Gitlin, Todd. *Inside Prime Time.* New York: Pantheon Books, 1983. An analysis of how television functions, through power plays made by small groups of top executives, writers, producers, and agents. Gitlin looks at what makes good shows good and why some catch on while others fail.

Goldstein, Fred, and Stan Goldstein. *Prime-Time Television.* New York: Crown, 1983. Combines text and pictures to present a vivid history of television from 1948 to 1983. Almost every program or series on the air for at least one season is included in this comprehensive work.

O'Connor, John E. *American History, American Television.* New York: Frederick Ungar, 1983. Television is presented here both as a force in recent social history and as a matter to be studied. This collection of essays came out of Columbia University's Seminar on Cinema, but they all relate to television. This book deals with a wide range of topics.

Rose, Brian G., ed. *TV Genres: A Handbook and Reference Guide.* Westport, Conn.: Greenwood Press, 1985. Attempts to explain to viewers how and why television shows fall into a limited number of formats. The cross-fertilizing of formats, or genres, is discussed. Genres from police shows to church services are discussed.

Michael R. Bradley

Cross-References

Situation Comedies Dominate Television Programming (1960's), p. 1835; *The Dick Van Dyke Show* Popularizes Situation Comedy (1961), p. 1908; *The Forsyte Saga* Is a Hit on Public Television (1969), p. 2168; *Dallas* Popularizes the Prime-Time Soap Opera (1978), p. 2418; *Hill Street Blues* Defines Hard-Reality Television (1981), p. 2470.

THE AUTOBIOGRAPHY OF MALCOLM X IS PUBLISHED

Category of event: Literature
Time: 1965
Locale: New York, New York

The Autobiography of Malcolm X *provided for the American white majority world a revealing version of life in black ghettos and the attraction of the racially exclusive Nation of Islam for African Americans*

> *Principal personages:*
> MALCOLM X (MALCOLM LITTLE, 1925-1965), a leader of the Nation of Islam who split from the group
> ELIJAH MUHAMMAD (ELIJAH POOLE, 1897-1975), the founder of the Nation of Islam, or Black Muslim, movement
> MARCUS GARVEY (1877-1940), the founder of the Universal Negro Improvement Association, a model for later Black Power movements
> ALEX HALEY (1921-1992), the author who collaborated with Malcolm X in composing the latter's autobiography
> BETTY SHABAZZ (1935?-   ), the widow of Malcolm X, active in the organization of the women's branch of the Nation of Islam

Summary of Event

Malcolm Little, better known by his adopted name of Malcolm X, published his autobiography in 1965, shortly after leaving the Black Muslim movement and scarcely a year before he was assassinated in the Audubon Ballroom in Harlem in 1965. The cultural and political significance of this autobiography by one of the most controversial leaders of the Civil Rights movement in the United States should be approached from several perspectives. In the immediate context of the Civil Rights movement of the mid-1960's, Malcolm X's account of the various stages of his life was quite significant. This was true because his autobiography represented personal insights into different aspects of black life in the United States that many Americans knew something about but could not picture accurately in their minds in relation to their own experience.

One very important aspect of his book was Malcolm X's description of the family life of African Americans. His family, like so many of their generation, had left the traditional rural setting of the southern United States to implant themselves in the very different environment of the northern states, first in Omaha, Nebraska, then in Milwaukee, Wisconsin, and Lansing, Michigan. The autobiography depicted elements of racism in small towns, ranging from patronizing social discrimination expressed through social services and foster-home arrangements to out and out violence in the activities of the Ku Klux Klan. Not only was Malcolm X's boyhood marked by firsthand witnessing of white-inspired racial violence, but it also exposed him to black-run movements that the average American had never before seen described with precise and personal details. A case in point was Malcolm's description of the Garveyists, who were the earliest movement to try to declare, in a very limited context, the superiority of black culture.

A second aspect of Malcolm X's autobiography that spelled out details of a milieu that many who lived in typical America could not have imagined came in the opening pages, in which he described his involvement as a young adult in the fast life of urban Boston and New York. Various forms of racial interaction, ranging from the "dance scene" and "zoot suits" of the early 1950's to the sleaziness of prostitution, drug trafficking, and robberies, were all parts of Malcolm Little's experiences until his criminal conviction and imprisonment. These sorts of interactions gave personal meaning to life-styles that affected hundreds of thousands of African Americans on a daily basis. Malcolm X's autobiography made it clear that many of them were unwilling to go on accepting such stereotypes as the 1960's progressed.

Without a doubt, however, it was Malcolm X's revelations concerning his exposure to the Black Muslim movement that sent shock waves across the United States when his autobiography appeared. His descriptions of the basic beliefs of the Nation of Islam as expounded by its original leader and prophet, Elijah Muhammad, opened a hitherto unknown world to readers of *The Autobiography of Malcolm X*. Few had realized that, for Black Muslims, white people were viewed as a satanic force whose influence was to be rejected vigorously by the Nation of Islam. Beyond the complexity of the adopted beliefs of the Nation of Islam, readers of Malcolm X's autobiography learned of the actual practical organization of the movement, including its almost puritanical elite units, the "Fruit of Islam." These groupings had been visible near Nation of Islam mosques and in the streets of large American cities, but until Malcolm X's book, few had any understanding of their rigorous code of ethics.

Something similar could be said for Malcolm's explanation of the place of women in the community of Black Muslims. His emphasis was on their extreme pride in propriety of appearance and behavior. This code was meant to belie widespread popular images of the depravity of ghetto existence in the 1960's.

Malcolm X's ultimate message concerning race relations, however, would turn away from the exclusivism of the mainly American-based Nation of Islam movement and call for a much wider view of the problems of injustice in the United States and in other areas of the world. He came to espouse, for example, what he believed were the universal principles of brotherhood contained in orthodox Islam, which rejected race as a form of identity in favor of an ideology calling for human justice in all societies and among all races. At the time of its publication, the autobiography thus became something more than an exposé of the American Black Nationalist movement: It was a personal witnessing by a black militant of the tenets of universal faith to which he, at least, attributed the potential to resolve the increasingly divisive struggle for civil rights all over the world. Possibly because his autobiography ended with a disavowal of the Black Power movement that was then gaining momentum, both in the Nation of Islam and in more radical violence-oriented groups such as the Black Panthers, he fell to assassins' bullets fired by rival African Americans.

Impact of Event

Whatever readers throughout the world may have learned from the diverse contents of Malcolm X's autobiography, whether these concerned "inside details" of black ghetto existence, the inequities of open or latent racism, or the declared principles behind the Nation of Islam movement, the book symbolized the unresolved dilemma which his career seemed to represent. Stated succinctly, the question remained: Which way should the Civil Rights movement turn?

Only months before Malcolm X's assassination, black leaders associated with the nonviolent Civil Rights movement, most prominently Martin Luther King, Jr., of the Southern Christian Leadership Conference, had riveted the attention of the world on their determined efforts to exercise the civil rights of thousands of civil rights demonstrators on a march between Selma and Montgomery, Alabama. Malcolm X, then still a fervent believer in the Nation of Islam, withheld his support from such movements, which were perceived to be a form of begging for the white majority's defense of minority rights. Instead, at that time Malcolm X preferred to support what he considered to be the courage of a different sort of champion of black rights, represented by the heavyweight boxing champion Cassius Clay. Clay, who had taken on the name Muhammad Ali when he joined the Nation of Islam, drew attention to the strength of conscious, but still pacifist, civil disobedience when he refused to be inducted into the armed forces as a statement of his opposition to United States interventionist policy in Vietnam.

Malcolm X's declared militancy on the issue of active application of black rights raised the question of appropriate boundaries and ethical as well as legal legitimacy. Before his "conversion" from the Black Muslims, he would have argued that black ethics existed as part of the identity of black people; no reference to a more universalist source of justice was necessary. In fact, what was not part of the Nation of Islam was by definition unjust through its suppression of black identity. The concept of "enemy" loomed large.

By his espousal of more universalist concepts of ethics in the orthodox Islamic religion, Malcolm's impact on the late 1960's and the decades that would follow cannot be said to have been clear. To the degree that African Americans chose to disavow the narrowness of Nation of Islam definitions and to search beyond extremist stands for more universal perceptions, his impact has had two sides to it: clarification of the true nature of Islam and increasing disinclination to couch all racial justice questions in terms of "us against them."

There seems, therefore, to have been several longer-term results that stemmed from Malcolm X's unique involvement in the Civil Rights movement. His autobiography opened a new, necessarily disconcerting world for the majority of Americans who had very little inkling of what black culture signified to those who lived it. This world contained both positive and negative features, although the latter tended to outweigh the former. Rejection of continuation of the status quo of racism assumed that these negative factors had to be eradicated, but few knew how to proceed.

Because the last stages of Malcolm X's career opened him to a philosophy that was based more on universal concepts of justice for oppressed peoples than on specific theories of racial inequities, there was some hope that there might be a gathering together of at least some of the many militant movements of the mid-1960's around a single positive social reform theme. The major drawback that promised to complicate such a drawing together was connected to the fact that Malcolm X's revised views reflected a clear association with the Islamic religion. Even though his eventual views espoused an Islam that was a reflection of a principal world religion, not a "devised" faith along the lines of the Nation of Islam movement, they were nevertheless religious views. This had two repercussions for those who might have considered, if he had lived, recognition of his leadership within a circle of civil rights movements and activist political reform groups.

On the black side, there definitely remained a strong insistence, at least among the more radical groups, on Black Power, which depended on a continuing exclusivist and confrontational perception of social justice. These African Americans would have rejected Malcolm X's last messages on racial bases. On the other hand, less racially radical, integrationist movements such as the Southern Christian Leadership Conference very obviously depended on their identification with specifically Christian religious principles as the basis of their racial reform policies. Here, Malcolm X's specific identification with Islam would have prevented, at least in the short run, a coming together of such integrationist groups around altered philosophical and religious principles.

Finally, one must consider that another aspect of Malcolm X's controversial position by 1965 would surge to the forefront in the year of his death and become, for the next five years at least, the overwhelming focal point of American political activists' efforts. That was the question of American involvement in Vietnam, which became a catalyst for racial and political ferment. Although it took Malcolm X's messages into consideration, activism tended to rush into a number of different ideological and organizational directions. His message and his ideals remained part of American culture, however, as exemplified by the positive response to Spike Lee's 1992 film *Malcolm X* and by the fact that such a film even was made.

Bibliography

Clark, Kenneth B. *The Negro Protest.* Boston: Beacon Press, 1963. This book consists of three sets of interviews with prominent black spokesmen of the period: James Baldwin, Malcolm X, and Martin Luther King, Jr.

Clarke, John Henrik, ed. *Malcolm X: The Man and His Times.* New York: Macmillan, 1969. This volume contains a wide range of contributions by persons who either knew Malcolm X or knew a great deal about him because of their association with the Civil Rights movement. It also contains some original speeches delivered by Malcolm X at various stages in his activist career.

Cronon, Edmund David. *Black Moses.* Madison: University of Wisconsin Press, 1969. An authoritative history of the career of Marcus Garvey, founder of the Universal

Negro Improvement Association (UNIA). Malcolm Little's father was involved in the ideas of the UNIA, and its principles of self-help and pride in African heritage were an inspiration for the Nation of Islam movement.

Goldman, Peter. *The Death and Life of Malcolm X.* New York: Harper & Row, 1973. This book deals primarily with the later stages of Malcolm X's life and the circumstances that led to his assassination. Although it focuses on Malcolm's "conversion" away from the Black Muslim movement and therefore is a complement to his own autobiographical reflections, it provides considerable insight into the ideas and attitudes of a number of different civil rights associations and analyzes their differences in light of what Malcolm X represented.

Warren, Robert Penn. *Who Speaks for the Negro?* New York: Random House, 1965. Underlines the diversity of leadership options faced by the militant black nationalist and more moderate integrationist movements.

Byron D. Cannon

Cross-References

The Harlem Renaissance Celebrates African-American Culture (1920's), p. 480; Wright's *Native Son* Depicts Racism in America (1940), p. 1185; Hansberry's *A Raisin in the Sun* Debuts on Broadway (1959), p. 1795; Baldwin Voices Black Rage in *The Fire Next Time* (1963), p. 1929; Baraka's *Dutchman* Dramatizes Racial Hatred (1964), p. 2000; *Do the Right Thing* Establishes Lee as a World-Class Director (1989), p. 2641.

THE ROLLING STONES RELEASE *OUT OF OUR HEADS*

Category of event: Music
Time: 1965
Locale: Great Britain and the United States

Out of Our Heads' *blend of cover versions and original songs both extended the Rolling Stones' reputation as traditionalists and established them as innovative writers, introducing new sounds and themes to rock*

Principal personages:
MICK JAGGER (1943-   ), the lead singer, harmonica player, and lyricist for the band
KEITH RICHARDS (1943-   ), a guitarist, backup vocalist, and cowriter of the band's original material
BRIAN JONES (1942-1969), a talented arranger and multi-instrumentalist who played guitar, harmonica, and keyboards on the album
CHARLIE WATTS (1941-   ), the band's drummer and percussionist
BILL WYMAN (1936-   ), the band's bass guitarist
ANDREW LOOG OLDHAM (1944-   ), the band's manager and record producer

Summary of Event

By 1965, the Rolling Stones had established themselves as an inventive cover band, introducing the music of black American blues and soul artists to a largely white international audience. *Out of Our Heads*, their fourth American album (their third English studio album), marked the transition of the group from interpreters and popularizers of other music to creators of their own, with five cover versions and seven original songs (three written under the band's collective pseudonym, "Nanker Phelge") on the album. Their next English release, *Aftermath* (1966; two compilations of assorted old and new material were released between the two albums in America), would consist entirely of original material written by Jagger and Richards. *Out of Our Heads'* punning title suggests that the band was entirely conscious of the change in direction. The title phrase suggests first the unpolished, high-energy sound that had come to characterize their early cover versions of songs and made of them not imitations but interpretations, frequently surpassing the original versions. The title also suggests that most of the material on the album was their own, created out of their own heads.

Side 1 of the album repeated the successful formula of their earlier records, with four covers of rhythm-and-blues songs: Don Covay's "Mercy Mercy," Marvin Gaye's "Hitch Hike," Otis Redding's "That's How Strong My Love Is," and Sam Cooke's "Good Times." The first two represented the Rolling Stones' talent as cover artists particularly well, constituting creative reworkings rather than mere covers. The side also featured two original compositions: "I'm All Right" was basically a throwaway, a live track meant to illustrate the band's rough and energetic performance style and highlight the screaming of the crowd, but "The Last Time," recorded in Los Angeles on January 17, 1965, was one of Jagger and Richards' best early songs. With "Play with Fire," another original song from the same recording session, as the B side, "The Last Time" was released as a single in February. It quickly went gold, selling more than a million copies worldwide and making it to number eight on *Billboard*'s pop chart by March 8; the record was the band's biggest hit to date. It also marked the first time that one of their own compositions had appeared as the A side of a single in England, another sign of the trend away from covers toward original material.

While the record's first side looked back to the band's earlier albums and built on their reputation as a cover band with blues and soul roots, side 2 looked ahead to their future as musical innovators. There was still one cover, a version of Solomon Burke's "Cry to Me." While Burke had had a mild hit with his own version, it had not crossed over to the pop charts, and it was the Rolling Stones' cover that made his music accessible to a large white audience. The other five songs were originals, the most the band had ever included on an album side; the most important was the song that opened the side and became the album's second single, "(I Can't Get No) Satisfaction." The song was written during the band's third American concert tour, which began on April 29. Richards came up with the basic musical riff on May 6, Jagger wrote the lyrics within a day or two, and they made an attempt at recording it on May 10 and 11 in Chicago's Chess Studios, where many of the classic blues artists they had been covering had recorded their own material. The band did get three other songs for the album finished at Chess ("Mercy Mercy," "That's How Strong My Love Is," and "The Under Assistant West Coast Promotion Man"), but the last five cuts for the album, including the final version of "(I Can't Get No) Satisfaction," were recorded May 12 and 13 at RCA Studios in Hollywood.

The band had originally recorded the song with acoustic guitar and harmonica, almost as a folk song, but Richards changed the song entirely by switching to an electric guitar, with electronic distortion provided by the newly developed Gibson "fuzz-box." The fuzz-guitar sound served the same function as had the horn sections that the band's rhythm-and-blues and soul influences had long been using on their Motown and Stax recordings, providing sustain and density and making the lead guitar the central component of the rhythm section. It seems likely that Richards had developed this guitar technique through his efforts to reproduce the horn textures on some of the material the band had been covering, and the guitar arrangement on "Mercy Mercy," clearly meant to fill the role played by horns on the original, bears a strong resemblance to the famous "(I Can't Get No) Satisfaction" riff. The vocals were buried under the instruments in the mix, making the lyrics hard to decipher, perhaps partly because of fears that censorship would hurt radio play. In 1965, the line "I'm trying to make some girl" would have offended many listeners, and numerous supposed allusions to sex and drugs have been read between the lines since the song's release.

On June 4, "(I Can't Get No) Satisfaction" entered *Billboard*'s top one hundred at number sixty-four; within two weeks, it had jumped to fourth, and the next week it went to number one, where it stayed until July 31. Their first number-one hit in the enormous American market, "(I Can't Get No) Satisfaction" established the Rolling Stones not only artistically but also financially. Ironically, Jagger and Richards, who had written the song, originally thought that it would make a strong album cut or B side but did not have hit potential. Fortunately for their careers, the band's other members and manager Andrew Loog Oldham outvoted them. The band's contract with Decca Records had expired in February, and the leverage of the hit single allowed their new business manager, Allen Klein, and Oldham to negotiate a lucrative long-term contract. While their first three albums had fared relatively poorly in America, the American release of *Out of Our Heads* in July was an immediate success, and the album quickly went gold.

Impact of Event

The evolution of the Rolling Stones from a resourceful cover band to important original songwriters in *Out of Our Heads* had a decisive impact on a generation of younger rock musicians and on the musical tastes of the popular audience. The Rolling Stones had begun by playing the music of black artists who had often been unable to cross over to be successful on the popular music charts; in fact, the band had come under occasional criticism that they were exploiting their sources. As Jagger pointed out in refutation, they had enabled those same black artists to cross over effectively by introducing them to a mass audience, in effect repaying the debt of influence. Perhaps the most striking immediate examples of this reversal of influence were the covers of "(I Can't Get No) Satisfaction" by soul artists. On *Out of Our Heads*, the Rolling Stones had covered two songs Otis Redding had recorded; a year later, Redding proved the viability of the band's own fusion of soul and rock by reaching the charts with his own version of "(I Can't Get No) Satisfaction," which Aretha Franklin also successfully covered. The Rolling Stones' success in creating mainstream acceptance of traditionally black music paved the way for other blues-based groups, notably the Doors, Cream, and, later, Led Zeppelin, and for innovative black artists such as Jimi Hendrix, who found his mass audience in white rock-and-roll fans.

The band's debt to blues and rhythm-and-blues music can easily be exaggerated, of course, and the album's innovative elements were probably as influential as its roots in traditional forms. While much of the album is conservative musically, it broke with convention lyrically. The narrator of the covered songs is always a suitor, either serious, pleading with his romantic interest to have mercy on him ("Mercy Mercy") and emphasizing his sincerity and depth of feeling for her ("That's How Strong My Love Is," "Cry to Me"), or else with self-deprecating humor recounting his many difficulties in pursuing the elusive, and perhaps not overly interested, woman of his dreams ("Hitch Hike").

The persona developed on the original songs is diametrically different, and the Rolling Stones reshaped the rock-and-roll love song into something less sentimental. "The Last Time" and "Play with Fire" are both warnings to a woman that the relationship with the singer will proceed on his terms or not at all, and "The Spider and the Fly" narrates a pseudoautobiographical tale of casual sex on the road. The male protagonist has the upper hand over the female addressed, and the songs have gone from pleas to threats, from submission to dominance. The undercurrent of misogyny implicit here seems obvious in retrospect, and it would become more evident in such later songs as "Stupid Girl" and "Under My Thumb," but the antifeminine stance attracted very little attention at the time. Instead, the attitude of defiance and independence was what struck contemporary audiences. The rebellious persona took on more generalized targets in "(I Can't Get No) Satisfaction," which railed against the vapidity of consumer society, and this vein of political protest would be more fully developed and explored in such subsequent songs as "Street Fighting Man" and "Sympathy for the Devil," which became activist anthems in the latter part of the 1960's. A version of this aggressively antisocial image would later prove potent for the Sex Pistols and other punk-rock bands.

Out of Our Heads was also an early example of the integrated "concept album," unified by sound, style, and theme and meant to be played as an album rather than as a collection of unrelated singles. In America particularly, the trend had been to buy albums merely to hear the singles, and the bulk of a typical album would be little more than cover versions put in as filler. The cover versions of soul songs in *Out of Our Heads*, however, were integral to the album and in fact provided the context within which the new sound of "(I Can't Get No) Satisfaction," described as "blues words with a soul sound in a rock song," could be fully understood and appreciated. Eight of the album's twelve cuts were recorded in a four-day period, which contributed further to the unity of effect. Some early reviews missed this point, finding the overall sound "samey" rather than focused, but the trend toward album-oriented radio play and record sales continued throughout the next decade, confirming the wisdom of the band's decision to forge a distinctive musical identity rather than search for variety or follow trends. These early concept albums would lead to such tightly unified works as the Beatles' *Sgt. Pepper's Lonely Hearts Club Band* (1967) and Van Morrison's *Astral Weeks* (1968) and eventually to the genre of the "rock opera," typified by the Who's *Tommy* (1968).

Out of Our Heads, in retrospect, established the Rolling Stones as one of the seminal influences on the course of rock music. Just as Bob Dylan had broadened and deepened rock music by bringing folk music and more introspective lyrics within its range, and the Beatles had created a distinctive rock version of contemporary pop music, the Rolling Stones were the most important group working to incorporate blues and soul music into the rock mainstream. The success of these early innovators in establishing the broadest possible definition of rock music has been undoubtedly one of the major reasons for the genre's longevity and popularity.

Bibliography

Dalton, David. *The Rolling Stones: The First Twenty Years.* New York: Alfred A. Knopf, 1981. In an indispensable book on the subject, Dalton has attempted to pinpoint the activities and whereabouts of the Rolling Stones virtually day by day from 1962 to 1981 by assembling and excerpting thousands of newspaper and periodical accounts in chronological order. He provides relatively little commentary and interpretation, preferring to present the evidence for the reader's own consideration, and the result is a virtually inexhaustible storehouse of interesting contemporary material, providing more information and a fuller picture of the times than any other source. An oversized book with some three hundred photographs. Contains a valuable "Sessionography" that documents all of the Rolling Stones' work in the recording studio.

Herbst, Peter, ed. *The Rolling Stone Interviews: Talking with the Legends of Rock and Roll, 1967-1980.* New York: Rolling Stone Press, 1981. Contains two interviews with Mick Jagger (1968, 1978) and one with Keith Richards (1971). The two earlier interviews include extended discussions of the band's early musical influences from blues and soul music, give biographical information on the period of *Out of Our Heads,* and detail the circumstances of the writing of "(I Can't Get No) Satisfaction." Photographs.

Palmer, Robert. *The Rolling Stones.* Garden City, N.Y.: Doubleday, 1983. An oversized book featuring more than 160 photographs, including a photograph of Jagger and Richards in the studio working on "(I Can't Get No) Satisfaction" and an outtake from the photo session that produced the cover for *Out of Our Heads.* Contains informative biographical and critical commentary, quotations from song lyrics, and selective bibliography and discography.

Ward, Ed, Geoffrey Stokes, and Ken Tucker. *Rock of Ages: The Rolling Stone History of Rock and Roll.* New York: Rolling Stone Press, 1986. Contains a total of some fifty pages concerning the career of the Rolling Stones through the middle 1980's; although the material is spread throughout the book, which is written in chronological order, the index is relatively (though not completely) accurate, and the chronological format functions to provide valuable context for the material on the Rolling Stones. Brief but informative discussion of "(I Can't Get No) Satisfaction" and *Out of Our Heads.* Photographs.

Wyman, Bill, with Ray Coleman. *Stone Alone: The Story of a Rock 'n' Roll Band.* New York: Viking, 1990. A loosely chronological history of the group by the band's bass player. More space is given to personalities and gossip than to the music, but the book still presents worthwhile inside information. The various appendices are extremely valuable and include copies of the original contracts signed with Klein in 1965 and lists of recordings, concerts, and media appearances through 1969. Several good photographs, inadequate index.

William Nelles

Cross-References

Berry's "Maybellene" Popularizes Rock and Roll (1955), p. 1635; Presley Becomes a Rock-and-Roll Sensation (1956), p. 1705; The Beatles Revolutionize Popular Music (1963), p. 1944; Brown Wins a Grammy for "Papa's Got a Brand New Bag" (1966), p. 2059; Hendrix Releases *Are You Experienced?* (1967), p. 2092; The Beatles Release *Sgt. Pepper's Lonely Hearts Club Band* (1967), p. 2098; The Monterey Pop Festival Inaugurates the "Summer of Love" (1967), p. 2104; The Woodstock Music Festival Marks the Climax of the 1960's (1969), p. 2180; Led Zeppelin Merges Hard Rock and Folk Music (1971), p. 2228; The Sex Pistols Spark Punk Rock's Musical Insurrection (1975), p. 2360.

THE SOUND OF MUSIC CAPTIVATES AUDIENCES

Category of event: Motion pictures
Time: 1965
Locale: The United States

Despite hostile film critics, The Sound of Music, *adapted from the stage musical and starring Julie Andrews, became the biggest box-office draw in film history*

Principal personages:
ROBERT WISE (1914-   ), the codirector of *West Side Story,* who replaced William Wyler as director of *The Sound of Music*
JULIE ANDREWS (JULIA ELIZABETH WELLES, 1935-   ), the actress who played the role of Maria, the postulant nun
CHRISTOPHER PLUMMER (1927-   ), the actor who played the role of the widower Baron Von Trapp
ELEANOR PARKER (1922-   ), an actress who, as the Austrian baroness, is Andrews' rival for Baron Von Trapp's affection
ERNEST LEHMAN (1920-   ), a veteran screenwriter who adapted the Richard Rodgers and Oscar Hammerstein II stage musical for film

Summary of Event

The phenomenal box-office success of *The Sound of Music* (1965), which replaced *Gone with the Wind* (1939) as the highest-grossing film of all time, resulted in large part from the casting of Julie Andrews as Maria, a postulant nun who leaves the convent to marry Baron Von Trapp. Andrews, who had won an Academy Award for her performance in the title role in *Mary Poppins* (1964), was again playing nanny to children who needed her love. In fact, Andrews was selected by William Wyler, who was originally slated to produce and direct the film and who was replaced by Robert Wise when Wyler asked for a release from his contract in order to direct *The Collector* (1965). Since Wyler had had reservations about the Richard Rodgers and Oscar Hammerstein II stage play's upbeat portrait of the 1930's as the "Golden Years" in Austria, Wise's selection as producer and director also contributed to the film's success. Fresh from his triumph in *West Side Story* (1961), for which he won an Oscar, Wise was an accomplished director with an excellent track record in film musicals.

The film was adapted from the last collaboration of Rodgers and Hammerstein, who did the score for the musical at the urging of actress Mary Martin, who had seen a German film about the Von Trapp family and who secured the necessary permission from the family members. Martin, who appeared as Maria, was rewarded for her vision when the musical succeeded not only financially but also critically, winning five Tony Awards. Twentieth Century-Fox bought the film rights, named Wyler to produce and direct, and contracted Ernest Lehman to write the screenplay. Although some songs were omitted and some added, the score remained largely the same. Lehman's major changes were in opening up the script to take advantage of the mountainous scenery around Salzburg and in eliminating the political conflict between Baron Von Trapp and Elsa Schraeder (the baroness in the film), Maria's rival for Von Trapp's affections.

As in *West Side Story*, Wise opened *The Sound of Music* with a helicopter shot, one of Maria singing and dancing in the Bavarian Alps. Because of her exuberance, she is not wholly compatible with life in the convent and leaves to become governess to the seven children of widower Baron Von Trapp, who whistles his children to attention, denies them music and beauty, and insists on discipline. The Von Trapp children do not play; they march. Under Maria's tutelage, they play, sing, and enjoy nature (as in the song "These Are a Few of My Favorite Things"). The rigid baron sends Maria back to the convent when Maria tells him that the children's uniforms are really straitjackets. In her absence, the baroness, who hopes to marry Von Trapp, attempts to win the children's affections but is unsuccessful. They visit the convent, and Maria soon returns to the Von Trapp household at the baron's urging because he realizes how important it was that she brought music back to his house.

Like most musicals, *The Sound of Music* concerns a conflict: the forces of music, dance, and life versus those of silence, rigidity, and death (or at least emotional numbness and sterility). Maria's mission is to encourage the baron to sing, dance, and enjoy life, things he had done before his wife died. When the baroness realizes that Maria has liberated Von Trapp, she retreats. Nazi Party influence continues to grow in Austria, however, and the earlier conflict is mirrored in one, again involving Von Trapp, concerning conformity and Nazi repression in opposition to freedom and Austrian patriotism. When Maria and Von Trapp return from their honeymoon, the conflict comes to a head as Von Trapp is ordered to assume command in the "new order."

Max Detweiler (Richard Haydn), the family's friend and an enterprising impresario charged with assembling a festival performance for the Nazis, provides the means by which the political and musical conflicts are resolved. Detweiler enables the aristocratic Von Trapp, who initially adamantly opposed his family's performing in public, to use the concert as a cover for their escape from Salzburg over the mountains to neutral Switzerland and safety. The only obstacle to their safe flight is Kurt (Duane Chase), the telegraph boy turned Nazi who is the admirer of young Liesl Von Trapp (Charmain Carr). He discovers the family's plan and informs on them despite his interest in Liesl. The family escapes nevertheless, and the film closes with a shot of the Von Trapps hiking through the Alps.

Despite the efforts of Wise and Andrews to "desweeten" the story, it has been the target of critics, both film and social, who have perceived a saccharine quality. The muted political message (especially in light of the Holocaust), the spectacular scenery, and the domestic and religious themes drew fire from critics but delighted filmgoers looking for the storybook world the film projects. Although the 1930's may not have been the "Golden Years" of Austria, it was a period before the horrors of the Third Reich were known to the world. The film does, especially in the character of Detweiler, present the dangers of accommodation and compromise. Although he sarcastically smells his hand after a "Heil, Hitler" salute, he does believe in survival. The treatment of the patriotic Austrian audience's response to the Von Trapp nationalism is more problematic, for the cheering audience is paradoxically also the audience that embraced the Nazi movement.

Impact of Event

Although *The Sound of Music* confirmed Julie Andrews as a major star following her Oscar-winning performance in *Mary Poppins*, it also resulted in her being typecast as a wholesome, pure heroine, exactly the antithesis of what film audiences wanted as societal disillusionment grew in the late 1960's and 1970's. Despite the popularity of *The Sound of Music* and its success at the Oscar ceremonies (it won five awards, including Best Picture), the Best Actress award for the year went to the more sophisticated Julie Christie, who starred in *Darling* (1965). Andrews starred in several more musicals (notably *Thoroughly Modern Millie*, 1967; *Star!*, 1968; and *Darling Lili*, 1970), but she never repeated her success in *The Sound of Music*. Despite the efforts of her husband, Blake Edwards, a successful producer and director, to find a more contemporary role for her talents, she did not, with the exception of *Victor/Victoria* (1982), appear in any significant films.

The impact of *The Sound of Music* on the careers of Robert Wise and Ernest Lehman was also negligible, except that the financial success of the film gave Wise considerable influence in Hollywood, especially since it so closely followed the popularity of *West Side Story.* Wise's next musical, *Star!*, also starring Andrews, was not as fortunate, and he turned his talents to science fiction (*The Andromeda Strain*, 1971, and *Star Trek: The Motion Picture*, 1979) and adventure films such as *The Sand Pebbles* (1966). Like Andrews, Wise was raised to the pinnacle of success by *The Sound of Music*, but he too could not sustain either his popularity or his performance. For Lehman, *The Sound of Music* was one in a string of hits dating back to *Executive Suite* (1954), which Wise also directed. Although he achieved success with the film musicals *The King and I* (1956) and *West Side Story*, Lehman had also written the novelette that was the source for the acclaimed *Sweet Smell of Success* (1957) and had scripted the Alfred Hitchcock thriller *North by Northwest* (1959). Following *The Sound of Music* were *Hello, Dolly!* (1969), another popular musical, and the dramatic *Who's Afraid of Virginia Woolf?* (1966).

The impact of *The Sound of Music* on Hollywood was also limited. Rather than pointing the film musical in a new direction, it marked the end of the era of traditional film musicals, though a few more were made (*Hello, Dolly!*, for example). The sentimental optimism they embodied quickly became anachronistic as the Vietnam War continued. In many ways, *The Sound of Music* is an archetypal film musical. It is a backstage musical in which the singer/dancer brings life to the initiate and affirms the power of mainstream music. Andrews' role is itself almost a cliché in the film musical; governesses in *The King and I* and *Mary Poppins* also bring music and life to the families they serve. The King of Siam in the former also resembles the baron in that both are rigid taskmasters who require only liberating nannies to be their real selves: spontaneous, emotional, and generous.

When *The Sound of Music* appeared, the American public was optimistic about the American incursion into Vietnam, though some observers were more apprehensive about American involvement. The storybook atmosphere of *The Sound of Music*, in which escape from Nazis is relatively easy and young Nazis such as Kurt are basically decent, appealed to a nation unwilling to confront harsh realities. Just seven years later, Bob Fosse's *Cabaret* (1972) had provided an effective contrast to the optimism of *The Sound of Music*. Both film musicals depict life in Germany just prior to the outbreak of World War II, but their images and their musical numbers attest changing musical and political tastes and perceptions. Rather than being the means of escape from Nazi Germany, music becomes the entrance to the cabaret world, which is controlled by money and which is characterized by perversity, deception, and degeneration. The young Nazis in *Cabaret* may be attractive when they sing "Tomorrow Belongs to Me," but Fosse shows his audience the violence they perpetrate on their opposition.

Many film historians identify the early 1960's as a transition period in American film, though there is understandable disagreement about which particular film heralded the arrival of a new kind of American film. The films often mentioned include *Bonnie and Clyde* (1967), *The Pawnbroker* (1965), *Dr. Strangelove: Or, How I Learned to Stop Worrying and Love the Bomb* (1964), *The Hustler* (1961), and *Psycho* (1960). All reflect changes in society's values. Offbeat protagonists who are alienated from their societies and plagued with explicit psychological and sexual problems respond violently in a morally complex world. Regardless of the exact film that marks the advent of the new film and the new society, *The Sound of Music* clearly was not the harbinger of a new American cinema. An indicator of the changing taste in film was Wyler's decision to direct the somber *The Collector* rather than *The Sound of Music*.

Other genres were changing as well. The traditional Western film was being replaced by the violent, experimental films that concerned the clash of country and city values and the end of the frontier. Rather than surrender to the new impersonal, industrial societies that make them anachronisms, the protagonists of *The Wild Bunch* (1969) and *Butch Cassidy and the Sundance Kid* (1969) go out fighting, even though it is futile. The excessive, almost ritualized violence in these films and in the other, more urban films of the late 1960's certainly reflects a growing American awareness of the Vietnam War violence and of the fundamental changes occurring in American society. *The Sound of Music* celebrated patriotism and the Austrian flag; within only a few years, American flags were being burned by Americans who were unwilling to follow orders. In the musical, escape from the enemy was relatively easy, but as the war in Vietnam continued, many people realized how difficult it was to extricate a country from a chosen course of action. Although *The Sound of Music* still has appeal for viewers who yearn for a better past, both the form and the content of the film seem out of touch with contemporary American life.

Bibliography

Brode, Douglas. *The Films of the Sixties.* Secaucus, N.J.: Citadel Press, 1980. Brode's chapter on the film contains the film credits, a synopsis of the film, some production details, a summary of the adverse critical reaction to the film, his own appreciative evaluation, and several still photographs.

Crist, Judith. *The Private Eye, the Cowboy, and the Very Naked Girl.* New York: Holt, Rinehart and Winston, 1968. Contains a lengthy review of the film, which is criticized for its "sweetness and light." Crist regards the stage original as the least inspired but most financially rewarding of the Rodgers and Hammerstein collaborations.

Druxman, Michael B. *The Musical: From Broadway to Hollywood.* South Brunswick, N.J.: A. S. Barnes, 1980. Druxman devotes a brief chapter to the adaptation of the theatrical musical to film. Critical responses to both media are included, as well as description of the major changes from the dramatic original.

Madsen, Axel. *William Wyler.* New York: Thomas Y. Crowell, 1973. Madsen's biography recounts the events preceding Wyler's decision to drop out as director of *The Sound of Music* shortly before production began. Anecdotes concern the Baroness Von Trapp's reactions to Adolf Hitler and the Austrians' support of the Nazi dictator.

Tynan, Kenneth. *Tynan Right and Left.* New York: Atheneum, 1968. Contains an unsympathetic film review characteristic of the critical response to *The Sound of Music.* Tynan, however, points out several interesting parallels between the film and *The King and I*, another film about a liberating governess and a rigid ruler.

Windeler, Robert. *Julie Andrews.* New York: St. Martin's Press, 1983. Windeler's biography, which features extensive quotations from Andrews and her associates, also contains production information about her films. Also includes helpful appendices regarding the credits for her films as well as a discography of albums featuring Andrews.

Thomas L. Erskine

Cross-References

Lubitsch's *The Merry Widow* Opens New Vistas for Film Musicals (1934), p. 941; *Gone with the Wind* Premieres (1939), p. 1154; *Casablanca* Marks the Artistic Apex of 1940's War-Themed Films (1942), p. 1245; Bernstein Joins Symphonic and Jazz Elements in *West Side Story* (1957), p. 1731; *Apocalypse Now* Is Hailed as the Ultimate Vietnam War Film (1979), p. 2428.

DYLAN PERFORMS WITH ELECTRIC INSTRUMENTS

Category of event: Music
Time: July 25, 1965
Locale: Newport, Rhode Island

Folk purists were outraged when folksinger Bob Dylan first performed with electric instruments, but he was forging a style that would affect the course of popular music for years to come

Principal personages:
BOB DYLAN (1941-   ), a folksinger/rock songwriter who brought a hitherto unknown intellectuality to rock music
MIKE BLOOMFIELD (1944-1981), a blues guitar player who played with Dylan at Newport and on the album *Highway 61 Revisited*
AL KOOPER (1944-   ), an organist who performed with Dylan at Newport and on the albums *Highway 61 Revisited* and *Blonde on Blonde*
PAUL ROTHCHILD (1935-   ), the sound engineer and producer who mixed the sound for Dylan's performance at Newport

Summary of Event

By 1965, Bob Dylan was the leading folksinger in the United States. He had recorded five albums, four of which fit squarely in the tradition of the folk music movement of the early 1960's. Folk music had its roots in hillbilly and country music; it was played on acoustic—that is, nonelectric—instruments, most often guitar and string bass. Dylan's protest songs of the early 1960's, such as "Blowin' in the Wind," "The Times They Are a-Changin'," and "Masters of War," were immensely popular, especially among young people beginning to question the values of American society. The solitary figure of Dylan, scruffily dressed and accompanying himself with only folk guitar and harmonica, had, in a few short years, come to symbolize the integrity of the folk movement's tradition and ideals. Dylan also represented the relevance of folk music to the times: His songs were sung at civil rights marches and rallies throughout the United States. His style, however, was about to change.

In July of 1965, Dylan was scheduled to perform at the annual Newport Folk Festival, the most important venue in the United States for performers in traditional and modern folk idioms. He had performed there before, in 1963 and 1964, to great acclaim; this time, however, his audience had a surprise in store. Dylan recently had returned from a trip to England, where he had been inspired by groups such as the Beatles; he had heard a group called the Animals perform the traditional folk song "House of the Rising Sun" with electric instruments and drums, which particularly impressed him.

The Paul Butterfield Blues Band, a band that performed with drums and electric instruments, was also on the bill at the 1965 Newport festival. Its presence marked one of the first times a band with amplified instruments had performed there (although blues played on nonelectric instruments had been a regular feature), and Dylan decided to have the band back him up. As Dylan took the stage on Sunday night, carrying an electric guitar, accompanied by a band, and wearing trendy English clothes rather than his characteristic simple attire, the festival's folk audience undoubtedly was perplexed and apprehensive.

Dylan's entire performance that night consisted of only five songs—three with the Butterfield band, then two as solo numbers. The band played the songs at a fast tempo. Its performance was driving and somewhat ragged; it was also loud. The sound was decidedly not that of folk music: The volume, fast tempos, and use of drums and electric guitar essentially turned it into rock and roll. The reaction of the audience went from stunned to confused to antagonistic—there were catcalls and boos. After three songs, Dylan said to the band, "Let's go, man—that's all." He was persuaded to return to the stage, however, and he calmed the audience by playing two more songs while accompanying himself on folk guitar.

Regardless of the Newport audience's response, Dylan knew that he was moving in the right direction. A month later, on August 28, he performed a concert in Forest Hills, New York, at which he first played a solo nonelectric set, then a second set with a band; again, the audience reaction was strongly negative. Dylan's next album also was released in August. A fully electric album, it was entitled *Highway 61 Revisited* and would become one of the most influential recordings of the 1960's.

The music of *Highway 61 Revisited* was in a bluesy rock-and-roll style that (as the Newport festival performance had) prominently featured the electric guitar work of Mike Bloomfield and the organ playing of Al Kooper. The songs' lyrics were like nothing ever heard before in rock, folk, or any other kind of music. Surreal, accusatory, relentless, even unabashedly angry, they continued for many long verses, sung over loud, repetitive music propelled by drums and electric guitars. The lyrics were so personal and abstract that, although one could experience them emotionally, one could never quite be sure what they meant. "The beauty parlor's filled with sailors/ The circus is in town," Dylan sang in "Desolation Row," a song in which "Einstein disguised as Robin Hood" wanders off "sniffing drainpipes and reciting the alphabet." The singing style that Dylan instinctively adopted in order to be effective over the sound of the amplified instruments also was unique. In an exaggeration of his husky and expressive folk style, he half-sang and half-shouted, gliding and swooping between notes. The album and the "new" Bob Dylan were fiercely loathed and equally fiercely loved.

These events created a furor in folk-music circles. Many people declared that Dylan was "selling out." Folk music aficionados perceived their music, with its traditions and its protests against racial and economic injustice, to be in sharp contrast to crass commercial music—either contrived "pop" songs with orchestras or, worse, vacuous teenage rock-and-roll songs. At the Newport festival in 1965, therefore, Dylan broke two cardinal rules of folk music: He was singing songs that lyrically had nothing to do with folk tradition or social protest, and he was performing them in a manner that sounded exactly like rock and roll.

In early 1966 came the recording sessions for the double album *Blonde on Blonde*, which was released in the early summer of that year. Both a consolidation and an extension of the rock sound of the previous record, it was an artistic and commercial success. Not long after its release, however, on July 29, Dylan suffered a motorcycle accident that compelled him to relax for the first time in five years. He withdrew from the public eye for nearly eighteen months; when he released the album *John Wesley Harding* in early 1968, his style had changed again, to a simpler sound with subtle elements of country music. The influence that Dylan had on the development of rock music stemmed primarily from the period beginning with the Newport Folk Festival in 1965 and ending with the release of *Blonde on Blonde* in 1966—a period of about one year.

Impact of Event

When Dylan "went electric" at the Newport Folk Festival and on his recordings, he may have alienated folk purists, but he gained a new audience that the purists never could have imagined. Dylan, it was soon said, spoke for a generation. This "generation" was the result of a particular moment in American history: the turbulent 1960's, with its Civil Rights movement, protests against the Vietnam War, and counterculture movement that claimed to reject materialism and turned to music, drugs, and meditation in an attempt to find meaning or at least consolation in life. Dylan's music was listened to, discussed, danced to, and written about in ways that no popular music had been before. It was analyzed and absurdly overanalyzed. The Dylan persona became a legend and a myth; he was even considered by some followers to be an oracle.

The primary impact of Dylan's entry into the genre of rock music, with its emphasis on electric instruments and dance beats, was that rock gained an intellectual respectability that it had not previously had. Dylan's surreal images provided the first body of work in this genre that could be considered poetry set to a rock beat. Its merits could be argued, for example, in the way that the merits of the Beat poetry of the 1950's were discussed. On a practical level, he also proved that rock artists could pursue serious themes and still sell a considerable number of records. Of the musicians of the rock era who were directly influenced by Dylan's combination of rock music and cerebral lyrics, the Beatles were the most important and influential.

Dylan and the Beatles became keenly aware of each other's music in 1965, and each influenced the other. It was from the Beatles and the other English groups of the era that Dylan took the idea of working with electric instruments. From Dylan, the Beatles in turn learned that they could expand their horizons and still be popular with their audiences. The lyrics of such Beatles albums as *Revolver* (1966) and *Sgt. Pepper's Lonely Hearts Club Band* (1967) clearly owe a debt to Dylan. Examples include the songs "Lucy in the Sky with Diamonds" (in which "cellophane flowers" tower overhead and "newspaper taxis appear on the shore") and "Eleanor Rigby" and "A Day in the Life," with their disturbing evocations of the emptiness of life and conventional values. Another extremely influential artist of the late 1960's, guitarist Jimi Hendrix, was strongly influenced by Dylan in his lyric writing, which gave his blues-based music a surreal cast.

The controversy over Dylan's turn to electric music overshadowed the fact that, by the time of his performance at the Newport Folk Festival, an electric version of Dylan's song "Mr. Tambourine Man" already had become a huge radio hit in a version by the Byrds, a group based in Los Angeles. It was the sound of the Byrds' recordings, with their pleasant harmonies and electric versions of folk classics (as well as a number of Dylan songs), that typified the genre that was quickly dubbed "folk rock." Folk rock used the rock rhythm section (drums and electric bass) but blended electric and acoustic instruments. Groups that fit within the folk-rock genre included the Mamas and the Papas as well as Simon and Garfunkel. "Sounds of Silence," the song that launched the latter's career, had first been recorded acoustically; after hearing Dylan's early electrified songs, Columbia Records, the label of both Dylan and Simon and Garfunkel, added drums and electric guitars to the song.

Although Dylan's entering and lyrically transforming the genre of rock, as symbolized by his appearance at the Newport Folk Festival, has generally been given most attention, his influence on popular music since the mid-1960's has been even more pervasive than that would suggest. When he recorded the album *John Wesley Harding*, for example, he helped initiate another new trend, "country rock," a genre that eventually would include such seminal artists as the Flying Burrito Brothers and such popular ones as the Eagles. The artists sometimes dubbed "singer-songwriters" (Joni Mitchell, James Taylor, and Jackson Browne among them) in the early 1970's often seemed to be defined by how they were like or unlike Dylan. The word "Dylanesque" became an unavoidable part of the rock lexicon; it could be applied to any artist with a gift for writing intelligent, dreamlike, or provocative lyrics. Any artist sufficiently Dylanesque was touted by a record company or reviewer as a new Bob Dylan. Among them were Loudon Wainwright III, John Prine, and Bruce Springsteen. (One reviewer dryly greeted a Dylan release in the late 1970's with a headline asking "Is Dylan the New Bruce Springsteen?") Leonard Cohen was the Canadian Bob Dylan; Patti Smith was the female Dylan. The Dylan influence on 1970's and 1980's artists as different as Elvis Costello (with his intense, literate, and angry lyrics) and Dire Straits (with their lyrics and singing style both reminiscent of Dylan's) is unmistakable.

The instrumentation that Dylan had serendipitously stumbled upon at Newport and in the recording sessions for *Highway 61 Revisited* and *Blonde on Blonde* also was influential. He frequently employed a piano and Hammond organ in addition to electric and acoustic guitars. This full sound, allowing a greater variety of moods and textures than rock and roll's typical guitar sound, was to be heard in the influential work of the Band (beginning with its 1967 album *Music from Big Pink*), a group that had toured and recorded with Dylan between 1965 and 1967 before recording its own work. The sound also appeared in the early recordings of Rod Stewart and on the influential album *Layla* (1971), by Eric Clapton's Derek and the Dominoes band.

The keyboards-plus-guitars combination later formed the cornerstone of the 1970's and 1980's sounds of Tom Petty and the Heartbreakers, Bob Seger, and Bruce Springsteen—all of whom freely admit their debt to Dylan in their songwriting as well.

It was Bruce Springsteen who inducted Bob Dylan into the Rock and Roll Hall of Fame on January 20, 1988. "Bob freed your mind the way Elvis freed your body," he said, and "changed the face of rock and roll forever. . . . To this day, wherever great rock music is being made, there is the shadow of Bob Dylan."

Bibliography

Cott, Jonathan. *Dylan.* Garden City, N.J.: Rolling Stone Press, 1984. An oversized book featuring a fine collection of photographs, including one of Dylan onstage at Newport with the Butterfield band. Cott's text is informative, providing both biographical details and critical commentary; he quotes from Dylan's songs and relates them to other music and literature. Contains a Dylan discography through 1983.

Dylan, Bob. *Tarantula.* New York: Macmillan, 1971. Dylan wrote most of this "novel" in 1965, then became dissatisfied and shelved it, finally publishing it in 1971. Represents Dylan at his most abstract and is therefore virtually impossible to decipher; wonderful flashes of absurdist humor, however, especially in its "letters" written by characters such as "Toby Celery" and "homer the slut."

Heylin, Clinton. *Bob Dylan: Behind the Shades.* New York: Summit Books, 1991. Deals extensively with Dylan's life and career after 1970 in addition to earlier years. Heylin includes lengthy quotations from many who have known Dylan and comments on earlier biographies. Interesting section on Newport, with quotes from eyewitnesses. Excellent notes, bibliography, glossary of interviewees, discography (including dates and songs of recording sessions), and index. Photographs.

Scaduto, Anthony. *Bob Dylan: An Intimate Biography.* New York: Grosset & Dunlap, 1971. The first serious book-length biography of Dylan. Especially valuable for quotations and anecdotes on Dylan's early years (contains a twenty-page interview with singer and Dylan paramour Joan Baez), although some events have been questioned by later writers. Dated, as biographical information ends at 1969. Photographs, discography (to 1970), and a brief index.

Shelton, Robert. *No Direction Home.* New York: William Morrow, 1986. Biography by a music critic and Dylan friend. In 1961, Shelton wrote a laudatory review in *The New York Times* that helped to make Dylan a success. Focuses primarily on the years up to 1970. Well written and informative, although Shelton's association with Dylan sometimes colors his view of events.

McCrea Adams

Cross-References

Guthrie's Populist Songs Reflect the Depression-Era United States (1930's), p. 810; The Rolling Stones Release *Out of Our Heads* (1965), p. 2027; Hendrix Releases *Are*

I SPY DEBUTS TO CONTROVERSY

Category of event: Television and radio
Time: September 15, 1965
Locale: The United States

I Spy, *an espionage drama, was controversial because it featured Bill Cosby, a black actor, in a starring role*

Principal personages:
BILL COSBY (1937-   ), a popular nightclub comic who with *I Spy* began a television career that was to make him a superstar
ROBERT CULP (1930-   ), an experienced stage and television actor who was Cosby's friend and costar on *I Spy*
SHELDON LEONARD (SHELDON LEONARD BERSHAD, 1907-   ), a film and television producer who recognized Cosby's talent and had the courage to cast him in a starring role

Summary of Event

The early 1960's were a tense time in the United States. The Cuban Missile Crisis, Vietnam, and the intensified Cold War produced a spate of books and articles that made the American public aware that the Central Intelligence Agency (CIA) was carrying on a secret war against foreign countries and rulers. This awareness was in sharp contrast to the American public's traditional view of the United States as the open and honest "good guy" of world affairs, but world conditions convinced most Americans such actions were necessary.

Television responded to this public interest by introducing spy programs, which fed on the public mood that the United States was under a secret attack and should respond in kind. Many of these shows were jingoistic and were unrealistic in the schemes they plotted for their characters. The National Broadcasting Company (NBC) broke out of this mold by developing *I Spy*, an hour-long weekly show to be filmed on location around the world. *I Spy* followed the exploits of two American agents, Kelly Robinson, played by Robert Culp, and Alexander Scott, played by Bill Cosby. Robinson was a world-class tennis player, and Scott was his trainer; their travels on the international tennis circuit provided the cover the pair needed to perform secret missions for the United States government. The cool, sophisticated nature of the acting, plots, and settings made the show a popular favorite during its three-year run.

The producer of the show, Sheldon Leonard, came to television after having achieved success as an actor in 1940's and 1950's films. His television record was impressive; he had produced and co-owned such hits as *Gomer Pyle, U.S.M.C.*, *The Dick Van Dyke Show*, and *The Andy Griffith Show*. Leonard had already contracted with NBC to produce *I Spy* and was looking for actors. The role of Alexander Scott was not written specifically for an African American, and Leonard actually had Dane Clark, a white actor, in mind for the role. Leonard, however, saw Cosby perform on late-evening television and decided that he would be perfect for the part. Leonard was especially attracted by Cosby's athletic agility and his sense of humor.

At the time, however, no black performer had had a starring role in a U.S. television series. Reflecting on Leonard's decision to cast him, Cosby later remarked that "no other producer would have had the guts to cast a Negro as Alexander Scott." Indeed, it took guts. Civil rights was a divisive issue in the United States at the time; large-scale demonstrations were the order of the day, and massive civil rights legislation was moving through Congress. In the midst of this, Bill Cosby was about to become the first black star of an integrated program on national television. As Cosby said, "This is the first time a Negro will play a spy instead of a problem."

The script for the show called for the characters played by Culp and Cosby to live, eat, and work together as complete equals. Culp summed up the attitude of the actors, and the point of view of the show, when he said, "We are two guys who don't know the difference between a colored man and a white man." The deliberate determination not to make an overt racial statement with the show was followed. In its three-year run, *I Spy* made only a handful of racial references. People were simply people, so far as the show's scripts were concerned.

That decision did not guarantee a dramatic hit. The first episode of the show was set in Hong Kong. Following the broadcast, a critic for *The New York Times* noted that "the setting was the real star. The actors wavered between strained suspense and a flirtation with James Bond. The show is searching for an attitude and the style to go with it."

Part of this initial problem was that Cosby was not yet a good actor. He had not made the transition from performing as a comic working alone to being a member of a team. Cosby recognized his lack of finesse and remarked that Culp "could have made mincemeat of me in front of the camera, but he has been a tremendous help instead." The genuine friendship between the two men became the show's greatest asset and helped Cosby to develop quickly as an actor.

A good working relationship among the cast did not mean the show was free of racial problems. Early on, Cosby raised complaints about the fact that his character did not date, while Culp's character was depicted as a playboy. The disparity was soon eliminated, and Cosby was shown romancing many of the leading black actresses of the day.

Impact of Event

I Spy, the first weekly network television drama to present an African American as a star, came on the air at the height of the civil rights struggle. The show was accepted for broadcast by more than 180 NBC stations; the only network affiliates to refuse to broadcast the program were in Savannah, Georgia, Albany, Georgia, Daytona Beach, Florida, and Alexandria, Louisiana. Stations in every Southern state carried the show, and its engaging presentation of integration as a fact of life was a powerful argument against segregation.

If a search had been made for the perfect black actor for such a role in such a situation, Cosby would still likely have been the choice. He grew up in the all-black Richard Allen housing project in Philadelphia. His father was a U.S. Navy mess steward—the only Navy job open to black men at the time. Although bright, Cosby was not a dedicated student. He dropped out of high school in the tenth grade and joined the Navy. Following his term of service, Cosby entered Temple University in 1961 on an athletic scholarship. During his sophomore year, Cosby began working part-time as a bartender and comic at a Philadelphia club. During this time, too, he met his future wife, Camille Hanks, on a blind date.

Cosby was so successful as a comic that he left Temple to perform full-time. His manager, Ron Silver, advised Cosby to eschew purely racial material and simply to develop his comic genius. Cosby followed Silver's advice in an effort to "reach all the people." It was this attitude that made Cosby the perfect costar for *I Spy*.

Cosby felt that *I Spy* was great fun; he commented that he had not had so much fun since he was in college. He worked hard, though, to make sure the show avoided the portrayal of black stereotypes. On the other hand, he did not want praise simply because the show took a liberal approach to race relations, noting that he wanted *I Spy* "to be judged on its entertainment value."

Culp, Cosby's costar, agreed. Culp felt that the plots for the episodes would prove to be secondary to the relationship between the people on the screen, and he remarked that "it is pretty obvious on screen as well as off that Bill and I have a great regard for each other." This regard brought the two together again to make *Hickey and Boggs* (1972), a detective film directed by Culp. Culp has also appeared as a guest on Cosby's television shows at various times.

I Spy also helped to change the public image of blacks in entertainment. When first offered the role of Alexander Scott, the trainer to a white tennis player, Cosby was hesitant; he feared that the role would prove to be merely another sidekick part. He was assured by Leonard, though, that he would play a character with special skills, would have equal prominence, and would be allowed to develop romantic interests. Once Cosby settled into the role, his performances were virtuoso, and his part became one of the most significant in television history. Cosby himself said of his character that Alexander Scott was "a Negro champion working for goodness and the law; a multi-lingual, highly educated man who is not the Negro stereotype." The old stereotype would never again be believable.

I Spy's success was largely the product of the charming on-screen interplay of its stars, who ad-libbed much of their dialogue. Together, Culp and Cosby brought a light touch to the show, even as the plots revolved around shootouts and superpower confrontation. Cosby's blackness made the series groundbreaking, but it was his skill as an actor that helped make the show a success. Having broken television's color line, Cosby opened the door for other serious black performers; moreover, the fact that a black actor had helped to propel a show to ratings success helped to ensure that television would never go back to offensive and demeaning portrayals of African Americans.

I Spy had an enormous impact on Cosby's career. For each season the show was on the air, 1965-1966, 1966-1967, and 1967-1968, Cosby won an Emmy Award for "outstanding continuous performance by an actor in a leading role in a dramatic series." Of course, such success brought other roles his way and boosted his earnings. He began to command $25,000 a week as a nightclub comic, and sales of record albums containing his comedy routines tripled. The experience on *I Spy* also turned Cosby into an accomplished actor. Before the series began, one television critic commented that seeing Cosby tied to a structured script and working with other actors would be like seeing Thelonious Monk play piano for Lawrence Welk. By the end of *I Spy*'s first season, no one doubted that Cosby could both improvise and work with a group.

Bibliography

Brooks, Tim, and Earle Marsh. *The Complete Directory to Prime Time Network TV Shows, 1946-Present.* 4th ed. New York: Ballantine Books, 1988. Gives the show's broadcast history, cast, and a brief summary. Useful for placing *I Spy* in a larger television context.

"I Spy." *Ebony* 20 (September, 1965): 65-66. A profusely illustrated magazine spread from the eve of the show's premiere. Text of the article, from one of America's leading black magazines, focuses on Cosby and his breaking of television's color line.

Karnow, Stanley. "Bill Cosby: Variety Is the Life of Spies." *The Saturday Evening Post* 238 (September 25, 1965): 86-88. Another magazine article from the time of *I Spy*'s debut, also centered on Cosby and the groundbreaking nature of his role. Its appearance in one of the institutions of Middle American publishing allows for an interesting comparison of perspectives with the *Ebony* piece cited above.

Lowe, Carl, ed. *Television and American Culture.* New York: H. H. Wilson, 1981. A collection of articles, addresses, and excerpts from books discussing television as a social force in American society. Helpful in understanding the broader implications of the *I Spy* controversy.

Smith, Ronald L. *Cosby.* New York: St. Martin's Press, 1986. A readable, though somewhat adulatory, popular biography of Bill Cosby, written after he attained megastar status with *The Cosby Show.* Chapters 7 and 8 cover *I Spy*, its creation, and its reception.

Michael R. Bradley

Cross-References

Poitier Emerges as a Film Star in *The Blackboard Jungle* (1955), p. 1650; Hansberry's *A Raisin in the Sun* Debuts on Broadway (1959), p. 1795; *Dr. No* Launches the Hugely Popular James Bond Series (1962), p. 1913; Le Carré Rejects the Fantasy World of Secret Agents (1963), p. 1934; *The Jeffersons* Signals Success of Black Situation Comedies (1975), p. 2339; *Roots* Dramatizes the African-American Experience (1977), p. 2397; *The Cosby Show* Makes Television History (1984), p. 2532.

THE NATIONAL ENDOWMENT FOR THE ARTS
IS ESTABLISHED

Category of event: Art
Time: September 29, 1965
Locale: Washington, D.C.

The burgeoning of the National Endowment for the Arts (NEA) began when first-time federal grant support for the development and support of the arts was offered to artists and art institutions

> *Principal personages:*
> NANCY HANKS (1927-1983), the chair of the NEA from 1969 to 1977
> LYNDON B. JOHNSON (1908-1973), the thirty-sixth president of the United States
> ROGER L. STEVENS (1910-   ), the first chair of the National Council on the Arts, which governed the NEA from 1965 to 1969

Summary of Event

Arts patronage in the United States developed intermittently and at a slow pace. Colonial Americans' support of the secular arts was very limited; however, by the second half of the nineteenth century, the United States aristocracy provided substantial patronage of the arts. Such wealthy individuals as Thomas Corcoran, Solomon Guggenheim, Henry Lee Higginson, Andrew Mellon, J. P. Morgan, William C. Ralston, and John Rockefeller offered significant support to individual artists and institutions.

During the Great Depression, private philanthropy could no longer fund many artists and cultural organizations. In November, 1933, the first form of federal support for the arts commenced; as part of President Franklin D. Roosevelt's New Deal, unemployed artists received financial assistance. This subsidized art program, the Public Works Arts Project (PWAP), lasted seven months. During that period, nearly four thousand painters and sculptors provided more than 15,600 works of art as decoration for federal buildings throughout the country. Early in 1934, the Federal Emergency Relief Administration (FERA) established another artwork program, administered by the states, which employed about a thousand artists.

In May of 1935, Congress created the Federal Arts Project (FAP), a branch of the Works Progress Administration (WPA). The primary emphasis of the program was to provide temporary economic relief, with a secondary focus on controlled artistic competence. Muralists, playwrights, architects, photographers, and novelists were employed to popularize New Deal programs and to memorialize administrative achievements. WPA projects included theater, literature, visual arts, and music projects and a historical survey. During World War II, however, federal subsidies for the arts plummeted. By mid-1943, only private philanthropy was left to sustain the arts.

Although early American political leaders recognized the importance of the arts to the strength of the nation, federal efforts to support art for art's sake were unsuccessful until the twentieth century. A formal study of the proper role of the federal government in advancing the arts initiated in 1951 by President Harry S. Truman and submitted to President Dwight D. Eisenhower in 1953 renewed interest in the arts. Various program proposals were made to Congress, but Congress failed to sustain them. Subsequently, presidents John F. Kennedy and Lyndon B. Johnson appointed special assistants on the arts for their own counsel.

Roger L. Stevens, a special assistant to President Johnson, observed that congressional support for public funding of the humanities was strong. Stevens suggested to the White House that the arts and humanities endowment be linked as a single legal entity. In 1964, to further investigate this idea, President Johnson signed a bill creating a twenty-six-member National Council on the Arts; Stevens was appointed the group's chairman.

This advisory body formally proposed a federal humanities and arts bill. The bill, which reflected the nature of Johnson's Great Society as a postwar monied, middle-class society seeking the amenities appropriate to its status, had its share of critics. During hearings on the bill, the wisdom of injecting federal bureaucracy into an area that traditionally had been left to the private sector was debated. Despite the criticism, on September 29, 1965, Johnson signed the National Foundation on the Arts and the Humanities Act.

The enactment of this federal arts bill provided for the creation of a single national foundation that included both the National Endowment for the Humanities (NEH) and the National Endowment for the Arts (NEA). The National Foundation on the Arts and the Humanities Act subsequently directed the NEA to distribute federal subsidies specifically for the development and support of the arts in the United States.

The bill's proponents hoped the prevailing cultural spirit of the legislators, the public, and the arts community would promote rapid advancement in artistic excellence and an enhanced national unity. Questions regarding how to develop a workable institutional system for making decisions and dispensing funds, however, slowed progress. Thorny issues about what type of art and which artists the government should subsidize were only the beginning of the conflicts. Many arguments ensued, including debates over what art was, what it should become, and for what purposes and which publics it should serve.

The hoped-for national unity was not enhanced. Elitists believed firmly that, because of the public's atrophied taste, only professionals in art or other fields should direct funding decisions. Populists saw the boundaries between the amateur and professional as inconsequentially arbitrary and therefore believed that equal grant support should be awarded to both traditional and nontraditional art forms. The artists who were potential recipients of federal funds feared that federal involvement in the arts would infringe on their artistic independence, and some predicted that government participation in the arts would lead to the establishment of an official national art form. Some projected that private donors would no longer be predisposed to support the arts, while others were confident that any void created by the withdrawal of private philanthropy would be filled by continual increases in federal subsidies.

The nature of the controversy between the proponents and opponents of the NEA subsidy program and the history of arts patronage in the United States illustrate the two conflicting themes that framed the funding legislation. The primary goal of the NEA, however, was to strengthen the role of arts in American life by promoting cultural and artistic excellence while preserving both artistic freedom and the private sector's role in the program.

Impact of Event

The endowment began with ten programs, in architecture, arts and education, creative writing, dance, drama, music, public media, miscellaneous art forms, visual arts, and the state. Later, seven more programs were added to cover museums, folk arts, expansion arts, opera and musical theater, interdisciplinary arts, local artists, and "challenge and advancement." Program grants are awarded to nonprofit organizations, state and local public agencies, and exceptionally talented individuals.

Congress specified at the outset of the endowment program that federal support for the arts was intended primarily to complement that received from local, state, regional, and private arts organizations. The first NEA budget of $8 million covered only a skeleton endowment staff, a few artists' fellowships, and some grants to states to launch their own art agencies.

In the NEA's first few years, chairman Roger L. Stevens' attention was directed toward rescuing elite institutions that were in dire financial straits. Nancy Hanks, the NEA's second chairperson, on the other hand, concentrated on awarding grants to grass-roots organizations throughout the country and to opera, theater, dance, and music groups that could then provide free performances. Her goal was to reach the culturally disadvantaged in economically deprived areas of the United States.

During Hanks's tenure, the NEA budget increased from $11 million to $114 million annually. By the 1990's, the NEA each year was processing nearly 19,000 grant applications in 115 categories and awarding nearly 4,500 grants. Most of the budget goes to nonprofit arts organizations such as symphonies; theater, dance, and opera companies; museums, arts festivals, arts centers, and arts colonies; literary magazines and small presses; film, video, and radio production; archival facilities; and service organizations.

At the NEA's inception, there were relatively few professional nonprofit performing arts organizations in the United States. Most such groups were located on the East and West Coast corridors, from Boston to Washington, D.C., and from Los Angeles to San Francisco, with a few organizations in Chicago and Texas. As a result of NEA patronage, professional performing arts organizations spread throughout the United States. The number of dance companies, opera companies, orchestras, and professional theaters in the United States grew dramatically. The granting of funds by the federal government to such organizations is for specified projects and requires at least a one-to-one matching grant from nonfederal sources. Nonmatching grants are given only as fellowships to individual artists for nonspecific projects.

Matching federal grants provided the incentive for many new state arts agencies. Before 1965, only seven states had arts agencies; in the wake of the NEA, every state in America as well as the District of Columbia soon had arts agencies. Over the years, the states themselves steadily increased their support for arts agencies; by the 1990's, state agencies were spending about $250 million a year on the arts.

The NEA has awarded tens of thousands of grants since 1966. Matching grants have stimulated private support and public interest in the arts. In fact, the federal funds have been more than matched by nonfederal sources. In 1990, total annual support for the arts was estimated at $6.8 billion, a figure that included contributions from the NEA, state agencies, private foundations, businesses, individuals, and bequests. The diversity of contributors seemed to provide the arts in the United States with protection against the establishment of an approved "official" style.

The NEA has contributed to unprecedented growth in virtually every field of the arts. Since 1965, the number of artists and the size of art audiences have increased dramatically. Symphony attendance, opera attendance, and nonprofit theater and dance audiences increased enormously. Art programming became a regular feature on television and radio networks. America's cultural heritage was both preserved and advanced with the funding of artists and organizations in folk-art traditions and in emerging art forms.

Despite the NEA's accomplishments, the grant-making procedures and the administration of the endowment have been sensitive political issues. Upon occasion, it has been charged that the endowment's policy of cultural populism has constituted an effort to democratize culture and to abolish aesthetic standards and artistic excellence. Over time, a small number of grants that were alleged to lack artistic import, to be political in content, or to be offensive, pornographic, or obscene have provoked significant controversy. In 1990, Congress created an independent commission to review the policies and management issues of the endowment. The commission's recommendations for increased efficiencies and improved oversight were instituted to make quality and accountability easier to achieve. The conclusion of the independent commission's report, however, noted that controversy over the direction of U.S. culture was only a continuation of the argument that had begun when the idea for the creation of a national endowment was introduced in the 1960's.

Bibliography

Netzer, Dick. *The Subsidized Muse: Public Support for the Arts.* Cambridge, England: Cambridge University Press, 1978. An economic analysis of public culture by a public-finance expert. Netzer's provocative evaluation includes case studies of symphony orchestras, theater groups, and ballet companies, yet omits museums. After examining the social and economic decisions made in the case studies, Netzer proposes what he considers to be wiser and more accountable ways to use government arts funding. Preface, appendices, index, and bibliography.

Robins, Corinne. *The Pluralist Era: American Art, 1968-1981.* New York: Harper & Row, 1984. A survey of the arts from the commencement of the NEA to 1981. Robins discusses political, cultural, and social trends and their role in shaping the art of the period. She does not, however, conclude that the NEA supported pluralist art thinking or helped to revolutionize the arts. Index and bibliography.

Russell, John. *The Meanings of Modern Art.* Rev. ed. New York: Harper & Row, 1981. A one-volume introduction to art from the 1870's to the end of the 1970's. No direct references to the cultural impact of the NEA, although some of the work discussed was publicly funded. Preface, photographs, index, and bibliography.

Straight, Michael. *Nancy Hanks, an Intimate Portrait: The Creation of a National Commitment to the Arts.* Durham, N.C.: Duke University Press, 1988. Little of this portrait of Nancy Hanks is intimate. Most of the text traces the NEA's public-funding increases for dance, theater, and education under Hanks's direction. Preface, photographs, sources, and index.

_____. *Twigs for an Eagle's Nest: Government and the Arts, 1965-1978.* New York: Devon Press, 1979. Personal anecdotes about formative years of the NEA. Straight, the former second-in-command to Nancy Hanks, provides an insider's perspective on the issues of public cultural policy-making from 1969 to 1978.

Wendy T. Olmstead

Cross-References

The Federal Theatre Project Promotes Live Theater (1935), p. 989; The Roosevelt Administration Creates the WPA/FAP (1935), p. 995; The Ford Foundation Begins to Fund Nonprofit Theaters (1957), p. 1736; *The Forsyte Saga* Is a Hit on Public Television (1969), p. 2168; Mapplethorpe's Photographs Provoke Controversy (1989), p. 2636.

WARHOL'S *THE CHELSEA GIRLS* BECOMES A COMMERCIAL SUCCESS

Categories of event: Motion pictures and art
Time: 1966
Locale: New York, New York

The Chelsea Girls *became the first underground film to play a long run in commercial theaters in Manhattan and eventually was distributed nationwide*

Principal personages:

ANDY WARHOL (ANDREW WARHOLA, 1928?-1987), an interdisciplinary artist who was inspired by popular culture and countercultures

EMILE DE ANTONIO, the agent who acted as mentor to Warhol in his career as a serious pop artist and introduced Warhol to the world of underground films

JONAS MEKAS, the head of the Film-Maker's Distribution Center, distributor of *The Chelsea Girls*

Summary of Event

On September 15, 1966, Andy Warhol premiered his film *The Chelsea Girls* at the Film-Maker's Co-operative's Cinematheque theater in Manhattan. This film had been shot during the previous summer at various locations in the city. The film lasted about three hours and consisted of segments approximately thirty-five minutes long, as that was how much film fit inside a film camera magazine. Each of the segments featured "Super Stars" regularly seen in Warhol's films, such as the Duchess, Hanoi Hanna, Pope Ondine, and International Velvet. The film was loosely constructed to show the different people one might find living at the downtown Chelsea Hotel, where many of the regulars who hung out at Warhol's studio, the Factory, actually lived. After hotel management threatened to sue, however, references to the hotel were omitted from the billing.

Prior to his filming of *The Chelsea Girls*, Warhol had experimented with popular music and supported a rock group called the Velvet Underground. To provide a place for them to perform, he rented a dance hall for a short time and had its walls painted white. While the band sang, Warhol experimented, creating different visual effects incorporated into the Exploding Plastic Inevitable media show. Acting as the projectionist, he showed his films side by side and explored the effect this created. This work predated the mixed-media shows held by Dr. Timothy Leary but were very similar to those used by Leary to simulate an LSD trip. This visual technique was the one Warhol used when screening *The Chelsea Girls.*

Film had never been displayed like this before. Rather than stringing the segments together one after another, Warhol chose to project two segments side by side. The segment on the right side of the screen was traditionally begun five minutes before the one on the left. Some segments were in black and white; some were in color. Some had sound and some did not. Each segment was a separate unit, or episode, and its companion did not continue or further illuminate its action. The effect was startling. Warhol had destroyed the narrative, or the storyline, in this film. He also disregarded the concept of filmic time, instead thrusting the visual and sensorial possibilities of the medium to the foreground. *The Chelsea Girls* shocked the senses of its viewers. It further disoriented them by not focusing their attention on what was meant to be important. Warhol's work was an interactive piece. For a viewer to concentrate on one thing, he or she had to forgo concentrating on something else. In this way, each individual in the audience chose a different experience and, in effect, saw his or her own movie.

As a major pop artist, Warhol received notice for his earlier films in the relatively small worlds of the visual arts and of independent film. Following the release of *The Chelsea Girls*, mainstream media started to take notice of the impact Warhol might have on film. Jack Kroll wrote a long review of *The Chelsea Girls* for the magazine *Newsweek*, and Bosley Crowther wrote a review of it for *The New York Times*. Other reviewers and critics followed suit. Media coverage generated enough popular interest in the film to move it to a commercial theater further uptown.

Many critics and reviewers who were trained to focus on the narrative in film were outraged by *The Chelsea Girls*. Not only was it nonnarrative, it also was not conventionally entertaining, thus violating two prerequisites for commercial films. Many reviewers focused on the content of specific segments and saw only the sordidness of the characters. They objected that homosexuality, sadomasochism, drug abuse, and nudity were too objectionable to be subjects for film investigation. Others, missing the point completely, complained that there was no definitive order in which the segments were shown. Lacking specific directions, projectionists were able to improvise, showing the segments in any order they chose, though the film usually began and ended the same way. These reviewers never knew if they were reviewing the same film that their colleagues had seen and so had difficulty entering into dialogue with one another. As Warhol himself wrote, however, "*any* publicity was good publicity." As the film finished its run at one commercial theater it would begin a run at another, and then another, with people standing in long lines waiting to buy their tickets. Warhol split the net profits evenly with the Film-Maker's Distribution Center, headed by Jonas Mekas.

The Chelsea Girls was the first underground film ever to play a long run in Manhattan. It was so successful that the Art Theater Guild arranged with the Film-Maker's Distribution Center to distribute it nationwide. Warhol, however, did not know for certain what he had done in *The Chelsea Girls* to make it so popular. For all he knew, viewers could have been attracted to it mainly for the nudity rather than for any great appreciation of its artistry. Still, it was the best known and the most often seen of Warhol's films. Film critic Vincent Canby of *The New York Times* compared *The Chelsea Girls* with Michelangelo Antonioni's *Blow-Up* (1966), with both eventually having important influences on commercial films. *Blow-Up* had been financed by Metro-Goldwyn-Mayer (MGM), which had formed a subsidiary company to release it, and Hollywood was just getting ready to shoot *Midnight Cowboy* (1969), a film very close in theme to Warhol's earlier production *My Hustler* (1965). What everyone wondered was whether Warhol would also get financing from a major studio and break into the business of commercial film.

Impact of Event

The Chelsea Girls marked a turning point in Warhol's career as a pop artist. It was also a turning point for American film, which had been floundering because of the popularity of television. A limbo existed in Hollywood, with executives not understanding the American film audience, especially the lives and tastes of American youth. The studios spent millions of dollars on more and more lavish (and perhaps tedious and boring) spectacles, featuring aging stars to whom young people could not relate. It became increasingly difficult for such films to break even at the box office.

Warhol's use of the medium of film was not inconsistent with the pop philosophy that everyone could do everything. In his career as an artist, Warhol had easily moved between illustration, painting, and silk-screen techniques. At first, film was just another medium in which he could do his work. He did not believe that work in the medium had to follow strict conventions. Especially to American youth, who had started to look at Warhol as a hero of the counterculture, Warhol's involvement with the medium reawakened the idea that American film could be art and not just lavish commercial enterprise. Warhol made going to films chic for some and "groovy" for others, depending on their age and vernacular. In *The Chelsea Girls*, there was subject matter to be viewed that never could be shown on television.

Warhol first gained notice as a commercial artist working as an illustrator for major women's magazines such as *McCall's*, *Ladies' Home Journal*, and *Glamour*, at a time when the fashion world was starting to take a serious interest in fine art. Paintings by Jackson Pollock and Willem de Kooning were used as backdrops for models and fashions. Artists were profiled in articles, and fashion photography became an art form in itself. Some artists found jobs as window designers for New York's large department stores. Warhol's agent, Emile de Antonio, encouraged him to start painting on canvas, frequently critiquing his early work. With de Antonio's encouragement, Warhol painted his first Coke bottles, which de Antonio and others found to be a strong symbol for American society.

By the time Warhol had his first New York show, at Eleanor Ward's Stable Gallery in November, 1962, movie cameras had become affordable. De Antonio was also a filmmaker and on the board of directors of the New American Cinema Group, started by Jonas Mekas to help finance and distribute independently made movies. Warhol accompanied his mentor to the Film-Maker's Co-operative to view underground films.

Movie cameras were also rampant at Eleanor Ward's seashore property, where Warhol spent some of the summer following his show in her gallery. It was there that Jack Smith, an underground filmmaker and actor, worked on his creation *Normal*

Love. Warhol watched Smith work and noticed how he continued shooting even after the actors got bored. This fascinated Warhol, who found it different from what he saw in commercial films, which had become so polished that they lacked all mystery, or in cinéma vérité, in which filmmakers self-consciously tried to capture real life. This bored time actually *was* real life and expressed themes similar to those of Warhol's pop art paintings and silk screens.

In 1963, Warhol bought a sixteen-millimeter camera. He also moved into the studio space that became known as "the Factory." In the spirit of the times, the doors to the Factory were always left open to anyone who wandered in, including dancers, artists, writers, poets, bohemian types, homosexual hustlers, aspiring actresses, and drug users. Some of these people were crazy or were made crazy by abusing drugs, but Warhol did not mind and admitted that he found creative inspiration in the insanity that surrounded him.

In 1964, Warhol purchased a better camera and was able to film with sound. More and more, the personalities of his "Super Stars" took over as subject matter for his films. This was consistent with his philosophy of pop and artist Marcel Duchamp's influential idea of "readymade" art. With inclusion of sound, there was more pressure on Warhol to come up with a script. Warhol kept scripting to a minimum, encouraging the "real" people to emerge improvisationally. Warhol gave the actors a situation, or "incident" as he called it, and then left them on their own. Warhol also worked from a stationary camera and shot continuously until he ran out of film, no matter what the actors did, although he admitted that at some times he was so upset with the action that he had to leave the room, camera still filming. In this way, his work resembled portraiture more than it did film, in which script traditionally determines the personalities of the actors and camera angles and camera work help establish the viewer's feelings or mood.

Negative reviewers accused Warhol of being a voyeur, of focusing his camera on people and situations that were raw and crude. Traditionally, however, artists have captured intimate moments that have titillated and moved their viewers. Warhol's "Super Stars" actually were often raw and crude, appearing to be individuals with very real problems. Setting this in motion and with sound, bigger than life, was more than some people's senses could take. Part of the problem was that Warhol saw his films as art and did not intend for viewers to sit through entire screenings but rather, in the manner of museumgoers, to wander in and out at will. When an audience paid to sit and view something, it actually sat and watched and listened to it all. It was unfortunate but not surprising that Warhol's material offended many people who were never able to see his body of work in any other light.

After the financial success of *The Chelsea Girls*, Warhol attracted more entrepreneurs to his filmmaking endeavors. They encouraged him to move away from the experimental or art component of his work and move in the direction of voyeurism and the pornographic, with the idea that this was what the American viewer wanted. The popularity of the film could be interpreted as showing the artistic credibility of pornography and sadomasochism. This focus on unusual sexuality alienated some but inspired many others, presaging a battle in American art over sexual politics and policies.

Warhol continued to shoot his artistic piece ★★★★*Four Stars* (1967), which took more than a day to screen and contained sections in which images were superimposed on one another on a single screen. More and more, Warhol gave up his artistic experimentation, wanting instead to make films that regular theaters would want to show. Unfortunately, Hollywood backing never materialized. Instead, Warhol saw the commercial film industry move into the underground filmmaker's territory, using its subject matter—counterculture, realistic scenes of life, formerly forbidden subjects of sexuality and drugs—and giving it a slick commercial treatment. Warhol saw actors Dustin Hoffman and John Voight play the Hollywood equivalent of hustlers in *Midnight Cowboy* (1969). He realized that without financial backing and good technicians, he could not compete. After he was shot and critically wounded in 1968 by a woman who claimed he had stolen her script, his interest in the production of film declined dramatically.

Bibliography

Coplans, John. *Andy Warhol.* Greenwich, Conn.: New York Graphic Society, 1990. An oversized collection of three essays written about the artist. Contains many black-and-white reproductions of Warhol's two-dimensional work as well as a filmography of Warhol's work prepared by Jonas Mekas, founder of the Film-Maker's Co-operative, where most of the films were screened.

Gidal, Peter. *Andy Warhol: Films and Paintings.* 1971. Reprint. New York: Da Capo Press, 1991. An unabridged reprint containing black-and-white photos of Warhol's paintings and silk screens, as well as wonderful stills from many of his early films.

Koch, Stephen. *Stargazer.* New York: Praeger, 1973. An early attempt to understand this pop artist. One gets the sense that the author was excluded from Warhol's inner circle of friends, and insecurity shows sometimes in the text.

Warhol, Andy. *America.* New York: Harper & Row, 1985. An oversized book filled with photographs and prose created by the artist. Quick and easy to read, it nevertheless provides a glance inside this enigmatic trendsetter.

_____. *The Philosophy of Andy Warhol: From A to B and Back Again.* San Diego, Calif.: Harcourt Brace Jovanovich, 1975. Warhol expounds on his theory of nothingness. The views might not have been worthy of publication had they not come from this cultural icon. Offers Warhol's interpretations of himself and of his work.

Warhol, Andy, and Pat Hackett. *POPism: The Warhol '60s.* New York: Harcourt Brace Jovanovich, 1980. Warhol speaks believably in the pages of this almost unillustrated book, offering insight into his roles and actions during his years at the Factory.

D. Tulla Lightfoot

Cross-References

Duchamp's "Readymades" Challenge Concepts of Art (1913), p. 349; The Dada Movement Emerges at the Cabaret Voltaire (1916), p. 419; Gance's *Napoléon* Revolutionizes Filmmaking Techniques (1925), p. 642; Rosenberg Defines "Action Painting" (1952), p. 1552; Jasper Johns Paints the American Flag (1954), p. 1590; McLuhan Probes the Impact of Mass Media on Society (1964), p. 1973; New York's SoHo Develops into a Center for Contemporary Art (1970's), p. 2191.

BROWN WINS A GRAMMY FOR "PAPA'S GOT A BRAND NEW BAG"

Category of event: Music
Time: March 15, 1966
Locale: Los Angeles, California

Master rhythm-and-blues and soul singer James Brown won his first Grammy Award for his 1965 recording "Papa's Got a Brand New Bag," signaling the invention of funk

Principal personages:

JAMES BROWN (1933-   ), a singer who broke new ground in rhythm and blues, soul, funk, and rap music with his raw singing, energetic dancing, and exciting live performances

SYD NATHAN (1904-1968), a Cincinnati native who founded the independent record company King in 1943 and who signed James Brown to a recording contract in 1956

BEN BART (1906-1968), Brown's agent, who became a sort of father figure for Brown

Summary of Event

On March 15, 1966, the National Academy of Recording Arts and Sciences (NARAS) awarded James Brown his first Grammy for his composition "Papa's Got a Brand New Bag" as the best rhythm-and-blues single of 1965. The recording had been a number-one soul hit and had even reached number eight on the *Billboard* pop chart. It was both a culmination of Brown's work since 1956, when he made his first recording for King Records, and a sign of a significant change in his music that would mark his work through the 1980's.

For Brown was inventing funk—a musical style that returned black music to its roots and eschewed some of the modified and more mainstream styles of the soul music of 1960's, which often dabbled in crossover styles, sweetened musical textures, and pop instrumentation. Funk music utilizes an instrumental sound based on a hypnotically riffing band working off a one-chord style. Brown himself developed his band's sound this way beginning in the mid-1960's, with reeds and horns doing staccato bursts and an electric guitar playing choked chords. From 1965 on, Brown experimented further with this kind of backing for his voice. His raw vocal style stemmed from hard black gospel influences and from the work of earlier rhythm-and-blues shouters. His rich baritone voice could reach into falsetto, could scream and shriek in the agony of his passionate love songs, and yet could also produce warm and caressing tones; his voice was an infinitely subtle and versatile instrument for his own compositions. By 1965, he was a major figure, live and on record, among black audiences. His kinetic live show featured large bands and many back-up singers, and his continuous movement and creative dancing had become the biggest draw in black show business. He could sing romantic, slow songs with a rich legato; he could do dance songs in which a minimum lyric was repeated over and over while his backing band built up tension with vamps and riffs and Brown gyrated all over the stage. He became famous as the "hardest working man in show business." A master of the one-nighter and the "chitlin' circuit" of black venues, Brown never rested on his laurels; he endlessly reinvented his music. From the early days of rhythm and blues, he moved on to write compositions in the early 1960's and later that would help to define soul music, including upbeat songs with a tone and message of pride in black culture. Along with such performers as Ray Charles, Otis Redding, Wilson Pickett, and Aretha Franklin, he would epitomize soul.

Still, Brown's music always remained rawer than theirs, his voice more astringent and uncompromising in its blackness. He refused to moderate his style to help his records cross over to the pop charts. An improviser who worked songs up live and then altered them in the studio, Brown was a protean creative singer, bandleader, dancer, and spokesman for rural and inner-city blacks—Soul Brother Number One, the Godfather of Soul.

From 1965 on, he evolved his style into its funk phase, using a polyrhythmic bass and chanted and semispoken vocals that anticipated the development of rap music. Yet he had always been inventive and gone his own way.

Born in rural poverty in Barnwell, South Carolina, in 1933 (just across the river from Augusta, Georgia, where he grew up), Brown was the child of a broken family. Imprisoned for petty theft in 1949, he spent three years rethinking the direction of his life and decided to pursue music. After his release, he joined a gospel group that became a local success; the band then altered its style to take advantage of the postwar popularity of rhythm and blues. Imitating the earlier jump-band stylings of Louis Jordan and His Tympany Five and heavily influenced by such performers as Little Richard and Hank Ballard and the Midnighters, Brown and his friends sought broader exposure than they could get around Augusta and Macon, Georgia. Their chance came in 1956, when a scout from King Records in Cincinnati listened to a demo of Brown's own "Please, Please, Please" and recommended them to label head Syd Nathan. Traveling to the Ohio studio, Brown and his vocal group, the Famous Flames, recorded the song with King studio musicians. "Please, Please, Please" made it to number five on the soul charts.

For Brown, Syd Nathan became both a father figure and a challenge. Nathan was more comfortable with the less raw talents of such performers on his label as Bill Doggett, Little Willie John, Hank Ballard and the Midnighters, and the Dominoes (with Clyde McPhatter), who were crossing over easily into the burgeoning rock-and-roll field. Nathan was an astute businessman who combined all the functions of recording and producing his records in one plant in Cincinnati. His producers scouted the South for talent and knew their market and its preferences. Yet Nathan simply seemed to think that Brown's music was not polished enough to merit much attention or publicity. Fortunately for Brown, his relentless touring and his development of a masterful stage show gave him a security and base on which to build, independent of the whims of Nathan and his release schedule for singles—which were often issued long after they were cut in the studio.

In 1959, Brown signed a contract with Ben Bart, the agent and founder of Universal Attractions in New York. Experienced with black artists—he had been an agent for Dinah Washington and Billy Eckstine—Bart would become a more benign father figure for Brown, an astute business partner, and, later, Brown's manager. Bart took charge of the complex bookings schedule Brown relied on and got him into larger venues. Brown and Bart wanted to capture on record the full force of Brown's live show so that his spontaneity and interaction with an audience could be conveyed to a wider home market. In 1962, they succeeded over the opposition of Syd Nathan. *Live at the Apollo* became a huge hit album, even reaching a pop audience as number two on the *Billboard* chart. New York's Apollo Theater was the mecca and testing ground for black performers, and the live album allowed Brown to do the kind of extended numbers (sometimes five to seven minutes in length) that best illustrated both his improvisatory talents and his ability to work an audience. Up to 1965, Brown continued to hone his band and show as he recorded a wide variety of material, often spread over two sides of a single disc. Dance pieces such as "(Do the) Mashed Potatoes" and "Good Good Lovin'" alternated with the slow, passionate vocals of "Try Me," "Bewildered," "Lost Someone," and the pop-inflected (with strings) "Prisoner of Love." With "Out of Sight" in 1964, he started to move his sound toward the funk style he would popularize in 1965. Nearly always writing and producing his own material, Brown was poised to take off to new national popularity and creative freedom.

Impact of Event

With the recognition he received as a Grammy winner, Brown started to appear on national television and to achieve more freedom at King Records, with which he remained affiliated until 1971. More live albums followed, and more pop success. A song such as "It's a Man's Man's Man's World" was easily a number-one soul music hit, but it also managed to be a number-eight pop success. Brown, though, had never been an artist to stick to the formulas guaranteeing continued crossover acceptance. Going his own way, he began to further intensify his funk groove, changing band members and writing pieces of social commentary often called "message" songs. As black popular music evolved in the 1960's and 1970's, Brown would be a pathfinder as well as an exemplar. Like other pioneer soul artists such as Ray Charles, Aretha Franklin, and Otis Redding, Brown helped to bring the passionate singing styles of black gospel into secular music of black pride and awareness, but he differed from them in his sense of the need for a controlled and totally integral musical experience: song, back-up instrumentation, dance, vocal backup, and audience interaction. The consummate live performer in black popular music, he tried hard to carry over to his recordings some of that mesmerizing power of communication. It was essentially out of this nexus that his later work came.

Brown's recordings continued to reflect the diversity of his repertoire. Upbeat dance songs and instrumentals as well as paeans to sensual love included chart successes like "Get Up (I Feel Like Being Like a) Sex Machine," "Super Bad," "Funky Drummer," "Make It Funky," "Mother Popcorn," and "Hot Pants." Intense funk pieces such as "Money Won't Change You" and "Cold Sweat" extended his experiments with heavy polyrhythms and emotion-laden vocals. His most enterprising material, though, turned out to be the socially conscious songs he wrote in the later 1960's and into the 1970's, when American blacks became increasingly involved with civil rights and initiatives and themes of black pride. Brown spearheaded the musical involvement of blacks in this era. Performing more as a chanting or talking preacher and testifier than as a singer, Brown created a series of classics in the funk groove: "Get It Together," "Talkin' Loud and Sayin' Nothing," "Get Up, Get Into It, and Get Involved," "Soul Power," "Say It Loud—I'm Black and I'm Proud," and most remarkably, "King Heroin" and "Public Enemy #1," in which he scorned drug-taking. In "Brother Rapp" and "Rapp Payback (Where Iz Moses)," from 1970 and 1980, respectively, Brown pioneered rap music. As early as 1966, he had put out his "Don't Be a Dropout," which addressed serious issues of black educational achievement.

After 1965, many of Brown's hits on the soul charts crossed over to register among the top one hundred in pop sales. Songs such as 1968's "Say It Loud" did turn away some of his white audience, who wrongly thought he had joined the militant wing of black activists who called for violence. Brown did become controversial as he advocated black capitalism and spoke proudly of his own rise within the system while acknowledging the importance of white men such as Syd Nathan and Bert Bart in the development of his career. Not an assimilationist, Brown did avow his belief in the efficacy of whites and blacks working together.

While expanding soul music into funk and rap, Brown continued to sing passionate songs about the tensions in male-female relationships. Truly prodigious in the reach of his music-making and enduring exploration of styles, James Brown expanded the possibilities of black expression and gave contemporaries such as Wilson Pickett the courage to take their hard gospel-based singing styles into a broader market. Never abandoning his African-American cultural and musical roots, Brown is a tradition-based "man of words" who has put an indelible mark on the American scene.

Bibliography

Brown, James, with Bruce Tucker. *James Brown: The Godfather of Soul.* New York: Thunder's Mouth Press, 1990. A fine autobiography: detailed, frank, and full, with attention to musical matters. Illustrated, full discography, indexed.

George, Nelson. *The Death of Rhythm and Blues.* New York: Pantheon Books, 1988. George offers a tough and critical assessment of popular music in America as it relates to the co-optation and dilution of black roots. Illustrated with index.

Gillett, Charlie. *The Sound of the City: The Rise of Rock and Roll.* Rev. ed. New

York: Pantheon Books, 1984. Seminal study of postwar popular music. Discography, indexed.

Guralnick, Peter. *Sweet Soul Music: Rhythm and Blues and the Southern Dream of Freedom.* New York: Harper & Row, 1986. A study, with interviews, of the major soul music figures of the 1960's and 1970's. Illustrated, bibliography, discography, index.

Hirshey, Gerri. *Nowhere to Run: The Story of Soul Music.* New York: Times Books, 1984. Using recent interviews with major figures, Hirshey conveys the tensions and changes in black popular music over two decades. Pays major attention to Brown. Illustrated, indexed.

Shaw, Arnold. *Black Popular Music in America: From the Spirituals, Minstrels, and Ragtime to Soul, Disco, and Hip-Hop.* New York: Schirmer Books, 1986. Encyclopedic, yet readable all through; Shaw is able to convey the complexity and richness of black music in an engrossing way. Provides a detailed picture of the interrelationships among types of music, helping to put soul music in perspective. Notes, bibliography, discography, index.

_____. *Honkers and Shouters: The Golden Years of Rhythm and Blues.* New York: Macmillan, 1978. An excellent in-depth survey relying on interviews and Shaw's longtime personal involvement in the field. Attention to the business side of music and the many small record labels involved. Discography, index.

_____. *The World of Soul: Black America's Contribution to the Pop Music Scene.* New York: Cowles, 1970. A more general survey, with attention to blues and jazz precedents. Discography, index.

Frederick E. Danker

Cross-References

Handy Ushers in the Commercial Blues Era (1910's), p. 252; Bessie Smith Records "Downhearted Blues" (1923), p. 572; Armstrong First Records with His Hot Five Group (1925), p. 670; Ellington Begins an Influential Engagement at the Cotton Club (1927), p. 739; Billie Holiday Begins Her Recording Career (1933), p. 930; Goodman Begins His *Let's Dance* Broadcasts (1934), p. 968; Berry's "Maybellene" Popularizes Rock and Roll (1955), p. 1635; Presley Becomes a Rock-and-Roll Sensation (1956), p. 1705; Gordy Founds Motown Records (1959), p. 1790; Wonder Releases *Innervisions* (1973), p. 2294; Rap Goes Platinum with Run-D.M.C.'s *Raising Hell* (1986), p. 2582.

BREUER DESIGNS A BUILDING
FOR THE WHITNEY MUSEUM

Category of event: Architecture
Time: September 28, 1966
Locale: New York, New York

Design of the Whitney Museum of American Art epitomized architect/designer Marcel Breuer's mature elaboration of constructivism as an architectural style and philosophy

Principal personages:

MARCEL BREUER (1902-1981), a distinguished, influential constructivist architect and designer

WALTER GROPIUS (1883-1969), a Bauhaus mentor of Breuer, later his American collaborator

FRANCIS R. S. YORKE (1906-1962), a leading British advocate of the International Style of architecture; Breuer's partner from 1935 to 1937

PIER LUIGI NERVI (1891-1979), a distinguished Italian engineer and an associate of Breuer in designing the UNESCO headquarters in Paris

BERNARD ZEHRFUSS (1911-   ), a leading French architect and one of Breuer's associates on the UNESCO project

LE CORBUSIER (CHARLES-ÉDOUARD JEANNERET, 1887-1965), a leading twentieth century architect and an early influence on Breuer

Summary of Event

In a unique building designed by Marcel Breuer, the Whitney Museum of American Art opened its exhibitions on September 28, 1966. Occupying a corner lot measuring 100 by 125 feet at New York City's East Seventy-fifth Street and Madison Avenue, with two levels below ground and only five above, the modestly sized museum nestles among the tall apartment and office buildings of what in 1966 was the city's gallery district. Evoking images of cubist sculpture, the structure offers bold evidence of Breuer's individualized constructivist architectural vocabulary and philosophy. It likewise emphasizes the museum's commitment to purchasing and exhibiting works of living American painters, sculptors, photographers, and other artists.

Breuer's design of the Whitney building reflected the museum directors' philosophy. Permanent collections were eschewed; instead, changes and variety in exhibition became the rule. Three floors therefore were configured as spacious, open galleries. Their ceilings are two-by-two-foot "egg crates" of suspended, precast concrete to which movable wall panels and a flexible lighting system can be attached to ensure maximum effectiveness for the gallery's showings. Detailing throughout the structure is meticulously modern and industrial, yet warmed to human sensibilities by

Breuer's hallmark selection of materials. Thus, gallery floors are bluestone while walls are dressed with white, painted canvas. Main stairwells are flanked by walls of bush-hammered concrete, and the stairs themselves are granite, with teak and bronze railings. Outdoor sculpture is displayed within a court formed by excavation one level below ground yet visible along Madison Avenue.

Breuer physically delineated the museum from its traditional neighbors by designing full-height, separating wing walls of poured concrete. The cubelike main structure he sheathed with mottled gray granite, dispelling potential monotony with six angled, protruding windows on the south side, each the shape of a truncated triangle, and one large, similar window several levels above the Madison Avenue entrance. The entrance itself is an inviting, partially covered concrete bridge leading into a warm lobby uniquely lighted by suspended aluminum disks reflecting illumination from specially devised lamp centers.

The museum can be interpreted as a pinnacle in the common artistic growth of the Whitney Museum directors and of Breuer. Evolution of the modernist museum and of Breuer's architectural career were nearly synchronous. Launched in 1914, only a few months after New York's famed Armory Show introduced Americans to the works of Europe's leading postimpressionists and cubists, the Whitney Studio (1914-1918) sought, without much initial success, to inspire American interest in modern art. The venture enjoyed two subsequent incarnations, as the Whitney Studio Club from 1918 to 1928 and as the Whitney Studio Galleries from 1928 to 1930. Neither catered to what then could be characterized as general tastes or sound investments.

Under the aegis of Greenwich Village sculptress Gertrude Vanderbilt Whitney, however, the galleries reopened in 1930 as the Whitney Museum of American Art, marking the increasing creativity, popular approval, and sales of contemporary American artists. By 1966 and Breuer's completion of the museum, what three decades earlier constituted mere acceptance of modern art had almost become a popular artistic and financial craze. To acknowledge the abundance of modern art, both the Guggenheim Museum, designed by Frank Lloyd Wright, and Huntington Hartford's Gallery of Modern Art, for example, had opened in New York (in 1958 and 1964, respectively). These two museums augmented the splendid impressionist collections of the older Museum of Modern Art (opened in 1929). Similarly, the paintings of Pablo Picasso, Marc Chagall, Paul Klee, Salvador Dalí, Wassily Kandinsky, Piet Mondrian, Amadeo Modigliani, Jackson Pollock, Andy Warhol, Robert Rauschenberg, and Jasper Johns, among other modernist painters, had won wide acceptance. Results of the concomitant architectural revolution initiated by Walter Gropius, Le Corbusier, Ludwig Mies van der Rohe, Tony Garnier, Frank Lloyd Wright, Josef Hoffmann, Louis I. Kahn, and Alvar Aalto had become manifest in furniture, homes, industrial buildings, airports, and public buildings throughout the world.

A doctor's son born in Pecs, Hungary, in 1902, Marcel (Lajos) Breuer trained at the chief source of twentieth century architectural change, the Bauhaus school, led by Gropius. Originally a strict functionalist or purist, Breuer, while master of the

Bauhaus cabinet and joinery shop, established himself in 1925 by designing a revolutionary tubular steel chair. He later designed other furniture and cabinetry that earned wide recognition. His early development paralleled that of Wright, Mies van der Rohe, R. Buckminster Fuller, and Aalto insofar as his mastery of craft, materials, and design (the essence of Bauhaus teaching) began with furnishings. To these Breuer soon added architectural works, such as the landmark Harnischmacher House and Dolderthal apartments. By the 1930's, his reputation augured well for his future importance.

After two years' association with England's pioneer of the International Modern style, Francis R. S. Yorke, Breuer joined Gropius in graduate teaching at Harvard University in 1937. They entered into a collaborative exploration of American regional architecture that lasted until Breuer entered private practice in 1947. Meanwhile, entranced with integrating a New England idiom into his International Style, he designed several classics: the Breuer House (Lincoln, Massachusetts), the Chamberlain Cottage (Wayland, Massachusetts), the Haggerty House (with Gropius in Cohassett, Massachusetts), the Cantilevered House (New Canaan, Connecticut), the Thompson House (Ligonier, Pennsylvania), the Robinson House (Williamstown, Massachusetts), and several other stunning "binuclear" homes and multiple dwellings. Thus, by 1963, when he received the Whitney commission, Breuer's constructivism had matured. His demonstrated philosophy was to exalt structure—simple materials, novel technology, and fine finishing—but to separate his requirements for structure (usefulness and longevity) aesthetically from the nonstructural elements of design in order to humanize his clients' immediate personal environments. The Whitney Museum satisfied these major criteria with distinction.

Impact of Event

An increasing public appreciation of functionalism, of the International Modern style (which was its American architectural counterpart), and accordingly of architects' signature variations on these themes coincided with the evolution of Breuer's career. Breuer benefited from this happy trend just as he contributed to it. Although the Whitney Museum bore Breuer's unique imprimatur, it also carried the stamps of its times.

The Whitney ultimately proved to be a success for its architect while simultaneously finding general favor in the artistic community. The museum's early days, as Breuer had expected, were beclouded by controversy, dramatized by one of the 1960's increasingly frequent bomb threats. Critic Ada Louise Huxtable reported, just prior to the museum's opening, that it was New York's most disliked structure, that nearly the entire community's sensibilities appeared violated by this brashly unconventional building. Her own views lauded its superb setting and its brutal beauty. Other complaints about Breuer's work, brought to focus by the Whitney, were of a cumulative nature. Several architectural historians, exemplified by Wayne Andrews and Carl Condit, had voiced disappointment either with the apparent derivativeness of Breuer's work as an associate of Gropius or, speaking to specifics, with Breuer's denial of his textures and his purported conservative shift—almost to Georgian style—in his translations of New England idioms into the design of his homes.

Completion of the Whitney, along with concurrent grand projects such as the Paris headquarters for the United Nations Educational, Scientific, and Cultural Organization (UNESCO), designed in collaboration with Pier Luigi Nervi and Bernard Zehrfuss, proved redemptive. Andrews, by 1973, included the Whitney (and Breuer's Tompkins House) among his selections of New York State's major architecture. Other professional observers, already impressed with Breuer's work, continued their applause. Foremost among these were architectural historian and critic Peter Blake, who had produced two studies of Breuer, and Gropius himself, who despite his previous quarrels with Breuer at Harvard praised Breuer's objectivity, boldness, and independence in meeting the challenges of technical and aesthetic problems.

By the late 1970's, a modicum of appreciation for the Whitney likewise had come from initially trenchant media pundits. Typical of them was *The New York Times'* former architectural critic, Paul Goldberger. Goldberger found the museum to be a defiance of common sense, an utterly abstract, arrogant granite fortress, overbearing and almost brutal in form, that blatantly cantilevered itself onto Madison Avenue. It could never be ideal either for its site or for its program, for in his judgment, like all Breuer structures, it could never banish the impression that it was more object than building. Nevertheless, more than a decade after the Whitney's opening, Goldberger accorded it "grudging respect."

Although it was no foregone conclusion that they would do so, Breuer's former associates praised both Breuer and his work. These associates included Hamilton Smith, who had worked with him on the Whitney as well as on the Priory of the Annunciation and Mary College (both in Bismarck, North Dakota) and New York University Technology Building II, in addition to other large undertakings. Similar approbation came from Tician Papachristou, who had become a Breuer associate (joining Herbert Beckhard and Robert Gatje) in 1965 and subsequently produced a major survey of Breuer's plans and projects undertaken during the 1960's.

Signals of his creative influences also came from Breuer's coterie of former Harvard graduate students. By the time that the Whitney was completed many of these had carved their own significant careers and were well-qualified assessors of their former teacher's concepts and designs. Among those who had earned international reputations by the 1970's were Eduardo Catalano, Emilio Duhart, Eliot Noyes, I. M. Pei, and Harry Seidler. All retained positive views of Breuer's corpus of works, the Whitney included. Seidler accurately synthesized their laudable evaluations of Breuer as an architect the validity of whose contributions—both visual and technical— were unequaled over the previous half century. Breuer was unrivaled in his handling of sunlight and shadow, unmatched for his juxtapositions of materials—natural woods against white industrial masonry, against indigenous stones, even against rubble—as well as for contrasting these materials with glass and smooth synthetics. He was praised not only for his furnishings but also for housing and building designs that had become prototypes worldwide, specifically, for the principles embodied in his binuclear and cantilevered homes, and for his famed "Y"-shaped and sculptured structures.

Breuer, in the Whitney Museum and in the larger body of his work, transformed brutalism into beauty. It was therefore appropriate that New York's Metropolitan Museum of Art dedicated its first one-man architecture show to Breuer's accomplishments.

Bibliography

Blake, Peter. *Marcel Breuer: Architect and Designer.* New York: Architectural Record in Collaboration with the Museum of Modern Art, 1949. Written before design of the Whitney, but an excellent introduction both verbally and visually to Breuer's earlier works. The author is a respected architectural historian and critic. An easy, enjoyable preview of Breuer before maturation of his work. Like many architectural studies, it includes many fine plates and designs. Standard in public, college, and university libraries.

_____, ed. *Marcel Breuer: Sun and Shadow, the Philosophy of an Architect.* New York: Dodd, Mead, 1955. Blake offers his own notes and a fine synthesis of Breuer's distillations of his own philosophy. Breuer's designs and structures, however, are clearer statements of his purpose and principles than are his words. Many plates and designs, happily including Breuer's furniture and a résumé of his early works. Indispensable and widely available.

Breuer, Marcel. *Marcel Breuer: New Buildings and Projects.* New York: Praeger, 1970. Outstanding visual and textual detailing of Breuer's work, including much on the Whitney, in the decade of the 1960's. Indispensable and delightful. Hundreds of photo plates and designs. Available in major libraries.

Dixon, John Harris. "The Whitney: Big for Its Size." *The Architectural Forum* 125 (September, 1966): 80-86. Detailed professional description of the Whitney, with pictures and text.

Goldberger, Paul. *The City Observed: New York.* New York: Vintage Books, 1979. Remarks on the Whitney and on Breuer are few but pithy. Goldberger, an architectural critic and historian, places the Whitney in the context of architecture in its own Manhattan neighborhood and the city's other major structures. Plenty of photos and diagrams; detailed index.

Hitchcock, Henry Russell. *Marcel Breuer and the American Tradition in Architecture.* Cambridge, Mass.: MIT Press, 1938. Old but prescient and interpretive. The only early treatment in English on Breuer's furniture, cabinetry, and homes. Good context. Photos and index.

Clifton K. Yearley

Cross-References

German Artists Found the Bauhaus (1919), p. 463; Le Corbusier's Villa Savoye Redefines Architecture (1931), p. 869; The Whitney Museum Is Inaugurated in New

York (1931), p. 885; Wright Founds the Taliesin Fellowship (1932), p. 902; Aalto Designs Villa Mairea (1937), p. 1067; Fuller's First Industrial Geodesic Dome Is Erected (1953), p. 1579; The Guggenheim Museum Opens in a Building Designed by Wright (1959), p. 1806.

CELAN'S INFLUENTIAL *ATEMWENDE* IS PUBLISHED

Category of event: Literature
Time: 1967
Locale: Paris, France

Atemwende *introduced Paul Celan's influential notion of the "breath-measure" to poetry and affirmed Celan's status as one of Europe's greatest modern lyric poets*

> *Principal personages:*
> PAUL CELAN (PAUL ANCEL or ANTSCHEL, 1920-1970), a Romanian-born, German-speaking lyric poet who showed that lyric poetry could survive the Holocaust
> GISÈLE LESTRANGE (1925-   ), a French artist and noblewoman who became Celan's wife
> OSIP MANDELSTAM (1891-1938), a Russian poet with whom Celan identified whose work had a great influence on European lyric poetry
> BEDA ALLEMANN, a friend of Celan who later became an important critic of Celan's work
> RENÉ CHAR (1907-1988), a French poet who explored Surrealism and one of Celan's oldest Parisian friends

Summary of Event

By 1967 and the release of *Atemwende*, Paul Celan had been living in Paris for nearly twenty years. Paris offered Celan a neutral ground for writing, one that allowed him to write in German while minimizing the memories of the Holocaust that his Jewish ancestry made particularly agonizing. In Paris, Celan could be close to who he was: a lyric poet deeply concerned with language's capacity to speak itself. For Celan, it seemed as though language might fail sometimes, that it might be content with silence.

Born to German Jewish parents in Czernowitz in what is now Romania, Celan was reared under the pressure of racism and identity that characterized Eastern Europe before World War II. By the time he was a student at the University of Czernowitz, his parents were deported to death camps, where they died not long afterward. Celan himself spent two years working in a labor camp until heavy snow forced it to close. His studies continued, as literature became a way of survival. When the Russian Army reinvaded his homeland in 1944, Celan went to Bucharest, the capital city of Romania, where he continued reading the great German lyric poets Georg Trakl and Rainer Maria Rilke. In a series of name changes, he sought an identity that would permit him to keep living, and thus the man who was born Paul Antschel became Paul Aurel and Paul Ancel before he became Paul Celan. His poem "Todesfuge" ("Death Fugue"), written during this time and widely read, would remain his most explicit expression of the Holocaust. Celan wrote his first book, *Der Sand aus den Urnen* (1948; sand from the urns), with the hope that lyric poetry, like humanity, could be preserved like ashes in an urn.

Risking everything, Celan escaped across the border to Vienna in 1947 and to Paris a year later, where his recognition was gradual. His friends included the poet René Char, with whom Celan shared an interest in Surrealism and expressionism, and Beda Allemann, who would later edit a five-volume edition of Celan's collected works. A lecturer in German literature, Celan began to concentrate on his work. In 1952, Celan married the graphic artist Gisèle Lestrange and was asked to read in Germany at the request of the prestigious "Group 47." Many of the poems that had appeared in his Bucharest collection were included in his first Western book of poems, *Mohn und Gedächtnis* (1952; poppy and memory), which was published in Germany later in the same year. The book attracted immediate attention, and Celan quickly became known as a difficult minimalist poet who ranked among the greatest lyric voices of Europe.

During the early 1950's, Celan's books of poems continued to receive wide acclaim, and he won a number of literary prizes, including the Literature Prize of the Free Hanseatic City of Bremen and the Georg Büchner Prize awarded by the German Academy for Language and Literature. His acceptance speech for the latter would become one of his very few statements of poetics and would provide one of the governing metaphors of his life: the meridian, the border between an overwhelmingly muted distance from life and a closer, more painful, proximity to life. *Von Schwelle zu Schwelle* (1955; from threshold to threshold) developed the ideas of the earlier works, focusing more on the idea of language as a mesh rather than as a crystal. Celan's work was also becoming known for its broken syntax and short length; many of the poems were less than fifty words. Increasingly, Celan would invent new words altogether, joining two previously existing expressions with a hyphen. While some critics objected to what they interpreted as an "aestheticizing" of the Holocaust experience, Celan continued to express his perception of the fragmented world in which he lived.

Celan's next two books, *Sprachgitter* (1959; *Speech-Grille and Other Poems*, 1971) and *Die Niemandsrose* (1963; the nobody rose), reflect his "middle" period, during which he composed poems that were increasingly subjective, muted, and concerned with the problems of language. In these poems, as in the earlier ones, there was no direct social commentary about Celan's experience; these were not confessional poems in the ordinary sense. Celan's poems were characterized in the early 1960's by fewer and fewer images, almost as if he could no longer trust metaphor to convey what he desired. Addressed to an unattached "you," the poems would grow increasingly remote from literal experience, from the "reality" that most people understood. The other person in the poems was at once someone close to the poet, a distant spiritual figure, and an anonymous stranger. Such a combination gave Celan's works the label of "resisting interpretation" throughout much of the academic community. Celan himself began to regard his earlier work as being too close to the experience, too explicit for the kind of distance he wanted to maintain.

Celan suffered from bouts of depression throughout the 1960's that made it increasingly difficult for him to write. When Claire Goll, poet Yvan Goll's widow, accused him of plagiarizing some of her husband's work, Celan suffered a nervous breakdown. Haunted by the past, he seldom made public appearances and received few visitors. *Atemwende* (breath-turning), his first book of poems in five years, became associated with the beginning of his "late" period, when the struggle to locate the meridian of language reached a heightened pitch. Scholars have pointed out that the breath unit, rather than the metrical or syllabic unit, became the basis for the late poems. The lines of the poems are short, as is their general length, and the broken syntax that characterized the early and middle work is fragmented to its limit. As one critic has said, the last work is written as if German were a foreign language to Celan. *Fadensonnen* (1968; thread-suns) followed a year later to mixed reception, as Celan was increasingly understood as being hermetic despite his own rejection of the term. In 1970, overcome with his struggle with language, Celan drowned himself in the Seine. His three posthumous books, *Lichtzwang* (1970; force of light), *Schneepart* (1971; snow-part), and *Zeitgehöft* (1976; time-stead), extended the range of his work well beyond his life and time.

Impact of Event

Paul Celan's work echoes strongly throughout the literature of Europe and America and continues to influence the way poetry is written. His early study of Rilke and Trakl links Celan's work to that of the great German lyric masters who preceded him and whose work stands on a level similar to his own. To be a lyric poet in Europe in the nineteenth and twentieth centuries meant a profound understanding of Stéphane Mallarmé's idea that "pure" poetry should reflect what was obscure, that it should reflect the subjectivity and uncertainty of life. French Surrealism, Russian Formalism, and German expressionism all sought to reflect such an ideology. The aesthetic focused on how something was perceived rather than what was perceived, and as such found common ground with avant-garde ideals. Poets that followed Trakl and Rilke in Europe, such as Yvan Goll, Osip Mandelstam, and Paul Valéry, sought to explore the boundaries of lyricism and language. In addition to writing his poems, Paul Celan worked at translating the works of many of these poets into German, spreading their work across the literary canon.

For Celan's contemporaries, the advent of World War II changed many of the assumptions that the previous generation seemed to have. Language could not be accepted as a given mantle of protection, and instead of saying "I," the poet should speak more broadly for the experience of the other. Celan's friends René Char, Nellie Sacks, and other poets all felt the restrictions placed on them by their identity and by the nightmare of history that the Holocaust represented. While some claimed that lyric poetry was dead, Celan and others showed through their work that it could indeed survive, although not in the same manner. As Celan said in his acceptance speech for the Georg Büchner prize, language must be set free from history.

Much the same idea came to have a tremendous impact in America during the

1960's and 1970's, when American poetry was undergoing dramatic change as a result of new theories of free verse as defined by poets such as William Carlos Williams. At first barely read by American audiences, Celan's work began to be translated by writers such as Michael Hamburger. During the shift of focus from English models of prosody to South American and European models, Celan was embraced as a poet whose minimalist work perfectly captured the tenets of the "organic" school of poetry: a poetry the form of which followed the form of the experience it reflected. Anthologized in collections of open-form poetry, Celan became associated with a historical consciousness, although his poems were clearly related to the archetypal mythic consciousness that other European writers were developing.

Celan's unit of the breath-measure offered an alternative to the metric, from which even free verse could not completely remove itself. The breath unit, while not unmetered, worked toward what Celan had called the freeing of the language. Already concerned with concentrating poetry to the essential core of the experience, free verse found Celan's radical minimalism to be an extreme form of lyricism, a form that developed out of the German lyric masters. For poets trying to find a new poetry in America, such achievement could hardly be assessed. A generation of American poets would follow Celan's minimal approach by concentrating away from narrative poetry and by avoiding the first person in their work, favoring instead the power of the single image. As such, contemporary poets the world over felt a Nietzschean distrust of metaphor and the very language through which they created their art. Celan's work helped Rilke interpretation as well, for passages that had once seemed difficult in Rilke began to seem penetrable after Celan's super-condensed lyrics.

The entire scope of what poetry was changed in Celan's wake. While some poets had come to be understood as confessional, Celan showed that a poet must never become too personal. His struggle with language was in another sense a struggle with the relationship that the poet must draw between the world and the poem. At his most personal, Celan was still at his most universal, writing poems that speak not only of the difficulty of surviving the Holocaust but also of the challenge of living while being so open to language that it seems ready to swallow those who seek to use it.

Celan's work created a much greater impact than his contemporaries realized and has continued to forge the definition of what lyric poetry is. His poems provide fertile ground for the ideas of contemporary theorists such as Emmanuel Levinas and Jacques Derrida (who wrote an essay about Celan's language). He was thus truly ahead of his time, already anticipating the problems of meaning that language in the poststructuralist world would come to express.

Bibliography

Celan, Paul. *Collected Prose.* Translated by Rosemarie Waldrop. Riverdale-on-Hudson, N.Y.: Sheep Meadow Press, 1986. Celan's few speeches and select letters for public audience are collected and translated here, although the original German is not provided. The text is nevertheless indispensable for any Celan scholar interested in interpreting the poems.

_____. *Last Poems.* Translated by Katharine Washburn and Margret Guillemin. San Francisco: North Point Press, 1986. This collection was designed to complement an earlier edition of Hamburger's collection by focusing solely on the late, posthumous works. The original German is provided along with the English translations. An introduction also illuminates this difficult period in Celan's career.

_____. *Poems of Paul Celan.* Translated by Michael Hamburger. New York: Persea Books, 1988. This collection of poems includes selections from all Celan's books, although the selection is greater for the books prior to *Atemwende.* Poems are printed in the original German, with English versions printed on facing pages. The introduction by the translator is a good foregrounding of the poems themselves and provides several insights that Amy Colin's biography does not.

Colin, Amy. *Paul Celan: Holograms of Darkness.* Bloomington: Indiana University Press, 1991. Colin's biography of Celan is the only up-to-date biography in English. Its many photographs and excerpts from letters, journals, and conversations greatly illuminate Celan's life and career.

Hollander, Benjamin, ed. "Translating Tradition: Paul Celan in France." *Acts: A Journal of New Writing* 8/9, 1988. Special double issue. An eclectic anthology of writings by and about Celan. Concentrates on the years Celan spent in Paris. In addition to essays by Celan's prominent translators, there are essays by a wide variety of writers whom Celan influenced, including Robert Duncan, Yves Bonnefoy, and Maurice Blanchot.

David Francis

Cross-References

Rilke's *Duino Elegies* Depicts Art as a Transcendent Experience (1911), p. 281; Sartre's *Being and Nothingness* Expresses Existential Philosophy (1943), p. 1262; Wiesel's *Night* Recalls the Holocaust (1956), p. 1700; Foucault's *Madness and Civilization* Is Published (1961), p. 1877; Lévi-Strauss Explores Myth as a Key to Enlightenment (1964), p. 1995; Derrida Enunciates the Principles of Deconstruction (1967), p. 2075.

DERRIDA ENUNCIATES THE PRINCIPLES OF DECONSTRUCTION

Category of event: Literature
Time: 1967
Locale: Paris, France

Jacques Derrida launched an assualt on what he viewed as the untenable linguistic underpinnings of all Western thought, thereby unfolding a "deconstructive" critique of rationalism and humanism

Principal personages:
JACQUES DERRIDA (1930-   ), the French professor of philosophy whose advocacy of "deconstruction" has had an immense impact on literary studies
PAUL DE MAN (1919? 1983), the leading American advocate of deconstruction, whose wartime pro-Nazi writings brought scandal to deconstruction when uncovered in 1988
FERDINAND DE SAUSSURE (1857-1913), an important early modern linguist whose concepts were transfigured by Derrida
FRIEDRICH WILHELM NIETZSCHE (1844-1900), the German philosopher whose prophetic tone, poetic fancy, and iconoclastic posture greatly influenced Derrida

Summary of Event

With the publication of the English edition of *De la grammatologie* (1967; *Of Grammatology*) in 1976, "deconstruction" catapulted into prominence on the highbrow American cultural scene, and by the 1980's the term had spread into the lexicon of journalism and popular culture. The French philosophy professor who coined this catchy neologism, Jacques Derrida, had grown up in Algeria along the margins of French culture. A fascination with giving overlooked, or "marginalized," phenomena their due has continued to infuse Derrida's prolific and prolix writings throughout his career. In particular, Derrida has repeatedly maintained that mainstream Western metaphysics has to be exposed as a sham, for it has been erected upon several supposedly erroneous assumptions: that writings have some connection with authorial intention and refer to things outside the text; that "man" is a meaningful and enduring concept; that such a thing as "presence" exists; and that spoken language precedes written language. Some two-thirds of *Of Grammatology* consists of Derrida's examination of the works of Jean-Jacques Rousseau in search of passages that betray the older writer's apparently benighted thralldom to one or another aspect of mainstream Western metaphysics. Through punning and rhetorical wordplay, confident pronouncements, clever flights of speculation, and a style of argumentation marked by conceptual leaps that defy logic, Derrida "deconstructs," or unmasks, texts as carrying within them the seeds of their own refutation.

Derrida has typically dismissed scholarly attempts from outside his movement to define either deconstruction or its central tenets. Rather than accepting the confining limits of definition and evidential argument, Derrida prefers to speak of deconstruction as an activity marked by the *jeu*, or "play," of untrammeled and often audacious thought. Arguing that "rationality" is a word that "should be abandoned," Derrida claims to have forged a "meta-rationality" and a "meta-scientificity" that can "be no more shut up within a science of man than conform to the traditional idea of science. In one and the same gesture," he adds, "they leave *man*, *science*, and the *line* [linearity] behind."

The ejection of the human subject from Derrida's model of language resonates with overtones of the works of other French antihumanist intellectuals such as Michel Foucault, Louis Althusser, Jacques Lacan, and Roland Barthes. Just as Barthes had dramatically proclaimed the "death of the author" within a brave new world of disembodied literary texts, Derrida insists that ordinary conversations as well as literary texts embody no intentionality on the part of a speaker. Using a Husserlian model to define "presence" in the narrow terms of a pure or absolute presence, Derrida claims that the inability to demonstrate the existence of absolute presence proves that presence itself is an untenable concept. "Logocentrism," this wrongheaded attachment to presence and yearning for immediacy that Derrida condemns as something of an insidious conspiracy pervading all Western writing and metaphysics, functions as a sort of bugbear or primal evil in deconstructionist thought.

Derrida claims that since there is no presence in which a speaker might formulate a thought or intention to speak, the idea of intentionality itself dissolves as an illusion. In effect, the Derridean model of discourse portrays the speaker as a passive and blank conduit for language, which itself stays in the driver's seat from start to finish. People do not use language to achieve their aims; if only humans could "free" their view of language "from the concept of man," they could perceive that language mechanistically uses humans to unfold its own dynamism. Similarly, flesh-and-blood human subjects do not desire things, for that would involve the impossibility of intentionality; instead, in the Derridean universe of passive humanoids and robust abstract forces, "Desire desires the exteriority of presence and nonpresence."

Another deconstructionist tenet that underlines the absence of the human subject is a radical view of "intertextuality," or the interchange of influences between various literary texts. Derrida makes a claim even more sweeping than Barthes' proclamation of the author's demise, insisting that "there is nothing outside the text." According to this model, there can be no presence of an external reality to which texts might refer. Derrida emphasizes the conviction with which he holds on to this model of an echo-chamber universe of texts reverberating with one another by anointing it an "axial proposition" of *Of Grammatology*. Quite a few of his followers have taken him at his word and discussed wars and famines as "texts" having a historical footing no different from that of a poem or an advertisement.

Although the disciplines of history and anthropology give evidence of many cultures with spoken languages that lack written counterparts, Derrida insists that the precedence of spoken language over written language is one of the grandest misconceptions of Western thought. He once again tweaks the nose of common sense, this time by redefining "writing" so that it is indistinguishable from "language," and then noting that since language ("writing") is a broader category than spoken language, it must have preceded spoken language in the scheme of things. According to Derrida, it is precisely the lamentable Western inclination to take the path of a phonetic-based alphabetic system that has wrongly valorized, or "privileged," speaking over writing by placing undue emphasis on the presence-besotten vocal aspects of language rather than on its pure and presence-free graphic features. He condemns the intransigence of the supposed Western "effacement" and "repression" of the written "signifier" by complaining that even after the West had become well aware of nonalphabet writing scripts in East Asia, the West stubbornly pressed on with its bad old logocentric ways. In order to back up his linguistically naïve claim that Chinese and Japanese are "largely nonphonetic scripts" and thus free of "logocentrism," Derrida earnestly cites the long-discredited and dilettantish views of Ernest Fenollosa and Ezra Pound about the purportedly "ideographic" nature of the Chinese script. By maintaining a tone of ebullient self-assuredness when discussing East Asian languages, an area about which he was almost totally ignorant, Derrida exposed a basic problem with his pungent and far-flung speculations—they are grounded on too thin a layer of sound scholarship to be very convincing.

Impact of Event

Without doubt, Derrida's ideas have exerted greater impact in the United States than in any other country. In many ways, then, the 1976 publication of *Of Grammatology* in English translation created a much larger and lengthier stir than the appearance of the original French edition in 1967 had. Derrida's subsequent publishing efforts in France were almost always made with an eye to getting the works out in English translation as rapidly as possible. Frequent lecture trips and visiting appointments to such U.S. universities as Yale, Cornell, and the University of California at Irvine have enabled Derrida to cast a larger shadow in U.S. academe than he had in France. In 1980, Derrida's university in Paris required that he appear in public to defend his dissertation, which he had been procrastinating over for more than a decade and a half. Had he been content to settle for a doctorate from an American university instead, several colleges would have probably lined up on a moment's notice to present him with honorary degrees.

"Grammatology," a term that Derrida had dug up from an obscure linguist named Gelb, never really caught on the way Derrida seems to have anticipated with the gushing proclamation in his preface that grammatology "shows signs of liberation all over the world." It was Derrida's coinage of "deconstruction" that would hit the jackpot for him within a cultural atmosphere as antinomian as America's had become by the 1970's and 1980's. The radical skepticism of Derrida's rhetoric appealed to the relativistic thought of large numbers of American academics in the humanities. Young professors, in particular, found it useful to draw on deconstructionist approaches to dismantle the ideas and studies of their forebears and peers prior to embarking on new tangents of their own. Even academics who disdained Derrida's general project or disapproved of his flamboyant and often Byzantine writing style often found the concept of deconstruction useful when overhauling or revamping a given conceptual framework.

Derrida's most pervasive influence may have been on the language of academic discourse in the American humanities. Many of his verbal mannerisms, whether personal idiosyncrasies or a shared tendency among Left Bank poststructuralists, soon became part of the stock-in-trade of upwardly mobile young professors and graduate students. The use of "privilege" as a pejorative transitive verb and "inscribe" as an ornate substitution for "write" or "impart" are but two examples of Derrida's influence on the increasingly arcane lexicon of the American humanities. The effect has been to make the field of literary studies radiate an increasingly inscrutable air, in which professional jargon serves to divide the insider elite from the rank-and-file citizenry on the outside.

Even though deconstruction has had little influence on Derrida's own field of philosophy, it has generated heated controversies in many American law schools, where the radical critical legal studies movement is active. A number of schools of architecture promote a deconstruction-inspired movement for asymmetrical construction methods known as deconstructivism. While the Paul de Man scandal that broke in 1988 brought public scrutiny to many deconstructionists' moral evasiveness and apathy toward history, the effects of deconstruction on American cultural life will no doubt continue to be felt for many years to come.

Bibliography

Abrams, M. H. *Doing Things with Texts: Essays in Criticism and Critical Theory.* New York: W. W. Norton, 1989. Expert and readable interpretations of Derrida and some other deconstructionist "Newreaders," as Abrams refers to them.

Defrancis, John. *The Chinese Language: Fact and Fantasy.* Honolulu: University of Hawaii Press, 1984. Explains how and why every written language, even those with a nonalphabetic script, such as Chinese, must be mainly phonetic in nature in order for the memory of flesh-and-blood speakers to be able to handle the requisite linguistic processing. Derrida's characterization of Chinese writing as "nonphonetic" and his yearning for the West to abandon the "logocentric" alphabet in favor of some supposedly nonphonetic script thus prove little more than uninformed fantasies.

Derrida, Jacques. *Of Grammatology.* Translated by Gayatri Chakravorty Spivak. Baltimore, Md.: Johns Hopkins University Press, 1976. The English edition has proven far more influential than the original French version. Spivak's correspondence with Derrida seems a double-edged sword: While the translation doubtless benefited from Spivak's attentiveness to Derrida's suggestions, the translator's introduction smacks of the disciple's unreserved embrace of the master's doctrines.

Dews, Peter. *Logics of Disintegration: Post-Structuralist Thought and the Claims of Critical Theory.* London: Verso Books, 1987. Discusses the theoretical disintegration of the unified subject in Derrida's work as compared with that of Foucault and Lacan, and contrasts all three approaches with Theodor Adorno's relatively cogent emphasis on intersubjectivity.

Ellis, John. *Against Deconstruction.* Princeton, N.J.: Princeton University Press, 1989. This succinct and lucid critique by a veteran literary theorist from the University of California guides the reader through the main threads of argument in *Of Grammatology* from square one. Ellis provides a strong case for doubting both the logical tenability and practical significance of Derrida's valorization of writing over speech.

Lehman, David. *Signs of the Times: Deconstruction and the Fall of Paul de Man.* New York: Poseidon Press, 1991. Explores the rise and fall in the scholarly standing of de Man, the second leading deconstructionist after Derrida. Lehman draws a compelling connection between de Man's cunning concealment of his wartime Hitlerite polemics and his deconstructionist credo that every theoretical position is unstable and is bound to contradict itself at some level.

Norris, Christopher. *Derrida.* Cambridge, Mass.: Harvard University Press, 1987. Unlike most books on deconstruction from a partisan perspective, this treatise does not simply dismiss Derrida's critics as too hidebound to be worth refuting but instead attempts to rebut critiques such as those by the speech-act theorist John Searle. Though Norris' arguments often fail to convince, his prose is much more readable than the norm for advocates of deconstruction.

Soper, Kate. *Humanism and Anti-Humanism.* La Salle, Ill.: Open Court, 1986. Explains how and why humanism and Western rationalism have come under such heavy fire from Derrida and other French poststructuralists such as Althusser and Foucault. These men deny not only the centrality but the very existence of the human subject, whose absence leaves *Homo sapiens* as little more than a conduit for the impersonal processes of textual interaction or insidiously concealed social manipulation.

Wiener, Jon. *Professors, Politics, and Pop.* London: Verso Books, 1991. The first three chapters of this book provide one of the most rigorous and fair-minded summaries of the late-1980's revelations about Paul de Man's wartime pro-Nazi writings. Also discusses reactions from de Man's critics and defenders, especially Derrida's vitriolic thrusts at the critics.

Philip F. Williams

Cross-References

Freud Inaugurates a Fascination with the Unconscious (1899), p. 19; Surrealism Is

Born (1924), p. 604; The New Criticism Holds Sway (1940's), p. 1169; Sartre's *Being and Nothingness* Expresses Existential Philosophy (1943), p. 1262; Foucault's *Madness and Civilization* Is Published (1961), p. 1877; Lévi-Strauss Explores Myth as a Key to Enlightenment (1964), p. 1995.

EXPO 67 PRESENTS INNOVATIVE ARCHITECTURAL CONCEPTS

Category of event: Architecture
Time: April 28-October 27, 1967
Locale: Montreal, Canada

Millions of visitors to an international exhibition in Montreal viewed futuristic designs from dozens of countries

   Principal personages:
   JEAN DRAPEAU (1916-   ), the mayor of Montreal whose tireless efforts secured the financing for the Expo
   R. BUCKMINSTER FULLER (1895-1983), a visionary American architect, engineer, and futurist who designed the Expo's U.S. pavilion
   MOSHE SAFDIE (1938-   ), an Israeli architect who designed both the master plan for the Expo site and Habitat 67, the exhibition's most acclaimed structure

Summary of Event

In the 1960's, the civic leaders of Montreal, one of Canada's oldest cities, made a concerted effort to transform the city into a modern world capital. As a key part of this effort, Montreal mayor Jean Drapeau, a man known for his creativity and resourcefulness, fought vehemently for the opportunity of hosting a world exhibition. In 1967, Canada would observe its centennial year, and Expo 67 was intended to mark the beginning of countrywide celebrations.

The first controversy that Drapeau met was in the selection of the Expo site. As a way of giving the exhibition full exposure, an unusual site was selected: the small island of Île Sainte Hélène in the St. Lawrence River. This created an uproar among environmentalists as well as among conservative city engineers. Drapeau's idea prevailed, but there was less than four years to prepare and build the exposition site, a short time for a project of such magnitude. Beset by the worst winter in thirty-three years, Canadian contractors managed to achieve almost impossible engineering feats in order to allow the Expo to open on time.

The Île Sainte Hélène was joined by a man-made island later named Île Notre-Dame, a reference to the famous island in the Seine in the heart of Paris. The name was chosen to emphasize that Montreal was the "new Paris" and that Canada was a worthy North American host for an exhibition that previously had been European in design and execution.

Officials organizing Expo 67 were quick to emphasize that this was a "first-category" exhibition. In the recent past, there had been smaller, "second-category" exhibitions such as the World's Fairs held in Seattle in 1962 and in New York in

1964-1965. Expectations ran high within government circles that Expo 67 would be a landmark event, one that would set the standard for all that followed.

"Man and His World" was chosen as the theme for the Expo. The theme was drawn from Antoine de Saint-Exupéry's book *Terre des hommes* (1939; *Wind, Sand, and Stars,* 1939); a key passage in the book stated that "to be a man . . . is to feel that through one's own contribution one helps to build the world." Three exhibition pavilions were devoted to variations on this central theme and were given the designations "Man the Provider," "Man the Producer," and "Man the Explorer." Designers placed these major structures at the entrance of the exhibition in an effort both to entice visitors and to remind them of the concept and vision behind Expo 67.

Each country participating in the Expo was given complete liberty to build a pavilion that best represented its culture and achievements. While the guidelines for those hosting the expositions were strict, such strictness did not impinge on the exhibitors. Most pavilions were designed with an eye to free-form construction, and geometric shapes with angular sides and pointed tops seemed to dominate the fair. All such fairs serve in some degree as testing grounds for new and innovative architectural designs; Expo 67 thus served to show what buildings might look like in the future—although many of the designs on display, of course, would never be built outside the Expo's environs.

Since the Expo was built on two islands in the middle of the St. Lawrence River, water played an important part in the ambience of the exhibition. Lakes, canals, lagoons, and inlets could be found in every corner of the site. If water was an obvious leitmotif of Expo 67, though, the individual pavilions were rather more difficult to classify. In general, each country attempted to reflect its essence in the design of its pavilion. Pavilions from Ethiopia, Thailand, and Burma appeared to be influenced by the design of those countries' religious buildings; each seemed to reflect the spiritual side of the country more than any other feature. A sense of African tribalism could be seen in the African Nations pavilion. Square, hutlike buildings with angular roofs facing inward reflected a sense of unity and togetherness. France's exhibit resembled a dome with sections that suggested at times the tiered levels of a high-rise apartment block. Great Britain, long known for its conservative architecture, allowed some surprising innovation; its pavilion consisted of square sections layered one on top of another to form a building in a somewhat distorted "E" shape. Near the water's edge, the British pavilion culminated in a tall cone with its top cut off at an angle.

More than fifty million visitors attended Expo 67. Prior to the opening, it had been predicted that the Expo would prove to be a financial loss for the Canadian government; instead, income generated by increased foreign tourism in Canada doubled the original investment. Much of this success resulted from the popularity of the fair's free intermixing of art and culture. One international pavilion in particular emphasized this view of accessible art; more than two hundred paintings from museums and art galleries around the world were hung in the main art building. There, for example, a work by the seventeenth century Dutch painter Rembrandt van Rijn hung near the stark work of the twentieth century American abstract artist Willem de Kooning; a sculpture by the nineteenth century French sculptor Auguste Rodin was placed opposite a piece of abstract sculpture by the American modernist David Smith.

Sculpture intermingled with buildings. Open-air dramatic performances and free-standing art allowed all who visited Expo 67 to get the distinct impression that culture was something to be experienced in the world at large and was not the exclusive property of museums and theaters. Expo 67 managed to offer a glimpse of what the world might be like if the arts were made accessible to everyone. The need for humanity to see itself as one was the strong theme that rang out from the many pavilions of the exposition.

Impact of Event

With its wide variety of cultural and architectural offerings, Expo 67 managed to achieve worldwide recognition. This success stemmed both from the fair's appealing and innovative site on the St. Lawrence River and from the popular and critical acclaim bestowed on many of the individual pavilions. A sense of accomplishment thus marked the closing of Expo 67 six months after the opening ceremonies.

Often, such government-sponsored events receive criticism. While society continues to evolve and change, actual discussion about such changes is often controversial. An event such as Expo 67, which displayed innovation in a wide variety of fields on a worldwide scale, thus invites cynics to lament progress and even invention. Such criticism was particularly directed at what were otherwise widely hailed as two of the Expo's most successful exhibits, the U.S. pavilion and Habitat 67. While most pavilions received only cursory mention by the media, both of these caught the imagination of the public and the critics; both, though, also prompted expressions of indignation from conservatives.

The U.S. pavilion, designed by the visionary architect R. Buckminster Fuller, was a twenty-story geodesic dome that epitomized experimentation. Fuller's futuristic creation pioneered the use of a special skin made of acrylic. During the day, the dome glittered in the natural light; by night, illuminated from within, it glowed like a large amber lamp. To maintain its internal temperature, the dome was constructed with 4,700 aluminized slides; as the ambient temperature in the structure rose, shades shifted position to keep the dome cool. Although Fuller's design drew wide praise, it was also the target of criticism from viewers who thought that the structure was not an appropriate reflection either of American culture or of the United States' position as a world leader.

While Fuller's dome was widely discussed, another structure at Expo 67 was receiving even greater scrutiny. Habitat 67, a collection of more than 150 prefabricated concrete apartment blocks, became the exhibition's crown jewel. Just as the Crystal Palace of the 1851 Great Exhibition in London and the Eiffel Tower of the 1889 Paris Centennial Exposition became symbols of their eras, Habitat 67 came to represent Expo 67.

In designing Habitat 67, Israeli architect Moshe Safdie was responding to the worldwide need for practical, inexpensive housing. Safdie chose the simple building block as a model. Each block that made up part of the dwelling space weighed eighty tons; special cranes had to be used to lift the blocks into place. The completed structure resembled an enormous ziggurat. Although the units appeared to resemble apartments, no dwelling was ever directly above another, and walkways connected the structure's various levels. Another important feature was the private terrace that was a part of every home. Arranged asymmetrically, each unit received the maximum view and space.

Expo 67 thus acted as an architectural laboratory for an experiment in living space, an important issue in a world with an escalating population. Habitat 67 opened up the possibility of looking at high-density living in a new way. Previously, large apartment blocks and high-rise buildings had sacrificed privacy for practicality. What Safdie achieved in the Habitat design was the use of precast concrete blocks in a more creative and people-oriented way.

What was perhaps most remarkable about the Habitat design was the infinite number of permutations that could be made from the basic box. Each Habitat dwelling was unique in the way in which the component boxes were put together. This freedom of design was what made the final exhibit so striking. Architectural critics who tried to find a model that Habitat 67 might resemble were unsuccessful; some sought precedent for the structure in such distant sources as the ancient mountain dwellings of the Pueblo Indians. Most, though, agreed that Safdie's design was both compelling and original.

Habitat 67 inspired architects to design with people in mind and opened up the whole question of people living in high-rise apartments. In its wake, public housing, particularly in Europe, began to incorporate different sizes of dwelling, meaning, for example, that a family of four might live next to a single retired senior citizen. Although experts pointed to some details of Habitat 67's design as flawed—for example, it was noted that much of the structure could have been built from materials lighter than the heavy concrete used—its overall success and influence on other public housing was undeniable.

The design of the West German pavilion also drew considerable attention. Architect Frei Otto designed the building in the shape of an enormous steel-mesh tent that drew wide praise for its exterior appearance; however, the interior of the tent, which exposed the structure's heavy supporting beams, was judged to be unimaginative. The overall success of the design, though, was soon confirmed in the summer of 1967, when Otto's firm won a competition to design a similar structure for a hotel for pilgrims to Mecca. The influence of Otto's project was also attested by many later large shopping malls that used a variation on the tent shape for roofing. Designs meant to serve only one function—in this case an exhibition—thus often get incorporated into mainstream architecture.

Expo 67 lived up to the expectations of the Canadian government and the people of Montreal. The fifty million visitors were exposed to innovative architecture, and the exhibition as a whole served as a useful reminder that architecture must serve human needs first.

Bibliography

Billard, Jules B. "Montreal Greets the World." *National Geographic* 131 (May, 1967): 600-621. Montreal has been a major French enclave in Canada for many years. Those who live and work in Montreal are zealous advocates for their city. This article puts those characteristics in the context of Expo 67. A clear and well-labeled pull-out diagram of Expo 67 is included.

Chamberlin, Anne. "Expo 67: The Big Blast Up North." *The Saturday Evening Post* 240 (April 22, 1967): 30-37. What is most striking about this article is that Chamberlin is able to convey the human side of the building of Expo 67. With wry humor, the obstacles that were overcome in getting the Expo built are discussed in detail. Through the use of anecdotes, a very real picture is given of the time preceding the opening day of Expo 67.

Jacobs, David. "What It's Like to Live in an Experiment." *Times Magazine* 6 (June 4, 1967): 50-81. Author David Jacobs gives a firsthand account of life inside the experimental Habitat 67 structure. Much of the article deals with the philosophy behind the project. There is enough description of the living conditions to give a real sense of what the experience was like for his family.

"Man and His World." *Time* 89 (May 5, 1967): 48-49. Despite the brevity of this article, the photographic display more than makes up for what is lacking in content. The approach is photojournalistic, and the choice of pictures is excellent.

Stagg, Anne. "Discoveries at Expo." *House and Garden* 132 (September, 1967): 192-197. Much of the space is devoted to photographs of the exhibits in each pavilion. A useful record of the artistic approaches adopted by the participating countries.

Richard G. Cormack

Cross-References

GARCÍA MÁRQUEZ'S *ONE HUNDRED YEARS OF SOLITUDE* IS PUBLISHED

Category of event: Literature
Time: May, 1967
Locale: Buenos Aires, Argentina

One Hundred Years of Solitude *brought Magical Realism and the "Boom" period of Latin American literature to the attention of an international audience*

Principal personages:
GABRIEL GARCÍA MÁRQUEZ (1928-   ), a Colombian novelist whose work *One Hundred Years of Solitude* marked the climax of the "Boom" period of Latin American literature
JULIO CORTÁZAR (1914-1984), an Argentinean novelist whose work inaugurated the "Boom"
CARLOS FUENTES (1928-   ), a Mexican novelist of the "Boom" era
ALEJO CARPENTIER (1904-1980), a Cuban novelist often considered to have been the founder of Magical Realism
MARIO VARGAS LLOSA (1936-   ), a significant Peruvian novelist of the "Boom" generation

Summary of Event

After years of writing fiction without attaining significant notice, Colombian novelist and journalist Gabriel García Márquez achieved enormous popular and critical acclaim with the publication of *Cien años de soledad* (1967; *One Hundred Years of Solitude*, 1970). The novel traces the rise and fall of the Buendía family from its harmonious beginnings (under founder José Arcadio Buendía) in a mythical Latin American town called Macondo to its increasingly chaotic decline through six generations of descendants.

One Hundred Years of Solitude, however, is not merely the story of the Buendía family and the town of Macondo. Critics have pointed out that the book is also a microcosm of Latin America: local autonomy yielding to state authority; anticlericalism; party politics; the coming of the United Fruit Company; aborted revolutions; the rape of innocence by history. The Buendías (inventors, artisans, soldiers, lovers, mystics) seem doomed to a biological tragedy from solitude to poetry to science to politics to violence back to solitude.

García Márquez himself describes the work as an apotheosis of the theme of solitude. The story of Colonel Aureliano Buendía—the wars he fought and his progress to power—is, in effect, a progress toward solitude. Not only is every member of Buendía's family solitary, but the entire town is also permeated by solitude (that is, antisolidarity); even people who sleep in the same bed are profoundly alone. This lack of solidarity, a consequence of individuals acting for themselves alone, precipitates the entire disaster of Macondo.

In *One Hundred Years of Solitude*, García Márquez gives solitude a uniquely political connotation. This connotation, to some critics, suggests a pessimism on the part of García Márquez concerning the fate of contemporary humankind. Humanity, it seems, has sealed its own destiny because of its consuming quest for power and material gain; the result is an incapacity to sustain a society based on love and solidarity with one's fellow beings.

Placing *One Hundred Years of Solitude* within the context of García Márquez's earlier work, it is apparent that almost all of García Márquez's previously published works are populated by people either from the imaginary town of Macondo or who have some relation to it. *La hojarasca* (1955; *Leaf Storm and Other Stories*, 1972) shows the effects of the short-lived "banana boom" and the subsequent depression on that small rural community. This event resurfaces in the thirteenth and fourteenth chapters of *One Hundred Years of Solitude*. The lonely unrewarded hero of *El coronel no tiene quien le escriba* (1961; *No One Writes to the Colonel and Other Stories*, 1968) and *La mala hora* (1962; *In Evil Hour*, 1979) re-create the climate of political violence that prevailed in the Colombian countryside in the 1950's, the former linking it to a long tradition of such violence and the latter depicting its corrosive effect on the community. Many of the characters of these early narratives are also forerunners of the Buendías of *One Hundred Years of Solitude* in that they are lonely, isolated individuals leading a solitary existence.

The short stories *Los funerales de la Mamá Grande* (1962; collected in part in *Big Mama's Funeral*, 1968) are vignettes of life in the town of Macondo. They portray the traditional dominance of the land-owning oligarchy through the mythical story of a legendary matriarch who ruled over the region for generations. With regard to style, this work marks a major evolution. In all of his fiction, García Márquez attempts to achieve a poetic transformation of reality, but in most of his early work, he does so in a style that is essentially realistic. In these stories, however, the author was to discover the narrative manner best suited to giving literary expression to the world he knew as a child. The narrator presents himself as a kind of spokesman for the community. Its Magical Realism is counterbalanced by an ironic, irreverent tone that subverts the very legend it is propagating. In *One Hundred Years of Solitude*, García Márquez was to perfect that narrative manner and to create an all-embracing fictional world incorporating the principal places, themes, and characters treated separately in his earlier work.

The town of Macondo is named after a plantation near the small town (Aracataca) on Colombia's Caribbean coast, where García Márquez grew up. Macondo has served as the location of his various narratives, and he has shaped and populated it from the stories told to him by his grandparents, in whose house he lived as a child. In the novel, Úrsula, the mother and grandmother of the entire Buendía family, is defined by her ability to recall and recount lives and situations otherwise threatened with oblivion or confusion.

In following the rise and fall of the Buendía family, García Márquez makes use of themes that have turned up often before in the literature of his continent. Futile revolution, imperialism, governmental lunacy, ludicrous *machismo*, doomed passion, and a voracious natural world are concepts of Latin-American private and political history that the writer uses. Although a self-proclaimed leftist, García Márquez has refused to use his art as a platform for political propaganda.

Impact of Event

Following its appearance in Latin America, *One Hundred Years of Solitude* received immediate acclaim and became the first Latin American novel ever to achieve international best-seller status. Although the novel provoked widespread debate among Latin-American literary critics who disagreed on the issue of whether the work presented a stereotypical portrait of Latin America in the manner of Latin-American Social Realist novels of the 1940's and 1950's, most agreed that the novel ranked as possibly the best Latin-American novel of its era. While some initial English-speaking reviewers asserted that García Márquez treated Macondo and its history as a microcosm of Latin America, others felt that the book's mythic and Magical Realist aspects combined to impart a more universal statement. Extensive critical commentary has since focused on many facts, particularly the novel's references to other texts and numerous allusions to biblical and classical myth.

The mixture of historical and fictitious elements that appear in *One Hundred Years of Solitude* places the novel within the Latin-American tradition of Magical Realism. The birth of this style of writing is often attributed to the Cuban novelist and short-story writer Alejo Carpentier, who elaborated the critical concept of *lo maravilloso americano*, the marvelous American reality, arguing that, geographically, historically, and essentially, Latin America was a marvelous and fantastic place. To Carpentier, to render that place was to render marvels.

García Márquez has also maintained that the Latin-American environment is marvelous, particularly the Caribbean. The coastal people were the descendants of pirates, smugglers, and black slaves; to grow up in such an environment, according to the novelist, is to have fantastic resources for poetry. In addition, García Márquez has argued, the mixture of many different cultures in the Caribbean has created an open-mindedness that looks beyond apparent reality.

Considered a masterpiece of contemporary Latin-American literature and a seminal example of Magical Realism, *One Hundred Years of Solitude* presents fantastic incidents in an objective style in an effort to obscure distinctions between illusion and reality. At the heart of the novel is its magic, a magic that moves from the simply phenomenal—a levitating priest, a flock of yellow butterflies that flit ominously around a young seducer, plants that bleed when cut, ghosts that are accepted as part of the natural landscape—to the core of García Márquez's world. In this world, beings shuffle back and forth in time, and the ordinary has been so clearly seen and followed to its conclusion that the world itself becomes more than natural; it becomes, instead, a wild conjuring of things that may seem to be anchored in reality but that slide imperceptibly into the fantastic.

Some critics maintain that García Márquez's particular gift for infusing the magical into the real is responsible for his international popularity. They assert that his utterly convincing tone has brought fantasy into the mainstream of world literature and has illustrated García Márquez's belief that reality is not restricted to the mundane. García Márquez once stated that he always writes in a serious tone because he can get away with anything as long as he makes it believable. Yet along with the fantastic elements appear the historical incidents and places that inspired them. An episode involving a massacre of striking banana workers is based on a historical incident. Although *One Hundred Years of Solitude* is first and foremost a story, the novel also has value as a social and historical document. A master of vision and language, García Márquez blends legend and history in ways that make the legends seem truer than truth. His scenes and characters are humorous, tragic, mysterious, and beset by ironies and fantasies. In his fictional world, anything is possible, and everything is believable.

Winner of the 1982 Nobel Prize in Literature, García Márquez is one of a small number of contemporary writers from Latin America who have given to its literature a maturity and dignity it never had before. *One Hundred Years of Solitude* is perhaps García Márquez's best-known contribution to the awakening of interest in Latin-American literature, since the book's appearance in Spanish in 1967 prompted unqualified approval from readers and critics. The 1960's "Boom" in Latin-American fiction reached its peak with the novel.

During the 1960's in Latin America, there appeared in different countries, almost simultaneously, a number of acclaimed novels and collections of short stories that dazzled a large reading public that had hitherto been virtually ignored by the literary world. This sudden flowering of writers (which has been labeled the "Boom" period of Latin-American literature) saw the emergence of such celebrated writers as Carlos Fuentes, Julio Cortázar, Mario Vargas Llosa, Jorge Luis Borges, and Gabriel García Márquez. The works of these writers began, almost at once, to be translated into foreign languages and to put Latin America on the international literary map for the first time.

One Hundred Years of Solitude has been translated into more than thirty languages and has sold more than ten million copies. The popularity and acclaim won by the novel meant that Latin-American literature would progress from capturing the exotic interest of a few to becoming essential reading. As a result, Latin-American culture itself came to be viewed less as an alien subculture and more as a fruitful alternative way of life. So great was the novel's initial popularity that the first Spanish printing of the book sold out within one week; for months afterward, Latin-American readers would exhaust each successive printing. Translations of the novel elicited similarly enthusiastic responses from critics and readers around the world. Chilean poet Pablo Neruda, himself a Nobel laureate, has referred to the book as the greatest revelation in the Spanish language since Miguel de Cervantes' *Don Quixote de la Mancha* (1605, 1615).

The novel owes its international success to several factors. Its plot is both fascinating and accessible to the average reader; its style is lucid, poetic, and rapidly paced; and in García Márquez's depiction of the people of Macondo, all basic human emotions and experiences are dramatized with extraordinary vividness. The riveting history of Macondo can be read as a metaphor not merely for Latin-American history but for all of Western civilization as well.

Bibliography

Bell-Villada, Gene H. *García Márquez: The Man and His Work.* Chapel Hill: University of North Carolina Press, 1990. In this excellent study of García Márquez's life and work, Bell-Villada asserts that the author stands in the tradition of nineteenth century novelists whose art combined the common touch with progressive and humane politics and who could inspire the affection of large audiences. Contains a useful and lengthy bibliography.

Donoso, José. *The Boom in Spanish American Literature.* Translated by Gregory Kolovakos. New York: Columbia University Press, 1977. A uniquely personal history of the "Boom" generation written by a prominent Chilean novelist of the period. Rather than defining the term, Donoso discusses why the rather misleading label was invented. He focuses his discussion on the "Boom" novels and novelists that merited international attention.

González Echevarría, Roberto. *Myth and Archive: A Theory of Latin American Narrative.* Cambridge, England: Cambridge University Press, 1990. This brief but scholarly work proposes a new theory about the origin and evolution of the Latin-American narrative and about the emergence of the modern novel. Argues that examining relationships the narrative establishes with nonliterary forms of discourse is more productive than examining relationships such literature has with its own traditions. Extensive bibliography.

Martin, Gerald. *Journeys Through the Labyrinth: Latin American Fiction in the Twentieth Century.* New York: Verso, 1989. First-rate interpretive history of the Latin-American novel in the twentieth century. Focuses primarily on the period from the 1920's to the 1980's. Combines a thematic with a historical approach and offers new readings of well-known writers and works. Intended for nonspecialists as well as specialists in the field. List of primary texts and critical bibliography.

Ortega, Julio, ed. *Gabriel García Márquez and the Powers of Fiction.* Austin: University of Texas Press, 1988. This collection of critical essays attempts to further the scholarship on García Márquez by offering new perspectives and fresh readings in order to provide a more complex and rewarding understanding of the texture and scope of his novels.

Swanson, Philip, ed. *Landmarks in Modern Latin American Fiction.* New York: Routledge & Kegan Paul, 1990. The aim of this series of insightful essays is to offer an overview of the evolution of modern fiction in Latin America via a study of key texts. Lengthy introduction and conclusion provide the background to the

"Boom" period and chart developments after its decline. Contains a useful bibliography.

Genevieve Slomski

Cross-References

Joyce's *Ulysses* Epitomizes Modernism in Fiction (1922), p. 555; Surrealism Is Born (1924), p. 604; *The Sound and the Fury* Launches Faulkner's Career (1929), p. 805; García Lorca's *Poet in New York* Is Published (1940), p. 1179; Borges' *Ficciones* Transcends Traditional Realism (1944), p. 1268; The "Boom" Captures Worldwide Attention (Late 1950's), p. 1689.

HENDRIX RELEASES *ARE YOU EXPERIENCED?*

Category of event: Music
Time: May, 1967
Locale: The United States and Great Britain

Rock music was changed when the heavy psychedelic blues and guitar virtuosity of Jimi Hendrix became a huge success, creating "acid rock" and pointing the way to fusion and heavy metal

Principal personages:
> JIMI HENDRIX (1942-1970), a guitarist and songwriter who fused blues with hard rock, surreal lyrics, and inventive, pyrotechnic sounds
> CHAS CHANDLER (1948-   ), a former bassist for the Animals who heard Hendrix playing in Greenwich Village, brought him to London, and became his manager
> MITCH MITCHELL (1946-   ), the drummer with Hendrix's first band, the Jimi Hendrix Experience
> NOEL REDDING (1945-   ), a guitarist who switched to bass to play with Hendrix

Summary of Event

When *Are You Experienced?* was released in Great Britain in May, 1967, the rock revolution of the 1960's in many respects had yet to reach its fullest flowering. Bob Dylan had recorded his classic trilogy combining visionary lyrics with folk rock, the Beatles had released *Revolver*, which fused a psychedelic pop sound with Dylan-influenced lyrics, and the Rolling Stones had recorded *Aftermath*, but nothing like the slabs of sound and feedback thrown from Hendrix's guitar had yet been heard.

The drug-influenced lyrics and aggressive sexuality of *Are You Experienced?* were accompanied by pounding rhythms and heavy guitar feedback, slashing power chords, and screaming guitar leads. Chas Chandler's production took advantage of recent advances in recording-studio technology to create stereo effects that complemented the otherworldly textures Hendrix summoned from his guitar. On the instrumental "Third Stone from the Sun," Hendrix created science-fiction paintings in sound over Mitch Mitchell's jazzy drums; on the album's title track, he played a howling guitar lead that sounded as if it were being played backward. It was a distinctive sound that some have labeled "psychedelic blues."

In the months prior to the album's release, Hendrix had become a sensation in England, guided by the careful management of Chandler, the former bassist for the Animals, a popular British rock band. Before Chandler heard him playing in Greenwich Village, Hendrix had honed his skills for years as a sideman for the Isley Brothers, Little Richard, and many others, listening to the great blues guitarists and taking what he liked from each of their styles. By the mid-1960's, the Seattle-born

Hendrix was living in New York City and playing small Greenwich Village bars. He became interested in the possibilities of guitar feedback after hearing recordings of the Who, while his discovery of Dylan influenced Hendrix's lyrics and convinced him that his voice was good enough to front a band.

When the Jimi Hendrix Experience played the Monterey International Pop Festival in June, 1967, Hendrix amazed an American audience only distantly familiar with his work by doing an innovative cover of Dylan's "Like a Rolling Stone," playing his guitar behind his back and with his teeth, and lighting his guitar on fire and smashing it at the end of his set. Sales of *Are You Experienced?* took off. The album stayed on the *Billboard* charts for 106 weeks and sold more than a million copies.

The rest of Hendrix's life is the archetypal story of the 1960's rock star. He toured incessantly, breaking box-office records, and continued experimenting with music. Hendrix saw the Mothers of Invention using a wah-wah pedal, a foot-controlled guitar attachment that radically changes the timbre of the instrument, and was soon using it so well that many automatically associate the device with his music. The wah-wah and Hendrix's songwriting skills were prominently featured on his more restrained second album, *Axis: Bold as Love* (1968).

On his third album, the double set *Electric Ladyland* (1968), Hendrix broke away from the formula of his first two albums. Several tracks are long jams with other musicians such as keyboard player Steve Winwood of Traffic, bassist Jack Casady of the Jefferson Airplane, and old friend Buddy Miles, a drummer. Some songs use multiple tracks of wah-wah guitar, while others display jazz and soul influences. Hendrix at this time was reportedly the highest-paid act in rock, with concerts grossing a minimum of $50,000 per show.

Yet Hendrix's personal life was falling apart. He was spending money on cars that he would quickly destroy in accidents; he often got violently drunk and was taking ever-larger amounts of drugs. Despite his artistic success, Hendrix was beginning to feel trapped in the role of guitar hero. He was tired of constant touring, of playing "Purple Haze" and his other early hits over and over again for audiences who were not interested in his newer material. He wanted to branch out and play with a variety of other musicians. His band and his management, however, did not want to tamper with a winning formula. Hendrix's desire to change styles led to disagreements with Chandler and fights with bassist Noel Redding, who barely appears on *Electric Ladyland*. In the wake of such controversy, the Jimi Hendrix Experience broke up, and Hendrix began playing with Miles and another old friend, Billy Cox, on bass.

At the Woodstock Festival in August, 1969, with the Vietnam protests in full swing, Hendrix gave one of his most memorable performances, one indelibly associated with the counterculture of the 1960's. On the final day of the festival, shortly after dawn, Hendrix climaxed a brief set by playing a free-form version of "The Star-Spangled Banner." Using his trademark feedback and vibrato bar ("whammy bar") effects, Hendrix caused his guitar to howl and explode with the sounds of jets and falling bombs, turning the patriotic anthem on its head to capture the frustrations and contradictions of the 1960's generation.

On January 1, 1970, Hendrix recorded the live *Band of Gypsys* album with Cox and Miles. Chandler was worried, fearing that this all-black band would alienate Hendrix's mostly white audience. The uneven *Band of Gypsys* included "Machine Gun," a virtuoso display in which Hendrix made his guitar sound like a machine gun and again imitated the sounds of falling bombs.

After Woodstock, Hendrix worked on concert films and began recording material for a new double album. He was in bad shape as the result of his constant drug use, however, and felt more trapped than ever by his earlier image. He wanted to straighten out his life by switching to new management and taking his music in a different direction. He had been playing with diverse musicians and wanted to continue to grow as an artist. Hendrix was interested in writing for and playing with a big band, and he had arranged for rehearsals to begin with Gil Evans and his orchestra in late September of 1970.

It never happened. On September 18, 1970, at the age of twenty-seven, Hendrix choked to death after taking too many sleeping pills. Many believe that he was on the threshold of a major new direction that may have found him playing with avant-garde jazz musicians. His last true studio album, *The Cry of Love*, taken from studio material recorded in the months before his death, was released shortly thereafter; the album found Hendrix turning away from hard rock and feedback in favor of bluesy songs.

Impact of Event

Hendrix's mature period lasted only four years, but his work has had a tremendous effect on rock and jazz, and to a lesser degree, blues and soul. Many critics believe that Hendrix was the single most important instrumentalist in the history of rock and consider the scope of his influence equal to that of musicians such as Elvis Presley, Chuck Berry, and Bob Dylan.

If Muddy Waters updated Delta blues by picking up the tempo and adding electric amplification, Hendrix updated Waters' urban blues by integrating it with rock and turning the amplification into howling feedback, using a whammy bar to mimic the glissando of the slide guitar favored by many old bluesmen, and modifying the tone with wah-wah pedals, fuzz boxes, and other technological tricks. While the hardware Hendrix used is primitive by later standards, he demonstrated persuasively that technology had much to offer musicians, and his constant experimentation with guitar sound and texture was the precursor to the work of Pat Metheny, David Gilmour of Pink Floyd, and Robert Fripp and Adrian Belew of King Crimson.

An entire generation of young guitarists was influenced by Hendrix. Hendrix's influence is easily discernible, for example, in the work of Robin Trower, Stevie Ray Vaughan, and Nils Lofgren, three prominent guitarists who rose to stardom after his death. Virtually anyone who modifies instruments with a wah-wah pedal is influenced by Hendrix's use of the device. Despite the excellent use of the wah-wah pedal by Eric Clapton and Frank Zappa at about the same time, the wah-wah's distinctive sound has become indelibly linked with the lead guitar style of Jimi Hendrix.

Hendrix imitators sprang up quickly. Blue Cheer, a power trio that was also fronted by overdriven guitar manipulated by whammy bar, put out its first album about a year after Hendrix did. The vicious wah-wah guitar on the first two Stooges albums, recorded in 1969 and 1970, shows how quickly some of the more superficial elements of Hendrix's style were assimilated by other guitarists. More than anyone else, he was the master, the standard by which other guitarists were judged. The long guitar solos of late 1960's and 1970's rock were partly an outgrowth of Hendrix's live style, as the guitar-hero image Hendrix helped create led to the glorification of guitar technique. Heavy-metal bands picked up on Hendrix's use of feedback, overdriven amplifiers, and power chords. Later guitarists such as Eddie Van Halen are flashy descendants of Hendrix.

In the early 1970's, bands with a guitar-centered sound inspired by Hendrix flourished. Frank Marino, the guitarist of the heavy-metal trio Mahogany Rush, even claimed to have been visited by Hendrix's ghost. While heavy metal evolved principally from the work of Eric Clapton and other British blues-rock musicians, the genre's heavy guitar sound is virtually unthinkable without Hendrix. Rock guitarists as diverse as Neal Schon of Journey and Brian May of Queen owe debts to Hendrix, as do jazz guitarists Pat Metheny and Lee Ritenour.

The funkier sound Hendrix used with the Band of Gypsys was an important influence on the psychedelic soul records of the late 1960's and 1970's, including the work of Curtis Mayfield and Sly and the Family Stone. Albums by the Isley Brothers from the late 1960's on also bear Hendrix's stamp. Funkadelic's free-form music, with its numerous guitarists playing over a groove, also was affected by Hendrix's sound, as was their flamboyant dress. The 1980's and 1990's star Prince owes a similar debt to Hendrix.

When *Are You Experienced?* was released, jazz had not assimilated the possibilities of electric guitar to anywhere near the degree that rock had. Many jazz musicians, however, took note of Hendrix's phrasings, the textures and sounds of his guitar, and the way he incorporated elements of jazz into rock. Hendrix, whose own guitar sound was influenced by the saxophone playing of John Coltrane, often played guitar in a way that made the instrument sound like a horn. This guitar/horn sound influenced a generation of jazz guitarists in the 1970's and 1980's.

By the time of Hendrix's death, jazz was beginning to explore the use of the electric guitar and other elements of rock. In the late 1960's, Miles Davis began to unite elements of rock with jazz, giving rise to the genre known as fusion. Hendrix played with many of the musicians who played on Davis' groundbreaking 1969 album, *Bitches Brew*. On *Bitches Brew* and on several albums from the 1970's, Davis is clearly influenced by Hendrix's work, even processing his trumpet and organ through a wah-wah pedal. Davis said at the time that he would have used Hendrix as the guitarist for his 1975 release *Agharta*.

James "Blood" Ulmer took Hendrix's ideas into a jazz context by playing with Ornette Coleman, while groups such as Defunkt took Hendrix's sounds into a realm where funk meets a heavily guitar-oriented sound. The fusion bass player Jaco Pastorius cited Hendrix as a major influence and incorporated quotations from Hendrix's "Third Stone from the Sun" into his bass solos. After Hendrix's death, Gil Evans recorded an album of arrangements of Hendrix songs and played many of them live.

According to the prestigious jazz magazine *Down Beat*, most jazz-rock fusion musicians cited Hendrix, along with John Coltrane and Miles Davis, as their major influence. Jazz guitarist Al DiMeola, who was a teenager when *Are You Experienced?* came out, has related how the sounds Hendrix wrung from his guitar were a primary influence. The funky, multitracked sound used for several pieces on *The Cry of Love* were an influence on the electric Prime Time band that Ornette Coleman formed during the 1970's. Subsequently, artists and groups including Material, Curlew, Bill Frisell, and James "Blood" Ulmer followed Coleman's example, exploring the edge of the jazz/rock divide.

Finally, Hendrix's skill as a song interpreter sometimes influenced even those who wrote the original songs. When Bob Dylan rerecorded his "All Along the Watchtower" in 1974, his new arrangement was clearly inspired by the powerful version of that song that Hendrix recorded on *Electric Ladyland*.

Bibliography

Henderson, David. *'Scuse Me While I Kiss the Sky*. Rev. ed. New York: Bantam Books, 1981. A long, worshipful biography containing many interviews with relatives and friends who provide many anecdotes. Takes a longer look at Hendrix's early years than some of the other biographies do. Includes many of Hendrix's song lyrics.

Hopkins, Jerry. *Hit and Run*. New York: Perigee Books, 1983. This biography contains the most material on Hendrix's family and childhood and makes some attempt to re-create the atmosphere in which he grew up. Hopkins examines Hendrix's early influences and brief Army service. The bulk of the book, on Hendrix's brief career, delves into how chaotic Hendrix's adult life was and dwells on the drugs and groupies that seemed to follow him everywhere.

Milkowski, Bill. "Jimi Hendrix: The Jazz Connection." *Down Beat* 49 (October, 1982). Examines Hendrix's influence on jazz. Includes a number of interviews with jazz musicians who discuss the effect Hendrix's work had on their music and that of their peers. A bit worshipful, but informative.

Murray, Charles Shaar. *Crosstown Traffic*. Boston: Faber, 1989. By far the best book examining the stylistic currents Hendrix absorbed and influenced. Murray devotes one chapter to Hendrix's biography and one chapter each to the musical currents with which he was involved: blues, soul, and jazz. Other chapters examine where Hendrix fit into the 1960's as a cultural movement and look at the contradictions in being a black artist performing for a mostly white audience.

Sampson, Victor. *Hendrix*. New York: Proteus Books, 1984. A brief biography that skips quickly over Hendrix's childhood, mostly covering the essential events of his career. Contains a large selection of black-and-white and color photographs. Also includes a thorough discography.

Scott M. Lewis

Cross-References

Berry's "Maybellene" Popularizes Rock and Roll (1955), p. 1635; Presley Becomes a Rock-and-Roll Sensation (1956), p. 1705; The Beatles Revolutionize Popular Music (1963), p. 1944; The Rolling Stones Release *Out of Our Heads* (1965), p. 2027; Dylan Performs with Electric Instruments (1965), p. 2038; The Beatles Release *Sgt. Pepper's Lonely Hearts Club Band* (1967), p. 2098; The Monterey Pop Festival Inaugurates the "Summer of Love" (1967), p. 2104; Davis' *Bitches Brew* Vitalizes Jazz-Rock Fusion (1969), p. 2153; The Woodstock Music Festival Marks the Climax of the 1960's (1969), p. 2180; Led Zeppelin Merges Hard Rock and Folk Music (1971), p. 2228.

THE BEATLES RELEASE *SGT. PEPPER'S LONELY HEARTS CLUB BAND*

Category of event: Music
Time: June 2, 1967
Locale: Great Britain and the United States

The Beatles retreated to the studio after three years of touring to revitalize their creative instincts and produced one of the most revolutionary records of all time

Principal personages:
JOHN LENNON (1940-1980), the Beatles' rhythm guitarist and lead vocalist
PAUL MCCARTNEY (1942-   ), the group's bass guitarist and lead vocalist
GEORGE HARRISON (1943-   ), the group's lead guitarist and vocalist
RINGO STARR (RICHARD STARKEY, JR., 1940-   ), the group's drummer and vocalist
GEORGE MARTIN (1926-   ), the producer and arranger of most of the band's albums

Summary of Event

After their last live concert in San Francisco, on August 29, 1966, the Beatles, weary from more than three years of constant, worldwide touring, retreated to the recording studio to work on an album that would become an aural scrapbook of their childhood days in Liverpool, England. Since early 1964, when they conquered the American audience, the Beatles had recorded six albums, each demonstrating a growing musical and lyrical sophistication, and audiences had come to expect that each new pressing would exceed the accomplishments of the last. Rumors had spread that the Beatles were preparing something different, but no one realized how revolutionary that next recording would be.

Work on the new record actually began in November, 1966, when John Lennon offered the first composition, "Strawberry Fields Forever," originally a simple, gentle song that took its title from an orphanage where Lennon and childhood friends attended garden parties. Through successive recordings, however, the song changed dramatically into a phantasmagoric recording accentuated by an eery, mildly slurred vocal track. The song was actually the product of two entirely different recordings in different keys that producer George Martin cleverly merged. The song clearly reveals the increasingly experimental nature of the Beatles' music and the indispensably significant role George Martin assumed in helping them create the particular sounds they heard in their imaginations.

The next song recorded was "When I'm Sixty-Four," a piece Paul McCartney had begun when he was sixteen years old and finished eight years later for his father's sixty-fourth birthday. A campy vaudeville-influenced tune, "When I'm Sixty-Four" gives ample evidence of Paul's considerable wit. Another McCartney composition, "Penny Lane," the title of which referred to a traffic roundabout in Liverpool, completed this first group of songs for their childhood album.

Pressured by Capitol Records in the United States, which had not had a Beatles release since *Revolver* in August, 1966, the band decided to issue the two strongest songs of the three—"Penny Lane" and "Strawberry Fields"—on a double-A-sided single record. Left now with only one song for their upcoming album, they reunited in Abbey Road Studios in February, 1967. Midway through the session, McCartney presented his song "Sgt. Pepper's Lonely Hearts Club Band" and suggested they make an album as though the Pepper band existed. Thus, as a result of happy accident, the concept was born.

In order to create a link between the first song, "Sgt. Pepper's Lonely Hearts Club Band," and the album's second, "With a Little Help from My Friends," McCartney invented the character of Billy Shears, a pseudonym for Ringo Starr, leader of the imaginary Pepper band. The suggestion is that the album presents tunes created and performed by this imaginary band during a performance. As George Martin has pointed out, the band members became so inspired that a spirit of friendly rivalry took over as each would arrive at the studio with a new composition.

McCartney's other songs—"Fixing a Hole," "Getting Better," and "Lovely Rita"— are cheerful, though not especially complex, pieces, songs that reflect a buoyant, optimistic point of view and aptly mirror the spirit of the time. His one remaining offering, "She's Leaving Home," is a melodramatic ballad describing a failure of parental love and a child's grim determination to run away from home.

Lennon, on the other hand, his imagination fueled by increasing amounts of psychedelic drugs that he would bring to the recording sessions, offered songs that abound in fantastic images and an often fractured point of view. "Lucy in the Sky with Diamonds" is one of the album's most original and controversial compositions. Beatle fanatics immediately seized on that idea that, because of its surreal imagery and because an acronym of the title revealed the letters "LSD," the song must surely be a celebration of drug-taking. Lennon, though, consistently denied such speculation and insisted that the title came from a remark his four-year-old son, Julian, had made when asked what a painting he had created in school was about. The child, Lennon said, had answered that the painting showed his friend, Lucy, in the sky with diamonds.

"Being for the Benefit of Mr. Kite" emerged as a kind of found poetry, its images derived entirely from an old circus poster Lennon had purchased. When Lennon decided he wanted to create a swirling circus atmosphere to accompany the lyrics, Martin randomly cut up and reassembled stock tapes of a steam organ to create a hurdy-gurdy sound.

"Good Morning, Good Morning" was inspired by a television advertisement for a breakfast cereal. Amid the blaring horns of Sounds Inc., a band that once toured America with the Beatles, Lennon, critic Nicholas Schaffner wrote, "parrots some of the vapid pleasantries most of us take refuge in to disguise a lack of real communication." As the music fades, dogs, barnyard animals, a fox hunt, and a screaming chicken conclude the piece and offer a smooth segue into a reprise of the title track.

The last song, "A Day in the Life," is a genuine masterpiece and a testament to Lennon and McCartney's collaborative skills. Each had a portion of a song he could not finish; through clever combination of the two fragments, the pair created a tale of a life of routines that ends in an auto accident. Lennon, Martin remembered, wanted to hire a symphony orchestra to create "a tremendous build-up, from nothing up to something absolutely like the end of the world." Settling on half an orchestra (forty-two musicians), Martin wrote a rough score that detailed only the lowest and highest possible notes the musicians were to play, and at the end of a cacophonous blast, the four Beatles hit three pianos simultaneously, while engineer Geoff Emerick manipulated the controls so that the final chord lasted a full forty-five seconds.

While all this was taking place, the Beatles, dressed in gaudy costumes and accompanied by friends such as Mick Jagger and Marianne Faithfull, wandered among the orchestra members (who had been requested to wear evening dress), passing out joints, sparklers, and novelty items. Thus, the orchestra leader wore a bright red clown's nose, a violinist held his bow in a gorilla's fist, and each member had a party hat. The recording had a festival atmosphere that the band would never recapture during subsequent recording sessions.

George Harrison's only contribution, "Within You Without You," is a song on which he plays sitar and on which none of the other Beatles appears. The piece marks Harrison's deepening interest in Eastern music, instruments, and philosophy; the song, though, does not age as well as the album's other compositions.

Buoyed by the knowledge that they had created something truly original, the Beatles decided that the album's cover had to match the music's uniqueness. To that end, they commissioned Peter Blake to stage an imaginary gathering of sixty-two personalities with whom the Beatles would be photographed. In addition, the cover shows wax effigies of the group from Madame Tussaud's studio and numerous marijuana plants circling what appears to be a grave with the name "Beatle" arranged in flowers upon it. The Beatles also hired Douglas Hayward, a popular tailor of the time, to create elaborate silk uniforms for the band.

Impact of Event

Sgt. Pepper's Lonely Heart's Club Band was overwhelming in its impact. In many ways, the album marked a departure from traditional rock songs, album production and packaging, fashion, and rock criticism, and as John Lennon tersely commented, "It was a peak."

Throughout the late 1950's and early 1960's, pop songs held to a rather strict formula—innocuous ditties of teenage love and angst that rarely exceeded three minutes in length. They were usually not topical in content and were musically rather pedestrian, three-chord tunes. In their steady improvement as writers and musicians, the Beatles had chafed against these restrictions and had expressed their frustrations in various ways, not the least of which was a suppressed cover for one American album release that featured the band in bloody butchers' coats, with pieces of meat and limbs of dolls draped over their shoulders.

With the release of *Sgt. Pepper's Lonely Hearts Club Band*, adherence to the formula for the Beatles and for other bands quickly went out the window. No longer limited exclusively to songs of teenage romance, they began to speak out on issues of the day with increasing sharpness, and songs of adolescent love soon gave way to hymns of adult passion. "A Day in the Life" demonstrated that audiences could not only sit through but also appreciate a longer song, and later releases such as "Hey Jude" pushed the limits of song length. As McCartney explained years later:

> We were always pushing ahead: *'louder, further, longer, more, different.'* I always wanted things to be different because we knew that people, generally, always want to move on, and if we hadn't pushed them the guys would have stuck by the rule books and still been wearing ties.

The notion of the concept album—a record unified by a dominant theme or motif or which offered a consistently unfolding narrative through its collection of songs— soon took firm hold in rock music circles. It is no surprise that the Who's *Tommy* and *Quadrophenia*, the Kinks' *Arthur*, and the Eagles' *Desperado* followed, and each in its separate way owed a debt to *Sgt. Pepper's Lonely Hearts Club Band*.

The group also created firsts in album packaging by printing the lyrics to each of the songs on the back cover and by making the album a foldout that featured a close-up photograph of the band on the inside. Within the sleeve itself was included a glossy sheet of cutout figures and patches, and the record jacket, in a departure from the usual staid jackets of white paper, was illustrated with a mass of swirling waves that range from bright red to white. In all, the album cost an unprecedented $100,000 and took four months to produce. For the time, these figures were staggering; in comparison, for example, the Beatles' first album had been completed in one day and for less than $2,000.

While the Beatles certainly did not inaugurate the explosion of fashion in the 1960's, they did seize on a trend and bring it to even greater popularity. Around this time, Patti Harrison, George's wife, introduced them to a group of Dutch designers whom they commissioned to make clothes, paint their pianos and cars, and run an exclusive boutique in a stuffy London neighborhood. The height of the band's elaborate costumes came with the photos included in their next release, *Magical Mystery Tour*.

For years, rock music was regarded with disdain by serious musicians and critics, and the idea of a probing rock record review was still a rather foreign concept in 1967. After *Sgt. Pepper's Lonely Hearts Club Band*, it became clear that rock music was changing, and so too the aesthetics by which it would be judged had to change. Magazines such as *Rolling Stone* and *Crawdaddy* addressed the challenges this new music posed. After 1967, rock criticism came of age as a serious form of aesthetic

analysis; increasingly, it drew accomplished writers who raised the level of evaluation of a medium theretofore not regarded as an art form.

George Martin summarized the effect of the album well when he wrote,

For my part, I felt it was the album which turned the Beatles from being just an ordinary rock-and-roll group into being significant contributors to the history of artistic
performance. It was a turning point—the turning point. It was the watershed which
changed the recording art from something that merely made amusing sounds into something which will stand the test of time as a valid art form: sculpture in music, if you
like.

Bibliography

Carr, Roy, and Tony Tyler. *The Beatles: An Illustrated Record.* New York: Harmony
Books, 1975. A book full of pictures and much detailed information. The authors
often make keen observations about the band and its songs, and the book is important for its notes on each of the Beatles' albums and their solo recordings.

Friede, Goldie, Robin Titone, and Sue Weiner. *The Beatles A to Z.* New York: Methuen, 1980. The book that presents everything one could want to know about the
band. Details are carefully researched, and the work is especially helpful in mentioning songs never released and the working titles of many pieces.

Lewisohn, Mark. *The Beatles Recording Sessions: The Official Abbey Road Studio
Session Notes, 1962-1970.* New York: Harmony Books, 1988. A scrupulously researched listing of all known Beatles recordings, listing where and when they
took place, how many takes were recorded, who participated in the sessions, and
the instruments played on each track. Includes an interesting interview with Mc-
Cartney.

Miles, Barry. *Beatles in Their Own Words.* New York: Quick Fox, 1978. An interesting collection of quotes from the band members on various subjects, compiled
from scores of publications. Divides material into seven principal subjects and
includes photos and sketches. Major drawback is a lack of bibliographic citations
to trace the origins of the remarks.

Norman, Philip. *Shout! The Beatles in Their Generation.* New York: Simon & Schu-
ster, 1981. In spite of the incongruous title (the Beatles never recorded the song
"Shout," though it does appear in the video of their performances on the British
television show *Ready, Steady, Go*), this remains the best history of the band.
Norman traces the Beatles from their beginnings to eventual success and decline.
An epilogue considers the impact of Lennon's murder.

Schaffner, Nicholas. *The Beatles Forever.* Harrisburg, Pa.: Cameron House, 1977.
Although written primarily for fans, this is a highly readable, documented, well-
informed look at the Beatles and their recordings. Schaffner brings a passion to
his study that few other publications can match.

David W. Madden

Cross-References

Berry's "Maybellene" Popularizes Rock and Roll (1955), p. 1635; Presley Becomes a Rock-and-Roll Sensation (1956), p. 1705; The Beatles Revolutionize Popular Music (1963), p. 1944; The Rolling Stones Release *Out of Our Heads* (1965), p. 2027; Dylan Performs with Electric Instruments (1965), p. 2038; Hendrix Releases *Are You Experienced?* (1967), p. 2092; The Woodstock Music Festival Marks the Climax of the 1960's (1969), p. 2180; Led Zeppelin Merges Hard Rock and Folk Music (1971), p. 2228.

THE MONTEREY POP FESTIVAL INAUGURATES THE "SUMMER OF LOVE"

Category of event: Music
Time: June 16-18, 1967
Locale: Monterey, California

The celebrated "Summer of Love" was inaugurated with the first large-scale pop music festival, an event that would serve as a prototype for similar festivals throughout the 1960's and 1970's

Principal personages:
LOU ADLER (1935?-   ), a prominent record producer and mastermind organizer of the festival
JOHN PHILLIPS (1935-   ), the leader of the Mamas and the Papas, who along with Adler planned the festival
OTIS REDDING (1941-1967), a soul singer who, backed by Booker T and the MG's, gave an inspired performance that brought him to greater attention among white audiences
THE WHO, a popular British band that catapulted to American fame after their destructive act at Monterey
JIMI HENDRIX (1942-1970), a guitarist and singer who competed with the Who for the honor of the most incendiary performance at the festival
JANIS JOPLIN (1943-1970), a blues singer with Big Brother and the Holding Company whose inspired performance at the festival launched her eventual successful solo career
RAVI SHANKAR (1920-   ), an Indian sitar virtuoso who mesmerized the audience with Eastern ragas

Summary of Event

On a damp weekend in June, 1967, an estimated fifty thousand music lovers gathered in Monterey, California, for the first and only Monterey International Pop Festival at the Monterey County Fairgrounds, site of an annual jazz festival. No one, including nervous city officials, knew what to expect, and to everyone's delight the event took place without any reported ugly incidents.

Originally, the festival was the idea of a pair of enterprising young men in Los Angeles who had raised seed money and secured a lease to the fairgrounds. Once the pair invited John Phillips, the head of the band the Mamas and the Papas, to join forces, however, he brought in his producer-manager, Lou Adler, at the time an influential power broker in the music business, and control quickly changed hands. A board of governors was enlisted, including such popular artists as Paul McCartney, Paul Simon, Smokey Robinson, and Brian Wilson, and a plan was hatched to donate the festival's proceeds to worthy charities.

The plan was to present the most important musical acts of the period, and although the event was billed as an international festival, the acts were primarily from California. In fact, every major California rock band was in attendance, with the notable exceptions of the Beach Boys (fearful they were passé in the psychedelic spirit of the times) and the Doors, who had recently released their first album. Rumors circulated that the Beatles, Donovan, Bob Dylan, and even the Rolling Stones might make surprise appearances (Rolling Stones guitarist Brian Jones was conspicuously present); none, however, took the stage.

The Friday evening show was an eclectic assemblage of new and veteran performers. An unknown Canadian group named the Paupers gave a surprising performance complete with the bassist creating waves of feedback and guitarists occasionally playing drums along with the drummer. Eric Burden debuted his new version of the Animals, and Johnny Rivers, an Adler protégé, gave a slick performance. The highlight of the night, though, came with an appearance by Simon and Garfunkel.

Saturday afternoon was devoted to the blues, with Los Angeles' Canned Heat starting the show and Country Joe and the Fish, the Paul Butterfield Blues Band, and the Steve Miller Band following. Al Kooper, recently departed from the Blues Project, gave a solo performance on the piano, and Mike Bloomfield, formerly of the Butterfield band, introduced his new group, the Electric Flag, which gave a rousing performance, with drummer-singer Buddy Miles called back for an encore.

Unquestionably, though, the highlight of the afternoon was the inspired performance of Janis Joplin, the lead singer of Big Brother and the Holding Company. Joplin was already a fixture in the clubs of San Francisco, but this one appearance brought her to the attention of a much wider audience and drove the crowd to hysterical appreciation. Joplin, in fact, made such an impression that her band made a reprise appearance Sunday night; D. A. Pennebaker's film *Monterey Pop* (1969) captures the impassioned energy of that second performance.

Saturday night's proceedings were begun by a newcomer, Moby Grape, a San Francisco band that gained a reputation for combining psychedelia with tight melodic structure. The Byrds, minus singer Gene Clark, gave a solid performance that included their recent hit, "So You Want to Be a Rock 'n' Roll Star," featuring the trumpet of South African Hugh Masekela, who appeared briefly with the band and later on his own. The Jefferson Airplane, featuring new singer Grace Slick, put on an excellent show, but the evening really belonged to Otis Redding, a veteran of the soul circuit who knew how to work an audience. Redding sang some of his standards, among them "Shake," and drove the crowd to distraction with a wrenching version of "Try a Little Tenderness."

Sunday afternoon featured a two-and-a-half-hour show by Indian sitarist Ravi Shankar, who mesmerized an audience largely unfamiliar with his ragas. Delighted but surprised at his reception, Shankar told the audience, "I love all of you, and how grateful I am for your love of me. What am I doing at a pop festival when my music is classical? I knew I'd be meeting you at one place, you to whom music means so much."

Sunday evening began with performances by the Blues Project and the Buffalo

Springfield, the latter without Neil Young but accompanied by David Crosby of the Byrds, and the Grateful Dead. Midway through the evening, the Who, a band which had enjoyed a few minor hits in the United States, worked themselves into a frenzy of smashed guitars, smoke bombs, and feedback that electrified the crowd. Two sets later, Jimi Hendrix and his band made their American debut, and in an effort to top the Who, Hendrix played the guitar with his teeth and behind his back and, for his finale, set his guitar on fire and then smashed it into his amplifier. The Mamas and the Papas closed the show with a selection of their most popular songs and called Scott McKenzie out to perform his recent hit "San Francisco."

Impact of Event

The festival was, quite simply, a seminal event in the history of American rock and roll. Although there were annual folk and jazz festivals across the country, there had never before been a carefully organized rock festival. San Francisco had provided precursor events—the Trips Festival in January of 1966 (at which the Grateful Dead and Big Brother and the Holding Company played) and the Human Be-In on January 14, 1967, in Golden Gate Park (at which the Grateful Dead, the Jefferson Airplane, and Quicksilver Messenger Service performed), for example—but a festival of such scope had never been attempted.

Monterey Pop became the touchstone by which later events would be measured. Before Monterey, it was typical for a collection of bands to tour a number of cities, putting on the same choreographed performances at each location, but the concept of a festival, a gathering at one site of a number of groups, quickly became the norm. Similar events followed in Miami, Fort Lauderdale, Atlanta, and the Isle of Wight, but the culmination came in 1969 at Woodstock in upstate New York, where many of the same bands gathered once again. In fact, the planners of the Woodstock festival saw the success at Monterey as an incentive to embark on their massive project. The idea of making a film to record the Woodstock event and a live album of the festival's performances was inspired by the production of *Monterey Pop* and the Monterey recordings of Hendrix, Redding, Ravi Shankar, the Mamas and the Papas, and the Jefferson Airplane.

The Monterey festival also brought national and international attention to a host of bands known primarily in the San Francisco region. The Jefferson Airplane had the strongest reputation, and the Grateful Dead and Moby Grape had each released their first albums shortly before the festival; however, their fans were still largely limited to San Francisco. Quicksilver Messenger Service, Steve Miller, Electric Flag, and Big Brother and the Holding Company managed to parlay their appearances into recording contracts. Suddenly, record companies were falling over one another to sign Northern California bands. Later groups such as It's a Beautiful Day, Creedence Clearwater Revival, Santana, the Sons of Champlin, Sly and the Family Stone, the Doobie Brothers, and Joy of Cooking received their own contracts and enjoyed a broader audience than they otherwise could have achieved outside the environs of Los Angeles or San Francisco.

Many San Francisco bands were initially wary of a festival engineered by Southern California masterminds that attempted to imitate the Bay Area's relaxed versions of outdoor concerts. Some bands such as the Grateful Dead, who refused to sign away film rights, found themselves excluded from the film; the Grateful Dead even staged a series of free concerts at the football field of nearby Monterey Peninsula College, where audiences were camping out. After the festival, San Francisco became an established music capital, with its own recording studios and a thriving community of musicians and producers, and promoter Bill Graham rose to international stature as the rock mogul who could put on any show, anywhere, with any band.

Other artists suddenly found themselves with an instant reputation and lucrative contracts. The career of Jimi Hendrix was launched by his Monterey show; his first album appeared later that summer, and he became a popular draw at concert halls. For a year or so, Hendrix continued to titillate audiences with his stage antics, until he grew weary of the clowning and decided to place emphasis on the music itself. Otis Redding likewise acquired a vast, adulatory white audience and considerable airplay on the growing number of white FM radio stations, and his popularity soared in the United States and Europe. His most famous song, the posthumously released "(Sittin' on) The Dock of the Bay," was written a few days after his Monterey appearance while Redding was resting on a houseboat in Sausalito. The Who, who had played to an audience of 250 in Ann Arbor, Michigan, a week before the festival, emerged with a two-night engagement at San Francisco's Fillmore Auditorium (thus beginning a long and productive relationship with promoter Bill Graham), a cross-country tour, and a new, appreciative audience in America.

As these bands grew in popularity, so too did the demands they could place on promoters and record companies. Suddenly, rock artists could choose their producers or oversee their records themselves; they could demand the best recording facilities and could take longer to prepare their records, as the Jefferson Airplane did in recording the eccentric *After Bathing at Baxter's* (1967). In fact, the band constantly battled with its record company and managed to prevail in using taboo language, which was left uncensored, on *Volunteers* (1969). The Grateful Dead, always a performance band, was allowed to release a series of rambling, utterly uncommercial recordings that would have been rejected before the post-Monterey euphoria with San Francisco bands. Live recordings multiplied, with Quicksilver Messenger Service's *Happy Trails* (1969), the Jefferson Airplane's *Bless Its Pointed Little Head* (1969), and Big Brother and the Holding Company's *Cheap Thrills* (1968) capturing the energy and dynamism of San Francisco concerts.

There was also a hidden, less savory side to all this new attention. Bands such as Moby Grape, which eagerly embraced the exaggerations of their publicity machines, suddenly saw their careers evaporate as they self-destructed. The history of Moby Grape's dissolution—its changes in personnel, reformations, and steady decline in artistry—forms one of the saddest yet most illustrative of rock's cautionary tales. When the band's first album was released in May, 1967, Columbia Records, in an unprecedented move, released ten of the album's thirteen songs simultaneously as singles. The band was a favorite with other musicians, but they could never match the artistry of their first recording, and subsequent albums marked a steady decline in performance. Many of the other bands at the Monterey concert rose to instant stardom and then fell apart as a result of jealousies, self-indulgence, or exaggerated expectations. Within three years, four of the principal performers—Hendrix, Joplin, Redding, and Al Wilson of Canned Heat—were dead, and most of the show's bands dissolved in the 1970's.

The best aspect of the festival was the general spirit of goodwill. The crowds were adoring of the bands and remarkably tolerant of one another. Even the Monterey police, who had planned for the worst, turned a blind eye on marijuana consumption and helped to ensure an atmosphere of harmony. Many band members calmly mingled with their fans, and Brian Jones of the Rolling Stones grandly strolled through the midway chatting with anyone. To most observers, this behavior seemed the perfect embodiment of the hippie ethos of peace and love, and it set the tone for the remarkably docile spirit of the Woodstock festival two years later—a spirit destroyed with the horror of the Altamont, California, festival in December of 1969, at which there was considerable violence and one audience member was murdered.

Never again would a nonprofit festival occur, and the social conditions that gave rise to such an event never again emerged. Festivals became money-making schemes, and bands that had freely donated their time now vied for increasingly outlandish contracts and amenities. Monterey Pop was remarkable, though, for showing that such generosity was possible and that such an assemblage of talent could be created. It was truly a one-time-only event.

Bibliography

Christgau, Robert. "Anatomy of a Love Festival." In *Any Old Way You Choose It: Rock and Other Pop Music, 1967-1973.* Baltimore, Md.: Penguin Books, 1973. Christgau brings the passion and knowledge of a firsthand account of the festival. Many of his observations are incisive and revealing.

Herman, Gary. *Rock 'n' Roll Babylon.* New York: Perigee Books, 1982. Initial chapter presents a dystopian view of the festival, emphasizing the personal and commercial exploitation of the artists.

McDonough, Jack. *San Francisco Rock: The Illustrated History of San Francisco Rock Music.* San Francisco: Chronicle Books, 1985. Provides excellent background information for the San Francisco music scene and the role that the city's bands played in the event.

Sanders, Ellen. *Trips: Rock Life in the Sixties.* New York: Charles Scribner's Sons, 1973. Offers an impressionistic, firsthand account of the event. Although thin on details about the bands and performances, the essay about the Monterey festival captures the unique ambiance of the event.

Santelli, Robert. *Aquarius Rising.* New York: Dell, 1980. A very good overview of the festival preparations, the bands that played there, and the event's significance.

Selvin, Joel. *Monterey Pop.* San Francisco: Chronicle Books, 1992. Twenty-fifth anniversary tribute offers the most comprehensive discussion of the preparations for the event, the bands that played, and the songs performed. Culled from numerous firsthand accounts by the musicians themselves.

David W. Madden

Cross-References

The First Newport Jazz Festival Is Held (1954), p. 1617; The Beatles Revolutionize Popular Music (1963), p. 1944; The Rolling Stones Release *Out of Our Heads* (1965), p. 2027; Dylan Performs with Electric Instruments (1965), p. 2038; Hendrix Releases *Are You Experienced?* (1967), p. 2092; The Beatles Release *Sgt. Pepper's Lonely Hearts Club Band* (1967), p. 2098; The Woodstock Music Festival Marks the Climax of the 1960's (1969), p. 2180; Live Aid Generates Millions for Famine Relief (1985), p. 2543.

MITCHELL FOUNDS THE DANCE THEATER OF HARLEM

Category of event: Dance
Time: 1968
Locale: New York, New York

The Dance Theater of Harlem became the first world-renowned African-American ballet company

Principal personages:
ARTHUR MITCHELL (1934-   ), a principal dancer with the New York City Ballet who became cofounder of the Dance Theater of Harlem
KAREL SHOOK (1920-1985), a ballet teacher and former director of the Netherlands Ballet who was a cofounder of the Dance Theater of Harlem

Summary of Event

Arthur Mitchell, a principal dancer with the New York City Ballet, was at a New York airport en route to Brazil on April 4, 1968, the day Martin Luther King, Jr., was assassinated. The idea to develop a black ballet company germinated that same day. Mitchell noted, "I sat there the whole time, thinking to myself, here I am running around the world doing all these things, why not do them at home?"

Mitchell was commuting to Brazil, where he was establishing that country's first national ballet company under the auspices of the United States. He was asked to head the Brazilian group as permanent artistic director; the event of April 4, though, lingered in his thoughts. Mitchell declined the offer and returned to New York. He felt that he should go to Harlem, the community of his youth, to open a school and pass on his knowledge to other blacks. He later wrote, "I realized from the start that there was little point in putting black kids through the rigors of development in classical ballet if, once trained, they had little chance to perform." Mitchell thus aimed both to open a school and to found a company in which the school's graduates could perform; he believed that, with talent and given proper instruction, African Americans could achieve success in ballet.

Mitchell approached Karel Shook, ballet master of the Netherlands Ballet and Mitchell's former teacher at the Katherine Dunham School of Dance, to assist in the undertaking. The two men established the Dance Theater of Harlem as a school of allied arts and as a professional dance company. Their goal for the Dance Theater was "to promote public interest in and support for the aims of the organization, while providing role models and professional goals for aspiring students." With the financial assistance of the Ford Foundation, the school opened in a garage and a church basement belonging to the Harlem School of Arts. The original student body of thirty increased to four hundred within two months' time. Many of the students had at first been curious onlookers, since the garage doors were left open for ventilation and light.

The primary purpose of the school was "to promote interest in and teach young black people the art of classical ballet, modern and ethnic dance, thereby creating a much-needed self-awareness and better self-image of the students themselves." The instructors at the school included Mary Hinkson, a renowned Martha Graham dancer who taught modern dance, and Pearl Reynolds, who instructed the ethnic dance classes. Classical ballet classes were conducted by Mitchell and Shook.

Strained relations with the Harlem School of Arts and the advice of George Balanchine and Lincoln Kirstein led to Mitchell's opening the school as an independent endeavor. The school and company moved to new premises.

The long-range goal of the Dance Theater was the production of dancers soundly trained in the classical tradition. Mitchell noted, "We have to prove that a black ballet school and a black ballet company are the equal of the best of their kind, anywhere in the world." The performing company was inaugurated in February of 1969, with Balanchine and Kirstein as members of the company's first board of directors.

Since funding from the Ford Foundation was provided via a matching grant, the Dance Theater of Harlem began performances as a means of raising money. The programs also provided the dancers with an opportunity for development as artists. In addition, frequent lecture-demonstrations were performed for a range of audiences, from neighborhood children to corporate executives.

The school also expanded to include classes in related aspects of theater production. Lighting, sound, music, costuming, stage management, and accounting became part of the curriculum.

During this period, Mitchell was still performing with the New York City Ballet. As he became increasingly involved with the operation of his organization, however, Mitchell's performances became fewer. In 1970, Mitchell resigned from the New York City Ballet, informing Balanchine of his need to stop dancing to devote his full attention to the Dance Theater of Harlem.

Early works performed by the company included Mitchell's own choreography of *Holberg Suite*, *Tones*, and *Fête Noir*. These pieces introduced the neophyte dancers to neoclassic ballets. With the inclusion of ethnic ballets, impossible technical difficulties were not imposed upon an embryonic company. The dancers, however, soon were dancing works by Balanchine with his encouragement and assistance.

The first extended performance of the Dance Theater of Harlem took place in August of 1970 at Jacob's Pillow, Lee, Massachusetts. The official debut of the company occurred in 1971 at the Guggenheim Museum in New York. The program included *Tones*, *Fête Noir*, and another Mitchell work, *Rhythmetron*.

In 1974, the Dance Theater of Harlem presented its first Broadway season at the Anta Theatre. Included in these performances was *Wings*, choreographed by Louis Johnson; *Dougla*, choreographed by Geoffrey Holder; *Design for Strings*, choreographed by John Taras, and *Caravansarai*, choreographed by Talley Beatty.

Impact of Event

Following the official debut of the Dance Theater of Harlem, the company built its international reputation. In 1971, the company participated in the Festival of Two Worlds in Spoleto, Italy, and played other Italian engagements. Cities in Switzerland and Holland were also included on the performance schedule.

The company played several seasons in England. Its 1976 appearance broke box-office records at the Sadler's Wells Theatre in London, with return engagements in 1979 and in 1980 resulting in full houses. In July of 1981, the company performed at the Royal Opera House in Covent Garden and in 1984 played a three-week engagement at the London Coliseum as part of an Anglo-American cultural exchange. In addition, the company performed for Queen Elizabeth II on two occasions.

In 1979, the Dance Theater of Harlem became the first major foreign classical ballet company to perform in Dublin, Ireland, since 1957. In 1980, the company's six-week tour of Australia met with sold-out audiences. That same year, the company performed in China. In 1981, the company toured Japan to full houses. The company participated in the International Festival of Dance in Paris and at the re-opening of the renovated Deutsches Theater in Munich, Germany, in 1982. European tours followed in 1985 and 1986, and a South American tour occurred in 1987. An invitation to participate in a government-sponsored cultural exchange resulted in the company's becoming the first major U.S. ballet to perform in the Soviet Union.

The Dance Theater of Harlem gained recognition within the United States through its touring. In 1977, the company participated in Columbia University's Summer Community Dance Series and performed to record-breaking audiences in San Francisco. In 1980, the company appeared at the Empire State Performing Arts Center in Albany, New York, and gave a special performance for the governor of New York. In February of 1981, the Dance Theater of Harlem debuted at the John F. Kennedy Center for the Performing Arts in Washington, D.C., and continued to perform there as part of the ballet subscription series sponsored by the Kennedy Center.

Starting in 1974, the company presented a New York season almost every year. The company has held New York seasons at the Anta Theatre, the Uris Theater, City Center, and the Metropolitan Opera House. In 1986, a "Harlem Homecoming Season" at the Theatre at Aaron Davis Hall, the first season presented by a major dance company in Harlem, was sold out. This was followed by Harlem Homecoming II in 1987, an equally successful undertaking.

Other milestone performances by the Dance Theater of Harlem include a White House performance on the occasion of the Ronald Reagan Administration's first state dinner honoring British Prime Minister Margaret Thatcher on February 26, 1982, and performance of the finale of Balanchine's *Stars and Stripes* at the 1984 Summer Olympics closing ceremony in Los Angeles as representatives of the United States.

The repertoire of the Dance Theater of Harlem diversified under the artistic direction of Mitchell. Balanchine ballets added to the repertoire included *Bugaku*, *The Four Temperaments*, *Serenade*, *Square Dance*, and *Stars and Stripes*.

The Dance Theater of Harlem's staging of *Creole Giselle* moved the locale of

Giselle from Germany to the bayous of Louisiana, where folk stories parallel the original libretto. While the costumes and settings were altered, Frederic Franklin's choreography remained unchanged. This production, first presented in London in 1984, won the Laurence Olivier Award for the Outstanding New Dance Production of the Year, the first award to an American dance company by the Society of West End Theatres. In 1987, the production was taped for television during performances in Denmark, and in 1988 won first prize for Best Television Production of a Classical Ballet at the First Grand Prix De Video Base in Nîmes, France.

The company's repertory diversified to include *Banda*, by Geoffrey Holder, *Billy the Kid*, by Eugene Loring, *Schéhérazade*, by Michel Fokine, *Les Biches*, by Bronislava Nijinska, *Fall River Legend*, by Agnes de Mille, *Fancy Free*, by Jerome Robbins, *Firebird*, by John Taras, and *A Streetcar Named Desire*, by Valerie Bettis.

Other acclaimed works performed by the company include *Voluntaries*, by Glen Tetley; *Troy Game*, by Robert North; *Footprints Dressed in Red*, by Garth Fagan; *Phoenix Rising*, by Mitchell and Billy Wilson; *John Henry*, commissioned by the 1988 New York International Festival, by Mitchell; and *Concerto in F*, by Wilson. In 1985, the National Choreography Project awarded the Dance Theater of Harlem a grant for a collaboration between David Gordon and the company, which resulted in *Piano Movers.*

Additional television credits include broadcasts in Europe and the United States of *A Streetcar Named Desire* and *Creole Giselle. Songs of Mahler*, sung by Jessye Norman and danced by the company, was shown by the British Broadcasting Corporation (BBC). A U.S. public television special, *"Firebird" by the Dance Theater of Harlem*, won the Peabody Award in 1982.

The Dance Theater of Harlem is acknowledged as one of the world's finest ballet companies. Initially predominantly composed of black dancers, the company has come to include several white dancers, underscoring its initial concept and attesting to the universality of classical ballet. In this regard, Mitchell has commented, "Blackness is now irrelevant in ballet."

Bibliography

Clarke, Mary, and Clement Crisp. *The History of Dance.* New York: Crown, 1981. Contains a paragraph on the company and includes a picture.

Clarke, Mary, and David Vaughan, eds. *The Encyclopedia of Dance and Ballet.* New York: G. P. Putnam's Sons, 1977. Contains brief descriptions of Arthur Mitchell and the Dance Theater of Harlem under separate headings. Includes a picture of the company in Beatty's *Caravansarai.*

Coe, Robert. *Dance in America.* New York: E. P. Dutton, 1985. Gives a brief account of Mitchell and the Dance Theater of Harlem.

Doeser, Linda. *Ballet and Dance.* New York: St. Martin's Press, 1977. Presents an overview of Mitchell's career and establishment of the Dance Theater of Harlem. Discusses the repertoire of the time. Presents listings of company members, the company's repertoire, and its tours. Includes pictures.

Emery, Lynn Fauley. *Black Dance from 1619 to Today.* 2d rev. ed. Princeton, N.J.: Princeton Book Company, 1988. Provides an interesting account of Mitchell's career and the emergence and rise of the Dance Theater of Harlem.

Haskins, James. *Black Dance in America.* New York: Harper Trophy, 1990. Takes an in-depth look at Mitchell's career and the Dance Theater of Harlem's growth.

Hodgson, Moira. *Quintet.* New York: William Morrow, 1976. Presents an insightful look at the early beginnings of the Dance Theater of Harlem. Discusses company members and repertoire. Replete with pictures of the company in rehearsal and performance.

Kraus, Richard, Sarah Chapman Hilsendger, and Brenda Dixson. *History of Dance in Art and Education.* 3d ed. Englewood Cliffs, N.J.: Prentice-Hall, 1991. Provides a brief description of the development of the Dance Theater of Harlem. References to the company are made in various sections of the book.

Long, Richard A. *The Black Tradition in American Dance.* New York: Rizzoli, 1989. Contains a concise overview of the Dance Theater of Harlem. Includes pictures of Mitchell, Shook, and the company.

Thorpe, Edward. *Black Dance.* Woodstock, N.Y.: The Overlook Press, 1989. Gives a generalized account of Mitchell's career and the development of the Dance Theater of Harlem. Provides a picture of Mitchell as a dancer with the New York City Ballet and one from *Creole Giselle.*

Mary Pat Balkus

Cross-References

The Harlem Renaissance Celebrates African-American Culture (1920's), p. 480; Baker Dances in *La Revue nègre* (1925), p. 665; Balanchine's *Serenade* Inaugurates American Ballet (1934), p. 974; Balanchine and Kirstein Make New York a World Center for Ballet (1946), p. 1301; Ailey Founds His Dance Company (1958), p. 1774; The New Dance U.S.A. Festival Celebrates Contemporary Dance (1981), p. 2480; Festivals Mark a Peak in the Dance Created by Black Artists (1983), p. 2521; Multiculturalism Dominates the Dance World (Late 1980's), p. 2559.

ROWAN AND MARTIN'S LAUGH-IN IS THE TOP SHOW ON TELEVISION

Category of event: Television and radio
Time: January 22, 1968-May 14, 1973
Locale: The United States

Rowan and Martin's Laugh-In, *a fast-paced, at times provocative comedy show, fully exploited the medium of television while conveying cultural upheavals occurring in American society*

Principal personages:
> DAN ROWAN (1922-1987), a "straight man" comedian who, with his partner Martin, helped to formulate and host the program
> DICK MARTIN (1923-), a "good-time Charlie" comedian who, with his partner Rowan, helped to formulate and host the program
> GEORGE SCHLATTER (1932-), the executive producer of *Laugh-In*
> EDWARD FRIENDLY (1922-), a former NBC vice president who formed a production company with Schlatter to generate the series and oversee its ancillary products
> JUDY CARNE (JOYCE A. BOTTERILL, 1939-), the "sock it to me" girl in the original cast
> ARTE JOHNSON (1934-), an original cast member whose roles included a guru, a German soldier, and a dirty old man
> GOLDIE HAWN (1945-), the stereotypical "dumb blonde" in the original cast
> RUTH BUZZI (1936-), an original cast member whose roles included Gladys, the man-hungry spinster
> HENRY GIBSON (1935-), an original cast member who played a parson and recited his own nonsense poetry
> JO ANNE WORLEY (1937-), a loud, brash original cast member

Summary of Event

By the early 1960's, the comedy team of Dan Rowan (a former used-car dealer, the straight man) and Dick Martin (a former bartender, the happy-go-lucky, "swinging" member of the duo), was headlining in Miami and Las Vegas lounges. After several guest appearances on variety shows, they broke into television programming by securing high summer replacement ratings while filling in for Dean Martin on his variety show in 1966; this success led to various network offers to star in situation comedies.

Rowan and Martin, however, wanted to push television comedy in a new direction, breaking out of both the situation-comedy format and the seat-in-a-comedy-club vantage of variety shows; instead, they wanted to develop something they referred to as a "cartoon humor approach." When the National Broadcasting Company (NBC) offered them a comedy-variety hour special in the autumn of 1967, the network put up $250,000, secured Timex Watches as a sponsor, and gave the duo free rein. After discussing their plans with George Schlatter, an enthusiastic, visionary producer also eager to try television-oriented visual techniques that would combine slapstick and social relevance, the three agreed to work together.

That first *Laugh-In* special aired September 9, 1967, receiving critical praise and ratings that pleased NBC. That network then moved on an option to develop the concept into a regular series, and soon Ed Friendly, a former vice president at NBC, and Schlatter had combined to form Schlatter-Friendly Productions to produce such a series. Although unsure about the sustainability of a *Laugh-In* show on a regular basis, Rowan and Martin agreed, and production ensued.

The series slipped into the NBC lineup in January, 1968, replacing *The Man from U.N.C.L.E.* Competition from 8:00 to 9:00 P.M. on Monday nights was certainly formidable; the show's time slot overlapped with both *I Love Lucy* and *Gunsmoke* on the Columbia Broadcasting System (CBS), at the time television's two top-rated shows. Nevertheless, American society responded quite favorably to *Laugh-In*; its subject matter, its style, its speed all spoke to current cultural concerns and needs. *Laugh-In* quickly climbed in the ratings, and it closed the season with the last four shows all in first place. It then garnered four Emmy Awards and was acclaimed as the most successful program of the season. In a reflection of the show's popularity and influence, *Time* devoted a cover story to the phenomenon of the show in October, 1968, and *Laugh-In*'s dominance continued through 1970.

Along with Rowan, Martin, and Schlatter, others integral to the creation of the program included head writer Paul W. Keyes and his colleagues, film editor Art Schneider and his crew, and the zany cast of regulars. The cast changed over time, more so as success brought options to members of the troupe, but the original comedic cast included Judy Carne, Goldie Hawn, Jo Anne Worley, Henry Gibson, Arte Johnson, Ruth Buzzi, and Gary Owens (as the announcer). Later additions and replacements included Dave Madden, Teresa Graves, Alan Sues, Johnny Brown, Pamela Rogers, Richard Dawson, and Lily Tomlin. For the 1969-1970 season, Schlatter-Friendly chose Mark Warren, a young African American, to take over directing responsibilities full time; the move was a step forward in breaking racial barriers in the American television industry.

What made *Rowan and Martin's Laugh-In* such a hit was its blend of personalities, the incredible number of jokes per episode, the editing style, the eclectic use of guest stars, and the popularity of some running gags and sequences combined to tickle America's funny bone, at a time when stress and discord concerning American involvement in the Vietnam War were running high.

Approximately 250 gags, skillfully edited together into a fifty-three-minute show, appeared in each of the 124 episodes produced over the five-year run of *Laugh-In*. A large portion of the audience fell into the twelve-to-eighteen age bracket. This generation, raised on television, found the sensory overload of the show's rapid-fire combination of skits, slapstick, blackouts, and one-liners quite stimulating. Some edited cuts were as brief as one eighth of a second—a closeup of graffiti on a go-go dancer, a funny face distorted by a camera lens.

The range of cameos was also impressive. Appearing on *Laugh-In* grew quite stylish in the late 1960's; guest stars included Jack Benny, Marcel Marceau, Truman Capote, John Wayne, Zsa Zsa Gabor, Harry Belafonte, Bing Crosby, Pat Boone, and Dinah Shore.

Sammy Davis, Jr., in a tribute to Pigmeat Markham's old vaudeville sketch, chanted "here comes de judge," and America joined the chant. Other catch phrases that entered the national idiom via *Laugh-In* included Johnson's "verrry interesting," Carne's "Sock it to me!" (a running gag that developed some sophisticated bits of punnery), the censor-testing "Look that up in your Funk and Wagnalls," and "You bet your sweet bippy," the exact meaning of which was left to the viewer's imagination. Popular recurring motifs included a psychedelic "joke wall," parodies of production numbers to introduce a satirical news segment, and a cocktail-party setting for stinging bits of provocative, topical humor.

Keyes took over as executive producer for the fourth and fifth seasons. During its prime-time run, *Laugh-In* spawned several merchandising spinoffs: a *Laugh-In* magazine selling 300,000 copies a month, a *Laugh-In* record album, a syndicated comic strip, and assorted products such as "sock-it-to-me" T-shirts and paperback jokebooks. The symbiotic relationship between product merchandising and television series would intensify in the decades to come.

The original freshness gone, the ratings down, in May, 1973, NBC canceled *Laugh-In*. Nevertheless, the show's vividly moving colors, its experimentation with cutting and sudden scene shifts, and its barrier-breaking thrusts in making fun of religion, politics, and traditional mores set it apart as one of the most distinctive programs of its era.

Impact of Event

The quick one-liner, fade to black, was pioneered by Ernie Kovacs in the early years of television. The creators of *Laugh-In* made such speedy delivery the *raison d'être* for the program. As an art form, television now could offer a young generation reared on the medium home entertainment with countercultural undertones that could only be conveyed in a finely edited, studio-prepackaged process. An argument could be made that the technological auditory and visual techniques Ken Kesey and the Merry Pranksters experimented with in Tom Wolfe's *The Electric Kool-Aid Acid Test* (1969) were, via *Laugh-In*, homogenized, commodified, and served to middle America by the National Broadcasting Company. America responded favorably, which hastened the inevitable production of some copycat programming.

One spinoff, a thirty-minute comedy game show entitled *Letters to Laugh-In*, appeared on NBC from September 29, 1969, to March 3, 1970. Gary Owens hosted this program, on which four guest celebrities took turns telling jokes submitted by home viewers. A panel of studio audience judges decided which jokes were successes or flops, the booby prize being a seven-day vacation in "beautiful downtown Burbank."

Programs that tried to simulate *Laugh-In*'s fast-firing style and chaotic mirth, duplicating its structure and format, did not fare well. *You Can't Do That on Television!*, a pilot for an American Broadcasting Company (ABC) series in the fall of 1968, shocked but failed to get the laughs. Schlatter and Friendly tried to re-create their success at NBC by generating an even hipper thirty-minute version of the show for ABC in February, 1969. Entitled *Turn-On*, it was canceled after one airing: 150 ABC affiliates registered protests, and the five other shows already taped were quickly abandoned.

Schlatter attempted to revive *Laugh-In* four years after its demise with a series of specials beginning September 5, 1977. Without the foundation of Rowan and Martin, in a post-Watergate era with disco on the rise, this version of the series did not click and soon petered out. The cast of virtual unknowns did include Wayland Flowers and his outspoken puppet Madame, who would eventually secure their own television program.

One great strength of *Rowan and Martin's Laugh-In* was its diverse ensemble. Many of the cast used the program as a springboard to other jobs in television and film. Most reached the level of game-show celebrities and television guest stars. A few, such as Hawn and Tomlin, went on to become powerful megastars in Hollywood and on Broadway. *Laugh-In*'s comedic ensemble format also paved the way for the Not Ready for Prime Time Players on *Saturday Night Live*. That program, which debuted in October, 1975, gave former *Laugh-In* writer Lorne Michaels the chance to test the limits of topical humor, pushing the barriers of acceptability in television comedy much as *Laugh-In* had.

Racy material was a legacy that *Laugh-In* left later television comedy. A contemporary program on CBS, *The Smothers Brothers Comedy Hour,* received much attention for its run-ins with the network censors, but unlike Tommy and Dick Smothers, Rowan and Martin carefully avoided conveying political messages. As a result, both conservatives and liberals, hawks and doves were fair targets. People of all political ideologies seemed to enjoy *Laugh-In.* Both Dick Gregory and Richard Nixon were welcomed as guests; Martha Mitchell did telephone jokes on *Laugh-In* amid the Watergate debacle. Yet despite its political neutrality, the show was still outspoken; for example, *Laugh-In* predated a national shift in public consciousness against smoking. Rowan noted that "The U.S. Public Health Service requested a clip of our Salute to Smoking piece, saying that we did more for their cause than they have been able to do in two years." *Laugh-In* also questioned racism, ethnic stereotyping, and the function of mainstream religion. It flirted with allusions to drug use; a wide range of topics related to the sexual revolution managed to slip by the censors. Antecedents of the multiculturalism movement that began to gather steam in the 1980's can be found on *Laugh-In*, both in practice and general philosophy. In the 1970's and 1980's, situation comedies would begin to confront many of these topics more readily, and late-night television more openly, but *Laugh-In* opened the door to such considerations.

The fast pace of delivery and film editing used to convey *Laugh-In*'s tried-and-true vaudeville skits, familiar old jokes, and classic bits of slapstick clearly foreshadowed a range of visual entertainment that would come. One genre of entertainment that has blossomed since the days of *Laugh-In* and that owes an artistic debt to the program for its blurring of imagery and its use of blackouts, quick editing, and very brief clips as a normative element—what Schlatter referred to as "energy film"—is the entire industry of music videos. Generations that have come of age on Music Television (MTV), many too young to remember *Laugh-In*, may not be aware that earlier viewers did not require rapidly changing, startling, often manipulative visual imagery to retain their interest. *Laugh-In* marked the beginning of the regular use of such techniques in television.

Bibliography

Archer, Jules. *The Incredible Sixties: The Stormy Years That Changed America.* San Diego, Calif.: Harcourt Brace Jovanovich, 1986. Useful introduction to understanding the historical and social context of America that created a need that *Laugh-In* filled in popular culture. Eloquent. Organized in topical chapters concerning such topics as the Vietnam War, feminism, rock and roll, literature, civil rights, and the sexual revolution. No attention to function of television. List of suggested further readings. Index.

Brooks, Tim, and Earle Marsh. *The Complete Directory to Prime Time Network TV Shows, 1946-Present.* 4th ed. New York: Ballantine Books, 1988. Gives a brief summary of the show's history and provides detailed information on broadcast history and cast members. Useful for placing the show in a broader television context.

Rowan, Dan, and John D. MacDonald. *A Friendship: The Letters of Dan Rowan and John D. MacDonald, 1967-1974.* New York: Alfred A. Knopf, 1986. Wonderful insights into Rowan's vision of what *Laugh-In* should be; also conveys his exasperation and glee at various points in the production process. Permits one to assess how success affected Rowan in his personal life. Some readers may find MacDonald's literary discussions extraneous. No index.

"Rowan and Martin's Laugh-In." The Burbank Edition. New York: World Publishing, 1969. Certainly not scholarly, but accessible in many libraries. Consists of gags and jokes used in scripts from 1968 and the spring of 1969. Presented with still photography taken from the television program. Range of fonts, layouts, and colors intended to convey *Laugh-In*'s frenzied pace and zaniness.

Winship, Michael. *Television.* New York: Random House, 1988. Companion volume to eight-part public television series *Television.* Wonderfully illustrated. Divides study of history of television into a series of reviews and interviews with forty-three diverse individuals involved in the business. Especially relevant: chapter 7, "Variety," which includes featured perspectives on George Schlatter and Dick Martin.

Scot M. Guenter

Cross-References

Variety Shows Dominate Television Programming (1948), p. 1383; Situation Comedies Dominate Television Programming (1960's), p. 1835; *Monty Python's Flying Circus* Captures Audiences Worldwide (1969), p. 2174; *The Sonny and Cher Comedy Hour* Brings Glitz to Television (1971), p. 2244; *Saturday Night Live* Is First Broadcast (1975), p. 2355; MTV Changes the Look of American Popular Culture (1981), p. 2475.

THE RADICAL MUSICAL *HAIR* OPENS ON BROADWAY

Categories of event: Theater and music
Time: April 29, 1968
Locale: The Biltmore Theatre, New York, New York

Hair *liberated Broadway from traditional musical comedy and introduced new music, new themes, and radical life-styles to the American musical stage*

Principal personages:
GEROME RAGNI (1942-1991), a veteran actor involved in the experimental theater and the coauthor of *Hair*, who first played the role of Berger
JAMES RADO (1939-   ), an experienced actor and coauthor of *Hair*, who played the role of Claude on Broadway
GALT MACDERMOT (1928-   ), the composer and conductor of *Hair*
TOM O'HORGAN (1926-   ), the director of the Broadway production of *Hair*
MICHAEL BUTLER (1926-   ), a wealthy Chicago liberal who became producer of the Broadway production

Summary of Event

"The uniqueness of *Hair*," declared critic Martin Gottfried, "proves just how backward Broadway really is." The controversial Broadway production, which mesmerized audiences with the authenticity of its presentation of the counterculture of the 1960's and which became a popular and international success, resulted from a number of fortuitous circumstances.

Hair, subtitled "The American Tribal Love-Rock Musical," originated with Gerome Ragni and James Rado, both actors, who talked about collaborating on a musical while appearing together in a Chicago production of *The Knack* in 1965. Ragni's experience was as an actor in the Off-Off-Broadway experimental theater; Rado had written musical revues and aspired to a composing career.

The youth culture of the 1960's, the "hippies," whose badge of membership was long hair, espoused ideals of freedom, love, and brotherhood, and became increasingly antiestablishment, anti-Vietnam War, and anti-President Lyndon Baines Johnson. Although not part of the hippie society, Ragni and Rado shared the antiwar sentiments and saw the possibility of transforming some of the counterculture's idealism into theater.

To amass material, the authors observed gatherings of East Village hippies and developed a script, which was unanimously rejected by mainstream producers. Fortunately, on a train back from New Haven, Ragni encountered Joseph Papp, producer of the New York Shakespeare Festival, who was seeking a production to open his newly renovated Public Theater. Papp agreed to produce *Hair* for a limited run, provided a composer was enlisted for the project. A fortunate choice was made in the selection of Galt MacDermot, a Canadian educated in South Africa who drew upon his knowledge of African rhythms as well as his formal musical education to compose what many critics acknowledged as a superb score.

The Broadway opening of *Hair* was preceded by two trial runs. The first, eight weeks at Papp's Public Theater, was mildly successful with a middle-aged audience and then closed. Again by chance, Michael Butler, the son of a wealthy Chicago family, attended a performance at the Public Theater under the mistaken assumption that the musical was written by or about American Indians (he was concerned about the mistreatment of Native Americans), and he opted to produce the show for a second run at the Cheetah, a discotheque in the Times Square area. The new production was more successful with a younger audience but was a commercial disaster. The choice facing the management was to move to Broadway or to close for good.

The decision was made to move to Broadway's Biltmore Theatre, and Tom O'Horgan, a colleague of the authors from the La Mama Company, was brought in to direct. The authors rewrote the book, the composer added thirteen new songs, a new choreographer joined the company, the director recast and restaged, and the show's emphasis shifted from a virulent antiwar theme to a celebration of the tribal nature of the hippie culture.

Critics later decided that *Hair* was a "concept" musical; that is, that ideas rather than story predominate. The characters include Claude, a young man who receives his draft notice; his friend Berger, a high school dropout who refuses to go to war; and Sheila, an antiwar activist college student. The rest of the "tribe" include Jeanie, a pregnant, somewhat mystical girl; Hud, a black hippie; Woof, a homosexual hippie, and a polyglot assortment of racial and ethnic young people. The virtually nonexistent plot concerns whether Claude will honor his draft notice or find another solution. At length, he joins the Army and is killed in Vietnam, and the tribe mourns his demise.

The music and creative staging lifted the show above its banal book and provided the controversy that surrounded the show throughout its many productions. The opening brings the cast through the audience onto the stage in slow, ritualistic movements. As Claude squats before a small fire, Sheila and Berger cut a lock of his hair and offer it to the fire. The lyrical "Age of Aquarius," promising the dawn of an era of harmony and understanding, is sung. Other numbers take note of environmental pollution, the breakdown of language, the benefits of drugs, and the obsolescence of parents. "Don't Put It Down," a paean to the American flag proclaimed by three cast members, was found offensive by some members of the audience. At the end of the first act, the sound of bells is heard offstage, and cast members bearing candles enter through the audience for a "be-in." As Claude contemplates the significance of not burning his draft card, the tribe crawls under a scrim spread out across the stage; the song finishes, and cast members appear, naked and motionless in a projection of light. The tableau is shattered by two policemen entering from the lobby who announce that the audience is under arrest for watching an obscene show.

The second act contains Claude's hallucinogenic trip through American history, emphasizing the absurdity of war and culminating in the ironic "What a Piece of Work Is Man," with lyrics by William Shakespeare. Sheila sings the wistful "Good Morning Starshine," which is followed by the tribe's awareness of Claude's unnecessary death. The production ends with "Let the Sun Shine In" and with an invitation to the audience to participate in a final dance. Frenetically paced, through the earnestness and energy of the young cast, the show celebrates both the fallibility and the nobility of humankind.

Impact of Event

Although the Broadway production of *Hair* was not universally acclaimed by the critics, several of whom pointed to its amateurishness and messiness and all of whom noted the obscurity of the book, most agreed that it was an engaging show despite its flaws. They found it "likable" and "unassuming, even in its pretensions," and they praised the score, "rich in melody" and with a "thoroughly contemporary musical sound." Further, as Gerald Bordman declared, "In every respect— commercial, historic, esthetic—it was far and away the most important musical of the season."

Commercially, the Broadway production was only the beginning of *Hair*'s success. Including the Public and Cheetah engagements, *Hair* played 1,844 performances in New York. Companies followed in Los Angeles, San Francisco, and Chicago, with appropriate local alterations to the book. Bernard Castelli, one of the coproducers, opened companies abroad in France, Germany, Belgium, Italy, Japan, Mexico, and elsewhere, playing in fourteen different languages. The London *Hair* ran for 1,997 performances. The backers of the show were repaid many times over.

Historically, *Hair* seemed to break the mold of the traditional Broadway musical, which was geared to middle-aged, middle-class taste. Audiences expected costumed, tuneful, apolitical productions that reinforced their own life-styles and values. They did not expect the torrent of sound, the irreverent characters, the obscene language, and the rock music that greeted them at the Biltmore. Perhaps it was the television critics, who raved about the show, perhaps it was the titillating prospect of viewing nudity, perhaps it was the emotional opposition to American involvement in the Vietnam War, or perhaps it was the show's message of peace, love, and equality that drew audiences, both young and old, to the Biltmore for four years.

Clive Barnes of *The New York Times* remarked that *Hair* is "the first Broadway musical in some time to have the authentic voice of today rather than the day before yesterday." Nevertheless, *Hair* did not, as some hoped, usher in a new era of musical theater that married musical comedy with rock music; *Hair* had a rock sound, but it was arguably not a rock musical. Although orchestrated for a rock band consisting of two guitars, a bass, and a keyboard, individual numbers were written in a variety of styles, from rock to country. With the exception of the writers of *Jesus Christ Superstar* (1971) and *Godspell* (1971), later rock composers chose to pursue the rock concert, rather than the Broadway musical, as their primary live venue. Nor was *Hair*'s structure new. The concept musical, with an unconnected, episodic plot revolving around a message, was in actuality an old form.

Nevertheless, *Hair*'s impact was considerable, in the theater and out of it. *Hair* liberated staging, subject matter, and language for productions that followed. In rehearsals, O'Horgan exhorted the tribe to "love the audience" and thus brought actors and audience together in close physical contact. Actors swung on ropes over the audience's heads, sat in their laps, talked to them in the lobby, and were sometimes indistinguishable from ticket holders, as casual dress style invaded middle-class culture.

Subject matter in the theater was another area expanded by *Hair*. Protest against the Vietnam War had climaxed when the show opened and had less pertinence through the run. Other issues, though, were current; the effects of marijuana and heroin were displayed, sexual freedom was encouraged, homosexuality was accepted, and racism was strongly protested. These were subjects played previously only in the experimental theaters.

Words concerning particular sexual acts, which some found offensive and unnecessary, were included liberally in songs such as "Sodomy" and in dialogue, the point being that language had lost its power through the doublespeak of the political establishment. After *Hair*, no subject or word was taboo in the theater.

Hair, rather surprisingly, influenced fashion. It brought attention to the dress of the hippies, to the long hair, beads, fringe, and loose clothing—which, above all, were comfortable and inexpensive. Lorrie Davis, a member of the cast, declared, "What *Hair* did to the fashion industry is history: it put bluejeans on the Establishment." It also helped to put them on every college student in the country (and they were no longer inexpensive).

Hair brought new and younger audiences into the theater; the show spoke to them with its opposition to the draft, the work ethic, and the life-styles of their parents. Further, the show's sound was contemporary and exciting.

Perhaps most important, *Hair* struck a blow for the right of free expression. The appearance of the cast in full frontal nudity at the end of the first act was highly controversial and outraged many people. Two cases eventually went up before the Supreme Court involving communities that wished to ban productions of *Hair*. A Boston district attorney objected to the nudity and to what he considered flag desecration, and Chattanooga, Tennessee, authorities were repelled simply by the production's reputation. In both instances, the Court ruled in favor of the show's producers.

Hair was a milestone in the theater in what it said and in how it said it. It was very much a product of its time; the flower children and their hippie friends vanished into suburbia within the next few years. A 1977 revival of the show was not successful; a 1979 motion picture version was deplored by the authors. Still, so long as there is a younger generation that rebels against its elders and so long as peace, love, and understanding do not rule the world, *Hair* has relevance.

Bibliography

Davis, Lorrie, with Rachel Gallagher. *Letting Down My Hair: Two Years with the*

Love Rock Tribe—From Dawning to Downing of Aquarius. New York: Arthur Fields Books, 1973. A cast member's unvarnished account of the rehearsal period and two years of the run of *Hair.* Apparently embittered by the commercial emphasis of the production, Davis provides an insider's view of backstage behavior, complete with drugs, sex, and conflicts with the management. Photographs.

Goldman, William. "Brave New World." In *The Season: A Candid Look at Broadway.* New York: Harcourt, Brace & World, 1969. A biting discussion of *Hair*'s journey from the Public Theater to Broadway, with a spate of negative quotations from other critics. Now a classic, the book places *Hair* in the context of other productions of the 1968 season. A valuable perspective. With index.

Gottfried, Martin. "*Hair*" and "What's New." In *Opening Nights: Theater Criticism of the Sixties.* New York: G. P. Putnam's Sons, 1969. The first article gives an unflattering review of the Broadway production, faulting the direction, the choreography, and the lack of a book. Gottfried acknowledges the value of the rock music and the uniqueness of the show. The second piece discusses *Hair*'s hippie perspective. Index.

Horn, Barbara Lee. *The Age of "Hair": Evolution and Impact of Broadway's First Rock Musical.* New York: Greenwood Press, 1991. Far and away the most thorough discussion of the evolution and significance of *Hair.* The book was developed through interviews with many of those involved with the show's creation. Contains cast lists from the Public Theater and the Biltmore productions, an index, and an excellent bibliography.

Richards, Stanley, ed. *Great Rock Musicals.* New York: Stein & Day, 1979. Contains the complete scripts of eight rock musicals, including *Hair.* Richards provides editorial notes, cast and staff lists, notes on musical numbers, and photographs. A good starting point.

Joyce E. Henry

Cross-References

The Beatles Revolutionize Popular Music (1963), p. 1944; Dylan Performs with Electric Instruments (1965), p. 2038; The Beatles Release *Sgt. Pepper's Lonely Hearts Club Band* (1967), p. 2098; The Monterey Pop Festival Inaugurates the "Summer of Love" (1967), p. 2104; The Woodstock Music Festival Marks the Climax of the 1960's (1969), p. 2180; *Jesus Christ Superstar* Establishes the Rock Opera (1971), p. 2254.

HANDKE'S *KASPAR* DRAMATIZES LANGUAGE THEORY

Category of event: Theater
Time: May 11, 1968
Locale: Frankfurt and Oberhausen, West Germany

Peter Handke's first full-length play, Kaspar *took Germany by storm and gave a new, postmodern voice to the Western world*

Principal personages:
>PETER HANDKE (1942-   ), a playwright and novelist who championed the postmodern aesthetic
>KLAUS PEYMANN (1936-   ), the director of *Kaspar* at the Theater am Turm in Frankfurt
>ULRICH WILDGRUBER, the actor who played the role of Kaspar in Frankfurt
>GUNTHER BUCH, the director of *Kaspar* at the Städtische Bühnen in Oberhausen
>WOLF R. REDL, the actor who played Kaspar in Oberhausen

Summary of Event

Until 1966, Peter Handke was a little-known author associated with the so-called Ganz Group, an assembly of young artists and intellectuals set to pull down the idols of modernism. The year 1966, though, was important in several ways to Handke. In addition to raising his voice in favor of a new aesthetic, he had published his first novel, *Die Hornissen* (1966; the hornets), and had his short play *Publikumsbeschimpfung* (1966; *Offending the Audience*, 1969) presented in Frankfurt. *Die Hornissen* received generally favorable reviews, and *Offending the Audience* was the hit of the "Experimenta I" drama festival at the Theater am Turm. For his new works, Handke was awarded the coveted Gerhart Hauptmann prize.

Offending the Audience had deeply startled its viewers by turning the tables on them; the actors stood in a row on a bare stage directly addressing the audience, forcing them to create the play by interacting with the performers. The mode established in *Offending the Audience* was followed by Handke in other short experimental pieces, notably *Selbstbezichtigung* (1966; *Self-Accusation*, 1969).

After having experienced such a startlingly new approach in Handke's short plays, the Frankfurt audience came to his first full-length play, *Kaspar*, with considerable curiosity and anticipation. They were not disappointed; *Kaspar* took the Frankfurt audience by storm. Despite some reactions of outrage, viewers continued to fill the house for each performance. Other theaters quickly followed with productions, and Handke's work became the year's most frequently produced play across Europe.

For all its popularity, *Kaspar* is not an easy play for audiences. It is mysterious and foreboding, completely without a traditional story line. A young man suddenly breaks through the rear curtain onto a stage filled with seemingly pointless properties. The young man is from the country. He is perplexed, indeed astonished, at his condition. He can hardly walk. He possesses nothing, knows nothing except a single sentence: "I want to be somebody like somebody else once was." Even this sentence is difficult for Kaspar to say; it comes out muffled and garbled.

Throughout the course of the next two hours, Kaspar grapples with the implications of his single sentence. At first he says it by rote, stumbling about. Under the influence of mysterious "prompters," though, he begins to elaborate, to use the sentence as a test against other sentences, in short to create a language.

As Kaspar develops language, the prompters give him advice. They point out that he has a great advantage, for he already possesses a sentence, which is better than a word, since a sentence can be spoken with style. Out of style, meaning can be expressed. A single sentence can make Kaspar an individual, for the sentence can be placed between Kaspar and everything else. It can encapsulate him.

Kaspar attempts to resist the prompters' advice, to master his single sentence by deliberately twisting the structure. His garbling results in new sentences, and Kaspar has now set a language between himself and the prompters. He has used language to create a solitary world of his own. The prompters, though, seize on this new development to teach Kaspar names for things and their functions, as well as old wives' tales about the behavior of things. In this way, Kaspar acquires wisdom and culture along with a mastery of language.

As becomes obvious to Kaspar, acquiring a language means acquiring order, but it is a mixed blessing. Language brings order, but it also brings its own imperatives. The speaker controls language only in the act of commencing to speak. Once initiated, a sentence follows its own logic. To demonstrate this phenomenon, Handke shows Kaspar arranging all the properties on the stage so that sets and suites are formed. When Kaspar attempts to list rules for the order he had built, however, the stage fills with other Kaspars who rearrange his designs and mock his logic. Similarly, life and reality are unrelated to language, which has an inherent order while existence remains chaotic. Now Kaspar is brought to a new, fundamental truth: Reality is not influenced by speech, but the speaker is. Life goes on freely, without oppression or order, while the speaker becomes a creature of his or her own speaking, a puppet to the order of language. Kaspar realizes that even in uttering his first sentence he was trapped forever. This is what Handke frequently refers to as the "nausea of language."

Handke based his play loosely on the German fascination with the "Kaspar legend." In Nuremberg in 1828, Kaspar Hauser, an autistic sixteen-year-old adolescent, appeared under mysterious circumstances. Apparently the young man had been kept in a closet, separated from human contact. He had difficulty moving, and at the time of his discovery, knew only a single sentence: "I would like to become a rider like my father once was." Appearing as he did at the peak of the Romantic movement, Kaspar Hauser became a *cause célèbre*. Karl Gutzkow, Georg Trakl, and Ernst Jandl are among the many writers who have treated the Kaspar legend; Handke chose a Jandl poem about Hauser as the epigraph to his play.

Impact of Event

With *Kaspar*, Peter Handke validated a new aesthetic that seemed to have sprung full-blown out of the decadence of an exhausted modernism that was clinging to the ideals of structure, ritual, myth, psychology, and moral socialism. To the "classic" modernist, structure was an intellectual truth. Peter Handke had battered at this truth with his two novels, *Die Hornissen* and *Die Hauserier* (1967; the peddler), but the first was too dense, and the other was at once too coy and too bold. *Die Hauserier* is a murder mystery without a plot. There are all the ingredients—a body, several possible murder weapons, a suspect—but nothing develops from these devices. They, like all reality, simply exist. Handke's point was that structure in itself, even such a traditional structure as the murder mystery, has no special value or function.

Offending the Audience came a step closer to making Handke's point, for it was presented in the most socialized art form, the theater. Theater is where people are gathered to share an art in public. It is the art, therefore, most dependent on structure, on shared conventions. In *Offending the Audience*, Handke eliminated all conventions. The audience did not view the play; they were the play. The piece was short and was performed as part of an experimental festival, however, and was thus limited in its impact.

Kaspar had to be considered a major drama; it was presented at a major theater as part of its regular season. Indeed, it was presented simultaneously at two theaters. It could not be blinked away. Postmodernism had arrived.

Not that Handke was unknown or unconsidered by 1968. He had already received the Hauptmann prize and had insulted the dignitaries gathered for the award with an outrageous speech about a notorious murder trial of the day. He had carefully cultivated a "bad boy" image and had sought out every controversy, deliberately outraging portions of his audience or reading public with each new work and then carefully fanning that outrage into open controversy. In fact, his frank manipulation of public controversy came to be known as "Handke-publicity," and his antics were compared to those of the Beatles, especially John Lennon, to whom Handke dedicated his first play.

Yet there was more than a simple seeking of notoriety to Peter Handke. He had something truly different to say, and he truly needed to be heard, because Handke's subject was speech itself.

Born into the chaos that was Austria between the wars, speaking German but a citizen of several different Germanies and Austrias, sent off to school to study law, a hated subject and profession, Handke became sensitized to the hopelessness of bringing order to reality. Ludwig Wittgenstein, the Viennese philosopher, had already set the stage for Handke's generation. Building on the work of Ferdinand de Saussure, Wittgenstein had taught that every problem was a matter of language. The semioticians who followed this premise laid out a world divided into signifiers (language) and the signified (reality), and by the late 1960's, postmodern philosophers such as Jacques Derrida and Michel Foucault were arguing that reality was imponderable in any case and that the signifiers invented by humans were all that remained to humans for study. The future study of humanity would be human language.

Handke met this challenge by creating a literature that matched the new philosophers' arguments. Language, not psychology or moral philosophy, is the subject, object, and total vehicle of Handke's plays. Kaspar, early in the play, asserts his belief in his own individuality and reality. Later, he realizes he has deceived himself, that he is only an eventuality of how he uses—or is used by—language. Finally, he admits that he is only a happenstance of speech, only accidentally himself.

Young writers in Germany such as Bazon Brock and Otto Piene were quick to follow in Handke's footsteps. Handke thus represents a leading edge of a wave of innovative writers that includes Kurt Vonnegut, Steve Katz, and Ronald Sukenick in the novel and Caryl Churchill in the drama. Audiences have found his plays simultaneously perplexing and compelling. When Joseph Papp produced Handke's second major play, *Der Ritt über den Bodensee* (1971; *The Ride Across Lake Constance,* 1972), at the Kennedy Center in Washington, D.C., the audience was outraged. Spectators booed and hissed, but they somehow sensed the significance of the event. Handke's plays have been performed frequently in the United States. In 1981, an English language video production of *The Ride Across Lake Constance* was created jointly by the University of Georgia and the Goethe Institute and distributed worldwide by the latter organization. At least in literature, Peter Handke is the person who most sharply defines the postmodern movement.

Bibliography

Handke, Peter. *Kaspar and Other Plays.* Translated by Michael Roloff. New York: Farrar, Straus & Giroux, 1969. Also includes *Offending the Audience* and *Self-Accusation.* A second volume from the same publisher, *The Ride Across Lake Constance and Other Plays* (1977) includes most of the remainder of Handke's dramatic works.

Joseph, Artur. "Nauseated by Language: From an Interview with Peter Handke." *The Drama Review* 15, no. 1 (Fall, 1970): 56-61. A good example of the primary material to be taken from an interview. Those interested in Handke's drama especially might also wish to consult Jack Zipes's "Contrary Positions: An Interview with Peter Handke" in *Performance,* September/October, 1976.

Klinkowitz, Jerome, and James Knowlton. *Peter Handke and the Postmodern Transformation.* Columbia: University of Missouri Press, 1983. A concise and clear study of Handke's early and middle career. An effort is made, successfully, to place him in the context of the postmodern intellectual climate. Handke's dramas are given a separate chapter, and *Kaspar* is analyzed thoroughly.

The New York Times Book Review. "Man, the Plaything of Language." August 7, 1970. An extremely informative consideration of Handke's impact. Clear, readable, and concise view of the author's achievement.

Schlueter, June. *The Plays and Novels of Peter Handke.* Pittsburgh: University of Pittsburgh Press, 1981. The best general study of the work and influence of Peter Handke. Most of Handke's dramatic works are considered.

August W. Staub

Cross-References

Wittgenstein Emerges as an Important Philosopher (1921), p. 518; Esslin Publishes *The Theatre of the Absurd* (1961), p. 1871; Foucault's *Madness and Civilization* Is Published (1961), p. 1877; Tawfiq al-Hakim Introduces Absurdism to the Arab Stage (1961), p. 1891; Derrida Enunciates the Principles of Deconstruction (1967), p. 2075; Guare's *The House of Blue Leaves* Combines Comedy with Horror (1971), p. 2239.

THE THEATRES ACT ENDS CENSORSHIP
OF ENGLISH DRAMA

Category of event: Theater
Time: July 26, 1968
Locale: London, England

On July 26, 1968, the centuries-old practice of censorship of the English stage came to an end thanks to the passage of the Theatres Act

Principal personages:
GEORGE R. STRAUSS, BARON STRAUSS (1901-   ), a Labour Party back-bencher who introduced the Theatres Act as a private member's bill and led the debate supporting it in the House of Commons
CAMERON FROMANTEEL COBBOLD, BARON COBBOLD (1904-   ), the last Lord Chamberlain, who, more liberal than most of his predecessors, was willing to see his position eliminated
JOHN TREVELYAN (1903-   ), the secretary of the British Board of Film Censors whose relatively liberal policies helped lay the foundation for the end of censorship of the stage

Summary of Event

Censorship of drama in England began in the sixteenth century as a means of ensuring that no pro-Catholic propaganda crept into scripts, England having officially embraced the Reformation. A secondary purpose was to control the influence of actors, whose morals and religious views generally were suspect. The latter attitude would linger at least through the nineteenth century. The role of the Lord Chamberlain, the chief officer of the royal household, as censor dates from 1737. In that year, Sir Robert Walpole, the chief political figure and head of government, responded to the political satire of Henry Fielding by securing passage of a new censorship law. Until 1968, the Lord Chamberlain had absolute power to determine what appeared on stage. Other than his staff of readers, he had no regular outside advice, and there was no appeal of his decisions. George Bernard Shaw reacted by saying that the Lord Chamberlain "robs, insults, and suppresses me as if he were the Czar of Russia."

Although never popular with intellectuals, journalists, and other writers, censorship did not become a matter of public debate until the late 1950's. There were at that time in Great Britain a number of barriers to artistic development, including lingering puritanism enforced by government censorship, limited public and private patronage, and the growth of television as home entertainment. In 1959, Penguin Books decided to publish an unexpurgated edition of D. H. Lawrence's *Lady Chatterley's Lover* (1928). Penguin's decision to publish Lawrence's book was a calculated challenge to the barrier of government censorship. The particularly active Lord

Chamberlain of the day, Lord Scarborough, brought a court case—one of his options in the situation—against Penguin Books. The defense introduced a series of experts to assert the literary and artistic value of the book, and the prosecutor made a fool of himself by asking jury members if the book were one they would want their servants to read. Although Mr. Justice Byrne, who presided, made his prejudices clear when addressing the jury, the decision to acquit came in three hours. The publication of the much more explicit *Last Exit to Brooklyn* (1964) by Hubert Selby, Jr., soon followed, but censorship continued. The *Lady Chatterley's Lover* decision had no immediate dramatic impact, but it did move Britain toward long-term easing of restrictions on expression. The question of censorship was to become a part of the series of retreats from Victorian policies that marked the 1960's.

The decade of the 1960's produced a new cultural tone that was a rejection of the establishment's somewhat staid and puritanical outlook. A series of reforms took place, particularly after the advent of a Labour Party government under Harold Wilson in 1964. Abortion became relatively easily obtainable, along with contraceptive materials and advice. Adult homosexuality was legalized, and restrictions on divorce were eased significantly. A woman's right to an equal share of family property in case of a marital breakup was established, and the principle (if not the practice) of equal pay was legislated. There was, then, a clear trend toward giving people more personal freedom.

Censorship, however, continued despite the attack on it in the late 1950's. Changing tastes made for some changes in what was acceptable, giving an appearance of more tolerance, but overt sexual activity and serious attacks on British and allied political figures both remained forbidden. The American play *Macbird*, a savage attack on President Lyndon Johnson, was denied access to the London stage by Cameron Fromanteel Cobbold, Lord Cobbold, Lord Chamberlain from 1963 to 1971. The cinema was less restricted. Harold Pinter's play *The Caretaker* (1960) did not measure up to the Lord Chamberlain's standards, but a film version was released in 1964 without trouble. The secretary of the British Board of Film Censors, a private agency, was John Trevelyan, formerly director of education for Westmorland County. Trevelyan was inclined to regard nudity and depiction of sexual activity, if actually germane to the plot line, as acceptable. He also was more tolerant of satire than was the Lord Chamberlain. The latter did show some flexibility, however. After the film version of *The Caretaker* was released, the story was resubmitted for presentation on stage and was cleared without difficulty. The playwright credited Lord Cobbold's reversal entirely to Trevelyan's position regarding the film.

Even as official policy seemed to become increasingly liberal, the principle of censorship came increasingly into question. A joint committee of the House of Lords and the House of Commons was appointed to study the matter. The committee's report, presented in 1967, recommended that censorship be ended. This did not, however, make the question of censorship a high priority with the government. The legislation was left to be a private member's bill. The introduction of such bills, given limited time at the ends of sessions in the House of Commons, is determined by a lottery that selects which members of the House of Commons will have an opportunity to bring forward their proposals.

Fortunately, George Strauss (later to be created a life peer as Baron Strauss), who favored legislation ending censorship of the theater, got a lucky draw and was able to introduce such a bill. Heated debate followed introduction of the bill. Among other things, Conservatives sought to protect the monarchy by forbidding any portrayal of a head of state, or possibly that of any living person, without his or her permission. Strauss jeered that in the past the Lord Chamberlain had banned W. S. Gilbert and Sir Arthur Sullivan's *The Mikado: Or, The Town of Titipu* (1885), George Bernard Shaw's *Mrs. Warren's Profession* (pb. 1898), Luigi Pirandello's *Six Characters in Search of an Author* (1921), and Tennessee Williams' *Cat on a Hot Tin Roof* (1955). Strauss urged that the bill be passed. He argued that "The present archaic, illogical and indefensible system of stage censorship . . . [has been] tolerated for too long. We are the only democratic and freedom-loving country in the world that has a censor." On February 24, 1968, the bill passed by voice vote, without, despite the vigorous debate, any recorded dissent. It went to committee, where it might have been altered fundamentally, but it was not. The Theatres Act became law on July 26, 1968. According to its terms, two months later the reign of the Lord Chamberlain as censor officially came to an end.

Impact of Event

Passage of the Theatres Act immediately prevented one struggle over censorship. James Vernor, a London producer, had proposed staging the rock musical *Hair* (1968), which includes liberal use of profanity and a brief nude scene. He submitted the script to Lord Cobbold, and it was returned marked "Unacceptable." A process of negotiation was expected, during which the producer and censor would seek agreement about changes required to allow the script to be granted a license. After the Theatres Act was passed, Vernor postponed the opening of *Hair* until late September. Although he insisted that this decision was made more for artistic reasons than to avoid censorship, Vernor did not deny that he was happy to be free of the Lord Chamberlain's oversight. The critical and popular reaction to the play was quite mixed and certainly suggested that English theatergoers would not be uniformly offended by either vulgarity or nudity.

There was, however, some concern about the long-term effect of the legislation even among theater managers and producers. The problem was that Strauss's bill did allow for prosecution in some situations. First, any citizen who regarded the content of a play as libelous could seek redress in the courts. Second, the attorney general might prosecute if, in his or her opinion, a script "tended to deprave and corrupt people likely to attend." Those who would be held responsible in the case of such prosecution were concerned that the threat of legal action would prove to be as restrictive as was the censor, or even more so. They had been protected from suit when a script had been licensed by the Lord Chamberlain.

Three months after the lifting of censorship, the concerns about the threat of prosecution had the possibility of being proven valid. On December 21, 1968, Rolf Hochhuth's play *Soldiers: An Obituary for Geneva* (1967) opened in London. The script intimated that Sir Winston Churchill had been involved in the death of Polish General Władysław Sikorski in 1943. As head of the Polish government in exile, Sikorski had been vigorously anti-Communist. According to the play's script, his attitude had endangered the Anglo-Soviet alliance against Nazi Germany.

The play premiered to critical and popular acclaim, but Winston Churchill, Sir Winston's grandson, asserted that it was an "infamous libel" against his illustrious ancestor. Churchill dismissed as spurious or as suppression of historical truth claims that evidence to support the charge was under lock and key for fifty years. Although many people insisted the charges were ambiguous, others previously had thought the work to be libelous. It had been rejected by the Lord Chamberlain unless written permission were to be obtained from survivors of all those portrayed. The controversy, bitter and lingering, was still making news a year later. It did not, however, keep the play from the London stage or result in any reduction in the freedom established by the Theatres Act.

The Theatres Act of 1968 was part of a wave of progressive change in the late 1960's. It opened the London stage to a variety of experimental drama that never could have been performed there previously. English arts, known since William Shakespeare's day for dramatic excellence, were given greater freedom to experiment and to explore previously forbidden topics. They did so, and despite occasional problems such as that concerning *Soldiers: An Obituary for Geneva*, the Theatres Act was a successful reform with, it seems, implications beyond the stage. Although it did not directly affect the cinema, censorship of that medium was greatly reduced after the act was passed, apparently as a response to the success of the uncensored theater.

Bibliography

Childs, David. *Britain Since 1945: A Political History.* New York: St. Martin's Press, 1979. An excellent survey of politics that is important for setting the Theatres Act in the context of policies of the Labour government of the day. Although more interested in politics than in fine arts, Childs does not ignore the latter.

Marwick, Arthur. *British Society Since 1945.* Harmondsworth, England: Penguin Books, 1982. Written by one of the preeminent scholars in the field, this volume is an important source for anyone studying British society. The chapter on culture in the 1960's is a stimulating essay on the decline of Victorian attitudes.

Morgan, Kenneth O. *The People's Peace: British History, 1945-1989.* Oxford, England: Oxford University Press, 1990. A recognized expert on the Labour Party, Morgan has created a work that is scholarly and readable. He does a good job of tracing the development of reform generally, and of censorship particularly, through the 1960's.

Thomas, Donald. *A Long Time Burning: The History of Literary Censorship in England.* New York: Frederick A. Praeger, 1969. Thomas traces questions regarding censorship in England from the fifteenth century. In his long, comprehensive volume, he looks at motivations for, methods of, and reform of censorship. Although his examples are sometimes obscure, his general points are clear.

Williamson, Bill. *The Temper of the Times: British Society Since World War II.* Oxford, England: Basil Blackwell, 1990. As suggested by the title, this book is an attempt to address the attitudes of the British in the latter half of the twentieth century. This is a difficult task and has not, in this case, been accomplished with complete success. The book is, however, a valuable look at the social scene in the 1960's.

Fred R. van Hartesveldt

Cross-References

Shaw Articulates His Philosophy in *Man and Superman* (1903), p. 85; Pirandello's *Six Characters in Search of an Author* Premieres (1921), p. 534; The Royal Shakespeare Company Adopts a New Name and Focus (1961), p. 1888; Great Britain Establishes the Royal National Theatre (1962), p. 1924; The Radical Musical *Hair* Opens on Broadway (1968), p. 2121.

60 MINUTES BECOMES THE FIRST
TELEVISED NEWSMAGAZINE

Categories of event: Television and radio; journalism
Time: September 24, 1968
Locale: New York, New York

*Don Hewitt and CBS brought an innovative format, the television newsmagazine, to
broadcast journalism, and the resulting program set the standard for years to come*

Principal personages:
DON HEWITT (1922-   ), the television producer and director credited
with inventing the newsmagazine format
MIKE WALLACE (1918-   ), a talk-show host and CBS correspondent
known for his tough interviewing style
HARRY REASONER (1923-1991), a television correspondent and anchorman known for his friendly, plodding, literate journalistic style

Summary of Event

The Columbia Broadcasting System (CBS) was at the pinnacle of its newscasting
authority in the fall of 1968. Starting first with radio news and shifting into television journalism, the work of correspondents Edward R. Murrow, Eric Sevareid, Bill
Shirer, Douglas Edwards, and Walter Cronkite had defined broadcast journalism.
The news divisions of the two competing networks, the National Broadcasting Company (NBC) and the American Broadcasting Company (ABC) were perennial also-
rans. Television "news," though, had a certain look to it—and that look was anything but entertaining. *60 Minutes* was about to change that perception, in the minds
of both network executives and network viewers.

Don Hewitt had begun working for CBS in 1947 as a television news assistant. His
tenure bridged CBS's illustrious radio past and the formative years of television. He
knew Murrow, directed the network's first nightly news show, made a name for himself directing the first John F. Kennedy-Richard M. Nixon debate in 1960, and produced several years' worth of the *CBS Evening News* with Walter Cronkite. Hewitt's
enthusiasm for his work and his animated behavior in a television control room
became another CBS legend. Still, he was taken off the *CBS Evening News* in 1965
when the corporation wanted its flagship newscast to have a more serious look—a
look executives felt Hewitt could not provide.

Hewitt was reassigned the executive producer chores for the long-running *CBS
Reports.* He worked in Murrow's shadow, producing several one-hour "documents
for television," and it was during this time that Hewitt came up with the idea for
60 Minutes. Recalling the inspiration for the program, Hewitt remarked, "No one
likes to read documents, so why would they want to watch something called a docu-

mentary?" Instead, he proposed a new kind of program—a television newsmagazine. The new show was to be a regularly scheduled series focusing on topics with broad appeal: politics, government, business, personalities, and features. Like Murrow, Hewitt believed that the best stories were those told through simple arguments and led naturally to a confrontation between people. The new program's stories would have to tell the audience something new, have a national dimension, run their course in thirteen minutes or less, and have an upfront punch to garner an emotional response from the audience. It was this format that Hewitt pitched to the network as *60 Minutes.*

The network brass watched the pilot episode Hewitt put together with CBS stock footage and narration by Harry Reasoner. They suggested a second correspondent be teamed with Reasoner, someone with an opposing demeanor. Hewitt picked the one man at CBS whose on-air personality was the antithesis of the easygoing Reasoner's—hard-hitting Mike Wallace. The network then agreed to try out *60 Minutes* on every other Tuesday night (it alternated with *CBS Reports*) at ten o'clock, where it could do little ratings damage; it was matched against ABC's top-rated *Marcus Welby, M.D.*

"This is *60 Minutes,*" Reasoner began on September 24, 1968. "It's a kind of a magazine for television, which means it has the flexibility and diversity of a magazine adapted to broadcast journalism." Less than one in five viewers watched it that night. With the exception of Don Hewitt, no one around CBS headquarters gave *60 Minutes* much of a chance—not even its hosts, Wallace and Reasoner.

After this dismal outing, Hewitt persuaded the news department executives to reassign several of CBS's top writer-producers to his show. Veterans of *See It Now*, Joe Wershba and Palmer Williams developed stories for *60 Minutes.* Mike Wallace, known for the 1950's talk show *Nightbeat*, was allowed to do what he did best—ask tough questions. His aggressive, almost inquisitional style brought a unique tone to the program's investigative pieces—and it brought ratings. Wallace and Reasoner played well off each other, with Reasoner's homey style lending itself to features and personality interviews. Just when *60 Minutes* was finding a small but steady audience, Reasoner left the program to anchor ABC's evening news in 1970. Hewitt replaced him with Morley Safer, CBS's London Bureau Chief, but in 1971 the entertainment executives finally got their way, and *60 Minutes* was pulled from the lineup in favor of a detective series.

For the next few years, *60 Minutes* bounced around the CBS schedule. In December, 1975, it was moved to Sunday evenings, where it finished fifty-second in the ratings that year. The move was not caused by a newfound confidence in the show but because the Federal Communications Commission was pressuring networks to program a "family hour" each night. The time shift also coincided loosely with the nation's heightened awareness of journalistic endeavors in the wake of the Watergate scandal and with the addition of future CBS anchorman Dan Rather to the program's lineup. Ratings began to climb; *60 Minutes* went into the top ten in 1977 and hit number one in the A. C. Nielsen ratings for the first time in November, 1979, the night after the U.S. embassy in Tehran was taken over by Iranian militants. The program soon had a lock on Sunday night ratings and became one of the longest-running and highest-rated series in television history.

Hewitt and his staff produce approximately one hundred stories for each television season. According to Hewitt, about half the stories aired on *60 Minutes* are generated in-house, thirty percent come from outside news sources, and twenty percent are suggested by viewers. Hewitt measures his work in stories completed, not programs aired (there are three stories to a program). In addition to Wallace and Safer, other CBS correspondents have passed through Hewitt's fold over the years. Dan Rather lent his investigative talents to *60 Minutes* from 1974 to 1980. The program's first black journalist, Ed Bradley, came aboard in 1981, and its first female, Diane Sawyer, served from 1984 to 1988. In the late 1980's several younger correspondents were brought in to help lay the groundwork for a second successful generation of *60 Minutes.*

Impact of Event

Don Hewitt's newsmagazine format had never been tried before on television, but its immense success assured decades of emulation. ABC's *20/20* and *Prime Time Live*, CBS's *Street Stories*, and the show-business oriented *Entertainment Tonight* all took their cue from *60 Minutes.* Geraldo Rivera and other investigative reporters have passed through doors *60 Minutes* opened. Network programmers once thought that news in prime time represented financial suicide, but *60 Minutes* changed that view. Unlike drama or comedy series, the newsmagazines are solely owned by the network that airs them, meaning that all the money they make stays with the network.

Over the years, *60 Minutes* has produced many memorable stories. Topics covered in the early telecasts included interviews with Eldridge Cleaver, the head of the Black Panthers, and Army Captain Ernest Medina, who was court-martialed for his part in the My Lai massacre. Also included were stories about ecology and minority issues. Several stories unleashed such public outrage that the parties involved mended their ways. There have been segments devoted to Middle East politics, the Vietnam War, and the plight of Jordanian Jews. Between 1974 and 1976, several stories and interviews were done about the Watergate scandal and the collapse of the Nixon White House. A 1976 story about brain damage suffered by workers at a chemical plant resulted in the filing of criminal charges against the company that owned the plant.

The program has also pioneered techniques necessary to produce a newsmagazine. As former NBC News president Reuven Frank once noted, the program has always been "star journalism, the reporter as hero." Don Hewitt's unique management style is the key to *60 Minutes'* success. Hewitt seldom has meetings and never sends memos; he prefers instead to conduct business with his producers, correspondents, and film editors in person—and often in office corridors. He is supported by a half-dozen associate producers based in New York, Washington, D.C., and other major news centers who pitch story ideas to Hewitt. Projected stories are checked for similarity to stories being produced for other CBS programs; once a story idea is approved, the producers go into the field to research and film. In the early stages of a story's development, producers are as much private investigator as producer; stories often mutate or die as more information is obtained. It is thus not at all unusual for a *60 Minutes* producer to have five or six projects in development at one time. Once the producers are sure a story will be filmed, a correspondent comes to the story's location; since so many projects are constantly in the works, the show's correspondents are forever aboard airplanes bound from one story to the next.

So much emphasis is placed on good film editing at *60 Minutes* that the editors' names, rather than the writers', appear on the credits. Editing is important because it expresses ideas, improves understanding, and shapes a story's progression. Hewitt shares Murrow's belief that a story is best told by letting those people involved tell the story. Yet editing is the most controversial aspect of *60 Minutes.* The fact that interviews and "reverse shots" (film of the show's correspondents asking questions) are put together at different times is disconcerting to news purists—and to those people who run afoul of a *60 Minutes* investigation. The success of *60 Minutes,* however, has made this type of content selectivity standard practice for all television newsmagazines.

Over the years, *60 Minutes* has taken on a distinctive "magazine of the air" look, with footage of a make-believe magazine cover, a verbal table of contents, an editorial page (the show's "Point-Counterpoint" and "Andy Rooney" segments), and letters from viewers. Its visual trademark is a ticking stopwatch that correctly shows the time remaining in each episode at commercial breaks.

In the show's most hard-hitting pieces, usually done by Mike Wallace (and more recently by Ed Bradley and Steve Kroft), the questioning is relentless and the program's tone almost inquisitional. Viewers tune in to watch an evasive politician, a dishonest corporate manager, or a shady businessman get hunted down like a big-game animal. Over the years, *60 Minutes* has been credited with uncovering numerous scandals and disreputable business practices and even with gaining freedom for citizens wrongly convicted of a crime. Yet the program does have its detractors. The National Rifle Association took offense after a 1982 broadcast about Teflon bullets. The same year, a doctor whose signature appeared on paperwork at a disreputable clinic investigated by the program sued CBS and the show's producers, and Dan Rather spent several days on the witness stand clearing *60 Minutes* of any wrongdoing. The program has also been criticized for paying H. R. Haldeman $100,000 for an interview about his experiences in the Nixon Administration. Still, in an industry in which executives, producers, and companies are often neutered by irate viewers and special-interest groups, it is a testament to *60 Minutes'* power that it has routinely been able to take on controversial issues without fear.

Bibliography

Frank, Reuven. *Out of Thin Air: The Brief Wonderful Life of Network News.* New York: Simon & Schuster, 1991. History of NBC television news, and broadcast journalism in general, as seen from its former president's perspective. Includes index and interviews.

Gitlin, Todd. *Inside Prime Time.* New York: Pantheon Books, 1983. Solid explanation of the programming decisions made by network executives in their search for a hit show. Includes interviews with producers, writers, agents, and executives. Includes footnotes and index.

Hewitt, Don. *Minute by Minute.* New York: Random House, 1985. Careless look into *60 Minutes* history by its executive producer. Coffee-table book, without index, treats subject too generally. Does include many photos.

Lesher, Stephan. *Media Unbound: The Impact of Television Journalism on the Public.* Boston: Houghton Mifflin, 1982. Looks at television news in general and *60 Minutes* in particular. Focuses on shortcomings of both and on the impact television news has on American culture. Includes index.

Madsen, Axel. *"60 Minutes": The Power and the Politics.* New York: Dodd, Mead, 1984. Unsanctioned history of the program that includes detailed information about the program's decision-making process, story content, and evolution. Indexed; includes interviews with staff and contributors

Metz, Robert. *CBS: Reflections in a Bloodshot Eye.* Chicago: Playboy Press, 1975. Dated history of CBS. Chronicles the network from Paley's acquisition through the growth of radio and television. Includes information on CBS's other businesses. An index is included.

Rather, Dan. *The Camera Never Blinks: Adventures of a TV Journalist.* New York: William Morrow, 1977. Autobiography that discusses Rather's coverage of 1960's civil unrest and his tenure as CBS White House correspondent. Dated; does not have information about his anchor position or later work with CBS.

Reasoner, Harry. *Before the Colors Fade.* New York: Alfred A. Knopf, 1981. Autobiography of Reasoner that covers his experiences with network news, the space program, the Civil Rights movement, *60 Minutes*, and journalism in general.

Wallace, Mike, and Gary Paul Gates. *Close Encounters: Mike Wallace's Own Story.* New York: William Morrow, 1984. Autobiography. Wallace writes about his early years in television (talk and game shows), his move into news, his experience on *60 Minutes*, and his views of news reporting.

Thomas C. Breslin

Cross-References

The Christian Science Monitor Is Founded (1908), p. 209; Luce Founds *Time* Magazine (1923), p. 577; Luce Launches *Life* Magazine (1936), p. 1031; McLuhan Probes the Impact of Mass Media on Society (1964), p. 1973; *USA Today* Is Launched (1982), p. 2507.

LAUREN CREATES THE "POLO" LINE

Category of event: Fashion and design
Time: October 18, 1968
Locale: New York, New York

The fashion and design worlds were changed when a young tie salesman from the Bronx developed a patrician clothing style to fit American notions of elitism, class, tradition, and luxury

Principal personages:
RALPH LAUREN (1939-   ), a tie salesman and onetime student at the
   City College of New York who longed to go to an Ivy League school
JERRY LAUREN (1934-   ), Ralph's older brother, who suggested the
   name Polo

Summary of Event

In 1967, with his time as a sales clerk at Brooks Brothers behind him, Ralph Lauren, the son of a Jewish house painter with artistic ambitions and a deeply religious Jewish mother, was working for the Abe Rivetz Company, under Mel Creedman, as a tie salesman. Lauren wanted to design wider ties than the ones then in fashion. Creedman allowed Lauren to make up some of his wider ties. Lauren naturally thought that he was doing more than just selling, so he asked for a bonus. Since tie salesmen were never given bonuses, Creedman turned Lauren down. Lauren began looking for another job and also began looking for backers for a tie line of his own. He was far more than an average tie salesman. He truly loved his merchandise, had a tremendous sense of color and style inherited from his father, and, although he had never attended an Ivy League school, had a love for the fine fabrics, exciting colors, hand stitching, rich stripes, and width (in lapels as well as ties) associated with the clothing worn by Ivy League students. His talent, low-key style, taste, personal commitment, and image of a world of elegance and comfort helped him to sell. Lauren quickly went from looking for a job to wanting to start his own company.

Lauren told Buddy Blake, an important New York tie maker, that he wanted to do more design and styling. Lauren, however, was trying to launch wide ties only seven years after many tie companies had suffered as a result of gambling on the wide ties of the "mod" look. Demographically, mod styles came just a little too soon and had an English look. People with longer memories than Lauren feared his wide-tie look, but he intended to Americanize it. He gave up his $13,000-a-year salary at Abe Rivetz; he had received one big order for his ties designed for the Abe Rivetz Company, but they had been returned by Abraham & Strauss, a division of Federated Department Stores.

Lauren was already looking for an investor by then. Although he was a natural salesman, he never feared telling people what he thought. He used an appointment with the Gant brothers, Marty and Elliott, to tell them that he used to wear their shirts and no longer did. This was not a comment likely to get one of the Gants to back his enterprise. Lauren, though, was attracted to their reputation for using good Oxford cloth, the original Ivy League look, and tradition. Gant Shirt Makers had begun their business in 1949 and had competed successfully with C. F. Hathaway and other major manufacturers, but Lauren, though young and comparatively inexperienced, was willing to tell them their business.

In 1967, ties typically sold for prices ranging from three to four dollars, but Lauren wanted to sell ties starting at $7.50. In Ned Brower, the president of Beau Brummell, a Cincinnati-based tie company, he found his first backer. Lauren quit Creedman's company a few days after agreeing with Brower to start a new division, which Lauren would run. The agreement was that Lauren would do the selling, and if the Beau Brummell salespeople had time to help with the line, they would. Jerry Lauren, Ralph's dapper older brother, came up with the name "Polo," and Ralph loved the suggestion. The name conjured up images of British society, a rich man's game, money, a patrician style, and exclusivity, concepts Lauren wanted to have associated with his ties.

Brower gave Lauren a small office in Brummell's Empire State Building headquarters. Lauren at first kept his ties in a drawer, then in a chest of drawers. He was president, chief executive officer, chief operating officer, packer, shipper, distributor, and top salesman, selling hand-blocked, brightly colored, diagonal-checked ties in exotic fabrics, including several made in Switzerland. These ties retailed at prices from $7.50 to $15.00. When Lauren was interviewed for the *Daily News Record*, a clothing publication, he wore one of his ties with a blue shirt, a jacket with four-inch-wide lapels, and deeply cuffed pleated pants. He was not above showing people what to wear with his ties, and the *Daily News Record* took notice. Lauren was already selling a total look even before he had his own line of menswear.

Lauren's first customers were Clifford Grodd at Paul Stuart and Roland Meledandri. Lauren's tie maker, George Bruder, could not make money on these first orders because they were so small, but he filled the orders anyway because he liked Lauren, as did many people. Lauren was able to sell to small stores, partly on the basis of his own presence and partly because he had Paul Stuart as a customer. Eric Ross in Beverly Hills, Louis of Boston, and Neiman-Marcus also became customers. More than anything else, however, Lauren wanted to sell to Bloomingdale's. Lauren opened only two dozen accounts his first six months, and he could not get Bloomingdale's to carry his ties. He had no advertising budget, so he spent hours talking to fashion editors. Robert L. Green, fashion editor of *Playboy* magazine, loved his ties and featured them with menswear by Bill Blass and Pierre Cardin. Finally, the Bloomingdale's Fresh Meadows store ordered some ties, and soon some appeared in the Bloomingdale's on Lexington Avenue. The ties had the Polo label, and Polo was launched. This was the beginning of a relationship between Lauren and Bloomingdale's that would seriously influence not only the menswear industry but also the fashion industry as a whole.

By April of 1968, Lauren was already refusing to sell to less prestigious stores, because he wanted to keep his exclusivity. He also wanted to advance beyond being a tie salesman. In the spring of 1968, Norman Hilton, a suit manufacturer, approached Lauren about designing a line of clothes, including suits, dress shirts, and sports clothes. Ned Brower was willing to let the Polo trademark go as long as Lauren would buy his remaining inventory. On October 18, 1968, Polo Fashions incorporated by filing papers in the state of New York.

Only four days later, Ralph Lauren showed a one-button suit with wide lapels and pleated pants at Robert L. Green's Creative Menswear Design Awards at New York's Plaza Hotel. Meledandri, Oleg Cassini, Pierre Cardin, John Weitz, and Bill Blass also showed at the Plaza. Lauren's inclusion in the show proved that he had become a menswear designer, but he was not happy stopping there. Eventually his lines would include home furnishings, linens, women's wear, and antiques. He even dreamed of marketing designer beef. At the time, however, he needed new offices and showrooms. Most menswear representatives had their showrooms crowded together at 1290 Sixth Avenue for the supposed convenience of the provincial buyers, but Lauren was not one to join a herd. He thought that the building was too commercial, noisy, and crowded. He had shown his suits at the Plaza Hotel with John Weitz, and Weitz had offices in a ten-story residential building. With Weitz's blessing, Lauren took a sixth-floor, two bedroom office, using one bedroom as a design studio and the other as his showroom. His father, from whom he got his sense of color and interest in interiors, painted his office.

Although Lauren still had no advertising budget, Bloomingdale's did. Polo ties sold quickly there, and Bloomingdale's placed a seven-column ad in *The New York Times* to encourage even more sales. The ad stressed the elegance and unique design of the ties and actually listed the $15.00 price. Some customers bought a half dozen at a time. The stock market was booming, business was good, and the times were optimistic, promising conditions for sales of expensive, stylish clothing. By the time Polo Fashions moved into its new offices, Lauren could not meet the demand for his ties. The young man from the Bronx who had never gotten closer to the Ivy League than the City College of New York had at least revived the Ivy League style. In the fall of 1957, he had dreamed of life on campus, and now he gave expression to that dream in his fashions.

Impact of Event

Beverly Hills retailer Berny Schwartz opened the first Polo Shop in September, 1971. By then, Lauren was designing ties, shirts, and suits, but the store and its constant need for more and different merchandise pushed Lauren to design more items, including a shoe collection, belts, raincoats, socks, and sweaters. Sales for his company's first fiscal year, ending March 31, 1969, had amounted to $400,000. For the next fiscal year, sales were $2.4 million, and the following year, the company sold $3.8 million in products. By the end of 1974, Peter Strom had joined Polo/Ralph Lauren Corporation, helping to raise its annual business from $7 million in 1974 to $925 million in 1988.

By 1974, Lauren's women's wear collection also was a success. Stores including I. Magnin in San Francisco, Bullock's Wilshire in Los Angeles, and Neiman-Marcus in Dallas had bought it in quantity. Department stores began building Lauren his own departments for fashion; later, they would build him his own departments for linens.

Lauren designed his women's wear collection for women who dressed to illustrate their success or who still were trying to achieve that success. Despite his original successes in *Playboy* magazine with his menswear, Lauren disdained sexually suggestive advertising while willingly appealing to status, family, permanence, belonging, and privilege. One never saw a woman with prominent cleavage in a Lauren ad, for he liked his models to look thin.

By 1972, Lauren had bought out his partner, Norman Hilton, at a time when Polo was highly undercapitalized and constantly late delivering goods. As a designer, Lauren was earning rave reviews, but as a manager, he was not doing as well. He got a lucky break in the form of an offer from Hollywood to costume the characters in the film *The Great Gatsby* (1974). Robert Redford, Mia Farrow, Bruce Dern, and Sam Waterston, as well as dozens of extras, wore his clothes. Woody Allen raided Lauren's closet and went away with an armful of clothes that he wore in *Manhattan* (1979). Lauren admits to having been influenced by films, particularly *The Thomas Crown Affair* (1968), which starred Faye Dunaway and Steve McQueen. One scene that particularly intrigued him and that he used in his ad concepts showed Dunaway sitting on a Ferrari with a big hat and a motion-picture camera while watching McQueen play polo. Other films that influenced Lauren include *Chariots of Fire* (1981), *To Catch a Thief* (1955), *The Philadelphia Story* (1940), and *The Godfather* (1972). Several of these suggest his love of sports, family, and family members at leisure together as well as showcasing characters with distinct styles. They also influenced his lines of tuxedos and evening gowns. Cary Grant's patrician stance clearly was another influence.

After a stormy partnership with old neighborhood friend Michael Bernstein, Lauren ran the business with his oldest brother Lennie, but Lennie needed help. That was when Peter Strom, who previously had worked for Norman Hilton, joined Lauren. By 1976, Lennie Lauren was out of the business and Strom was ensconced. Polo began making the fragrances Polo and Lauren, and the business as a whole was on a better financial footing. By 1984, Lauren was a multimillionaire. The man who had once come close to closing his business was forming partnerships everywhere, particularly with The Gap. There was a new problem, however. Less expensive knock-offs of his own designs were beginning to appear, particularly in his casual wear line and Chaps. This situation influenced him to develop his own less expensive casual wear featuring denim. The Gap provided funding for the Polo Westernwear line. By that time, Lauren was interested in New Mexico and Colorado and actually bought a ranch in Colorado. His New West look had clothes inspired by Navajo blankets and Indian jewelry, chamois shirts, turquoise hoop earrings, jacket-sized Navajo sweaters, and suede skirts. Also called "the Santa Fe look," it was a tremendous success. The age of the yuppie had come, and young people took comfort in the status symbols and symbols of success that Lauren designed. Among them were an alligator notebook selling for almost a thousand dollars.

Lauren's bold experiments in the world of fashion first brought back the Ivy League look, then through their successes encouraged other designers to take more chances with innovative looks. His Polo fashions were some of the first with appeal that spread down from the upper to the middle classes, and his was one of the first fashion companies to branch out into a varied product line including such things as colognes. Polo fashions also brought Lauren's name to prominence as a designer. Soon status-conscious shoppers would learn to look for clothes imprinted with a particular designer's name. In all these ways, Lauren changed the fashion world.

Bibliography

Black, Susan. "The Scarf Company That Could." *Bobbin* 31 (June, 1990): 48-54. An important article that deals specifically and at some length with important issues of the clothing trade and the psychology of success in the industry. The text is informative, providing details and critical commentary, although it is clearly an appreciation of Lauren's company.

Buck, Joan Juliet. "Everybody's All-American." *Vogue* 182 (February, 1992): 202-211. One of the lengthier articles on Ralph Lauren. An excellent article, it deals with Lauren and his "All-American" style. A helpful addition to an understanding of Ralph Lauren and his contributions. Includes a fine collection of photographs.

Donaton, Scott, and Pat Sloan. "Lauren at Work on Lifestyle Magazine." *Advertising Age* 63 (April 27, 1992): 1, 54. Although this article is informative, one would expect that a field that owes Lauren so much might have afforded him a more complete examination in terms of his use of advertising. Shies away from an analysis of his life-style as he portrays it in ads.

Shao, Maria. "Everybody's Falling into the Gap." *Business Week* 3232 (September 23, 1991): 36. Discusses Lauren's deals with The Gap. Although brief, it is a fine report on the relationship between Lauren and The Gap. Jeffrey Trachtenberg (see below) treats his subject more thoroughly.

Trachtenberg, Jeffrey. *Ralph Lauren: The Man Behind the Mystique.* Boston: Little, Brown, 1988. Deals extensively with Lauren's life and career after 1968 as well as the earlier years. Includes lengthy quotations from people who worked closely with Lauren. The best source on the subjects of Ralph Lauren, his enterprises, and the development of his style. Notes, bibliography, index, and photographs.

Merrilee Cunningham

Cross-References

Brooks Brothers Introduces Button-Down Shirts (1900), p. 24; Chanel Defines Modern Women's Fashion (1920's), p. 474; *The Great Gatsby* Captures the Essence of the Roaring Twenties (1925), p. 626; Schiaparelli's Boutique Mingles Art and Fashion (1935), p. 979; Dior's "New Look" Sweeps Europe and America (1947), p. 1346; Punk's Antifashion Style First Appears (1974), p. 2299.

KAWABATA WINS THE NOBEL PRIZE IN LITERATURE

Category of event: Literature
Time: December 12, 1968
Locale: Stockholm, Sweden

Catching most Western observers by surprise, the selection of Yasunari Kawabata as the Nobel Prize winner in literature for 1968 ushered in a trend of genuine cosmopolitanism for the West and the Swedish Academy

Principal personages:

YASUNARI KAWABATA (1899-1972), a novelist and short-story writer who was the first Japanese author to be honored by the Nobel Committee
ANDERS ÖSTERLING (1884-1981), the permanent secretary of the Swedish Academy, the presenter of the award
EDWARD SEIDENSTICKER (1921-   ), the principal translator of Kawabata's work into English

Summary of Event

The Nobel Prize in Literature was presented to Yasunari Kawabata on December 12, 1968, by Anders Österling, the permanent secretary of the Swedish Academy. To aid the Westerner unfamiliar either with Kawabata's work or with Japanese literature in general, Österling pointed out that, for all his peculiarly Japanese ideas and sensibilities, Kawabata seemed to share certain features with some European writers. Among those Österling mentioned was the Russian novelist Ivan Turgenev, who, like Kawabata, sensitively portrayed the social scene at a time of transition between old and new.

Such comparisons between Kawabata and familiar Western figures were not, however, enough to convince many in the West who reacted to the selection of Kawabata with wonderment and surprise. Most who had speculated had expected the prize to go to one of several well-established European writers: Samuel Beckett, Günter Grass, Eugène Ionesco, or André Malraux. The selection of a Japanese writer genuinely shocked the unsuspecting.

This general reaction of disbelief rested largely on the simple fact that Kawabata, whose oeuvre had only been partly translated into a handful of languages—the best translations are arguably those in English by Edward Seidensticker—had languished in near obscurity. What is more, faithful translations were in themselves insufficient to explain what seemed to many Westerners weaknesses in plot construction and characterization.

Comparable though Kawabata may be to certain European writers, overwhelmingly it is his peculiarly Japanese qualities that best define him. Like his elder contemporary Jun'ichirō Tanizaki, who was similarly influenced by Western literature, Kawabata still very much represents a continuity, not a break, with the tradition of Japanese culture. His worship of beauty, fascination with nature, and obsession with death are all treated with keen observation and a visual immediacy recalling Japanese painting. His prose style, as the academy itself remarked, calls to mind *haiku* poetry.

Fortunately, the part of Kawabata's oeuvre most accessible to the academy (and to the West in general) was that handful of novels that distinguish the mature Kawabata: *Yukiguni* (1947; *Snow Country*, 1956), *Sembazuru* (1952; *Thousand Cranes*, 1958), *Yama no oto* (1957; *The Sound of the Mountain*, 1970), *Kyoto* (1962; *The Old Capital*, 1987), and—though an early work, written in the mature style—*Izu no odoriko* (1926; *The Izu Dancer*, 1955). All of these novels are episodic in nature, and all in fact were published in serial form before appearing in single volumes. Also, the novels all end on notes seemingly lacking resolution or closure, a feature of Kawabata's oeuvre that has caused some consternation. It can be said that this distinctive characteristic results from the fact that Kawabata records life as a process; the form or structure of his novels is more musical in quality than architectural, more temporal than spatial. He has a sharp eye for physical description, as attested by his sensitive and highly charged renderings of the Japanese landscape. It is probably significant that Kawabata, one of whose passions was collecting Japanese art, had originally wanted to be a painter.

Perhaps because the Swedish Academy cited *Kyoto*, which can be interpreted as Kawabata's most undisguised lament over Japan's Westernization, in making the award, it was only logical that the academy emphasized the underlying conflict between East and West, old and new, in the laureate's works. In *Kyoto*, the dignity imparted to the ancient capital by its Shinto and Buddhist temples, centuries-old artisan shops, and botanical gardens is beclouded by increasing signs of Americanization.

Snow Country, a novel also specifically cited by the academy, characteristically links beauty with the evanescent. The protagonist, a disillusioned dance critic trying to rejuvenate himself at a hot-spring resort in the snowy region of Hokkaido, gets involved with two geisha. The young one is pure and virginal and perishes suddenly before her beauty has been defiled; the older woman declines in vigor and beauty in slow, inexorable stages.

The Sound of the Mountain has in microcosm practically all the main characteristics—motifs, images, themes—of Kawabata's oeuvre as a whole. The main character, Shingo, is an elderly businessman obsessed with death. As old friends and acquaintances die, and as he experiences the frailties and debilities of old age, his observation of the world around him takes on new dimensions. His senses, despite his marked physical decline, seem sharpened, and he becomes more acutely aware of the cyclical nature of time. The symbolism of the novel is arguably the most intricate of any of Kawabata's works. Flora, fauna, and inanimate objects of nature turn up mostly as symbols and emblems; for example, the mountain of the title is a harbinger of death, and one-thousand-year-old lotus seeds represent a promise of eternal life. Stylistically, too, *The Sound of the Mountain* may be the most satisfying of Kawabata's novels. The remarkably simple syntax is still capable of bearing multiple meanings. Short paragraphs, sometimes only a single sentence long, capture not only impressions of the external world but also the internal associations of the protagonist. This technique recalls the traditions of Japanese *renga* verse.

Kawabata's acceptance speech, published as *Utsukushii nihon no watakushi* (1969; *Japan, the Beautiful, and Myself,* 1969), discusses his influences and approach as a writer. The speech consists mainly of quotations from Japanese classics and reflections thereon, strung together in what practically amounts to free association. Among those quoted are such past masters of verse as Myōe and Dōgen, poets who attend to the details of nature and who, by so observing, penetrate the veil of the temporal and contingent and glimpse into eternity.

Impact of Event

By selecting Kawabata as 1968's Nobel Prize winner in literature, the Swedish Academy took a dramatic step away from Western parochialism. As the translator and scholar of Japanese literature Donald Keene noted, it also went some way toward integrating the tradition of the Japanese novel, the oldest in the world, into the mainstream of world writing. The occasion of the award was highly symbolic, coming as it did exactly one hundred years after the Meiji Restoration, which marked the end of Japanese isolation.

Perhaps the most tangible result of Kawabata's elevation to the rank of Nobel laureate was the simple fact that he grew immensely in popularity in the West. This was no mean feat, given the fact that Kawabata, whom the Japanese themselves had some trouble understanding, was generally thought to be impenetrable to the Western mind. (Much of Kawabata's work may, in fact, be untranslatable.) Much of Kawabata's output was, after years of neglect, at last translated. One such work was *The Sound of the Mountain,* published in translation in 1970; *Meijin* (1954; *The Master of Go,* 1972), was still another. Other translations, meanwhile, were reprinted and saw second and even third editions. Moreover, translations also began appearing in German, French, and other Western European languages. It had been a source of embarrassment for Kawabata that the Swedish Academy members who made the selection knew only a handful of his works, and those only in English translations or in Swedish translations based on the English.

Indeed, the Swedish Academy's selection of Kawabata seemed to awaken an interest in Japanese literature in general. Westerners with no previous exposure to Japanese culture were now reading and discussing such uniquely Japanese literary forms as the *waka* and *haiku,* to which Kawabata's writing style was in fact often compared. Younger and older contemporaries alike were swept in on the coattails of Kawabata and were finally granted the worldwide recognition that was their due. Among the older Japanese writers whose fame increased in the wake of Kawabata's Nobel selection were Jun'ichirō Tanizaki and Ryunosuke Akutagawa. Yukio Mishima, a young protégé of Kawabata who was one of the few Japanese writers popular in the West before Kawabata's selection, was catapulted into the ranks of the world's literary superstars.

Critics, too, redoubled their efforts at trying to come to grips with the slippery phenomenon that was Kawabata's work. They observed that Kawabata explored such universal themes as love, death, aging, beauty, and innocence and that such themes are often treated in dichotomous fashion. For every example of virginity or purity, there is an example of decay or corruption of equal weight; for every example of beauty, there is an equal and opposite example of ugliness. Yet discussions of Kawabata tended to center on his Asian or Japanese qualities. Noted were his sharp eye for physical description and his evocative renderings of the Japanese landscape. Gradually, it also came to be appreciated that the episodic nature of Kawabata's novels was not peculiar to him but was a basic characteristic of Japanese literature in general. Also—with some help from Kawabata himself, who in his acceptance speech called attention to the fact—critics noted that the beautiful in Kawabata is intimately linked with the evanescent and the impermanent; that, however, beyond this there is the ultimate beauty of nothingness. This nothingness is Buddhist in conception and is not to be confused with the nihilism of the West.

Kawabata was not only the first Japanese to be awarded the Nobel Prize in Literature but was also only the second Asian to be so honored (the first was the Bengali poet Rabindranath Tagore, who won in 1913). Moreover, in retrospect it is clear that the 1968 award, in stark contrast with the 1913 Prize given to Tagore, signaled the start of an important trend. Since 1968, the year of Kawabata's award, the once overwhelmingly Western European bias of the Swedish Academy has given way to a genuinely cosmopolitan orientation. Only three years later, in 1971, the Nobel Prize was awarded to the Chilean poet Pablo Neruda; in 1978, to the Yiddish-language author Isaac Bashevis Singer; in 1979, to the Greek poet Odysseus Elýtis; in 1980, to the Polish poet Czesław Miłosz; in 1982, to the Colombian novelist Gabriel García Márquez; in 1984, to the Czech poet Jaroslav Seifert; in 1986, to the Nigerian poet, dramatist, and novelist Wole Soyinka; in 1988, to the Arab novelist Naguib Mahfouz; in 1991, to the South African author Nadine Gordimer; and in 1992, to West Indian poet Derek Walcott.

Finally, it should be noted that the Nobel Prize had an important consequence of an entirely personal nature. Kawabata, who was a very private man, was after the award encumbered with several public duties. As a Nobel laureate, he traveled widely, giving lectures, visiting the many foreign academies to which he had been elected a member, and even receiving (at the University of Hawaii) an honorary doctorate.

On April 16, 1972, Kawabata committed suicide by inhaling gas. He left no note of explanation, and he had gone on record that he did not approve of suicide. It has been reasonably surmised that the growing number of public activities, an onerous burden to one so used to privacy, may have contributed to that state of mind that led to his suicide.

Bibliography

Buckstead, Richard C. *Kawabata and the Divided Self.* Taiwan: China Printing, 1972. A fine book that addresses the symbolic and allegorical features of *Snow Country* and *Thousand Cranes.* Also discussed are the symbolic and emblematic aspects of Kawabata's female characters.

Keene, Donald. *Fiction.* Vol. 1 in *Dawn to the West: Japanese Literature of the Modern Era.* New York: Holt, Rinehart and Winston, 1984. A groundbreaking book by perhaps the most outstanding Western scholar of Japanese literature. His chapter on Kawabata gives an overview of the author's oeuvre that is perfectly balanced between richness in detail and prudent concision.

Lippit, Noriko Mizuta. *Reality and Fiction in Modern Japanese Literature.* White Plains, N.Y.: M. E. Sharpe, 1980. The chapter on Kawabata is a consideration of his numerous dilettante characters. The author sees Kawabata's dilettantes as in a limbo between life and death.

Miyoshi, Masao. *Accomplices of Silence: The Modern Japanese Novel.* Berkeley: University of California Press, 1974. Kawabata is one of six authors covered in this volume. Although the chapter devoted to him presents an overview of his entire career, it is mostly concerned with discussing some themes and motifs of his mature years.

Petersen, Gwenn Boardman. *The Moon in the Water: Understanding Tanizaki, Kawabata, and Mishima.* Honolulu: University Press of Hawaii, 1979. The section on Kawabata provides an introduction to his works, exploring their incorporation of traditional Eastern aesthetics, Buddhist philosophy, and Japanese literary symbols. Includes an extensive (but dated) bibliography and a detailed biographical chronology.

Swann, Thomas E., and Kinya Tsuruta. *Approaches to the Modern Japanese Short Story.* Tokyo: Waseda University Press, 1982. The section on Kawabata considers three of his novellas: *The Izu Dancer, Nemureru bijo* (1961; *The House of the Sleeping Beauties,* 1969), and *Kataude* (1965; *One Arm,* 1967).

Takeda, Katsuhiko. *Essays on Japanese Literature.* Tokyo: Waseda University Press, 1977. Includes a short chapter on the Nobel laureate entitled "Kawabata Literature: Harmony and Conflict." Dealing mostly with influences, it argues that Kawabata's writings reflect not only Buddhist and Shinto traditions but also the Old and New Testaments of the West.

Tsuruta, Kinya, and Thomas E. Swann. *Approaches to the Modern Japanese Novel.* Tokyo: Sophia University, 1976. Includes a section on Kawabata made up of analyses of three of his novels: *Snow Country, The Sound of the Mountain,* and *The Master of Go.*

Ueda, Makoto. *Modern Japanese Writers and the Nature of Literature.* Stanford, Calif.: Stanford University Press, 1976. This volume, which takes up the critical and aesthetic views of several modern Japanese writers, includes a chapter on the theory and practice of Kawabata. Includes extensive Japanese and English bibliographies.

Gregory Nehler

Cross-References

The First Nobel Prizes Are Awarded (1901), p. 45; Kurosawa's *Rashomon* Wins the Grand Prize at Venice (1951), p. 1476; Singer Wins the Nobel Prize in Literature (1978), p. 2423; Soyinka Wins the Nobel Prize in Literature (1986), p. 2594; Mahfouz Wins the Nobel Prize in Literature (1988), p. 2625; Gordimer Wins the Nobel Prize in Literature (1991), p. 2668.

DAVIS' *BITCHES BREW*
VITALIZES JAZZ-ROCK FUSION

Category of event: Music
Time: 1969
Locale: The United States

Miles Davis' jazz-rock fusion album Bitches Brew *shook jazz out of its commercial doldrums and spawned a style that characterized much of the jazz produced during the 1970's*

Principal personages:
MILES DAVIS (1926-1991), a distinctive and influential trumpeter responsible for many innovative approaches to jazz
CHICK COREA (1941-   ), a *Bitches Brew* keyboardist whose later groups reflected jazz-rock tendencies
JOHN MCLAUGHLIN (1942-   ), the *Bitches Brew* guitarist who later led the Mahavishnu Orchestra, an important fusion band
WAYNE SHORTER (1933-   ), the *Bitches Brew* saxophonist who was later a coleader of the creative jazz-rock combo Weather Report
JOE ZAWINUL (1932-   ), a *Bitches Brew* keyboardist who was later a coleader of Weather Report

Summary of Event

The integration of jazz and rock—long awaited and often prematurely announced during the 1960's—was fully achieved for the first time on Miles Davis' *Bitches Brew* album in 1969. Making frequent use of electronic instruments and sophisticated studio techniques, the resulting "fusion" jazz style was based upon a synthesis of modern jazz with elements of rock, pop, and soul music of the 1960's. A trumpeter known for his influential tone and distinctive improvisations, Davis had been a dominant force in jazz since the late 1940's, changing jazz perhaps more deeply and in more varied ways than anyone else. Though fusion jazz had forerunners prior to the appearance of *Bitches Brew*—for example, the music of Soft Machine and the Gary Burton Quartet—Davis was influenced very little, if at all, by those artists. His work had always demonstrated his compulsion to explore new musical territory on his own terms. By the time he recorded *Bitches Brew*, he had played in the classic bebop style with Charlie Parker, broken new ground with the cool style of his Capitol band in the late 1940's, played first hard bop and then a pioneering modal style during the 1950's, and then had experimented in the 1960's with a style that was based on modal concepts but was more open in its harmonic structure and was played with sharper accents.

By the late 1960's, Davis' creativity was by no means exhausted. He was listening to many rock and rhythm-and-blues artists, especially James Brown, Jimi Hendrix, and

Sly and the Family Stone. Electronic instruments caught his ear as early as 1967. By 1968, Davis was incorporating electronic instruments and rock rhythms into his music. The effect varied—sometimes the new approach produced a collage of sound, at other times a danceable ostinato, or "ground," beat with garish harmonies and exotic melodies floating above it.

Although Davis' *In a Silent Way* (1969), with its multiple percussionists and electric piano players, came first, his *Bitches Brew* (1969), which was recorded six months later, represents the full flowering of the jazz fusion style. Breaking radically with tradition, this two-disc album captures a collage of jam sessions characterized by impressionistic soloing over shifting, rock-influenced rhythms and a continuous interplay of electronic keyboards, guitar, and percussion instruments. *Bitches Brew* pulled out all the stops, as Davis superimposed the sophisticated, modally based harmonies and more flexible phrasings of jazz upon rock's intensity. Furthermore, Davis produced new, brilliantly colored sound surfaces through his combination of sonorities, as in "Spanish Key," which features a soprano saxophone over a bluesy electric piano and guitar with a rich bass clarinet droning underneath.

The working principles of the *Bitches Brew* band—like those of all the previous Davis groups—were spontaneity and Davis' uncanny ability to capitalize on every idea, no matter how small, that he encountered. Davis was as much influenced by his sidemen as they were by him, but for Davis, such influence meant that he used creatively everything he heard. There were virtually no rehearsals for the *Bitches Brew* sessions, and the resulting music reflects the unpredictability and boldness of its methodology.

The most tightly organized track on the album is "Miles Runs the Voodoo Down." It is perhaps the track most likely to appeal to fans of Davis' earlier styles. Davis' melodic trumpet lines dovetail well with the rock-like beat underneath (a characteristic not to be found in the looser structure of the twenty-minute-long "Pharoah's Dance"). Davis' solo on "Voodoo" varies effectively quick phrases and long tones, a recognizable element in his straight-ahead jazz playing. The track is punctuated heavily with the sounds of South American and African percussive instruments (percussion would blossom throughout the 1970's).

By contrast, "Bitches Brew" is an impressionistic and expansive twenty-seven-minute vamp-plus-improvisation. Davis' open trumpet sound reverberates through an electronic Echoplex unit, surrounded by chord splashes from a guitar and an electric piano. On top of an ostinato bass, Davis' trumpet pierces and unites the various elements of a Charlie Mingus-like instrumental conversation. Sustained energy and sensitivity characterize Wayne Shorter's "Sanctuary," which elicits one of Davis' longest solos. "Spanish Key," by John McLaughlin, features straight-out rock rhythm with numerous stop-time breaks that became a formula for the fusion style in later years.

In 1968, Davis had announced his intention of forming the best rock and roll band in the world. As far as jazz-rock was concerned, he succeeded in gathering the most original and prolific one. Musicians apply the term "bitch" only to the finest of improvisers. Given the *Bitches Brew* sessions' improvisational nature and assembled talent, the album's title proved quite appropriate. The album quickly sold 400,000 copies, four times the number sold for Davis' previous best-seller, *Sketches of Spain*, another fusion of sorts done with composer-arranger Gil Evans. So-called pure jazz had never fared so well commercially, especially since the rapid development of rock and its commercial domination of the music business.

Impact of Event

Davis received equal amounts of praise and scorn for *Bitches Brew.* Some saw his fusion style as little more than inspired mercantilism. Yet objective critics, who judged the music on its merits rather than on Davis' intentions, recognized it as coherent, highly improvisational, exciting, and evocative. Unquestionably, it jolted jazz out of its commercial doldrums and expanded jazz's horizons. The ingredients of *Bitches Brew*—though Davis' combination of them was unmatched—became the recipe for much of the jazz produced during the 1970's. The success of the personnel of the *Bitches Brew* band and of those that had preceded it during the 1960's—many of whom became well known individually—serves as a barometer of Davis' impact on yet another generation of jazz musicians.

The degree and consistency of the fusion synthesis is attributable in part to the unprecedented impact of rock and soul music on American listening habits. Jazz musicians have always absorbed the sounds around them, and the aesthetic development of rock and soul, along with the increased availability of electric pianos, guitars, and synthesizers, thus made the cross-fertilization that led to *Bitches Brew* inevitable. Fusion developed more purposefully than earlier jazz styles, with bands making significant use of electronic instruments and overdubbing and editing separately recorded tracks—factors that had played a minimal role in jazz prior to 1969. The advantages of electronic sound, noted enthusiasts, were multiple. It captured the tones, timbres, and energy of much rock and soul music; it became easier to play louder and faster, an asset in the cavernous halls needed to house fusion audiences; and, given programmable synthesizers, it offered new tone colors with which to work.

Some argued that electronic instruments, which abandoned the subtlety and nuances of the acoustic for volume and gadgetry, could not communicate the personality of the musician. Fusion musicians, however, having discovered the power of modern recording equipment to improve upon what had been played in a studio or even to record music that was physically unplayable by a band performing live, insisted that the electronics were just as appropriate to fusion as acoustic instruments had been to modern jazz.

Fusion exploded on the music scene after the appearance of *Bitches Brew.* Davis continued to play fusion until ill health and an accident led to a seven-year retirement beginning in 1974 (after his return in 1981, he performed a pop-oriented type of jazz-rock). In 1973, keyboardist Herbie Hancock, a Davis alumnus (from the 1963-1968 bands), recorded jazz's first gold album by combining funky and danceable rhythms with a modicum of jazz melodic and harmonic feeling. Fusion's commercial peak was reached as early as 1976, when George Benson, a superb improvising jazz guitarist of the 1960's who had played briefly with Davis, was transformed into a semipop vocalist with the album *Breezin'*, which went on to sell four million copies by 1980.

The leaders of the major fusion bands of the 1970's—Chick Corea of Return to Forever, John McLaughlin of the Mahavishnu Orchestra, and Joe Zawinul and Wayne Shorter of Weather Report—all came from the ranks of the *Bitches Brew* group. The Mahavishnu Orchestra, led by British guitar virtuoso McLaughlin, proved that precise interplay and challenging improvisation were entirely compatible with the high-decibel, high-energy sound of hard rock. The group's music was a synthesis of various elements: the impassioned guitar style of Jimi Hendrix, the muscular drumming and electronics of rock, and the modes, or scale patterns, found in classical Indian ragas and in the work of John Coltrane and Miles Davis. The band's sound frequently seemed to have a spiritual aura expressed in the musical unison of amplified violin and guitar. The Mahavishnu Orchestra was the first band to prove that jazz-rock could fill large concert halls. *The Inner Mounting Flame* (1972) captures the group's compelling enthusiasm and urgency.

No jazz musician used the fusion concept during the 1970's with more variety, intelligence, and taste than Chick Corea. The second incarnation of his Return to Forever band was based quite consciously on the Mahavishnu Orchestra, thus departing radically from the jazz-combo sound of the first version. With drummer Lenny White, a *Bitches Brew* alumnus, and guitarist Bill Connors, Corea's new band breached the walls of hard rock. *Hymn to the Seventh Galaxy* (1973) and *Where Have I Known You Before?* (1974) capture the group's heavily electronic, high-energy jazz-rock. *Hymn to the Seventh Galaxy* is raw and primitive, while the 1974 album is more polished, featuring Corea's first outing on synthesizer.

The most innovative and improvisational fusion band of the 1970's was Weather Report, organized in 1971 and led by Joe Zawinul and Wayne Shorter. While the band's harmonic sophistication and improvisations came from the highest levels of 1960's jazz, its rhythmic drum and electric bass patterns were more akin to rhythm and blues and occasionally to rock. After 1976, Weather Report's albums acquired a nearly orchestral density provided by Zawinul's use of multivoiced synthesizers. The band's two-disc *8:30* (1979), recorded live, provides an ideal overview of its work and reveals its ability to combine the agility of an improvisational quartet with the solidity of a big band.

Fusion, the dominant strain of jazz during the 1970's and 1980's, has been both lucrative and controversial. Critics maintain that its profits and popularity have far exceeded its durability, aesthetic value, or contribution to the development of jazz. Defenders point out that, for all of fusion's limitations, it helped overcome the uncommunicative and elitist image that jazz had projected in the 1960's, thus gaining a much wider audience for jazz in the era of rock. Fusion is an eclectic rather than an innovative jazz style, and its coupling of repetitive rhythms with electronically amplified instruments led in time to the creation of a formulaic music characterized by a finely detailed yet passive musical fabric. Nevertheless, jazz fusion was responsible for some undeniably exciting music in its heyday during the 1970's.

Bibliography

Berendt, Joachim. *The Jazz Book: From New Orleans to Jazz Rock and Beyond.* Rev. ed. New York: Granada, 1983. Translated by Helmut and Barbara Bredigkeit with Dan Morgenstern. Fusion trends in the 1970's—including the work of Miles Davis, Chick Corea, the Mahavishnu Orchestra, and Weather Report—are discussed in conjunction with other contemporary developments in jazz and rock.

Carr, Ian. *Miles Davis: A Critical Biography.* New York: William Morrow, 1982. Highly recommended. Provides a detailed examination of Davis' life and musical development. Sees Davis' 1969-1974 work as unquestionably expanding jazz's horizons.

Cole, Bill. *Miles Davis: A Musical Biography.* New York: William Morrow, 1974. Cole's negative view of Davis' post-1968 work, including *Bitches Brew*, provides a good example of the lingering hostility to Davis' jazz-rock, even among Davis scholars and aficionados. Cole finds Davis using technology for its own sake.

Davis, Miles, with Quincy Troupe. *Miles: The Autobiography.* New York: Simon & Schuster, 1989. In his discussion of *Bitches Brew*, Davis recalls the president of Columbia Records urging him to reach out to the youth market.

Gridley, Mark C. *Jazz Styles: History and Analysis.* 2d ed. Englewood Cliffs, N.J.: Prentice-Hall, 1985. Chapters 19 and 20 contain excellent discussions of the workings of the Miles Davis bands of the 1960's and early 1970's and of the continuing importance of jazz-rock during the 1970's and 1980's. Also good material on Weather Report, the Mahavishnu Orchestra, and Chick Corea.

L. Moody Simms, Jr.

Cross-References

Parker's Playing Epitomizes Bebop (1946), p. 1318; Davis' *Birth of the Cool* Recordings Spawn 1950's Cool Jazz (1949), p. 1438; The Beatles Revolutionize Popular Music (1963), p. 1944; The Rolling Stones Release *Out of Our Heads* (1965), p. 2027; Brown Wins a Grammy for "Papa's Got a Brand New Bag" (1966), p. 2059; Hendrix Releases *Are You Experienced?* (1967), p. 2092; The Beatles Release *Sgt. Pepper's Lonely Hearts Club Band* (1967), p. 2098; The Monterey Pop Festival Inaugurates the "Summer of Love" (1967), p. 2104; Wynton Marsalis Revives Acoustic Jazz (1980's), p. 2454.

EASY RIDER CAPTURES THE SPIRIT OF 1960'S YOUTH

Category of event: Motion pictures
Time: 1969
Locale: The United States

Easy Rider *was released to popular success, spurring a series of films about the generation gap*

> *Principal personages:*
> DENNIS HOPPER (1936-   ), the director of and a leading actor in *Easy Rider*
> PETER FONDA (1939-   ), the actor who played Wyatt, the Captain America character, and produced the film
> JACK NICHOLSON (1937-   ), an actor who gave a critically acclaimed performance
> BOB DYLAN (ROBERT ZIMMERMAN, 1941-   ), a folk singer who wrote lyrics to "The Ballad of Easy Rider"

Summary of Event

In 1969, the film *Easy Rider* expressed the sensibility of the 1960's, a decade of violence, assassination, protest, and social upheaval. It also played on a nation's yearning for a better country.

The plot and the filmmaking of *Easy Rider* were simple. It was the story of two hippies searching for the real America. Wyatt (Peter Fonda) and Billy (Dennis Hopper) smuggle drugs out of Mexico, sell them to a pusher in California, and head east on their motorcycles to New Orleans and the Mardi Gras, searching on the way for the spirit of America and the dream of freedom. On their journey east, they encounter a farmer and his family, visit a commune about which they express different attitudes, and go swimming with two girls from the commune. In a small Southern town, they meet George Hanson (Jack Nicholson), an amiable, drunken, liberal lawyer and black-sheep aristocrat who goes along with them, grinning under the football helmet he wears instead of a motorcycle helmet. In another small Southern town, locals and the police mock them. At night, asleep outdoors, they are attacked, and George is beaten to death. Wyatt and Billy go on to New Orleans and join two prostitutes on an acid trip. Later, on the road to Florida, they come upon two rednecks in a pickup truck. Billy responds to an insult with a disparaging gesture and is shot. After Wyatt stops to tend to his friend, the rednecks return and kill him as well. The film ends with an almost apocalyptic vision of a burning motorcycle. An aerial shot of a river, accompanied by lyrical music, offers peace.

Wyatt and Billy were the voices of the 1960's—hopeful and innocent, though not untainted. *Easy Rider* had a passion that appealed to its audience. Although Wyatt and Billy were outsiders, their trek was in the mainstream of the American Dream.

Easy Rider is in the tradition of Huck Finn, Jack Kerouac, the Joads, Nick Adams, and all those who sought the dream of freedom by going on the road. Wyatt and Billy, modern outlaws and descendants of Wyatt Earp and Billy the Kid, were in pursuit of a fading frontier. They were trying to reclaim the frontier and were trying to discover America as a land of spiritual values. The audience, even if it did not always affirm Wyatt and Billy, affirmed those values.

There was also a theme of human fallibility in *Easy Rider*, along with an underlying theme of personal responsibility. Wyatt's comment of "We blew it" after the two leave New Orleans did not register strongly with most audiences, who were involved in the emotional catharsis of the annihilation of Wyatt and Billy and the indictment of the society that cost them their lives in 1969. *Easy Rider* was a portrait of the hippie life-style, with its communes, drugs, rebellion, and alienation. Although the portrait often suffered because of oversimplification, Wyatt's self-doubt because he and Billy had gone the way of materialism and sold drugs gave the film a depth and resonance.

Easy Rider was a box-office phenomenon. Made for $375,000, it brought in more than $16 million. It had been developed independently, from an original idea by Peter Fonda. Terry Southern wrote the screenplay with Fonda and Hopper. Bert Schneider and his BBS Productions financed the film, which was released by Columbia.

Even though they were uneasy about the film's broadness and obviousness, most critics were affected by its sincerity and emotion. Even critics with usually strict, demanding standards, such as John Simon and Stanley Kauffmann, were moved by *Easy Rider*. Critics agreed that the film was flawed, but almost all affirmed the film's spirit.

Hollywood was not so willing to applaud the film's independence. Although it was released by a Hollywood studio, and even though it made a lot of money—a Hollywood criterion for approval—*Easy Rider* received no Academy Awards and only two nominations, for script and for Nicholson as best supporting actor. The award did not go to Nicholson; it went to Gig Young for *They Shoot Horses, Don't They?* The Oscar for best film of 1969 went to *Midnight Cowboy.* Outside Hollywood, *Easy Rider* was more successful. Hopper won the Cannes Film Festival award for best film by a newcomer, and Nicholson won the best supporting actor award from the National Society of Film Critics.

Originally the film was to be shot by Barry Feinstein, but in a struggle for control, Hopper had a fistfight with his cameraman. Hopper turned to cinematographer Laszlo Kovacs and editor Donn Cambern, two skillful professionals, and his vision survived.

The film's small budget sometimes showed, especially in the footage shot at the Mardi Gras with a hand-held camera. Fonda had gotten the dates of the Mardi Gras wrong, which complicated matters. Overall, some of the amateurish effects added to the film's sense of authenticity. *Easy Rider* is as frenetic, impassioned, and erratic as Dennis Hopper.

The music in *Easy Rider* was a statement of a generation's values. The film's sound track featured the Byrds, Steppenwolf, the Jimi Hendrix Experience, and Roger McGuinn singing compositions written by Bob Dylan, though the lyrics of "The Ballad of Easy Rider" are uncredited to him in the film. Dylan convinced Hopper that *Easy Rider* should end with hope instead of nihilism, and he wrote lyrics that bring spiritual peace to the ending.

Easy Rider went outside the Hollywood system to find its voice, much as the young people of the time were trying to go beyond the system to find theirs. *Easy Rider* amplified the political and spiritual call of a generation, a cry for a better society and a freer world but a recognition of lost opportunities and human failure.

Peter Fonda and Dennis Hopper offered the images and voices of an embattled time in American culture. With *Easy Rider*, they made a document that captured both the fervent idealism and the shattered hopes of a generation.

Impact of Event

Easy Rider was a phenomenon in 1969. Coming at the end of a tumultuous and violent decade, it captured a significant time in American cultural history. Many of its reverberations were dissipated as protest in America was replaced by corporate America in the 1980's, but though its political impact was short-lived, *Easy Rider* was influential in several ways and remained an artistic landmark.

After the success of *Easy Rider*, Hollywood and the United States seemed primed for a revolution in filmmaking. Political films seemed to be the wave of the future in 1969. Along with *Easy Rider*, Haskell Wexler's *Medium Cool* was very popular. Using *cinéma vérité* techniques, Wexler employed the 1968 Democratic National Convention in Chicago as a background for his film. He shot footage of the bloody conflicts when protestors clashed with the police in the streets of the city. The French import *Z*, a political thriller, won an Oscar as best foreign film.

If Hollywood seemed on the brink of embracing politics, the promise never was fulfilled. Instead, Hollywood turned to a youth audience, with youth becoming the arbiter of taste. Protest and generation gap films abounded in the 1970's. Many of the films that followed *Easy Rider*, such as *The Strawberry Statement* (1970), about riots at Columbia University, and *Getting Straight* (1970), with Elliott Gould as a graduate student exploring his values, seem exploitative, a stigma that *Easy Rider* had transcended. A few were interesting, such as *Zabriskie Point* (1970) and *Alice's Restaurant* (1969), but most simply were inept. Hollywood had tried to tap a resource, but it quickly had gone dry.

Another illusion that *Easy Rider* had helped promote was that there would be a boon for independent filmmakers. *Easy Rider*'s tremendous success at the box office gave hope to independent filmmakers, since Hopper and Fonda had gone outside the Hollywood system to create their film. That hope proved fleeting. Hollywood has always viewed the independents suspiciously, and though *Easy Rider* was successful, it was viewed somewhat as an aberration and did not change Hollywood's attitude toward independents.

The next film by Hopper was *The Last Movie* (1971), which he made in Peru. *Easy Rider* was an experiment that rewarded Hopper with bankability, but he quickly exhausted it. *The Last Movie* was a fiasco that was quickly withdrawn and shelved. It took Hopper almost twenty years to direct again in Hollywood, with the controversial *Colors* (1988). That film, ironically, was photographed by Haskell Wexler.

Peter Fonda, the son of Henry Fonda and brother of Jane, seemed to have great potential, but he reached his apogee with *Easy Rider.* He went on to direct *The Hired Hand* (1971) but never recaptured the image and appeal he had in *Easy Rider.* The film poster from *Easy Rider* featuring him looking for America became a classic, but his career leveled off.

Easy Rider introduced Jack Nicholson to a mass audience. Previously he had been in low-budget Roger Corman films, but his performance in *Easy Rider* received an Academy Award nomination for best supporting actor, and his career as a bankable star began. He won audiences with his trademark grin and his mixture of charm and neurosis. He became the prototypical alienated man in films of the 1970's. If anyone benefited from getting an identity and a persona from *Easy Rider*, it was Nicholson, who became one of Hollywood's finest and best-known actors.

Easy Rider was also important in its use of a rock music score that commented on the action. The music was written and performed by some of the major rock figures of the time. Films about rock concerts themselves, as counterculture events, became both popular and artistic. Donn Alan Pennebaker's *Monterey Pop* (1969), Michael Wadleigh's *Woodstock* (1970), and David and Albert Maysles' *Gimme Shelter* (1970) saw rock music as a metaphor and captured memorable performances. *American Graffiti* (1973) and *The Big Chill* (1983) were classic films that used music to capture eras much as *Easy Rider* had done.

Easy Rider was one of the films that embodied the new cinematic violence, which was both unpredictable and stunning. Sam Peckinpah released *The Wild Bunch* (1969) to great controversy. Two years earlier, *Bonnie and Clyde* (1967) had expressed the new visceral style of violence. In all three films, the violence was sudden and shocking, but there was a lyricism to it. It was painful but eloquent. Violence was no longer sanitized and conventional. *Easy Rider* and *The Wild Bunch* were two cinematic poems that ended in carnage. After 1969, violence was never to be the same in films.

Despite the controversy concerning it, *Easy Rider* is one of the seminal works that helped promote the personal film. Directors such as Robert Altman, Sam Peckinpah, and Martin Scorsese, like Hopper, espouse personal films that express opposition to materialism and current social institutions. *Easy Rider* captured the antiestablishment feeling of the time. In 1967, *The Graduate* had also struck a chord with that theme. What is ironic about both films is that years later viewers were much more critical of both Ben Braddock in *The Graduate* and Wyatt and Billy in *Easy Rider.*

The Reagan era of the 1980's rejected the antiestablishment attitude that had been so much a part of the 1960's. Many of the young were no longer antiestablishment and were likely to desire a Mercedes instead of a motorcycle. Corporate America had reclaimed the American Dream. For many viewers, however, *Easy Rider* remains a visual poem and an unforgettable memory of the struggle that once had been.

Bibliography

Guillaumont, Antoine, et al., eds. and trans. *The Gospel According to Thomas.* New York: Harper & Row, 1959. Hopper believed in this work, which contains the "sayings of Jesus," recorded by Didymos Judas Thomas, that had been lost for sixteen centuries and were discovered in 1945 in a ruined tomb in Upper Egypt. A copy of the book was given to Hopper and Fonda by a friend and influenced *Easy Rider.*

Kauffmann, Stanley. *Figures of Light.* New York: Harper & Row, 1971. In his review, Kauffmann places *Easy Rider* in social and artistic perspective, saying that its portrayal of hippie life is the most believable he has seen in a fiction film. He applauds Hopper's multifaceted contribution, predicting that he could be an important talent in the future.

Morganstern, Joseph, and Stefan Kanfer, eds. *Film 69/70.* New York: Simon & Schuster, 1970. An anthology of the National Society of Film Critics, with reviews of *Easy Rider* and other significant films of 1969 that show the cultural sensibility of the time.

Schickel, Richard. "Easy Rider." In *Second Sight: Notes on Some Movies, 1965-1970.* New York: Simon & Schuster, 1972. A reprint of critic Schickel's initial *Life* magazine review of the film, supplemented by his later reaction to his own comments. Interesting, though brief and somewhat dated.

Springer, John. *The Fondas.* New York: Citadel Press, 1970. A pictorial history emphasizing the career of Henry Fonda, also including the career of Jane and Peter. It is interesting to compare Henry Fonda in *The Grapes of Wrath* (1940) with his son almost thirty years later in *Easy Rider,* since both films were effective American odysseys and offered significant social criticism.

Tony Macklin

Cross-References

Westerns Dominate Postwar American Film (1946), p. 1313; The Beat Movement Rejects Mainstream Values (1950's), p. 1460; Dylan Performs with Electric Instruments (1965), p. 2038; The Monterey Pop Festival Inaugurates the "Summer of Love" (1967), p. 2104; The Woodstock Music Festival Marks the Climax of the 1960's (1969), p. 2180.

ROTH PUBLISHES *PORTNOY'S COMPLAINT*

Category of event: Literature
Time: 1969
Locale: New York, New York

Rabbis and Jewish community leaders denounced novelist Philip Roth for being an anti-Semitic Jew when his sexually explicit novel exploited Jewish stereotypes with ruthless humor

Principal personages:
>PHILIP ROTH (1933-   ), a novelist whose books have generated ethnic and political controversies and tested censorship limits
>IRVING HOWE (1920-   ), a literary critic, the founder and editor of *Dissent*
>NORMAN PODHORETZ (1930-   ), a literary journalist and an influential spokesman on Jewish affairs
>JOHN UPDIKE (1932-   ), a distinguished novelist of contemporary urban and suburban life, whose books blend sexual and theological themes

Summary of Event

When Philip Roth published *Portnoy's Complaint* in 1969, he set off a furious controversy among literary scholars and journalists and sent a shock wave through the American Jewish community. The novel, which consists of a ranting, first-person monologue delivered by an obsessive patient to his psychoanalyst, is sexually explicit and depicts certain stock Jewish character types in lurid colors. Roth's defenders and admirers believed he had accomplished an artistic breakthrough, but to his detractors, he seemed no better than a pornographer and a betrayer of his people. Like John Updike's *Couples* (1968), however, *Portnoy's Complaint* quickly proved to be a critical and commercial success.

Roth was born in 1933, the son of an insurance salesman, and grew up in Newark, New Jersey. He attended college first at Rutgers University and later at Bucknell University, where he earned a bachelor's degree in English in 1951 at the age of eighteen. He studied for a doctorate at the University of Chicago in the mid-1950's, but he was already writing fiction. He had his first major success with *Goodbye Columbus* (1959), which won the National Book Award and several other prizes. He taught creative writing in the Iowa Writers' Workshop, at Princeton University, and at the University of Pennsylvania in the early 1960's, and he produced two more novels, *Letting Go* (1962) and *When She Was Good* (1967), along with numerous short stories.

Portnoy's Complaint (1969), much zanier and more hectic than its predecessors, marked a stylistic change that, coming from an established writer, drew widespread attention and immediate controversy. The book grew out of four fragmentary works

Roth had begun in the preceding years, one of which, a play entitled *The Nice Jewish Boy*, had had a public performance with Dustin Hoffman in the principal role. Roth had reworked many aspects of the text and felt pleased with the finished result. Based in part on incidents from his own life, the novel was more than a *Bildungsroman*; Roth was too artful to rely on his own experiences alone, and he contrived numerous scenes to squeeze the maximum dramatic impact from his characters.

Alexander Portnoy, the book's narrator, is on the couch of his psychoanalyst, Dr. Spielvogel, pouring out his soul. Portnoy speaks like a stand-up comedian, often making himself the butt of his own jokes. He presents himself by turns as pitiable, comic, and disgusting, but he is always very knowing and able to anticipate the criticisms that might be leveled against him. His is the only point of view given in the entire book, and Roth lets the reader see all the bizarre skewing of realities that Portnoy's obsessions have created.

As Alex tells it, most of his life has been dedicated to yearning for, and trying to have sex with, *shiksas*, or Christian girls. Overpoweringly alluring, through most of his adolescence they were also hopelessly beyond his reach. Spying on them, following them, masturbating to visions of them, Portnoy found such girls a complete obsessive fantasy, fragments of which he was able to live out in later years, but always with unsatisfactory results. When he has real *shiksa* girlfriends, he feels too guilty to enjoy them, and the disapproving presence of his mother, Sophie Portnoy, looms in his imagination.

Alex knows, and he shows, that he has been unfair to many of his girlfriends. Admiring their good qualities, he still cannot stop himself from despising them, imagining insults from their families, and feeling smugly superior to them in a way that completely contradicts his outward life as a defender and uplifter of the underprivileged. He gives each one a deprecating nickname such as "The Monkey," "The Pumpkin," and "The Pilgrim." When, as a young adult, he goes to Israel, he meets a tough Jewish Marxist woman. She renders him impotent, but he gets a petty revenge by thinking of her as "The Jewish Pumpkin." Israel upsets him; accustomed to being one of the Jewish minority in America, in Israel Portnoy finds that even the bus drivers are Jews, and he is deprived of the chance to blame everyday misfortunes on the *goyim*.

Sophie Portnoy, his mother, is the bane of Alex's life, first in childhood but no less when he is an adult, a law-school graduate and a political aide to New York Mayor John Lindsay. She is the stereotypical Jewish mother, smothering Alex with love but stifling him with constant surveillance, nagging, and criticism, always making him feel guilty and indecent, and completely overpowering Alex's father, who is a shadowy, constipated insurance salesman. In one of many humiliating scenes, Alex recounts the time when, as a growing boy, he wanted to buy a jock strap in an athletic equipment shop. Far from indulging him in this symbolic aspiration to maturity, his mother mocks loudly that his penis is far too small. The agonizing memory of this and other humiliating episodes from his childhood and adolescence will not leave him; he circles back to miserable incidents again and again.

The book ends with a heading in block capitals, "PUNCH LINE," which is followed by the doctor's telling Alex that the analysis can now begin. The reader realizes that the book's 274 exhausting and hilarious pages have been only the preliminaries from Portnoy; luckily, readers do not have to overhear the item-by-item analysis itself.

Impact of Event

Portnoy's Complaint was heralded as a product of the "swinging 1960's" in which the media had developed a new frankness about discussing sexuality, in which the "sexual revolution" was in full swing, and in which much of "counterculture" regarded monogamous marriage as a repressive institution rather than as the logical goal for every mature adult.

There was nothing new about sex in literature. From their development in the eighteenth century, novels had always, overtly or covertly, discussed sex, sometimes in a very straightforward way. The novels of Honoré de Balzac, for example, were saturated with eroticism. In English novels, eroticism was usually elliptical rather than direct, at least until D. H. Lawrence, Henry Miller, and James Joyce began writing straightforward descriptions of sex in the early twentieth century. Such writing was met with censorship through the middle decades of the century, but court cases largely put an end to such censorship in the early 1960's. Lawrence's *Lady Chatterley's Lover* (1928) was the *cause célèbre*, and removal of American censorship of that book in 1960 opened the door for many more candid depictions of sex in the following years.

In 1968, John Updike's *Couples* charted new ground for a major novelist's treatment of sex. The book's central character has an explicitly described sexual affair with his neighbor's pregnant wife, which continues after she has given birth and includes a scene in which he drinks her breast milk. *Couples* was a literary and commercial success. Although Roth, in interviews, always denied that he was writing for the new sex-receptive market, he was surely aware of being able to get away with *Portnoy's Complaint's* most daring passages in a way he could not have done a few years previously.

The American Jewish community was, by the mid-1960's, a wealthy and influential part of society. Having achieved rapid upward social mobility in the decades since their mass migration from Germany and Eastern Europe, American Jews filled prominent positions in academic, business, and political life. Proud of their accomplishments, their artistic creativity, and the large number of eminent citizens drawn from their ranks, they still exhibited some of the defensiveness common to ethnic immigrant groups. They were fiercely protective of Israel, the Jewish state that had been fighting for its life since 1948; it was American Jews' money, donated in extravagant amounts, that helped secure Israel against its encircling Arab enemies. A powerful Jewish lobby in Washington ensured that presidents and members of Congress, all kept their eyes fixed on Israel as an object of special solicitude for American foreign policy.

American Jews had prospered in (among other places) the entertainment industry and had long been willing to make jokes at their own expense. By and large, however, American Jews did not take kindly to others making such jokes. The extremely daring way in which Roth touched on, and exploited, the most sensitive areas in American Jewish life caused some Jews to see him as a betrayer. Many rabbis who had earlier been disturbed by *Goodbye Columbus* warned their congregations not to read the new book and said that Roth was a Jew who was damaging the good name of Jews in America. Some critics said even that he was an anti-Semite. Another strand of intra-Jewish criticism came from Norman Podhoretz, editor of the influential magazine *Commentary*. Formerly a political liberal and a sympathetic admirer of Roth, Podhoretz had become an outspoken neoconservative at the end of the 1960's. He wrote in 1972 that Roth's work was getting steadily worse and that Roth had only one point to make: "that Americans are disgusting people." Podhoretz, eager to revive American patriotism from its low ebb in the Vietnam era, deplored what he saw as Roth's pandering to anti-American sentiment and what he took to be Roth's air of unearned moral superiority.

To Irving Howe, one of the most distinguished critics in America, Roth seemed to have run out of ideas early in his career and no longer belonged in the company of Saul Bellow and Bernard Malamud, the novelists with whom he had most often been compared. Howe's judgment of *Portnoy's Complaint* was harsh: He said that Roth had nothing to offer but "a thin-lipped animus against Jewish woes, Jewish mothers, Jewish sentiments, Jewish aggrandizements." Howe admitted that Roth's complaining "could sometimes be very funny, as in his assemblage of skits called *Portnoy's Complaint*, but too often it dropped into a mere wail for release from the claims of Jewish distinctiveness and burdens." To call the carefully constructed novel a series of skits was itself, of course, to damn with faint praise.

Roth did not want to be thought of as a Jewish novelist but rather as a novelist whose background simply happened to be Jewish. In *When She Was Good*, the novel that preceded *Portnoy's Complaint*, he took as his subject a midwestern Christian family, of the sort among whom he had been living in Iowa, and made no reference to Judaism. He was often at pains to emphasize that he was more than a local or ethnic writer and that he belonged in the mainstream of American literature. Critics who agreed with this claim pointed out that Alexander Portnoy could be compared to such characters in American fiction as Huckleberry Finn, Captain Ahab, and Holden Caulfield, all isolated males seeking satisfactions the real world would never be able to offer.

The film version of *Portnoy's Complaint* was a flop. It could not match the obsessive quality of the book and still had to tread warily in treating the masturbation and orgy scenes if it were to gain commercial release; the brazen zestiness of the novel was completely missing. Although Roth continued to treat sexuality with total frankness in *My Life as a Man* (1974) and *The Professor of Desire* (1977), none of his later works was explosive in quite the same way. Sex in literature proliferated so rapidly that it quickly lost both its novelty value and its ability to shock, making Roth a less distinctive character in the 1970's and 1980's than he had been earlier. Roth himself was also tempted, in the vertiginous years of the early 1970's, to turn from fiction to grotesques, parody, and satire, notably in *Our Gang* (1971), a satire on President Richard Nixon that seemed funny in its day but that quickly became obsolete. Nevertheless, Roth continues to hold an honored place in American literature, with such excellent subsequent novels as *Zuckerman Unbound* (1981). Like Norman Mailer (who is in some ways a parallel figure in his treatment of sex and in his methodological daring), Roth has achieved his objective of being as much an American as a Jewish writer.

Bibliography

Baumgartner, Murray, and Barbara Gottfried. *Understanding Philip Roth.* Columbia: University of South Carolina Press, 1990. A more up-to-date account of Roth's work than Rodgers' and refreshingly jargon-free. Heavy on text explanation, light on biographical details.

Howe, Irving. "Philip Roth Reconsidered." *Commentary* 54 (December, 1972): 69-77. The most persuasive analysis of what is wrong with Roth, full of harsh judgments but free of cheap shots. Especially useful as a source of second thoughts for readers who find Roth breathtakingly good.

Milbauer, Asher Z., and Donald G. Watson, eds. *Reading Philip Roth.* New York: Macmillan, 1988. A collection of essays by critics of Roth, emphasizing his connections to other Jewish writers, his debts to Franz Kafka, and his use of themes in popular culture, asceticism, and psychoanalysis.

Rodgers, Bernard F., Jr. *Philip Roth.* Boston: Twayne, 1978. A sensible introductory summary of Roth's life and works, explaining the author's intentions and methods while evaluating his place in literary history. Rodgers is also author of a large bibliography on Roth.

Roth, Philip. *Reading Myself and Others.* New York: Farrar, Straus & Giroux, 1975. A collection of Roth's essays, interviews, and occasional pieces for newspapers. Witty, politically engaged, and knowing, they give an excellent general impression of Roth as a thinker and working writer.

Patrick Allitt

Cross-References

Dreiser's *Sister Carrie* Shatters Literary Taboos (1900), p. 39; Miller's Notorious Novel *Tropic of Cancer* Is Published (1934), p. 963; Mailer Publishes *The Naked and the Dead* (1948), p. 1373; Young Readers Embrace *The Catcher in the Rye* (1951), p. 1493; Wiesel's *Night* Recalls the Holocaust (1956), p. 1700.

THE FORSYTE SAGA IS A HIT ON PUBLIC TELEVISION

Category of event: Television and radio
Time: 1969-1970
Locale: The United States

The broadcast of The Forsyte Saga *led to additional imports of British television programs and the evolution of the miniseries*

> *Principal personages:*
> ERIC PORTER (1928-   ), an English actor who portrayed Soames in *The Forsyte Saga*
> KENNETH MORE (1914-1982), an English actor who portrayed Jo in *The Forsyte Saga*
> NYREE DAWN PORTER (1940-   ), an English actress who portrayed Irene in *The Forsyte Saga*
> SUSAN HAMPSHIRE (1942-   ), an English actress who portrayed Fleur in *The Forsyte Saga*
> STANFORD CALDERWOOD (1920-   ), the president of television station WGBH in Boston, who helped create *Masterpiece Theatre*
> CHRISTOPHER SARSON (1935-   ), the first producer of *Masterpiece Theatre*
> HERBERT SCHMERTZ (1930-   ), the Mobil Oil executive responsible for funding *Masterpiece Theatre*
> ALISTAIR COOKE (1908-   ), the host of *Masterpiece Theatre*

Summary of Event

Although what has come to be seen as the British invasion of American television began with the first broadcast of *The Forsyte Saga* on what was then called National Educational Television (NET) in October, 1969, British imports had long appeared on American commercial television. The most significant of these programs were *The Avengers*, a spy spoof that ran on the American Broadcasting Company (ABC) from 1966 to 1969, and *The Prisoner*, an allegorical drama dealing with a British spy banished to an island from which he cannot escape, which appeared on the Columbia Broadcasting System (CBS) in 1968 and 1969. These programs, produced by Independent Television (ITV), the United Kingdom's commercial alternative to the state-supported British Broadcasting Corporation (BBC), were notable for showing that entertainment programming could be created with a style, wit, and intelligence missing from typical American series.

Attempts at so-called quality television also did not begin with *The Forsyte Saga*. Television adaptations of famous plays and novels were common on American television in the 1950's. As ratings became more and more important, however, commercial television broadcast fewer such dramas and fewer arts programs as well.

Public television in the 1960's was known as "educational" television and consisted mostly of instructional programs, interview shows, and occasional dramatic programming such as *NET Playhouse*, which presented classic and contemporary plays, a few of which were purchased from the BBC. Clearly, something more was needed.

A report by the Carnegie Commission calling for a publicly funded network offering the type of public-service and cultural programming unavailable on the commercial networks led to the Public Broadcasting Act of 1967 and the creation of the Corporation for Public Broadcasting (CPB). In 1970, the CPB formed the Public Broadcasting Service (PBS) to replace NET and link these local systems into a network.

The effort to change the public's perception of public television was given impetus by the broadcast of the twenty-six episodes of *The Forsyte Saga* over the 167 stations affiliated with NET from October 5, 1969, to March 29, 1970. Written and produced by Donald Wilson and directed by David Giles and James Cellan Jones, *The Forsyte Saga* was a monumental undertaking. Featuring 120 characters speaking 300,000 words of dialogue, the series was adapted from six novels published by Nobel Prize winner John Galsworthy between 1906 and 1928.

A television version of these novels seemed striking in the late 1960's; the program, which over a period of several months presented the slow decline of generations of a large family, had a scope unprecedented on television. *The Forsyte Saga* was shown once on the BBC without much fanfare, but when it was repeated, the series became a national passion, attracting seventeen million viewers each week. Since the program was shown on Sunday nights, churches throughout the United Kingdom scheduled their services earlier. Following the last episode, one London newspaper published an article about the death of the protagonist as if Soames Forsyte were a real person. Similarly enthusiastic responses occurred abroad after the BBC sold the series to fifty countries, including the Soviet Union.

When *The Forsyte Saga* was first offered to broadcasters in the United States, however, there was no interest. American commercial broadcasters understood programming only in terms of series that might continue for years and one-time-only specials. If *The Forsyte Saga* were successful on a commercial network, American executives wondered, how could the broadcaster follow up on something that had an irreversible conclusion? (The series was also rejected because it was in black and white.)

NET purchased the American rights to *The Forsyte Saga* for only $140,000, and the program duplicated the interest displayed in other parts of the world. As in the United Kingdom, the series was more popular when repeated than it was during its initial showing. The repeat broadcasts in Washington, D.C., for example, were shown three times a week for the convenience of viewers with busy schedules. *The Forsyte Saga* began the public-television tradition of attracting viewers who watched few if any programs on the commercial networks. Critics praised the drama for offering writing, characterizations, insight, and acting of a quality rarely seen in American programs. The popularity of the series in the United States may also be attributed to the show's characters, who had recognizably human failings and clearly defined motives, and its setting in the comfortably distant past. *The Forsyte Saga* seemed somehow reassuring at a time of political, social, and sexual turmoil.

The Forsyte Saga presents the divergent destinies of two sides of the wealthy Forsyte family. Soames (Eric Porter), a successful lawyer, lives according to the conservative, materialistic values of the older generation of Forsytes. Soames sees acquiring and keeping property as the purpose of life. His cousin Jo (Kenneth More) conducts his life at the other extreme, taking risks the other Forsytes find shocking. An unsuccessful painter, Jo leaves his first wife for his daughter's governess. Meanwhile, Soames marries the beautiful but poor Irene Heron (Nyree Dawn Porter). Irene longs to escape her oppressive home life, but she finds living with the cold, humorless Soames even worse. When Soames hires the architect Bosinney (John Bennett) to build a mansion, Irene finds someone to share her passion for living. After Bosinney is killed in an accident and Soames rapes Irene, she runs away.

Years later, Jo and Irene meet and marry. Soames, meanwhile, acquires a second wife, who leaves him after giving birth to their daughter. Fleur (Susan Hampshire) grows up to marry the dull politician Michael Mont (Nicholas Pennell) and then initiates an affair with Jon (Martin Jarvis), the son of Jo and Irene, bringing the two sides of the family into conflict. Fleur attempts to dominate Jon the way her father had his mother, but Jon leaves her alone with her selfishness.

The Forsyte Saga captivated audiences by combining the best elements of soap opera, the irony and symbolism common in literature but unusual on television, and social history. It showed how the class represented by Soames was doomed for refusing to change with the times. The series was also praised for the excellence of its casting and performances; Susan Hampshire won an Emmy Award for her portrayal of Fleur.

Impact of Event

With PBS supplanting NET, more such programs were needed to continue the momentum created by the Galsworthy dramatization. Stanford Calderwood, a former Polaroid executive who became president of WGBH, Boston's PBS station, in 1970, was impressed by the quality of BBC programs he had seen in London. Calderwood and Christopher Sarson, a British-born producer at WGBH, sought a corporate sponsor for a series of BBC dramas. After several rejections, they found a sympathetic executive in Herbert Schmertz, a vice president for public affairs at the Mobil Oil Corporation. The subsequent agreement with Mobil occurred at a time when corporate sponsorship of public broadcasting was unknown. (NET had received funds from the Ford Foundation.)

With $400,000 from Mobil, WGBH began acquiring BBC serials, and *Masterpiece Theatre* was born. In 1990, Mobil's commitment to the program had risen to $10,000,000 a season. By that time, *Masterpiece Theatre* had changed the American conception of the quality and format of dramatic programs.

With Alistair Cooke, a veteran British journalist and broadcaster, as host, *Masterpiece Theatre* debuted on January 10, 1971, with the first of twelve episodes of *The First Churchills*. The program was followed by dramatizations of novels by Henry James, Fyodor Dostoevski, Honoré de Balzac, Thomas Hardy, Leo Tolstoy, and Stella Gibbons. In its early years, the program emphasized adaptations of classic novels and historical dramas and was immediately a hit with discriminating viewers and the critics. Susan Hampshire won another Emmy for *The First Churchills*; Keith Michell received one for starring in *The Six Wives of Henry VIII*; and *Elizabeth R*, with Glenda Jackson as Queen Elizabeth I, won five Emmys.

Over its first twenty seasons, the most highly regarded *Masterpiece Theatre* presentations were *Upstairs, Downstairs*, shown in fifty-five episodes from 1974 to 1977; *I, Claudius*, thirteen episodes shown in 1977 and 1978; and *The Jewel in the Crown*, fourteen episodes broadcast in 1984 and 1985. *Upstairs, Downstairs* was a departure for *Masterpiece Theatre*, since it was not based on a literary or historical source and was not produced by the BBC but the commercial London Weekend Television. A soap opera with a sense of humor and irony, *Upstairs, Downstairs* depicts changes in the lives of a wealthy London family and their servants from 1904 to 1930, encompassing many of the social and political upheavals during the period. *I, Claudius*, from the novel by Robert Graves, was another departure, since this depiction of four Roman emperors deals with a much earlier and more exotic period than other *Masterpiece Theatre* productions—and also because of the series' emphasis on sex and violence. Many American viewers received their first glimpses of televised nudity from *I, Claudius*. *The Jewel in the Crown*, based on novels by Paul Scott and produced by the commercial Granada Television, focuses on tensions between British colonials and native Indians in the years leading up to India's 1948 independence, offering yet another look at the broad sweep of history.

The success of *Masterpiece Theatre*, which averaged 4.7 million viewers a week by 1991, led WGBH and Mobil to create a sister series in 1980. *Mystery!* was designed to feature stories of murder, detection, and espionage. The backbone of *Mystery!* was formed by series with recurring characters such as Peter Lovesy's Sergeant Cribb, John Mortimer's Horace Rumpole, Arthur Conan Doyle's Sherlock Holmes, Dorothy L. Sayers' Lord Peter Wimsey, and Agatha Christie's Miss Marple and Hercule Poirot. *Mystery!* has also included highly regarded closed-end series such as *Malice Aforethought, Charters and Caldicott, Mother Love*, and *Prime Suspect*.

Many popular and critically acclaimed British imports have appeared on PBS independent of *Masterpiece Theatre* and *Mystery!*, including *War and Peace, Jenny, The Pallisers, Brideshead Revisited*, and *Mapp and Lucia*. Many popular British series on public television have not been PBS acquisitions but programs purchased independently by public stations. These include *Monty Python's Flying Circus, Dr. Who, All Creatures Great and Small*, and *The Sandbaggers*. Several acclaimed closed-end series have also appeared on public television exclusive of PBS funding. Notable for their daring social, political, sexual, or aesthetic content are Frederic Raphael's *The Glittering Prizes*, Troy Kennedy Martin's *Edge of Darkness*, and Dennis Potter's

Pennies from Heaven and *The Singing Detective.*

The British imports on public television have not all been dramatic programs. Such fare as art historian Sir Kenneth Clark's *Civilisation*, BBC science documentaries on *Nova*, and several natural history series hosted by David Attenborough became familiar to PBS viewers in the 1970's and 1980's.

American commercial television was not immune to the British invasion. *The Six Wives of Henry VIII* appeared on CBS before it was broadcast on *Masterpiece Theatre*, and that same network created the ill-fated *Beacon Hill* as an American version of *Upstairs, Downstairs.* The most profound influence of these programs, however, was to convince commercial executives of the value of multi-episode, limited-run series. Such American miniseries as *O.B. VII, Rich Man, Poor Man*, and *Roots* would not have existed had not *The Forsyte Saga* and *Masterpiece Theatre* preceded them.

The success of *The Forsyte Saga* also led to the further internationalization of American television. Many programs have been imported from countries other than Great Britain. In the 1970's, PBS showed a French miniseries about the playwright Molière, and CBS broadcast an Italian series about Leonardo da Vinci. *Masterpiece Theatre* has also included productions from Australia, Canada, and Ireland.

Beginning in the 1980's, public television began having competition for such programs, as the growing cable-television industry started purchasing foreign dramas, situation comedies, and documentaries. The Arts and Entertainment (A & E) network made an agreement with the BBC in the 1980's to acquire first American broadcast rights to BBC programs. From a black-and-white dramatization of Soames Forsyte's greed grew a major component of the American television industry.

Bibliography

Cooke, Alistair. *Masterpieces: A Decade of Masterpiece Theatre.* New York: Alfred A. Knopf, 1981. A collection of Cooke's introductions to *Masterpiece Theatre* series. Heavily illustrated with photographs, drawings, and stills from *Masterpiece Theatre* productions. A chronology of the series unfortunately has omissions and misspellings in the program credits.

Coppa, Frank J. "The Global Impact of Television: An Overview." In *Screen and Society: The Impact of Television upon Aspects of Contemporary Civilization.* Chicago: Nelson-Hall, 1979. Excellent overview of how broadcasting systems worldwide export and import programming and how the imported programs affect these systems. Bibliography.

Green, Timothy. *The Universal Eye: The World of Television.* New York: Stein & Day, 1972. Explains how television broadcasting evolved in various countries with the emphasis on Europe. Traces the development of the BBC and ITV in Great Britain. Shows the effect of American and British programs abroad.

Macy, John W., Jr. *To Irrigate a Wasteland: The Struggle to Shape a Public Television System in the United States.* Berkeley: University of California Press, 1974. A brief but thorough history of the creation and early years of public television. Traces how *The Forsyte Saga* and *Masterpiece Theatre* came to public television.

Mayer, Martin. *About Television.* New York: Harper & Row, 1972. A lengthy chapter on public television outlines its creation, goals, strengths, and weaknesses. The effects of the popularity of *The Forsyte Saga* and *Masterpiece Theatre* are discussed. Mayer argues that such dramas should be only on commercial television.

O'Connor, John J. *"Masterpiece Theatre*: A Retrospective." *Television Quarterly* 22 (1986): 31-37. An account of the origins of *Masterpiece Theatre* and a critical overview of its first fifteen years, with particular attention to *Upstairs, Downstairs* and *The Jewel in the Crown*. Analyzes the program's influences on the concepts of television held by audiences and broadcast executives.

"Saga." *The New Yorker* 45 (January 10, 1970): 15-17. Excellent account of *The Forsyte Saga* phenomenon in Great Britain and the United States. Includes numerous statistics.

Zukerman, Ed. "The Legacy of *Masterpiece Theatre.*" *American Film* 3 (December, 1978/January, 1979): 10-15. A history of *Masterpiece Theatre* based on interviews with Stanford Calderwood, Christopher Sarson, Herbert Schmertz, and Joan Wilson, Sarson's successor. Explains how the series was created and how the programs are selected.

Michael Adams

Cross-References

The British Broadcasting Corporation Is Chartered (1927), p. 712; *Peyton Place* Brings Serial Drama to Nighttime Television (1964), p. 2017; *Monty Python's Flying Circus* Captures Audiences Worldwide (1969), p. 2174; *Sesame Street* Revolutionizes Children's Programming (1969), p. 2185; *Roots* Dramatizes the African-American Experience (1977), p. 2397; *The Civil War* Rivets the Attention of the United States (1990), p. 2657.

MONTY PYTHON'S FLYING CIRCUS
CAPTURES AUDIENCES WORLDWIDE

Category of event: Television and radio
Time: 1969-1974
Locale: Great Britain

Monty Python's Flying Circus, *an unconventional comedy program, ran on British television from 1969 to 1974 and captured worldwide attention, earning the Monty Python troupe and its work an enduring cult status*

Principal personages:
JOHN CLEESE (1939-), a member of Monty Python who acted as straight man in many sketches
TERRY GILLIAM (1940-), the animator for Monty Python
ERIC IDLE (1943-), a member of Monty Python
MICHAEL PALIN (1943-), a member of Monty Python
TERRY JONES (1942-), a member of Monty Python
GRAHAM CHAPMAN (1941-1989), a member of Monty Python famed for his depictions of dim-witted, stuffy police and military officers

Summary of Event

Monty Python's Flying Circus first appeared on British television on October 5, 1969, and ran for forty-five shows through December 5, 1974. The last six shows in the series bore the shortened title of *Monty Python*, differed somewhat in style from the first thirty-nine, and were performed without John Cleese in the cast. The program was written and performed by Graham Chapman, John Cleese, Terry Gilliam, Eric Idle, Terry Jones, and Michael Palin, all of whom had worked in British television in one capacity or another (chiefly writing, except for Gilliam, whose specialty was animation) prior to their involvement in the Monty Python troupe. *Monty Python's Flying Circus*, however, was as a whole like nothing that had come before it. It featured an unconventional brand of comedy as well as an unconventional presentation. It did not rely on one-liners or punch lines, or, for that matter, jokes, at least not in the traditional sense of the word. It eschewed standard sketches with a beginning, middle, and end, musical interludes, guest stars, and linear and logical progression. It instead flowed without interruption from one idea to another in stream-of-consciousness fashion, mixing film sequences with sketches performed before a live studio audience as well as animation and stock footage. The film sequences and sketches most often took a concept or situation and stretched it to comically absurd extremes and/or completely removed the predictable contents of a concept or situation and replaced said contents with totally unconventional, unpredictable material. Sequences were linked most often—if in fact there was a link at all—by comically strange animation, much of which consisted of the creative superimposition of several pictures that appeared to be clipped from art books, magazines, and catalogs, or by the loose theme of a particular episode. The program was absurd, bizarre, even near anarchic, but once its audience caught on to its style, it was an unmitigated success and the beginning of what would become the Monty Python phenomenon.

The Pythons themselves were an eclectic group, six young writer/performers who came together to invent, with the blessing of the British Broadcasting Corporation (BBC), a comedy program. The most prominent member of the troupe was John Cleese, for whom the BBC supposedly had been searching for a comedy program when the soon-to-be Pythons came together. As a Python, Cleese excelled at playing the educated, cultured, prim and proper, establishment character, but always, in true Python fashion, with a twist. His characters included, to mention but a few, a lawyer who questions a deceased witness, a BBC newsreader who continues to read the news even as he and his desk are wheeled out of the studio by gunmen, and Mr. Teabags of the Ministry of Silly Walks, whose job it is to consider grants for those who wish to develop silly walks of their own.

The members of the troupe performed together as a group but wrote segments of the shows in smaller teams or individually. Cleese's writing partner for the show was Graham Chapman, who had collaborated with Cleese on pre-Python projects and who, like Cleese, excelled at playing establishment characters, though most of Chapman's most memorable characters were not simply establishment but authority figures. These included numerous police inspectors, such as Inspector Dim of the Yard, who, in a courtroom, breaks into a song and dance to a recurring colonel character who frequently interrupted sketches to declare them either too risqué or too silly.

Cleese and Chapman wrote rather tight, though by no means conventional, sketches that relied heavily on verbal humor, in the University of Cambridge tradition. Michael Palin and Terry Jones, who also had written together prior to the show, regularly produced more nonsensical, visually oriented segments, more in the tradition of the University of Oxford. As a performer, Palin played a wide range of characters, both male and female. Almost all female characters in the program, except those for whom an obvious female appearance was vital, were played to comic and screechingly high-pitched absurdity by the Pythons themselves. Some of Palin's most popular characters were either a combination of dishonest and phony, such as his frequent shop-owner characters and his numerous television hosts, or downright stupid, such as the Gumbies, idiotic characters who appear in various roles and whom Palin polished to perfection. Jones also played a wide variety of roles, including numerous female characters—perhaps most frequently middle-aged suburban housewives—and one of the program's most bizarre characters (which is saying something, given the program in question), a nude organist who helped open most of the shows of the third season of the program.

While Cleese and Chapman and Palin and Jones paired off and wrote together, Eric Idle wrote primarily on his own. The comic weight of Idle's characters frequently lay in their verbal excess, from his man on trial who delivers an impassioned speech on the issue of freedom, all in defense of his citation for a parking violation, to his popular "Mr. Nudge" character, who, in a conversation full of insinuation concerning a fellow bar patron's wife, repeatedly nudges the other man in the ribs and utters the phrase "Say no more! Say no more!" Terry Gilliam, the only American of the troupe, performed only on occasion, usually in relatively minor roles, though his role as a performer grew as the program progressed. He was instead responsible for creation of the program's animation, which he created largely without contact with the other members of the troupe, frequently revealing his work only on the day of each show's taping. This animation, known both for its unusual style and its comic violence, was yet another element that separated *Monty Python's Flying Circus* from its comedic predecessors. The fortuitous teaming of these six talented individuals produced a program that in both its form and its content lived up to the program's and the troupe's popular catch-phrase: "And now for something completely different."

Impact of Event

The success of *Monty Python's Flying Circus*, first in Britain, then in the United States, beginning with the first airings of the program by stations of the Public Broadcasting System in 1974, and then around the world brought the Monty Python troupe legions of loyal fans who could recite their favorite segments from the shows word for word. These favorites included sketches such as "The Dead Parrot," also known as "The Pet Shop," in which a man (Cleese) attempts to return a dead parrot to the pet shop from which he purchased it and is told by the shop owner (Palin) that the parrot is only sleeping. In "The Ministry of Silly Walks," a man (Palin) seeking funding to develop a silly walk is told that his walk is not silly enough by Mr. Teabags (Cleese), who works for the Ministry of Silly Walks and whose walk, as well as that of his secretary, are far sillier. "The Spanish Inquisition" is known primarily for its intentionally poor acting by Palin, Jones, and Gilliam. In "The Architect," Cleese presents plans for a slaughterhouse to a group that wishes to build a block of flats. A frustrated customer (Cleese) attempts to purchase cheese in "The Cheese Shop." After running through a list of cheeses he would be willing to purchase, the customer finds that the shop in fact has no cheese for sale. At this point, he produces a gun and shoots the cheese-shop proprietor.

Python fans embraced favorite characters from the program as well, such as the aforementioned Gumbies, and even songs from the show, for example, "The Lumberjack Song," which praises the virtues of being a lumberjack, which, in the case of the lumberjack in the song, includes dressing in women's clothing.

The success of the television program allowed the Monty Python troupe to branch out into other media. The Pythons took their act on tour, performing many of their most popular sketches, as well as some new material and their unique animation (projected on large screens), on stages from those in Great Britain to the Hollywood Bowl. The troupe also made films. *And Now for Something Completely Different* (1972) collected skits, much like a longer version of the television show. *Monty Python and the Holy Grail* (1974) was a sketch-driven, Pythonesque look at medieval England, loosely connected to King Arthur's search for the Holy Grail. *Jabberwocky*

(1977), directed by Gilliam and starring Palin but no other Pythons, offered another look at medieval England. *Life of Brian* (1979) follows the life of a man (Brian, played by Chapman) whose life parallels that of Jesus Christ. Although intended by the troupe as an attack on those who follow blindly, the film drew considerable protest from those who thought it ridiculed the life of Christ. *Monty Python Live at the Hollywood Bowl* (1982) was a filmed performance of the troupe's stage act. *Monty Python's The Meaning of Life* (1983) was a series of bizarre—even by Python standards—sketches on everything from birth control and sex to gluttony.

The troupe recorded numerous records as well, such as *Monty Python's Flying Circus* (1970), *The Monty Python Matching Tie and Handkerchief* (1973), *The Monty Python Instant Record Collection* (1977), and *Monty Python's The Final Ripoff* (1988). The troupe even produced a number of books, such as *Monty Python's Big Red Book* (edited by Eric Idle, 1971), which appropriately has a blue cover, and *Monty Python's Flying Circus: Just the Words* (1989), which contains the scripts of the television program. Numerous books by outsiders have attempted to chronicle and explain the Python phenomenon.

The members of the Monty Python troupe continued to work in television and film after the group disbanded. Many of the members, along with numerous others, appeared in two film productions that benefited Amnesty International: *The Secret Policemen's Other Ball* (1982) and *The Secret Policeman's Private Parts* (1984). Terry Gilliam directed several films starring troupe members, including *Time Bandits* (1981), starring Cleese and Palin and with a screenplay by Gilliam and Palin; *The Adventures of Baron Munchhausen* (1989), with Eric Idle in the cast; and *Brazil* (1985), probably his most famous directorial effort, for which he also cowrote the script.

Cleese perhaps had the most successful career following *Monty Python's Flying Circus.* He starred in another British television program, *Fawlty Towers*, and won a 1987 Emmy Award for an appearance on the American *Cheers* television series, as Outstanding Guest Performer in a Comedy Series. Cleese wrote the script for *A Fish Called Wanda* (1988), in which he starred with Palin. Kevin Kline won an Academy Award for his role in that high-profile film. Cleese also appeared with Chapman and Idle in *Yellowbeard* (1983).

Palin starred in various roles in *Ripping Yarns* (1978), a spin-off film from his British television series. He wrote material for that film along with Jones. He also hosted a travel special, *Around the World in Eighty Days?* Idle continued to perform on American television, most notably as a frequent host of *Saturday Night Live.*

One of the strongest influences of *Monty Python's Flying Circus* can be seen in *Saturday Night Live.* Monty Python certainly helped popularize the skit-oriented style of show. *Saturday Night Live* was one of the first American shows to exploit this rediscovered genre, and a host of other skit-oriented comedy shows followed through the 1970's and 1980's and into the 1990's.

Monty Python's Flying Circus not only broke with but virtually obliterated all conventions of both content and presentation in its comic style. Once its audience learned to expect (and accept) "something completely different," both the program and its troupe went on to earn an enduring cult status. Most important, the program influenced numerous writers, performers, and programs that followed it, as well as the comic taste of an entire generation and beyond.

Bibliography

Johnson, Kim "Howard." *The First 200 Years of Monty Python.* New York: St. Martin's Press, 1989. The number "200" is not a misprint in the title. In true Python tradition, the final zero is simply crossed out on the book's cover and title page. This may be the definitive book on both *Monty Python's Flying Circus* and the troupe itself. Includes a synopsis of each show, discussion of the films, and behind-the-scenes information from the Pythons themselves on everything from how the members of the troupe interacted to how certain sketches came about. Also includes a profile on each Python as well as trivia questions, a collection of quotes on various subjects taken from the sketches, and an annotated list of records, books, videos, and other items by or about Monty Python. Numerous photos.

McCall, Douglas L. *Monty Python: A Chronological Listing of the Troupe's Creative Output, and Articles and Reviews About Them, 1969-1989.* Jefferson, N.C.: McFarland, 1991. Provides what the title indicates as well as a record of numerous personal events in the lives of the Pythons, including their work outside the group. Index.

Nathan, David. "Monty Python's Flying Breakthrough." In *The Laughtermakers: A Quest for Comedy.* London: Peter Owen, 1971. The book as a whole examines the development of postwar comedy in Great Britain. Most of this nine-page chapter focuses on John Cleese, also discussing the nature of *Monty Python's Flying Circus* and how it differs from programs before it. Written while the program was still in production.

Perry, George. *Life of Python.* Boston: Little, Brown, 1983. Includes an opening chapter entitled "Birth," which discusses British humor from around 1950 up to the formation of Monty Python. Considerable attention is paid in this chapter to each of the Pythons' work prior to *Monty Python's Flying Circus.* Subsequent chapters are dedicated to insightful profiles of each Python. The final chapter traces the history of the troupe's work, from *Monty Python's Flying Circus* through its films. Includes a "Pythonography" (compiled by Lucy Douch) of the troupe's creative production both together and individually. Numerous photos.

Wilmut, Roger. *From Fringe to Flying Circus: Celebrating a Unique Generation of Comedy, 1960-1980.* London: Eyre Methuen, 1980. Includes a thirty-seven-page chapter on *Monty Python's Flying Circus.* Discusses the history of the program, with considerable attention paid to the types of sketches, the evolution of the program, and the distinctive characteristics of each performer. More analysis than simple description. Also discusses the group's films, records, and books.

Keith H. Brower

Cross-References

The British Broadcasting Corporation Is Chartered (1927), p. 712; *Rowan and Martin's Laugh-In* Is the Top Show on Television (1968), p. 2115; *The Forsyte Saga* Is a Hit on Public Television (1969), p. 2168; *Sesame Street* Revolutionizes Children's Programming (1969), p. 2185; *Saturday Night Live* Is First Broadcast (1975), p. 2355; *The Civil War* Rivets the Attention of the United States (1990), p. 2657.

THE WOODSTOCK MUSIC FESTIVAL MARKS THE CLIMAX OF THE 1960'S

Category of event: Music
Time: August 15-17, 1969
Locale: Bethel, New York

An estimated 400,000 young people gathered to hear rock music at the Woodstock Music and Art Fair, one of the most significant events in the history of the counterculture of the 1960's

Principal personages:
THE BAND, one of the greatest rock groups to emerge from the 1960's
COUNTRY JOE AND THE FISH, a San Francisco band whose "I-Feel-Like-I'm-Fixin'-to-Die-Rag" became an anti-Vietnam War anthem
CREEDENCE CLEARWATER REVIVAL, a Bay Area band whose critical reputation would outlast that of other San Francisco acts
CROSBY, STILLS, NASH, AND YOUNG, an emerging vocal quartet who would achieve prominence in the years following Woodstock
JANIS JOPLIN (1943-1970), a charismatic singer who attained the peak of her fame in the aftermath of the festival
THE GRATEFUL DEAD, one of the newer acts at Woodstock, who would go on to embody many countercultural values
JIMI HENDRIX (1942-1970), the dazzling virtuoso rock guitarist whose Woodstock rendition of "The Star-Spangled Banner" would earn lasting fame
THE JEFFERSON AIRPLANE, a key band in the San Francisco music scene of the late 1960's
SLY AND THE FAMILY STONE, perhaps the most successful racially integrated rock group to perform at Woodstock—or, for that matter, anywhere else
THE WHO, the only major British band to play at the festival

Summary of Event

The road to Woodstock began in Monterey California. It was there from June 16 to 18, 1967, that approximately seven thousand fans who bought tickets—and an estimated fifty thousand who did not—heard some of the most famous rock acts of the 1960's, including the Who, Otis Redding, Simon & Garfunkel, and others.

Monterey was a success on a number of levels. First, the affair made money. Second, the 1968 documentary film that recorded the event, *Monterey Pop*, reached a wide audience and introduced many fans to some exciting new talent (notably Jimi Hendrix, who created a sensation). Third, as a showcase for San Francisco talent—Janis Joplin (who performed with Big Brother and the Holding Company), Country Joe and the Fish, and the Jefferson Airplane, all of whom would appear at Woodstock two years later—Monterey captured the key symbols of the emerging counterculture in the idyllic Summer of Love.

In the wake of Monterey, rock festivals became common, at no time more so than in 1969. Successful events were held in Toronto (attended by an estimated fifty thousand people) and Atlanta (with an attendance of 140,000). The Rolling Stones performed for about 300,000 people in England that year, an especially notable figure in light of the country's relatively small population. Yet not all such festivals went smoothly. A concert during Easter week resulted in extensive rioting in Palm Springs, California; another in Denver ended in clouds of tear gas.

It was in this context of growing musical excitement on the part of young people, and growing concern and distaste on the part of older people, that a large festival was planned in upstate New York for August of 1969. Contrary to popular belief, the event did not take place in Woodstock; resistance by residents of the town forced a change of venue. When promoters paid farmer Max Yasgur fifty thousand dollars for the use of his six-hundred-acre farm in the town of Bethel, local opposition also arose, but the town of twenty-seven hundred people imagined that the event would help generate needed revenue; 150,000 people were expected.

This proved to be a gross underestimate. By Friday morning, August 15, the roads approaching the farm were so congested that state police told motorists to avoid the area entirely. The volume of people strained basic services such as food, water, and sanitation at the site, a problem complicated by the steady rain that made the farm a mud puddle. Gatecrashers made it impossible to restrict the flow of people, and before long, the promoters gave up and declared the festival a free event. At the event's height, an estimated 400,000 people gathered in Bethel, making the small town temporarily the third largest city in New York State. Ebullient participants dubbed themselves "the Woodstock nation."

To most observers and participants, it was an amazing experience. Woodstock seemed to be a world unto itself: There were three deaths, three births, countless drug overdoses, and rampant nudity. Despite food shortages, a lack of shelter, and the absence of police at the site (they refused to come at the last minute), the crowd managed to live in relative harmony. For one weekend, sex, drugs, and rock and roll became a way of life.

Rock and roll, moreover, had never been better. Jimi Hendrix and Janis Joplin, both of whom would die the following year, were among those who gave acclaimed performances. Established acts such as the Who shared the stage with newer ones such as Crosby, Stills, Nash, and Young. Other bands, including Creedence Clearwater Revival and the Band, articulated the doubts and fears of baby boomers with a complexity that would win them lasting reputations. Such performances were captured on *Woodstock* (1970), a film and sound-track album that more than offset the promoters' losses. (The promoters' financial success, however, did not prevent them from descending into squabbles and lawsuits.)

The success of Woodstock engendered euphoria among the nation's youth and even won the grudging admiration of institutions such as *The New York Times*, which followed a condemnation of the event on Monday, August 18, with a reversal on Tuesday, August 19, that praised the participants for the event's success. For a while, it seemed, a genuine youth culture had defined itself as a compelling alternative to the status quo.

Alas, the road from Woodstock led to Altamont Speedway, forty miles outside San Francisco. The Rolling Stones had decided to host a free concert, but the band changed the location less than a day before the event was scheduled to begin. By the time it did, 300,000 people had gathered in a space a fraction of the size of Woodstock. The Rolling Stones and the Grateful Dead had hired the Hell's Angels to perform security for the show and paid the motorcycle gang with five hundred dollars' worth of beer. This proved to be a foolish, tragic mistake. Amid space, toilet, and temper shortages, a black man drew a gun and was knifed to death by members of the Hell's Angels. When the lead singer of the Jefferson Airplane tried to halt the beating of another black man, he was assaulted on stage. In falling far short of the Woodstock experience, Altamont suggested that, by December of 1969, the 1960's were indeed coming to an end.

Impact of Event

To many observers at the time, Woodstock seemed to embody the values of 1960's youth culture—personal freedom, political pacifism, and social optimism in what seemed to be a land of plenty—and the power of those values in a time of social upheaval. For these people, there was considerable hope that the United States was undergoing a fundamental, permanent change and that rock music was a potent symbol of that change. For its critics in the "establishment" (a fuzzy term that seemed to connote the status quo in any number of forms), Woodstock was also a symbol of the power of youth culture, but that culture was one of permissiveness and flaccidity in a nation in decline.

Years later, Woodstock remains an important symbol. In retrospect, however, it is the weaknesses of youth culture, and the contradictions that would ultimately lead to its unraveling, that are more apparent. It now seems that if Woodstock was indeed a beginning, it was the beginning of an end.

To understand why, one needs to consider the political and cultural climate in the years preceding the festival. As the decade drew to a close, it seemed that the forces of change loosely called "the movement"—an amalgam of allies centered in promoting civil rights and opposing the Vietnam War—were winning some important victories. The walls of segregation that had seemed impregnable ten years before were collapsing, and it appeared that radicals had convinced mainstream America that the war had to end. Rock-and-roll music, which had seemed at best a trivial (and, at worst, barbaric) diversion, had come to be recognized as a political and artistic force in its own right, a key institution around which young people, black and white, could rally.

Yet all these victories, real as they were, came at a price. As the decade wore on, white America became increasingly resistant to yielding ground in race relations.

The antiwar effort had helped to force President Lyndon Johnson to give up a reelection bid, but in the process, the Democratic Party was so badly split that it would not recover for a generation. Meanwhile, there remained many Americans who were willing to prosecute the war—which would drag on for years—and who were angry about "traitors" who were ruining the country. Here was the core of Richard Nixon's "Silent Majority" that rejected all for which Woodstock would come to stand.

This polarity in American society led to sharp confrontations, most notably at the 1968 Democratic National Convention in Chicago, where protesters were met with violence by police. Amid a growing sense of young people as troublemakers—and amid the chaos that had surrounded the rock festivals preceding it—Woodstock became a litmus test as to whether the counterculture could be true to its principles. It did so, but by that point, the movement that participants celebrated had become so diffuse, and its contradictions had become so glaring, that the unity of the counterculture was beginning to break down. The audience at Woodstock embodied these problems, though the fact was not clear to many at the time.

The first contradiction was the sense of the counterculture as a youth movement. To be sure, the overwhelming majority of people involved were young—but by no means were all young people members of the counterculture. To some extent, the counterculture was increasingly marked by class fissures: Working-class youths who could not get college deferments went off to war, while middle-class youths in schools with money to burn listened to music and attended protests.

Such differences led to another tension. By the end of the 1960's, some people thought of the counterculture as a political movement. Others saw it as a life-style revolution. Increasingly, the two views were at odds. Never was this more clear than during the Who's performance at Woodstock, where angry guitarist Pete Townshend chased hippie leader Abbie Hoffman off the stage for proselytizing during the band's performance. By the early 1970's, most young people had concluded that the counterculture was more about good times than about radical politics, while radical politics reached such extremes that few could take such views seriously.

Meanwhile, the youth movement had its own race problem. The original energy for reform in the 1960's had come from the Civil Rights movement, but by the end of the decade, the antiwar movement, the women's movement, and the struggles of gays, Hispanics, and other minority groups were increasingly competing for attention on the left. However worthy each of these issues may have been, they sapped the strength of the youth movement, which grew more fragmented. At the same time, many whites on the left became progressively less interested in racial issues. In this, as in so many other ways, Woodstock was telling: Relatively few of the acts were African American, and only one—Sly and the Family Stone—practiced what it preached with a lasting interracial makeup.

Whether by luck, goodwill, or an unusual sense of discipline on the part of the young people there, Woodstock was able to avoid the pitfalls implicit in all these issues. Fans at Altamont would not be so lucky. Meanwhile, the growing power of Richard Nixon, violence at Kent State, the failure of George McGovern, and economic recession would eviscerate the counterculture to the point where it became a memory. In the 1970's and 1980's, a number of rock festivals were held, some of them quite successful (but not a 1979 Woodstock reunion, which was held on Long Island—towns in upstate New York refused to host it). Perhaps the most notable of these was Live Aid, a 1985 Anglo-American effort for famine relief that probably did more concrete good than Woodstock did. Yet neither this event nor any other was able to articulate a social critique the way Woodstock did, however implicitly.

Yet if Woodstock is only a memory, it remains a powerful one. Perhaps a sense of history—and a strong desire to prevent the tactical mistakes of a remarkable decade—will help a future youth culture to fulfill the promise of the 1960's.

Bibliography

Baritz, Loren. "Culture War." In *The Good Life: The Meaning of Success for the Middle Class.* New York: Harper & Row, 1989. Although the discussion of Woodstock is brief, Baritz, a social historian, does a good job of placing the festival in context.

Jones, Landon. "The Road to Woodstock." In *Great Expectations: America and the Baby Boom Generation.* New York: Ballantine Books, 1980. A concise history not only of the events leading up to the festival but also of the attitudes that brought people there.

Morthland, John. "Rock Festivals." In *The Rolling Stone Illustrated History of Rock and Roll*, edited by Jim Miller. New York: Rolling Stone Press, 1980. A superb distillation of the culture of rock festivals, focusing on Woodstock.

Reich, Charles. *The Greening of America.* New York: Random House, 1970. This best-selling book is not about Woodstock, but it typifies the mindset of many people who attended the festival. An amazingly dated document, and thus an amazingly revealing one.

Tucker, Ken. "Woodstock . . . and Altamont." In *Rock of Ages: The Rolling Stone History of Rock and Roll*, by Ed Ward, Geoffrey Stokes, and Ken Tucker. New York: Rolling Stone Press, 1986. A diffuse treatment of the subject, which is both a strength and a weakness. Very good background material, though one must skim a bit to get to (excellent) treatments of the festivals in question. See also Tucker's handling of Monterey in his chapter "Love for Sale."

Jim Cullen

Cross-References

The First Newport Jazz Festival Is Held (1954), p. 1617; Hendrix Releases *Are You Experienced?* (1967), p. 2092; The Beatles Release *Sgt. Pepper's Lonely Hearts Club Band* (1967), p. 2098; The Monterey Pop Festival Inaugurates the "Summer of Love" (1967), p. 2104; The Radical Musical *Hair* Opens on Broadway (1968), p. 2121; Live Aid Generates Millions for Famine Relief (1985), p. 2543.

CHRONOLOGICAL LIST OF EVENTS

VOLUME I

VOLUME II

VOLUME III

VOLUME IV

CHRONOLOGICAL LIST OF EVENTS